THE READING NATION IN THE ROM

CW00684971

During the four centuries when printed paper was the only means by which texts could be carried across time and distance, everyone engaged in politics, education, religion, and literature believed that reading helped to shape the minds, opinions, attitudes, and ultimately the actions, of readers.

William St Clair investigates how the national culture can be understood through a quantitative study of the books that were actually read. Centred on the romantic period in the English-speaking world, but ranging across the whole print era, he reaches startling conclusions about the forces that determined how ideas were carried, through print, into wider society.

St Clair provides an in-depth investigation of information, made available here for the first time, on prices, print runs, intellectual property, and readerships gathered from over fifty publishing and printing archives. He offers a picture of the past very different from those presented by traditional approaches. Indispensable to all students of English literature, book history, and the history of ideas, the study's conclusions and explanatory models are highly relevant to the issues we face in the age of the internet.

WILLIAM ST CLAIR is a Senior Research Fellow of Trinity College, Cambridge University. He is the author of award-winning books, including *That Greece Might Still Be Free* (1972), *Trelawny, the Incurable Romancer* (1978), *The Godwins and the Shelleys, The Biography of a Family* (1989), and *Lord Elgin and the Marbles* (1967, third revised edition, 1998). Formerly a senior official in the British Treasury, he uses his experience of economic matters to analyse the whole political economy of texts, books, reading, and its consequences.

THE READING NATION IN
THE ROMANTIC PERIOD

WILLIAM ST CLAIR

CAMBRIDGE
UNIVERSITY PRESS

CAMBRIDGE UNIVERSITY PRESS
Cambridge, New York, Melbourne, Madrid, Cape Town, Singapore, São Paulo

Cambridge University Press
The Edinburgh Building, Cambridge CB2 2RU, UK

Published in the United States of America by Cambridge University Press, New York

www.cambridge.org
Information on this title: www.cambridge.org/9780521699440

First published 2004
Reprinted 2005 (twice)
First paperback edition 2007

Printed in the United Kingdom at the University Press, Cambridge

A catalogue record for this book is available from the British Library

Library of Congress Cataloguing in Publication data
St Clair, William.
The reading nation / by William St Clair
p.   cm.
Includes bibliographical references and index.
ISBN 0 521 81006 X (hardback)
1. Books and reading – Social aspects – History.   2. Book industries and trade – History.
3. Literature and society – History.   4. English literature – History and criticism.
5. Books and reading – Social aspects – England – History.   6. Book industries and
trade – England – History.   7. Literature and society – England – History.
8. England – Intellectual life.   1. Title.
ZI003.S77   2004
028′.9 – dc22   2003060795

ISBN 978-0-521-81006-7 hardback
ISBN 978-0-521-69944-0 paperback

Contents

Figures

All figures, except number 9 are reproduced from the author's collection.

Tables

Acknowledgements

I should like to record my thanks to the following organisations and institutions for kindly giving me access to their books, manuscripts, and archives, and for much other help. American Antiquarian Society, Worcester, Mass., Bodleian Library, Bristol Central Library, British Library, British Museum, Brontë Museum, Haworth, Calderdale Record Office, Halifax, Codrington Library, All Souls College, Oxford, Cambridge University Library, Cambridge University Press, William Clowes and Company, Edinburgh City Archives, Glasgow University Library, Gloucester Public Library, Guildhall Library, London, Hertfordshire Record Office, Hornell Museum, Kirkcudbright, Keats House, Hampstead, Keats-Shelley Memorial, Rome, John Rylands University Library, Manchester, Library Company, Philadelphia, Lincoln Public Library, London Library, Lowestoft Record Office, Mitchell Library, Glasgow, John Murray (Publishers) Ltd, National Library of Scotland, National Library of Wales, Newberry Library, Chicago, Northampton Central Library, New York Public Library, including Arends, Berg, Pforzheimer, and other special collections, Public Record Office, Kew, Reading University Library, St Bride's Printing Library, London, Stationers' Company, Library of Trinity College, Dublin, Library of University College, London, Frederick Warne and Company, Westminster City Archives, Wren Library, Trinity College, Cambridge.

I record my warm thanks to the many individuals who have helped me during the long time when the book was in preparation and production, of which the following is an incomplete list:

Bathsheba Abse, Christine Alexander, Betty Bennett, Michael Bott, Sue Bradley, Linda Bree, Rimi Chatterjee, Jonathan Clark, Peter Cochran, Stephen Colclough, Patrick Collinson, Keith Crook, Robert Darnton, Paul David, Gernot Doppelhofer, Ian Donaldson, Simon Eliot, Paula Feldman, Doucet Fischer, Ian Gadd, Stephen Gill, Abijit Gupta, Tanya Hagen, Michael Harris, Anne Henry, Boyd Hilton, Mary Hilton, Debbie Hodges,

xi

Clive Hurst, Heather Jackson, Robin Jackson, Paulina Kewes, Ian King, Sally King, Maureen Leach, Iain McCalman, the late Don McKenzie, Irmgard Maassen, Giles Mandelbrote, Scott Mandelbrote, John Marenbon, the late Colin Matthew, James Raven, Jean Maxwell-Scott, Patricia Maxwell-Scott, John Murray, Virginia Murray, Robin Myers, Judith Pascoe, Robert Picken, Mark Reed, Charles Robinson, Richard Serjeantson, Miranda Seymour, John Simmons, Jon Stallworthy, Michael Suarez, Michael Turner, David St Clair, John St Clair, Melissa Sydeman, Marc Vaulbert de Chantilly, Stephen Wagner, Jack Wasserman, Paul Watt, Steve Weissman, Tim Whelan, Donald Winch, Karen Waring, Teresa Webber, Bill Wexler, Frances Wilson, Linda Woodward, and William Zachs.

Special thanks are due to Anne Barton, Richard Holmes, David McKitterick, Emma Rothschild, and the anonymous readers of Cambridge University Press who commented at various stages of draft.

I also wish to thank the many antiquarian and second-hand booksellers who have shared their specialist experience with me, and who, over the years, have enabled me to examine a huge range of books. Without the knowledge I have gained from them, the book could not have been attempted.

Trinity College
Cambridge
ws214@cam.ac.uk

Abbreviations

Ac	from the author's collection of books, advertisements, other print not available or easily discoverable elsewhere, and manuscript commonplace books.
Accardo	Peter X. Accardo, 'Byron in America to 1830' in *Harvard Library Bulletin* 9, 2, (1998).
Ackers ledger	*A Ledger of Charles Ackers*, edited by D. F. McKenzie and J. C. Ross (Oxford 1968).
add. mss.	additional manuscripts.
Aldis	H. G. Aldis, ed., *A List of Books Printed in Scotland before 1700* (1904, updated 1970).
Altick	Richard D. Altick, *The English Common Reader* (Chicago 1957).
Altick, *Writers*	Richard D. Altick, *Writers, Readers, and Occasions* (Columbus, Ohio 1989).
Arber	E. Arber, *A Transcript of the Registers of the Company of Stationers of London, 1554–1640* (1875–94).
Arber, *Transcript*	*A Transcript of the Registers of the Worshipful Company of Stationers, 1640–1708 AD* (1913).
Armstrong	Elizabeth Armstrong, *Before Copyright: the French Book-privilege system 1498–1526* (Cambridge 1990).
Ashton	John Ashton, *Chap-Books of the Eighteenth Century* (1882).
Austen, *Letters*	*Jane Austen's Letters,* collected and edited by Deirdre le Faye (third edition 1995).
BL	British Library.
Baldick	Chris Baldick, *In Frankenstein's Shadow* (Oxford 1987).

Barnes and Barnes	James J. Barnes and Patience P. Barnes, 'Reassessing the Reputation of Thomas Tegg, London Publisher 1776–1846' in *Book History* 3 (2000).
Bennett, *1558 to 1603*	H. S. Bennett, *English Books and Readers 1558 to 1603* (Cambridge 1965).
Bennett, *1475 to 1557*	H. S. Bennett, *English Books and Readers 1475 to 1557* (second edition, Cambridge 1970).
Bennett, *1603 to 1640*	*English Books and Readers 1603 to 1640* (Cambridge 1970).
Bentley, 'Copyright Documents'	Bentley, G. E. Jr, 'Copyright Documents in the George Robinson Archive: William Godwin and Others 1713–1820' in *Studies in Bibliography* (1982).
(*Bennet and Clements*)	Norma Hodgson, and Cyprian Blagden, *The Notebook of Thomas Bennet and Henry Clements* (Oxford 1956).
Besterman	Theodore Besterman, *The Publishing Firm of Cadell and Davies. Select Correspondence and Accounts 1793–1836* (1938).
Bew	John Bew, 'Chapmen's Books' printed list in a copy of *The New History of the Trojan Wars* (n.d., late eighteenth century), Ac.
Black Book	*The Black Book or Corruption Unmasked* (1820).
(Blackwood)	Mrs Oliphant and Mrs Gerald Porter, *William Blackwood and his Sons* (Edinburgh 1897 and 1898).
Blagden	Cyprian Blagden, *The Stationers' Company, A History* (1960).
Blakey	Dorothy Blakey, *The Minerva Press, 1790–1820* (1939).
Blanning	T. C. W. Blanning *The Culture of Power and the Power of Culture, Old Regime Europe 1660–1789* (Oxford 2001).
Blayney	Peter W. M. Blayney, *The First Folio of Shakespeare* (Washington 1991).
Bloomfield	B. C. Bloomfield, 'The Publication of *The Farmer's Boy*' in *The Library* (1993).

Blunden	Edmund Blunden, *Keats's Publisher, A Memoir of John Taylor* (1936).
Bodleian	Bodleian Library, Oxford.
Bonnell, 'John Bell's Poets'	Thomas Bonnell, 'John Bell's Poets of Great Britain' in *Modern Philology* 85 (1987).
Bonnell, 'Bookselling'	Thomas Bonnell, 'Bookselling and Canon-Making: The Trade Rivalry over the English Poets, 1777–1783' in *Studies in Eighteenth Century Culture* (1989).
Bowyer	W. Bowyer, *Biographical and Literary Anecdotes of W. Bowyer, and of many of his learned friends* (1782).
Brack	O. M. Brack, Jr., ed., *Writers, Books and Trade, An Eighteenth-Century Miscellany for William B. Todd* (New York 1994).
Bradsher	Earl L. Bradsher, *Mathew Carey* (New York 1912).
Burney	Joyce Hemslow *et al.*, eds., *The Journals and Letters of Fanny Burney* (1972–).
Byron, *Letters and Journals*	*The Letters and Journals of Lord Byron*, edited by Leslie A. Marchand (1973–82).
Byron, *Poetical Works*	*The Complete Poetical Works of Lord Byron*, edited by Jerome J. McGann (Oxford 1980–93).
Byron, *Prose Works*	*The Complete Miscellaneous Prose*, edited by Andrew Nicholson (Oxford 1991).
CBAW	Hugh Amory and David D. Hall, eds., *The Colonial Book in the Atlantic World* (Cambridge 2000).
CHBB iii	*The Cambridge History of the Book in Britain iii: 1400–1557*, edited by Lotte Hellinga and J. B. Trapp (Cambridge 1999).
CHBB iv	*The Cambridge History of the Book in Britain iv: 1557–1695*, edited by John Barnard and D. F. McKenzie, with the assistance of Maureen Bell (Cambridge 2002).
CUL	Cambridge University Library.
Capp	Bernard Capp, *Astrology and the Popular Press, English Almanacs, 1500–1800* (1979).

Cavallo and Chartier	Guglielmo Cavallo and Roger Chartier, eds., *A History of Reading in the West* (1999).
Chambers	*Memoir of William and Robert Chambers* (twelfth edition with supplementary chapter 1883).
Chilcott	Tim Chilcott, *A Publisher and his Circle* (1972).
Christianson	C. Paul Christianson, *Memorials of the Book Trade in Mediaeval London* (Cambridge 1987).
Clare's *Autobiographical Writings*	*John Clare's Autobiographical Writings*, edited by Eric Robinson (1983).
Clegg	Cyndia Susan Clegg, *Press Censorship in Elizabethan England* (1997).
Clive	John Clive, *Scotch Reviewers* (1957).
Cochrane	J. A. Cochrane, *Dr Johnson's Printer, The Life of William Strahan* (1964).
Coleridge, *Letters*	*The Collected Letters of Samuel Taylor Coleridge*, edited by Earl Leslie Griggs (Oxford 1956–72).
Collins, *Authorship*	A. S. Collins, *Authorship in the Days of Johnson* (1927).
Collins, *Profession of Letters*	A. S. Collins, *The Profession of Letters. A Study of the Relation of Author to Patron, Publisher, and the Public, 1780–1832* (1928).
Constable	*Archibald Constable and his Literary Correspondents* (Edinburgh 1873).
Conway	Moncure Daniel Conway, *The Life of Thomas Paine* (one-volume edition 1909).
Cooper	*The Life of Thomas Cooper Written by Himself* (1872).
Cruse, *Shaping*	Amy Cruse, *The Shaping of English Literature* (1927).
Cruse, *Englishman*	Amy Cruse, *The Englishman and his Books in the Early Nineteenth Century* (1930).
Cruse, *Victorians*	Amy Cruse, *The Victorians and their Books* (1935).
Curwen	Henry Curwen, *A History of Booksellers* (n.d. 1873).
DNB	*Dictionary of National Biography*.
Darnton, *Underground*	Robert Darnton, *The Literary Underground of the Old Regime* (Cambridge, Mass. 1982).

Darnton, *Forbidden*	Robert Darnton, *The Forbidden Best-Sellers of Pre-Revolutionary France* (1995).
Darnton and Roche	Robert Darnton and Daniel Roche, eds., *Revolution in Print, The Press in France 1775–1800* (Berkeley 1989).
David, *Intellectual Property*	Paul David, *Intellectual Property Institutions and the Panda's Thumb* (Stanford 1992).
Davidson	Cathy N. Davidson, ed., *Reading in America* (1989).
Deloney	Francis Oscar Mann, ed., *The Works of Thomas Deloney* (Oxford 1912).
Dibdin	T. F. Dibdin, *The Library Companion, or The Young Man's Guide and Old Man's Solace in the Choice of a Library* (second edition 1824).
Dickson and Edmond	Robert Dickson and John Philip Edmond, *Annals of Scottish Printing* (1890).
Dodsley	*The Correspondence of Robert Dodsley 1733–1764*, edited by James E. Tierney (Cambridge 1988).
Dorne	John Dorne, bookseller in Oxford c. 1520, *Daybook*, edited by F. Madan (Oxford Historical Society, 1885). See also Henry Bradshaw, 'A Half Century of Notes on the Day-book of J. Dorne' in *Collected Papers* (1889).
Dunton	*The Life and Errors of John Dunton* (1818 edition).
Duppa	(Richard Duppa), *An Address to Parliament on the Claims of Authors to Copyright* (1813).
Duval	Gilles Duval, *Littérature de colportage et imaginaire collectif en Angleterre à l'époque des Dicey (1720–v. 1800)* (Bordeaux 1991).
ESTC	*English Short Title Catalogue.*
Elfenbein	Andrew Elfenbein, *Byron and the Victorians* (Cambridge 1995).
Eliot	Simon Eliot, *Some Patterns and Trends in British Publishing, 1800–1919* (1994).
Evans	Charles Evans, *American Bibliography, A Chronological Dictionary of all the Books, Pamphlets, and Periodical Publications Printed*

Geduld	Harry M. Geduld, *Prince of Publishers, A Study of the Work and Career of Jacob Tonson* (Bloomington 1969).
Gettman	Royal A. Gettman, *A Victorian Publisher, A Study of the Bentley Papers* (1960).
Gilmont	Jean-François Gilmont, ed., *The Reformation and the Book*, translated by Karin Maag (Aldershot 1998).
Gilmore	William J. Gilmore, *Reading Becomes a Necessity, Material and Cultural Life in Rural New England, 1789–1835* (Knoxville 1989).
Gilson	David Gilson, *A Bibliography of Jane Austen* (1982).
Glasgow	Glasgow University Library.
Gohdes	Clarence Gohdes, *American Literature in Nineteenth Century England* (Carbondale, Ill. 1944).
Gomme, *Bibliographical Notes* and *Literary Curiosities*	George Laurence Gomme, ed. *The Gentleman's Magazine Library, Being a Classified Collection of the Chief Contents of the Gentleman's Magazine from 1731 to 1868* (Boston n.d., c. 1868) Volumes entitled *Bibliographical Notes* and *Literary Curiosities and Notes.*
Goodhugh	William Goodhugh, *The English Gentleman's Library* (1827).
Goodrich	S. C. Goodrich, *Recollections of a Lifetime* (New York 1856).
Graham	George MacGregor, ed., *The Collected Writings of Dougal Graham* (Glasgow 1883).
Green	Ian Green, *Print and Protestantism in Early Modern England* (Oxford 2000).
Greg, *Companion*	W. W. Greg, *A Companion to Arber* (Oxford 1967).
Greg and Boswell	W. W. Greg and E. Boswell, *Records of the Court of the Stationers' Company, 1576 to 1602* (1930).
Gregory	Benjamin Gregory, *Autobiographical Recollections* (1903).

Griest	Guinevere L. Griest, *Mudie's Circulating Library and the Victorian Novel* (1970).
Groom	Nick Groom, *The Making of Percy's 'Reliques'* (Oxford 1999).
HBA i	Hugh Amory and David D. Hall, eds., *The History of the Book in America i: The Colonial Book in the Atlantic World* (Cambridge 2000).
Hackwood	Frederick William Hackwood, *William Hone, His Life and Times* (1912).
Hansard	T. C. Hansard ed., *The Parliamentary History of England from the Earliest Period to the Year 1803 xvii: AD 1771–1774* (1813).
Harlan	Robert Dale Harlan, 'William Strahan, Eighteenth Century London Printer and Publisher' (unpublished Ph.D. thesis, University of Michigan 1960).
Harriette Wilson	*Memoirs of Harriette Wilson* (1831) Stockdale's eight-volume edition, with much detailed additional information about the trials for piracy and libel. BL.
Herbert	A. S. Herbert, *Historical Catalogue of Printed English Bibles 1525–1961* (1968).
Herford and Simpson	C. H. Herford and Percy Simpson, *Ben Jonson* (Oxford 1927).
Hernlund	Patricia Hernlund, 'Three Bankruptcies in the London Book Trade, 1746–61, Rivington, Knapton, and Osborn' in O. M. Brack, Jr, ed., *Writers, Books and Trade, An Eighteenth Century Miscellany for William B. Todd* (New York 1994).
Houston	R. A. Houston, *Literacy in Early Modern Europe* (1988).
Hughes	Thomas Hughes, *Memoir of Daniel Macmillan* (1883).
Hunt, Mandelbrote, and Shell	*The Book Trade and its Customers, 1450–1900: Historical Essays for Robin Myers,* edited by Arnold Hunt, Giles Mandelbrote and Alison Shell (Winchester 1997).
Jackson	William A. Jackson, *Records of the Court of the Stationers' Company, 1602 to 1640* (1957).

Jerdan	*The Autobiography of William Jerdan* (1852–3).
John Rylands	John Rylands University Library, Manchester.
Johns	Adrian Johns, *The Nature of the Book: Print and Knowledge in the Making* (1998).
Johnson	C. R. Johnson, *Provincial Poetry. 1789–1839* (1992).
Francis R. Johnson	Francis R. Johnson, 'Notes on English Retail Book-Prices 1550–1640' in *The Library* (1950).
John Johnson	John Johnson collection of printed ephemera, publishers' announcements, circulating library catalogues, book club labels, book plates, and other material relating to books and reading, Bodleian.
Jordan and Patten	John O. Jordan and Robert L. Patten, eds., *Literature in the Market Place. Nineteenth Century British Publishing and Reading Practices* (1995).
Judge	Cyril Bathurst Judge, *Elizabethan Book-Pirates* (Harvard 1934).
Kaser	David Kaser, ed., *The Cost Book of Carey and Lea, 1825–1838* (Philadelphia 1963).
Kaufman	Paul Kaufman, *Libraries and their Users, Collected Papers in Library History* (1969).
Keats Circle	*The Keats Circle, Letters and Papers 1816–1878*, edited by Hyder Edward Rollins (Harvard 1848).
Kewes, *Authorship*	Paulina Kewes, *Authorship and Appropriation, Writing for the Stage in England, 1660–1710* (Oxford 1998).
Kewes, *Plagiarism*	Paulina Kewes, ed., *Plagiarism in Early Modern England* (2003).
Keir	David Keir, *The House of Collins* (1952).
King and Stuart	Arthur King and A. F. Stuart, *The House of Warne, One Hundred Years of Publishing* (1965).
Knight, *Old Printer*	Charles Knight, *The Old Printer and the Modern Press* (1854).
Knight, *Passages*	Charles Knight, *Passages of a Working Life* (1864).
Knox	'Henry Knox and the London Book-store in Boston 1771–1774, transcriptions of

correspondence by the editor', *Proceedings of Massachusetts Historical Society,* June 1928.

Korte, Schneider, and Lethbridge — Barbara Korte, Ralf Schneider, and Stephanie Lethbridge, eds., *Anthologies of British Poetry, Critical Perspectives from Literary and Cultural Studies* (Amsterdam and Atlanta, Ga. 2000).

Kubler — George A. Kubler, *A New History of Stereotyping* (New York 1941).

Lackington — *Memoirs of the Forty-Five First Years of James Lackington. The Thirteenth Edition, Corrected and Much Enlarged* (n.d. c. 1810).

Leavis — Q. D. Leavis, *Fiction and the Reading Public* (1939).

Lee — (Lee, John) *Memorial for the Bible Societies in Scotland* (Edinburgh 1824).

Lehmann-Haupt — Hellmut Lehmann-Haupt, *The Book in America* (1952).

Liber A — Typed transcription of the unpublished Stationers' Company confidential ledger known as Liber A. Pollard papers 304, Bodleian.

Linton — W. J. Linton, *James Watson, A Memoir* (1880).

Linton, *Memories* — William James Linton, *Memories* (1895).

(Lister) — *I Know my own Heart, The Diaries of Anne Lister, 1791–1840,* edited by Helena Whitbread (New York 1992).

Liveling — Edward Liveling, *Adventures in Publishing, The House of Ward Lock, 1854–1954* (1954).

Livingston — Carole Rose Livingston, *British Broadside Ballads of the Sixteenth Century: A Catalogue of the Extant Sheets and an Essay* (1991).

Lockhart — J. G. Lockhart, *Memoirs of the Life of Sir Walter Scott, Bart* (one volume edition 1842).

Love — Harold Love, *Scribal Publication in Seventeenth-Century England* (Oxford 1993).

Loewenstein — Joseph Loewenstein, *The Author's Pen, Printing and the Prehistory of Copyright* (Chicago 2002).

Lowndes — William Thomas Lowndes, *The Bibliographer's Manual of English Literature* (new edition 1857–64).

McCalman	Iain McCalman, *Radical Underworld, Prophets, Revolutionaries and Pornographers in London 1795–1840* (1988).
McDougall	Warren McDougall, 'Smugglers, Reprinters and Hot Pursuers' in Myers and Harris, *Spreading.*
MacGillivray	J. R. MacGillivray, *Keats, A Bibliography and Reference Guide with an Essay on Keats's Reputation* (Toronto 1968).
McGrath	Alister McGrath, *In the Beginning, The Story of the King James Bible* (2001).
McKenzie	D. F. McKenzie, 'The Economies of Print, 1550–1750' in *Produzione e Commercio della Carta e del Libro secc. XIII–XVIII.* Istituto Internazionale di Storia Economica (1992).
McKitterick i	David McKitterick, *A History of Cambridge University Press* i: *Printing and the Book Trade in Cambridge, 1534–1698* (Cambridge 1992).
McKitterick ii	*A History of Cambridge University Press* ii: *Scholarship and Commerce, 1698–1872* (Cambridge 1998).
McKitterick 'Ovid'	David McKitterick, '"Ovid with a Littleton"; the Cost of English Books in the Early Seventeenth Century' in *Transactions of the Cambridge Bibliographical Society* (1997).
Manby Smith	Charles Manby Smith, *The Working Man's Way in the World* (1857 reprinted by the Historical Printing Society 1967).
Mann	Alastair J. Mann, *The Scottish Book Trade 1500–1720* (East Linton, 2000).
Marotti	Arthur F. Marotti, *Manuscript, Print, and the English Renaissance Lyric* (Cornell 1995).
Marston	E. Marston, *Sketches of Some Booksellers of the Time of Dr Samuel Johnson* (1902).
Mary Shelley, *Letters*	*The Letters of Mary Wollstonecraft Shelley* edited by Betty T. Bennett (Baltimore 1980–8).
Maxted	Ian Maxted, *The London Book Trade, 1775–1800, A Preliminary Checklist of Members* (1977).

Merriam	Harold G. Merriam, *Edward Moxon, Publisher of Poets* (New York 1939).
Michael	Ian Michael, *The Teaching of English from the Sixteenth Century to 1870* (Cambridge 1987).
Minto	John A. Minto, *History of the Public Library Movement in Great Britain and Ireland* (1932).
Mokyr	Joel Mokyr, *The Gifts of Athena: Historical Origins of the Knowledge Economy* (Princeton 2002).
Morison	Stanley Morison, *John Bell, 1745–1831* (Cambridge 1930).
Moulton	W. F. Moulton, *The History of the English Bible* (n.d.).
Mumby	Frank Arthur Mumby, *Publishing and Bookselling, with a Bibliography by W. H. Peet* (first published 1930, reissued 1934).
Mumby, *Routledge*	F. A. Mumby, *The House of Routledge 1834–1934* (1934).
Myers	Robin Myers, ed., *The Stationers' Company, A History of the Later Years 1800–2000* (2001).
Myers and Harris, *Spreading*	Robin Myers and Michael Harris, eds., *Spreading the Word, The Distribution Networks of Print, 1550–1850* (1990).
Myers and Harris, 1550–1990	Robin Myers and Michael Harris, eds., *The Stationers' Company and the Book Trade, 1550–1990* (1997).
na	information not available.
NLS	National Library of Scotland.
NYPL	New York Public Library.
Neuburg, *Diceys*	Victor E. Neuburg, 'The Diceys and the Chapbook Trade', in *The Library* (1969).
Newberry	Newberry Library, Chicago.
Newcomb	Lori Humphrey Newcomb, *Reading Popular Romance in Early Modern England* (New York 2002).
Nichols	J. Nichols, *Literary Anecdotes of the Eighteenth Century* (1812–16).
PMLA	*Proceedings of the Modern Languages Association of America.*

Plant	Marjorie Plant, *The English Book Trade* (third edition 1974).
Plomer, *Wills*	Henry R. Plomer, *Abstracts from the Wills of English Printers and Stationers from 1492 to 1630* (1903).
Pomeroy	Elizabeth Pomeroy, *The Elizabethan Miscellanies* (Berkeley 1973).
Potter	Esther Potter, 'The London Bookbinding Trade: From Craft to Industry' in *The Library* (1993).
Pottinger	David Thomas Pottinger, *The French Book Trade in the Ancien Régime, 1500–1791* (Cambridge, Mass. 1958).
Raven, *London Booksellers*	James Raven. *London Booksellers and American Customers* (Charleston, SC 2002).
Raven, *Export*	James Raven, 'The Export of Books to Colonial North America' in *Publishing History* 41 (1997).
Rees and Britton	Thomas Rees, *Reminiscences of Literary London from 1779 to 1853* (1896).
Remer	Rosalind Remer, *Printers and Men of Capital. Philadelphia Book Publishers in the New Republic* (Philadelphia 1996).
Richardson	Brian Richardson, *Printing, Writers and Readers in Renaissance Italy* (Cambridge 1999).
Roberts	William Roberts, *Memoirs of the Life and Correspondence of Mrs Hannah More* (1834).
Robinson	Charles E. Robinson, 'Percy Bysshe Shelley, Charles Ollier, and William Blackwood' in *Shelley Revalued*, edited by Kelvin Everest (1983).
Rogers	Pat Rogers, 'Classics and Chapbooks' in *Literacy and Popular Culture in Eighteenth Century England* (1985).
Rollins, *Phoenix Nest*	*The Phoenix Nest, 1593,* edited by Hyder Edward Rollins (Cambridge, Mass. 1931).
Rollins, *England's Helicon*	Hyder Edward Rollins, *England's Helicon, 1600, 1614* (Harvard 1935).
Rose	Mark Rose, *Authors and Owners* (1993).

Roston	Murray Roston, *Biblical Drama in England* (1968).
Rotemberg and Salone	Julio J. Rotemberg and Garth Salone, 'The Cyclical Behavior of Strategic Inventories' in *Quarterly Journal of Economics,* 104: 1 (1989) 73–97.
Ruff	William Ruff, *A Bibliography of the Poetical Works of Sir Walter Scott* (Edinburgh 1936).
Russell's *Moore*	Lord John Russell, *Memoirs, Journal, and Correspondence of Thomas Moore* (1853).
STC	*A Short Title Catalogue of Books Printed in England, Scotland and Ireland: and of English Books Printed Abroad 1475–1640*, first compiled by A. W. Pollard and G. R. Redgrave (second edition, revised and enlarged 1976).
St Clair, *Godwins and Shelleys*	William St Clair, *The Godwins and the Shelleys* (1989).
St Clair, 'Godwin as Bookseller'	William St Clair, 'William Godwin as Children's Bookseller' in Gillian Avery and Julia Briggs, eds., *Children and Their Books* (Oxford 1989).
St Clair, *Byron*	William St Clair, 'The Impact of Byron's Writings, An Evaluative Approach' in Andrew Rutherford, ed., *Byron, Augustan and Romantic* (1990).
Scherer and Ross	Scherer, F. M., and David Ross, *Industrial Market Structure and Economic Performance* (third edition Boston c. 1990).
Select Committee	*Minutes of Evidence Taken before the Select Committee on the Copyright Acts* (House of Commons 1818).
Seng	Peter J. Seng, *The Vocal Songs in the Plays of Shakespeare* (Harvard 1967).
Shaylor	Joseph Shaylor, *The Fascination of Books with Other Papers on Books and Bookselling* (1912).
SC	*Shelley and His Circle: 1773–1822*, edited by K. N. Cameron and others (Cambridge, Mass. 1961–70).
Shelley, *Letters*	*The Letters of Percy Bysshe Shelley*, edited by Frederick L. Jones (Oxford 1964).

Shenfield and Stelzer	John H. Shenfield and Irwin M. Stelzer, *The Antitrust Laws, A Primer* (fourth edition, Washington, DC 2001).
Silver	Rollo G. Silver, *The American Printer, 1787–1825* (Charlottesville 1967).
Smiles	Samuel Smiles, *Memoir and Correspondence of the late John Murray* (1891).
Smith's *Wealth of Nations*	R. H. Campbell, and A. S. Skinner, general eds., W. B. Todd, textual ed., *An Inquiry into the Nature and Causes of the Wealth of Nations* (1976).
Southey, *Life*	Charles Cuthbert Southey, *The Life and Correspondence of Robert Southey* (1850).
Sparke	(Sparke, Michael) *Scintilla, or A Light Broken into darke Warehouses* (1641), reprinted by Arber iv, 35–8.
Spinney	G. H. Spinney, 'Cheap Repository Tracts: Hazard and Marshall Editions' in *The Library* (1939/40).
Spufford	Margaret Spufford, *Small Books and Pleasant Histories* (1981).
Stewart-Murphy	Charlotte A. Stewart-Murphy, *A History of British Circulating Libraries* (Newtown, Pa. 1992).
Stockdale	Eric Stockdale, 'John Almon and the Stockdales 1760–1840', typewritten ms. BL add. mss. 71220.
Stoker	Stoker, David, 'William Procter, Nathaniel Ponder, and the Financing of *Pilgrim's Progress*' in *The Library* (2003) 66.
Strout	[John Gibson Lockhart] *John Bull's Letter to Lord Byron* edited by Alan Lang Strout (Norman Okla. 1947).
Sutherland	Kathryn Sutherland, 'Events . . . have made us a world of readers', chapter 1 of *The Penguin History of Literature, The Romantic Period*, edited by David B. Pirie (1994).
Tegg's *Select Library*	*A Select Library of Books . . . now offered at greatly reduced prices, By Thomas Tegg* bound in a copy of Locke's *An Essay on Human*

	Understanding . . with notes (Twenty-fifth edition 1825), Ac.
Thin	[James Thin] _Reminiscences of Booksellers and Bookselling in Edinburgh in the Time of William IV_ (privately printed 1905).
Thomson	Robert S. Thomson, 'Transmission of English Folksong' (unpublished Ph. D thesis, University of Cambridge 1974).
Thompson	Ralph Thompson, _American Literary Annuals and Gift Books_ (New York 1936).
Tieken-Boon van Ostade	Ingrid Tieken-Boon van Ostade, ed., _Two Hundred Years of Lindley Murray_ (Münster 1996).
Timperley	C. H. Timperley, _A Dictionary of Printers and Printing_ (1839).
Todd	William B. Todd, _A Directory of Printers and Other Allied Trades in London and Vicinity, 1800–1840_ (1972).
Todd and Bowden	William B. Todd and Ann Bowden, _Sir Walter Scott, A Bibliographical History, 1796–1832_ (Oak Knoll, Del. 1998).
Townley	James Townley, _Biblical Anecdotes_ (1813).
Typographia	T.C. Hansard, _Typographia_ (1825).
Vincent	David Vincent, _Literacy and Popular Culture, England, 1750–1914_ (Cambridge 1989).
Vizitelly	Henry Vizitelly, _Glances Back Through Seventy Years_ (1893).
Watt	Tessa Watt, _Cheap Print and Popular Piety, 1550–1640_ (1991).
Webb	R. K. Webb, _The British Working Class Reader, 1790–1820_ (1955).
Welsh	Charles Welsh, _A Bookseller of the Last Century_ (1885).
Wheatley	Henry B. Wheatley, _Prices of Books: An Inquiry into the Changes in the Price of Books which have occurred in England at Different Periods_ (1898).
White	Newman Ivey White, _Shelley, A Biography_ (1947).

Williams	Jane Williams, *The Literary Women of England* (1861).
Wills	Elizabeth Carter Wills, *Federal Copyright Records, 1790–1800* (Washington, DC 1987).
Wing	Donald Goddard Wing, *Short-Title Catalogue of books Printed in England, Scotland, Ireland, Wales, and British America, and of English Books Printed in Other Countries, 1641–1700*, compiled by Donald Wing (second edition, revised and enlarged 1982–98).
Wise	Thomas J. Wise, *A Bibliography of the Writings in Verse and Prose of Lord Byron* (1932).
Wordsworth, *Letters*	*The Letters of William and Dorothy Wordsworth*, edited by Alan G. Hill (Oxford 1988).
Wroot	Herbert E. Wroot, 'A Pioneer in Cheap Literature, William Milner of Halifax' in *The Bookman* (March 1897).
Wroth	Lawrence C. Wroth, *The Colonial Printer* (New York 1931).
Zachs	William Zachs, *The First John Murray* (1998).

CHAPTER I

Reading and its consequences

During the four centuries when printed paper was the only means by which complex texts could be carried in quantity across time and distance, almost everyone believed that reading had vital consequences. Reading, all were sure, shaped the knowledge, the beliefs, the understanding, the opinions, the sense of identity, the loyalties, the moral values, the sensibility, the memories, the dreams, and therefore, ultimately, the actions, of men, women, and children. Reading helped to shape mentalities and to determine the fate of the nation.[1]

But was their assumption correct? Can it be historically validated? And, if so, what are the implications for our understanding of the antecedents that have taken us, as societies, to our present mental states? If the assumption that reading has wide social and political consequences is even only partly valid, then should we not expect the reading of written texts to feature strongly in our explanations of how and why societies change? And, since we can be certain that mentalities are always changing, should we not take a close interest in the governing structures? Although there has always been much interest in the meaning of certain texts, how they came to be written, and in the lives of their authors, little attention has been paid to the processes by which the texts reached the hands, and therefore potentially the minds, of different constituencies of readers. Could histories of reading help us to understand how knowledge was constituted and diffused, how opinions were formed and consolidated, how group identities were constructed, and, more generally, why ideas that at one time seemed mainstream and unassailable could suddenly lose credibility, while others persisted for centuries largely unchallenged? Can we find explanations which apply to the print era as a whole? Can we begin to model the links between texts, books, reading, changing mentalities, and wider historical effects?

[1] For the texts that set out these beliefs in the romantic period see chapters 7, 14 and 16.

The questions I ask are not only of historical interest. The political and economic arrangements governing the production and sale of copies of written texts today (and the production of the many other cultural media invented later) are essentially unchanged since they were devised and put in place in the late fifteenth century and altered in the late eighteenth.[2] These include a presumption that, in addition to some offered free, the supply of copies of written texts should be largely determined by a market divided into two sectors, one for older texts, where the prices, and therefore the extent of access, are set in conditions of economic competition, and another sector for more recent texts, where the prices are set by private intellectual property owners in conditions of state-guaranteed monopoly. The governing structures which began as an economic response to the technology of paper, ink, moveable type, and hand-powered printing presses, are still in place in an age when copies of texts can be reproduced and circulated instantaneously direct from person to person, in limitless numbers, at infinitesimal unit cost. If an historical investigation reveals identifiable systemic links between texts, printed books, reading, mentalities, and wider consequences in the past, we may be able to take a more informed view of the public and private choices that we face in the digital age.

The main tradition of literary and cultural history has been to consider the texts of those authors whose works have subsequently been regarded as the best or the most innovative in a chronological order of first publication.[3] The printed writings of the past have been presented as a parade of great names described from a commentator's box set high above the marching column. Early Modern gives way to the Enlightenment, and then Romanticism. Here come the Augustans, to be followed by the Romantics, and then the Victorians, or whichever other categories are chosen. According to the conventions of this approach, those texts of an age which have later been judged to be 'canonical' in a wide sense, are believed to catch the essence, or some of the essence, of the historical situation from which they emanated. In recent decades this parade model has been supplemented by studies which present the printed texts of a particular historical period as debating and negotiating with one another in a kind of open parliament with all the members participating and listening. Under both the parade

---

[2] The date of the effective outlawing of perpetual intellectual property in printed texts in England and the colonies. Discussed in chapter 6.

[3] The contradictions implicit in traditional literary history are well illustrated by David Perkins, *Is Literary History Possible?* (Baltimore 1992).

and parliament conventions, the historian makes his or her own selection of texts to be included and may draw on other evidence besides the written word. Both approaches can be linked, although they need not be, with critical and hermeneutic analyses which are not time specific, employing, for example, psycho-analytic theories to excavate hidden meanings, or applying theories of myth to explain the enduring appeal of certain texts and narratives.[4] And all can be situated in their specific historical contexts.

However, as methodologies for understanding how mentalities may have been formed by reading, none of these approaches is satisfactory. For one thing, any study of the consequences of the reading of the past ought to consider the print which was actually read, not some modern selection, whether that selection is derived from judgements of canon or from other modern criteria. Nor can these approaches normally accommodate the fact that the impact of a text on its readers invariably occurred at a different time from when it was first written, and often in very different circumstances, the writing and the reading being separated in some cases by a few days or weeks, but in many others by years or by centuries. Secondly, in describing the reading of a particular period of the past, it cannot be enough to draw solely on the texts written during that period, specially significant though these may have been. Readers have never confined their reading to contemporary texts. Much of the reading that took place in the past, probably the majority, was of texts written or compiled long ago and far away. In both parade and parliament models, newly written printed texts succeed their immediate predecessors, engage intellectually with them, and in some cases defeat or supersede them, and it can be convincingly shown that this happened in certain cases. As far as readers were concerned, however, chronological linearity was not the norm. Not all readers had access to all newly published texts as in the parade or parliament models, nor did they necessarily give equal attention to those texts which they did read.

Furthermore, no historical reader, whatever his or her socio-economic or educational status, read printed texts in the chronological order in which they were first published. This was true even of modern texts. During the romantic period in Great Britain, for example, many readers read the texts of the Enlightenment only after they had been subjected to an intensive school education in the texts of the Counter-Enlightenment, and many

---

[4] For a discussion of author- and text-based approaches, see James Chandler, *England in 1819* (Chicago 1998), part 1.

others, including many women, read the Counter-Enlightenment without having read the Enlightenment at all. If, as we must posit in any historical inquiry into the effects of reading, the engagement between competing texts occurred mainly in the minds of readers, we must expect the trajectories of development to be different from those of the first writings or of the first printings of texts.

But the problem of relating printed texts to reading, cultural formation, and changing mentalities goes deeper than the need to find ways of off-setting the shortcomings of the parade and parliament conventions. While text-based studies can recover an understanding of what it was possible for their authors to think at the time when the texts were composed, they do not necessarily reveal what was thought by their readers. Nor can text-based studies enable us to judge impact. All exclusively text-based approaches, because they either ignore readers altogether, or they derive their readers from the texts, are caught in a closed system. Although they may help us to understand the meanings that the readers of the past may have taken from a text, or ought to have taken if they had been perceptive enough, they cannot, by themselves, without circularity, reveal the meanings that readers historically did construct.

Older readers of newly printed texts had memories going back to their childhood reading and education, and brought expectations to their reading acquired much earlier, whereas others were children whose minds were less fully formed. Any inquiry into the impact of the printed writings of any particular historical period must, therefore, span the reading of a minimum of two or three generations, as individual readers passed through the whole cycle from first reading as a child to ceasing to read in old age or at death. Text-based studies cannot by themselves recover the processes whereby readers filled in the gaps that exist in all texts, how they made their interpretations from their previous base of knowledge and expectations, or how their attitudes and actions may have altered as a consequence. We may find it useful to reconstruct the 'implied reader' addressed by the author, hoped for by the author, or implicit in the rhetorical strategy of the text and paratext. We may helpfully utilise notions of the 'critical reader' who is alert to the multiple meanings and effects of words, knowledgeable about the generic conventions of texts and intertextuality, and who picks up veiled allusions, hidden metaphor, ambiguities, underlying ideologies, and other subtleties. We may confidently accept the existence of 'communities of interpretation' who bring shared preconceptions and expectations about texts and genres to the act of reading, and accept as a premise that readers were normally much constrained in the meanings they created and accepted.

We may reasonably assume too that strategies were often successful in pre-setting expectations and responses, and that some readers may have devoted considerable efforts to trying to build a full and balanced critical understanding of the meanings of the texts which they read.[5] However, the general point seems to me to be incontestable that we cannot, without circularity, recover the range of actual responses to the reading of printed texts without information from outside the texts.

Without implying that the reactions of readers were independent of the texts being read, we need to grant them autonomy. If we wish to investigate the consequences of reading, we need to recognise that readers had freedom, within their circumstances, to choose which texts to read and which passages to give most attention to, to skip, to argue, to resist, to read against the grain, to be influenced by irrelevancies, to be careless, to misunderstand, to be distracted, to slip into dreams, to disagree but to continue reading, to stop reading at any time, and to conclude that the reading had been a waste of time. Readerly autonomy also included the opportunity to pass on opinions and impressions, even if they were ill-informed, confused, or irrelevant, to anyone willing to listen. As far as children were concerned, if our own experience of real children is any guide, their mental responses to the reading of the texts chosen for them by adults were even less constrained.

Reports of individual responses to reading as recorded in letters, diaries, or other documents can help us to break out of the closed circle implicit in exclusively text-based approaches. For that purpose they are invaluable. But anecdotal information raises methodological difficulties of other kinds. When records are plentiful, it is easy to slip into the belief that they are a reliable record of actual acts of reception. It is easy to forget that, however many of such reports are found and collected, they can never be, at best, anything beyond a tiny, randomly surviving, and perhaps highly unrepresentative, sample of the far larger total of acts of reception which were never even turned into words in the mind of the reader let alone recorded in writing.[6] Even if we are willing to regard the written records of individual responses as reliable, as we probably normally should, they too are written texts which were produced by their authors, within the generic conventions of a specific historical time, with implied readers and intended

---

[5] For 'reception theory' and the notion of 'horizons of expectations' as developed by Jauss and Iser, see the summary by Robert Holub, 'Reception Theory, School of Constance' in *The Cambridge History of Literary Criticism*, 8 (1995) 319. An essay by Wolfgang Iser, 'Interaction between Text and Reader' is reprinted in Finkelstein and McCleery 291. For a discussion of different approaches, see William Sherman, *John Dee, The Politics of Reading and Writing in the English Renaissance* (Amherst 1995) 53.

[6] A fuller discussion of the unrepresentative quality of anecdotes is given in chapter 20.

rhetorical effects in mind. The same methodological difficulties apply to the use of published reviews which are often taken as surrogates for 'reception' more generally. Although such reviews may be useful for some purposes, such as reconstructing horizons of readerly expectations, or the dominant discursive frameworks within which a particular text was understood and debated at the time of publication, they cannot be assumed to be representative records of the actual reception of the reviewed text by its many other readers. Nor can we recover actual reading from contemporary advice on reading that is to be found in, say, conduct literature, or by examining literary and visual representations of reading, useful though these sources may also be.[7] In crucial respects, the champions of modern reception theory, which emphasises that it is the reader who makes the meanings, have not yet faced the full implications of their insights. The concept of 'the reader' is needed for any investigation and analysis of a culture just as we need 'the investor' when we try to understand an economy. But whereas the 'investor' of economics is normally deduced from empirical quantitative studies of how real investors have been observed to behave in practice, the 'reader' of modern literary studies is seldom more than the reader implied by the text and the paratext.

How then can we trace the influence of texts, books, and reading without becoming presentist, determinist, circular, or anecdotal? How can we break free from the residual power of the fallacy that readers are the inert recipients of meanings created by authors? If, as I suggest, we conceive of a culture as a complex developing system with many independent but interacting agents, including authors and readers, into which the writing, publication, and subsequent reading of a printed text were interventions, then we need a systems approach to understand it.[8] From a scrutiny of the consolidated empirical records of historic reading we may be able to perceive patterns, to identify hierarchies, and to generate models, partial and provisional though they may have to be. We may be able to develop a conceptual framework from which provisional conclusions can be drawn, the data interrogated and re-interrogated, and the models themselves tested and refined.

The difficulties of applying such an approach in practice are severe. Although concepts such as idea, attitude, opinion, belief, feeling, value,

---

[7] Discussed in chapters 14 and 19.

[8] The basic notions of systems thinking are summarised by Peter Checkland, *Systems Thinking, Systems Practice* (revised edition 1991). 'The central concept of system . . . embodies the idea of a set of elements connected together to form a whole, this showing properties of the whole, rather than properties of its component parts. Systems thinking is . . . the use of a particular set of ideas to try to understand the world's complexity – an epistemology which, when applied to human activity, is based upon the four basic ideas: emergence, hierarchy, communication, and control, as characteristics of systems.'

world-view, cultural change, and mentality are serviceable within their limits, there are few easily identifiable units which can be traced through the system. In the case of texts which contain an identifiable cluster of new ideas, such as Adam Smith's *Inquiry into the Nature and Causes of the Wealth of Nations*, we can use normal historical techniques to try to trace how the ideas were spread within society, advocated by converts, adopted by policy-makers, and carried into effect, just as we can to trace the invention, development, and industrial application of a newly invented technology such as the printing press or the steam engine.[9] In the case of most texts, however, and especially the texts of imaginative literature, that were always amongst the most often read, it is hard to identify any but the loosest clusters of ideas, and when we try to trace them into the busy world of mentalities, we quickly lose sight of them in the crowd. Even when we believe we can trace the ideas of one text, we know that readers seldom, if ever, read only one text, and that the meanings offered by the range of texts that they read was seldom fully consistent with one another. Then there is feedback, perhaps the most intractable of all the methodological problems that arise in tracing ideas. Printed texts are the products of their times as well as helping to shape them, authors have potential readers in mind when they write, readers bring expectations to their reading, the environment in which ideas prosper and perish is itself, to a large extent, an outcome of mental factors, including reading, and the notion of a national or group 'culture' implies that there is a large measure of shared stability, as well as development, across the generations.

However, in writing histories of ideas, we have a unit which can be more readily identified and traced. If we could trace print, and understand how certain texts came to be made available in printed form to certain constituencies of buyers and readers, we would have made a good start in narrowing the questions to be addressed in tracing ideas. Books, furthermore, are material goods which were manufactured, sold, rented, and distributed by processes which are receptive to economic as well as to historical analysis. Indeed, since the production and sale of print was the business of an industry with its own economic characteristics, it is to the disciplines and methodologies of the social sciences that we should initially turn. In advocating and adopting this approach, I emphasise that I do not wish to imply that printed books can or should be regarded simply

---

[9] The early publication history of Adam Smith's two main works is summarised in appendix 9 'Adam Smith.' For indications of readership in the romantic period see chapter 13. For an example of a case in which an innovative text which is admired today failed to make much of an impact when it was first published, see the discussion of Wollstonecraft's *Rights of Woman* in chapter 14.

as material goods which were manufactured for sale, nor that the governing structures and customary practices of the printed-book industry were the only, or even the main, determinants of the texts which were made available to be read in printed form. The whole literary system of writing, texts, books, and reading, has to be conceived of as existing within wider historical contexts, including what Bourdieu calls the *habitus* of literary production within which, by the interplay of numerous agents, including authors, publishers, and critics, certain texts are accorded value.[10] Nor do I wish to imply that the authors of the past should be regarded principally as economic agents, or to exclude or downplay the contribution of individual agency at any point of the chain that linked authors with readers. To attempt to match the production of printed texts with the weight of influence of that print or to equate numbers of acts of reading with numbers of transfers of textual meaning would be to revert back to the notion of readers as inert recipients of textual meanings which my approach is intended to correct. It would be simplistic too to expect that models which may help to explain the production, distribution, and sale of books can also explain the states of mind which caused texts to be written or which resulted from the reading of those texts and the subsequent diffusion of the ideas.

But just because a model cannot be run mechanistically to provide a full answer to my questions, to take us, as it were, all the way from the minds of authors, through the materiality of print, to the minds of readers, that does not mean that it cannot produce worthwhile results, let alone that the traditional parade or parliament conventions are to be preferred. There are many other advantages. Although it is always likely to be extremely difficult to judge the extent to which the readers of a particular text may have been influenced by it, we can be certain that those persons who had no access to that text cannot have been directly influenced by it at all, but may have been influenced by many other texts to which they did have access. The possible links between texts, print, reading, and mentalities are not symmetrical. If we could discover who read what, we would have a far more secure basis than exists at present upon which to employ other approaches, including traditional critical scrutiny of texts, to try to understand the appeal and assess the effects. An analysis of the printed-book industry, furthermore, can proceed initially without reference to the nature of the texts being produced, the personal characters or motives of individual participants, the rise and fall of firms, or the claims and explanations offered by contemporaries, however honest and sincere they may have been. If we could elucidate and

---

[10] See Pierre Bourdieu, *The Field of Cultural Production*, edited by Randal Johnson (1993).

model the factors which determined which constituencies of readers had access to which printed texts at which times, we would have advanced from explanations which are textual, local, and time-specific to a fuller and more theoretical understanding. Since much of the study will be concerned with attempting to elucidate the long-term constraints and determinants which affected the materiality of texts, I ask to be excused from repeating these qualifications on the many occasions where they arise.

The largest practical obstacle to writing histories of reading has been the absence, in readily accessible form, of the consolidated and comparative quantitative information that is indispensable to any analysis of the kind I suggest. Although, for Great Britain, we have excellent descriptive bib-liographies and library catalogues of the titles of English-language books known to have been printed since the fifteenth century, we lack information on costs, prices, print runs, and sales. We have no reliable indices of book prices, even in general changes, for periods before the nineteenth century.[11] As the late D. F. McKenzie, one of the founders of modern book history, wrote in his posthumously published work, 'There is still no satisfactory model of the economics of the London [book] trade', and he picked out the lack of information about edition sizes as amongst the worst of many 'crip-pling deficiencies' from which the subject suffers.[12] I know of no studies of how the changing internal trade customs of the book industry, its market-ing policies, and the private intellectual property regime have influenced texts, availability, prices, access, and readerships.

The standard, indeed the only, book on readerships that includes more than a sprinkling of quantified information, remains Richard D. Altick's *The English Common Reader, A Social History of the Mass Reading Public 1800–1900*, an excellent and pioneering work on which I have frequently drawn and which can still be warmly recommended. But Altick wrote nearly half a century ago; he did no archival work but relied on scattered mentions in printed sources; and he made no claim to be offering consoli-dated information or economic analysis. That modern writers on reading have made little or no attempt to update, add to, or look behind Altick is a tribute to the strength of his work, but also shows an unfamiliarity with what would be regarded as the indispensable minimum demanded by prac-titioners in disciplines that attempt to describe, understand, and theorise complex systems. The history of reading is at the stage of astronomy before telescopes, economics before statistics, heavily reliant on a few commonly repeated traditional narratives and favourite anecdotes, but weak on the

---

[11] See Eliot.   [12] *CHBB* iv, 553, 556.

Figure 1. 'Industry'. An allegory of how all knowledge in the arts and sciences depends upon printed books. On the right is an English printing shop in the age of moveable type, showing the writing, composing, type-setting, inking, drying, and pressing. From George Bickham, *The Universal Penman* (1735–41).

spade-work of basic empirical research, quantification, consolidation, and scrutiny of primary information, upon which both narrative history and theory ought to rest.[13]

Although, in the present state of knowledge, it is impossible to write general histories of reading, we may be able to answer at least some of the main questions by making a formal case study of the reading of a particular historical period in a specific culture. Provided it is large enough to encompass both the long-term governing structures and the long-run consequences, a study of one historical period may yield results which have a wider applicability. The period which I have chosen as the central case for my inquiry is the romantic period in Great Britain, roughly the years between the 1790s and the 1830s, a remarkably rich and distinctive period of literary and intellectual history, as contemporaries knew, and one of great change. Suddenly, towards the end of the eighteenth century, the number of men, women, and children who read printed texts began to grow rapidly. The more highly educated members of society read more books, journals, and newspapers

---

[13] See the useful collection of Finkelstein and McCleery.

than ever before and on a wider range of subjects. Lower-income groups, whose reading had long been the English-language Bible, short chapbooks, and ballads, now had access to other print including book-length literary texts. When, at around the same time, school education began to make the reading of extracts of English literature a central part of the curriculum, whole communities were able, by means of reading, to make new imaginative escapes from their immediate here and now. The rapid expansion in reading occurred across all strata of society, whether categorised by income, by occupation, by educational attainment, by geographical location, by age, or by gender.[14] If there are links to be found between texts, reading, and resulting mentalities, that is a time when they are likely to be visible.

It was also a time when reading and its likely consequences caused much worry to those in power. During most of the previous three centuries of the print era, the authorities of the state and church had attempted to influence the textual content of the printed material available to be read within their jurisdictions. In general, they advocated that certain mandatory, approved, or recommended texts should be read carefully, regularly, and frequently, preferably under supervision. Although large numbers of texts which provided stories, news, and entertainment were permitted to circulate so long as they did not pass certain limits, reading was seen mainly as a means of advancing religion, morality, and knowledge. There seems always to have been a large, politically powerful, constituency that wished to discourage reading altogether, particularly among the less-well educated.[15] By the end of the eighteenth century, however, not only was more reading occurring in Great Britain than ever before but there appeared to be a change in reading practice. There was no slackening in the rapid expansion of newspapers which had begun in the early eighteenth century, and they now sometimes offered political comment and literary reading.[16] As far as books were concerned, many readers seemed now to prefer to read one after another, without giving them much attention, and for pleasure rather than for instruction. Readers were, it appeared, abandoning the ancient practice of 'intensive reading' in favour of 'extensive reading'.[17] Furthermore, some of the books were textually near or beyond the limits which those in authority regarded as desirable. Similar changes have been noted as

---

[14] For a fuller discussion of the growth of reading in Great Britain see chapter 6, and in English-speaking North America, chapter 19. For the change in the nature of textbooks used in school teaching, see chapter 7.

[15] See chapter 17.   [16] See chapter 5 and the statistics of periodical production in appendix 8.

[17] The originator of this useful distinction was Rolf Engelsing, *Der Bürger als Leser, 1500–1800* (Stuttgart 1974). Some of the contemporary German comments on the point are quoted and translated by Blanning 133.

occurring at around the same time in other countries in northern Europe and America.[18]

For the romantic period we also have a body of contemporary comment on the effects of reading on minds and on subsequent behaviour. Surprised by the suddenness and scale of the change, the politicians, churchmen, teachers, authors, and journalists of the time anxiously weighed the benefits and the dangers. Should the prospect of a more informed population be welcomed as a liberation from ignorance? Could reading help to bind the nation into a more secure cultural and political consensus, and so enable it to escape the violent revolutions which had engulfed France and other countries? Or, as others feared, would the spread of new ideas carried by print destabilise the precarious constructions of belief on which existing political, economic, social, and gender relationships were founded?[19] Would the result be unrealisable demands for greater participation from groups hitherto excluded from decisions which affected them, leading to disappointment, unrest, violence, and national disaster? The romantic period was to see the last sustained attempt by the British state to control the minds of the British people by controlling the print to which they had access.[20]

Among those whose views are recorded, who were mostly from the higher-income groups, there was much common ground. They were more worried about book-length texts than by newspapers, partly because the state had taken effective fiscal measures to discourage them and had tried to outlaw some altogether.[21] The reading of books about ancient history, geography, science, and technology would, many considered, produce benefits, as would the reading of the English-language Bible and associated religious works. They disliked the philosophical and historical works of the European Enlightenment which questioned or undermined accepted beliefs, and the pamphlets on current topics which encouraged readers to believe that they could contribute to public debates. Feared too was the reading of plays, poetry, and novels, and other 'romance' which offered readers means of escape into attractive alternative worlds. When literature elevated the feelings of readers, many believed, it could help to sustain

---

[18] See Reinhard Wittman, 'Was there a Reading Revolution at the End of the Eighteenth Century?' in Cavallo and Chartier 284. For the sharp increase in titles published in Germany from about 1760, see the summary by Blanning 142. For North America see chapter 19.

[19] The general anxieties about reading can be seen most vividly in conduct literature, in prefaces to books intended for children and young people, and in school textbooks. See chapters 14 and 17.

[20] For the fear of the political effects of literacy and reading, and the attempts of the British state in the romantic period to control minds by controlling reading, see chapter 16.

[21] For state measures against newspapers, see chapter 16. For newspaper societies, chapter 13.

religious and moral values. But when it conferred an apparent legitimacy on ideas, emotions, and types of behaviour which readers had not previously seen articulated and fixed in print, it became dangerously unsettling.

By the 1820s, it was clear that the surge in reading was not a temporary blip which would soon level off or go into reverse. The romantic period marked the start of a continuing, self-sustaining, expansion, a take-off in the nation's reading equivalent to the take-off in manufacturing production which accelerated at about the same time. By the turn of the nineteenth century, virtually everyone read books, magazines, and newspapers on a regular basis. In the single century Great Britain became a reading nation, one of only a handful to do so at that time.[22] The change had occurred in spite of a rapid growth in the size of the population as a whole, and was well under way long before the industrialisation of print manufacturing, universal primary education, and free public libraries.

The take-off in reading in Great Britain has not yet, I would say, been satisfactorily described, nor do we yet have adequate explanations for how or why it occurred when it did. I hope that my study will help to elucidate the issues. However, in order to identify the governing structures which determined the texts that were made available for reading in the romantic period, I have to start several centuries before. I also need to carry the analysis briefly through to the end of the Victorian period, which is when we should expect the effects on mentalities of romantic-period reading to be most visible, and which, as it happened, was also the time when the most famous authors of the romantic period were most read.[23] By 1914, with the arrival of cinema and radio, the uniqueness and hegemony of print was being rapidly eroded, so making any attempt to trace texts and ideas even harder.

In the phrase 'reading nation', I include the men, women, and children in Great Britain, and to a lesser extent, other English-speaking communities in Ireland, North America and elsewhere, who regularly read English-language printed books. Within this English-speaking and English-language-reading world there was both a large degree of political and cultural common-ality and a constant exchange both of texts and of books. The reading nation, in the sense I have chosen, was probably always far smaller than the 'literate nation', among whom I include those many others whose reading was largely confined to the reading of commercial documents, manuscript ledgers, accounts, and letters directly associated with their employment, and

---

[22] For the continuing growth of literacy and of reading in the Victorian age, see especially Vincent.
[23] See chapter 21.

to the reading of newspapers.[24] The non-reading nation consisted of those members of society whose experiences of written texts were mainly oral and visual, although almost all were also influenced, at school or in church, by texts which derived from printed books. For many men, women, and children of the print era, reading was the only escape from the mental village into which they were born. The boundaries between the non-reading, the literate, and the reading nations as I have defined them for the purposes of the present study, were unmarked, unpatrolled, and constantly shifting, as children, men, and women extended the range of their reading. While concentrating on the romantic period in Great Britain, therefore, the study spans several centuries of the print era in the wider English-speaking world.

It would, of course, have been possible to draw these chronological, geographical, and conceptual boundaries at different places. The largest long-term change brought about by the coming of print, the archival record shows, was the astonishingly rapid growth of periodical publications, journals and newspapers.[25] I believe however that my approach of concentrating on books, not only enables long-run systemic features to be identified, but it also allows for the dynamism which occurs both within social groups, as cohorts of children learned to read long texts for the first time and older people ceased to read, and between groups, as new constituencies joined the expanding reading nation. For the romantic period the number of readers, particularly among the higher income groups, was still small compared with later, and a great deal is retrievable about their reading, values, opinions, and attitudes. In attempting to write quantified histories of reading and its effects, and developing a fuller understanding of the political economy of texts, books, readers, cultural formation, and resulting mentalities, the romantic period in the English-speaking world is as promising a central case as we are likely to find.

The first task, without which the inquiry could not have been attempted, has been to establish and consolidate a reasonably comprehensive foundation of quantified information on the production, prices, edition sizes, sales, and circulation of books and other print. I have, accordingly, searched for and examined as many primary sources as I could discover in which such information is to be found, mainly the commercial records of publishing and printing firms. It turns out that over fifty relevant manuscript archives

---

[24] For the difficulties of measuring literacy and relating literacy to reading, see Roger Chartier, 'The Practical Impact of Writing' in Finkelstein and McCleery 118. For the extent to which orality interacted with literacy in early modern England, see Fox.
[25] See appendix 8.

have survived, far more than is generally realised, that most have seldom been explored, and some never.[26] In addition I have studied the printed or microfilmed transcripts of other relevant archives, including those of the Stationers' Company.[27] As far as the romantic period is concerned, with the exception of the specialist books of the university presses, on which I have relied on secondary reports, I am not aware of the existence of any archival sources which are likely to yield information on the kind needed besides those on which I have drawn in the study.

Although most of the printing and publishing archives which survive are incomplete or fragmentary, and in some cases consist of a single ledger, taken as a whole the record of books produced in the romantic period, is astonishingly full.[28] It has also been possible to find archival information about the comparative sales of periodicals including newspapers.[29] There are, in addition, numerous individual records scattered in printed books, such as collections of printed letters and biographies of authors, on which I have also drawn. Although, except when nothing else has survived, scattered anecdotal information, whose representative quality is necessarily always suspect, can be no substitute for information systematically collected from archives, it has helped to fill gaps. For distribution, renting, and circulation, I have examined the manuscript archival records of a number of commercial lending libraries, book clubs, and mechanics institute libraries, which can be linked to the quantified information now becoming available online on the Library History Database. I have also examined several hundred early nineteenth-century manuscript commonplace books, another primary source which, partly because these private self-made books are seldom found in institutional libraries, has never previously been systematically considered.[30]

For retail book prices, I have used the printed trade catalogues of the book industry, some of which only survive in unique copies.[31] Also highly relevant have been the collections of printed prospectuses, advertisements, and other ephemeral print relating to the marketing and sales of books in the libraries of Reading and Oxford universities and elsewhere.[32] These can, to some extent, be matched with the printed catalogues of titles and prices which were sometimes bound into books or were printed on their

---

[26] See bibliography: 'Manuscript archives of publishers, printers, and booksellers'.
[27] See bibliography: 'Transcribed archival sources, and printed works containing archival information'.
[28] See appendices 7 and 9.   [29] See appendix 8.
[30] See bibliography: 'Libraries' and individuals' manuscript archives and other collections of manuscripts relating to books and reading', discussed in chapter 12.
[31] See bibliography: 'Book trade catalogues' and 'Book trade catalogues. Popular literature'.
[32] See bibliography: 'Rare and ephemeral printed sources'.

temporary covers but were usually removed when the books were rebound, and are, as a result, seldom found in institutional libraries. This source is particularly valuable for the large quantum of book production which took place outside the mainstream London industry, including pirate and offshore publishing, which were not included in trade catalogues or regularly acquired by libraries.[33] Central too to the analysis of the economic behaviour of the industry are the catalogues of the closed trade sales at which the London publishing syndicates auctioned intellectual properties among themselves, of which a few copies, with the achieved prices marked in manuscript, survive in different locations, but which together make a reasonably complete run.[34] These catalogues have enabled me to calculate the changing monetary value of particular intellectual properties, such as those in Shakespeare.[35]

Taken together, the archival and trade sources have not only enabled me to build the quantified factual foundation of costs, prices, print runs, textual controls and intellectual property which is indispensable to my approach, but they also permit a reasonably full analysis of the economics of the book industry during the age of print to be carried out. Rather than referring my readers back, unassisted, to the scattered sources, I have digested the information into a series of appendices. These appendices offer quantified information on all the main genres of printed texts produced during the periods with which I am principally concerned of a comprehensiveness never previously attempted. Extensive although they are, however, they are still necessarily a selection, and the information can be added to by anyone who chooses to do the spade-work.[36] My aim in making and publishing the present appendices has not been to pile up pieces of information for its own sake but to provide the indispensable factual basis which enables the archival and printed record to be interrogated, patterns discerned, trends and turning points identified, and emerging conclusions offered and tested. In many cases I have included worked examples selected for their potential usefulness in filling gaps.

By constructing a standard for a typical income of a gentleman in the romantic period, I offer an easy methodology for my readers to assess the impact of the book prices of that time against the then prevailing levels of income and distribution of wealth.[37] I also set out in what I hope is easily

---

[33] Discussed in chapters 16 and 17.
[34] See bibliography: 'Closed book industry marked auction sale catalogues with achieved prices marked in manuscript'.
[35] See chapter 8.   [36] For my suggestions see chapter 22.
[37] See chapter 11. See also 457 for a note about money.

usable summaries consolidated information on some of the main economic and regulatory features which determined, or greatly influenced, the nature and behaviour of the printed-book industry, and therefore the nature of texts made available, prices, access and readerships. They include information on production costs, book-renting facilities, the effects on texts of changes in manufacturing technologies, such as the introduction of stereotyping, and the constantly changing regime of state textual controls, fiscal disincentives, and private intellectual property. By engaging directly with this material and the patterns it reveals, I have, on many occasions, come to conclusions which differ from those of literary, cultural, or book historians whose methodological approaches have been different and whose informational base has necessarily been more limited. By including plentiful cross-references in the narrative, I hope to enable my own readers to appreciate the interlocking characteristics of the historic reading system, and to assist them in their intellectual engagement with the evidence. Since they provide information not previously available or consolidated, the appendices are therefore a resource which can be used for helping to answer questions other than those addressed in the present study. Tabular presentation, although seldom used in traditional literary history, has many advantages. It enables factual and statistical material to be presented in non-hierarchical form in ways which reveal long-term historical developments; it provides opportunities for both my empirical foundation and my provisional results to be assessed, added to, replicated, or modified.

The information I have collected and consolidated has enabled my study to proceed systemically, bottom-up from empirical data to identification of patterns to general conclusions, rather than in the top-down mode of proffering generalisations illustrated by examples adopted by predecessors. They not only liberate both me and my readers from a dependency on the univocalism of linear narrative, but unlock the material for other research purposes, so that, my readers, if they choose, can make their own creative searches for other long-run structures, emerging patterns, historical conclusions, and potentially usable models.

For material of this kind, web publication, as a medium, has advantages over print, notably the comparative ease with which additions, corrections, and modifications can be incorporated, and the opportunity an electronic medium gives readers to make searches. I have considered publishing it separately online. Such a method of publication would have enabled the database which I am able to present to be larger and fuller. However, since not all my readers will either have ready access to an online medium or feel the need to consult the factual data base to the same extent, I have decided to include the appendices at the end of the book, with occasional summarising tables in text. Although I may decide to put the fuller information online later, and so enable the appendices to become the core of a growing research resource, my chosen method of presentation gives my readers the advantages and conveniences of the printed codex, a form of text-copying whose demise has long been predicted but which still appears to be in robust good health.

CHAPTER 2

Economic characteristics of the printed-book industry

When we examine the statistics of British book production, book prices, and book sales collected and consolidated in the appendices and tables, the patterns that emerge suggest two general economic propositions, neither of which should cause surprise.[1] First, for books sold by willing sellers to willing buyers in reasonably open markets, there is a strong correlation between the price at which a particular book was offered for sale and the number of copies sold. In general, across the whole print era, the higher the price, the smaller the sales, with a few exceptional titles in high demand even at high prices, and a few others unsaleable at low prices except as waste paper. The demand curve facing sellers of new books has normally been of much the same shape as that for other manufactured goods.

In the case of many individual titles, by comparing recorded print runs with sales, we can reconstruct both the demand curve that producers judged that they were facing at the time of publication or reprinting, and the demand curve they turned out to have faced in practice. In a few cases, the demand proved higher than expected, in others lower. Usually a high proportion, often as much as half, of the sales of any edition occurred soon after publication, a factor which was built into the publishers' commercial judgements, but copies were sometimes kept available for years or decades, selling slowly until stocks were exhausted. Titles which were printed more than once seem always to have been a small minority. With some exceptions, the archival record suggests that the response of buyers and readers could seldom be confidently predicted.

The demand curve for printed books as a whole looks very steep in Great Britain in the century before the romantic period, showing that the reading nation was at that time concentrated among the higher income groups and the number of additional copies which were sold if the price was reduced was

---

[1] This emerges from the information in appendices 1, 6, 7, 10, 12, 13, and elsewhere.

modest.[2] In the romantic period, the curve became progressively less steep as more books were sold in smaller formats in the lower price ranges, and this trend seems to have continued right through the nineteenth century. By late Victorian times, aided by productivity improvements in the technology of book manufacture and by the reduction in some of the factor costs such as paper and taxes, we see printed texts of out-of-copyright authors such as Shakespeare being profitably sold at 10 per cent or less of the minimum price of a century earlier, while at the same time the real price of copyrighted titles continued to rise.[3] In general the statistics suggest that books offered at appropriate prices helped to build demand, inducing a virtuous circle of growth in reading. However, they do not suggest that the size of the reading nation always grew as a proportion of the population, the economy, or the potential market, as is often assumed. On the contrary, the increases in the price of books of the seventeenth century and the trade practices of the eighteenth may have caused the reading nation to contract.[4]

It is sometimes said that it was not until the eighteenth century that a 'reading public' developed, and that only then did the commercial market replace aristocratic patronage as the main driving force.[5] The 'growth of the reading public' has been a common theme since Q. D. Leavis used the phrase in 1939.[6] As far as England is concerned, however, the archival record shows that, already by the early seventeenth century, printer/publishers were amongst the main commissioning agents of new titles, investing their own money in publishing almost all of the texts printed for sale, including Bibles.[7] By that time not only was the English printed-book industry financially self-sufficient, with most of its products being sold commercially without subsidy, but the industry also made substantial payments to the state exchequer, in the form both of taxes and occasional levies, and as payments to the state in the form of investments for the purchase of franchises for exclusive manufacturing and selling rights.[8]

---

[2] See table 11.2 'An indication of the shape of the demand curves, copyrighted books, romantic period. Sales of Moore's *Lalla Rookh*' 198, below.

[3] For Dicks's Victorian paperback editions of Shakespeare, Scott, Byron, and many others, which sold at 1s or 6d (1 or 0.5 shillings), see chapter 21.

[4] Discussed in chapters 5 and 6.

[5] For example, Blanning 9. 'So for the first time, in the eighteenth century, a reading public developed. one sign of this, among many others, was the replacement of aristocratic patrons as commissioning agents.'

[6] Q. D. Leavis, *Fiction and the Reading Public* (1939).   [7] Discussed further in chapter 3.

[8] For example, through taxes on paper but also, in the case of the many compulsory and semi-compulsory texts, by paying capital sums to the state upfront for the monopoly franchises. See chapter 3.

Many printed books, the records show, were not sold in markets involving willing sellers and willing buyers. Since the sixteenth century, it was compulsory for certain purchasers to buy certain texts, such as English-language Bibles and other mandatory religious books, at centrally set prices. There were also other classes of printed texts, notably schoolbooks, which were willingly bought by certain groups, such as parents and teachers, to be compulsorily read by others. Indeed when we look at print runs, one of the largest constituencies of readers during the whole print era has been young people, much of whose reading has been prescribed by adults. Throughout the print era, the archival record also shows that many books were not commercial in the sense that the full costs were recouped from final buyers. During the romantic period, for example, many sermons, political pamphlets, and books of verse were printed at the expense of their authors or their supporters, to be given away free or sold at heavily subsidised prices, a fact that is not usually revealed by the text or paratext of the book.[9] The listing of a printed text in a bibliography or in a library catalogue, this feature should warn us, does not imply that there was any interest in it on the part of buyers or readers.[10] Indeed, in the many cases where we are able to check from archives, it turns out that many of the texts whose printing was paid for by authors seldom reached beyond the author's family and friends.

As far as English print runs of the early modern period are concerned, although the record is fragmentary, a range of 250 to 2,000 copies per edition seems to have been normal, with a few editions with runs as low as 100 or 50 copies, and only very occasionally 5,000 or more.[11] The range was also wide in the case of sixteenth- and seventeenth-century French, and German, and Netherlands printers for whom the archival evidence is fuller.[12] Although the range of print runs per printed edition was quite wide, the range within which edition sizes were chosen looks remarkably steady. The figures for British edition sizes of books in the early nineteenth century were not all that different from those found in the two previous centuries, when the population, the economy, and the market for books were only a fraction of the size it had become. Only in the mid nineteenth century, does the archival record reveal much of a change. In

[9] For non-commercial printed texts, see chapters 11 and 17.
[10] For the example of how the inclusion of privately financed books of verse has tended to distort later opinion about readerships and readerly taste in the romantic period see chapter 9.
[11] See appendix 1.
[12] See 'Print runs, early modern period, examples recorded in archives from elsewhere in Europe', appendix 1, 460.

the age of stereotyping, which coexisted with moveable type for more than a century, the archival record suggests that the range of edition size widens considerably, from 250 to 20,000 from the same plates.[13] Indeed the very concept of 'an edition' loses much of its meaning. If we take the era of the hegemony of the printed book in the English-speaking world as having lasted from around 1500 to around 1900, there are substantial differences between the first three and a half centuries, when the technology was exclusively moveable type and hand presses, and the half century before 1900 when much of the manufacturing consisted of reimpressions from existing plates.

The figures for edition sizes, which appear to be characteristic of the era of moveable type and hand presses throughout Europe, suggest an immediate general conclusion which has far-reaching consequences for our understanding of long-term patterns of reading and of their potential effects.[14] During the manuscript age, when ecclesiastical and university institutions had great influence over the manuscript texts to be copied, hired out, and read by members and students, when many of the books were read on the premises, and when there was little distinction between newly copied and existing books, the total stock of books in use grew with each act of manuscript copying. Furthermore, although there was much new writing, and many institutions and individuals were eager to obtain and copy manuscripts of works to which they did not previously have access, most of the additions to the stock of books brought about by manuscript copying appear to have been further copies of existing texts, especially biblical, patristic, liturgical, homiletic, and ecclesiastical texts.[15] The growth in books and reading brought about by the coming of print, by contrast, took the form of the production of more texts rather than of more copies of existing texts.

That result, if it can be confirmed, was not intrinsic to the system of texts, books, and reading as such. Indeed, we may be sure that at the time of the transition, many political and ecclesiastical leaders would have preferred that the invention should be used to cheapen the cost of access to centrally approved texts and so enable more readers to read them. Since the leaders of the time claimed a monopoly of truth, there was no need to encourage the

---

[13] Discussed in chapter 21.
[14] See chapters 10 and 21.
[15] I make this judgement, which is necessarily highly provisional, from my reading of the descriptions of mediaeval *scriptoria* by Thompson, and Richard H. Rouse and Mary A. Rouse, *Manuscripts and their Makers* (2000), and from the information collected in the *Corpus of British Mediaeval Libraries*.

creation or diffusion of newly written texts as such. Indeed, except within elites, they may have actively preferred the opposite. This sharp change in the trajectory of reading that occurred between the manuscript and the print eras helps to explain why so many of the governments of early modern states, including England, not only tried to control the textual content of printed texts but limited the size, and therefore the total productive capacity, of the printed-book industries that operated within their jurisdictions.

There was, however, an insistent techno-economic fact about moveable type that pushed in the direction of more texts rather than more copies. In deciding the length of the print run to order, the commercial publisher knew that, in general, the longer the run, the lower the unit cost to him of manufacturing a copy of the text, and the wider his profit margin on each copy of the text sold. There was a minimum print run below which a switch to the new technology would not be worthwhile as compared with manuscript copying, but above a certain number the fall in the unit cost to the producer of manufacturing copies by print became much less steep.[16] Of the main cost components that the printer/publisher faced, only the contribution to fixed capital (types and press) and the costs of composing (labour of printers) diminished with scale, the cost of the materials (paper) and the cost of final manufacturing into the books (labour of pressing, folding, stitching, and binding) being largely proportionate to the number of copies ordered. There was also the problem of the pressing. Even when worked by teams of men, hand-pulled presses were always slow. A printer might, if he expected a follow-up order, incur the opportunity costs of keeping the type standing, but neither the printers nor the publishers could avoid the problem of the time taken by hand-pressing. At the margin the problem they faced was always the same. Should the printer/publishers order the manufacture of a large edition right away, so as to be able to catch the market, but risk being left with unsold stocks on their hands, or should they, by going for a more cautious initial print run, risk being unable to supply if demand proved strong?

If reading does indeed play an important part in shaping mentalities, then the transition from manuscript to print offers an immediate case for consideration. If, as is a general impression, mentalities in the European middle ages were more uniform and the speed of innovation and change less dynamic than the early modern period that followed, then the change may be partly attributable not only to the coming of print as such, but

---

[16] See appendix 5.

to the historically specific techno-economic conjuncture of moveable type and hand presses which encouraged the new industry to produce more texts rather than more copies of existing texts.

As far as book prices are concerned, in order to enable comparisons to be made and trends detected, it is useful to translate the records of costs and prices into a single monetary denominator, for which in the English-speaking world during the print era, the English sterling shilling is the most suitable.[17] Despite some short-term fluctuations, throughout the print era, the prices of the commodities which constituted the cost of living in England were remarkably stable, and book prices denominated in shillings can tell us a good deal about relativities, even over quite long time spans, without the need for deflators.[18] As far as new books are concerned, prices throughout the print era ranged from extremely expensive publications to short pieces available to be bought for little more than the cost of the paper. The range of book prices is much wider than that for edition sizes. Throughout the print era, there was also normally a second-hand market, in which the prices of the books were usually at levels below the initial sale price.[19] But sometimes, when a text was not available new, or was only available new in an expensive format, the price of second-hand copies could rise far above the original price, even without any premium for antiquarian rarity. This seems to have happened to printed play texts, including plays by Shakespeare, in the seventeenth century, and to Byron's *English Bards and Scotch Reviewers* in the nineteenth.[20]

The number of titles or editions of which copies have survived, virtually the only measure of output in use by historians, turns out to be a poor indicator of book production. Nor can it be easily reconciled with the other indicators. Measured by the number of surviving titles, English book production between the mid sixteenth and late seventeenth century shows an exponential growth, but we know from the official records of the numbers of presses and of the recruitment of apprentices, that is from reliable measures of the physical capital and human resources employed, that the overall capacity of the industry changed little during the period.[21] The huge difference between the two measures can be best explained by postulating that many more items of print have been lost without trace

---

[17] See 'Currency units', appendix I, 457.
[18] See, for example, B. R. Mitchell, *British Historical Statistics* (1988).
[19] For example through the printed catalogues produced by Lackington and Tegg. See chapter 11 and examples in the bibliography.
[20] See chapters 3 and 9.   [21] *CHBB* iv, 17.

than is generally realised, a finding which, if confirmed, implies that all modern work which uses titles as a measure of book output or of reading is misleading.

The variation in print runs per edition revealed by the archival record has many other implications for our understanding of historic reading patterns. If we wish to estimate the size of the total readership of any printed text, we need to take account of the fact that each book may have been read many times over, by being given or lent to friends, inherited, rented out commercially, sold to the second-hand market, or passed down from one class of school children to its successors. As a matter of simple arithmetic, any differences in print runs per edition, and in cumulative print runs across editions, may have to be multiplied, sometimes by many hundreds of times, when we come to make estimates of total readerships or comparisons between the readerships of different texts.[22] If we wish to trace the diffusion of texts we should, therefore, resist the false appeal of averaging, or of treating recorded numbers of book titles, or of editions printed, as satisfactory measures in any cases when better measures are retrievable or can be more reliably estimated. If we wish to write histories of the reading of texts, the archival record tells us, we need to know as much as we can about the prices and print runs of the books in which the texts were inscribed, information which is seldom to be found either in traditional literary history or in descriptive bibliography.[23]

In many of the cases where the archives enable us to check, publishers and authors turn out to have exaggerated the numbers of copies they say have been sold, especially when the numbers were, in fact, unusually large. In the romantic period, for example, the publisher John Murray seems habitually to have claimed to have sold more editions of works by Byron than his ledgers show were manufactured.[24] Routledge and Warne, competing reprint publishers in Victorian times, seem both to have claimed more than double their actual sales of Longfellow, enormous though they were.[25] Some of the claims made, such as the million and a half copies of part II of Paine's *Rights of Man* (1792) defy credibility when seen in the publishing circumstances of the time as revealed in the archival record, and the historical narratives which have been built on them, and then repeated in secondary historical writings, need to be heavily revised.[26]

---

[22] Discussed further in chapter 13.
[23] The recent bibliography of Scott by Todd and Bowden contains much information on print runs.
[24] See 'Lord Byron', appendix 9, 586.   [25] See appendix 13.
[26] Altick, 70, 381. For a summary of what can be recovered about the publishing of Thomas Paine's main works see 'Thomas Paine', appendix 9, 623–4.

A printed book, whether new or second-hand, might reach the end of its material life by being accidentally or deliberately destroyed, but, in economic terms, the main occasion was when the maximum obtainable price for the book as a carrier of a potentially readable text approached its financial value, or its alternative use value, as waste paper. Throughout the print era, paper was a commodity in its own right. Book-binders used paper from unsold new books to stiffen bindings, box-makers and trunk-makers needed it for linings. Indeed so dependent were the trunk-makers on the book industry that they were located in the same district of London, and we hear of dynastic marriages between the leaders of the two industries.[27] Byron may have been telling the truth when he said he read the eleventh book of Sir James Burgess's epic poem, *Richard the First*, from the lining of his trunk when he was ill in Malta in 1811, 'If this be doubted', he wrote, 'I shall buy a portmanteau to quote from.'[28] Grocers and bakers too liked book paper, preferably new, for wrapping butter and cakes. James Lackington, an outsider bookseller at the end of the eighteenth century whose frank *Memoirs* were much disliked by his colleagues, tells that when customers tried to buy his book at the regular bookshops, they were refused. Their shops did not stock it, the booksellers sneered, they already had too much waste paper; 'and some kindly added, "You need not be in haste to purchase, as in the course of the Christmas holidays, Mr Birch in Cornhill will wrap up all his mince pies with them."'[29] Wordsworth's poems were frequently remaindered as Byron wrote gleefully to Thomas Moore.[30]

> Of Turdsworth the great Metaquizzical poet
> A man of vast merit, though few people know it;
> The perusal of whom (as I told you at Mestri)
> I owe, in great part, to my passion for pastry.[31]

The jibe about pastry cooks was already common in first-century Rome, and need not be taken literally.[32] But the value of books as paper sometimes did exceed their value as material carriers of readable texts. In the American Revolution, most of the 3,000 copies of Saur's 1776 German Bible were

[27] Simon Roscoe, *John Newbery and his Successors, 1740–1814* (1973) 14.
[28] In *Some Observations* (1820) in Byron, *Prose Works* 106. See also Byron, *Letters and Journals* viii, 12. Sometimes Byron said it was the first or the tenth book he read.
[29] Lackington. Preface to the second and subsequent editions.
[30] For the modest sales and heavy remaindering of Wordsworth see 'William Wordsworth', appendix 9, 660–4.
[31] Written in 1821. Byron, *Poetical Works*, no. 363. Mestri was one of the places where travellers went by ferry to Venice. The name was chosen for reasons of rhyme. Byron later admitted that it was while on the other ferry, that from Fusina, that he made his joke.
[32] It is made, for example, by Martial, *Epigrams* vi, 61.

used to make cartridges for muskets.[33] In Britain during the Revolutionary and Napoleonic wars, when shipping was expensive and uncertain, many older books went to the grocers and cheesemongers – the 'old long winded folio divines were unmercifully sacrificed, along with Greek and Latin fathers, saints, schoolmen, physicians, &'.[34] When William Hone was a boy, he hung around the cheesemongers' shops in hopes of finding occasional printed pages to read – one was an account of the seventeenth-century regicide John Lilburne, which helped decide him on his future career as a political publisher.[35] Until the mid twentieth century every house had an insatiable need for twists of paper for kindling fires, for lighting lamps, relighting the tobacco in pipes, and for innumerable other household uses, including especially lavatory paper. The exit of many unsold new books from the world of texts was assisted by another ancillary industry, the dealers who supplied paper for the 'necessary houses'.[36] Many books ended their existence, as the polite Lord Chesterfield said, as a 'sacrifice to Cloacina'.[37]

Survival rates turn out not to be closely related to the length of time that has passed. Of the many hundreds of broadside ballads recorded as having been printed in the sixteenth century, only a handful have survived, and, with few exceptions, they are ballads produced for special occasions which, when unsold, were used as paper for book binding, rather than the best or the steadiest sellers, the great majority of which are entirely lost or are known only from later reprints.[38] Studies of seventeenth-century ABCs, psalters, and primers, on which we have archival information, show an inverse relationship between price and survival rate, the more expensive versions surviving in far larger numbers proportionally than the cheaper versions. In the year 1676/7, 84,000 school primers are archivally recorded as having been printed, but only one copy is known still to exist.[39] In the eighteenth century, if an account book of Ackers the printer had not fortuitously survived, we would probably not have guessed from the five extant copies of the school textbook, Dyche's *Guide to the English Tongue*, that 265,000 copies were printed during the years when Ackers held the printing contract.[40] Of the many hundreds of thousands of copies of the

---

[33] Timperley 652.   [34] Lackington 261.   [35] Hackwood 40.

[36] See, for example, the reference to the late-seventeenth-century Mr Tyson in Dunton 257.

[37] Lord Chesterfield, *Letters to his Son*, edited by Oliver H. G. Leigh (1926) i, 37.

[38] See Livingston.

[39] See John Barnard, 'The Survival and Loss Rates of Psalms, ABCs, Psalters and Primers from the Stationers' Stock 1660–1700' in *The Library*, 1999.

[40] Quoted by McKenzie 394. Also in *Making the Meaning, "Printers of the Mind" and Other Essays*, edited by Peter D. McDonald and Michael Suarez (Amherst 2002) 85. More copies were produced after Ackers ceased to be the sole printer. Hence the larger estimate I offer in appendix 1, 474.

sixpenny *Soldier's Companion* (1803) which are known to have been printed, all that survive are singletons from the thirty-fifth and sixty-fifth editions.[41] Scarcely any of the many hundreds of thousands of texts which the archives show were sold serially in cheap parts, have survived in that form. Many low-priced editions of Byron's *Don Juan* only survive in single copies, which implies that others are likely to have been lost altogether, and there are records of at least two Victorian editions of Mary Shelley's *Frankenstein* of which no copy has yet been found.[42] In general, we can take it as a stable economic pattern of the whole print era, almost a model which we can use in estimating readerships, that the more common and less expensive a printed text was when it was produced, the greater its readership and the poorer its survival rate to the present day.[43]

The second strong pattern which emerges from the statistics is that there is close correlation between the price of a book when it was first put on sale and the intellectual property regime under which it was produced. In both the eighteenth and the nineteenth centuries, the moment any title still in demand went out of copyright restriction and other publishers were free to reprint it, the minimum price fell and the print runs rose, often by substantial amounts.[44] We also find occasional examples of intellectual property rights being successfully reasserted after a period when no copyright had been enforced, resulting in the price being forced up and sales reduced.[45] Given the correlation with print runs, these differences in prices cannot be dismissed or discounted as of little consequence in the task of retrieving historic reading patterns. On the contrary, the relationship between price and intellectual property status is a long-term stable characteristic of the printed-book industry which has helped to determine the size and composition of readerships throughout the print era. As with price and quantity, the relationship is also as we should expect.

Many writers on the history of books have assumed that it was the costs of manufacture of a book, that is the printing, paper, binding, taxes, plus any payments made to the author, that determined the price.[46] Of course, no industry which sells its products commercially can be indifferent to

---

[41] Blakey 20.   [42] The examples of *Don Juan* and *Frankenstein*, are discussed in chapters 16 and 18.

[43] For an attempt to assess comparative popularity among readers by postulating a positive correlation with survival rates, see *Shakespeare's Sonnets* edited by Katherine Duncan-Jones (1997) 8.

[44] See chapter 5 for the late eighteenth/early nineteenth century. For the spectacular case of Byron's *Don Juan* see chapter 16.

[45] For example the case of the Shelley copyright reasserted in 1839, see appendix 11, 682.

[46] For example Altick 262; Sutherland, ch. 1; Feather, *Publishing* 130; Lee Erickson, *The Economy of Literary Form* (1996) 20, and Peter Garside in Garside, Raven, and Schöwerling ii, 44. For the guild period, when price controls were in operation, the link between costs and prices was more direct.

its costs, and we can be certain that cost considerations always influenced decisions on whether to invest in printing a particular text for sale. However, the records suggest that, in England, at least since the abolition of effective price controls in the early seventeenth century, the relationship between the cost and the price of a book has seldom been a direct one, nor have publishers always, or even normally, chosen the least costly methods of manufacture available to them even within a cost structure in which many of the components, such as printers' wages, were not determined by competitive markets. This is seen most obviously from the wide range of sizes of format adopted, from the varied quality of the printing and of the paper, from the presence or absence of illustrations, and from other optional design features of the books which were offered for sale by producers who were facing the same choice of manufacturing technologies and the same choice of costs. During the romantic period, for example, when some of the factor costs of book manufacturing, including paper, printing, and taxes, were rising, publishers were able to reduce the unit cost of manufacturing out-of-copyright titles in book form by printing them in smaller type and smaller formats, and were able to offer lower retail prices. During the same period, the prices of newly printed copyrighted titles were raised far more steeply than the increase in factor costs of manufacturing would have warranted.[47] In Victorian times, while some book prices fell to levels which made them extremely cheap in real terms by any standard, some others, such as those for newly published novels, stayed high, even after the factor costs of book manufacturing had fallen drastically.[48]

Nor were these differences small. During the romantic period, for example, the cheapest retail price of a book containing a literary work of roughly equivalent length could vary by ten times or more, and by the late Victorian period by sixty times.[49] Nor, the records show, can the large differences in price be explained by differences in the extent to which producers may have spent money on advertising and other selling costs, nor on payments to authors, significant though these often were. Within wide limits, the costs and prices of books, including the extent to which payments were made to authors, were chosen by the publishers, not dictated by circumstances over which they had no control.

What, we therefore need to ask, were the characteristics of printed books which led to these patterns of costs, prices, and therefore of access and readerships? At the risk of stating the obvious, I note that the main asset

---

[47] Discussed in chapter 11.   [48] See chapter 21.   [49] See chapters 11 and 21.

which was sold was the text, that is the readable words inscribed on the paper of the book, or, put another way, the folded paper, the ink, and the binding would have had little sale value if they had not been assembled into a system of readable signs. Since, once created, the text did not have to be recreated with each book manufactured, or each new edition printed, in economic terms the text was a capital asset not an item of consumption, and the income taken was mainly a rent from the text not a profit on the manufacture of the book. The receipts taken by book producers were, therefore, essentially different from those taken by, say, a baker on the baking and sale of bread, where new goods had to be created after each new sale.

The explanation for the relationships between cost, price, and intellectual property revealed by the archival record is straightforward. Intellectual property conferred a monopoly and the right to charge a monopoly price. The producer of a copyrighted book could therefore set whatever price he or she chose, knowing that any customers who wished to buy could not shop around. The publisher of a copyrighted text was therefore in an entirely different commercial situation from that of the publisher of an uncopyrighted book who needed always to take account of the prices being offered by rival producers of the same text. Furthermore, although it is helpful to distinguish the 'producer interest' (authors, publishers, manufacturers, and distributors) from the 'consumer interest' (book purchasers and readers), the material books in which the texts were inscribed were not 'consumed' by the act of reading. On the contrary, many books were highly durable, capable of providing, and often in fact providing, a stream of acts of reading (including acts of listening to a text being read aloud) to many persons over decades and even centuries. Although book production, in economic terms, can therefore be regarded as an accumulation of capital assets, with additions being netted against losses, we cannot equate cumulative production with cumulative reading, let alone with cumulative influence. Many books, although materially durable, lay on the shelves unread, and therefore culturally inert, although capable of quickly reasserting their efficacy if picked up by an interested reader.

Another clarification which may be helpful relates to the concept of 'commodity', a word which, in literary studies, is commonly used to mean goods which were sold commercially, sometimes with the additional connotations suggested by Marx.[50] And, of course, to turn a text written in

---

[50] For useful discussions and applications of the Marxist meaning of 'commodity' to specific cases, see Alexandra Halasz, *The Marketplace of Print, Pamphlets and the Public Sphere in Early Modern England* (Cambridge 1995) and Newcomb.

one copy on paper into a book of which multiple copies are commercially sold is to make a commodity of the text, whether copies are made by manuscript or by print. But the word 'commodity' can also be used in the more precise sense favoured by traders, as a type of primary good, such as coal or sugar, whose characteristics remain much the same however much of it is produced. In the romantic period publishers, authors, and others, the record shows, were sometimes successful in persuading book buyers to regard gothic thrillers, society romances, and the Waverley novels of Walter Scott as reasonably predictable in textual content, uniform in material appearance, and sufficiently mutually substitutable to be 'consumed' week after week like bottles of wine. Historically, however, as a glance at relative sales figures shows, book producers seldom succeeded in 'commodifying' texts in this precise sense to any great extent. On the contrary, although the main texts of the printed copies of a particular work or edition were normally much the same, this was not true of texts or of books as a whole. One of the key economic characteristics of both texts and books is that they are highly differentiated and only mutually substitutable within such wide limits as to make the notion of 'commodity' of limited value.

To regard books as highly differentiated capital assets from which reading services were taken by purchasers and others enables us to form a better understanding of the structures of production, distribution, price, and access that were put in place early in the development of the industry and continued throughout the moveable print era. Since, once bought, books retained not only a value as potentially readable texts, but a resale financial value as material objects, the producers could not assume that they would be able to sell separate copies to every individual who wished to read.[51] This was true even if they had a monopoly and were able to supply the book at a price acceptable to the chosen market. In this respect the book monopolist differed from a monopoly baker who, provided he or she could supply loaves at an acceptable price, could sell them to everyone in the locality who wished to eat bread. With consumption goods, once the initial producers have made their sale, they usually have no interest in the subsequent fate of the product. The baker, for example, having sold his bread to a purchaser, does not have much interest in whether it is the initial purchaser who eats it or someone else, because the bread once sold can only be eaten once. Producers of books, however, always aware that books could be used by many people without diminishing their efficacy as carriers of

---

[51] For a 1514 Italian paratextual plea by an author not to lend, see Richardson 60.

readable texts, could not ignore what happened to their products after they left their hands.

Monopolists who wish to maximise their receipts at minimum risk usually prefer to sell a smaller number of their goods at a higher price than they would in conditions of price competition, the loss of potential income from the lower volume of sales being more than offset by the higher receipts made on each sale. As far as books are concerned, we see from the records that the monopoly owners of texts often first set their prices to take the maximum rent from the topmost tranche of the market, that is the richest buyers, and only when they had satisfied, 'exhausted', that market, did they move down the demand curve to a new position of less high prices and larger sales. When their receipts from that second tranche were exhausted, they sometimes reduced prices further in order to sell to a third, even larger, group of potential customers. In the case of printed books manufactured from hand-made moveable type, that is virtually all books from the fifteenth to the early nineteenth centuries, the selling practice of moving prices in discrete stages down the demand curve, which I propose to call 'tranching down', often coincided with moving from a larger to a smaller manufacturing format as a text was reprinted for a later edition. We find examples of such economic behaviour from the early days of printing, for example with Luther's German Bible of 1522, and successive Italian editions of Dante's *Commedia*.[52] The different formats, which were normally identified by the number of times a printed sheet was folded in the manufacture of the book (folio, quarto, octavo, and duodecimo), can be regarded as descending points on a demand curve, although there might be other differences, for example in the size and readability of the type, the quality of the paper, and the presence or absence of illustrations. Texts printed in England could start their book life as folios, quartos, octavos, duodecimos, or as single sheets. By the eighteenth century, with an increase in the standard size of a manufactured sheet of paper in England, the folio format had become more unwieldy and was largely reserved for books of maps and illustrations. The normal formats then became quarto, octavo, and duodecimo. When, shortly before the middle of the nineteenth century, the printing industry changed much of its manufacturing technology from moveable type to stereotype plates, the selling practice of tranching down by price continued, even although the text of the

[52] For Luther see Mark U. Edwards, Jr, *Printing, Propaganda, and Martin Luther* (Berkeley 1994) 126. See another example, from folio to quarto quoted by John L. Flood, 'The Book in Reformation Germany' in Gilmont 49. For Dante's *Commedia* and other early Italian examples, see Richardson 128.

books as inscribed on the paper remained identical in every tranched-down edition.[53]

For certain texts there were sometimes further tranches to be taken by abridging them into shorter versions, including epitomes, selected extracts, and ballad and chapbook versions, which were manufactured in even smaller formats, and sold at even lower prices. Since abridged texts were usually, in effect, different texts, they were sometimes put on sale simultaneously with the more expensive unabridged versions, the markets for the two versions being sufficiently separate.[54] Other texts were divided into parts which were sold to purchasers at intervals, a form of marketing which can be regarded as tranching down financed by consumer credit. Many books which were commercially disappointing to their producers, in the sense that the whole edition did not sell out, were 'remaindered', that is sold off wholesale after an interval, to become available to be bought retail at reduced prices by customers lower down the income scale than those at whose purses they were initially aimed.

Any selling strategy which involves large differences in price for what is essentially the same object of sale (meaning, in the case of printed books, the same text), can normally only be successful if the customers at the lower price are well separated by time, and preferably also by distance, from those who had earlier been willing to pay the higher price. With English-language Bibles, it was commercially possible for the monopoly producers to offer the same texts at a range of prices simultaneously, but, in general, the owners of a printed text were only able to sell it simultaneously at both high prices and low prices if they could find remote or isolated markets at home or overseas, and prevent the goods sold at the lower price from being brought back for sale in the higher price market. This producer's need to separate the market tranches geographically is particularly acute in the case of the monopolist of durable, but also small and easily moved, capital assets such as books which have a continuing second-hand resale financial value after they are first sold.

Historically, the record shows, book producers in England went to great efforts to control the retail price at which the books were sold, even although they themselves usually sold the books to intermediaries, and not to final customers. As was common with book markets from the manuscript age until the late eighteenth century, we see the producers attempting to combine the new and the second-hand book trades into a single enterprise in

[53] See the discussion of stereotyping and its effects in chapters 10, 15, 16, and 21.
[54] See chapter 4.

which the supply to the market could be managed and price differentials controlled.[55] We see them offering to buy back books in part exchange for new, in order to remove them from the market.[56] We see them, during certain periods, attempting to prevent the growth of a renting sector, and at other times actively promoting one provided it remained within pricing structures which they controlled.[57] As far as the lowest tranches of the market are concerned, where the risk of undermining higher-priced sales may appear disproportionate to the potential returns, we see the producers sometimes withdrawing altogether, or leaving the market to specialists.[58] We also find them destroying books, even when they had a resale value higher than that of waste paper, in order to protect their general pricing and selling structures.[59] All these selling and pricing strategies, which derive from the underlying economics of the book industry in the days of moveable type, are in line both with the generally accepted economic theory of monopoly and competition and with the practices of other monopolistic industries. They all had profound effects on potential access to printed texts and therefore on the nature and composition of readerships.

In order to protect their monopolistic price structures, book producers needed the active co-operation of colleagues in the industry, including both fellow producers and the distributive sector of retail bookshops and commercial lending libraries. From the earliest days, in response to such economic pressures, the English printed-book industry developed strong centralising industry-wide corporate institutions, operating many internal self-imposed regulations and trade customs, particularly relating to restricting competition and maintaining prices. The mutual trust between colleagues in different sectors of the book industry which these structures required often took the form of financial interdependence, particularly overlapping lines of credit. The early printer/publishers, for example, exchanged printed sheets of the books which they produced to colleagues across Europe, preparing advance lists of their publications for industry-wide negotiation at annual trade fairs. The first mention of the first folio edition of Shakespeare of 1623, for example, occurs in a Frankfurt trade catalogue printed a year before publication.[60] The practice of exchanging printed sheets and offering mutual credits, so that expected liabilities were offset in advance by promises to buy, was adopted by every newly founded printed-book industry for which we have archival records, including

---

[55] Notably in the arrangements for supplying commercial lending libraries and book clubs. See chapter 13.
[56] See chapters 5 and 13.   [57] Discussed in chapter 13.   [58] Examples in chapters 4, 5, 8, and 19.
[59] As happened in the high monopoly period and less often later. See chapter 5.   [60] Blayney 8.

fifteenth-century Italy, sixteenth-century England, eighteenth-century Scotland, and the book industry of the newly independent United States.[61]

Much of the credit created within the industry took the form of post-dated promissory notes, which could sometimes be traded for cash in money markets. The book industry was therefore able, to some extent, to create money, markets, and therefore readerships. In those geographical areas where there were few members of the book industry to whom credit could be confidently accorded, such as rural Ireland in the romantic period, books did not reach their markets, even if there were eager customers.[62] In other areas where credit was more reliable, such as colonial America, on the other hand, we see that a large two-way trade could be financed by lines of mutual credit stretching over many years with no need for every purchase to be paid for as such.[63] The development of the English, and later the British, printed-book industry, and the resulting nature of readerships, was, therefore, coincident with, and to a large extent dependent upon, the parallel development of the credit and other financial institutions of modern capitalism. Those countries such as Spain which, for whatever reasons, did not permit such market and credit arrangements to evolve, found their book industries shrink relative to those of others, so slowing the advance of modernity in ideas as well as in economic development.

Under the conventions of property as practised in Europe in recent centuries, the owners of moveable tradeable goods, whether monopolists or not, are usually permitted to sell them, as and when they choose, at whatever price they can get, to any customer they can find willing to buy. With landed property too, the practice of entail, which limited the right to sell, was phased out. Modern capitalism also discourages business practices which restrict the ability of newcomers to enter the industry or inhibit price competition. Many of the customs of the historic book industry in England were, therefore, what, in modern economic parlance, are formally and legally regarded as restrictive trade practices which require to be justified on public-interest grounds if they are to be permitted. For most of the print era, the right to do what one wants with one's own moveable property was central to constructions of Englishness, property and liberty being as ideologically inseparable as love and marriage. The trade practices of the printed-book industry were, therefore, for most of its history also often

---

[61] Incidentally I use the term 'printer/publisher' which is appropriate to the period when the printer was sometimes himself also the publisher or part publisher, for example, John Danter was the printer and also the publisher of the first printed edition of Shakespeare's *Romeo and Juliet*. During the romantic period, many printers were again also the publishers.
[62] See chapter 11.   [63] See chapter 19.

at odds with the prevailing ideologies and philosophies of property in the wider society in which they were operated.[64]

With distribution, as with manufacture, the industry had to operate within the economic and physical constraints imposed by the available technology. How could the producers of highly individuated manufactured products, which were each of high value relative to their weight, find and supply markets which, outside the metropolitan centres, were thinly spread across wide geographical areas? Until the coming of the railways in the mid nineteenth century, by far the most economical way to transport books was by water, either in the semi-manufactured state of unbound printed sheets or bound and ready for final sale, and once a consignment was put on board a ship or a barge it could be taken cheaply to virtually any town that stood on a navigable river or canal.[65] The time that it took for information to be sent from the production centres to arrive, for orders to be placed, and for the goods to reach their destinations, varied with the distance, but, contrary to what is sometimes assumed, the costs of transporting books by water over long distances were seldom high relative to their financial value. Even in wartime, when insurance for ocean voyages was particularly expensive, transport costs from Britain across the Atlantic from dockside to dockside seem normally to have been only a small proportion of the final retail price of a book.[66] Nor did transport costs rise proportionally with distance. Until the end of the romantic period, the economics of sending books from London or Edinburgh to English-speaking markets in North America, the West Indies, India, and later Australasia, was little different from sending them to the main provincial cities in Great Britain and Ireland.

Not all towns had ready access to water transport. Horses could be hired to haul loads in carts or wagons, but only between places connected by satisfactory roads, and the prices of all forms of land haulage were high, even for short journeys. It was, the archival records show, almost as expensive to send books by land from Edinburgh to the port of Leith a few miles away as it was to send them from the dockside in Leith to the dockside in Philadelphia.[67] At least since Elizabethan times, certain types of books manufactured in London were sent to distribution points round the country, where they were sold to chapmen, who then carried them

---

[64] A point made explicitly by the judge Lord Campbell when the lawfulness of the booksellers' pricing practices was adjudicated in 1852. Quoted by Shaylor 31.
[65] Examples in appendix 1 and 5.　　　[66] Discussed also in chapter 19.　　　[67] Examples in appendix 5.

physically on their backs, or on a pack animal, until they were able to sell them to the final buyers. Similar chapman networks existed in Scotland, Ireland, and English-speaking North America, as well as in many other European countries.[68] In addition to the print sold by the English chapmen, the 'walking stationers' of the country, another branch of the network served the towns. The 'flying stationers' and 'mercuries', many of whom were women, ran through the streets, crying and selling the latest ballad or broadside to passers-by. The printed accounts of the latest fatal accidents, crimes, mysteries, and judicial executions, the street literature of the urban poor, were hurriedly written and printed and sold week by week.

Chapmen, pedlars, packmen, hawkers – the words have often been used, more or less interchangeably, with varying degrees of distaste and condescension. In some modern writings it is implied that chapmen were casual vagrants, alongside whom they tended to be classified in statistical surveys, and such direct information as we have confirms that many lived in conditions of near poverty. Some drank, stank, were not too honest, and were unwelcome visitors.[69] In the country areas, however, chapmen were as much a part of the rural economy as blacksmiths, carpenters, or carriers, and they enjoyed traditional rights and privileges, such as a barn roof over their head for the night and the right to lick the porridge pot. It would be a mistake, too, to regard chapmen as near the lowest strata of society. Book chapmen could read and write, skills which were by no means universal. Many young men joined the trade in hopes of becoming rich and at least some succeeded.[70] To become a chapman could be a sign of ambition, a

---

[68] Discussed by Fontaine.

[69] See Spufford, Thomson, and Watt. The most detailed accounts of the actual life of chapmen in the romantic period mainly come from Scotland. Dougal Graham, author of many chapbooks and other works, was himself a chapman in the latter eighteenth century. Some of his experiences are related in *John Cheap the Chapman* in Graham. William Cameron was part chapman part beggar in the first half of the nineteenth century. See John Strathesk, ed., *Hawkie, The Autobiography of a Gangrel* (1888). William Love, another chapman who left an account of his life, claims to have walked twenty miles a day, six days a week, for twenty-five years. *The Autobiography of William Love* (Paisley 1857). For David Love of Nottingham, author of *The Life, Adventures, and Experience of David Love* (Nottingham 1825), see Michael Harris, 'A Few Shillings for Small Books: the Experiences of a flying Stationer in the 18th Century' in Robin Myers and Michael Harris eds., *Censorship and the Control of Print in England and France, 1600–1910* (1992). Harris also makes use of another autobiography, *Some Account of the Travels of John Magee Pedlar* (Paisley 1826).

[70] The examples of chapmen's inventories of the late seventeenth century quoted by Spufford 121, net assets of £20 or £30, seem to me to show that in the circumstances of the day the individuals concerned were not as poor as she assumes. Love and *John Cheap the Chapman* both mention the hopes of riches. For William Urquhart, an example of a 1751 Aberdeenshire chapman found at the time of his death to have been rich, see *Notes and Sketches Illustrative of Northern Rural Life in the Eighteenth Century* (1877), noted by Neuburg, *Diceys* 226.

determination to escape the stultifying monotony of an agricultural worker immobilised in the village of his birth.

Many of the 'walking stationers' or the 'travelling stationers', 'the 'Honourable Company of Walking Stationers' – as they liked to call themselves in contrast with the stationary and flying stationers of the towns – travelled the rural areas on set routes agreed with their local suppliers which, by the eighteenth century, seem increasingly to have coincided with the radial distribution networks for locally published newspapers.[71] The father of Thomas Holcroft, who was a casual chapman in the mid eighteenth century, walked from Ascot Heath to London and back on the same day, a distance of thirty miles between his source of supplies and his market.[72] As much as in the mainstream book industry, the chapman distributors were tied in and new entrants kept out. Some chapmen were almost an employed workforce, travelling salesmen with exclusive dealerships, each with a recognised territory and circuit of fairs which he would defend against any wandering incomers who attempted to poach on his market. In the seventeenth century when all pedlars required a licence, we find references to booksellers being fined for enticing chapmen from colleagues, that is for poaching markets by poaching sales staff.[73]

The constraints on what forms of print could be profitably produced and sold in such circumstances as a regular business were severe. In the mainstream industry, the distributors added about a third to the price at which they bought from the producers. In the chapbook sector, the final retail price was far above the wholesale buying price.[74] In the mainstream industry, financing was by lines of credit. In the chapbook sector, although it seems likely that some chapmen were given some credit, the distributors seem to have provided much of their working capital themselves. They also carried most of the risks, often literally, on their backs. An unexpected rainstorm or an animal tumbling over in the mud could physically ruin a week's stock of unsold books and lose a week's income. Only 'small books', ballads and chapbooks, could normally be fitted within the competing constraints

---

[71] 'Printed for the Company of Walking Stationers' in a copy of *Valentine and Orson* (Nottingham n.d.). 'Printed for the honourable Company of Walking Stationers' in a copy of *London Prentice* (Nottingham n.d.). 'Printed for the benefit of the Travelling Stationers' in a copy of *Friar Bacon* (Derby n.d.). 'Printed for the Walking Stationers' in a copy of *Robinson Crusoe* (Burslem n.d.). 'Printed by C. Sutton for the Flying Stationers' in a copy of *Rhyming Dick* (Nottingham n.d.). All in the Lauriston Castle chapbooks collection.

[72] [William Hazlitt] *Memoirs of Thomas Holcroft* (1816) i, 13. As an incomer trying to break in, Holcroft's father was unsuccessful.

[73] For example Jackson 460, 1617. Licensing under Letters Patent was introduced in England in 1618.

[74] Some figures for the high monopoly period quoted in appendix 1.

of weight, volume, cost, transport cost, and price.[75] The popular rural market was therefore concentrated on the lower tranches of print which included abridgements and books sold in parts or serially in 'numbers'.

The chapmen who distributed and sold books also supplied the scissors, ribbons, perfumes, medicines, and other small manufactured goods which were not made locally. Indeed the alliance between books and pharmaceuticals, industries that shared many economic characteristics, operated continuously from the age of manuscript to the twentieth century.[76] Since no transport system likes to run with an empty load, the chapmen bought as well as sold. They would buy, for example, the hair of village girls, cut off to be sold on to the wigmakers of the towns.[77] Such transactions helped to balance the payments between the urban production centres and the rural periphery. In economic terms, the chapmen were the principal agents in a sophisticated high-volume, low-price, narrow-margin, sector of the book and pharmaceutical industries, sending manufactures to the rural areas and bringing back primary products. For much of the print era the chapbook sector was so different both in its texts and in its production and distribution structures as to constitute a separate sector of the book industry operating in parallel with the mainstream industry. The chapman network was therefore itself a political and cultural as well as economic asset of great potential value to any producer who was able to control the initial sources of supply. The frequent attempts by the state, and later by private groups, to influence the mentalities of the people by controlling the textual content of popular reading frequently involved attempts to monopolise the supply of print passing through the chapman networks.[78]

The long-term effect on reading of these techno-economic structures of production, pricing, and access was to separate the different tranches of the book market, and therefore the texts available to be read by different constituencies of readers, by length of time from first production as well as by socio-economic and educational status. The more substantial the text, the higher up the demand curve it was likely to start its material life. By the time such texts were reprinted for the next tranche down, if they ever were,

---

[75] 'Small books' is the term normally used in the Stationers' Company Registers. The term 'Chapmen's books' is used in the London trade catalogues during the high monopoly period described in chapter 17. 'Chapbook' appears to be a more modern usage.

[76] Graham ii, 100. Hair features in the inventories for an earlier period quoted by Spufford.

[77] An example from 1470 noted by G. H. Putnam, *Books and their Makers during the Middle Ages* (New York 1896) i, 232.

[78] See chapter 4 and appendix 4 for the Ballad Partnership, and chapter 17 for the attempts to change the nature of popular print by taking over the network.

they were usually no longer new, and by the time they reached the lowest socio-economic tranches, as they seldom did, they could be far out-of-date. The archival record shows that these time differences were sometimes to be measured in years, sometimes in decades, and over a large range of popular literature, in centuries.[79]

Book purchasers could, of course, have chosen to spread their book purchases among the newer/more expensive and older/cheaper texts in a mix of their own choosing, and many readers from the higher income groups bought cheap as well as expensive books. But, as far as newly printed texts were concerned, the evidence confirms what we would expect from the width of the price differentials, that such individual book-purchasing strategies were highly exceptional. It is unlikely, for example, that a skilled craftsman in the romantic period, earning two shillings a day, would have spent forty two shillings to buy the latest verse romance of Walter Scott.[80] During an era when the time available to be spent on reading texts of any kind was limited in the case of most readers of the lower income groups to a few daylight hours per week, the opportunity costs were high, both in terms of other texts left unread and other activities foregone. Price, the record suggests, is a good indicator of access.

The layering of readership by time that these structures encouraged not only meant that different socio-economic groups read different texts at intervals of different lengths from the time they were first written, edited, or compiled, but it created a self-reinforcing pattern in which the readerly horizons of expectations also diverged, the economically less-well-off being, on the whole, held back in various stages of obsolescence in their horizons of expectations as well as in the texts they read. On those rare occasions in which the normal structures of intellectual property on production, pricing, and access broke down, and groups of readers from the lower socio-economic groups could read a newly written text soon after it was first printed, the historical impact could be dramatic, as we see from the astonishing spread and influence of the cheap pirated editions of works by Byron and Shelley during the romantic period. Incidentally, by using the word 'obsolete', I do not wish to imply that older texts were *ipso facto* of less literary, or even informational, value, although in such matters as medical advice, or the value of astrological prognostications compared with scientific observation, this was the case.[81]

Ultimately, in economic terms, the producer and consumer interests depended intimately upon each other – without a commercially

---

[79] For the long time gaps see chapters 4 and 17.   [80] See chapter 11.   [81] Discussed in chapter 17.

successful book industry there would have been no books, or fewer books published, distributed, and otherwise made available to be read. Historians of the Stationers' Company have tended to equate the interest of the Company and of its members with the presumed wider public interest.[82] Book historians too have silently assumed that, with some give and take here and there, what was good for authors and publishers was also good for readers. Many have adopted the rhetorical stance of the publishers, repeating, for example, their indignation at 'disorder in the trade', 'interlopers', and 'absurdly low prices', and, in general, uncritically endorsing the producer interest.[83] Biographers too, have often assumed, as Wordsworth did, that copyright was 'good for literature' and 'good for authors.'[84] Intellectual property has existed for so long that it is difficult to imagine a world without it, but it is not intrinsic to authorship, books, or reading as such, but it too came into existence in response to a conjuncture of economic circumstances which came together in the late fifteenth century.

As far as the English-speaking world is concerned, as appendix 2, and the summary in table 3.1, show, the intellectual property regime has changed frequently and drastically over the centuries. The balance struck among the competing interests of the three main producer agents (authors, publishers, and manufacturers), has sometimes been steady for long periods but has frequently moved in favour of one or another, sometimes drastically. The balance between the producer interest and the consumer interest (book purchasers and book readers) has also frequently moved, sometimes to the lasting detriment of large constituencies of readers.[85] The relationship between the industry and the state has also been unstable, textual controls being particularly restrictive in the early modern and in the romantic periods. During the intervals when the normal intellectual property structures temporarily broke down, we can see that the whole economy of writing and reading immediately changed, usually with a proliferation of short new topical printed texts at the expense of longer works.[86] The same phenomenon has been observed in France after intellectual property controls were abolished in 1793.[87] But we can also see that it has often taken decades, and sometimes centuries, for the effects of some changes in the governing

---

[82] Notably Blagden, but similar the assumptions run through much other writing on book history. Arnold Hunt in Hunt, Mandelbrote, and Shell is a notable exception.

[83] Typical quotations taken from Greg, *Companion* 230, Feather, *Publishing*, Blagden, and Hernlund 89. Other writers, e.g. Besterman vii, look back with nostalgia to an eighteenth-century 'golden age of publishing'.

[84] For example Feather, *Publishing* 8.   [85] See chapters 3 and 4.

[86] Notably after 1695. The breakdown in 1641 was corrected almost immediately. See appendix 2, 483.

[87] See Carla Hesse, 'Economic Upheavals in Publishing' in Darnton and Roche 83. See also chapter 22.

intellectual property structures to work their way through into the nature of texts, production, prices, access, reading, and therefore, potentially, into mentalities.[88]

Any investigation into the effects of reading, these patterns suggest, needs therefore to address questions which are both long-run and structural, and chronologically, locally, and culturally specific. Although much has been written about the origin and development of the modern notion of plagiarism, authorial copyright, and the emergence of 'the author' as the perceived prime creator of literary production, almost all of it is written from the producer point of view. I am not aware of any published quantitative or economic analysis of the effects of the changing intellectual property regime on texts, prices, access, and readerships.[89] If we start with the aim of my inquiry, the argument runs as follows. To help to understand and trace the possible effects of reading on mentalities, we need to trace historic reading. To trace readership, we need to trace access. To trace access, we need to trace price. To trace price, we need to trace intellectual property, and to trace intellectual property, we need to trace the changing relationship between the book industry and the state. Most of the texts being read in the romantic period were produced long before. It follows that any study of the determinants of the reading patterns in the romantic period cannot start at the beginning of that period nor even fifty years before. It must explain the historical invention and later development of the concept of intellectual property, examine how it developed and was applied in practice at different times, and attempt to assess how the changes influenced the nature of the texts that were historically made available in printed form to different reading constituencies.

---

[88] See, for example, chapter 4.

[89] For authorial copyright, see the excellent book by Rose. For the increase in complaints about 'plagiary' by authors in the Restoration theatre, see also Kewes, *Authorship*.

CHAPTER 3

Intellectual property

The history of copyright is usually told from the point of view of authors. It is often presented as a grand narrative of prehistory, struggle, set-back, and eventual success.[1] Dickens devoted much effort to the cause of authorial copyright. Wordsworth, late in life, wrote sonnets on the subject. In writing histories of reading, however, it is necessary to investigate the effects of the changing intellectual property regime without preconceptions, paying particular attention to the economic effects on texts, production, prices, and access. The key feature of intellectual property, seen as a business practice, is that the owner of a property has the exclusive right to make copies of a text for sale, a monopoly respected by colleagues in the industry and guaranteed by the state. Infringing intellectual property is a commercial offence, the appropriating of some of the potential financial income which would otherwise accrue to the owner of the monopoly. Intellectual property is different from plagiarism, in which what is appropriated is authorial reputation, although there is an overlap.

The invention of intellectual property in Europe in the fifteenth century can, I suggest, best be explained as part of an economic and business response to the new text-copying technology of print. With manuscript copying, virtually no fixed capital was employed. The owner of a manuscript might charge a fee for allowing it to be copied, or refuse access altogether, but, if agreement was given, all that was needed was the working capital required to finance the work in progress while the text was being copied (pens, ink, paper or vellum, and payment for the labour of the copyist).[2] With copying by print, by contrast, the technology required two new forms

---

[1] Loewenstein describes how some early modern English authors, such as Jonson, were able to take control of their texts and how they should be published, and in that sense, to 'own' them, but they had no formal rights.

[2] Examples of donors to libraries laying down in their wills that the manuscripts books they donated should be made available for copying suggest that permission was not automatic. See G. H. Putnam, *Books and their makers during the Middle Ages* (New York 1896) i, 240.

of capital which were unknown in the manuscript age. It required fixed capital in the form of plant (a stock of hand-made types and a printing press) and also a new form of working capital (the financing of the stocks of copies of manufactured books or of semi-manufactured unbound sheets, as they awaited sale). Unless the pricing structures of the industry enabled all these costs to be recovered over a reasonable time, the advantages of moving to the new text-copying technology could not be realised.

In order to maintain book prices at a level that would allow a profit to be taken, the printer needed the cooperation of other printers. Otherwise, whenever a particular printed text was in demand, another printer might also print it, overstock the market, bring down the price, reduce the profitability of the industry as a whole, and discourage future investment both in the printing of new texts and in print technology as such. Indeed, if unrestricted competition had been permitted, any printer who had paid a fee for a manuscript of an as-yet unprinted work, that is any printer who became an enterprising publisher, would have been put at a cost disadvantage. Although in England, for a short time after the arrival of the new technology, there appears to have been some competitive printing, the first English printer/publishers seem soon to have established internal mutual no-poaching agreements aimed at giving the first printer of any text a monopoly in manufacturing and selling copies.[3]

English authors, editors, and compilers could, as the fragmentary records show, occasionally enjoy a share of the revenues available from making printed copies of the texts they had composed or compiled, but only if they could obtain payment for the outright sale of their manuscript, or some equivalent in kind. But they held no share in the equity of the investment, neither benefiting financially by its commercial success nor losing by its failure. In England, authors and editors soon became, in economic terms, sub-contractors to the text-copying industry. If they shared in the returns from the printing of the texts they had provided, it was capitalised in the fee they received for their manuscript, that is for a material not an intellectual property. Since the English language was almost entirely confined to England and parts of Scotland and Ireland, with most of the potential market within the jurisdiction of the English state, the English industry was able to pre-empt the practice of authors in continental Europe who

---

[3] There may have been competitive printing of *The Ship of Fools*, *Dives and Lazarus*, and Latin–English dictionaries. See Loewenstein 67. In the 1520s there seems to have been still some competition in the printing of texts which made available information on English law, a self-evidently public matter, but all competition had been brought to an end by 1553. *CHBB* iii, 427.

wrote in Latin, such as Erasmus, who sold manuscripts of essentially the same texts to different printer/publishers in different jurisdictions.[4]

Early in the history of the English industry, the ownership of texts passed from the printers to the booksellers, that is from the manufacturers to the investors. The pioneering printers with their highly visible, immobile investments in fixed capital thus soon found themselves, as authors already were, reduced to being fee-paid contractors to entrepreneurs within the book industry who owned and dealt in assets which existed only in the virtual world of agreements, claims, obligations, and promises.[5]

To a greater extent than the producers of consumption goods, the printed-book industry also needed the cooperation of the government, and of the geographically wide enforcement institutions which only the state could provide or guarantee. They needed the state's cooperation, for example, both inland and at the frontiers, to protect the monopoly of their intellectual properties in relation to other producers. The state, in its turn, needed the industry to print and distribute its own texts, including the statutes and decrees by which it governed. Furthermore, however liberal or illiberal the state may have been at different times, it has always felt compelled, as part of its governing function, to delimit, and often to prescribe, the nature of the written texts permitted to circulate within its jurisdiction. Although the state was seldom as monolithic as it later became, but consisted of separate and usually competing institutions, alliances, and individuals, and the degree of coordination and control which it was able to exercise was always incomplete, in the English-speaking world the main branches, governmental, ecclesiastical, and judicial, normally shared a common interest in utilising the medium of print to promote a core official ideology on whose essentials they agreed. If, for convenience, I refer to 'the state' in the many cases where it is not essential to differentiate the different branches, I ask to be excused from repeating these qualifications.

The system of royal 'privileges', another adaptation of a practice well established in other European jurisdictions, gave an English state guarantee

---

[4] David R. Carlson, *English Humanist Books* (1993) 84.

[5] See, for example, the complaint of 1582, which notes that the owners of the best copies 'keepe no printing howse' quoted by Mumby 79, from Arber. George Wither's *Schollers Purgatory* (1623) complains that the booksellers have turned the other members of the industry into slaves, quoted by Mumby 117. For examples of the changing balance of the printers' business, see Bennett, *1558–1603* 272.

to the monopoly right to sell a particular text in printed form.[6] Here again, the fact that use of the English language was limited to countries within the British isles, gave the English industry a strong local advantage. In Italy an author or printer often had to obtain separate privileges from the governments of all the main Italian-speaking states where his text might be printed.[7] In Germany the printer/publishers of Wittenberg had divided the market in the printing of the works of Martin Luther, with each work having the 'privilege' of the local ruler, but that could not prevent Luther's works being quickly reprinted in other jurisdictions.[8] In France, the monopoly privileges granted by various state organisations were, in the early decades of print, invariably for a limited period of around three years and there is evidence of competitive reprinting occurring the moment the privilege expired.[9] The English printer/publishers thus found themselves in a far more favourable position than their equivalents in other European jurisdictions. The main features of a private intellectual property regime were not only in full operation by the early sixteenth century but they could be effectively enforced.

Although, in England, the intellectual property in a text came formally into existence with the act of printing, some of the rights and responsibilities started a little earlier, during the interval between the decision to copy it by print and the actual act of printing. For during that interval it was the duty both of the author and of the prospective intellectual property owner to ensure that the text was in conformity with the current textual controls and industry regulations and to obtain any necessary permissions.[10] Again, the limited use of the English language was an advantage to the English industry and the English state. Whereas in France, the system of textual controls and intellectual property protection formally coalesced so that many books were published 'avec Approbation et Privilège du Roi', in England the state's wish to control texts remained formally separate from the industry's wish to record and police its private property rights, and gaps could

---

[6] The texts of early 'privileges' which were frequently granted in the name of authors or which referred to named book titles, were sometimes printed as part of the paratext, or their existence noted on title pages. For the misreading of these privileges, as guaranteeing the authority of the texts, see Johns 251. For the privileges given in other European jurisdictions see Armstrong.

[7] For the example of Ariosto who obtained at least eight separate privileges see Richardson 41.

[8] See John L. Flood, 'The Book in Reformation Germany' in Gilmont 38.

[9] Armstrong 21 and 199.

[10] For the complex, and changing, relationship between the obtaining of permission, authority, or 'allowance' to print, the granting of a printing licence, and the entering of copies of plays in the Stationers' Company register, see Peter W. M. Blayney, 'The Publication of Playbooks' in *A New History of Early English Drama* edited by John D. Cox and David Scott Kastan (New York 1997).

develop between the two regulatory systems as the romantic period was to reveal.[11]

In England, all of the participants in the textual clearance process, authors, printer/publishers, licensors, and Stationers' Company registrars, shared the responsibility, and all laid themselves open to penalties if they were subsequently judged to have made a wrong decision.[12] Decrees of the seventeenth century extended that shared responsibility to every man or woman who worked in the industry, including binders, sewers, stitchers, retail booksellers, country chapmen, and the men and women who sold printed news in the streets.[13] These arrangements were often compared with those of the pharmaceutical industry with which the book industry was economically similar and commercially closely allied. As George Wither wrote in 1624, a stationer was entrusted to supply the needs of the soul and, like an apothecary who supplied the needs of the body, he was under an obligation not to sell any thing harmful.[14] Throughout the print era, those who wished to forbid the reading of certain texts have used metaphors of poison and disease. The effect of these structures was to encourage personal and corporate self-censorship at all stages in the writing, editing, publishing, manufacturing, selling, distribution, holding, and reading of printed texts.

Long after the arrival of printing in England, when many printed texts still had to be imported, the two commercial text-copying technologies of manuscript and print were able to co-exist.[15] As the local English-printing industry developed, however, the professional scribes or scriveners, who had previously supplied copies of texts by transcribing by hand from manuscript to manuscript, could no longer compete in price terms with the printers for large orders for long texts. Commercial copying by hand became gradually confined to the copying of private, mainly legal, documents for which the number of needed copies remained small, and for which personal authentication was especially important.[16] Some of the printers who did the text-copying soon extended their operations into the commissioning,

[11] See especially the cases of Shelley and Byron discussed in chapter 16.
[12] For the author's responsibility, examples of printer/publishers seeking and paying for the licences, and an example of a licenser in trouble, see W. W. Greg in 'Samuel Harsnett and Hayward's *Henry IV*, 4' in *The Library*, 1956.
[13] See, for example, the 1623 'Proclamation against the disorderly Printing' noted in appendix 2, 482.
[14] Comparing the 'honest stationer' with the 'mere stationer' in *Schollers Purgatory*. Quoted by Arber iv, 16.
[15] Examples in appendix 2.
[16] To provide honest copies of legal documents was the main function of the Scriveners' Company when it was incorporated in 1616. See Francis W. Steer, *History of the Worshipful Company of Scriveners of London* (1973).

financing, storage, distribution, and marketing of printed books, becoming publishers as well as printers, and greatly increasing their economic role. Although in England as elsewhere, therefore, the adoption of text-copying by moveable print was a shift from a more private to a more public culture of books and reading, another result of the change, which has seldom been remarked upon, was to put the beneficial intellectual property ownership of all long written texts into the private hands of the text-copying industry.[17]

But, although, until 1710, intellectual property did not apply to manuscript, we should not assume that 'scribal publication' was always available as an alternative to print, or that it coexisted with print.[18] Although occasional copying for private use could not be prevented, it would be consistent with what we know of the guild system if the two text-copying industries, the scriveners and the printers, had no-poaching agreements. Foregoing his right to make manuscript copies was, for example, a feature of Milton's contract for the publication in print of *Paradise Lost*, nearly two hundred years after the arrival of printing in England.[19] The few seventeenth-century manuscript miscellanies produced by professional *scriptoria* that have survived appear to emphasise on their title pages that the texts have not been printed.[20] With short texts such as songs and music, where it was cheap and easy to make manuscript copies for sale, the printer/publishers were especially concerned that printed texts should not be copied into manuscript for commercial sale. During the eighteenth century, many music publishers paid a large fee to obtain a royal licence forbidding 'copying out in writing', or 'copying out in writing for sale'.[21]

Although the public and the private spheres increasingly came to be separated by the two text-copying technologies, print for publicly available texts sold commercially, manuscript for personal domestic documents kept privately within a household, the regime was not symmetrical. As the prefaces to many English printed books proclaim, their authors welcomed the opportunities offered by print, since it enabled their writings to be made

---

[17] In France, according to Francis M. Higman, 'French-speaking regions, 1520–62' in Gilmont 128. 'Throughout the *ancien régime* editors and printers owned the rights to the text, as can be seen from privileges, almost always granted to an editor or printer, not to an author.'

[18] That until 1774 no intellectual property right, either in law or in customary practice, existed in any literary work before it was printed was made explicitly by Lord Mansfield in his judgement of 1774. See Duppa 49.

[19] Quoted by Rose 27.

[20] For example, *a collection of poems and lampoons/not yet printed: a collection of choice poems . . ./ never printed*. Quoted by W. J. Cameron, 'A late seventeenth-century scriptorium' in *Renaissance and Modern Studies* vii, 1963, 25.

[21] Many examples in the list given in Shef Rogers, 'The Use of Royal Licences for Printing in England, 1695–1760: A Bibliography' in *The Library*, 7th series 1, 2, (2000).

more publicly available and therefore potentially more influential.[22] But those authors who wished to select their readerships by sending manuscript copies to chosen readers, 'scribal publication', could no longer do so with confidence. For it was often then impossible to prevent a manuscript copy falling into the hands of a printer who would print it, assume the intellectual property rights, sell copies to the general public, and frustrate the author's wish to restrict access.[23]

In England, the twin processes of creation and privatisation of intellectual property quickly extended to all written texts for which there was a commercial demand for copies. The owners of manuscripts of the works of Chaucer, Langland, Malory, Gower, and of the other English authors who wrote before the arrival of printing, are unlikely to have realised that, by permitting them to be copied by print, they were allowing the creation of an intellectual property which others would then privately own in perpetuity. An English printer/publisher could also make a reprint, translation, or adaptation of any text printed in Latin or in any of the European vernaculars, and by the act of being the first to print it in England, take it into his private possession. He could take over the intellectual property rights in England of English-language texts first printed in Scotland. The works of Sir David Lindsay, for example, were registered as owned by a member of the London industry when reprinted in London.

One effect of the coming of print to England that has not, as far as I know, been previously noticed, was therefore simultaneously to invent and to privatise the intellectual property rights implicit in much of what is now called popular culture. A ballad singer who, for a small fee, wrote down the text of an old song that had hitherto existed only in manuscript or oral performance, and sold it to a printer, or if he sang it to a printer who wrote it down in manuscript and printed it, had established in that printer's hands a monopoly in the subsequent printing and sale of the printed text of that song. The ballad singer could sell his knowledge only once, and if even one other singer had already been to any printer's shop with the same song, that market was already closed for ever. If the ballad singer attempted to sell

---

[22] Examples quoted in Bennett, *1558 to 1603*.

[23] For 'scribal publication' see Love and Marotti. Many examples of printing purportedly against the wishes of authors are quoted in the three books by Bennett. Other authors, however, whatever their public statements, seem to have welcomed unauthorised printing which enabled them to keep their hands clean of the social stigma with which commercial writing for money was at first associated. For examples of scribal publications which were appropriated and sold commercially by printer/ publishers, see Francis Osborne's *Advice to a Son*, and the Marquis of Halifax's *Advice to a Daughter*, discussed by William St Clair and Irmgard Maassen, ed., *Conduct Literature for Women, 1640–1710* (2002).

manuscript copies, he might find himself in trouble with the printed-book guild, and in any case it was difficult for manuscript copies to compete with either the price or the legibility of printed copies. The first man to print an ancient text took it into his private ownership, and that of his heirs or assigns, for ever, and the only room for dispute later was who had been the first to print it. Here too, the English printers found themselves in a highly favourable position compared with that of their colleagues in France where the whole body of mediaeval romance appears to have been regarded as being in the public domain and its texts sold in conditions of economic competition.[24]

Across the whole range of popular oral and manuscript culture, the English printers of the fifteenth and sixteenth centuries thus found themselves like the first European colonists arriving in a territory which had hitherto been free from European ideas of private property. Just as the first immigrant to fence a tract of ground in a new-found-land became the owner, and his rights of ownership were then guaranteed to him and to his heirs by the colonising state, so the English printers were able to take hitherto unprinted texts into the virtual world of private intellectual property. Or like the English landowners who, step by step, sometimes under ineffectual protest, enclosed the real property of English common lands, and then charged the villagers a rent for grazing their animals on them, the London book industry took into its private ownership much of the traditional common culture of England, and then charged a rent for using it. As the old rhyme put it:

> The law doth punish man or woman
> That steals the goose from off the common,
> but lets the greater felon loose
> Who steals the common from the goose.

Much of the ancient oral ballad culture of England, including pre-Reformation Christmas carols such as *The Holly and the Ivy*, was evidently printed, and the intellectual property rights created and taken into private hands, in the earliest decades of print.[25] And we can catch occasional glimpses of these processes at work. In 1568, for example, the printer Robert Copland advertised for owners of manuscripts and oral performers of stories and songs to come to his printing shop, so that he could buy their manuscripts or write down their words to make a manuscript for printing.[26]

---

[24] I draw this conclusion from remarks in Armstrong 93, but the point requires further research.
[25] See the notable cases of *Guy of Warwick* and *Bevis of Hampton* discussed in chapter 4.
[26] Robert Copland, *Poems* edited by Mary Carpenter Erler (Toronto c. 1993) 87.

Thomas Deloney, a performer of traditional orally transmitted songs, noted one which he caused to be printed and thereby privatised for the first time, 'the Commons of England made this song'.[27]

For a time it seems to have been part of the cooperative arrangements within the print industry that the exclusive right to print and sell copies of a particular text lapsed when all the copies of a particular edition of that text had been sold out. These arrangements can be seen as analogous to other forms of manufacturing in a guild system – who would allow a baker to retain his or her monopoly if he or she had no more bread to sell and other bakers with flour and ovens were ready to supply the market? An author could also contract for a certain number of copies of a text to be manufactured for an agreed price, whether positive or negative, and if and when all the copies had been disposed of, he could reserve the right to contract again for another edition, normally with the same printer. Contracts of this kind are to be found throughout the print era.[28] Milton's contract for the print publication of *Paradise Lost* provides for a payment to Milton and his heirs on every edition in perpetuity.[29] Defoe's contract for the publishing of *Robinson Crusoe* enabled him to benefit from every edition of 1,000 copies.[30] But since, without a specific disclaimer, the act of printing by itself created a private intellectual property, the English printers seem to have preferred to leave the matter unspecific, in effect assuming the exclusive right to reprint a text as part of the initial right to print it. Although an author could own a manuscript, and might complain of plagiarism if another copied his or her words, until 1710 no author could, under English law or customary practice, own a text.

By the early seventeenth century, we see examples of shares of an intellectual property being accepted for official entry in the registers, as well as translation rights, rights to publish a book in some formats only, or for a term of years only, further stages in a continuing process of separating ownership of texts from ownership of books.[31] Gradually the implied private property in an out-of-print title seems to have become normally regarded

[27] In *Jack of Newbury* (1597) 'now first imprinted'. Reprinted from the tenth edition of 1626, reprinted in Deloney 25.
[28] See chapter 8.
[29] The full text, from the original in the BL, is transcribed by Mumby 120. Quoted in part by Rose 27.
[30] The conditions are set out in the trade sale catalogue of 3 October 1725 when the assets of W. Taylor, the original publisher, were sold.
[31] For half shares, see, for example, the entry of 4 August 1608, Arber iii, 386. For a potential translation, registered in 1611, Arber iii, 473. For a 1609 transfer of a right to publish only in sextodecimo (sixteenmo), Arber iii, 412. For a 1619 example of intellectual properties being transferred for a few years only, see Jackson 112.

as an absolute one, which continued dormant in the hands of the original printer and his or her heirs and assigns even if they were unwilling, or unable, to supply the market by reprinting.[32] The 1660 will of the stationer Humphrey Moseley, for example, mentions 'Coppies or Coppies of Books', that is, apparently distinguishing his intellectual from his material properties, among his heritable assets.[33] An inventory made in 1732 of all the assets of Midwinter and Ward, carefully distinguished their 'copies' from their books, and some of the 'copies' were valued at nil.[34] If, as happened in the eighteenth century with Milton's prose works, a text had been so long out of print that no publisher could easily establish an ownership claim, a new property right could be established in a newly printed text.[35] By the romantic period, and probably earlier if the archival record were more complete, we find examples of dog-in-the manger refusals to give permission to others to reprint an out-of-print title, even if the owner of the text was unwilling to do so himself. This happened with Keats and with Mary Shelley.[36]

Quite early in the history of the printed-book industry, all intellectual property rights which had any continuing value, even only potential value, thus became in practice, ever more like other private property rights, such as land: personally or corporately owned, heritable, divisible, able to be held in trust, saleable, leaseable, and mortgageable, liable to revert to worthlessness, but open to offers for redevelopment, in perpetuity.[37] In England, under these arrangements, during the whole period between the early sixteenth century and the effective outlawing of perpetual copyright on the eve of the romantic period, there was no way in which the intellectual property in any text, once created by the act of printing, could pass out of the possession of the printed-book industry guild. Nor, with only a handful of partial exceptions, such as English-language Bibles, was there ever a time when books inscribed with the same printed texts were sold in competition

---

[32] Any intellectual properties owned by members who died intestate passed into the collective ownership of the Stationers' Company.

[33] Transcripts of wills of stationers, Guildhall Library, London, ms. 2571. This formulation can be contrasted with that of Johanne Woolfe, who died in 1574, who left the physical capital and the books to her son but without mention of intellectual properties except for a promise/contract to publish made by her late husband and not discharged before his death. Plomer, *Wills* 20. John Audlie, who died in 1575, left to his wife the residue of his 'wares, copies, and other things', which may already imply intellectual property. Plomer *Wills* 23. Robert Dexter 1603 directed that his 'copies' be sold. Plomer *Wills* 38.

[34] BL add. mss. 44,849. See also the article by W. Roberts in *The Times Literary Supplement*, 4 January 1936.

[35] Noted in 1801 in John Nichols, ledger, CUL, add. mss. 8226.   [36] Details in appendix 9.

[37] For an example of the mortgaging of intellectual property rights in 1629 see Jackson 211. The Stationers' Court records contain many examples of elaborate arrangements by which shares in the English stock were used to provide for a shareholder's dependents after his death.

with one another. These business conventions had immense effects on the nature of the texts made available for reading in the English-speaking world during the first three centuries of the age of print.

There are, of course, many essential differences between real property and intellectual property. One is physical and visible. The other is immaterial and invisible. The custom and practice of real property have existed throughout recorded human history, in essentials unchanged at any rate in the western tradition. Intellectual property is a European invention of the fifteenth century which has subsequently been subject to many changes in law and in customary practice. Real property is normally sold in an open market. Intellectual property was only transferable within the printed-book industry. With a piece of real property, say a house, the owner can make drastic alterations and the result will still be recognisably the same house, and be accepted as the same house by others. But the owner of a house cannot make a second house for rent by making an abridgement of the first. Nor, if he builds a new house which closely resembles the house of one of his neighbours, can that neighbour claim that he has been robbed. If a piece of real property, a piece of land or a house, is divided among a number of people, each can only enjoy a share, and the more the property is divided the smaller the share that each one gets. With intellectual property, on the other hand, division need not lead to any diminution of utility. My experience of reading Shakespeare is not diminished if you read Shakespeare.

No one, whether author or intellectual property owner, can reasonably claim that any substantial text has been compiled solely from privately owned materials. By its use of language, which is essentially social, by its appeal to memory and readerly notions of genre, and by its repetition of recognised old as well as new sentiments, all texts inescapably draw on knowledge which they share with their readers. Indeed, without the shared public element, texts would have little or no appeal to readers. The intellectual property in every newly printed text is, in effect, the asserting of a private ownership claim over part of a language and intellectual domain which has previously been both open to the public and free. However, by the seventeenth century, the whole discourse of property as it applied to real property, including the penalties for stealing it, damaging it, and trespassing on it, the political rights and privileges attached to the possession of it, and the legal protections against confiscation, was being applied to this recently invented form of private wealth. A summary of the changing intellectual property regime, which introduces some of the terms which I intend to use later in the study, is in table 3.1.[38]

---

[38] Summarised from the fuller version in appendix 2.

Table 3.1 Summary of the changing intellectual property regime,
sixteenth to nineteenth century

ENGLAND
Guild period. Arrival of printing until around 1600
Perpetual intellectual property in the hands of printer/publishers. Monopoly rights in
many texts franchised or guaranteed by the state. The main objective of the regime is to
prevent competition between similar texts in the market. Licensing. Price controls.

Early monopoly period, around 1600 to 1640
The Stationers' Company, a London guild, is endowed by the state with many valuable
intellectual properties, and other properties are taken into the industry's collective
beneficial ownership by inheritance, assignment, and purchase within the industry.
Licensing continues. Prices rise. The popular sector is separated from mainstream
industry. Intellectual property becomes more narrowly textual, leading to a clamp-down
on anthologies, abridgements, and adaptations of previously printed texts.

Civil war, Commonwealth, and Protectorate, 1640 to 1660
Few books are printed but many pamphlets. Textual and intellectual property controls
temporarily break down but are quickly re-imposed.

State licensing period, 1660 to 1695
Tight pre-censorship by state and ecclesiastical officials. When the Licensing Act lapses in
1695, a legal hiatus is created.

GREAT BRITAIN
High monopoly period, 1710 to 1774
The Act of 1710 declares that intellectual property comes into existence with the act of
composition by an author, who can then transfer the right to the book industry for a
period of time that is limited by the statute to fourteen years, with provision, if the author
is still alive, for another fourteen. All existing intellectual properties are maintained for a
transitional period until 1731.

In practice, despite the Act, the English industry maintains perpetual copyright in all
printed texts old as well as new in its own hands. In Scotland the courts uphold the
provisions of the Act. The English industry becomes highly cartelised. Textual controls are
light. Price controls abandoned.

Brief copyright window, 1774 to 1808
Following a House of Lords judicial decision that perpetual copyright had been illegal in
England since 1710, a competitive market is established in the sale of out-of-copyright
texts, leading to lower prices, larger sales, and expanding readerships in these texts. In the
case of most other texts, prices rise steeply. Texts only have copyright protection for the
brief period laid down by the act of 1710. Tight textual controls are re-introduced in the
1790s.

UNITED KINGDOM OF GREAT BRITAIN AND IRELAND
Long copyright re-established, acts of 1808, 1814, 1836, and 1842
Copyright is extended from fourteen to twenty-eight years, and later to author's lifetime
plus seven years or forty-two years from date of publication, whichever is the longer.
Textual controls remain tight until the 1840s.

Table 3.1 (*cont.*)

Long copyright internationalised and further lengthened

1844. The British government is empowered by parliament to make reciprocal copyright treaties with foreign states. Between 1846 and 1886 sixteen treaties are concluded with European governments.

1911. Copyright is extended to life of author plus fifty years. The act enables the United Kingdom to join the Berne International Copyright Convention with a uniform copyright regime throughout the British Empire. (Canada did not ratify until 1924.) At the time of this consolidating Act there were twenty-two separate Acts of Parliament relating to copyright in force in the United Kingdom. Registration is abolished.

1891. With the accession of the United States to the international copyright treaties, offshore publication of English language texts as a means of evading intellectual property ceases, although pornographic and other texts which would have been prohibited by the British textual controls continue to be produced in Paris.

Soon after the arrival of print in England, as in other European jurisdictions, the authorities of state and church realised the potentialities for advancing their own political, religious, and cultural objectives. In Germany, the ecclesiastical authorities of the Roman Catholic Church had been caught off guard by the speed with which the ideas of the Reformation were carried across Europe, and the archival record shows that it was not only the technology of print as such that enabled texts to be widely read, but the fact that, in the absence of an effective international intellectual property regime, the price of books and, with it, the cost of access to the texts, fell rapidly. The printer/publishers of Wittenberg, where Luther's works were first published in print form, were unable to stay at the top of the demand curve when reprints for sale at lower prices were produced elsewhere.[39] In England, however, although some offshore printing of English-language texts occurred, the state and the book industry, acting in concert, had a high degree of control over the texts which circulated. From the mid sixteenth century, as part of the ambitious national agenda, each of the nine thousand parishes in England was required, from its own local resources, to buy and use a range of centrally selected English-language printed texts, including officially authorised English-language Bibles, psalters, and prayer books, books of homilies to be read out aloud, expository texts whose reading by the clergy was made mandatory, statements of the law, and occasional compulsory printed sermons prescribed, for example after a rebellion had been put down. Other books, for example Foxe's *Acts and Monuments of the*

---

[39] Between 1522 and 1526, for example, for every Wittenberg imprint, there were five reprints in other jurisdictions. Noted by John L. Flood, 'The Book in Reformation Germany' in Gilmont 51.

English Martyrs, which provided the new Protestant order with an illustrated mythic history, were, if not formally compulsory, expected to be purchased with locally raised funds by bishoprics and larger parishes throughout the country.[40] The professions of law, medicine, and education were obliged or encouraged to use only the centrally approved texts. The same broad pattern can be seen in Scotland where the Scottish state attempted to make certain Bibles, catechisms, and other printed texts of the official Scottish religion mandatory for households as well as for parishes.[41]

Monopolies conferred by privilege or letters patent, that is the right to take a stream of future income from state-conferred, state-guaranteed, and state-enforceable monopolies in texts which were compulsory or semi-compulsory to large constituencies of buyers and users, were high-yielding, low-risk, properties both at the time they were first granted and at any time later when the franchisees wished to onsell them within the industry.[42] From the point of view of the state, they were a costless way of rewarding political supporters which was far easier on the national treasury than, for example, granting them rent-yielding real property such as land, the means by which Oxford and Cambridge colleges had been initially financed. Indeed, it was soon realised that conferring such intellectual properties was not only costless but potentially profitable.[43] By accepting a fee for granting the right to take a stream of future revenue from intellectual property, the state itself acquired a share of the economic rent which could not only help to finance the enforcement system but produce a net income which it could use for its own purposes. If, as became increasingly frequent, the granting of privileges and letters patents was set for a limited period, the state could take successive capitalised streams of revenue from the intellectual property each time the monopoly was renewed.[44]

Since disputes over invisible intellectual property were harder for the courts to administer than visible real property rights, new enforcement institutions

---

[40] In the case of some of these long-lived compulsory or semi-compulsory texts, the manufacturers who were franchised to supply the books were able to continue to sell the same texts in a range of book formats simultaneously, without the need for much tranching down. They were able, for example, to sell English-language Bibles simultaneously both in folio and quarto versions (which were required for lecterns in churches) and in more portable octavo and duodecimo versions (which were suitable for family or for individual reading).

[41] Mann 210.

[42] See Arnold Hunt, 'Book Trade Patents 1603–1640' in Hunt, Mandelbrote, and Shell 27, with a list of patents.

[43] In 1626, for example, Caleb Morley, the producer of a Latin schoolbook offered to pay an annual fee in exchange for a state endorsement. See this and other examples in appendix 2.

[44] For example, in 1603, a printer/publisher paid King James's government £300 plus £20 (later £40) annually for the exclusive right to print the public statutes over the following twenty two years. See Timperley 433.

were invented. What was put in place early in the development of the industry was a register of private intellectual property rights, equivalent to a land registry for real properties, including a register of transfers of property rights, administered by officials experienced enough to smell out and deal with infractions at an early stage. Under its founding royal charter of 1557, which formalised arrangements which appear to have been in operation long before, the Stationers' Company was granted general powers to supervise the manufacture and selling of books throughout England.[45] If a printer/publisher was willing to incur the expense of registering his property with the Stationers' Company, his claim to exclusiveness was quickly upheld against any rival by the institutions of the industry and of the state. Although the registers only began after many English-language texts had already been printed and the implicit intellectual properties created and established, many older titles, especially those which were commercially most valuable, including traditional popular ballads, were re-registered as they changed hands. Occasionally whole classes of books conferred by the state under letters patent were entered as a kind of belt-and-braces legitimacy.[46] The registers of printed texts kept at Stationers' Hall were, therefore, a developing, though always incomplete, record both of private intellectual property rights, and, at the same time, a national, self-financing, state-guaranteed system for the surveillance, recording, and control of the dissemination of printed books in England.

As a chartered guild, the Stationers' Company soon became ever more fully integrated into the state's fiscal structures, becoming liable, like other London guilds, to contribute to the state's occasional demands for arms, armed men, provisions, financial contributions, and the compulsory loans with which the state's foreign wars and colonial conquests and settlements were increasingly financed. As early as 1591, as its secret archive noted, the company was required to contribute £80 to a total of £7,400 being levied at that time from the London guilds, a figure which indicates its small relative economic weight at that time.[47] But as the industry grew, and its fiscal as well as potential cultural usefulness increased in proportion, it was accorded ever greater opportunities to take rents from state-conferred intellectual property.[48] In 1603, for example, the Stationers' Company, as a corporate body, was granted a perpetual monopoly on the printing and selling of

[45] The first surviving recorded reference to the guild of 'Writers', i.e. copiers of manuscripts, appears to be in 1403. Mumby 41, quoting records in Arber. Others are in Greg, *Companion*.

[46] Two examples of 1615 are given in Arber iii, 576.

[47] The so-called Liber A, so far unpublished. See D. F. McKenzie, 'Stationers' Company Liber A; An Apologia' in Myers and Harris, *1550–1990*.

[48] Liber A. Typed copy 304.

ABCs, primers, psalters, and almanacs and prognostications, monopolies which had previously been franchised to individual members.[49]

To take the example of almanacs, in exchange for its continuing cooperation with the state, the main collective institution of the book industry was thus granted the right to take a rent every year in perpetuity from all of the wide range of economic activities and religious and cultural practices which depended upon participants having access, each year, to the printed information which almanacs contained. Almanacs gave the dates of the monthly and annual fairs held in the larger towns, essential information for an agricultural economy. They gave information about the tides on which all sea-borne and much river-borne trade depended. They set out the dates of church festivals, used to recommend the best times for crop planting and harvesting, as well as for the renewals of labour contracts, the collection of tithes, taxes and rents, and for scheduling religious festivals. They also set out the dates of law and university terms. The almanac monopoly appears to have produced an income to the industry of several hundred per cent on the manufacturing costs of the books every year on sales of several hundred thousand copies, and for nearly two hundred years the company was engaged in a constant struggle against the producers of unauthorised almanacs, of local piracies, and of almanacs printed abroad.

Many other prime intellectual properties were added to the company's initial corporate endowment, by grant, purchase, and inheritance, to create a collective portfolio known as the 'English stock'.[50] In 1616 came the establishment of the 'Latin stock', initially the monopolisation of the arrangements for the importation of scholarly, scientific, and medical books in the international language of European high culture. The 'Irish stock', established in about 1618, was primarily a means of monopolising the export of books to the then semi-colonial market of English-speaking Ireland. The near monopolisation of popular literature, and its separation from the market in other literature, culminated in 1624 with the formal establishment of the Ballad Partners and their 'Ballad stock'. By the 1630s, with the bringing into the 'English stock' of Bibles, prayer books, and other texts of the English official supernatural, as well as a range of educational and law books, the company as a whole, or groups of company members acting

---

[49] Full text in Arber iii, 42. The universities of Oxford and Cambridge were also given the right to print almanacs, but, with certain exceptions, they later waived their rights in return for an annual fee from the Stationers' Company. Some of the monopolies had previously been granted, as time-limited franchises, to certain leading members of the industry such as the king's printer.
[50] A list of the English stock as it stood in 1620 is given in Arber iii, 668.

in partnership, held the monopoly franchises on all the most important compulsory and semi-compulsory texts in use throughout England.

Only those members of the industry who were sworn members of the official English church, and whose loyalty to the state was unquestioned, were permitted to share in these arrangements. In 1644, for example, the £160 share in the English stock owned by Mrs Alice Smith was sequestered and sold to another member because she was a Roman Catholic.[51] From 1684, all officials of the Stationers' Company had to be practising members of the Church of England and to take various oaths.[52] The monopoly of knowledge claimed by the English political and ecclesiastical state now coincided with a commercial monopoly in the supply of the texts in which the truth in all branches of knowledge was to be inscribed. The process of dividing the supply of written texts into sectors coincided with the drive to divide the whole London economy into guilds, of which a great number, including the Scriveners, were incorporated in the early seventeenth century.[53]

The economic benefits which their alliance with the state brought to the book industry took many forms. The regular printing work which the almanac monopoly provided, for example, was divided among the printers so that each was given a share in the massive annual orders. To judge from later practice, a printer might receive an order to print just a single sheet of a single almanac title, but with such long and regular print runs, this was a valuable order.[54] The profits of the English stock portfolio financed the collective operations of the industry, including the arrangements for apprenticeships and training, the inspection system which backed up the registration arrangements, social activities, internal charities, and the ongoing costs of maintaining a close political relationship with the state, including political lobbying.[55] The English stock also paid dividends to members. Yielding around 6 or 7 per cent when the portfolio was established at the beginning of the century, dividends were raised until they reached 12.5 per cent, a level at which they remained unchanged although the nominal capital was greatly increased. The industry had created, in effect, a high-yielding, fixed-price, and fixed-interest bond, available only to be bought by members of the Stationers' Company in amounts calculated in accordance with their changing share of the industry, and which

[51] Liber A. [52] Blagden 168.
[53] See Francis W. Steer, *Scriveners' Company Common Paper 1357–1628* (1968) vii.
[54] Ackers, for example, regularly printed a single sheet of *Poor Robin's Almanac*. Ackers ledger.
[55] For the 'English stock' and other corporate holdings of the Stationers, see Blagden. The type of some almanacs may have been kept standing to be updated each year.

could always be rapidly liquidated without loss. When a member of the industry died or went out of business, or if a widow wished to liquidate her shares, the company or its members bought the most valuable properties to be added to the various portfolios and partnerships as part of an ongoing process of ever more closely held ownership of texts.[56]

The state for its part also benefited from the alliance. It was, for example, able to mobilise private capital for its political and cultural purposes. The 1611 'authorized', 'King James', translation of the English-language Bible took about 84 per cent of the readings from earlier English-language versions, and especially from Tyndale's Bible that had been produced offshore, and the translator judicially put to death at the instigation of the English ecclesiastical authorities, nearly a hundred years earlier.[57] All the fees to scholars over nearly a decade and the upfront costs of type, printing, and paper, were financed by what is now called 'public/private partnership', private capital offered to the state in exchange for future monopoly selling rights.[58] Instead of having to pay English printers to manufacture and distribute its preferred texts, as in the early years of print, the English state was now able to accept bids for what was, effectively, a private franchise to levy a small tax in perpetuity on all the parishes and many of the individuals in the kingdom. The sharp increase in price which this change brought about emerges from the fragmentary record of the prices of English-language Bibles summarised in appendix 1.[59]

The few textual changes from the earlier English-language versions which were included in the 1611 translation seem in many cases to have been made in order to reinforce the authority of the English state from whom the industry received its monopoly franchise. To take one example, if there was one topic above all which the English monarchs of the early modern period did not want to see publicly debated in print, it was whether citizens had a right to rebel against the political and ecclesiastical authorities. Until the time of King James, whose claim to legitimacy under a hereditary system was a little more secure, every recent English monarch had come to power as a result of some form of rebellion or recent *coup d'état*, or was the child of a marriage whose legitimacy was disputed, and all monarchs used all the resources available to them, to assert the validity of their claims. The

---

[56] See, for example, the huge transfer of music, plays, romances, ballads, sermons and many other properties made in 1626. Arber iv, 152. The ballads, such as *Bevis of Hampton*, became part of the Ballad stock.

[57] See Andrew Hope, 'Plagiarising the Word of God' in Kewes, *Plagiarism* 93–105.   [58] McGrath 197.

[59] Appendix 1. 'Raising the price of English-language Bibles, early modern period, prices on first publication, with a few recorded print runs'.

mandatory 'Great Bible' of 1539, for example, included an engraved frontispiece showing the people of England pledging their allegiance to Henry VIII, so associating his claim to political legitimacy directly with the holy book. The words 'God save the King' and 'Vivat rex' appear no less than nineteen times.[60] Its successor, the 'Geneva Bible', however, which included many expository printed glosses intended to help the reader to understand the meaning of the prime text, seemed in a number of places to imply that the obedience which subjects owed to their monarch was not absolute or unconditional.[61] Among the reasons why, immediately on his succession, King James's government had pressed ahead with plans for a new version, was to remove these offending glosses and to strengthen the usefulness of English-language Bibles as instruments of political legitimation. Although the translators were mostly given a free hand, they were ordered to render the Greek words 'ekklesia' and 'episkopos' as 'church' and 'bishop', and so to imply, anachronistically, that modern ecclesiastical and episcopal institutions existed in the time of the early Christians.[62] The King James version of the English-language Bible, destined to be, by far, the most often printed and most widely read text in the English-speaking world, was a product of the cultural and economic bargain between the English state and the book industry at a specific political conjuncture of the early modern period.

By the early seventeenth century the Stationers' Company had become the English state's principal enforcement authority.[63] It was given power to limit the numbers of printing presses and the amount of types which could be manufactured, that is, to determine the amount of physical capital, and therefore the maximum production, of the printed-book industry throughout England. The company regulated the entry arrangements for apprenticeships and advancement through membership of the company, so determining the supply of trained manpower, another way of controlling the maximum output of print. The company set maximum book prices, maximum edition sizes, and made regulations governing the imports of printed books, and much else. Their officials carried out frequent searches in printing houses, shops and ships for books that infringed state textual controls, state-conferred monopoly franchises, and private intellectual property conventions.[64] They had powers to fine members and

---

[60] Reproduced by Moulton, frontispiece.
[61] Notably in its comments on passages in the book of Daniel where duty to God was represented as overriding duty to the sovereign.
[62] For the instructions to the translators, see McGrath 173.
[63] See the Proclamation of 1623 summarised in appendix 2, 482.   [64] Timperley 413.

non-members, to arrest apprentices who left their masters, to destroy types
and presses, to imprison alleged offenders without trial, and to obtain the
severest penalties from the courts, including death, for some publishing
offences.[65]

The key to the long success and stability of the alliance between the industry
and the state was pricing. During the sixteenth century, the price control
arrangements of the manuscript era and guild system seem to have served
the interests of book buyers and readers quite well.[66] Until the early seventeenth century we find examples of the controls being enforced and price
reductions ordered.[67] From 1560 until early in the seventeenth century,
a period for which some estimates have been made, book prices seem to
have been kept steady in nominal terms even although other prices in the
economy were rising. In other words the controls brought about a fall in
real and in relative terms. During these decades, which coincided with an
increase in population, we see more titles being published, more books
being produced, and probably, bigger sales, wider access, and a growth in
the absolute size, and probably also of the proportionate size, of the reading nation.[68] The rise of literature in the English language in the English
Renaissance, it seems likely, was assisted by a fall in the real price of access
to English-language texts imprinted in books.

After the change in the controlling structures of around 1600, however,
we can discern the beginning of a steep rise in book prices. The price
control provisions of the guild system seem to have been lifted, ignored,
or the limits raised so high that they ceased to matter in practice, and the
maximum sizes of editions, a guild feature intended to protect the jobs of
print workers, were also raised.[69] Although it is as yet impossible to offer
full and reliable quantification, it seems likely that, in the course of the
seventeenth century, the real price of English printed books of all kinds
was raised to a much higher level than it had previously been. Nominal
prices of newly printed plays, for example, seem to have doubled from
sixpence at the time of Shakespeare to one shilling when the theatres were

---

[65] Summarised in Blagden. For control of edition sizes see the order of 1587 reprinted by Arber ii, 43.
See also Clegg. As far as appenticeships were concerned, the records of the Court of Stationers are
full of cases of irregularities being punished.

[66] For an example from Paris of price and margin controls in the manuscript era see F. Somner
Merryweather, *Bibliomania in the Middle Ages* (1933) 59.

[67] See 'Price controls', appendix 1, 457–8.   [68] Examples quoted in Francis R. Johnson.

[69] I can find no documentary evidence for the price controls being formally lifted, although they
had clearly ceased to be effective. See the example of the *Ten Commandments* in 'Price controls',
appendix 1. The controls were formally renewed in the 1710 Act.

reopened after the restoration of the monarchy.[70] Ballads at least doubled from the controlled price of 1598.[71] Most of the 'penny merriments' and 'penny godlinesses' which Pepys bought in the 1680s, then cost him two pence.[72] Since there was some inflation of the prices of commodities which constituted the cost of living during the first part of the seventeenth century, the real terms increase was less than the nominal increase. However, during the seventeenth century, the retail price of London books rose from three times to five times the manufacturing cost, a ratio which implies the transfer of a large quantum from prices to profits at any cost and price level.[73]

The most noticeable increase was in the prices of books produced under formal, state-conferred, monopoly franchises, that is all the mandatory print of religion, law, and education. Indeed the buying-up of many of the patents by the Stationers' Company in the years after 1603, and the rise in the fees which the company was able to charge its members, appear to have been a preparation for the large price rises which followed. In 1641, Michael Sparke, a book-industry insider who revealed the secrets of his trade, declared that the monopolists had raised the prices of Bibles, prayer books, school books, and law books by from 50 to 100 per cent.[74] In the case of Bibles alone, Sparke gives figures which enable us to calculate that the transfer from consumer to producer, that is from prices to profits, which took place shortly before 1641 was over £5,000.[75] Over the seventeenth century the prices of standard law books appear to have risen by several hundred per cent.[76] The university press at Cambridge, although a partial beneficiary, protested that it could profitably produce some of the standard mandatory texts at less than half the London prices.[77] In 1690, John How, an outsider bookseller, claimed that some standard titles could be profitably produced for sale at half the current prices and others at less than a tenth.[78] Over the seventeenth century, the income taken by the book industry had shifted from a regulated profit relating to manufacturing costs, as under a

[70] See appendix 12.   [71] For the maximum prices per sheet see Greg and Boswell 59.
[72] Noted by Watt 273. A discussion of rising prices is in Spufford 48. It was reported that ballads which had been profitably sold at about 10 shillings a ream were now only obtainable from the cartelised Ballad Partners at 13s 3d (13.3 shillings). Hunt, Mandelbrote and Shell 35, quoting a contemporary document.
[73] *HBA* i, 39.   [74] (Michael Sparke) *Scintilla* (1641) reprinted in Arber iv, 35.
[75] My calculation is based on the figures per impression quoted by Sparke.
[76] This emerges from prices quoted by J. H. Baker in 'English law books and legal publishing' in *CHBB* iv, 484 and 496.
[77] Bibles sold at 4 shillings in quires in London could, they said, be profitably produced for 2 shillings, metrical psalms sold at 37 shillings (£1 17s) a ream could be profitably produced for sale at 15 shillings. McKitterick i, 202.
[78] In an original document quoted by Don-John Dugas, 'The London Book Trade in 1709' in *Papers of Bibliographical Society of America*, 95: 2 (2001).

guild system, to a rent on intellectual property levied by an unregulated private commercial monopoly operating in cooperation with the state.

The complex interlocking pricing, fiscal, and regulatory arrangements, which were put in place in England in the early seventeenth century, and which lasted in many of their essentials, with only brief interruptions, until the eve of the romantic period, turned an industry whose institutions had been loose and voluntary, into a tight corporate cartel. They bound the leaders more closely together, and they bound them to the state. Although, therefore, in England, as elsewhere in Europe, the coming of print introduced certain written texts to a wider readership, and so speeded up the dissemination of ideas, the main effect, once the potentiality was understood by the authorities of state and church, was to strengthen their power to promote their own religious, political, and cultural policies.[79] The technology of text-copying by moveable print, with the associated development of private intellectual property, enabled a large number of newly written English texts to be published by many authors, indeed it encouraged the supply of a flow of new texts to elites. But it also enabled the state and the book industry, acting together, to take a rent from the intellectual property rights in the official supernatural whatever that was declared to be at any time (Bibles, prayer books, printed sermons), from the officially approved system of personal ethics (prayers, commandments, catechisms, conduct literature), from the practice and enforcement of law (printed statutes, official publications, and law books), from science, medicine, and scholarship (still mainly Latin language texts imported from abroad), from knowledge of the geography of the country and of countries abroad (maps, navigation charts, and globes), from all branches of education (ABCs, primers, school textbooks in English, and texts in Latin and Greek), from music (including psalters and sung ballads), from leisure activities (theatre advertisements, playing cards, and printed games), from various forms of popular entertainment (from the licensing of chapmen who distributed ballads and chapbooks), and from many other activities which depended upon printed texts.

Although the nature of the texts which the state and the official churches of England and Scotland wished to prescribe or to proscribe depended upon which political and ecclesiastical groups were in power, the instruments of control were much the same, and the state could take an income from

---

[79] For Luther's highly innovative use of the printing press to spread his ideas in pamphlets both in German and Latin, and the initially ineffective response of the Catholic hierarchy who mainly printed in Latin, see Mark U. Edwards, Jr, *Printing, Propaganda and Martin Luther* (Berkeley 1994). See also R. A. Houston, *Literacy in Early Modern Europe* (1988).

all of them. As a form of taxation, the sale of publishing and printing privileges and patents was invisible because the effects were buried in general price levels. It was inescapable because it was applied monopolistically across a wide range of essential or mandatory goods and services; and it was easily collected, because the proceeds came into the exchequer in the form of capitalised payments made upfront by businessmen with access to financial capital. The occasional hanging, mutilation, imprisonment, public pillorying, and ruination of printer/publishers who remained outside the structures, or who trespassed beyond the tolerated textual limits, provided reminders of the advantages of keeping within them. The text-based culture of the people of England, taking both 'text' and 'culture' in their widest senses, was thus simultaneously centralised, controlled, and made more uniform, in a regime of regulated printed-book production that was both financially and culturally self-reinforcing.

CHAPTER 4

Anthologies, abridgements, and the development of commercial vested interests in prolonging the obsolete

Besides the effects on texts, books, prices, and access considered in the previous chapter, I discern the putting in place around 1600 of three other changes that also profoundly influenced the reading of the English-speaking world right through to the romantic period and beyond. They are, first, a clamp-down on the publishing of printed anthologies which drew on previously printed sources; secondly a clamp-down on abridgements; and thirdly, the development of a range of vested commercial interests in prolonging the reading of obsolete texts. The third change was, to an extent, a consequence of the other two.

Anthologies, abridgements, and adaptations are part of the means by which texts and ideas are diffused. They enable longer texts to be made available, in some form, to wider readerships, including the less well educated and the economically disadvantaged. They help to bind a society together, enabling texts of different writers to be easily compared, uniting the reading experiences of one generation with that of others, introducing children to texts which they may later read in fuller or more sophisticated versions, and helping to maintain a shared memory across time, place, and social situation. To forbid anthologies, abridgements, and adaptations was therefore further to divide the reading nation both by socio-economic class and by the degree of obsolescence of the texts to which different constituencies had access.

As far as I am aware, none of these changes has previously been explicitly noticed nor their effects explored, except possibly occasionally in terms of changes in taste. As the study progresses, the pervasive effects of the changes made around 1600 across the reading of the whole English-speaking world will become ever more apparent.[1] It would not be an exaggeration to say

---

[1] In order to enable my conclusions to be tested, and I hope replicated, by future research, I have set out the evidence in detail in appendix 3. Although it mostly relates to literary writings, there is every reason to believe that the changes applied across the whole of print.

that the changes discussed in this chapter were amongst the most decisive events in the history of reading.

The clamp-down on anthologising can be seen most obviously from the record of the printing of English verse miscellanies.[2] Between 1557, the date of the first printed publication known as *Tottel's Miscellany*, and the end of the sixteenth century, we find a flurry of printed English verse anthologies, many consisting only of newly composed and hitherto unprinted pieces, and others containing pieces which had previously been printed. These miscellanies can be seen as a carrying into the new text-copying technology of print a tradition of anthologising which had long been normal in the manuscript era. They were the printed equivalents of the individually chosen manuscript miscellanies which a gentleman or lady might compose or compile for his or her own reading, for the entertainment of friends, or for distributing to chosen patrons or readers as a form of 'scribal publication'.[3]

The English printer/publishers also printed collections of the short pieces from selected texts used in education. During the manuscript era, anthologies of brief extracts from biblical, classical, and patristic texts had been among the staples of religious teaching throughout Europe, and *florilegia* ['collections of flowers'] continued to be produced in large numbers across Europe far into the print age.[4] In England, in the years before 1600 we find a flurry of printed collections of short quotations, proverbs, maxims, adages, and apothegms known as *sententiae*, or in English 'select sentences', most of which purport to have been derived from ancient classical and biblical texts but which also draw on modern authors. As Francis Meres, the editor of one of the collections, *Palladis Tamia* (1598) advised in a *sententia* on reading itself: 'Out of hearbs and plants the best things are to be extracted: so the best sayings are to be gathered out of Authors.'[5] These were part of a common European assortment of pieces of wisdom, carried all over Europe by the widespread reprinting and translating of the *Adagia* compiled by Erasmus.[6] Intended for all constituencies of readers, including children, *sententiae* were, apart from single words, the irreducible common

---

[2] See 'Anthologies. The pre-1600 flurry of printed literary anthologies which draw on previously printed works. Poetry miscellanies', appendix 3, 490–2.

[3] See, for example, the discussions by Love and Marotti.

[4] See, for example Ann Moss, *Printed Commonplace-Books and the Structuring of Renaissance Thought* (Oxford 1996) chapter 2. Among the first texts to be printed in England was *Dictes and Sayinges of the Philosophres* (1477), a translation of a Latin anthology of the Bible by Nicolaus Hanapus (St Albans 1481), STC 2093 and 12742.

[5] 'The vse of reading many Bookes' 269 in the 1598 edition.

[6] See Fox 117, drawing on the work of Margaret Mann Phillips, *The 'Adages' of Erasmus* (Cambridge 1964).

atomic units of thought put into textual form, of which longer literary and dramatic texts could be regarded as rearrangements, embellishments, variations, or enlargements. Such *sententiae* were spoken, heard, printed, read, carved on mantelpieces, sewn on wall hangings, quoted in plays, songs, and daily speech, and recommended in education.[7] The printing of English collections of *sententiae* was the taking into the copying technology of print of the centralising and authoritarian educational practice recommended by the contemporary English *Book of Common Prayer*, 'to read, mark, learn, and inwardly digest'.[8]

By the end of the sixteenth century, however, the producers of English printed anthologies were confronting a contradiction between two previously coexisting, but now increasingly opposed, ideas about what constitutes the essential function of literature. It was among the commonly accepted roles of the imaginative writer to capture in concise and memorable form the shared ideas and experiences, literally the 'common places', of the shared culture, which were regarded as universally and perennially true. Euripides, for example, was much praised as having been the most 'sententious' of the ancient authors.[9] Modern poets, it was sometimes declared, needed such anthologies in order to know the existing stock of metaphors and conceits from which their predecessors had built the culture and which they in their turn were to celebrate and to continue.[10] Men of humanist education needed such texts if they were to learn to behave with the polite manners which were expected from their breeding and status.[11] Anthologists themselves had their own stock of metaphors, such as that of the honey-bee who selects from the sweetest flowers of the garden.[12] However, at the same time, we find examples of an alternative view which was later to become dominant, the author as creator. Poets, following the *sententia* of Horace, were born not made. Spenser in *The Shepheards Calendar* (1591), picking up another piece of ancient wisdom, described poetry as 'a divine gift and heavenly instinct, not to be gotten by labour and learning'.[13] But, if an author was inspired by God, did he have the right to treat the manuscript

---

[7] Examples quoted by Juliet Fleming, *Graffiti and the Writing Arts of Early Modern England* (2001).
[8] Collect for second Sunday in Advent.
[9] For example in (Francis Meres) *Palladis Tamia* (1598). Euripides' works were not available in English translation at this time.
[10] The explanation given by Edward Bysshe, *The Art of English Poetry* (1702).
[11] As in *Wits Commonwealth*. See C. T. Onions, *A Shakespeare Glossary* (Oxford 1911) 251 for the contemporary meaning of 'wit.'
[12] For an example of this metaphor see Augustine Vincent, *A Discouerie of Errours in the First Edition of the Catalogue of Nobility* (1622), epistle to Raphe Brooke.
[13] In the Argument for 'October'.

on which the divinely inspired words were inscribed as a commercial property from which he and printer/publishers could make money? Before 1600, there were many complaints by authors that their best passages were stolen by lesser men, and the word 'plagiary' made its first appearances in the English language.[14]

Until around 1600, the English industry's intellectual property regime seems to have been mainly a business practice whose purpose was to prevent duplication and competition in the market. In 1581, for example, the Stationers' Company required that a proposed book on education by Richard Mulcaster, should not contain 'any thinge preiudiciall or hurtful' to Roger Ascham's *Scholemaster*, the work on the subject then on sale.[15] By 1600, however, day-to-day tensions within the discourse of private intellectual property precipitated the shift in publishing practice. Was the printing of a new anthology containing quotations from existing books the creation of a new property in which the printer/publisher could claim a monopoly ownership? Or was it rather an invasion, or as would soon be said, a 'pirating', of a property which already existed? An anthology was, by etymological derivation, a selection of flowers, but did anthologists have the right to open flower shops which sold flowers picked from other people's private gardens?

How far, in the years after 1600, the book industry faced these questions overtly is not known. It was obvious that the printer/publishers of anthologies could legally quote from longer texts that they happened to own, or they might obtain permission. However that does not appear to have been the norm. The editor of *Englands Helicon*, of which about three-quarters of the materials had previously appeared in print, felt obliged to defend in advance his encroachment on the intellectual property rights of other printer/publishers, by claiming that he drew his materials from manuscript copies supplied by authors, not from printed versions. At the same time he appealed to the notion that authors are themselves simply repeating truths taken from elsewhere.[16]

But it was probably business considerations which forced a resolution. As objects of sale, the printed miscellanies competed commercially with one another as well as with the printed books from which they drew their quotations, so that even their titles were difficult to distinguish. *The Paradise of Dainty Devices* was challenged by *A Handful of Pleasant Delights* and *A Banquet of Dainty Conceits*. *Englands Helicon* was followed by *Englands*

[14] For authorial plagiarism in the early modern period see Kewes, *Plagiarism*.   [15] Arber ii, 390.
[16] Pomeroy 23. See also the quotation in appendix 3, 492.

Parnassus. Such books were a 'disorder' in the trade. The Court Book of the Stationers' Company in which an overt policy change may have been recorded has not survived.[17] In addition to the change of business behaviour discernible in the archival record, however, there are scattered indications that a regime to prevent more than a line or two of previously printed texts from being anthologised without the explicit consent of the owner of the main text was being developed. By 1615, when we have a record of a fee being paid for the right to quote from a printed book, it seems clear that a regime to control the anthologising of more than a line or two from previously printed works was already fully in place.[18]

Margreta De Grazia has written perceptively of how the convention of enclosing a passage in quotation marks, which began as an indication that the sentiment was literally a common place open to all, was transmuted into an indication that the phrase was a private property 'created' by another writer.[19] What had once been free commons, at the disposal of all members of the community as a birthright, were transformed into carefully fenced-off parks situated in the midst of large private estates. Writers could still use them, without charge if they did not take much, but only as a favour, with an explicit acknowledgement, say by a footnote reference, that they gratefully acknowledged that they were encroaching on the property of another.

The effects on reading of this shift were profound and long-lasting. After 1600, for about 180 years we find only a handful of newly compiled printed collections of quotations of English literature, mostly widely separated by time of first publication.[20] It seems likely that the industry decided collectively that, while existing titles could continue to be reprinted, there was commercial room for just one, or occasionally two, printed collections in the market at any one time.[21] The owners of Shakespeare, Milton, and other classics, who guarded their intellectual property rights jealously, seem to have given their consent to the use of extracts in such works, provided they were kept short, and to have agreed that after each printed collection had

---

[17] Arber ii, 876.

[18] See 'Indications that a regime intended to control the use of quotations from printed books *unauthorised by the intellectual property owners* is being put in place, appendix 3, 493.

[19] Margreta De Grazia, *Shakespeare Verbatim: the Reproduction of Authenticity and the 1790 Apparatus* (Oxford 1991) 214.

[20] If there had been an explicit decision, a record might have existed in the Stationers' Company 'Liber A', their archive of internal confidential document decisions, to which the company long denied access to all outsiders, but I have found nothing there.

[21] See 'Printed "common places", in the form of substantial quotations continue to be produced occasionally', appendix 3, 494.

exhausted its potential sales, including new editions at lower prices tranched down, another would be permitted. These collections never became selections from the corpus of English literature, like Palgrave's *Golden Treasury* or of the *Oxford Book of English Verse*. Arranged alphabetically by topic or sentiment, they remained sources of advice to literary practitioners looking for a striking image for a particular occasion. Between 1600 until after 1774, English printed anthologies failed to perform the selecting, canonising, and memorialising role which had been theirs in the manuscript age and which has often been seen as among the essential purposes and characteristics of the genre.

The publication of newly compiled printed collections of short *sententiae* was not affected to the same extent, and many collections of maxims, proverbs, and apothegms, mostly composed of passages of not more than a sentence or two in length, continued to be printed and published. With these collections too we see the same tendency to have only one main title in the market at any time, to keep it in print for as long as possible, and then to replace it with another printed text which could be given a similarly long life in its turn. After *Wits Commonwealth* (1597) had been in production as a school teaching text until 1722, for example, the two standard school books of the eighteenth century, Dyche and Dilworth, which also taught by *sententiae*, were reprinted for a century or so in their turn. Such compilations were sometimes presented by their producers not as literature but as an alternative to literature – ancient well-tested wisdom which could counter the poison to be found in modern romance, songs, and plays.[22] They exemplified an authoritarian catechetic attitude to education, in which children were given instructions on how to answer standard questions in accordance with centrally set norms, not attempts to equip them with the ability to think critically about texts and meanings.

The 1600 changes cannot be explained adequately in terms of changing demand by buyers or of a sudden shift in readerly taste. Manuscript commonplace books which draw on both printed and manuscript sources are plentiful for a century or more, and some of the printed collections which had been first printed before the change continued to be reprinted.[23] Miscellanies compiled from previously unprinted works continued to be

---

[22] See, for example, the preface to *Select Proverbs* (1707) 3.
[23] See Hilton Kelliher, 'Contemporary Manuscript Extracts from Shakespeare's *Henry IV, Part 1*' in *English Manuscript Studies* i (1989) 144, which contains more than its title suggests, and Mary Hobbs, 'Early Seventeenth-Century Verse Miscellanies and their Value for Textual Editors' in *English Manuscript Studies* 182.

produced and were among the main literary media of the following two centuries. There was no turning away from literary anthologies as such. And, as the archival record shows, the moment that the restrictions on reprinting extracts from certain older printed texts were lifted in 1774, with the effective outlawing of perpetual intellectual property in England, we see a flood of verse and prose anthologies compiled almost entirely from those printed literary texts which were then released into the public domain.[24] The cultural effects on the reading of the romantic period were to be immense.[25]

The second change which I discern from the archival record, a clamp-down on abridgements, also seems to have occurred quite suddenly around 1600 and to have produced similarly long-run effects on texts, books, access, and reading. As with anthologies, although the main evidence is again the patterns which emerge from the industry's behaviour, there is also a good deal of scattered corroborative historical documentary evidence. The pattern is similar to that for anthologies, a flurry of printed abridgements of literary, dramatic, and historical works, commonly known as 'ballad versions', towards the end of the sixteenth century, a sudden cessation around 1600, a continuation of the ban until after 1774, and then a sudden flood.[26]

Many ballad versions, that is abridgements of a story put into verse and sung to a familiar tune, are directly drawn from the mainstream printed literary culture of the English Renaissance. Taken from romances, histories, and plays, they seem to have been produced as part of normal tranching down. Ballad versions followed strong generic conventions. Ballad versions of plays, for example, seem usually to be divided into two parts, maybe to mark intervals in a performance, and are not so much adaptations of the plays as alternatives, simpler to perform and to listen to, but also, as print, far cheaper to buy, and more widely circulated. By the 1590s, the Stationers' Company registers are recording separate entries for main texts and ballad versions, implying that, by that time, they recognised that a separate intellectual property right existed in an abridged version, and that the ownership of the full text could be separated from that of the abridgement, either at the time of entry or later. Some registrations at this time claim ownership of ballad versions yet to be written, an advance in notions of intellectual

<hr />

[24] See chapter 6.   [25] Discussed in chapter 7.
[26] See 'Abridged "ballad versions" of longer literary works common before 1600, but only a few later', appendix 3, 496–8. For the resumption after 1774 see chapter 6.

property into potential spin-offs from main texts. By the 1630s, however, when we have specific recorded examples of abridgements being forbidden both on commercial grounds and on the perceived need to prevent certain texts from reaching popular readerships, a regime to control abridgements was evidently fully in place. One of the compliments that could be paid to a bookseller by a colleague was that 'he never abridged another man's copy'.[27]

After the beginning of the seventeenth century, with less than half-a-dozen known exceptions for which there are likely to be specific explanations, not a single seventeenth- or eighteenth-century mainstream English literary work was abridged into a ballad or a chapbook version.[28] It would not be easy to abridge the long novels of Fielding and Richardson into twenty-four pages and a woodcut, but there are no books even of famous episodes in texts such as *Don Quixote* which look good candidates. We can also see evidence of the stresses which the restrictive policy caused. In the eighteenth century many of the royal licences, equivalents of the belt-and-braces 'privileges', and 'letters patent' of earlier centuries, related to encyclopaedias, presumably to protect their publishers from the risk of being accused of infringement of property. Other royal licences which guarantee the copyright of longer works, declare that extracts are not permitted.[29] Chapbooks exist called *Paradise Lost* and *Paradise Regained*, two famous texts which had attained near-biblical status among many Christians, but the chapbooks are not abridgements of Milton and may have been deliberately produced to give a false impression.[30] As with anthologies, the change cannot be adequately explained in terms of readerly taste. Here again, the

[27] Timperley 719 quoting Dunton.
[28] The exceptions known to me are Bunyan's *The Pilgrim's Progress* and *Grace Abounding*, Defoe's *Robinson Crusoe* and *Moll Flanders*, and, more doubtfully, Swift's *Gulliver's Travels*, and (Combe's) *The Devil on Two Sticks*. The abridgement of *Robinson Crusoe*, to judge from the long list of publishers, was probably commissioned by the owners of the main text which, being three volumes long, is too long to be suitable for children's reading. For *Moll Flanders* see David Goldthorpe, 'Textual instability: The Fortunes and Misfortunes of Moll Flanders', unpublished doctoral thesis, Open University 1995. I am grateful to Dr Bob Owens for drawing this work to my attention. The intellectual property status of *The Pilgrim's Progress* was disputed. See Hansard column 1082. An intellectual property in *The Pilgrim's Progress* was enforced in the eighteenth century when Luckman of Coventry, who printed an edition, was obliged to hand over all copies and pay all costs. Augustine Birrell, *The Law and History of Copyright* (1899) 133. In the case of Bunyan, one of the apparent exceptions may have been Methodist versions prepared by Charles Wesley in the 1740s. See Altick 36.
[29] See the list in Shef Rogers, 'The Use of Royal Licences for Printing in England, 1695–1760: A Bibliography' in *The Library*, 7th series, 1, 2 (2000). The full text of the one granted to Newbery for *The Circle of the Sciences*, a compilation for children, is quoted by Welsh 111.
[30] In the collection of Harvard University, numbers 78 and 79. Both titles appear in the Ballad Partners' trade catalogue of 1764.

moment that intellectual property restrictions were lifted after 1774, we find an outpouring of abridgements of older texts which, along with anthologies, were to become one of the largest components of the reading of the romantic period.

With all other English printed texts, too, the same general patterns emerge. With the translated texts of the ancient Greek and Roman classics, for example, until about 1600 we find a range of ancient fictional or mythic stories taken, abridged, and adapted from texts of ancient authors, some spurious, such as *The Seven Wise Masters of Rome*, *The Seven Wise Mistresses of Rome*. In this pre-Renaissance unscholarly tradition, Hercules took part in the siege of Troy, and Don Bellianis of Greece married the daughter of the Sultan of Babylon. But we find few, if any, abridgements of the works of the genuine ancient authors, such as Homer, Virgil, or Ovid, rich potential sources for retelling in simpler form, after the full and accurate texts of these authors became widely available. When Chapman and later Pope translated Homer, and when Dryden translated Virgil, the translations remained unabridged.

The same patterns can be discerned in the case of the English-language Bible, namely a continuation for a while of the freedom of the manuscript era, a sudden clamp-down around 1600 which lasted for nearly 200 years, and a flood in the romantic period.[31] During the period of restriction the English official church prescribed its own anthologised abridgements of the English-language Bible to be read aloud in its church services in a cycle throughout the year, in the prayers which were to be repeated in order to internalise the lessons, and in the paraphrases and catechisms to be used in religious teaching. In the sixteenth century, we find references to numerous printed stories and ballads abridged or adapted from the Bible and the Apocryphal Bible, including 'Joseph and his Brethren', 'Potiphar's wife', 'David and Bersheba', and the 'Constancy of Susanna' as well as stories which had clustered round the main biblical narratives in the remoter past, *Joseph of Arimathea*, *The Gospel of Nicodemus*, *The Wandering Jew of Jerusalem*, texts which, in some cases, had been printed, and intellectual property rights established, before the texts of the Bible itself were easily available in English translation.[32] Henry VIII is reported

---

[31] Noted also by Ian Michael, *Literature in School, A Guide to the Early Sources, 1700 to 1831* (Swansea 1999) 60.

[32] *Joseph of Arimathea* may have been abridged and adapted from longer texts printed by Caxton's successor Wynken de Worde and by Pynson 1520, 1520. *The Gospel of Nicodemus* may derive from Wynken de Worde's editions of 1509, 1511, 1512, 1518, or 1532. See Ashton 27, 31.

to have complained that the Bible which he had given to his subjects for their private edification was instead 'disputed, rimed, sung, and jangled in every alehouse and tavern'.[33] In the decades before 1600 we still find many biblical abridgements taken specifically from named chapters of the Bible being officially entered in the registers, but there is then a sudden and complete stop.[34] Until the end of the sixteenth century, too, a high proportion of dramatic performances were adaptations of themes drawn from biblical texts, with the stories often substantially changed from the originals.[35]

At some time around 1600, however, the use of the Bible as source material by other writers seems to have ended altogether, although playwrights continued to use stories from the Apocryphal Bible and from Josephus for some time longer.[36] Paraphrases of passages of the Bibles, that is rewriting of the old texts in new words, had been one of the ways in which English writers such as Spenser and Sidney began their literary careers.[37] But after 1597, when Middleton's paraphrase of the *Book of Solomon* was printed, the publication of new printed paraphrases also seems to have ceased altogether. With music, too, the Bible, which had provided about a quarter of the themes for Byrd and Ravenscroft, could no longer be used.[38]

After the clamp-down on biblical anthologies, abridgements, and adaptations, the changes of practice seem to have lasted as long as those that applied to other texts, with only a few children's versions permitted as exceptions, under special dispensation.[39] I have been unable to discover exactly when the restrictions were relaxed or lifted in law or in practice, but as with other types of printed text, the restrictions seem to have become inoperative as part of the changes which followed the decisions of 1774. After

---

[33] Quoted by David Starkey, *Elizabeth* (2000) 56, no source given.
[34] See 'English-language biblical and apocryphal biblical printed texts. Evidence of a clamp-down on abridgements and adaptations, around 1600', appendix 3, 495–6.
[35] See Roston.
[36] See 'The end of dramatic adaptations of biblical and apocryphal biblical texts', appendix 3, 496.
[37] See Christopher Hill, *The English Bible and the Seventeenth-Century Revolution* (1993) 338.
[38] *Ibid.*
[39] See STC 2993 and following list 'Selections from the Bible'. Those few after 1600 appear to be reprints. In Wing, which lists books from 1640, there is again no section on selections from the Bible. Green notes almost no abridgements after 1600. For the verse adaptations for children, see Green 155. In 1726 John Harris, a publisher who specialised in religious text books, sold *A Compendious History of the Old and New Testament, extracted from the Holy Bible, with 120 Copper Engravings.* The Ballad Partners trade wholesale catalogue of 1764, for which see chapter 17, lists among its 'small histories' adorned with a great variety of cuts and neatly stitched up in blue paper, 'The Holy Bible in Verse, Ditto in prose'. In 1755 John Newbery, an approved children's bookseller, obtained a state monopoly to produce biblical abridgements.

that date, we see a spate of abridgements and adaptations. In the 1790s, for example, Sarah Trimmer produced a series of illustrated simplifications of Bible stories, to be followed in 1802 by William Scolfield's *Scripture Stories* which, I have shown elsewhere, was pseudonymously written by William Godwin, the philosopher.[40]

The editor of *Christian Terence* (1592) noted that: 'There is an old familiar proverb, *It is not good to play with sacred things*. And what is holier and more sacred than the divinely inspired canonical scriptures? Therefore, to add, subtract, to omit anything from them, to insert speeches and characters, as poetic license permits, becomes a scruple in the eyes of some whom we do not want to offend needlessly.'[41] And it is easy to see the attraction of such arguments. However, we can note too that the English-language biblical texts were recent, commercially extremely valuable, intellectual properties created by private capital in exchange for a monopoly franchise. Whatever the theological justifications offered, the patterns of restriction and freedom are almost identical with others that were applied to mainstream printed texts for purely commercial reasons, and no theology is necessary in order to explain them.

In the decades before 1600, the astonishing originality, versatility, and vigour of the English Renaissance was helped by a large measure of overlap within and among texts, genres, and performance. Anthologies, abridgements, and adaptations are frequent. Performed plays are adapted from older plays, printed and unprinted, and from biblical and classical texts, long printed histories, novels, and poems, long and short, from works written at home and abroad. Printed verse plays and prose histories are frequently abridged into ballad versions, which are sung, and some of these versions give rise to new plays. Players perform ballads, some previously printed, others not, during the course of plays, and at times they carry the texts of these ballads into print with the main text. Performance and text draw freely from one another. Collaborations among authors are common, and the borrowings and appropriations move freely across the social spectrum. Prices are falling and access is widening. But what to modern eyes may look like admirable flexibility, diversity, and inclusiveness may, at the time, have seemed like a jungle of 'disorder' in the media, a worrisome loosening of

---

[40] For the attribution of this book to Godwin, see St Clair, *Godwins and Shelleys*, and 'William Godwin as Children's Bookseller' in Gillian Avery and Julia Briggs, eds., *Children and Their Books* (Oxford 1989). More details of Godwin's publications are given in 'William Godwin'. appendix 9, 603.
[41] Quoted by Roston 119.

control, a threatening tangle of competing intellectual property claims, and an unnecessary loss of income.

The tightening of the intellectual property regime after 1600 brought this artistic freedom to an end, and it was never to be regained. As private intellectual property ownership became more narrowly textual, printed texts increasingly stand on their own, unabridged, unanthologised, and closed off by price from the lower tranches of the reading nation. The adaptation by a playwright of an earlier play or a well-known story, was no longer to be seen as a compliment to a predecessor and to the continuity of the tradition and the audience's memory, but rather as evidence of the writer's lack of originality. Adaptation was plagiarism, a more generalised form of theft of intellectual property than textual copying.[42] By 1700 the notion of private ownership had spread even to the most intertextual and sententious of printed texts such as conduct books, texts which purported to offer immutable and timeless truths based on biblical precepts.[43]

The discouragement of anthologies, abridgements, and adaptations, affected printed texts of all kinds, including those concerned with religion, history, philosophy, scholarship, science, and medicine. Since after 1600 permission to quote from, abridge, or adapt long works seems seldom to have been sought or given, the changes held back the development of many of the genres of printed books which are most appropriate for carrying new texts, new discoveries, and new ideas to wider readerships. Taken with the general rise in mainstream book prices of the seventeenth century, they had the effect of dividing the reading nation into two, cutting off the majority from participation in modern culture, widely defined. From around 1600, all the main conduits for the spread of ideas from elites to the wider public, including children, were effectively blocked up, with only a small trickle, whose flow was carefully controlled by the textual owners, permitted. And when the dam broke in the years after 1774, the resulting flood was overwhelming.

The third change which I detect in the years after 1600 is, to some extent, a result of those already discussed. This was a tendency to create vested commercial interests in the continued production of older, and intellectually obsolete, forms of print. This trend too is also fully in line with what we

---

[42] For the increase in complaints about plagiarism by authors in the Restoration theatre, see Kewes, *Authorship*.

[43] See, for example, the complaint by the publisher Royston Meredith in *Mr Steele Detected* (1714), that Richard Steele had, in *The Ladies Library* (1714), plagiarised the works of Jeremy Taylor, of which, in accordance with the industry's practice, he claimed to hold the intellectual property rights.

would expect from the economic and intellectual property structures, and one which is most easily explained in such terms. Because they were privately owned properties, printed texts were treated, from a regulatory point of view, differently from other forms of cultural production. When, for example, as part of the English Reformation, the official supernatural was more closely delimited, and many elements declared to be illegitimate (for example, prayers for the dead, doctrines of purgatory, the cult of Mary, and non-biblical Christian myths), the state and church were able to ban them immediately. The employed priests in the parishes were simply instructed by their ecclesiastical superiors to change the content of the official supernatural which they taught to their parishioners or face penalties. Ballad singers could be prevented from singing ballad versions of biblical texts, at any rate in public. Visual images could also be removed or replaced. As far as the printed texts of the superseded official supernatural were concerned, the priests in the parishes and the fellows in the colleges could be ordered to destroy the old and to buy the new. When, however, the religious and cultural policies of the government and the church came into conflict with the private property rights of the intellectual property owners of the texts, the English common law tended to favour the rights of private property. Intellectual property having been conceived of as equivalent to real property, to stop an owner from taking an income from a private property would have been regarded as a confiscation. Changes in publishing practice were, therefore, generally not retroactive.

The book industry might voluntarily forgo the right to reprint a particular text of no great economic value, and the state sometimes encouraged owners not to reprint texts which had earlier been accepted as lawful. But when substantial commercial interests were at stake, the laws and customs of property weighed more heavily.[44] It was one thing to agree to renounce a belief in the doctrine of Purgatory, quite another to compel owners to give up an income-yielding property. Just as Roman Catholic and non-conformist families continued to enjoy their inherited real estates, albeit under restrictions, so too the owners of the intellectual property estates were allowed to continue to keep their possessions and to take their rents.

With many intellectual properties, the record suggests, the book industry successfully insisted on a right to reprint texts that were officially declared to

---

[44] For the state's 1623 request to the producers to adhere to the current textual policies, in spite of their legal property rights, see *A Proclamation against the Disorderly Printing* noted in appendix 2, 482.

be invalid and untrue. The ancient law book known as Bracton continued to be reprinted long after it was superseded.[45] In the years after 1600, the Ballad Partners continued to sell the older abridgements of biblical stories and non-biblical Christian myths even although they were no longer officially regarded as legitimate. Although the English state and church forbade the printing of new texts that offended against the current official supernatural, they did nothing to stop the reprinting of older texts, many of which were pre-Reformation. Nor did they clamp down on the continued production of books of fortune-telling, prognostications, and other ancient forms of supernatural which had long since been pronounced illegitimate, even although they had assumed the legal powers to do so. And the effects on the minds of readers were detectable two hundred years later. As the late eighteenth-century antiquarians discovered when they first took an interest in English rural popular culture, it was permeated with the remains of popery.[46]

For those at the lower tranches of the book market, the result was a cultural lock-in. The supply of abridgements of new texts having been cut off by the changed intellectual property regime, the Ballad Partners continued to produce the same, increasingly obsolete, titles year after year. On the eve of the romantic period, the printed literature available to a large constituency of readers was not much different from what it had been 200 years before.[47] This popular canon contained many texts which were already ancient at the time of the 1600 freeze. Three stories admired by Wordsworth, *Robin Hood, Jack and the Giants, St George and the Dragon*, and others, had a continuous history back to the oral and manuscript tradition of mediaeval romance.[48] Two of the most often-mentioned favourites, *Guy of Warwick* and *Bevis of Southampton*, predated printing by many centuries.[49] Of the dozen or so favourite romances condemned by Francis Meres in his printed anthology of 1598, the majority were still in print in abridged versions in 1774.[50] It was often part of the formula to begin by noting the reign during which the events occurred. Many stories, including *The King and the Miller* and *Fair Rosamond* are attributed to the time of Henry II. Another group cluster round Henry VIII: 'In the time of Henry Eighth, there was born

---

[45] Noted in *CHBB* iv, 490.
[46] Fox 407 quoting John Brand, *Observations on Popular Antiquities* (Newcastle 1771).
[47] See chapter 17.
[48] Victor E. Neuburg, *Popular Education in Eighteenth-Century England* (c. 1971) 116.
[49] Summarised in appendix 4, 503.   [50] (Francis Meres), *Palladis Tamia* (1598) 269.

in Lancashire a Maid (for her excess in height) called Long Meg.' Many of the stories are pre-Reformation and only a few refer to reigns after Elizabeth. They made little distinction between factual history and abridged romance.[51] King Arthur, King Leir, and King Alfred were as real as King Edward and King Henry. David and Goliath vied for attention with Jack and the Giants. In its 'godly books', fortune telling, its spells and love remedies, its astrological and magic almanac, its dream books, the chapbook made no distinction between the legitimate and the illegitimate supernatural, between history and myth, between science and magic. A similar freezing of popular reading seems to have occurred at much the same time, perhaps for similar reasons, in France, Spain, and probably Germany.[52]

Some historians of eighteenth-century popular culture have attributed the long survival of the ancient ballad and chapbook tradition to the innate conservatism of the rural mind.[53] However, such general factors, even if valid in some sense, cannot, by themselves, account for the patterns of book production which emerge from the record. The rural mind is unlikely to have suddenly become conservative in 1600 and suddenly ceased to be conservative within a few years of 1774, any more than a readerly taste for literary anthologies and abridgements suddenly disappeared in 1600 and suddenly revived in 1774.

The freezing of the popular canon after 1600, and the creation of a strong vested interest in prolonging it, can be correlated with a move to formal monopoly ownership of the main texts of the whole popular literature sector and the control of the chapman network. New, locally composed, titles could be run off on provincial presses, and if any proved successful, they were often bought in and added to the portfolio, but, contrary to what has been assumed in much modern writing on popular culture, none of the old favourites could be legally printed outside London.[54] During the course of the seventeenth century, the sector moved from no-poaching agreements to informal cartel, and then through formal cartel to the near complete monopoly which operated until after 1774. By inheritance and purchase, under the pre-emption conventions, the partnership took over all the printed stocks of their predecessors, the types and the wood blocks from

---

[51] See also Vincent 221, quoting Rogers.
[52] See, for example, Roger Chartier, 'Reading Matter and "Popular" Reading: from the Renaissance to the Seventeenth Century' in Cavallo and Chartier 274, 279.
[53] E.g. Rogers.
[54] Of recent writers Watt and Thomson are notable exceptions. For the huge change after 1774, see chapter 17.

which the books were made, the ballad warehouse, and all their exclusive rights to reprint them. The ballad and chapbook canon may have been read by the 'folk', that affectionate but condescending term, but they were not produced by the 'folk'. They were designed, manufactured, and supplied by a consortium of businessmen and portfolio investors in metropolitan London as part of a large, mature, and sophisticated sector of a centralised, cartelised, national book industry.

The same development and consolidation of vested commercial interests in prolonging the obsolete can be seen in many types of text besides the literary and the historical. *Solomon's Sentences*, an anthology of purportedly biblical *sententiae*, first produced in pre-Reformation days, continued to be supplied to the popular market during the whole of the long period of restriction. With books on medicine, too, the discouraging of abridgements meant that older texts continued to be reprinted and sold, sometimes with paratextual guarantees of their scientific validity. *Dreams and Moles, with their Interpretation and Significance*, for example, a long-lived chapbook which contained much nonsensical advice, claimed in the eighteenth-century editions, to have been 'first composed in Greek, and now faithfully rendered into English by a Fellow of the Royal Society, and a True lover of Learning'.[55] *Aristotle's Compleat Masterpiece*, a book about women's bodies which derives from an ancient pseudo-Aristotelian text and from Albertus Magnus's thirteenth-century *De Secretis Mulierum*, continued to be monopolistically sold until 1774.[56] Again, it is neither fair nor convincing to blame the poor for their ignorance, which was, to a large extent, simply knowledge which was mainstream and modern at various times before it was frozen in 1600.

The same long-run tendencies towards creating vested commercial interests in prolonging the obsolete can be seen with especial vividness in the case of almanacs, a group of texts which, along with the texts of the official supernatural, lay at the heart of the political and economic alliance between the state and the book industry. At the time when printed almanacs were first produced, the distinction between astronomy and astrology was not clear-cut. Officially produced almanacs in the early modern period could, therefore, legitimately include astrological forecasts without transgressing

---

[55] Ashton 77.
[56] See Paul-Gabriel Boucé, 'Some Sexual Beliefs and Myths in Eighteenth-Century Britain' in Paul-Gabriel Boucé, ed., *Sexuality in Eighteenth-Century Britain* (Manchester 1982) 28. Boucé notes that in 1743/5, when the Aristotle book had reached a twenty-third edition, the most up-to-date book, Robert James's *Medical Dictionary* cost £4 (80 shillings). The Aristotle seems to have been available from chapmen for about a shilling.

the limits of what was officially legitimate mainstream scientific knowledge. When, however, many features were later officially declared to be untrue and incompatible both with the discoveries of science and with the reformed religion, there was no easy way for private property rights and official cultural policies to be reconciled. In almanacs, the legitimate and the illegitimate supernaturals depended so intimately on one another that they often coexisted within the covers of a single book. Almanacs contained, for example, both the official state and ecclesiastical calendar and the astrological forecasts, prognostications, and advice on auspicious days whose efficacy depended upon knowing the date. The solution arrived at, as with other types of text, seems to have been, broadly, for the state and church to encourage the production of newly written types of almanac, but with no retrospective effect. Although formal pre-censorship of almanacs was introduced soon after the restoration of the monarchy in 1660, and from time to time the ecclesiastical authorities protested at the continued toleration of such 'magic' and 'superstition', the English state tacitly accepted the continued publication of a wide range of texts of what we may call the tolerated illegitimate supernatural. In the eighteenth century the almanac publishers cleared their astrological and magical texts with the ecclesiastical authorities, but provided they contained nothing politically dangerous, such as forecasts of social unrest, riots, dearth, or of a second fire of London, they were allowed to be printed under the royal arms and much Latin, traditional guarantees of authority and truth. As an instrument of control, the unofficial supernatural was a useful adjunct to the official. As late as 1800, on the basis of 'the brumal ingress', the *Vox Stellarum*, by Francis Moore, Physician ('Old Moore'), offered a detailed forecast of the course of European politics month by month for the coming year, including the foiling of a Popish plot.[57]

The practice of tranching down by price in the sale of newly written printed texts tended to divide the reading nation into layers which were differentiated by the length of time which had passed since first publication of the texts as well as by socio-economic class. This was a long-term continuing effect of the economic and intellectual property structures associated with text copying by moveable print. The effect of the 1600 tightening was to separate the constituencies of the reading nation by even larger time differences. Those at the top of the income scale had access to the most recently produced texts as well as to others. Those who had to wait for the

---

[57] See the facsimile in Robin Myers, ed., *The Stationers' Company, A History of the Later Years 1800–2000* (2001) 87.

effects of tranching down, had access to texts of varying degrees of modernity and obsolescence produced in the fairly recent past. But, as for those who, by lack of money, by remoteness, or by lack of education, were at the lower boundaries of the reading nation, many, on the eve of the romantic period, were still reading, or were listening to others reading aloud, a body of printed texts which were produced in the pre-modern age. For nearly 200 years a large constituency of the English reading nation was locked into the print of the early years of the reign of King James.[58]

[58] Discussed further in chapter 17.

CHAPTER 5

The high monopoly period in England

Lord Macaulay, whose *History of England* (1860) helped to establish many English national myths, attributed the rise of English literature in the eighteenth century to the abandonment of state censorship in 1695.[1] To win her freedom, France had to wait for the violent revolution of 1789, an event marked by declarations of rights and annual celebrations. England, with what Macaulay saw as her unique genius for pragmatic adaptation, simply allowed the Licensing Act of 1690 to lapse.[2] Once literature was 'emancipated', according to Macaulay, the good sense of the English people saw to the rest: English readers demanded more and better books and English authors came forward to supply them. The 1695 decision, Macaulay noted, was passed without a word being said about the liberty of the press. Petty excisemen grumbling about the frustrations of rummaging for illegal books had more impact on government policy than all the philosophical arguments of Milton's *Areopagitica*.[3]

Nowadays we rightly distrust grand narratives which flatter a nation's view of its own distinctive characteristics.[4] Nor is it clear that when the Whig parliament abandoned the legislation that required texts to be licensed before they could be printed, they intended to abolish textual

---

[1] Thomas, Lord Macaulay, *The History of England from the Accession of James the Second* (1860) i, 394; iv, 542; iv, 609; i, 281. See also Feather, *Publishing*, in which the key dates for changes offered are 1695 and 1800. The latter date is also chosen as signalling the 'democratisation of literature' by Kathryn Sutherland in *Penguin History of Literature v, 5: The Romantic Period* (1994).

[2] As Michael Treadwell points out in *CHBB* iv, 755, the act was normally referred to at the time as the 'Printing act'.

[3] Although against state licensing, Milton appears to have been in favour of perpetual intellectual property, 'the just retaining of each man his several copy, which God forbid should ever be gainsaid'. Quoted by William Dougal Christie, *A Plea for Perpetual Copyright* (1840) 6.

[4] Macaulay's narrative was broadly followed by Feather, *Publishing*, who calls the period until 1695 'The Press in Chains', and talks, at p. 105, of the ending of official controls 'opening the flood gates'. The Macaulay narrative has been repeated more recently by Marilyn Butler, 'Hidden Metropolis: London in Sentimental and Romantic Writing' in Celina Fox, *London, World City 1800–1840* (1992).

controls. By abolishing the requirement for texts to be pre-censored, the government was not, either in law or in practice, allowing the printing presses to be used for free discussion. General laws which put the onus on authors, publishers, and printers, have often proved more effective in controlling texts than pre-censorship by officials, and for a time after 1695, the penalties for infringement continued to be draconian. In 1720, for example, an eighteen-year-old apprentice, who had accepted a contract to print a pamphlet which questioned the Whig government's legitimacy, was put to death.[5] And all through the eighteenth century the penalties for printing texts that were judged libellous of politicians were severe.[6]

But, seen from a longer perspective, in one respect Macaulay was clearly right. During the eighteenth century, the British state largely withdrew from controls on the textual content of print. There continued to be boundaries beyond which no text could be printed without falling foul of the law, and banned books were still occasionally publicly burned by the common hangman, but, except during crises, such as the 1715 and 1745 rebellions, the limits of what was permissible were progressively widened and the penalties lessened.[7] The writings of the English deists, of Hume, Gibbon, and of other sceptical philosophers, historians, and moralists were printed, published, and sold without state interference, although in their various ways their writings undermined respect for governmental and ecclesiastical institutions. In this regard the experience of Great Britain differed from that of most other European countries whose governments continued to keep a tight, although seldom fully effective, textual control over the printed materials available for reading within their jurisdictions. In *ancien régime* France, for example, the writings of some of the most innovative thinkers, such as Rousseau and Voltaire, were banned; nearly a thousand persons, about 17 per cent of the total, went to the Bastille for publishing offences; and books were being sent for burning until the very eve of the Revolution in 1789.[8]

Modern accounts of the history of reading in England tell another story of national progress. During the eighteenth century, it has often been said, there was a growth in the number of schools and Sunday schools. As the English population became better educated, authors came forward to meet

---

[5] Timperley 623.   [6] Many examples in Timperley.
[7] For book burning of which examples are found during all but the last decades of the century, see Charles Ripley Gillett, *Burned Books* (New York 1932).
[8] See Daniel Roche, 'Censorship and the Publishing Industry' in Darnton and Roche 23 and Pottinger 77.

the new demand.[9] However, one of the many difficulties with this account is that, with the large exception of Scotland, there is little evidence of any general or steady rise in educational provision during the eighteenth century, even among the higher income groups.[10] Nor should we assume that for there to have been more reading, there had to have been more schools. The increase in national literacy which undoubtedly occurred in England in the nineteenth century has been shown to have preceded the provision of compulsory state primary education and was not caused by it.[11] The expansion in the use of computers which occurred in the 1980s and 1990s was not driven by state-financed teaching programmes, although there were some, but by large numbers of individuals responding to the drastic fall in the price of computers and educating themselves in the necessary skills.

It is sometimes suggested that, until the late eighteenth century, the growth of reading in England was limited by a shortage of capital. As long as the market for printed books was not yet fully mature, so it is said, the publishers had insufficient money with which to finance new publications and the expansion of the industry was therefore held back.[12] However, explanations relating to capital availability carry little conviction. A prosperous country with a growing economy which built the spa towns of Bath and Cheltenham as well as innumerable country houses, which settled colonies in North America, founded cities in India, sent fleets of ships to China every year, and dominated the slave trade, all from private funds, did not suffer from any shortage of capital nor from the means of mobilising it.[13] Although, as far as I know, the statistical work on the comparative rates of return on capital available in the various investment media has not yet been done, it is evident that some of the highest rates of return were available on those types of investments that catered for the richest constituencies of society, of which books were likely to be part. Indeed there is plentiful information, such as the rising asset prices of intellectual

---

[9] For example Collins, *Authorship* 51, and *Profession of Letters, passim*; Leavis 131; Altick 30; Plant 53, although she sees the growth occurring despite the low education levels. S. H. Steinberg, *Five Hundred Years of Printing* (1955) 16; and Raymond Williams, 'The Rise of the Reading Public' in *The Long Revolution* (1961) 156. See also Alvin Kernan, *Printing Technology, Letters, and Samuel Johnson* (Princeton 1987) 48, repeating the view of Terry Belanger, 'Books and Writers in Eighteenth Century England' in Isabel Rivers, ed., *Books and their Readers in Eighteenth-Century England* (Leicester 1982); and Sutherland.

[10] As late as 1816, of 12,000 English parishes, about 30 per cent had no schools of any kind and about 40 per cent only minimal provision of varying quality. See Williams, *Long Revolution* 135, no source given.

[11] For the growth of literacy and of reading in the nineteenth century, see especially Vincent 4.

[12] For example, Collins, *Authorship* 18; Cochrane 54; McKitterick ii, 167.

[13] See, for example, M. J. Daunton, *Progress and Poverty, An Economic and Social History of Britain 1700–1850* (Oxford 1995) 237.

properties, and the personal wealth of the intellectual property owners, to suggest that high rates of return were both obtainable and obtained.[14]

Another frequently repeated modern explanation relates the perceived growth in reading to the industrialisation of the manufacture of books. According to this account, the invention of the iron printing press, the mechanisation of papermaking, the use of steam power, and other productivity improvements reduced the cost, and therefore the price, of print, and so created a new 'mass audience' for reading.[15] Many recent discussions of reading in the romantic period offer variations of this view. However, without a single known exception, all of the books produced during the surge in book production in the late eighteenth century were manufactured by traditional hand-craft methods largely unchanged since the fifteenth century.[16] It was not until the 1820s and 1830s, a full generation and a half later, during which time the surge had continued, that we see significant mechanisation of book production. The technological changes, the evidence suggests, came after the expansion of reading was already well under way, and were more a result than a cause. Furthermore, although certain classes of books fell in price during the romantic period, the newly written books which traditional literary and cultural history regards as the most representative of the romantic period did not fall in price. On the contrary, in nominal as well as in real terms, the price of this type of print rose steeply and continued to rise even when cheaper methods of book manufacturing became available.[17]

So what did happen? Until more quantitative work is done, any conclusions must remain provisional, but from the data which I have gathered and consolidated, some patterns emerge. After 1695, and the simultaneous ending of the Stationers' Company's controls on the numbers of printing presses, we can trace a rapid, and reasonably steady, expansion of printing capacity, both in London and in the English provinces.[18] In London alone, during the eighteenth century, the number of active presses rose by at least 400 per cent, and it is easy to understand why Macaulay and others have seen such figures as evidence of a rise in book production.[19]

[14] Discussed further in chapter 7.
[15] For example R. A. Houston, *Literacy in Early Modern Europe* (1988) 196; Feather, *Publishing, Piracy, and Politics*; Jon Klancher, *The Making of English Reading Audiences, 1790–1832* (Madison, Wis. 1987); Sutherland; Lee Erickson, *The Economy of Literary Form* (1996); and William G. Rowland, Jr, *Literature and the Marketplace: Romantic Writers and their Audiences in Great Britain and the United States* (Lincoln, Nebr. 1997).
[16] See chapter 10.   [17] Chapter 11.
[18] Twenty-eight printing presses were counted in various English towns outside London, Oxford, and Cambridge, by 1728, just one generation after the lifting of the restrictions, Bowyer, *Anecdotes* 535.
[19] See McKitterick ii, 4, table 1.

However, much, probably most, of the increase seems to have consisted of legal documents, commercial stationery, advertisements, newspapers, and other printing besides books, and the growth was probably inhibited by taxes and stamp duties.[20] As far as printed books were concerned, the picture is less clear.[21]

The measurement of such a large quantum as book production is fraught with practical and definitional difficulties, for example, whether to include dictionaries, religious books, school textbooks, occasional sermons, and pamphlets, how to deal with the fragmentary nature of the sources, and which time frames to choose. Titles known to have been printed is a poor indicator of book production, and even on this measure I know of no series compiled on a consistent basis. Estimating the size of the potential market is also difficult. Population figures include minorities who did not speak English. We need to take account of Ireland which was both a market for British books and an offshore reprinter of British texts for illicit sale into the British markets. We need also to take account of the fact that North America was a growing market for British books until 1800 after which local American production increasingly displaced imports.[22]

However, making a number of assumptions, what seems to emerge is that during most of the first three-quarters of the eighteenth century, book production in England showed at best only a modest increase, some of which can probably be directly related to the expansion of commercial circulating libraries from the 1760s onwards.[23] When we put the estimates into a broader economic context, however, and look at trends rather than absolutes, the pattern is more clear. During the first three-quarters of the eighteenth century, a period in England when population, markets, transport, gross domestic product, and real incomes per head were all growing steadily, a modest increase in book production in absolute terms represents a fall in real terms.[24] The pattern that emerges is of a long, slow, downward trend in real terms, during which time the market for books became more concentrated in the upper-income groups, followed by a sharp change of direction upward towards the end of the eighteenth century, a trend that continues for the next hundred years. As far as I can see, with the partial exception of Raymond Williams, none of the modern authors who claim

---

[20] For the rapid growth in English provincial newspapers see Hannah Barker, *Newspapers, Politics, and Public Opinion in Late Eighteenth-Century England* (Oxford 1998).

[21] I have summarised some of the information which is most relevant to considering the issues in 'Markets' and 'Book production', appendix 1, 453.

[22] Some print runs in appendix 1. Discussed further in chapter 6.   [23] See chapter 10.

[24] See estimates from Floud and McCloskey in appendix 1, 455.

that the eighteenth century saw a steady rise in reading in Great Britain has appreciated that a rise in absolute levels may be a fall in real terms.

The traditional narratives about the growth of reading in eighteenth-century England do not fit the archival record at all well. Instead, they point to another set of questions. How could there have been a real terms' stagnation in book production, and presumably therefore in book reading, during the period which we think of as the Enlightenment, when so many innovative works of history, philosophy, and literature were being published, and when most other indicators of economic and social welfare were rising? Why too, we need to ask, did the growth rate in books and reading suddenly accelerate in the late eighteenth century and not at some other point before or later? A starting point for addressing such questions is the event to which Macaulay took as his turning point, the abolition of state censorship in 1695.

As far as the industry was concerned, after the lapsing of licensing in 1695, the question was not whether pre-censorship or general laws were to be preferred as a means of controlling the textual limits of acceptable print, but how, in the absence of state licensing, the industry could protect its private intellectual property rights in mainstream legitimate texts. For in 1695, as in 1641, by abolishing the institutions of textual pre-censorship, parliament had also, in effect, abolished the state guarantee of intellectual property. The ancient bargain between the industry and the state had been unilaterally, if inadvertently, abrogated.

The effects of the legal hiatus were soon seen. In a number of well publicised cases, including some involving Addison, Pope, and Dryden, a bookseller paid an author for a manuscript and took the commercial risk of printing and putting a new title on sale, only to find his prices undercut and his market seized by a rival who had done nothing but exploit a commercial opportunity created by somebody else. Although, in these cases, the courts upheld the rights of the first publisher against the reprinter, it was no longer clear under what legal authority they did so. Authors too found that publishers could again print their unprinted works without their consent.[25] In the absence of a law of licensing or of intellectual property, the two main agents of literary production, publishers and authors, were both in danger of being unable to recoup their investments. It was around this time that the stealing of intellectual property acquired the vocabulary which it has retained to the present day. Addison, adopting the commercial metaphors

---

[25] Formal authors' rights were still quite recent. See the summary in appendix 3.

of international trade, compared an expensive education and the personal efforts needed for the writing of a book to the fitting out of a ship for a long hazardous voyage. 'Those few investors who have the good fortune to bring their rich wares into port are plundered by privateers under the very cannon that should protect them.'[26] The word 'pirate' soon became the most common image in the book industry to describe the stealing of intellectual property by one member of the industry from another.

If a new legal regime of intellectual property was to be introduced, what form should it take? After the political settlement of 1688/9, no acts of previous governments which conferred monopoly, including monopolies relating to printing, were regarded as legal unless they had been explicitly approved by parliament. The Stationers' Company's collection of ancient vellum royal charters and letters patent, many of them bestowed by capricious and tyrannical monarchs, were no longer enough to persuade the Whig parliament to maintain and guarantee the industry's monopoly privileges.[27] The prerogative to grant monopolies over printing which the English crown had exercised, it was now remembered, had itself been a usurpation. Caxton, the first English printer, had not needed royal permission to set up his printing press any more than he would have needed royal permission for a new bakery. If the monopolies implicit in intellectual property and those conferred or guaranteed by the state were to be permitted to continue, they had to be seen to be serving some public policy purpose.

Rights in real property, according to the concept of property whose philosophical justification the Whigs adopted from the writings of John Locke, had been won by gifted individuals using their talents to tame a piece of nature. But could a formal new regime of intellectual property rights be constructed on Lockian principles? The answer lay with the now fully emerged 'author'. Was not an author who composed a literary work, where nothing had existed before except words, paper, pen, and ink, also a pioneer? Was not the writing of a new literary work equivalent to the creating of a real property, a farm say, or an orchard, from a piece of ground which had previously been untamed and unowned? And did not the English common law uphold the rights of the owners of such anciently pioneered properties, and of their heirs, to enjoy them in perpetuity? Historically, intellectual property rights had not been 'created' by the author by the act of writing a text, but by the printer by the act of copying it on to paper

[26] See Richmond P. Bond, 'The Pirate and the *Tatler*' in *The Library*, 1963.
[27] See, for example, 'On the Crown Privilege of Printing Bibles and Common Prayer Books' in *Quarterly Review*, 1819.

with moveable type. However, having themselves increasingly accepted the discourse of 'originality' which credited Shakespeare and others with having taken their works 'from Nature', the industry opened the way for a shift in the regulatory regime.

The 1710 Act of the Parliament of Great Britain, 'for the encouragement of learning', the outcome of a period of negotiation between the industry, the government, and parliament, enacted that the author of any book not yet published had the sole right of printing it for a term of fourteen years from first publication. If the author was still alive at the end of the first fourteen year term, the act made provision for a second term of fourteen years, making a maximum of twenty-eight years in all circumstances. Books for which the right to copy by print had already been assigned by an author to a bookseller, or was assumed to have been assigned, that is all books ever printed in England, were copyright-protected for twenty-one years. As the wording of the act made explicit, this new legal property right applied, after the expiry of the transitional period, within the time limits of the act 'and no longer'. The short time span of fourteen years matched the limit for patents for new industrial inventions which were also based on the need to provide economic incentives to encourage innovations which would benefit the public.

By the act of 1710, the theory of intellectual property as being essentially and originally an authorial right was, for the first time, made explicit in the statute law of Great Britain. The act of Queen Anne, as it was often called, on which many other countries later modelled their copyright laws, was a decisive step in the formalisation of a new jurisprudential theory of intellectual property. Under the 1710 formulation, copyright was held to come into existence with the act of composition by the author, that is the writing of a text in manuscript on paper, and the right was then available to be ceded by the author to a publisher, with or without payment. The act therefore marked not only the culmination of a change in thinking about the nature of texts, but also a conceptual shift, and therefore potentially an economic shift, in the relationship between the two main agents of literary production, the author and the publisher.

The 1710 Act gave the London book industry much of what they most wanted, the establishment of a legal intellectual property right enforceable in the courts. However, the time-limited period of the monopoly was a severe disappointment. The industry had hoped that the new law would give them a statutory right of copyright in perpetuity, and so confirm in statute law the actual practice in England which had existed, largely unbroken, since the coming of print. In their many memoranda and petitions they claimed that the owner's rights to his or her literary property were, like other property rights, common law rights, as ancient as the institution of property itself, and therefore not limited or limitable in time. In 1724 and again in the 1730s, when the transitional period had expired, the industry's leaders promoted parliamentary bills aimed at extending the time limit, or gaining further transitional relief. However, in every plea that came before parliament in the eighteenth century, the industry's pleas for perpetual or long copyright were rejected. Even Locke, whose writings did much to give a philosophical underpinning to the claimed rights of real property, could see that intellectual property was essentially different and argued for a limited time period.

For a time after 1710 there seems to have been no doubt in the minds of parliament, of the publishers, or of the lawyers who advised them, that the act meant what it plainly said.[28] Pope's contract for the sale of the copyright of his translation of *The Iliad*, agreed in March 1713/14, was limited to 'such time and terme of years as he or his heirs enjoyed such rights', the only rights which he had the legal power to sell under the recent act.[29] Even when a bookseller obtained a private act of parliament, the rights were limited to those accorded by the 1710 statute.[30] In 1735, however, the Master of the Rolls, one of the two most senior judges in England, gave an injunction to prevent the reprinting of a standard conduct book, *The Whole Duty of Man*, even although the date of the book's first publication, 1657, was well outside all the time limits set out in the act.[31] In 1739 the Lord Chancellor granted an injunction to prevent R. Walker from reprinting Milton's *Paradise Lost*, first published in 1667, also well outside the time limits of the act. The English courts, it emerged, were reluctant to enforce a statutory provision which, in the vocabulary of real property, could be represented as an uncompensated confiscation. By granting injunctions, the English courts only conceded that a point of law had been raised which needed to be considered in a full trial but, for practical purposes, an injunction was as good as a determination. We hear of litigants being offered money by their opponents' lawyers to let the injunctions stand unchallenged.[32] When a

---

[28] For the legal advice see Collins, *Authorship* 54, 68, and 73.

[29] See James McLaverty, 'The Contract for Pope's Translation of Homer's Iliad: An Introduction and Transcription' in *The Library*, 1993.

[30] For example an act which granted Samuel Buckley exclusive rights to print and reprint the 'Histories of Thuanus' in 1714. Quoted by Collins, *Authorship* 65.

[31] Rose 51. Example quoted by Lord Hailes in the Court of Session Judgement of 1773. The name, and even the gender, of the author were unknown, although it is now well established that he was Richard Allestree. See also William St Clair and Irmgard Maassen, eds., *Conduct Literature for Women, 1640–1710* (2002) in which (Allestree's) *Ladies Calling* is reproduced.

[32] Most notoriously in the case of almanacs in 1775. See Blagden 36.

copyright case occurred, the book industry's specialist lawyers stood ready to quote earlier injunctions, to threaten expensive legal actions against anyone who challenged its interpretation, and to obscure the whole institution of copyright in such an impenetrable fog that even the judges were unable to see their way. 'Rent seeking', that is, the devising of imaginative means of enhancing and maintaining the monopoly, is a well-attested feature of modern monopolistic industries.[33]

In disregarding the unambiguous words of the statute, the English courts may have been attempting to continue to exercise the regulatory role of balancing the producer and consumer interests that had been theirs under the guild system, but in practice the consumer interest was scarcely considered.[34] Those who had framed the act of 1710, foreseeing the possibility of the abuse of monopoly, provided for appeal against excessive book prices, and gave powers to enforce price reductions. But the price control provisions of the 1710 Act appear never to have been used, and in a further act of 1739, the last legal safeguards against excessive prices were abolished without replacement. At some point, whose date I have not found, the limits on maximum edition size were also abolished. All these decisions appear to have been taken with at least the tacit approval of the political institutions of the English state which made no attempt to ensure that the 1710 Act was implemented. At the beginning of the eighteenth century, the London book industry thus found itself with all the privileges and institutions of the guild system, but without any of controls which normally accompanied such a regime. They were able to act as an unregulated and unrestrained private commercial monopoly over the whole text-based culture of England, and this is what they proceeded to do.

The London industry consisted of a changing association of publishing firms, some large, some small, together covering all aspects of publishing, printing, and wholesale bookselling.[35] It excluded all members of the industry operating in England outside London, notably the publishing presses in Cambridge and Oxford and the provincial retail sector, as well as a large and shifting fringe publishing/printing industry in London. From 1710 until 1774, a time I call the high monopoly period, the London book industry operated an elaborate regime of restrictive trade practices, of which the foundation was the private beneficial ownership of all printed texts.

Intellectual property, or 'literary property' as it was then called, was heritable, transferable, and divisible, and held in perpetuity. Contracts made

---

[33] Scherer and Ross 668.   [34] The stages in the transition are well described and analysed by Rose.
[35] For the involvement of the print makers in the cartel see the letter of Horace Walpole to Mason of 15 May 1773 quoted by Cochrane 140.

between publishers and authors and between publishers now provided for the sale of copyrights 'in full' and 'for ever'.[36] Some contract documents contain phrases like 'to have and to hold for ever', piling up the same tautologies as are used in marriage contracts, and with the same aim.[37] Other contracts illegally required authors to waive their statutory rights 'all Acts of Parliament to the Contrary in any way Notwith Standing'.[38] When a manuscript of what was then believed to be an unknown play by Shakespeare was sold, Theobald the owner and editor of the manuscript assigned the intellectual property rights 'for ever, notwithstanding any Act or Law to the Contrary'.[39]

Property rights were accorded to all printed texts, to music, to songs, to new editions of previously published works, to translations, to anthologies, to abridgements, to printed collections of private letters, to maps, engravings, and woodcuts. The beneficial ownership of the whole of the printed literature of England, old and new, from the Bible to the ballad, lay in the hands of private monopolists, partnerships of monopolists, or individuals or institutions granted monopoly franchises by the state. For some older printed works, the industry's claim to textual ownership was supported by a written record of inheritance, assignment, and trade sales going back to the time of the original publishing contracts. With older English-language authors, such as Chaucer, records went back to the time when the registers were first established and it could reasonably be assumed that the line of ownership went back to the act of first printing by Caxton. As for the ancient Greek and Latin authors, it was hard to believe, as the Lockian theory of property required, that Homer and Virgil had made contracts transferring their authorial intellectual property rights to a publisher, but in all cases, the current English owners were able to construct a pedigree of trade transfers or of state privileges or patents back to the printing firms who had created such rights in England by being the first to copy them with the technology of print.

The second characteristic of the industry was that it was highly cartelised. The large and growing portfolio of prime intellectual properties, known

---

[36] Examples from the Robinson archives, transcribed by Bentley.

[37] Words used, for example, in a receipt by A. Millar of 1751 in Bodleian, ms. Eng. Misc. b 44. Millar's contract with Robertson for *The History of Scotland* was in the same form. The custom was explained by a spokesman for the industry to a parliamentary inquiry in 1774. See Hansard, column 1081.

[38] Stagg to Bowyer, 28 April 1740. Letter inserted in Nichols, ledger. In 1729, Thomas Walker assigned his play *The Fate of Villany* (sic) 'to John Watts, his Heirs and Assigns for ever, notwithstanding any Act or Law to the contrary.' William Upcott collection, BL add. ms. i, 206.

[39] Theobald's contract dated 31 July 1728, quoted from the manuscript in the Folger library, by Peter Seary, *Lewis Theobald and the Editing of Shakespeare* (Oxford 1990) 220.

as the 'English stock', which continued to be held collectively by the Stationers' Company, enabled members to hold shares in proportion to their changing weight within the industry, and gave the whole industry a strong economic interest in maintaining the current arrangements.[40] But now, in addition to the formal 'stocks' similar arrangements for common ownership were extended to many other types of text by an elaborate system of overlapping partnerships. When a new book was to be published, only members of the cartel were permitted to participate in the arrangements by which shares in the new venture were divided, and only members were permitted to participate in the shared credit, advertising, and distribution facilities. These arrangements, by sharing both risks and rewards, helped to bind the industry together, and ensure that all important decisions were taken collectively. When an obituary noted that someone was a 'respectable' bookseller, always scrupulous in his business dealings, that is code for 'member of the cartel'.[41] The first so-called 'conger' was formed around 1719, with another, 'the new conger' shortly afterwards, but the practice had existed before the word was generally in use and all the separate congers were soon amalgamated.[42] According to those left outside, congers were the giant eels which gobbled up the smaller eels, but etymologically the name derived from a 'conjure', or sworn agreement, of the kind which guilds had enforced to protect the trade secrets or 'mysteries' of their trade.

The publishers enforced strict pre-emption rights, a classic feature of cartels, which is designed to keep the assets in the hands of the members. When any intellectual properties owned by a member came to be sold, say when he or she died, ended a partnership, or retired from business, they could only be sold to other members, at special sales arranged for the purpose.[43] If, as occasionally happened, a non-member, usually a candidate member, was permitted to buy the assets of a member, he was required to sell any shares in the cartel's intellectual properties back to the cartel. John Murray the first, for example, who had made a success of publishing specialist medical books written in Edinburgh, was permitted to buy a London bookselling business, but only on condition that he immediately sold all the intellectual properties to the members of the cartel at a pre-emption trade sale which

---

[40] For a list of stockholders of the Stationers' Company in 1785, a group who coincided to a large extent with the members of the cartel, see Michael L. Turner, 'A List of Stockholders in the Worshipful Company of Stationers, 1785' in Hunt, Mandelbrote, and Shell 141.

[41] Many examples in Timperley.

[42] *The Notebook of Thomas Bennet and Henry Clements* gives many glimpses of how the 'congers' worked in practice in the late seventeenth and early eighteenth centuries. The account by Robert Dale Harlan (see Harlan, which quotes many original documents), is also particularly useful.

[43] See 'Closed book-industry sale catalogues' in bibliography.

he did not attend.[44] Any member buying intellectual properties at one of these sales also bound his widow and his heirs to onsell only within the cartel, a sworn condition which may have been the original 'conjuration'.

It was because of the need to preserve the pre-emption rights in a guild system that women, especially widows, but also unmarried daughters, had played a part in the book industry from the earliest days. Women who inherited property were highly marriageable, and there were many jokes about the apprentice marrying the widow.[45] Under the guild system as it operated in the book industry, this had been more than a custom – any widow who married a man from outside the ranks of the Stationers' Company forfeited her rights. The theory of real property emphasised the freedom which possession conferred – a man could do what he liked with his own. Of all the restrictive practices, which contradicted the business norms operating in other areas of the economy, pre-emption rights were the most obvious, and the cartel maintained a fiction that the sales were open to all, even although in practice the catalogues were only sent to cartel members and no outsiders were admitted to the meetings.[46]

The industry guarded the demarcation arrangements between the different trades. Printers, for example, were barred from publishing and retail bookselling, even in cases where the author was paying all the costs.[47] New entrants to both the publishing and to the manufacturing sectors were required to serve seven-year apprenticeships, and then to follow a long career progression through the ranks of the Stationers' Company.[48] These guild limits on the human resources employed in the industry had remained even although the restrictions on the number of printing presses, that is the capital stock, had been abolished in 1695, and they were legally enforceable. Thomas Gent, a printer, for example, records that in 1715 he was arrested for breaking his apprenticeship, and later when he had succeeded in obtaining his freeman's livery, he was accused of having broken the apprentice's obligation not to marry.[49] Anyone who practised printing

[44] Zachs 24 notes the sale of intellectual properties Murray had acquired by taking over Sandby's business. Once admitted he was then able to buy at the restricted trade sales as noted by Zachs 35.

[45] The remarrying widow was a well-known figure in the comic theatre from *Roister Doister c.* 1550 to Massinger's *A New Way to Pay Old Debts*, Wycherley's *Plain Dealer*, and Congreve's *The Way of the World*. See Barbara J. Todd, 'The Remarrying Widow, a Stereotype Reconsidered' in Mary Prior, ed., *Women in English Society, 1500–1800* (1985). The statistics in the sample, p. 83, suggest a decline in the proportion of widows who remarried, perhaps an indicator of the decline in the guild system and the rise of the commercial economy.

[46] Collins, *Authorship* 18.   [47] Collins, *Authorship* 16, quoting Johnson.

[48] See figures in Cyprian Blagden, 'The Stationers' Company in the Civil War Period' in *The Library*, 1958.

[49] Thomas Gent, *The Life of Mr Thomas Gent, Printer, of York* (1832) 50, 67.

without having served his full apprenticeship was liable to prosecution, even if he was skilled at the craft, as Cheney of Banbury discovered as late as 1771.[50]

Those who had passed through the necessary gradations of apprenticeship could practise within the industry in London or in the English provinces and colonies. In order to join the cartel, however, a London bookseller had first to make himself acceptable to the existing members either by being a family member or by showing a track record of commercial success. For a bookseller who wished to publish, this usually meant having successfully published a number of new titles on his own account, often titles declined by members of the cartel. If any of these properties still had value, he would offer shares to the members of the cartel, indeed he seems to have been obliged to offer them. Once accepted into the cartel, he then had the right to buy shares in other intellectual properties as they became available at the closed pre-emption sales in competition with other members. The risks associated with innovative and risky publications thus tended to be left to newcomers and outsiders, with any intellectual properties which proved successful being quickly taken over and brought into the existing industry's structures. To obviate the potentially stultifying effects which usually result from such a closed, and to a large extent, hereditary system, the cartel picked out its own potential leaders, likely 'high fliers' – the term used as early as 1724 – including some men from the provinces.[51] The talented young John Robinson, for example, who was given unlimited credit by Longman when he began in business as a bookseller, was to become the biggest publisher of his generation.

During the high monopoly period the English publishing industry operated almost as a single firm with a limited measure of internal competition. The leaders were rich, well organised, commercially ingenious, and politically powerful. Many became members of parliament and five were lord mayors of London.[52] William Strahan, who had extensive private publishing and printing interests, as well as a formal monopoly, as king's printer in England, over the main required texts of the official supernatural, bought his seat, kept silent except when book-industry interests were under threat, voted consistently with the government, and accepted money from the secret service vote.[53] He and many of the others were not uninterested

---

[50] *John Cheney and His Descendants, Printers in Banbury since 1767* (Banbury, privately printed 1936) 6. Examples from 1734 in Timperley 651.
[51] They included Cluer of Northampton who later took over the management of the whole chapbook industry. See Timperley 631.
[52] Timperley 806   [53] Cochrane 190.

in literature. Indeed many publishers were highly regarded by authors, such as Samuel Johnson, for their personal generosity. But personalities mattered less than structures. Whoever was in charge, the industry as a whole behaved as a classic private corporate interest group, like the East India Company or the West India sugar planters, combining together to maximise their privileges, actively excluding outsiders, maintaining a close alliance with the state, and, incidentally, creating a dependent and well-rewarded branch of the legal profession to help uphold their privileges and practices.[54]

Key to all the operations of the industry, as at other times, were the arrangements for the pricing of books. The industry moved effortlessly from the price regulation of the guild period, in which price controls aimed to keep prices low, to price-fixing which aims to keep prices high. The industry seems to have had in place agreements for setting the prices of manufacturing, such as printing, binding, engraving, and perhaps paper.[55] Equally important was vertical price-fixing, especially resale and retail price maintenance, strict limits on discounts, including discounts on exports, internal rules on the financing of credit, and tight conditions for supplying books to circulating libraries. As Adam Smith noted, 'People of the same trade seldom meet together, even for merriment and diversion, but the conversation ends in a conspiracy against the publick, or in some contrivance to raise prices.'[56] Indeed, he said, one reason why guilds and corporations were so eager to maintain internal charities was that they provided legitimate occasions for such meetings.[57]

What were the consequences for texts, books, prices, access, and reading? The benefits which the industry's structures and practices brought to the producer interest were not only well spread among the publishers and printers, the investors and manufacturers, but were shared to an increasing extent with the authors and editors of texts. Those authors whose writings could command a sufficient number of sales at high prices were, for the first time in history, able to demand not only large payments but a rising share of the total receipts. Whereas, in the seventeenth century, authors,

---

[54] When the elder Tonson died in 1735 his estate, which included lands in three counties, was valued at £100,000, a figure which put him among the richest men of the time. Timperley 652.

[55] See Ellic Howe, *The London Compositor, Documents-Relating to the Wages, Working Conditions, and Customs of the London Printing Trade, 1785–1900* (1947). The first fully formal price-fixing agreement covering the whole industry seems to have been put in place in 1775, the year after 1774 when the cartel was trying to regroup, but less formal agreements seem to have existed before that date.

[56] Smith's *Wealth of Nations* 145.   [57] Ibid. 45.

including Milton, parted with their manuscripts and with their intellectual property rights for a few pounds, Dryden and Pope, Johnson and Smollett, Gibbon, Hume, Robertson, Adam Smith, Hugh Blair, and many others, were able to command hundreds and even thousands. William Blackstone was able to sell the copyright of his *Commentaries on the Laws of England* for over £3,000, an immense fortune.[58] Even when, as was normal, an author had parted with all rights at the time of the first edition, the booksellers might make an *ex gratia* later payment if a book did well, even although they were under no contractual obligation to do so, a practice which enabled them to claim that they were not so much commercial agents as patrons of literature.[59]

In the high monopoly period all the main producer interests, the authors and the editors, the publishers, the printers, the papermakers, the cutters of the types, the binders, and the booksellers, and many of their employees, all benefited from the carefully managed structures of costs, prices, and margins. These arrangements enabled the publication of an impressive range of innovative texts, some very long, in philosophy, history, travel, political economy, and many branches of learning and imaginative literature. It is easy to sympathise with those who, from the time of Macaulay, have seen the eighteenth-century London book industry as among the glories of the European Enlightenment. However, the structures which produced benefits for some, tended to disbenefit others. One by one, the avenues which made printed texts available, other than to the topmost tranches, were closed off. To protect their prices, the publishers preferred to 'waste' unsold stocks rather then remainder them.[60] The renting of books from bookshops and coffee houses was discouraged, reversing a trend of the previous century.[61] Abridgements were seldom permitted, and the reprinting of passages from printed books in periodicals outlawed. As for the selling of books in parts, the industry seems over the period to have phased out practices which had been quite well developed earlier.[62] Gibbon refused permission for *The Decline and Fall of the Roman Empire* to be made available in numbers.[63] Although the great philosophical and historical books of the century, which in previous centuries might have been banned or censored, were all

---

[58] The Strahan archives, 48,804, record the purchase from the author in 1772 of a one-third share for £1,096 18s. 6d.

[59] See, for example, Blair's *Sermons* in chapter 14 and appendix 9.

[60] Lackington says that this was done before his time. There are also examples in the romantic period, see, for example Burney's *The Wanderer* in appendix 9. Most of the books wasted would probably have still been in sheets, unbound.

[61] See chapter 13.　　[62] See R. M. Wiles, *Serial Publication in England before 1750* (Cambridge 1957).

[63] See Horace Walpole's sneering story quotated in appendix 9 'Edward Gibbon'.

published as commercial productions without state restriction, they were all expensive and remained out of the reach of many readers for a long time after publication.

Physically, in the high monopoly period, the typefaces of English books grew larger, paper became whiter and thicker, and the margins on the page widened. Many titles were published in the larger formats of folio, and quarto, beautiful to the eye, but uncomfortable to the wrist. Octavos too were frequent, and short texts were made to appear longer by splitting them into more than one volume.[64] By contrast the convenient duodecimos and smaller formats that had been common in the previous century were no longer favoured.[65] Large and heavy books which remained immobilised in aristocratic and institutional libraries had slow velocities of circulation both new and second-hand, an arrangement which kept second-hand prices high and access restricted. Monopolists are well known for offering unnecessary luxury as a way of justifying high prices, and the display of art and belles-lettres was part of the eighteenth-century culture of conspicuous politeness. But, to an extent, the control over access to ideas which had previously been exercised by state censorship was now effected by the weight, price, and immobility of modern books. Only in the area of newspapers and period-icals do we see a compensating trend towards a widening of the reading nation. Although most newspapers stuck closely to political, military, and economic news, the literary reviews of the high monopoly period, notably the *Monthly Review* and the *Critical Review*, not only offered comment on recently published works but usually included extensive direct quota-tions. During the high monopoly period the literary reviews were a way of enabling knowledge of newly published texts to circulate among the higher tranches of the market rather than as a tranching down to readers of lower socio-educational status.

There is plentiful evidence of other effects commonly associated with monopoly. If the cartel was to continue to deliver monopoly profits to all participants, there could be no breaking of ranks between the publishers and the printers, that is between the investors and the manufacturers. As has been observed in many monopolistic industries, the industry resisted technological innovation.[66] The technology for making stereotype plates, for example, was already well developed in the Netherlands by the end of the

---

[64] For example, Dodd's *Beauties of Shakespeare*, Goldsmith's anonymous *Vicar of Wakefield*, and Sterne's anonymous *Sentimental Journey* were issued as two volumes.

[65] Bowyer *Anecdotes* 503. For the small format offshore piracies of Thomas Johnson of the Hague see appendix 1, p. 476.

[66] For the weak record of innovation in such firms see Scherer and Ross 682.

seventeenth century, and was later adopted and refined in France.[67] However, in England, since it put traditional hand-printing at risk, attempts to introduce stereotyping were discouraged and sabotaged, and it was not until the 1810s and 1820s, when outsiders and pirates led the way, that we see that technology was being slowly adopted in the mainstream industry. Another effect was to cause a relative rise in the investment returns available from, and therefore the asset value of, older, safer, well-tried copyrights, compared with those of new copyrights. Rising asset prices acted as a financial barrier to entry even for members of the cartel. Nevertheless such financial figures as have been found suggest that, even after paying these entrance costs, investment in the older intellectual properties often proved more profitable than new publications.[68] The industry, by building up vested interests in the supply of certain favoured titles, and by its constant awareness of the need to maintain the share price of these properties by rationing the supply, encouraged a tendency towards cultural as well as towards technological obsolescence. In the supply of school textbooks, for example, the same two texts, Dyche's *Guide to the English Tongue* and Dilworth's *New Guide to the English Tongue* were commercially and therefore culturally entrenched in the school system for a century or more.

During the high monopoly period, the London book industry was as perfect a private monopoly as economic history can show. Examples of every restrictive trade practice known to modern regulators can be found, including cartel, conspiracy, price-fixing, predatory pricing, rent seeking, repetitive and baseless litigation, entry barriers, market division, credit-fixing, collective refusal to deal, exclusionary joint ventures, resale price restrictions, tying, and vertical non-price constraints. Commercial practices aimed at restricting output and raising prices which nowadays attract heavy criminal penalties including prison, were not only openly practised but were built into the day-to-day operating structures of the industry.[69] And all these practices rested upon the perfect monopoly of perpetual intellectual property. The economic and welfare consequences of such business practices were, of course, less well researched and theorised than they are now. However, even at the time, the main point was well understood. Monopoly leads to unnecessarily high prices which restricts access and reduces the potential benefits to the public.

---

[67] For stereotyping in the Netherlands, see McKitterick ii, 176. For the effects of stereotyping, see chapters 10, 16, 17 and 21. For the French stereotypes of Firmin Didot see chapter 15.
[68] This emerges from the account of the sale given by Zachs.
[69] Usefully summarised by Shenfield and Stelzer.

As far as the producers were concerned, the constantly changing pattern of interlocking obligations of the high monopoly period enabled members to share in the general prosperity of the industry in proportion to their stake, spreading the ups and downs of economic cycles, and providing a measure of insurance against business disasters.[70] Members of the industry and new entrants could, for a price, increase their relative share quite quickly, buy into the collective assets, and increase their influence over the industry's collective policies, while others could retire, disinvest, or withdraw from business altogether, with minimum commercial disturbance to themselves, to their colleagues, or to the commercial strength of the industry as a whole. As far as book buyers and readers were concerned, it was a system which allowed many new long texts to be researched, written, and published, advancing knowledge and understanding in many fields. But these benefits were only available to the wealthiest readers at the highest tranches of the market, with some of the biggest reading constituencies increasingly confined to texts which were both stable and obsolete. The literary system as a whole, producers and consumers, was self-perpetuating and self-reinforcing, both financially and culturally, and could only be changed as a result of some drastic external shock.

[70] Bankruptcies were infrequent and sometimes voluntary. See the table in Ian Maxted, *The British Book Trades 1731–1806, A Checklist of Bankruptcies* (Exeter 1985) iv, and chapter 6, below.

CHAPTER 6

The explosion of reading

Industries operating a profitable cartel usually find themselves challenged.[1] Outsiders who undercut the artificially high prices have to be stopped or co-opted. Insiders who break the rules have to be disciplined or expelled. Instances of all the main types of challenge and response observable in modern monopolistic industries can be found in the eighteenth-century London book industry. Rivington, who broke ranks on a wide range of practices, including offering larger-than-normal discounts on exports to the American colonies, selling intellectual properties in contravention of the pre-emption conventions, and having books printed cheaply outside England, was driven into bankruptcy by predatory pricing.[2] Osborn, another publisher was also obliged to go into bankruptcy, but in his case this was a state he could enjoy, for he was given a large lifetime pension as compensation for withdrawing from business.[3] Edmund Curll, one of the pirates whose reprints during the legal vacuum after 1695 led to the passing of the 1710 Act, seems to have been accepted into the cartel, his name appearing, for example, as one of the authorised publishers of works by Pope. He must have looked out of place at the meetings of the board, since, during his earlier career as a pornographer, he had had his ears sliced off.[4]

In modern conditions, studies suggest that cartels seldom manage to maintain their effectiveness for long periods. Often their dominance is undermined by the development of substitutes. In the 1920s, for example, the artificially high price of rubber was successfully challenged by the

---

[1] For a modern discussion of cartels and the various welfare losses they cause see Scherer and Ross.
[2] See Hernlund. Some details and transcribed documents are given in Cochrane 86, although, like Hernlund, he equates the producer interest with the wider public interest. Among the attempts to break the power of the booksellers during the high monopoly period, the Society for the Encouragement of Learning wished to finance publication outside the industry structures. See Marston 19.
[3] See Terry Belanger, 'Tonson, Wellington and the Shakespeare Copyrights' in (Graham Pollard), *Studies in the Book Trade in Honour of Graham Pollard* (Oxford 1975). See also Michael Harris, 'Paper Pirates: The Alternative Book Trade in mid-18th Century London' in Robin Myers and Michael Harris, eds., *Fakes and Frauds* (1989) 47–69. For Osborn see Collins, *Authorship* 82.
[4] Examples from Collins, *Authorship*.

development of synthetic products. In the 1950s, the aluminium industry ended the hegemony of the cartelised producers of tin-plated steel cans.[5] As far as printed books were concerned, however, until the arrival of radio and film in the early twentieth century, there was no substitute with even remotely similar characteristics. Moreover, it was not only the industrial structures and practices which were monopolistic, but the monopoly implicit in intellectual property, guaranteed by the state, which prevented competition between books, except where the texts were sufficiently different to be regarded as separate properties.

However, the London industry's power extended only to England and, to a diminishing extent, to the British colonies overseas. Ireland, which contained a large English-speaking population in Dublin and elsewhere, was then a separate jurisdiction, not part of the United Kingdom, and one where there was no intellectual property law and little customary practice. During the high monopoly period, many titles first printed in Great Britain were reprinted offshore in Ireland, with no financial benefit given to the author, and put on sale in both countries at prices far below those prevailing in London. The ledgers of Daniel Graisberry, a Dublin printer, the only archival source known to me which gives production figures, and one which, as far as I know, has not been previously used, suggest that, in terms of titles, the Irish offshore industry may have reprinted more English books, notably novels, than is commonly estimated, and that the print runs were much the same as those in Great Britain.[6] How far the circulation of books printed in Ireland was confined to the local Irish market and how far they were illegally smuggled into Great Britain and the British colonies cannot be easily judged. What we can say is that, during the eighteenth century, as a result of its offshore status, English-speaking Dublin had access, at highly favourable prices, to a wide range of English-language books, from the long philosophical and historical works of the Enlightenment to the latest circulating library novels, a factor which may have contributed to the intellectual vigour of the city at that time. There was also some offshore English-language reprinting in the Netherlands and in Switzerland, but there is little evidence that the books concerned reached Great Britain in significant numbers.[7]

---

[5] For these and other examples, see Scherer and Ross 355.

[6] Some print runs from the Graisberry ledgers, in appendix 1, 470, include novels which are otherwise unrecorded. See also Warren McDougall, 'Smugglers, Reprinters and Hot Pursuers' in Myers and Harris, *1550–1990* 173, which contains some quantified information taken from legal records.

[7] Notably in the Netherlands by Thomas Johnson, a Scottish printer. See appendix 1, 476 for a summary of his list.

By far the biggest external challenge came from Scotland. Although a separate Scottish printing/publishing industry had existed since the first years of the sixteenth century, its output had been small and its sales local. There had been some competitive offshore reprinting between the two countries, and although Sidney's *Arcadia*, a book much in demand in England, was reprinted in Edinburgh in 1599 and Shakespeare's *Venus and Adonis* in 1627, and the *Works of Sir David Lindsay*, a Scottish writer, were reprinted several times in London, there appears later to have been some understanding between the two industries, notably in the case of Bibles.[8] By the terms of the 1707 Act of Union which established the United Kingdom of Great Britain, freedom of trade was guaranteed, and the 1710 Act applied to both countries.[9] But although the two countries were politically united, they retained separate legal systems and judiciaries, and it was this feature of the union which enabled a divergence to occur.

The English judges, operating a system of law which relied heavily on property, precedent, and custom, gave great weight to the fact that the English book industry had operated perpetual intellectual property since the earliest days of printing. Their approach to legal decision making was essentially backward-looking. The Scottish judges, by contrast, operating a legal system derived from Roman law, attempted to judge cases in accordance with general legal and moral principles, and by their willingness to consider the likely economic, social, and cultural effects of their decisions, took a forward-looking approach. When the first cases came before the Scottish courts, the judges declared that the law of Great Britain was as set out in the act of 1710 which declared that copyright should extend for fourteen years from the date of first print publication 'and no longer.'[10]

In making their assessment, the Scottish judges were advised by their Edinburgh friend and neighbour Adam Smith, whose *Inquiry into the Nature and Causes of the Wealth of Nations* had not yet been published but whose main ideas were already known.[11] The effect of all monopolies, Smith told his students in his lectures at Edinburgh University, is to reduce the wealth of any nation which is ignorant enough of its own interests to grant, to permit, or to tolerate them. By bringing about unnecessarily high prices, Smith showed, monopoly restricts what he called the 'comeatability

---

[8] For Sidney see appendix 1. For *Venus and Adonis* see H. G. Aldis, ed., *A List of Books Printed in Scotland before 1700* (1904, updated 1970) 667.

[9] Those modern authors, such as Feather, Mann, and Michael F. Suarez, 'Poetic Miscellanies' in Isabel Rivers, ed., *Books and their Readers in Eighteenth-Century England: New Essays* (Leicester 2001) 230 who say or imply that the 1710 Act did not apply to Scotland, or who describe the Scottish reprints of out-of-statutory-copyright titles as 'piracies', have misunderstood the legal position.

[10] See appendix 2.   [11] Production figures for Smith's two main books are given in appendix 9.

[come-at-ability]' of the monopolised goods to the nation's citizens. With silver and silk, the industries Smith studied, the avoidable losses which monopoly brought about took the form of the people of Great Britain having less silver and less silk than would otherwise have been the case. The only monopolies for which there could be any economic, or indeed moral, justification, Smith argued, were those granted for a short time for specific public policy purposes in order to reward and encourage innovation from which society as a whole would later benefit. The statutory limited monopoly privilege of fourteen years for industrial patents given for inventions and for copyrights for newly written works of learning, Smith noted, were exceptions which 'can do no harm and may do some good, and are not to be altogether condemned'.[12]

At the time the Scottish judges made their first decisions, there was no substantial book industry in Scotland, nor any powerful constituency of intellectual property owners. The effect was therefore not only to create a difference in what was legally permitted in the two countries of the union, but to set up economic incentives for the development of a Scottish book industry, as a kind of offshore rival to England but without any of the usual legal, physical, or tariff barriers. To reprint a title which had passed into the public domain under the terms of the 1710 Act was not illegal, nor subject to injunction, in Scotland, nor was it illegal to sell such books in England or in the British colonies in America and elsewhere. By the middle of the eighteenth century, a substantial Scottish book industry had grown up in Edinburgh, and others in Glasgow and Aberdeen, publishing a variety of newly written texts under statutory copyright, but mainly reprinting works which lay outside the limits of the 1710 Act. The Scottish publishers were able to do this profitably at prices which were between half and two-thirds of the levels of the London industry.

By the 1750s, as the Customs records show, Scotland was exporting a large quantity of books, mainly Bibles and religious and educational textbooks, to the American colonies, a market hitherto the preserve of London.[13] Most worrying of all from the point of view of the London cartel, Scottish books were increasingly to be found on sale not only in the north of England, where there were few bookshops, but in the southern heartlands, including

---

[12] *Adam Smith. Lectures on Jurisprudence*, edited by R. L. Meek, D. D. Raphael, and P. G. Stein (1978) 83. Smith did, however, contrive a device to extend the copyright of *The Theory of Moral Sentiments*. See *The Correspondence of Adam Smith*, edited by Ernest Campbell Mossner and Ian Simpson Ross (1977) 256.

[13] See Warren McDougall, 'Copyright Legislation in the Court of Session, 1738 to 1749 and the Rise of the Scottish Book Trade' in *Transactions of the Edinburgh Bibliographical Society* (1988).

the university towns of Oxford and Cambridge, and on credit terms which were three or more times more favourable than those offered by London. In 1759 the London cartel decided that, since the arrangements for tying-in the retail bookshops in England were breaking down, they must take strong measures against any which handled Scottish reprints. It emerges from a few archival records, moreover, that some members of the London book industry secretly dealt in 'pirated' Scottish books, including reprints of Shakespeare, and the measures which the leaders of the cartel decided upon were also directed at English colleagues who might be tempted to evade the rules of the cartel.[14] In a circular letter to the English retailers, the London publishers demanded that any Scottish books should be sent to London for inspection and destruction, to be replaced by the (more expensive) London versions. In exchange for the lifting of the threat of ruinously expensive legal proceedings, the retailers were required to give an undertaking not to handle Scottish books in the future. As the Scottish publishers noted of their colleagues in London, 'Like all rich dealers', they could 'afford to throw away a little money to destroy those who incroach upon their Trade.'[15] Donaldson, the leader of the Edinburgh industry, who was making a fortune from selling his reprints, seems at one time to have been ready to join the cartel, in effect offering to extend the English industry's hegemony over the whole of Great Britain. But when the London cartel decided on a policy of resistance rather than co-option, it soon emerged that they had misjudged the relative strength of the opposing forces. When they refused to admit Donaldson to their pre-emption sales, he opened his own retail shop in London, selling out-of-statutory-copyright books direct to the English public at about half the London prices.[16] At around the same time the Scottish industry began to undercut London prices not only for books but for printing equipment.[17]

Faced with such direct challenges, the London publishers turned to their steady friends, the English courts. In 1770 an English court required a bookseller in Berwick-on-Tweed, the town on the English–Scottish border, to account to the 'proprietors' for the sale of copies of Thomson's *The Seasons*, printed in Scotland.[18] They also started a lawsuit against Donaldson in the English courts for 'piratically' reprinting the book. A legal action

---

[14] John Nichols ledger.

[15] In the *Memorial for the Booksellers of Edinburgh and Glasgow . . . Relating to the Process against them by Some of the London Booksellers* (n.d., c. 1770).

[16] Collins, *Authorship* 18.

[17] In 1769, for example, the university press at Cambridge decided to switch suppliers for its typefaces from London to Glasgow, on grounds both of price and quality. McKitterick ii, 219.

[18] Timperley 722.

which focused on the same issue was brought in the Scottish courts in Edinburgh. Thomson's *Seasons*, first published in 1730, was a steady seller, an intellectual property which had produced large profits and could be expected to continue to do so.[19] It was probably chosen as the site for the struggle because the details of the transactions were well documented and the financial interest in the outcome well spread across the London industry.[20] Half a century after the 1710 Act, the pieces were at last all in place to force a conclusion. Either the Scottish book industry would be compelled to back off by the sheer expense of pursuing its statutory rights through the courts, or the English courts would be obliged to come off the fence where they had sat for half a century and to make a clear decision about the lawfulness of perpetual intellectual property in England.

The stakes were high. In terms of the value of property in dispute the case was by far the largest ever to come before a Scottish court. On one side, if perpetual copyright was declared to be lawful, the growing Scottish book industry would be declared to be a pirate operation, it would have to contract, with many men and women thrown out of work.[21] On the other side, if the perpetual private ownership of texts was declared illegal in England, the way would be open for price competition throughout Great Britain on all except recently published titles, the prices of out-of-statutory-copyright books would fall, and the London publishers' portfolio of older intellectual properties would become worthless.[22] A figure of £200,000 was quoted by the *Annual Register* as the value of the intellectual property at risk. The *Scots Magazine*, which favoured abolition, estimated £100,000. In 1774 the conger's clerk told parliament that £50,000 had been paid in the closed trade auctions since 1755, a figure which excluded transactions by private sale.[23] Since the marked sale catalogues show that the perpetual copyright of Shakespeare alone had been valued at between £2,000 and £3,000 in the 1760s, and that the most valuable intellectual properties of all, the texts of Bibles and almanacs, were not included in this estimate, none of the figures look exaggerated.[24]

In the legal and political debates of 1773 and 1774, besides the producer interests of the Scottish and English book industries, there was now a third

---

[19] The London publisher Millar had bought the copyright in two lots in 1729 and 1738 for a total of about £250. After Millar's death the copyrights were sold to a group of fifteen members of the cartel of whom Beckett was the leading shareholder, for double that amount.
[20] See Rose 120.   [21] Women were employed to do the stitching.
[22] Figures quoted by Collins, *Authorship* 100.   [23] Hansard, column 1085.
[24] For the changing market value of the intellectual property in Shakespeare see chapter 8.

party whose voice was occasionally heard, the book purchasers and book readers of both countries of the United Kingdom on whom ultimately all costs fell and from whom all profits were taken. An occasional voice was also heard on behalf of a fourth party, the many citizens of England who, unlike their fellow citizens in Scotland, were excluded by the high prices from access to many of their nation's printed writings. The more the London booksellers were tempted to exaggerate the value of their portfolio, the more they proclaimed the benefits of abolition.

The scene was now set for the most decisive event in the history of reading in England since the arrival of printing 300 years before. It was a struggle between the ancient guild approach to economic management and the emerging world of free trade and economic competition, between entrenched interests and challenging innovatory forces, between elegant old money and vulgar business, between the fuzzy talk of common-law rights and the clear words of modern statute law, between a static *ancien régime* view of society based on hierarchy, heredity, property, and allocation of roles, and the new Enlightenment science of political economy that aimed to use the power of reason to bring about social and economic improvement. According to the Lockian view of property, the booksellers' portfolio was the intellectual property equivalent of a rich real estate originally tamed from a wilderness by the ancestors of the present owners, and subsequently improved and added to over the centuries by careful stewardship. Seen in terms of political economy, the portfolio was a fortune amassed by monopolistic businessmen derived from centuries of monarchical usurpation, restrictive trade practices, and price exploitation.

The high monopoly period regime not only suited the producer interest of the book industry: a powerful political constituency in England liked the results on reading and mentalities. Among the main arguments put forward in the parliamentary bill that introduced a stamp duty on periodicals in 1701 was that the resulting higher prices would help keep such print from 'the poorer sort of people', and so reduce the allure and enticement of reading among their children.[25] In 1757, Soame Jenyns argued that to 'encourage the poor man to read and think, and thus to become more conscious of his misery, would be to fly in the face of divine intention'.[26] George Hadley of Hull declared in 1788, in resisting moves to improve elementary schooling in his locality, that the people of Scotland had been more industrious before reading had become universal earlier in the century. Servants in England, he claimed, were reading when they ought to have been 'renovating their

---

[25] Timperley 584.   [26] Altick 32.

faculties' by sleeping. 'What ploughman who could read the renowned history of *Tom Hickathrift, Jack the Giant-Killer*, or the *Seven Wise Men*, would
be content to whistle up one furrow and down another, from the dawn in
the morning to the setting of the sun.'[27] William Playfair, the unsympathetic editor of Adam Smith's *Wealth of Nations* appointed by the industry
after the author's death, advised against policies which encouraged workers
to learn to read.[28]

The hearing before the Court of Session in Edinburgh took place in July
1773. The Scottish judges quickly confirmed their predecessors' view that
no right of perpetual copyright had ever existed in Scotland. They then
offered their opinions on the underlying principles which governed their
decisions. Literary property, they were clear, could not be regarded as a law
of nature or of nations. If spoken language is common, indeed the main
faculty which holds human beings together in society, why should written
or printed words be regarded as private property? Why was man made a
social being, asked Lord Kames, but to benefit society in its progress toward
perfection? Monopoly, he declared, so far from being founded on common
law, is contradictory to the first principles of society.[29] The Scottish judges
were concerned about the effects of their decisions on prices, on access
to reading, and on the progress of civilisation. The author of a text, they
accepted, like the inventor of a new industrial process, was entitled to be
rewarded by society for his work and his talent, but the judges could see
that, as a simple matter of arithmetic, the wide disparity between the prices
of English and Scottish books had little or nothing to do with payments
to authors. In the case of some of the most valuable intellectual properties,
the authors had been dead for hundreds of years, and in the case of some
of the most valuable of all, the Bible and classical texts, for thousands. For
newly written texts, as Kames pointed out, the publishers gave very little
more for a perpetual copyright than they did for a copyright for a single
edition, a point soon to be proved by Adam Smith's own experience in
selling the rights to *The Wealth of Nations*.[30] In a fine example of the ideas
of the Scottish Enlightenment in action, the Scottish judges confirmed,
by a majority of eleven to one, that perpetual copyright was unlawful in
Scotland.

---

[27] George Hadley, *A New and Complete History of Kingston-on-Hull* (1788) 381.
[28] See Emma Rothschild, *Economic Sentiments* (Harvard 2001) 97.
[29] Summarised and paraphrased from the account in James Boswell, *The Decision of the Court of Session
upon the Question of Literary Property* (Edinburgh 1774).
[30] For the production and price of *The Wealth of Nations* see appendix 9 'Adam Smith.'

The discussion of the judges in the House of Lords, the supreme court for civil cases for the whole of Great Britain, took place the following February. The judges focused on the English rather than on the Roman conception of law, and were less interested in the (forward-looking) effects of their decisions than on the (backward-looking) records of privilege, property, precedent, and customary practice. The London publishers mounted a well-financed political campaign to defend the *status quo* – the archives of Strahan the printer show that they printed a thousand copies of *The Case of the Booksellers*, presumably mainly for free distribution – but the judges remained reluctant to make any judgement, as they had been for the past sixty years, or to take any step which would upset the old economic–cultural bargain between the state and the industry. The discussion in the court itself, unlike that in the Scottish court, was conducted in a hermetic legal language in which the issues were kept narrow and difficult for non-lawyers to follow, and the declared outcome was almost incomprehensible. It is not even certain which way the judges voted on the three questions on which they had been asked to give a ruling, but a majority seem to have wanted to allow perpetual copyright to continue. As was then the practice, however, the ultimate decision was not exclusively for the judges but for the whole House of Lords, acting as a political as well as a legal body, and they took wider considerations into account. Perpetual copyright, the Lords declared in a clear decision, was unlawful in England as well as in Scotland.[31] With some exceptions, the only allowable intellectual property was the short statutory copyright provided for in the act of 1710.

The 1774 legal judgement, it can be seen in retrospect, was a decisive moment for the whole subsequent development of notions of intellectual property, for the price of books and of access to texts, for the progress of reading, and for the subsequent course of the national culture widely defined. After 1774, the terms of the act of 1710 were enforced by the courts in England, as in Scotland, and we hear no more of alleged common-law property rights.[32] But there was no guarantee at the time that 1774 would not turn out to be just another passing occurrence which would soon be set aside in law or in practice. The London book industry had quickly reversed the loss of intellectual property rights in 1641 and again in 1695.

[31] The exceptions related to the printing of the Bible, and to certain privileges accorded to the universities and to Eton College which were reaffirmed by an Act of Parliament in 1775.
[32] For example, in the case of Beckford *v.* Hood, 1798, described by Peter Thorogood, 'Thomas Hood, a nineteenth century author' in Robin Myers and Michael Harris, eds., *Development of the English Book Trade, 1700–1899* (1981).

Having successfully ignored the intentions of parliament and the precise words of the law in 1710, why not again in 1774? As soon as the decision was announced, the industry brought forward a parliamentary bill to claim transitional relief. With the help of its large corporately financed campaign fund, commonly known as bribery, a procession of apologists, including some well-known authors, came forward to warn of a dark age of Gothic barbarism if the decision was not reversed.[33] Some of the speeches delivered in the debate in the House of Commons show that in England too the effects on access and employment were now considered relevant.[34] The Attorney General described the booksellers as 'a set of impudent monopolizing men, that they had combined together and raised a fund of upwards of £3,000 in order to file bills in Chancery against any person who should endeavour to get a livelihood as well as themselves'.[35] Parliament received a petition against the bill from the sector of the industry which remained outside the cartel, dismissed as 'sellers of books on walls, at the corners of streets, and at the doors of alehouses'.[36] The parliamentary reporter noted too a petition against the bill from representatives of those who sold printed texts to the lowest tranches of the reading nation, 'weavers, old clothes-folks, chandler's shop men and women, a person who keeps a stall upon Parliament Street, &c', but he recorded too that 'the House was almost a scene of laughter during the whole of the evidence, which was very long'.[37] The bill passed the Commons, but it was defeated in the Lords.

   The industry then drew up proposals for turning themselves into an even tighter syndicate. The proposals included the setting up of a well-capitalised association, 'The United Company . . . for the Preservation of the Trade and the Security of Literary Property', consisting of all the holders of putative copyrights. The proposal provided for sanctions against any member of the industry, whether in or outside the association, who did not cooperate in a system of perpetual copyright, in effect a return to earlier guild practice whereby owners who did not keep their intellectual properties in good repair by reprinting them forfeited them to their colleagues.[38] Given the political and economic weight of the industry, and the personal wealth and parliamentary influence of its leaders, it was only a matter of time, many people believed, before the *status quo* of perpetual intellectual property

---

[33] The best-known writer who prepared a pamphlet was Catherine Macaulay, but the booksellers' cause was also supported by Hume, Hurd, Robertson, and Beattie. See Hansard, column 1098.

[34] See, for example, the speech of Lord Camden quoted in Augustine Birrell, *The Law and History of Copyright* (1899) 137.

[35] Hansard, column 1086.   [36] *Ibid.* column 1100.   [37] *Ibid.* column 1093.

[38] Quoted in full in *Bennett and Clements* from the document among the William Strahan papers.

would again be fully restored, in practice if not in law, if indeed it need be interrupted at all. Something like that appears to have happened in France where edicts of 1777 which aimed at reducing the monopolistic powers of the book industry guilds were only partially effective.[39]

The London publishers continued to deal in legally unenforceable perpetual intellectual properties for at least forty years after 1774.[40] Some contracts with authors for new works still required them to transfer their rights 'for ever'.[41] Some new entrant publishers, relying now on what they called 'the customs of the trade', paid good money for the right to reprint titles which had passed out of statutory copyright. The Longman archives contain examples of letters to other publishers reminding them of Longman's claim to hold 'honorary copyrights', for example in Walpole's *Castle of Otranto*. In 1805 was established a cooperative of twenty booksellers, calling themselves the 'Friends of Literature', who produced editions of older standard texts such as *Walker's Classics*, as if they were still privately owned.[42] Well into the nineteenth century, many titles continued to be published by consortia of what I call 'pretender' copyright holders in much the same way as they had been before 1774, and the archival record shows that some intellectual property asset prices, such as the pretender rights in Shakespeare, initially held up well.[43] There appears also to have been a deliberate policy of subdividing the ownership of the pretender rights. The 1790 edition of Shakespeare, for example, was published by a consortium of no less than thirty-two London firms.

If a new edition of a title, specially revised for the occasion, was published at the moment of expiry of the statutory copyright, the rights could be effectively renewed for another period. As Longman, who had bought the copyright of the works of Gibbon from the first publisher, warned Gibbon's executor and editor Lord Sheffield in 1812, 'the Miscellaneous Works [of Gibbon] already published, being already out of time as to Copy-right, are open to others to print, & will consequently be printed, (1) if your Lordship does not soon bring forward your Lordship's improved edition, (2) by some Scotch or country bookseller'.[44] As had occurred during the

[39] Darnton, *Underground* 189.
[40] Many examples of post-1774 transactions in out-of-statutory copyrights are to be found in the Upcott collection.
[41] Examples quoted by Bentley 'Copyright Documents', from the Robinson archives.
[42] See the article 'The Friends of Literature' in Marston 84, based on archival material whose present whereabouts I have been unable to discover. I do not know if the Walker of the title was the Robert Walker who had been driven out of the business of reprinting the English classics by predatory pricing.
[43] See chapter 8.   [44] Longman to Sheffield 1 January 1812. Longman archives i, 97, 274.

transitional period of the 1710 Act, the records show many titles being reissued with revisions, the purpose being to enable the purchasers to claim a new copyright. Publishers who threatened to reprint at lower prices could also be bought off. As Joseph Johnson told Lackington in 1805, if he declined to sell 'pirated' editions of Enfield's *Speaker*, a best-selling school textbook, he would supply him with 1,000 copies at a special price. 'On these terms no capital is employed and you have yr. genuine edition.'[45]

But such measures were of little use against the Scots. By 1775, a visitor to Edinburgh declared that the most profitable trade was that of bookseller. As Lord Mansfield, one of the judges himself noted, titles such as Thomson's *Seasons* and Young's *Night Thoughts* were being reprinted in Scotland by five or six separate publishers. Cobblers were throwing away their awls, weavers their shuttles, to join the printing boom. Scotland teemed with men carrying books from town to town, and they now crossed to England.[46] One of these Scottish pedlars made a deep impression on the mind of the young Wordsworth.[47]

Tens of thousands of volumes printed in Edinburgh, Glasgow, Aberdeen, and Perth, were sent for sale in London.[48] A bookseller in Berwick-on-Tweed, who took a share in many books printed in Scotland, provided a general service for the coastal trade between Edinburgh and London.[49] Bookshops run by Scotsmen opened in London specially to sell books printed north of the border.[50] By the 1790s, the Perth firm of Morison alone was producing about 14,000 volumes annually.[51] The Scottish publishers were able to undercut English prices in all markets for out-of-copyright books. Until 1774, with the exception of some titles first printed by the university presses, the intellectual property rights in all texts ever printed in England had been held by the London publishers. But now the gates of the great private estates had been thrown open, and anyone could enter free of charge. With the dismantling at around the same time of the other entry barriers, such as control of apprenticeship numbers, the way was open to free trade and competition in all but the most recent works. By the early 1780s we see the English book industry adapting to the changed circumstances,

[45] Johnson to Lackington, 7 December 1805, Johnson ledger.   [46] Hansard, column 1099.
[47] 'The Wanderer' in *The Excursion*. See also chapter 17.
[48] [E. Topham] *Letters from Edinburgh Written in the Years 1774 and 1775* (Dublin n.d. c. 1776) 200. Letter dated 23 February 1775.
[49] See Phorson's list summarised in appendix 6, 539.
[50] The advertisement list of Ogilvy and Speare of Holborn in the mid 1790s, inserted in *The Poems of Ossian* (Edinburgh 1792), Ac, lists 183 titles 'printed for Ogilvy and Speare' which appear to be mostly of Scottish manufacture.
[51] See Judith A. Entwistle, 'A Notable Scottish Printing Firm, Morisons of Perth'. Unpublished dissertation, University of Strathclyde (1975).

mainly from newly founded firms entering the industry. A revolution in the production, selling, and in the reading of books in Great Britain had begun.

In 1774, the year of the decision, Adam Smith offered a theoretical comparison, and a predictive model, of the effects on prices of the two types of economic regime:

The price of monopoly is upon every occasion the highest which can be got. The natural price, or the price of free competition, on the contrary, is the lowest which can be taken, not upon every occasion, indeed, but for any considerable time together. The one is upon every occasion the highest which can be squeezed out of the buyers, or which, it is supposed, they will consent to give: The other is the lowest which the sellers can commonly afford to take, and at the same time, continue their business.[52]

With both of these economic regimes now coexisting in the British book industry, it was soon evident that his observation was valid in both sectors. After 1774 a huge, previously suppressed, demand for reading was met by a huge surge in the supply of books, and was soon caught up in a virtuous circle of growth. All the older printed texts first printed in England entered, or returned to, the public domain, available to be legally reprinted by anyone in Great Britain for sale throughout the country at whatever price their publishers chose to set. The new freedom applied to almanacs, maps, textbooks, law books, medical books, school and university educational books, texts and translations of the ancient classics, and to virtually all printed knowledge and the print of virtually all text-based cultural practices.[53] The huge corpus of traditional stories, poems, and songs, which had been appropriated into private ownership in the early years of printing were returned to unrestricted common public use. Of older texts, only the texts of the official religions of England and Scotland remained unliberated in the hands of monopoly franchisees, but, even in this area, new English-language Bibles which were produced by other publishers created some economic competition with the commercial monopoly in the supply and sale of the word of God.

The decision of 1774 transferred, through lower prices, a huge quantum of purchasing power from book producers to book buyers. With more firms entering the business, increasing price competition, and the prices of

---

[52] Smith's *Wealth of Nations* 78.
[53] The monopoly franchises on the printing and selling of the 'Authorised' version of the English-language Bible continued, but when many other translations entered the market, they were not stopped.

pretender copyrights plummeting towards zero, the British book industry as a whole moved to a faster growth rate. Bankruptcies tripled, a sign of boom, and the industry as a whole prospered as never before.[54] From about 1780, the minimum price of access to certain much demanded out-of-copyright texts fell to about a half, and then to a quarter, of previous levels. Editions grew three or four times as long, and there were also many more editions, often on sale at the same time. From 1774, when the first cheap reprint publisher, John Bew, moved into Paternoster Row, the centre of the London book industry was transformed from what a later observer called 'old bookselling, or the issuing only of large and important new works, to general publishing, and particularly of periodicals', among which he included books sold in parts.[55] Within a generation we see a doubling of the size of the book-binding industry – an indicator of the growth of book production which is more reliable than that of printing capacity or of titles published.[56]

In the public domain sector, the economic pressures which had encouraged producers of the high monopoly period to stay at the top of the demand curve now went into reverse. Instead of books becoming larger and more expensive, they now became smaller and cheaper. The duodecimo (12mo) made a spectacular come-back, and other even smaller formats were invented or reinvented, the sextodecimo (16mo), the vicesimo-quarto (24mo) and even the tricesimo-secundo (32mo), made possible by producing paper sheets of larger size and folding them more times.[57] In the new circumstances after 1774, but only as far as out-of-copyright texts were concerned, the link between marginal manufacturing cost and price was re-established for the first time since the abolition of the price controls, and, as economic theory would predict, the competitive pressures to offer lower prices moved inexorably towards lowering the costs of manufacturing. We see the invention and harnessing of new technologies, stereotyping, machine-made paper, ready-made bindings, steel engraving, all major changes with huge economic and cultural effects, some at least of which can be regarded as innovations previously prevented or postponed by the industrial structures of the high monopoly period.[58]

Although some of the factor costs of book manufacturing, such as paper and taxes rose as a result of the war which began in 1793 and continued until 1815, the fall in minimum retail prices of books containing out-of-copyright texts was not much affected. In 1823, when it seemed as if prices could fall

[54] See Ian Maxted, *The British Book Trades 1731–1806, A Checklist of Bankruptcies* (Exeter 1985) iv.
[55] Timperley 838.   [56] Figures in appendix 5. Binding included trade binding in boards.
[57] See appendix 6.   [58] Discussed in chapters 11 and 21.

No. 2.   **Price 6d.**

CHEAP, ELEGANT, and less than ONE FOURTH the price of any other 8vo. Edition!! uniform and designed as a Companion to Jones's Edition of **SHAKSPEARE**, **BRITISH THEATRE** and **BRITISH CLASSICS.**

To be completed in about 32 weekly Nos. price 6d. or 16 Parts 1s. each, beautifully printed on the finest Vellum paper, hotpressed,

THE

MODERN POETS

OF

Great Britain:

COMPRISING

THE WHOLE OF SOME, AND THE SELECT WORKS OF OTHER OF THE MOST POPULAR AND ESTEEMED AUTHORS;

INCLUDING

PETER PINDAR,	COLEMAN,	BYRON,	ROBINSON,
KIRK WHITE,	SOUTHEY,	CRABBE,	BEATTIE,
COWPER,	MOORE,	SHERIDAN,	HAYLEY,
BURNS,	DARWIN,	CH. SMITH,	&c. &c. &c.

The whole forming one elegant Library Volume, closely and beautifully printed in double columns, with a clear, bold Type,

AT ONCE UNITING TASTE, UTILITY AND ECONOMY.

☞ *Some idea may be formed of the cheapness of these Editions, by the following comparative view:—*
COWPER's complete WORKS, usually published in 8vo. at 18s. the whole here comprised in 7 Nos. at 6d. each—say 3s. 6d.!!

LONDON:
Published by JONES & Co. 3, Warwick Square, and Sold by their Agents, and all other Booksellers in Town and Country.

1823.

☞ Each Number of this Work will contain more Reading for Sixpence, than was originally published at 5s.!!

Figure 2. A 'number' sold for sixpence, 1823.

no further, the leaders of the mainstream industry remonstrated with the outsider Limberd for selling whole novels at six pence (half a shilling) a volume, or two pence (0.17 per cent of a shilling) in numbers, probably the lowest price in real terms hitherto achieved for texts of this length. By that time one could buy a beautifully illustrated edition of *Robinson Crusoe* for one penny (0.08 shillings) a week.[59]

After 1774 we see a sharp rise in the annual growth rate of book titles published nationally, much of it accounted for by reprints of older titles, as well as a rise in the rate of growth of provincial book publishing, provincial bookshops, and provincial circulating libraries.[60] There was a boom in anthologies, abridgements, adaptations, simplified and censored versions, and books sold in parts. We see the rapid growth of a new children's book industry, which also drew on, anthologised, and abridged the out-of-copyright authors, and which drove out or absorbed the long frozen ballad and chapbook canon within a few years.[61]

The quantified estimates I have assembled match the more impressionistic judgement made by the remainder bookseller Lackington writing in 1791:

According to the best estimation I have been able to make, I suppose that more than four times the number of books are sold now than were sold twenty years since . . . In short all ranks and degrees now READ.[62]

The industry at the time estimated a fourfold increase in output during the last quarter of the century. We need another multiplier to convert sales of books to acts of reading.[63] If we take the contemporary estimate of an average of four, this implies an increase in acts of reading of books of about fifty times. An increase in book production and in acts of reading does not necessarily imply that there was a corresponding increase in the absolute size or composition of the reading nation. Many of those social groups who read before may simply have taken advantage of the lower prices to buy and to read more, and it was said that, for many noblemen and gentlemen of the time, 'a mansion without a library is like a castle without an armoury'.[64] Taken as a whole, however, the evidence suggests that it was not only ownership of books and acts of reading among existing reading constituencies which increased, but readerships, and the size of the whole reading nation.

---

[59] See 'An example of the effects on print runs of the 1774 decisions (Defoe's) *Robinson Crusoe*', appendix 5, 507.
[60] See appendices 6 and 10.   [61] See chapter 17.   [62] Lackington 257.
[63] Discussed in greater detail in chapter 11.   [64] Dibdin xxi.

In the case of Defoe's *Robinson Crusoe*, which had been commercially successful the moment it was published in 1719, and which the publishers of the high monopoly period regarded as a steady bestseller, within five years of the start of the explosion it had already sold more copies than in the seventy years since it first appeared.[65] As for Thomson's *Seasons*, by 1777 it was said to be found among shepherds who had previously never seen any other book but the Bible.[66] Within eight years of the 1774 decision, Carl Moritz, a visitor from Germany, was amazed at how cheap and how plentiful the English classics had become, on sale even on stalls in the streets. His landlady, he noticed, the widow of a tailor, was reading Milton. Lackington, writing a few years later, noticed the collapse of boundaries which had previously divided the oral, literate, and reading nations:

The poorer sort of farmers, and even the poor country people in general who before that period spent their winter evenings in relating stories of witches, ghosts, hobgoblins, &c now shorten the winter nights by hearing their sons and daughters read tales, romances &c and on entering their houses you may see *Tom Jones*, *Roderick Random*, and other entertaining books stuck up on their bacon racks.[67]

By 1825, as was noted by Thomas Dibdin, who travelled round the country looking at libraries and bookshops, the continuing transformation was unmistakeable:

The growth of knowledge is daily increasing in rapidity and strength. In this wonderful country it is barely possible for those who lead a quiet and uniform life far beyond the reach of the hum of our great Metropolis to form a correct notion of the various channels by which knowledge is so swiftly and so widely diffused.[68]

It was probably at some time towards the end of the romantic period that the curve of the growth of book production in Great Britain at last caught up with the growth of population, of incomes, and of the economy as a whole from which it had diverged at some time in the seventeenth century, and it then continued to outstrip it until universal reading was achieved around the end of the nineteenth century.

In 1774 the London book industry had been found by the supreme civil court of Great Britain to have been conspiring to disobey the statute law for sixty-four years. In modern circumstances, it would be open to those who

---

[65] See 'An example of the effects on print runs of the decisions of 1774 (Defoe's) *Robinson Crusoe*', appendix 5, 507.
[66] Quoted by Stephanie Lethbridge, 'Anthological Reading Habits in the Eighteenth Century: the Case of Thomson's *Seasons*' in Korte, Schneider, and Lethbridge.
[67] Lackington 257.   [68] Dibdin xi.

had been damaged by the long illegality to claim compensation. All the illegally obtained excess profits which the cartel had taken during the high monopoly period could be forfeit, especially in the many well-documented cases of bullying. In investigating what would now be regarded as an abuse of economic power, the public regulatory authorities would also take an interest. In modern conditions the industry would have been liable for fines of up to 10 per cent of turnover for every year of infringement.[69] The damages which the British nation suffered from sixty-four years of illegality can also be estimated by comparing what went before with what came after. In economic terms we can note the income losses of everyone forced to buy overpriced books, the foreclosing of opportunities to authors, manufacturers, and traders, the loss of potential jobs. The losses include less literature of all kinds being written and published, less reprinting, less reading, a slow-down in the pace of the diffusion of new ideas, less access to the discoveries of science and medicine by those at the lower tranches of the book market, less education, more obsolete education, more illiteracy, more ignorance, more unwanted children.

Equally important for an understanding of the effects on reading patterns is realising what 1774 did not do. The British courts had struck down extra-statutory perpetual copyright, but they did nothing about the publishers' cartel or about the many other restrictive practices with which the former perpetual, but now time-restricted, regime had been buttressed. These not only continued uninterrupted, but they intensified as Adam Smith had predicted. As far as new titles were concerned, we see the Scottish book industry being quickly incorporated into a national British industry, which operated a number of no-poaching agreements and other market-sharing devices. During the romantic period, the minimum price of out-of-copyright books halved, halved again, and went on falling, and the print runs and sales soared and went on soaring. Over the same period, the price of newly published copyrighted books rose and went on rising, most vividly seen in the price of new novels whose prices doubled and then trebled.[70]

In 1808, when the economic and cultural consequences of 1774 had not yet worked their way through, the publishers' campaign to reverse the decision had its first success. The statutory copyright period was extended from fourteen years to twenty-eight years in all circumstances. In 1814 the period was extended to cover the life of the author. In 1838 a proposal to lengthen the copyright period to sixty years was defeated, but in 1842, when

[69] Shenfield and Stelzer 128.   [70] Discussed in chapter 11.

most of the famous works of the romantic period were still in copyright, a new Copyright Act extended the copyright period to author's lifetime plus seven years or forty-two years from publication, whichever was the longer. Taking account of the lag after 1774, while the industry wondered whether the decision could be made to stick, the short legal copyright set out in the act of 1710 was, therefore, only observed in England for about twenty-five years. In practice only a limited range of texts slipped through what I call the brief copyright window. We can regard them as forming a canon, which I propose to call the 'old canon', the characteristics of which will be discussed in the following chapter, on which 1774 conferred the gifts of low and falling prices, widening access, and larger readerships.

When it was first made available during the brief copyright window, the old canon, although mainly the print of a remoter past, also contained a proportion of works which had been written only a few decades earlier. If the 1710 Act had continued in force, the old canon would have been continuously replenished, refreshed, and updated by works falling out of copyright. However, when, after 1808, the brief copyright window came to an end, the number of titles coming out of copyright dropped sharply. As the publishers drove up the price of new books to ever higher levels, the old canon, held fast within the ever tightening economic constraints, stood unchanged, gaining in authority, falling in price, gradually extending its penetration ever deeper and wider into the expanding reading nation, but becoming more obsolete with every year. The closing of the window meant that most of the books written during the romantic period would have to wait until middle or late Victorian times to become as cheap, as accessible, or as widely read within the nation.[71]

---

[71] See chapter 21.

CHAPTER 7

The old canon

By 1780, the publishers of Great Britain were free, both legally and in practice, to reprint any texts they chose from the hundreds of thousands which lay outside the copyright restrictions of the 1710 statute. Apart from English-language Bibles and some other texts where the previous arrangements were permitted by statute to continue, the public domain now included everything first printed in England or Scotland before 1746, and some even more recent publications. For the first time, English publishers who wished to enter the out-of-copyright reprint business could do so without encroaching on private intellectual ownership rights or having to pay permission fees. They could choose the text, format, design, print run, and price, and attempt to sell their books in competition with any others who had already entered the same market or who might choose to do so. They could also use materials from out-of-copyright texts to prepare and sell anthologies, abridgements, and adaptations.

But which texts should they choose? In particular which literary texts should they choose? The tradition of identifying and classifying the best writers of the past was already under way in the mid seventeenth century, when Jonson, Shakespeare, and Fletcher were enshrined as the 'Triumvirate of Wit', the three masters of the English drama.[1] By the end of the seventeenth century, we also see the beginnings of a more historical, more unified, more comprehensive, and more critical approach to the nation's past written literature, beginning with brief biographies. By the high monopoly period there were many books which summarised the lives of authors, offered descriptions of their writings, and commented on their merits.[2] But, for

---

[1] First, I believe, in the 1647 folio edition of Francis Beaumont and John Fletcher's *Comedies and Tragedies*, but repeated frequently later, sometimes as the 'Trinity of Wit'. See Kewes, *Authorship* 181.

[2] The tradition included (Francis Meres's), *Palladis Tamia* (1598), [Edward Phillips's] *Theatrum Poetarum* (1675), W. Winstanley's *Lives of English Poets* (1687), Gerald Langbaine's *An Account of the English Dramatick Poets* (1691), Joseph Addison's 'Account of the Greatest English Poets' (1694); Sir Thomas Pope Blount's *De Re Poetica; or Remarks upon Poetry* (1694), Charles Gildon's *Lives and Characters of*

readers of that time, it was one thing to know the names in the long pedigree of English literature, quite another to be able to buy or to read the works. Before 1774, the London publishers re-issued the works of Chaucer, Spenser, Shakespeare, Milton, Swift, Dryden, Pope, Prior, Thomson, Young, and some others, at intervals, but the great majority of the older authors were never reprinted. In many cases, the only copies of their works in existence were the original editions, obtainable, if at all, only at high prices after a search in the antiquarian book market.[3] Many works of the sixteenth and seventeenth centuries could only be read by those able to obtain a personal introduction to one of the noblemen's houses or university libraries where copies might have been preserved.

Perpetual copyright separated the making of reputations from the supplying of texts. In particular it prevented formal canonising, the publication of the works of authors in a uniform series of 'English Poets'. Before 1774, a proposal to publish such a series, from, say Chaucer to Thomson, would have involved research among the records of the Stationers' Company, publishers' wills, and the book trade's closed sales catalogues, to find all the current shareholders of the much-divided intellectual properties and then persuading them to engage in a jointly financed enterprise, and the idea seems never even to have been contemplated.[4] Given that the Scottish book industry was able to operate under the 1710 Act long before 1774, it is not surprising that the first formal canons of the classics of the English language should have been produced not in England but in Scotland.

---

the *English Dramatick Poets* (1699), Elizabeth Cooper's *The Muses Library* (1737); and [Giles Jacob's] *Poetical Register* (1723). The five volumes of Theophilus Cibber's *The Lives of the Poets of Great Britain and Ireland* (1753), published at the height of the high monopoly period, and which drew on the large private collection of a Mr Coxeter, began with Chaucer, Langland, and Gower and included over 200 names before ending with Swift. Cibber also included a long list of *Dramatic Authors and their Works* as part of *An Apology for the Life of Colley Cibber* (1740). The tradition of writing *Live* was continued with John Berkenhout's *Biographica Literaria* (1777), Samuel Johnson's *Lives of the English Poets* (1779–81); and, for Scottish poets, J. Sibbald's *Chronicle of Scottish Poetry* (1802), and David Irving's *The Lives of the Scottish Poets* (1804). In 1758 Horace Walpole produced a six-volume *Catalogue of the Royal and Noble Authors of England, with Lists of their Works*. For an account of the development of a canonical tradition through such works, but without discussing availability, price of access, or readership, see Richard Terry, *Poetry and the Making of the English Literary Past* (Oxford 2001).

[3] The high price of second-hand copies was emphasised by Goodhugh.

[4] For the difficulties of determining ownership, see the remarks of Thomas Mortimer, 1763, quoted by Raven in Garside, Raven, and Schöwerling i, 86. When Robert Dodsley, a leading publisher of the high monopoly period, published his *Collection of Old Plays* in 1743, most of the plays had not been reprinted for over a century, but he acknowledged that permission had been given by the then owner, Tonson. Prefatory remarks to Sir John Suckling's *The Goblins* reads: 'I was willing to enrich my Collection with a Comedy from this Author, for which Mr. Tonson gave me his Consent.' I am grateful to Tanya Hagen for this reference. For the procedure for keeping ownership within the industry in such circumstances see chapter 5.

The Scottish book publishers began by reprinting, at cheaper prices, those out-of-statutory-copyright titles for which demand was high in both Scotland and England.[5] Since their reprints were often printed by the same firms, and were alike in their appearance, it was an easy step to present them as a uniform multi-volume series, to give them a unifying title, and to market them as a formal canon.[6] The forty-three volumes of *The British Poets* published by Kincaid of Edinburgh in 1773, which grew out of a list of individually published volumes printed by Foulis of Glasgow, was the first publishing venture in Great Britain to offer a named canon of English-language poetry in a uniform format. The selection, made by Hugh Blair, Edinburgh professor, literary polymath, and editor, was limited to works that were out of statutory copyright.[7] The books were well printed in handy size on good paper, well bound, at a price of 1s 6d (1.5 shillings), or one shilling on less good paper, very cheap for anyone used to London editions. 'It is such productions as these that do honour to a country', wrote a visitor to Edinburgh in 1775.[8]

When Kincaid first planned his series, he offered to cooperate with the London publishers, but when they refused and he went ahead, he was treated as an offshore pirate and denied facilities in the English market. Even after 1774 his books seem to have been sold mainly in Scotland. It was only a few years later, when it was clear that the 1774 decision was not going to be rapidly reversed, that the full implications of Scottish reprint publishing for the canonisation of English literature made themselves felt. In 1778 Kincaid's successor, John Bell, produced an even cheaper series, opening his own shop in London to sell direct to English customers. Bell's edition of *The Poets of Great Britain*, like Kincaid's, was well printed on good paper, and illustrated with engravings, and each volume carried a short biographical and critical introduction.[9] His 'British Classics', Bell announced in his prospectus, were worthy to stand alongside the classics of Greece and Rome, of France and of Italy. The classics of the English language were to be produced from his Apollo Press in 'delicate size', Bell stated, to resemble Elzeviers, the famous books in which the seventeenth-century Dutch publisher Elzevier had made them accessible to large new readerships all over Europe. Never before had

---

[5] See appendix 6. [6] See the full accounts by Bonnell.

[7] For Blair's involvement I rely on the preface to Anderson's edition of *The British Poets* volume i (1795 edition). For Blair's sermons see chapter 14.

[8] [E. Topham] *Letters from Edinburgh Written in the Years 1774 and 1775* (Dublin n.d. c. 1776) 203. Topham nevertheless disapproved of the law which allowed the books to be sold so cheaply.

[9] Bell is said to have been the first publisher to abandon the printer's long 's', so easy to mistake for an 'f'.

English-speaking readers been offered such a literary and artistic feast for their sixpence.

Bell, like Kincaid, was treated as a pirate by the London publishers who stopped him advertising in the English book-trade publications, tried to prevent English retailers from handling his books, and called him a red-faced drunken Scotchman. But with the law, and many English book buyers, now on his side, Bell's business prospered. Soon he was producing attractive, illustrated editions of plays, *Bell's British Theatre* and *Bell's Shakespeare*, and he started to move into publishing new titles and newspapers. In the later 1770s, Bell arranged to print his books in London, and this seems to have been the last straw for the English publishers. An outsider had established himself at the heart of their empire, manufacturing as well as selling, publishing as well as reprinting, and stealing the market for the English national classics, whose share prices they had carefully nursed, from under their noses. It was only then, when bullying and smear tactics failed, that they decided that they would have to meet Bell's challenge face on and produce their own directly competing uniform series. Faced with the crisis, almost all the leading firms agreed to take a share, binding the whole consortium into the long-term success of the project. Acting together, the London publishers would, they hoped, drive the Scottish interlopers out of their market. To ensure that their series would be superior, they invited Samuel Johnson, the foremost English literary figure of the time, to write the *Lives*.

Samuel Johnson's edition of *The English Poets*, which appeared after many delays in 1779, was the first attempt at a formal canon of English poetry to be produced by the London literary- and book-industry establishment. The English publishers had many advantages. Bell, like Donaldson, Kincaid, and the other Scottish publishers, was boxed in by the terms of the 1710 Act. Johnson and the London publishers, by contrast, with their claims to own all the copyrights of all the texts that had ever been printed in London, had the whole of recent as well as older English literature from which to make their choice. The negotiations were hard but the need for unity keenly felt. In the end, only in the case of Oliver Goldsmith, a poet still much in demand, did any of the owners or pretender owners refuse to cooperate.[10]

The Lives of the Most Eminent English Poets, as Johnson's publishers later called the biographies appended to the works, was a highly misleading

---

[10] The owner, Carnan, had been responsible for breaking the monopoly on almanacs. A bill to restore the monopoly was defeated in 1779.

claim, as was pointed out at once.[11] The series was not a canon of the best poets in English chosen by Johnson, but a miscellaneous list of mainly eighteenth-century authors which emerged from a multilateral commercial negotiation conducted behind closed doors by the London publishers. In essentials the list given to Johnson, after his fee was agreed, was largely copied from Bell's. At first the publishers wished to exclude Thomson's *Seasons*, ready in their pique at the Scottish victory in 1774, to ignore the bestselling poet who happened to be Scottish. Johnson persuaded them to add Thomson and three others to the list, but the publishers then discovered that they had too much material. Determined to prepare their edition in a larger format than Bell's, the economics of the project soon became unmanageable. In the competition for space the modern in-copyright poets and a few weak early eighteenth-century poets for whom there was said to be a continuing demand, were given priority. Even Chaucer, whom Bell had included, was squeezed out. No poet earlier than Milton was included. As Elizabeth Barrett wrote later, catching the general disappointment of innumerable readers at the time and since, 'Johnson wrote the lives of the poets and left out the poets.'[12] The title by which the series was presented, 'Johnson's Edition of the Poets', was another misnomer. Johnson did not edit the texts or see the book through the press. 'He never saw a sheet of it', a contemporary wrote.[13]

Five years after 1774, however, with the appearance of 'Johnson's Poets', the scene looked set for a decisive fight between Edinburgh and London, between the invaders and the defenders, between the 'English' poets of England and the 'British' poets of the United Kingdom. Compared with Bell, a one-man business with one shop in London, the London publishers, with their enormous financial resources and their hold over the English retail and renting sector, looked by far the stronger. At first they had in mind only to sell the edition as a traditional, immobile, multi-volume, 'library' edition, an idea which showed how little they had as yet understood the forces set free by 1774. Soon however they agreed to sell individual volumes as well as the whole set and lowered the planned price. Having lost the legal war of 1774, they could still win the commercial war of 1779.

---

[11] See, for example, the comments by Chalmers the editor of a fuller Scottish edition, 'It has often been objected to Dr Johnson's Collection that it includes authors who have few admirers . . . but it ought always to be remembered that the collection was not formed by the illustrious scholar, but by his employers, who thought themselves, what they unquestionably were, the best judges of vendible poetry' in *The Works of the English Poets from Chaucer to Cowper, including the Series edited by . . . Dr Samuel Johnson . . . the Additional Lives by Alexander Chalmers* (1810) preface.

[12] In *The Book of the Poets* (1842).   [13] Edmund Malone, quoted by Knight, *Old Printer* 228.

In the event, the outcome was different from what either side had expected. Both the Bell and the Johnson editions quickly sold out, and both were reprinted.[14] The demand released by the lowering of prices, and the more convenient size, was, it turned out, larger than either camp had expected. In such a market, with both rivals emerging as winners, the business response might have been for the two parties to agree to cooperate, for the Scottish interlopers to be co-opted into the London cartel, and prices forced back up. Indeed in 1804 Archibald Constable of Edinburgh suggested that the English and Scottish publishers should act together in an enlarged consortium to prepare a more considered and grander collection of *The British Poets,* old and new, to be edited by Walter Scott, which would include the works of many English and Scottish poets who had been missed by the initial sift, and a set edited by Thomas Campbell did eventually appear many years later.[15] However it was too late. Even although Campbell was an industrious researcher and had the backing of the whole industry, he found it difficult to find the books he wanted, as his complaining letters to the publishers constantly reaffirm. By 1808, with the closing of the brief copyright window, the Scottish as well as the English publishers were now locked within the same new limits and the opportunity for compiling an authoritative and comprehensive canon had passed. As events turned out, the initial commissioning of 'Johnson's Poets' was the only occasion ever when a comprehensive canon of old and new poets could have been selected and made available in a uniform series, and the opportunity was missed.

Both the Bell and the Johnson editions themselves went out of copyright before the end of the brief copyright window and became available to be reprinted by others. Meanwhile, as a result of the closing of the brief copyright window, the texts of the newly published romantic-period poets mostly remained in private ownership and could not join the lists.[16] The result was a lock-in of the original Kincaid/Bell/Johnson canon. And although Thomas Warton's *History of English Poetry,* which appeared in three volumes from 1774 to 1781, offered a fuller understanding of the extent and variety of literature in English than anything which had existed earlier, it made no discernible difference to the formal canons produced for reading.

From the 1780s onwards, publisher after publisher produced an English or British classics poetry series of his own. The books were different in

---

[14] See appendix 6.
[15] Quoted in Constable i, 176, correcting a misstatement in Lockhart.
[16] With the exception of the poems, but not the novels, of Scott. See chapter 21.

design, in format, in illustrations, in paratextual material, and in price, but scarcely at all in the choice of the texts which they offered. Although the weakest of the poets infiltrated into the Johnson canon by the London publishers were soon dropped, there was no resurrection for the stronger older poets who had been left out, although there was now no intellectual property barrier against doing so.[17] The poets of the 1790s such as William Hayley and Charlotte Smith did not join the canon even when their works fell out of copyright, perhaps because of pretender copyright.[18] The eighteenth-century lists of Kincaid, Bell, and Johnson, were followed by those of Cooke, Sharpe, Whittingham, Jones, and Dove in the romantic period, by Scott and Webster in the 1830s, Pickering in the 1840s, Nichol in the 1850s and 1860s, Nimmo in the 1860s, and many others.[19] With *The Classic Poets*, a series launched in 1870 by Robert Bell (no relation of John) at the time when the poets of the romantic period were at last all coming out of copyright, the old canon of the British poets finally came to an end.[20] It had lasted more than a hundred years.

It was the first formal canon of poetry in English to be made widely and cheaply available, the most stable, the most frequently reprinted, and the longest lived. The old canon began with Chaucer and ended with Cowper. In some old-canon lists there are more than fifty authors, in others a dozen or less, but the core was nearly always the same. It consisted, alphabetically, of Samuel Butler, some works of Chaucer, Collins, Cowper, Dryden, Falconer, Gay, Goldsmith, Gray, Milton, Pope, Shakespeare, Spenser, Thomson, and Young. The canon contained no Gower, no Marlowe, nor any of the other contemporaries of Shakespeare, no Drayton, no Herrick, no Lovelace, no Marvell, no Herbert, and no women writers. Donne was reprinted once in Scotland and once in England, but did not feature in the many collections which followed. In this canonising process, literary historians, critics, and editors had played only a small part. The old canon of poetry owed its birth and its long life more to the vagaries of the intellectual property regime, than to any carefully considered judgements. Its demise as a formal canon too owed more to the coming out of copyright of the romantic poets in the 1850s and 1860s and the resulting opportunities for them to be published together in a uniform canonising series, than to any sudden change of readerly taste.

---

[17] The weaker eighteenth-century poets who had crept in as a result of the negotiation sold in smaller numbers and more slowly, but some copies seem to have been kept, unwasted, in order to make up sets. Copies of the works of the minor poets in Bell and Sharpe's editions are found in publishers' remainder bindings of about 1830. Examples in Ac.

[18] See the 1790s list of Cadell and Davies in appendix 7, 563.

[19] See appendix 6.   [20] For the Victorian canon see chapter 21.

COOKE'S
Cheap and Elegant Pocket Editions
Of the most esteemed Works in the
ENGLISH LANGUAGE,
SUPERBLY EMBELLISHED.

To gratify the admirers of *beautiful Printing* and *decorative Elegance*, as well as accommodate the general class of Readers, the Proprietor has submitted to their choice *Two Editions*.

SUPERIOR EDITIONS

These Editions are printed with the utmost *neatness and elegance* on fine wove *Vellum Paper* of the most delicate colour and texture, glazed and *hotpressed*, and contain highly finished *Scenic Representations*; *Portraits* of the respective Authors; *Vignette Frontispices*; to every Volume; and other *additional Engravings* by the first Artists in the kingdom. They also possess the advantage of the *first Impressions* of the Plates, which are worked off in the manner of *Proofs* From the distinguished *merit* of the Engravings, and the peculiar *beauty* of the Typography, they embrace the united efforts of the Press and Pencil. It is therefore presumed that these Editions will not only gain admission into the Cabinets of the *Curious*, but the libraries of the *Literati*, and the most fashionable of the present age. To these Editions is affixed the additional price of only *Sixpence* each Number, which is double the price charged on the

CHEAP EDITIONS.

These Editions, from the unprecedented *low Charge*, might be considered as abridgments, but the Proprietor assures the public that they are printed *verbatim* from the original copies; they also contain *numerous Embellishments*, and, from the *unusual* quantity of Letter-Press, given at the price, are rendered *less expensive* than the most common and unadorned; as is exemplified by the following charges.

SELECT POETS-

Authors.	Price.	Authors	Price.	Authors.	Price.	Authors	Price.
Gray	0 6	Lyttleton	1 0	Cunningham	1 0	Watts	2 0
Collins	0 6	Goldsmith	1 0	Lansdowne	1 0	Glover	2 0
Otway	0 6	Falconer	1 0	Addison	1 0	Somerville	2 0
Rochester	0 6	Congreve	1 0	Blackmore	1 0	Thompson	2 6
Walsh	0 6	Fenton	1 0	Shakspeare	1 6	Prior	3 6
Sheffield	0 6	Rowe	1 0	Waller	1 6	Butler	3 6
Pomfret	0 6	Mickle	1 0	Langhorne	1 6	Milton	3 6
Dodsley	0 6	Broome	1 0	Savage	1 0	Gay	3 6
Armstrong	0 6	Mallet	1 0	Parnell	2 0	Young	4 0
Smollet	0 6	Moore	1 0	Shenstone	2 0	Pope	5 0
Johnson	0 6	Tickell	1 0	Akenside	2 0	Dryden	5 6
Garth	0 6	Warton	1 0				

The Price of binding the respective works in Cooke's Pocket Editions, is Ninepence per Volume, Sheep, lettered; and Sixteen pence in Calf, gilt and lettered; except the Drama, Two pence a Volume more.

BRITISH CLASSICS.

Titles.	Price.	Titles.	Price.
Goldsmith's Essays	1 0	Johnsons Idler	3 0
Shenstone's Essays	1 6	Adventurer	5 6
Citizen of the World	3 0	Rambler	6 6

To compleat the British Classics, the following Works are preparing for the Press, viz. Spectator, Guardian, Tatler, Connoisseur, World, Mirror, &c.

Figure 3. The old canon. First page of a four-page catalogue of Cooke's editions of inexpensive reprints, c. 1810.

The same general patterns emerge in the case of many other types of text. With prose fiction, for example, we see an initial selection to take advantage of the new copyright freedom, a rapid formal canonisation of this selection into a uniform series, a sharp and continuing reduction in minimum price, with an accompanying surge of production and sales, and a subsequent locking in as the intellectual property regime changed.[21] As with the verse, the initial selection then continued to be reprinted, dropping the weaker titles but unchanged in its essential core, with an astonishing conservatism, far into the nineteenth century. The old canon of prose fiction consisted of a long list of mainly eighteenth-century novels, especially *Robinson Crusoe, Gulliver's Travels*, the many works of Richardson, Fielding, and Smollett, Goldsmith's *The Vicar of Wakefield*, Johnson's *Rasselas* and Sterne's *Tristram Shandy*, and included many translations from French, Spanish and German. *Don Quixote* and *Gil Blas* were so wholly absorbed into the old canon as to be regarded almost as English works.[22]

To some readers, all fictional writing was abhorrent, a telling of lies. To others the novels of Fielding and Richardson might purport to teach religion and virtue, but their effect was to glamorise the alternatives. Some of the main publishers, notably Longman who took over *Walker's Classics*, a copyright pretenders' series, seem to have responded to this mood by stressing in their advertisements that the books make suitable gifts and school prizes for young ladies. We thus see the emergence of a more restricted formal canon of prose fiction, within the wider canon, centred upon *Don Quixote*, Fielding's *Joseph Andrews*, Richardson's *Sir Charles Grandison*, Goldsmith's *The Vicar of Wakefield*, Johnson's *Rasselas*, Le Sage's *Gil Blas*, St Pierre's *Paul and Virginia*, and Smollett's *Roderick Random, Peregrine Pickle, Humphrey Clinker, Count Fathom*, and *Sir Launcelot Greaves*.[23]

The word 'classics' seems not to have been normally applied to English prose fiction until later. In the romantic period the word was, however, often used to describe another type of writing which was also canonised into editions in uniform series, reprinted in numerous large editions by all the main old-canon publishers, and then locked in. The 'English classics' were the short essays and stories, with an overtly moral didactic purpose,

---

[21] This emerges from the table in James Raven, *British Fiction, 1750–1770, A Chronological Checklist* (Newark, NJ 1987) 15, which shows a doubling of editions compared with the previous twenty years during which the titles had first been published.

[22] After the decision to encourage the circulating libraries and the boom in reading which followed 1774, there were not yet enough novels in the English language to satisfy the growing demand for prose fiction.

[23] My judgement is based on those most frequently made available in the same series as old-canon poetry by mainstream copyright-pretender publishers, such as *Walker's Classics*, led by Longman.

which had originally appeared in periodical form (Addison and Steele's) *The Spectator* (Addison and Steele's) *The Tatler* (Johnson's) *The Rambler* (Johnson's) *The Adventurer* (Johnson's) *The Idler, The Mirror, The Observer, The Lounger, The Guardian, The World,* and *The Connoisseur,* all texts which could safely be commended to women and safely read aloud within a family.[24] These 'classics' too were immediately published in formal canonising series, their prices fell, their print runs soared, and they became boxed in as the intellectual-property regime changed.

Amongst the largest group of prose texts to be reprinted were conduct literature, reprints of books that gave advice on how to lead a pious life, that offered comfort in tribulation, guidance on how to prepare for approaching death, and consolation in time of illness or bereavement, many reprinted from texts of the seventeenth and early eighteenth centuries. In addition we find later titles which are more concerned with manners than with morals, with behaviour in society more than with internal virtue, and increasingly with advice on reading. The explosion of reading in the romantic period included an explosion of warnings against its dangers.[25]

To judge from advertisements, from printed prospectuses, and from archival records of print runs, I judge that the titles which were produced in the largest numbers were probably, in alphabetical order, Baxter's *Saints' Everlasting Rest*; Bunyan's *Pilgrim's Progress*; Chapone's *Letters on the Improvement of the Mind*; Chesterfield's *Letters to his Son*; Doddridge's *Rise and Progress of Religion,* and *Sermon on the Care of the Soul*; Dodd's *Reflections on Death* and *Thoughts in Prison*; (Dodsley's) *The Economy of Human Life, with Precepts on Practical Morality*; (Fénelon's) *Telemachus*; Benjamin Franklin's *Essays*; Gessner's *Death of Abel*; Gregory's *A Father's Legacy to His Daughters*; Hervey's *Meditations among the Tombs*; Mason's *On Self Knowledge*; Melmoth's *Great Importance of the Religious Life*; Mrs Rowe's *Devout Exercises of the Heart,* and *Friendship in Death*; Sherlock's *Practical Discourse concerning Death*; Sturm's *Reflections on the Works of God*; Watts's *On the Improvement of the Mind*; and Zimmerman's *On Solitude*.[26]

Cooke, in many ways the most innovative and entrepreneurial of the publishers who entered the new competitive reprint business after 1774, began his career by reprinting religious publications, and there were a few other 'Sacred classics'.[27] The range of conduct and courtesy books was, however, too wide for them to be corralled into a single canonising series,

---

[24] For the practice of reading see chapter 20.   [25] Discussed more fully in chapter 14.
[26] Many reprints of these editions do not appear to have found their way into libraries or catalogues. See also chapter 12.
[27] Rees and Britton 26.

and many entered the general 'English classics'.[28] Outside London too, it is noticeable that when printers in provincial towns began to join in the boom by publishing books on their own account, it was often to conduct literature that they first turned. Since the provincial printer/publishers who produced these books for local sale were closely in touch with their customers, we may have a glimpse here of the mentalities of one of the new constituencies which were joining the reading nation at this time and of the horizons of expectations against which they judged their reading.

The same pattern can be seen in the print publication of music, including operas, and songs. In 1777, the courts ruled that such texts were legally the same as literary texts and that the perpetual intellectual property exercised by the music sellers in defiance of the 1710 act was unlawful. Harrison who had produced novels and plays at a fraction of previous prices immediately started to sell a wide range of musical texts, at about a third of the previous price.[29] Not only did most of the nation read the print, they played the tunes and sang the popular songs that had been written for earlier generations.

Taken as a whole, however, the old canon, although a direct result of the legal judgement of 1774, and only made possible by 1774, is not wholly explainable as an economic response to an economic opportunity. Some authors who might have joined the cheaper reprint series are absent. There were, for example, few if any reprints in smaller format and cheaper prices of the philosophical works of Hume, Adam Smith, Gibbon, Wollstonecraft, or Godwin, even in abridged versions, although the texts of these authors came out of statutory copyright before the closing of the brief copyright window. These publishing decisions stand in sharp contrast to the frequent reprinting and anthologising of the works of Hugh Blair and William Paley, who were, ideologically, safely mainstream.[30]

In the case of some the absentees, we may be seeing an effect of the operation of the pretender copyrights. Cadell who held the copyrights of some of the great philosophical and historical works of the Enlightenment, continued to reprint them in expensive editions right through the romantic period, re-editing them from time to time in order to claim a new copyright in practice if not in law, with only occasional competition from cheaper reprints. At the same time the firm was publishing the works of Hannah More and Thomas Gisborne, authors of counter-Enlightenment conduct

---

[28] See appendix 6.
[29] See Nancy A Mace, Litigating the *Musical Magazine*, in *Book History* 2 (1999). A recorded print run is given in 'Music', appendix 6, 538.
[30] See chapter 14.

books which warned against Hume, Gibbon, and other authors on his list.[31] When, however, in the 1830s, Scott and Webster's *English Classics* edition, the successor to the copyright pretenders' editions, did eventually admit Gibbon, it was in an abridged and censored version edited by a clergyman which omitted Gibbon's chapters on Christianity. The old-canon offered a set of texts which was not only of the past but was ideologically selected from that past. What we seem to be seeing is self-censorship on the part of the publishers, a continuation and reassertion of the old bargain between the state and the book industry to patrol the textual limits of the print they made available in the lower price ranges.

Although taken together, the poetry, the novels, the essays, the conduct literature, and the other works were by no means a fully coherent body of texts, they shared many common features. The old-canon writers had written mainly about their own times and about England, especially about life in the country villages in the southern counties. The poets had written on topics regarded as particularly suitable for poetry: love of God, moral lessons, family love and affection, elegies for the dead. They celebrated, or occasionally satirised or lamented, the values of the (still largely pre-industrial) society as it had existed at the time the poems were written. The benevolence of God, the poetry of the three favourites, Young, Thomson, and Cowper, implied and proclaimed, is proved by the design of the natural world, especially by the extraordinary variety and beauty of living things. God is good and so is Nature, and by extension agriculture and rural life which has its own beautiful rhythms which follow the rhythm of the seasons. God made the country, man made the town.

Poetry, as many editors pointed out, inspired awe, wonder, a sense of the sublime, and – therefore according to the theory of natural religion – a sense of piety. The purpose of literature, as set out explicitly by innumerable editors, schoolmasters, clergymen, politicians, and other opinion formers, is to refine the heart and elevate the soul. Reading good literature, it was declared, makes men and women morally good and socially content. In a broad sense all old-canon literature was conduct literature. Old-canon anthologies still on the whole classified the selected passages not by author, as had now become normal in most newly published works, but by their expected effects on the reader – whether a piece of writing was lyrical or dramatic, humorous or pathetic, by whether it stirred patriotism or sympathy or awe, by its efficacy in promoting the right emotional and moral responses, and by its reinforcement of what were regarded as the larger

---

[31] For the huge print runs of the books written by these authors, see appendix 9.

truths of natural religion.[32] The publishers of the old-canon lists, whether mainstream or newly joining outsiders, not only ignored the discoveries of the Enlightenment, but offered a Counter-Enlightenment to readers who knew nothing of the Enlightenment.

When we survey the huge quantities of reprinted out-of-copyright books which were printed in the new conditions after 1774, one point stands out which, as far as I know, has not been noticed before, nor its implications explored. Of the millions of volumes which became cheap and plentiful, almost every one is illustrated with at least one engraving, and some with many. The editions of the poets published by Bell, Cooke, Whittingham and most others, for example, often provided a portrait of the author, an engraved title page, and sometimes a frontispiece, and these were an intrinsic part of the book's design. We find illustrations too in the reprints of the novels, the essays, the conduct books, and Shakespeare. The reprint publishers thus opened up new opportunities for painters and engravers, and many of the artists who were later to become famous as painters of individual works, including Fuseli, Opie, Smirke, Stodhart, Turner, and Westall, reached their first viewers around 1800 when they were employed to provide illustrations to be engraved. Even the cheapest versions, such as the series of novels sold by Harrison and Hogg, which are on poor quality paper, have tiny print, and double columns, are generously illustrated. Cooke, one of the first and most successful of the reprinters, displayed the originals of the illustrations in a picture gallery at the rear of his shop, sold the engravings separately from the books, and offered his books at two prices, with or without illustrations, but the illustrated versions seem to have been by far the more popular.[33]

The explanation for this feature is not obvious. There was no change in technology which suddenly made illustrations cheaper in absolute terms, and newly published books continued, for the most part, to be unillustrated. The explanation may be that, the lower down the demand curve at which the publisher chose to position himself, the lower the unit cost of illustrations within the overall costs of manufacturing, and that plates of illustrations once made could be used for later editions at low marginal cost. In economic terms, plates for illustrations shared some of the characteristics of woodcuts for ballads and chapbooks and stereotype plates for text.[34] Whatever the explanation, as far as readers were concerned, the explosion

---

[32] Examples in appendix 6.   [33] Rees and Britton 27.   [34] For stereotyping, see chapter 10.

of reading of literary texts was accompanied by an explosion in the viewing of engraved pictures. There was, however, a temporal mismatch between the written and the read texts, which was often old, and the engraved and viewed illustrations, which were contemporary. Within a few years of 1774 much of the older English literarature, including Shakespeare and Milton, was being illustrated in the neo-classical style of the later eighteenth century (classical deities especially Athena or Minerva, classical architecture, lyres, laurels), features which may have helped to convey a false impression of unity, timelessness, and contemporaneity. This anachronising mismatch between text and illustration was also to be a feature of the Victorian canon when it superseded the old canon in the 1860s.[35]

One of the most far-reaching consequences of 1774 was to allow a revival of the types of printed text which had been discouraged after 1600: abridgements, adaptations and, above all, anthologies. 'Beauties', selected from old-canon verse and prose, the archival record shows, were amongst the largest components of the reading explosion of the romantic period whether measured by number of titles, lengths of cumulative print runs, or by accessibility to widening constituencies of readers, including children.[36] Many were produced in provincial cities by local editors, often schoolmasters or clergymen, sometimes the first books ever to be printed there. In addition to the general move down the demand curve represented by the lowering of the minimum price of access to whole texts, these anthologies took printed texts to tranches even lower down, indeed to the whole reading nation of the time.

A typical example, selected because it mentions the anthologised authors in the title, is

Roach's Beauties of the Poets of Great Britain, Carefully Selected & Arranged from the Works of the Most Admired Authors, Particularly Milton, Pope, Dryden, Thomson, Addison, Goldsmith, Johnson, Young, Blair, Gray, Prior, Shenstone, Mallet, Cowper, Collins, Parnell, Beattie, Moore, Chatterton, Buckingham, Duncombe, Armstrong, Percy, Cotton, & In Six Volumes.

The book was first put on sale in 1793 in duodecimo, and sold in twenty-four parts of about sixty pages each, at sixpence. Each part was illustrated. The arrangement, as in the old miscellanies, was by topic not by author.[37]

---

[35] See chapter 21.   [36] See appendix 6.
[37] Ac. 'Moore' is the eighteenth-century John Moore, not Byron's friend Thomas Moore.

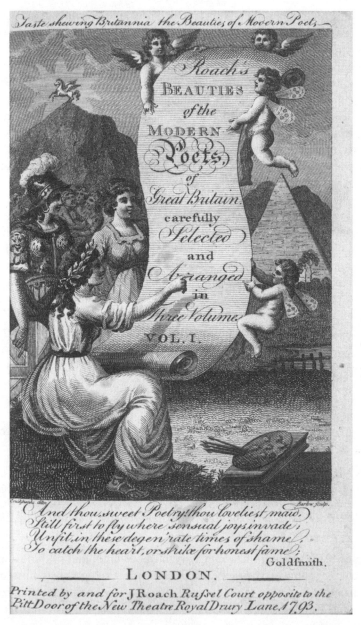

Figure 4. 'Taste shewing Britannia the Beauties of Modern Poets'. Frontispiece to
Roach's selection of eighteenth-century verse sold in 1792 at sixpence a part.

The decision of 1774 also made possible a new generation of textbooks and school books, 'readers', 'speakers', 'classbooks', 'preceptors', 'instructors', 'monitors', and other print for children of all ages which drew on, anthologised, and abridged the out-of-copyright authors and which quickly superseded the bestselling books by Dyche and Dilworth.[38] William Enfield's *Speaker*, Lindley Murray's *English Reader*, and William Mavor's *Classical English Poetry for the Use of Schools and Young Persons*, to mention only three among many rivals and imitators, were reprinted in large editions every year, and sold in hundreds of thousands of copies throughout the romantic period. Murray's *English Reader* alone was selling 10,000 copies a year during much of the period, and sales of all his textbooks have been estimated to have totalled three million in the first half of the nineteenth century.[39] We also see simpler literary anthologies being prepared, for the first time, for younger children learning to read.

Through such school anthologies, English literature entered the educational and imaginative space which had traditionally been occupied by the Bible, and by the anthologised readings from the Bible, laid down for Sunday reading in church. The balance between the two locations outside the home where younger children had previously encountered literary texts, the local church and the local school, was now shifted decisively towards school. Quite suddenly, in the course of a few years from about 1780, English literature became the principal source of texts for English education, aiming to associate learning with reading, reading with pleasure, pleasure with beauty, and beauty with virtue. Instead of centrally approved *sententiae*, or as we might say nowadays, 'clichés', children were now offered substantial passages from famous English authors, often passages of great beauty and literary quality. Instead of catechetic question-and-answer methods, in which pupils were presented with single questions to which they were expected to give a single correct answer, the new school books offered texts which had to be read critically. For the many men and women who entered the reading nation as children in the romantic period and a generation later, these anthologies of old-canon English literature were not only the first books they were asked to read and to admire, but were likely also to have been culturally the most formative. Of all the many changes brought about by 1774, the one with the most long-lasting consequences was to steep British children of the post-Enlightenment urban and industrialised nineteenth century in the pre-Enlightenment rural religious culture as it had been imagined and celebrated by writers of the previous century.

[38] See the lists in Michael 191.   [39] Tieken-Boon van Ostade 39.

Figure 5. Tabart's Juvenile Library. From S. W., *A Visit to London* (1808).

Almost everyone in the romantic period about whose reading we know anything, from lord to cottager, appears to have been familiar with old-canon authors. It was the first truly national literature, available not only to men and women of the traditional reading classes but to a rapidly growing constituency who could choose to find sixpence (0.5 shillings) from their income to buy a book. Reprinted on local provincial presses, anthologised, abridged, incorporated into schoolbooks, and carried to the villages by chapmen and 'numbers' salesmen, the old canon reached far more deeply into the reading nation than any texts actually written during the period.[40] The old-canon texts made their way into the village school room, to the smoke room of the ale house, to the ingle nook of the shepherd, to the wallets of ploughmen in the fields, the weaver at his handloom, and artisan at his bench, the bored lady and the unhappy schoolboy. During the romantic period the reading nation was probably, to a large extent, commensurate with the reach and availability of these texts.

The jagged, constantly shifting, border between the literate nation and the reading nation was closing. A man of limited education who had previously been restricted to an ancient chapbook with a few pages and a crude woodcut, could afford to buy *Robinson Crusoe*. A woman who could not herself read with ease could hear Thomson's *Seasons* read aloud by a member of her family. She might have on her dresser a copy of some anciently

[40] For books sold in parts and numbers see chapter 11. For *Queen Mab* and *Don Juan* see chapter 16.

written, but recently reprinted, book of advice on religious practice and moral conduct, and an anthology or two of old-canon verse. Now that a range of attractive reading material was available and affordable, persons of all ages, whether previously literate or not, could teach themselves to read. A parson might quote Young's *Night Thoughts* to a congregation of farm workers in his Sunday sermon. A shoemaker or tailor might read aloud to his fellow workers in their workshop. The expanding print of ever cheaper old-canon literature now entered the long frozen culture of the English-language Bible, the ancient ballad and chapbook, and the magical or astrological almanac, within which the reading of the poor had been constricted since the early seventeenth century.

CHAPTER 8

Shakespeare

Who read Shakespeare? Scholars, attempting to answer this question, have drawn on the numerous references in the historical and literary record. We have bibliographies, editions, studies of the growth of Shakespeare's reputation, including bardolatry, accounts of the ways in which Shakespeare's plays were later adapted, as well as histories of Shakespearian editing and scholarship as such. However, there has, as far as I am aware, been no systematic attempt to reconstruct readerships that is based on archival information about prices and print runs. Nor has much attention been paid to the many ways in which the changing intellectual property regime helped to influence the texts, the books in which they were made available, and the changing composition of the readerships.[1] In many ways it turns out that Shakespeare exemplifies the patterns discovered in the study so far, providing further confirmation of their validity.

In the case of Shakespeare's *Sonnets*, a reference to Shakespeare's 'sugred Sonnets among his private friends', in a book printed in 1598 suggests that some at least had circulated in manuscript as a form of scribal publication.[2] The phrase 'sugared sonnets' occurs not long after in reference to another poet, Samuel Daniel.[3]

> Sweete hony dropping *Daniell* may wage
> Warre with the proudest big Italian
> That melts his heart in sugred sonnetting.

---

[1] Appendix 12 sets out the scattered information, much of it assembled and consolidated for the first time. To avoid repetition, I offer a selection of examples rather than a comprehensive account.
[2] (Francis Meres) *Palladis Tamia* (1598).
[3] *The Three Parnassus Plays (1598–1601)* edited by J.B. Leishman (1949) 238. This parallel appears to have been overlooked.

The comparison is with Tasso and the phrase 'sugred sonnetting' is evidently a cliché. To judge by Shakespeare's own usage, 'sugared' was not a compliment.[4]

The title of the first printed book in which the sonnets appear *Shakespeare's Sonnets, never before imprinted* (1609) implies that readers were already familiar with the work and the author.[5] It also appears to emphasise the book's status as a newly created intellectual property, although some sonnets had already been printed elsewhere.[6] It has been common among some Shakespeare editors to discuss the pre-1609 printing of Shakespeare sonnets in terms of 'piracy', meaning that they may have been printed without Shakespeare's involvement or consent, but that is anachronistically to project back notions of an authorial intellectual property right that did not yet exist in law or in custom.[7] Whether or not Shakespeare had given his consent for the sonnets to be circulated in manuscript, the printed book proclaims that they had decisively passed from one text-copying medium to another.

Poems Written by Wil Shake-speare, Gent. (1640), the next occasion on which the sonnets are known to have been printed, offered a different text from *Sonnets* (1609). The references to homoerotic love were removed by changing he to she in most cases, and the whole book was presented as a miscellany, with some sonnets being given titles, such as 'True Admiration'. In a paratext, the editor claimed that the sonnets were being presented 'in the same purity, the Author then living avouched', a claim which, biographically, is highly implausible. In recent times the 1640 edition has been universally despised, but talk of 'piracy' is again anachronistic and explanations based on changing readerly taste inadequate. As the legitimate owners of the text, the 1640 publisher and printer not only had a right to alter it, but under the severe textual controls of that time, they had the civic duty to do so. Cornelius Cotes, the printer of the book, it has not, I believe, previously been noticed, was one of the twenty printers appointed by the state to clean up and control the whole printed-book industry.[8]

---

4 Compare 'By fair persuasion mix'd with sugared words' *1 Henry IV* iii, 3, 180; 'Hide not thy poison with such sugared words' *1 Henry VI* iii, 3, 18; 'Your grace attended to their sugared words, but looked not on the poison of their hearts' *Richard III* iii 1, 15.
5 A point made by Katherine Duncan-Jones, 'What are Shakespeare's sonnets called?' in *Essays in Criticism* xlvii (1997). Duncan-Jones notes that 'Shakespeare's sonnets' is like 'Greene's Groatsworth of Wit', 'Tarleton's Jest Book', 'Coryat's Crudities', a form that implies that the author, and maybe the works, are already well known, rather than, say, '*Sonnets* by William Shakespeare'.
6 In *The Passionate Pilgrim*, and in the quarto edition of *Love's Labour's Lost*.
7 For example, the discussion of *The Passionate Pilgrim* in Katherine Duncan-Jones, ed., *Shakespeare's Sonnets* (1997) 3.
8 Timperley 490.

Like a house that had been altered to meet an official health and safety regulation, the 1640 text then became the owned property, subject to further alteration and modernisation by the new proprietors on any occasion when it came to be reprinted.[9] Although Shakespearian scholarship rediscovered *Sonnets* (1609), of which only thirteen copies survive, in the eighteenth century, most eighteenth-century readers still only saw the 1640 text and its derivatives. It was, essentially, the 1640 text which was reprinted by Bell in 1774, in a large edition, sold at an unusually cheap price, and then reprinted and sold even more cheaply in parts or 'numbers'.[10] The texts of the sonnets to which most readers of the eighteenth century and romantic period had access was a product not of Shakespeare's time, nor of their own time, but one adapted to fit the policies of King Charles and Archbishop Laud on the eve of the English Civil War.

As far as the Shakespearian plays are concerned, there is now no sure way of establishing how far the printer/publishers of the quarto editions did so with the consent of, or at the instigation of, the author or the players of the theatre companies. Authors and players, although they had no formal power to stop the printing of a manuscript, could protest, and call on the help of powerful supporters, and they were sometimes able to have their complaints printed in a later edition.[11] But, as with other texts, authors and players had no means of reversing the creation of the new privately owned intellectual properties which the first act of printing *ipso facto* brought about. If a textually poor text was printed, with or without their consent, the only recourse they had was to offer the printer/publisher who then owned the text a manuscript of a better text, and give him the opportunity, if he chose, to bring out a textually superior edition, and this seems to have been done in some cases.[12]

As with the English-language Bible of 1611, we can see how careful the first printer/publishers of the Shakespearian texts had to be if they included any discussion of political legitimacy. In the first quarto edition of *Richard II*,

---

[9] See the discussion of the changes made in Gildon's edition (1710) and of others derived from it, in Hyder Edward Rollins, *New Variorum* (1944) ii, 29.

[10] *Ibid.* ii, 31.

[11] For example, in 'To the Reader' printed in later editions of Thomas Heywood's play, *The Rape of Lucrece*, the author explained that it had been first printed without his permission in 1608. The title page of Jonson's *Every Man out of his Humour* (1600) notes that the play contains 'more than hath been Publickely Spoken or Acted.' See the facsimiles in Herford and Simpson iii, 419. In his preface 'To the Readers' to *Sejanus* (1605), Jonson declares that 'this Booke, in all numbers [i.e. verses], is not the same with that which was acted on the stage' Herford and Simpson iv, 351. For possible authorial revision in Shakespeare, see John Jones, *Shakespeare at Work* (Oxford 1995).

[12] This appears to have happened with *Hamlet, Romeo and Juliet*, 1597 and 1599, *Love's Labour's Lost*, and others.

printed in 1597, the scene in which Richard hands over the crown to Bullingbrook (Bolingbroke), was not printed. Whoever it was who decided that the passage should be omitted, the author, the printer/publisher, the licenser, or the registrar, his decision was soon vindicated. A few months later, a historical work, Hayward's *Henry IV*, that included an essay on the deposition of Richard II, was suppressed by royal command despite its having been regularly licensed and entered, and not only the author and the printer/publisher but the licenser were all punished.[13] The deposition scene in *Richard II* was added in the 1608 fourth quarto, without the need for a new licence, at a time when the topic was becoming less sensitive. One reason, I suggest, why *Antony and Cleopatra*, *Julius Caesar* and *Macbeth* were among the Shakespearian plays that were not printed in Shakespeare's lifetime is that, in one way or another, they discussed political usurpation.[14]

The early printing history also illustrates the general move upmarket and the separation of the reading nation into mainstream and popular sectors that began after 1600 and continued until the eve of the romantic period. It was said in Shakespeare's time, for example, that law students who bought the light and portable quarto playbooks on their visits to London, sold them soon afterwards in order to buy more recent plays, evidence that such texts were read extensively, and that the velocity of circulation from reader to reader was rapid.[15] There is good evidence too that quarto playtexts were sold nationally through the chapman network, at any rate as remainders.[16] Although, at sixpence each, they were not expensive compared with many other books, that was also the price of a pair of shoes.[17]

The publication in 1623 of *Mr William Shakespeares Comedies, Histories, & Tragedies*, the first folio edition, the book which brought together almost all of the Shakespeare plays already printed and added seventeen others, was a defining event in the history of Shakespeare and of English literature. The negotiations to buy in the intellectual properties, which stretched over several years, were evidently not welcomed by some of the existing owners who stood to lose. In 1619, for example, when the idea of an expensive folio edition of Shakespeare's collected plays was already being discussed, one

[13] Discussed by W. W. Greg, 'Samuel Harsnett and Hayward's *Henry IV* ' 3, in *The Library*, 1956. See also W. W. Greg, *Licensers for the Press, & c. to 1640* (Oxford 1962) 42. For another example of a licenser finding himself in trouble see S. Wilton Rix, ed., *The Diary and Autobiography of Edmund Bohun* (Beccles 1853) 105.

[14] *Antony and Cleopatra*, although regularly entered in 1608, appears not to have been printed.

[15] For the sale of plays by country chapmen see the quotation in 'Early play quartos. Indicators of price and extent of circulation', appendix 12, 692.

[16] *Ibid.* 692.   [17] Plant 244.

of the quarto publishers, Pavier, surreptitiously printed some new quarto editions with false dates, probably in order to pass them off as existing stocks not yet sold. From the manufacturing composition of the folio, it emerges that the owners of *Troilus and Cressida* only parted with their intellectual property in that play at the last minute after the printing of the folio had already begun. The owners of *Pericles*, then a commercially successful printed text, that was not included, may have refused to transfer their intellectual property, and some other owners, including those of *Othello*, seem to have negotiated a right to publish in quarto before the folio came out, and to continue to do so later, a form of intellectual property not previously recorded.[18]

Many of the members of the book industry involved in the plans for the Shakespeare folio, both as publishers of the new edition and as owners of the texts already printed, participated in the wider changes in the industry which I discern as occurring after 1600. Some owners had been in trouble with the authorities for printing texts whose monopoly was guaranteed under letters patent. Some had printed ballads that were textually unlawful. They were part of the 'disorder' which both the state and the Stationers' Company, acting together, began successfully to bring to a halt after the endowment of the Stationers' Company in 1603.[19] The negotiations for the Shakespeare folio also overlapped with those which are likely to have occurred before the promulgation of the fierce *Proclamation against Disorderly Printing* (1623), with later proclamations regulating the textual contents of permitted books, and with the reorganisation of the popular sector of the market into a closely owned syndicate within the structures of the Stationers' Company.[20]

To judge from later parallels, the prospective publishers of the folio are likely to have had to pay the previous owners for their properties.[21] Attempts

---

[18] For the late addition of *Troilus and Cressida* see Charlton Hinman, *The Printing and Proof-Reading of the First Folio of Shakespeare* (Oxford 1963). The rights to sell certain plays independently are recorded in the later records of intellectual property trading. See 'The market value of the Shakespeare copyright', appendix 12, 706–9.

[19] Ling was fined in 1595 for selling Psalms, Arber ii, 821. White was fined in 1594 for printing a ballad without licence, Arber ii, 822. Jones had an edition destroyed in 1597, Arber ii, 396. Sims was fined for printing 'a thing disorderly' 1598, Arber ii, 829. White was fined for printing a ballad belonging to Jones in 1579, Arber ii, 850. Infringements in 1599 by some of the same publishers are noted in Liber A.

[20] The culmination was marked by the entry of their joint portfolio of properties in the Stationers' Register on 14 December 1624, but the partnership must have been formed before that date.

[21] The publishers of the first folio edition of Beaumont and Fletcher (1647), faced with the same problem of gathering a range of properties held by different printer/publishers, note that they joined 'in the purchase and the printing', implying that fees had to be paid. Preface by Humphrey Moseley quoted by Bennett, *1475 to 1557* 195.

to estimate the print run by relating the recorded price to estimates of the manufacturing cost of the book are therefore unlikely to be valid, quite apart from the fact that, with the loosening of price controls, the new intellectual property owners could choose their price.[22] What we see is a move upmarket, such as was occurring across the whole printed-book industry at this time, that took Shakespeare from a popular, rough, readership, whose political restlessness the authorities feared, to a readership among the political elites.[23] In 1616, Ben Jonson, who had supervised the publication of the folio edition of his *Works*, on which the Shakespeare folio was modelled, had declared contemptuously that he intended that the book would not be read by the ignorant playgoers.[24] Special interest therefore attaches to the words of the corresponding preface to the Shakespeare folio, which proclaims the opposite

'To the great Variety of Readers.

From the most able to him that can but spell: There you are number'd. We had rather you were weighd. Especially, when the fate of all Bookes depends vpon your capacities: and not of your heads alone, but of your purses. Well! it is now publique, & you wil stand for your priuiledges wee know: to read, and censure. Do so, but buy it first. That doth best commend a Booke, the Stationer saies. Then, how odde soever your braines be, or your wisdomes, make your licence the same, and spare not. Iudge your sixe-pen'orth, your shillings worth, your five shillings worth at a time, or higher, so you rise to the iust rates, and welcome. But what ever you do, Buy.

The preface appears to sustain an elaborate and playful conceit about privilege, censorship [censure], licensing, rising book prices, and perhaps the sale of letters patent, all of which were highly topical when the book was first put on sale. But how could the prospective buyer of a twenty-shilling folio assess its value in sixpences? The passage can be read as an encouragement to readers not to be put off by any one play, but it implies that readers could decide how much to spend. The comedies, histories, and tragedies are paginated separately which may mean that they could be purchased separately. There is a record of the book being sold with a promise to buy it back at a third of its price.[25] The folio preface may

---

[22] For example, the estimates by Anthony James West, *The Shakespeare First Folio* (2001) 68.
[23] A similar case is Jonson's *Poetaster* in which the folio included passages not printed in the quarto. Herford and Simpson iv, 193.
[24] In 'To my bookseller.'
[25] Noted and signed on copy no. 60 in the Folger Shakespeare Library, Washington: 'at ye Returne to allow 5s 6d.' Blayney 29.

even imply ironically that the book could be bought in 'numbers', that is in instalments, although that pun does not quite work.[26] One explanation that has not, as far as I know, been suggested is that the folio publishers simultaneously sold some of the texts in quarto until stocks ran out. No printer/publisher of any texts with unsold stocks would normally have assigned his intellectual property rights to another publisher without simultaneously assigning to him his remaining unsold stocks, a convention which the Stationers' Company were sometimes called in to enforce.[27] Whatever the passage means, we can be sure that the folio did not in fact enable Shakespeare to be read by 'the great Variety of Readers'. The folio, at forty times the price of an individual play, took Shakespeare to the very top of the demand curve.[28] The main buyers at that price are likely to have been noblemen, high ecclesiastics, gentry, and institutional libraries, a point which the pedigrees of surviving copies tend to confirm.

For nearly a century after 1623, when only folio versions were available, no chapman who may previously have sold individual Shakespeare plays in quarto could easily have found a market for a collection of thirty-six plays, carrying the heavy and unwieldy book from fair to fair or house to house, until he found a buyer, even if, as is unlikely, the folio publishers had been willing to sell him copies at trade discount.[29] No printed plays, whether old or newly written, are found in the lists of the Ballad Partnership or in the trade catalogues of 'chapmen's books' sold through the national chapman network.[30] Instead, as part of the general move upmarket, we see the prices of second-hand copies of out-of-print quarto plays rising to 200 or 300 per cent of their original price.[31] At the same time, the price of buying

---

[26] The sentence, whose surface meaning is that the readers are to be counted like, say, eggs rather than weighed like, say, corn, besides implying that they are the commodities on sale rather than the purchasers, makes less sense without a pun on both key words. Compare the joke 'Mr Clench . . . has a folio coming out in numbers' in Samuel Foote's short comedy, *The Author*, first performed 1757, and the reference to Voltaire being '*number'd* through the town' in George Crabbe's *The Library* (1781) quoted in appendix 6. 'Weighd' appears to be used in the sense of having value, as used by Shakespeare in *Coriolanus* ii, 2, 79 'I love them as they weigh.' Other examples of figurative uses in C. T. Onions, *A Shakespeare Glossary* (Oxford 1911).

[27] This was made an explicit condition of a reassignment in 1603, implying perhaps some attempt to avoid it, Arber iii, 249. A spokesman for the industry told a parliamentary inquiry in 1774 that at that time successor publishers frequently bought the stocks but 'they never reprint a book under that predicament until the books remaining are sold off'. Hansard, column 1084.

[28] An indication of those who bought folios is the printed subscription list in *A catalogue and true note of the names of such persons which . . . haue receaued the etymologicall dictionarie . . . from the handes of Maister Minsheu the author* (1617), CUL.

[29] More plays, some not Shakespearian, were added to the later folios.   [30] See chapter 17.

[31] Examples in appendix 12. None refers to Shakespeare quartos.

the folio edition new appears to have been raised. The fourth folio of 1685 sold so badly that in 1688 stocks had to be sold off in bulk at discounted prices.[32]

In terms of authors, the Shakespeare first folio has, rightly, been seen as one of the most magnificent achievements in English literary history. As far as readers were concerned, however, the effect was to bring him in from the playhouses, the law courts, and the country fairs to the hall and the library, to take him from the coat pocket and the satchel to the table and the lectern, to immobilise him indoors. The book which celebrated and monumentalised Shakespeare as a great English author simultaneously removed him from most of the nation's readers.

Shakespeare's career as an author spanned the period when the changes that I discern relating to anthologies, abridgements, adaptations, and quotations were put in place.[33] And here too Shakespeare both illustrates and confirms the validity of my conclusions. Until about 1600, the intellectual property regime was more concerned with anticipating and forestalling competition than with preventing copying of textual content as such. In terms of intellectual property, therefore, the anonymous play *The Taming of a Shrew*, that was entered in the Stationers' Company register in 1594 and was printed several times by successive owners, was the same intellectual property as *The Taming of the Shrew* by William Shakespeare, although *The Shrew* differs in so many respects from *A Shrew* as to be textually almost a different play.[34] The reason why *Romeo and Juliet* was not entered in the Stationers' Register when it was first printed may be that it was regarded as the same intellectual property as the (textually very different) *Tragicall Historye of Romeus and Juliet* which had been entered in 1562.[35]

Shakespeare, more than any other author, exemplifies the growing association between notions of the author as individual genius and the increasingly textual nature of the intellectual property regime. As early as 1592, Shakespeare was accused by a rival playwright of being an 'upstart crow, beautified with our feathers', implying that it was only by plagiarism that

---

[32] See *A Catalogue of Latin, French, and English Books, to be sold in numbers, to the Booksellers of London and Westminster, by Auction: . . . By Benjamin Walford* (1688). Copy in CUL. This includes the entry under 'English Books in folio'. '*Shakespears* Works'. As far as I can see this point has not previously been noted.

[33] See chapter 4.

[34] *The Shrew* was not entered among the plays not hitherto entered in the registration of the folio in 1623.

[35] Arber i, 203. *Romeo and Juliet* first appears as a transfer of ownership in 1607.

he had been able to succeed.[36] But within a few years, Shakespeare was said to have drawn his materials direct from Nature. By the time of the much despised 1640 *Poems Written by Wil Shake-speare, Gent*, the owners were claiming that he never adapted the work of others or even used *sententiae*

> Next Nature onely help him for looke thorow,
> This whole Booke, thou shalt find he doth not borrow
> One phrase from Greeks, nor Latins imitate
> Nor once from vulgar Languages Translate
> Nor plagiari-like from others gleane.

Shakespeare was thus, with considerable violence to the historical record, constructed as a romantic genius, inspired, unique, and unassisted by tradition.

The making of such claims may have helped to justify the advance of intellectual property to include short pieces and quotations. *Poems Written by Wil Shake-speare, Gent* did not have to be re-entered in 1640, but the then owners carefully registered their ownership of the poems by other named authors, some quite short, included in the volume.[37]

Extracts from Shakespeare's works appear in many of the printed verse miscellanies of the late sixteenth century, including the last *Loves Martyr* (1601), thereafter only being anthologised in the carefully controlled single stream that the publishers permitted in the 180 years that followed.[38] That the sudden change resulted from a change in the regime of printed books and not simply from changing readerly taste is confirmed by the fact that extracts from Shakespeare, mostly copied from the printed texts, occur in many manuscript miscellanies.[39] The intellectual property owners of the high monopoly period also produced Dodd's *Beauties of Shakespeare*, the only permitted Shakespeare anthology before 1774. Dodd, incidentally, was hanged for forging a bank note, the only case so far of a literary scholar being put to death for appropriating someone else's text.

As soon as the intellectual property restrictions were lifted in 1774, Shakespeare immediately became one of the authors most quoted from

---

[36] S. Schoenbaum, *William Shakespeare, A Compact Documentary Life* (revised edition, Oxford 1987) 151.
[37] Arber iv, 487.
[38] It is not known how his poem, later called *The Phoenix and the Turtle*, came to be printed along with works by Jonson, Chapman, Marston, and Chester. At that time, the regime would not have prevented the poem from being printed from a manuscript copy without authorial consent.
[39] See Peter Beal, *Index of English Literary Manuscripts, 1450–1625, Part 2* (1980) 452.

in the printed anthologies of the romantic period. Within a few years of 1774, anthologised Shakespeare had also reached the school room, being among the authors most often drawn on for the school 'readers' and 'speakers' that proliferated in the romantic period.

With abridgements too, Shakespeare both illustrates and confirms the patterns identified earlier.[40] A ballad version of *Titus Andronicus* was entered, as a newly created intellectual property, along with Shakespeare's play of that name, simultaneously to a printer/publisher who operated in both the mainstream and the ballad markets, on 6 February 1594.[41] There are direct parallels with ballad versions of plays by Marlow composed and registered at this time. The author of *Titus Andronicus's Lament* is likely to have been Richard Johnson who, along with Thomas Deloney, seems to have been a jobbing writer.[42] A new ballad of *Romeo and Juliet* was entered in 1596, that is before the play was first printed, of which no trace has been found.[43] But with the exception of *Titus Andronicus*, and the uncertain case of *Romeo and Juliet*, no other play by Shakespeare was printed in a ballad version, although *Hamlet*, *Macbeth*, *Antony and Cleopatra*, *Othello*, and many others look excellent candidates, and there is record of a manuscript version of a ballad version of *Othello*.[44] We may even have a documentary record of the exact moment of clamp-down on ballad versions of Shakespeare's plays in 1596.[45]

As with other texts, the freeze continued until after 1774. Besides the ballad version of *Titus Andronicus*, that of *King Leir and his three Daughters*, an old play which predated Shakespeare's, continued to be reprinted and sold over the same long timespan, without challenge or rival, probably wrongly believed by many readers to have been derived from Shakespeare's *King Lear*. The first abridged version of a Shakespeare play since the 1594 ballad version of *Titus Andronicus*, appeared in 1808 when William Godwin published *King Lear*, the first of Mary and Charles Lamb's *Tales from Shakespear*, and many other abridgements, adaptations, and children's versions followed.

---

[40] See chapter 4.
[41] Details in 'Clamp-down on ballad versions and abridgements', appendix 12, 695.
[42] See 'Did Richard Johnson compose the ballad versions?', appendix 12, 697.
[43] To White 'these twoo ballades the followinge, viz. The one intituled. A newe ballad of Romeo and Juliet', Arber iii, 68.
[44] Printed from the manuscript allegedly discovered by Collier in *Othello. The New Variorum Edition*, edited by Horace Howard Furness (Philadelphia 1886, New York reprinted 2000) 398.
[45] See 'Possible explicit documentary evidence for the sudden cessation of ballad versions of Shakespeare's plays', appendix 12, 696.

Just as the clamp-down on anthologies kept Shakespeare out of the school room for 200 years, so the clamp-down on abridgements and adaptations kept him out of the playground.

There is another respect in which the first Shakespeare texts that we have may have been affected by the intellectual property regime that has not, as far as I know, been previously considered. Editors, I think it is fair to say, have assumed that the decision on whether to include a song in a play was taken by Shakespeare and the players solely on artistic grounds, and that the printed texts replicate, more or less, what was done in performance. Editors may not have sufficiently appreciated that songs were as much subject to private intellectual property ownership as longer texts, and indeed were a large and valuable part of the stock in trade of the printer/publishers who first printed the Shakespeare plays. The first documentary record I have found of a printer being fined for printing part of an intellectual property belonging to another refers to a ballad.[46] It is worth considering, therefore, whether there is any evidence that the tightening of the regime on quoting from previously printed texts may have impinged on the texts of the songs and ballads included in the printed texts of Shakespeare as they have come down to us.

A key feature of the intellectual property regime until the mid nineteenth century was that it applied only to texts that had been printed. There was no intellectual property right either in manuscript or in performance, such as the singing of a song, the oral delivery of a sermon or lecture, or the performance of a play, even although such performances might have been transmediated from a printed text or from a manuscript.[47] A player in one of the acting companies could therefore be scripted to sing a ballad transcribed from a printed ballad, if the needs of the play required it, without any obligation to obtain permission from the owner.[48] It was only if and when the time came for the play to be printed, that is to move from the medium of material manuscript through performance back into the medium of printed text, that questions of intellectual property arose. If the prospective owner, that is the printer/publisher of a previously unprinted play, printed the text of a performed song or a ballad which had

[46] See 'Indications that a regime intended to control the use of quotations from printed books unauthorised by the intellectual property owners is being put in place', appendix 3, 493.

[47] Discussed further in the case of *Frankenstein* in chapter 18.

[48] Manuscripts were subject to other controls not associated with intellectual property. For example if an obscene, profane, seditious, or libellous ballad was passed from hand to hand or posted in a public place, the penalties could be severe.

already been printed, he might, unless he himself owned the property or had obtained permission from the colleague who did, be at risk of breaching the industry's customary practice. If such restrictions were in place, we would expect to see the main evidence in the later texts, and especially in the 1623 folio.

A possible example is in the witches' song 'Come away Hecate' in *Macbeth*, of which only a snatch is given as it was first published in the folio of 1623.[49] Since a longer version is included in *The Witch*, a play by Middleton, written around 1615, of which a manuscript fair copy version survives, it has been commonly assumed that the existence of the prior Middleton version means that Shakespeare wrote *Macbeth* in collaboration with Middleton, or that Shakespeare's *Macbeth* was added to or adapted by Middleton. What does not appear to have been considered is that both Middleton and Shakespeare may have been using a song which had already been printed. Since the intellectual property regime applied only to texts which had been reified into printed books, a player could be scripted by a playwright to sing an existing printed song without having to obtain permission, and he could sing it on stage as scripted. By quoting the song in a manuscript, Middleton would not have breached intellectual property, but he might have run into problems if his manuscript of *The Witch* had ever proceeded to print. If I am right, then the modern view that the witches' song shows that Middleton had a hand in the writing of *Macbeth* may have to be reviewed.[50]

When we consider the Shakespeare plays as a whole, almost all the songs of any length, in both the quarto and folio versions, appear to be sufficiently unlike anything known to have been printed for us to be reasonably sure that they were specially composed. There is no evidence for example, that the songs of Autolycus, the ballad singer in *The Winter's Tale*, had appeared in print. As far as songs which already existed are concerned, on the other hand, they are usually given in the printed plays only in snatches.[51] If intellectual property considerations were present, the first printer/publisher

---

[49] Discussed in Nicholas Brooks's edition of *Macbeth* (Oxford 1990).

[50] See Elizabeth Schafer, ed., *Thomas Middleton, The Witch* (1994). The title of the manuscript, 'A Tragi-Coomodie Called the Witch; long since Acted by his Ma.ties Servants at the Black Friars. written by Tho. Middleton' does not imply that Middleton wrote the songs. The point may have been understood by the dramatist William Davenant, the main link with practice before the closure of the theatres, who in 1673, in the first quarto edition of the play printed in the different regulatory conditions of the Restoration, included the whole song.

[51] The point that existing songs 'are seldom actually sung in the plays or sung only in snatches' was noticed independently by Edward J. Dent, 'Shakespeare and Music' in Harley Granville-Barker and G. B. Harrison eds., *A Companion to Shakespeare Studies* (Cambridge 1934) 158, but he offered no explanation.

of a Shakespeare play, if he did not own the intellectual property himself, might, of course, avoid potential difficulties by omitting the texts altogether or by including only short extracts, and there are examples of plays of the time where the texts of the ballads are omitted from printed versions, and others where they were added in later printings.[52] Alternatively, the printer/publisher could include a newly composed piece or a version of an existing piece which was sufficiently different from the printed version to be a separate property just as various versions of *Greensleeves* appear to have been separately owned.

But there are cases where the play demands that the song being sung is well known to the audience or readership. It is possible that Falstaff's words in the first quarto of *2 Henry IV* (1600) 'When Arthur first in court empty the iourdan [chamber pot] and was a worthy King; how now Mistris Doll?' were enough to signal to the early audiences and readers that Falstaff is singing from *Sir Lancelot du Lac*, an old romance of violent chivalry that is in line with Falstaff's assumed but not his actual character, and that even a few words were enough to make that excellent dramatic point.[53] If so, this shows much confidence by the author in the sophistication of the audience in the theatres and the readership across the whole country. A similar example occurs in *Twelfth Night*, where Sir Toby Belch's sung words, 'There dwelt a man in Babylon', may have been enough to remind the audience/readership that he was singing the ballad of *Constant Susanna*, a text which dated from before the restrictions on making ballad versions of biblical and Apocryphal Bible texts, and whose ownership was carefully guarded.[54] The theatre audience of *Twelfth Night*, knowing the story of the putting to death of the Elders for the sexual harassment of Susanna, may have regarded it as a foil to the action of the play, but again a great deal of knowledge and sophistication on the part of audiences and readerships is implied. Other examples where the dramatic needs of the play seem to demand the singing of songs which were both already known to the audience but in the ownership of others occur in *The Taming of the Shrew*, first printed in the folio of 1623. The then famous song which Petruchio is

---

[52] See *Songs from the British Drama*, edited by Edward Bliss Reed (New Haven 1925) 280, 346, and Phyllis Hartnoll, ed., *Shakespeare in Music* (1964) 10.

[53] Seng 45.

[54] Probably first entered in the Stationers' Register in 1562/63. Arber i, 211, and it is not known whether the entry of 1592 noted in appendix 3 is for the same title. A reprint by the Ballad Partners, which is likely to preserve the text of the earlier printed versions circulating in Shakespeare's time, from which he quotes, has survived: *An excellent ballad intituled, the constancy of Susanna* (1640), *STC* (second edition) 23436.

singing when he is interrupted, of which only a line and a half is printed, 'Where is the life that late I led? Where are those . . .' may have been an encroachment on the ballad entered in 1578 to Thomas Man 'The lamentacon of a yong man confessinge his former lyfe that he hathe led'.[55] The same may be true of the two lines of his song beginning 'It was the Friar of Orders Gray', first printed in 1550, where, unless the audience was exceptionally alert and well informed, the two first lines by themselves would not have given much of the flavour of the long, bawdy, story, written partly in joking Latin, of the seduction of a nun.[56] In the many plays printed between 1603 and 1641 there are dozens of examples where the play calls for a song that is not printed, where the play appears to have been altered to remove a song, where songs are printed not at the places where they would have been performed in the play but at the beginning or the end of the printed text, where the songs are added in later editions, and other indications that songs were regarded as separable from the plays in which they were sung.[57]

If intellectual property considerations did influence the nature of the quotations of ballads in the printed texts, it would resolve the famous textual puzzle in *Othello*, Desdemona's singing of the willow song. The singing of that song is universally regarded as one of the highest points of the drama, the moment of quiet pathos that prepares us for the violence. The song does not appear in the quarto version of 1622, the first time *Othello* was printed, but it is in the 1623 folio, although not at any length. Most editors have assumed that the willow song was an addition made to the folio, in the opinion of Dr Johnson, 'the only addition which improved the play'. However, it looks more likely that the willow song was cut out of the quarto than added to the folio. But if so, why? The abridgement was only about 5 per cent. In the negotiations which led up to the publishing of the folio, Walkley, who evidently controlled the manuscript of the previously unprinted *Othello*, drove a hard bargain, insisting on a right to print the play as a separate property both before the folio came out and after. The agreement that he made influenced the extent of readerly access to *Othello* for nearly 200 years. But he did not own the willow song, and he appears

---

[55] In iv, 1, 143. Arber ii, 341. In the printed version of *The Taming of a Shrew*, originally the same intellectual property as *The Taming of the Shrew*, no songs are transcribed even in snatches.

[56] Transcribed by Seng 3 from a manuscript version.

[57] This emerges from the survey by William R. Bowden, *The English Dramatic Lyric, 1603–42* (New Haven 1951) 87–114 and 133–209.

to have been denied permission to include even a snatch until after the publication of the folio.[58]

If I am right, then both editors and producers of performances, should, in some cases, consider reinstating fuller versions of the old songs which may have been truncated from the earliest printed texts.

Shakespeare vividly illustrates the operation of the restrictive trade practices, and the effects on texts, books, prices, access, and readerships, of the changes in publishing practice that took place in the seventeenth and eighteenth centuries. By the high monopoly period, the firm of Tonson had, as a result of judicious buying, built up a controlling interest in the Shakespeare plays that was eventually to reach about 65 per cent, although the intellectual property in the sonnets and other poems remained in other hands.[59] And again, Shakespeare not only confirms the general patterns but enables us to illustrate them in detail.

In 1731, for example, the transitional period allowed by the 1710 Copyright Act came to an end, and Shakespeare's works along with innumerable other old texts, entered the public domain. In 1734 an enterprising printer/publisher called Walker began to offer Shakespeare plays at a third of the existing price. He even added illustrations. At fourpence a play, less than the quartos of the sixteenth century, Shakespeare was again affordable by a wide readership and it is recorded that Walker's books were distributed by country chapmen. Walker took Shakespeare back to the popular market from which he had been removed in 1623, as had been the intention of parliament in framing the 1710 Act. However, when Tonson and the other 'proprietors' used their deeper pockets to print huge editions of 10,000 copies of each play and to sell them at below cost at predatory prices, Walker accepted money to go away.[60] With the challenge beaten off, the 'proprietors' resumed their *de facto* monopoly, raised their prices back to the previous levels, and then took them higher. At some point, if we are to judge from the industry's trade catalogues, Tonson ceased to supply the market with single plays altogether, although some rights to reprint some plays remained in other hands and were occasionally exercised.[61] Instead

---

[58] For indications that the willow song was privately owned see 'The willow song, evidence for its being privately owned', appendix 12, 697.

[59] See Terry Belanger, 'Tonson, Wellington and the Shakespeare Copyrights' in (Pollard) *Studies in the Book Trade in Honour of Graham Pollard* (1975).

[60] For Walker's costs and prices, and extracts from the altercation with Tonson, see appendix 12. For the offer to pay him for not printing Shakespeare, see Geduld 1940.

[61] See bibliography: 'Book trade catalogues'. I can find no reference to Tonson advertising the sale of individual plays in any of the catalogues where one would expect to find them.

Table 8.1 Shakespeare. Minimum prices

Individual plays		Shillings
Before the 1623 folio		0.5
After 1623 until early eighteenth century single plays mostly not on sale		
1730s. Tonson's price		1
Walker's price, attempting to exercise his statutory rights		0.3
Tonson's predatory price		0.25
Tonson's price after Walker is driven out of business		1
Element of price exploitation		0.7 (70%)
After 1730s (single plays mostly not on sale)		
1774. End of perpetual copyright		
After 1780.		0.5

Collected editions on first publication	Number of volumes	
1623. First folio. One volume, but paginated so that it could also be sold as three separate volumes	1	20
1685. Fourth folio. Later remaindered. One volume, but paginated so that it could also be sold as three separate volumes		?24
1709/10. Rowe	6	30
1725. Pope	6	126
1733. Theobald	8	42
1744. Hanmer	6	210
1747. Warburton	8	48
1765. Johnson	8	48
1767. Capell	10	42
1773. Steevens	10	60
1790. Malone	11	88
1774. End of perpetual copyright		
1773/75. Bell	5	15
1784. Stockdale	1	15

he kept the unsold copies as a strategic reserve ready to flood the market at predatory prices if another Walker were ever to appear.[62]

As the summary in table 8.1 shows, as the high monopoly period advanced, the minimum price of access to Shakespeare's printed works

---

[62] The existence of these large stocks of single plays is noted in the trade catalogue of Tonson's assets sold in 1767. See bibliography: 'Closed book industry marked auction-sale catalogues with achieved prices marked in manuscript'. For the practice by cartels of holding strategic reserves in order to be able to flood a market, see Rotemberg and Salone.

Table 8.2 Shakespeare. Market value of the intellectual property in the 'Dramatic Works', as sold at closed auction (simplified and rounded, pounds)

1707	a small fraction of	280
1709	a small fraction of	200
1734	much more than	200
1737	less than	675
1737	less than	351
1737/38	less than	340
1741		439
1756		1,630
1759		1,717
1760		1,717
1761		1,361
1762		1,291
1765		3,462
1765		2,997
1767		2,838
1768		1,087
1769 The Shakespeare Jubilee		
1774 End of perpetual copyright		nil

became ever more expensive and readerships ever more limited.[63] The owners moved ever higher up the demand curve, producing one expensive, immobile, multi-volume, library edition after another, in large format with editorial annotations that grew in scale with every relaunch.

Between 1737 and 1767 the market value of the intellectual property in Shakespeare, which I have calculated from the prices obtained at the cartel's closed sales, rose sharply, as is shown in table 8.2 summarised and simplified from the more complete and complex evidence given in appendix 12. The prices paid were the cost to a partner of being allowed to participate in the publishing of the work to the extent of his shareholding, excluding all the publishing costs of manufacturing and selling, which were shared by the partners in the intellectual properties in accordance with their relative shareholdings. The figures represent the closed market capitalisation of Shakespeare seen as a rentable property in conditions of expected perpetual monopoly in which the supply to the market would be carefully controlled.

---

[63] Summarised from the fuller data in appendix 12.

We have an excellent example here of long or perpetual intellectual property monopoly in action. In the end, in order to preserve the rising share price, the owners had to abandon almost the whole of the potential market.

Once perpetual intellectual property was ended in England in 1774, and Shakespeare was sold in conditions of economic competition, the effects were dramatic. The number of editions rose sharply, print runs lengthened, and minimum prices fell. It had taken nearly 200 years for the minimum price of access to a Shakespeare play to fall back to what it had been in Shakespeare's day. When we add in the anthologies, the abridgements, the sale in parts, the inclusion in school books and all the other innovations of the post-1774 public domain, we can say that, by about 1800, Shakespeare at last became available to readers of all classes and ages.

After 1800 the price of buying a Shakespeare play continued to fall until, by the end of the nineteenth century, excellent annotated editions could be bought for a penny each.

CHAPTER 9

Literary production in the romantic period

Authors of the romantic period normally wrote their drafts on paper with a quill pen while seated at a desk. A few, notably Walter Scott, dictated to an amanuensis. Shelley preferred to compose in the open air, writing his thoughts down later. Whatever the initial transfer from mind to paper, the creation of a text was seldom a solitary activity. Wordsworth's compositions normally involved several stages of draft, discussion, revision, and fair-copying in which his sister and wife participated.[1] Byron liked to imply that all his writings were dashed off, but when parts of *Don Juan* were fair-copied by Mary Shelley, her suggestion that the 'indelicate' word 'breast' should be changed to 'heart' was accepted.[2]

Many works remained in manuscript, sometimes sent to friends or transcribed into a commonplace book.[3] Others were not printed until long after they were first written. Coleridge's *Christabel*, for example, was passed from hand to hand in numerous manuscript copies for a decade or more, as a form of scribal publication, before it was published in print in 1816. Southey believed that Scott, who had read the piece in manuscript, had plagiarised it in *The Lay of the Last Minstrel*, which was published in print in 1805.[4] The novels of Jane Austen and Susan Ferrier were initially composed to entertain their families without any expectation of having them published in print, or so the authors claimed.

Authors who aspired to a larger readership could send short pieces to a newspaper or a literary review. Wordsworth, Southey, and Coleridge all started their literary careers this way. By the end of the romantic period there were many dozens of periodicals in Great Britain offering to consider short

---

[1] Discussed in Stephen Gill, *William Wordsworth, A Life* (1989).
[2] Discussed in Byron, *Poetical Works* vi, and T. G. Steffan, E. Steffan, and W. W. Pratt, eds., *Byron's Don Juan, A Variorum Edition* (Austin, Tex. 1957).
[3] For scribal publication see chapter 3. For manuscript commonplace books in the romantic period see chapter 12.
[4] Southey, *Life* ii, 316.

poems and stories, and payment could be good. All except one of Southey's *Metrical Tales*, had, for example, already been published in the *Morning Post* before they appeared in book form, earning Southey nearly £1,500, far more than the book.[5] When Thomas Campbell visited Walter Scott in 1825, he remarked that 'every magazine now contained such poetry as would have made a reputation for a man twenty or thirty years ago'. 'Ecod', Scott replied, 'we were in the luck of it to come before all this talent was at work.'[6] If, however, an author wished to see his or her works printed in book form, he or she needed to find a publisher to arrange the financing, the manufacture, the distribution, and the sales. The main publishing centres were London and Edinburgh, but although postage was expensive, authors no longer needed personal meetings. Felicia Hemans, for example, who lived in Wales, built her literary reputation first with Murray in London and later with Blackwood in Edinburgh, without visiting either city.[7]

Most manuscripts were turned down. Byron's *Childe Harold's Pilgrimage, A Romaunt*, soon to be the most admired literary work of the age, was rejected by Longman and by Constable, the two leading publishers, and by others, until in 1812 a friend managed to place it with Murray, who was then still on the fringes.[8] By 1817, Murray was rejecting 700 poetry manuscripts a year.[9] Austen's *Pride and Prejudice* was rejected by return of post.[10] Nor did having a contract necessarily ensure that a work was published. Austen bought back the manuscript and intellectual property rights to *Northanger Abbey* six years after they had been sold to a publisher who did nothing.[11] By taking out options in this way, publishers could, if not quite corner a market, put a squeeze on competitors, but on the whole, the record suggests, most works which were accepted were published not long after.

Longman, the biggest firm, known as the 'establishment publisher', was reluctant to accept any text that was not safely mainstream.[12] To have done so would not only have risked upsetting the customers of the firm's main business in religious and school books, but might have strained the bargain between the book industry and the state, which resumed much of its

[5] *Ibid.* 313.   [6] Russell's *Moore* 391.   [7] Feldman.
[8] See Byron's reference to 'the Crafty' in Byron, *Letters and Journals* x, 70. For evidence that it was Constable who was known as 'the Crafty' see Lockhart 167, 363, 374, and Blackwood i, 121.
[9] Smiles i, 342.
[10] The letter to Cadell and Davies is printed by Besterman xxi.
[11] Bloomfield's *The Farmer's Boy* was another work only printed with reluctance as a result of pressure from the poet's influential patron. The circumstances of the first publication are described in successive versions of the preface. For the huge sales see chapter 12 and appendix 9.
[12] The phrase used by Thomas Moore. Russell's *Moore* 562.

importance after the French Revolution.[13] Among the literary works which Longman turned down were Shelley's *Laon and Cythna* and Mary Shelley's *Frankenstein*.[14] Longman also tried to protect the reputation of his authors, turning down not only Byron's *English Bards and Scotch Reviewers*, a satire rejected by ten or twelve other publishers, but also *Rejected Addresses*, a book of gentle and witty parodies by James and Horace Smith that was soon to be a bestseller.[15] Murray too became more cautious in his publishing policies when he was given the government contract for publishing the *Navy List*, as Byron was quick to point out.[16]

In the romantic period, as the industry expanded, roles became more specialised. In the larger firms we see the emergence of professional 'publishers' readers', paid employees who read the submitted texts in manuscript, guessed at the market appeal, and advised the publisher on how to respond. Murray, who at first relied on the opinions of a group of friends who dined regularly in his house, found that he received so many unsolicited manuscripts that he had to employ 'a porter to carry, an author to read, and a secretary to answer them'.[17] Authors too began to employ specialists to help them judge the likely reactions of publishers and we see the first emergence of the literary agent. It was, for example, at the insistence of his adviser, John Ballantyne, that Scott rewrote twenty-four pages of *St Ronan's Well* before sending it in. If 'the author of Waverley' insisted on keeping the episode in which a modern lady enjoyed sex before marriage, Ballantyne advised, he would damage the reputation, and therefore the sales, of the Waverley novels as a whole. And we can see from the archival record how percipient Ballantyne was.[18] For nearly a hundred years the Waverley novels were to be virtually the only novels that were universally recommended, without reservation, to be read by men, women, and young people.

Publishers had their own views about what would make a marketable book, proposing subjects to be written about, whether the work should be in prose or verse, and advising on the desirable length. Hemans normally asked her publisher which subjects would appeal to the market before putting pen to paper.[19] It was partly at the urging of Longman that first Wordsworth and then Moore wrote long continuous verse romances of the kind popularised by Scott and Byron. In the event Wordsworth's *The White Doe of Rylston* (1815) was not a commercial success, and Wordsworth

[13] See chapter 16.   [14] For *Frankenstein* see chapter 18.
[15] For the turning down of *English Bards*, see Byron, *Letters and Journals* x, 60. For Smith, Arthur H. Beavan, *James and Horace Smith* (1899) 114. Longman is not mentioned directly.
[16] In 'Strahan-Tonson-Lintot of the times'. Byron, *Poetical Works* iv, 326.
[17] Smiles i, 342.   [18] Edgar Johnson, *Sir Walter Scott, the Great Unknown* (1970) 853.   [19] Feldman.

soon resumed writing the collections of short poems for which he was best known, but Moore's *Lalla Rookh* (1817) fully vindicated his publisher's judgement. Publishers and their advisers also had views about linguistic propriety, decency, Scotticisms, provincialisms, and other factors that might detract from sales, and often asked for changes. 'The two passages cannot be altered without making Lucifer talk like the Bishop of Lincoln', Byron protested at Murray's suggested alterations to *Cain*.[20] The rhetoric of romanticism, mainly devised and developed in Victorian times, stressed the uniqueness and autonomy of the 'creative' author, and some writers who did not depend financially on their pens, notably Byron, fiercely defended their independence. In practice, however, most authors were obliged to operate within a commercial system in which they, their advisers, and their publishers attempted to judge what the market wanted and how best to supply it.

A common type of contract, as it had been for centuries, was for the author to sell the copyright to a publisher outright for a lump sum. Under this type of contract, the publisher met all the costs of manufacture and publication, and the author had no further financial claim. When the Bristol publisher, Joseph Cottle, bought *Lyrical Ballads* from Wordsworth in 1798, he made a poor bargain, for when he transferred all his business assets to Longman not long after, the copyright was valued at nil. By contrast when, in the same year, a Glasgow publisher agreed to print *The Pleasures of Hope* by the twenty-year old Thomas Campbell in return for the right to buy copies at the trade discount, fortune favoured the publisher. The poem was an instant and continuing bestseller, netting thousands of pounds over the following decades, but nothing more for Campbell except an occasional *ex gratia* payment which did more to enrage than to soothe his feelings.[21] Campbell never overcame his sense of having been cheated. Publishers, he said, were ravens feasting on their victims.[22] He sent one of them a Bible in which the phrase 'Now Barabbas was a thief' was altered to 'Now Barabbas was a publisher.'[23] He admired Napoleon, Campbell liked to tell his friends, because he had once ordered a bookseller to be shot.[24]

Authors with a record of good sales on their first or later books could command large sums. After *The Lay of the Last Minstrel*, Scott was offered

---

[20] Byron to Murray, 3 November 1821. Byron *Letters and Journals* ix, 53. See also Jack Stillinger, *Multiple Authorship and the Myth of Solitary Genius* (1991) and Zachary Leader, *Revision and Romantic Authorship* (Oxford 1996).
[21] Details in appendix 9.   [22] William Beattie, ed. *Life and Letters of Thomas Campbell* (1849) i, 234.
[23] Smiles i, 336, denies that Byron was the originator of the joke.   [24] Jerdan i, 143.

over £1,000 for *Marmion*, unseen and unfinished. For *The Lady of the Lake*, he received over £2,000 plus a share in the equity.[25] For *Lalla Rookh*, Thomas Moore agreed with Longman, before a word was written, 'That upon your giving into our hands a poem of yours of the length of *Rokeby* [a long romantic poem by Walter Scott], you shall receive from us the sum of £3,000.'[26] Byron received nearly £20,000 in total from Murray over the nine years of their association. At first he felt it was unbecoming to a nobleman to accept money at all, and grandly gave away the copyright of *Childe Harold's Pilgrimage, A Romaunt*, to a friend, but when he discovered that Murray had bought it back for £525, he quickly learned to accept the humiliation. By the end, when he estimated the profits that Murray was making from his writings over the copyright period, Byron too felt exploited. The five hundred guineas (£525) he was receiving for each of his poems was no more than Murray paid to the Reverend Henry Milman for religious verse dramas which sold far less well.[27] Hannah More, the author of many bestselling conduct and religious books and tracts, is said to have made £30,000 from the sale of her copyrights. In financial terms, she was the most successful British author of the romantic period, although that money came from subsidies from supporters not from the market.[28] Robert Bloomfield, the bestselling verse writer of the period, who parted with his intellectual property rights on unfavourable terms, died in penury.[29]

Publishers usually paid authors, if at all, in bills post-dated to three, six, or twelve months in the future. Most authors, however, preferred to sell their bills at a discount for immediate cash to a money-market dealer, or to accept a discounted payment from the publisher. The actual amounts received by authors were, therefore, usually less than the nominal amounts mentioned in contracts.[30] Since the writing of a book took time, and the income of authors was lumpy and unpredictable, some publishers made money advances against works not yet written. It was only the flexibility of the financing arrangements that enabled Godwin, De Quincey, Hazlitt, Keats, Peacock, and others to go on writing at moments of financial crisis. However, since advances were netted against past and future obligations, the cumulative effect was often to tie authors to publishers in a relationship of continuing financial dependency. Wollstonecraft, for example, was, for

---

[25] Lockhart 144, 192.   [26] Russell's *Moore* 127.

[27] Some sales figures for Milman are given in appendix 9.

[28] From the anonymous *Books and Authors* (n.d.c. 1860) 66, probably from figures made public by Tegg at the time of the copyright debates of 1836–42. See chapter 11.

[29] See Bloomfield.

[30] In the figures given for authors' returns I have normally given the nominal, i.e., post-dated, amount.

most of her writing career, an indebted employee of her friend and publisher Joseph Johnson, acting as editor, compiler, reviewer, and translator, as his business needs developed, rather than as an independent author deciding which books she would like to write.[31]

Another common type of contract involved the publisher buying the copyright for an edition of a certain agreed size, say 500 or 1,000 copies, another fee to be negotiated if a second edition was agreed. From the author's point of view, such a contract could be preferable to an outright sale of copyright, although in practice only a few authors benefited. Hemans, for example, repossessed the copyrights of her books when the first editions sold out and sold them again on similar contracts.[32] Because Hazlitt's contracts were for single editions of agreed size, his family were able to regain the copyrights and reprint his books in mid Victorian times, a rare instance of authors and their children benefiting from the 1842 Act. Authors with such contracts were, however, inclined to suspect that publishers printed and sold more copies than they acknowledged in their accounts, and they were sometimes right.[33] For example, when in 1809 ten or more mainstream London publishers turned down Byron's *English Bards and Scotch Reviewers*, the not-yet-famous poet contracted with Cawthorn, an outsider, for an edition of 1,000 copies to be published anonymously.[34] When the secret of Byron's authorship came out, Byron authorised a second edition with amendments; then a third and a fourth, each of 1,000 copies. By 1812, however, when Byron was the famous author of *Childe Harold's Pilgrimage*, he realised that he had been unfair to many writers who were now his friends. He refused Cawthorn permission to print a fifth edition, and ordered the poem to be suppressed. The price of second-hand copies soared.[35] Manuscript copies written by professional copyists appeared on

[31] That Wollstonecraft received advances long before her books could be published is confirmed by an unpublished letter of Joseph Johnson, her publisher, to Charles Wollstonecraft, 15 November 1796, in which he also notes that 'she deserves more than most women, & cannot live upon a trifle'. Johnson letter book, NYPL. When her affairs were finally wound up, ten years after her death, her estate owed her publisher over £75, Joseph Johnson to Everina Wollstonecraft, 8 April 1807, Johnson letter book.

[32] Feldman.

[33] For Landor's row with Taylor on sales figures see Chilcot. Authors were also distrustful of Moxon's use of stereotype plates. Examples discussed by Merriam.

[34] Byron *Letters and Journals* x, 70. The reason for Longman's refusal is confirmed in a letter to Revd. Mr Card, 8 May 1815, 'some of our friends were hardly treated in it'. Longman archives 99/98.

[35] An advertisement of 1818 by the Paris offshore pirate Galignani claimed that 'this work is so scarce in London that copies have been sold for five guineas [105 shillings] and upwards', a huge premium over Cawthorn's price of 5 shillings. Shelley's friend Jefferson Hogg noted that the book 'became so exceedingly scarce that a large price was often given for a copy, and some curious people even took the trouble to transcribe it. I have met with such MSS.' Thomas Jefferson Hogg, in his *Life of Shelley* (1858) i, 300.

the market, carefully reproducing the title page, the preface, and even the printer's imprint, in expensive morocco note books.[36] When an Irish publisher put on sale a printed pirated edition, Cawthorn took legal proceedings to have him stopped.[37] But the real pirate was Cawthorn himself. Denied permission to print a fifth edition, he went on reprinting third and fourth editions. About twenty such fakes have been identified, all claiming on the title page to have been issued in 1810 or 1811, but all manufactured from paper on which the manufacturing dates of 1812, 1815, 1816, 1817, 1818, and 1819 are visible in the watermarks.[38] Cawthorn probably sold 20,000 more copies of *English Bards* than he was allowed to by his contracts, all without payment to the author.[39]

A third common type of contract was for a sharing of the net profits between publisher and author, either by half or in some other proportion, after all the costs of publishing had been met. Under this arrangement the publisher accepted the costs and risks of production, but paid no advance. Scott, when not yet famous, made a contract for half profits for the first edition of *The Lay of the Last Minstrel*. When that sold well, he accepted Longman's offer of £500 for the copyright outright. Profit-sharing contracts were attractive to publishers, but for authors they also raised suspicions. Since, in striking the declared profit to be divided, all costs of every kind, capital and current, were netted against the receipts from the sales of the declared first edition, publishers had an incentive to understate the income and to overstate the costs.[40] It was especially difficult for authors to judge whether the stated figures for the costs of printing and paper were reasonable, and they were often taken in. Coleridge's publisher offered figures for the costs of printing *Biographia Literaria* and *Sibylline Leaves* which were several times above the norm.[41] The accounts that Murray prepared for Austen, in calculating her share in the profits of *Emma*, are as fictional as the novel.[42]

---

[36] They are commonly found. Several copies Ac; others seen in various private collections, and noted in booksellers' catalogues. As an indication of copying costs, the cost for transcribing of a whole three-volume Waverley novel was regularly £18 18s (378 shillings). Longman archives.

[37] I know of no surviving copy of this alleged edition.

[38] There are also fakes of the first edition, and of the third edition with paper watermarked 1808, Ac.

[39] Many of his customers, we may be sure, were the users of his large circulating library in London which was his main business.

[40] Examples of complaints in Johnson letter book and Longman archives.

[41] *Biographia Literaria* £5 3s 6d (103.5) shillings a sheet and *Sibylline Leaves* £5 8s 6d (108.5 shillings) a sheet, exclusive of paper. Coleridge, *Letters* iv, 658. The normal cost was less than £2 10s (50 shillings).

[42] See appendix 5. 'Printing costs of three volume novels, setting per sheet' and 'Paper per ream, standard quality as used for novels, shillings per ream'. Printing prices could legitimately differ in accordance with comparative difficulty in setting, length, readability of handwriting, and other factors, but

Finally, for authors who could not find a publisher willing to risk any of his own money, there was publishing 'on commission'. As Longman explained the arrangement in 1816, the publisher 'gets the book printed at the trade price, purchases the paper at the best market, superintends the general interests of the W[or]k, & takes upon himself the risk of Bad Debts for which he charges a commission of 10% on the Sales'.[43] With publishing 'on commission', it was the author who was the investor who accepted all the costs and the risks, and the publisher who took a royalty on sales. 'On commission' publishing was therefore the reverse of normal modern publishing practice, in which the publisher accepts the costs and the risks and the author receives a royalty, a type of contract which was virtually unknown in the romantic period. The invoice for payment presented to Shelley for the printing of *Laon and Cythna* 'on commission' has survived.[44] Comparing the cost figures with the figures officially offered by the publishers' representatives to parliament in the same year, it can be seen that, in this case, far from benefiting from low trade prices for printing and paper, Shelley was overcharged.

Publishing 'on commission', nowadays called 'vanity' publishing, was the recognised way for an aspiring author to take a first step on the literary ladder. Many of Shelley's works were published at his own expense, and he seems to have put up the money for Keats's first volume.[45] The great majority of authors of verse, including some, such as Shelley, who later become famous, were never commercially published in their lifetimes.[46] Thomas Campbell told the story of how God came to London to offer to sell the copyright of the Bible. Colburn, the first publisher he approached, whose main line was in society novels, disliked the mangers and carpenters,

Austen appears to have been charged about double the going rate. The paper used in novels was a fairly uniform commodity. The paper from which *Emma* was manufactured, surviving copies show, is of ordinary unwatermarked quality, and at £1 17s (37 shillings) Austen was heavily overcharged. Letters among the Longman archives show the firm making frequent orders for paper of this type at about £1 3s (23 shillings). Longman told an author who complained about overcharging for paper that 'it is a universal rule to charge into our accounts with authors exactly the same as we pay ourselves'. Letter to John Burns, 24 January 1810 (actually 1811) Longman archives i, 97, 6. The usual method of exaggerating paper prices seems to have been to enter them in the accounts at nominal catalogue prices rather than the discounted prices actually paid. According to an insider in the book trade 'It is possible for the publisher to take discounts in which the author does not share.' Shaylor 231. I have made no calculations about the extent to which paper quantities may also have been overstated, a way of overcharging authors under net profit contracts which was even more difficult for authors such as Austen to detect. That publishers routinely inflated their costs by such devices is also noted by James Spedding, *Publishers and Authors* (privately printed 1867) 11. Spedding had found it impossible to have his pamphlet published by normal methods.

[43] Longman to Renshaw, 20 November, 1816, Longman archives i, 100, 34.
[44] Bodleian, ms. Shelley adds. c 12, folio 7. Transcribed in *SC* x, 160.   [45] A suggestion by Robinson.
[46] See, for example, Shelley's letter to an unknown publisher, Shelley *Letters* i, 563.

wanted the characters to be made aristocratic, and asked for the story of King Herod and Salome to be expanded. Longman, to whom God went next, said he did not think sales would be high. He told Him 'that he would be very happy to print it at his Lordship's expense on commission'.[47]

Besides books published from London and Edinburgh, new works of many kinds, especially locally written verse and sermons, were published in dozens of towns all over the country, probably mostly 'on commission'. Coleridge started in this way in Bristol, Byron in Newark, Shelley in Worthing. In many provincial towns, some quite small, members of the local community could be persuaded to put up money to enable locally written literary texts to be printed. Subscription had been a common method of publication in the previous century not only for titles which needed patronage, and in which lists of the subscribers' names were often printed, but for mainstream commercial titles.[48] When it survived during the romantic period, there was often an element of charity, raising money for a widow or giving a start to a local lad or lass without a patron, and the subscribers were often local nobility and gentry.[49] Lady Penfeather, a character in Scott's *St Ronan's Well*, who pesters visitors to subscribe for the books of her coterie of poets, was probably a well-known type in many localities where the leisured classes were to be found. During the romantic period, few village Miltons lay unprinted in country churchyards.

The initiative for deciding how a literary text should be published normally lay with the publisher. It was he who took the decisions on format, design, print run, and price which determined access, sales, and therefore potential readership. The main limiting factors which he faced were not technological but commercial, particularly how to finance his capital and make the needed rate of return on his outlay while minimising his risks. By juggling the financing instruments he could ensure that many of the costs of production, such as paper and printing work and payments to authors, did not have to be met until they were covered by income from sales. He could also spread much of the risk to other publishers and booksellers, although they expected reciprocity. He could usually make a profit, or at least cover his costs, even if a book was a commercial flop. Even when he made a spectacular misjudgement, as when Longman paid Fanny Burney £3,000 for *The Wanderer*, or Murray paid Crabbe the same sum for *Tales of the Hall*, the loss was widely spread throughout the industry. As far as can be

---

[47] Quoted by Gettman 9.
[48] Surviving examples of printed subscription slips are to be found in the file of Booksellers' autographs, Bodleian ms.
[49] See Johnson.

seen, none of the publishers had any deliberate policy of cross-subsidisation among titles, among editions, or among authors.

Under all four of the main types of contract commonly used in the romantic period the interests of the publishers and the authors were sharply divergent. Under outright sale of copyright contracts, the competition was for a share of net profits, measured as an amount not as a proportion, as it was estimated in advance at the time of the contract. It was not for a share of actual achieved profits. Net profit contracts, which gave the author a share of actual achieved profits, reduced the element of unpredictability, but the author was at the mercy of the cautious high price/low sales policies which such contracts encouraged, and of questionable and sometimes fraudulent accounting practices. From the point of view of the publisher, the key to commercial success lay in the extent to which he could obtain an equity stake in titles which were commercially successful and likely to be reprinted. He could afford to buy many copyrights if they were cheap, in the hope that a few would turn out to be money-spinners, and he would take on the costless distribution of locally produced works on repayment in hopes of finding an occasional winner. He might buy shares in titles that were already well established and which could be expected to produce good returns, although the price would be high and the returns only a little above what he could expect from investing in, say, government bonds. He would also take a keen and active interest in books published on arrangements for shared net profits. With all such books he had an equity share and would do his best to promote publicity and sales.

By contrast, with books published by subscription, on commission, or otherwise at the expense of others, the publisher had little financial interest either way, whether the book sold well or not. Accepting books on commission enabled him to say yes to an author at minimal risk to himself and gave work to the printers.[50] But most books published on commission had fulfilled their commercial purpose simply by being manufactured, and there was no need for them to be promoted or sold, let alone read. It was normal for the provincial publisher to make an arrangement with a London publisher, whose name would appear on the title page. But if copies were sent to London, it seems to have been normally on a 'sale or return' basis, which usually meant return. The first John Murray, for example, acted as

---

[50] If a book published 'on commission' turned out to sell well the publisher would expect a share of the equity in the later editions. See, for example, the acrimonious correspondence from the publisher about the copyright of *The Farmer's Boy* which was reprinted without a new contract having been made. 'No Bookseller what ever prints another man's property and pays for it himself.' Quoted by Bloomfield 81.

partner for books published on commission in Newcastle, but his archives show most copies he received from Newcastle made the long journey back.[51]

The differing relative incentive effects of the different forms of contracts helps to explain why publishers seem to have shown scant interest in selling some of their own publications.[52] Their archives contain many letters from authors complaining of what they saw as neglect and carelessness, but which was probably sabotage. Anna Seward, 'the swan of Lichfield', claimed that her books were deliberately left out of the trade catalogues, and when people asked for her books, they were told they were not available.[53] A letter from C. Simeon of 1831 complains that he spent eight thousand hours and £1,500 on his book, but had not received a farthing of payment three years later.[54] In a letter of 1830, A. Burton offers to exchange 400 or 500 unsold copies of his 1819 'on commission' poem, *Linstein*, for two second-hand text-books.[55] According to Lackington, who revealed many of the secrets of the book trade, thousands of books listed as being in print were ordered by customers every year, but the orders were not delivered.[56] The archives of Whittingham the printer/publisher list the stocks of a number of poetry books published in editions of 500 of which typically 300 or 400 remain unsold.[57] The guilds, from which the commercial book industry had emerged, believed that the amount of luxury goods, such as silver or silk, produced in the economy, and therefore the amount of work available to be done by their members, needed to be closely rationed by the guild, 'the lump of labour fallacy'. Publishers of the romantic period who knew that the main market for books was confined to a narrow tranche at the top, suffered from what we can now see was a lump of reading fallacy.

Figures for the costs of book publication, said to be typical, were offered by Owen Rees, a partner of Longman, on behalf of the London publishers, to the 1818 Parliamentary Select Committee.[58] They allow calculations to be made of the implied average and marginal unit cost, both of manufacturing and then of selling a book, on the edition sizes assumed in Rees's answers.

[51] Examples in Zachs, e.g. 263.
[52] Lackington says that the regular publishers deliberately held back the sales of successful books published at author's expense in order to pick up the copyrights cheap, 236. Murray's offer to Austen for the copyrights of her novels was far below the value, as she recognised.
[53] In a letter of 1796, referring to the 500 copies of her *Ode on General Eliot's Return from Gibraltar*, Cadell and Davies papers, NYPL. She also mentions having commissioned an edition of *Louisa*, of which 344 copies (presumably out of 500) remained 'on hand' years later.
[54] Cadell and Davies papers.
[55] Quoted by Shaylor 206. Perhaps a joke. The book is not mentioned in the official *London Catalogue*.
[56] Lackington, 229, quoted by Collins, *Authorship* 44 with other, mainly eighteenth-century, examples.
[57] BL add mss. 41. 956.   [58] Collected and summarised in appendix 5.

Rees's answers also enable us to deduce some of the economic assumptions which lay behind the industry's practices. Although the publishers regarded copyrights as capital assets in the valuation of their businesses, they always treated any payments they made for copyrights as current costs in calculating the profit or loss made by each edition. Advertising too was always presented as a current cost. A rule of thumb for the target rate of return, offered by someone with inside knowledge of the business, was that 'Every edition of a book of 750 is calculated to pay all the expenses *of every kind* when half the number are sold.'[59] Every edition was expected to make a target rate of return equivalent to at least 100 per cent of manufacturing costs if the whole edition sold out. If about half of the copies of an edition were sold within a year of publication and the whole edition was sold out in five years, a book was reckoned to have done well, and the various rules of thumb that publishers used for calculating costs, prices, profits, and rates of return appear to have been devised on this basis. The publishers were concerned to convince parliament and authors that they were operating on tight profit margins. If the edition size was, say, 1,500 instead of the 750 given as an example by Rees, the unit costs are lower and, if the edition sold out, the gross margins are higher. If a book no longer needed to be advertised, the gross margins quickly reached several hundred and even thousands per cent. The publishers, as their costings and business practices showed, had a lively sense of the difference between average and marginal costs and revenues, both within editions and in successive editions, but in their public representations, the costs that they quoted were usually total or average costs of a small first edition, capital and current, and the stated profitability correspondingly modest.[60]

To publish a book required no heavy start-up investment in fixed or working capital. Longman, who maintained a huge business in wholesale bookselling as well as in publishing new and older titles, was a proud family business whose money had been made by fathers and grandfathers, but which was now run by Rees, a non-family partner. The other leaders of the industry were mainly new men. Murray operated from his house in Albemarle Street, London, with minimal overheads. Constable began by serving an apprenticeship as an antiquarian bookseller in Edinburgh. Other publishers, such as Lackington, Tegg, and later the Chambers brothers had started with a few second-hand books on a stall, building start-up capital from retained profits, but they were not welcomed into the industry's

---

[59] Duppa 21.
[60] For example, in measuring the costs of the copies deposited by law in the national copyright libraries, or of paying authors in kind, the publishers valued their books at full retail price.

corporate bodies. Many firms had scarcely any employees other than the owner/managers. In the firm of Taylor and Hessey, for example, which published books by Hazlitt, Charles Lamb, De Quincey, Clare, and Keats, Taylor did the publishing and Hessey ran the retail side. Charles and James Ollier, who published Shelley, also ran a retail bookshop and a circulating library, all unsuccessfully.[61] Publishers still called themselves booksellers and some were both publishers and wholesale booksellers.[62] Most of the sales made by publishers were either wholesale to other publishers or to retail booksellers who were supplied at a fixed discount below retail prices.[63]

But the industry, deeply conservative in many of its other practices, permitted a good deal of fluidity within its structures. Printers diversified into publishing, book publishers into newspapers or literary magazines, retailers into publishing and book renting, renting libraries into book publishing. Other publishers preferred to integrate publishing with manufacturing. Oliver and Boyd of Edinburgh, for example, who published school books, owned their own bindery. Murray, realising he was essentially an entrepreneur who selected and put together packages of text, finance, and marketing, withdrew from bookselling altogether, to become the first publisher in a modern sense.[64]

The networks of overlapping obligations offered opportunities for manipulating transfer prices. The charges for printing the Waverley novels levied by Ballantyne, the publishing and printing firm of which Walter Scott was a principal owner, appear to be several hundred per cent above the normal rate, deliberately inflated, it would seem, to exploit cross-ownership as a means of transferring profits.[65] When the rights to new Waverley novels were being negotiated, Scott's agent was also able to insist that the London partners took quantities of slow-moving Ballantyne publications, valued at full price.[66] For a time, Scott and his partners achieved an ownership of the whole literary production and distribution process from author to reader, controlling or influencing the initial choice of subjects, the writing of the texts, the editing, the publishing, and the printing of the books, the reviewing in the local literary press, the adaptations for the theatre, and the putting on of the theatrical adaptations at the theatre in Edinburgh which Scott also owned.[67] Such a close vertical and horizontal concentration of media ownership has seldom been seen in Britain even in recent times.

---

[61] See Robinson.   [62] See Chilcot.
[63] The discounts were larger if they subscribed before publication or if they took the books in a semi-manufactured state, unbound in sheets.
[64] Smiles i, 49.   [65] See the accounts for *Rob Roy* in appendix 5.
[66] Some details in Blackwood i, 58.
[67] Discussed in most books about Scott, and especially John Sutherland, *The Life of Walter Scott* (1995).

When most firms were sole traders or partnerships with unlimited liability, there was no unambiguous distinction between a firm's capital and private wealth, or between pay, expenses, and profit. Taylor and Hessey attributed costs to the firm, such as the rising costs of supporting their growing families, which would not be recognised as such by a modern economist, auditor, or tax inspector.[68] Constable, Scott's publisher, allowed him to draw huge advances from the business almost at will for the purpose of buying land, building Abbotsford, and supporting a large extended family in aristocratic style.[69] Constable, Robinson, Tegg, Lackington, Whittaker, and other publishers and booksellers were known for their ostentatious lifestyle which contrasted sharply with that of most of their authors, but which helped to maintain the illusion that they were credit-worthy. As owner/managers in a booming industry, they were media moguls, inclined to pay themselves large salaries, to borrow heavily, to understate their net profits, to distribute cash surpluses immediately to themselves, and to complain that trade was bad.

With multiple interlocking credit arrangements, it was however easy in a time of boom for a firm to be profitable and still find it difficult to finance its cash flow. Publishers were most vulnerable when they diversified into periodical publication which required heavier capital investment in payments to authors and staff, and where the interval between incurring liabilities and covering them from income was longer than for books. It was, for example, the *London Magazine*, the most distinguished literary journal of the romantic period, which forced Taylor and Hessey to go out of business. Murray narrowly escaped a similar fate by starting *The Representative*, which failed almost at once. Publishers were especially vulnerable when, for reasons of national monetary policy, credit was suddenly squeezed, and it became difficult to discount commercial bills for cash or roll them over. The failure in 1826 of the London firm of Hurst Robinson was precipitated by a string of banking failures, and a decision of the Bank of England to cease to act as lender of last resort. Although the Bank's decision was soon reversed, the collapse in credit brought down Constable, Ballantyne, and the huge commercial empire of Walter Scott and his partners. A succession of post-dated bills, issued against the security of yet-to-be-written Waverley novels, some for as long as three years ahead, had been given to Scott and encashed on the money markets.[70]

The collapse of 1826, the figures show, was not due to losses in publishing, let alone to any falling away in the public demand for Waverley novels, and

---

[68] Chilcot.   [69] See, for example, Johnson 764.   [70] Johnson 807.

when the effects are quantified, they appear only as a blip on the steadily expansionist growth pattern which began after 1774 and was to continue with few interruptions until 1914.[71] Despite virtually continuous wars from 1793 until 1815 and high taxes on paper and advertising for long afterwards, the British book industry boomed as never before. In the year 1822 Longman was reported to have sold five million volumes, employed sixty clerks, and given employment to two hundred and fifty printers and bookbinders.[72]

For the period between the 1780s and the 1830s, we have records of about 5,000 new books of verse, 10,000 new editions, written by about 2,000 living poets, as well as of a vast amount of reprinting of old-canon poetry written earlier.[73] About fifty poets, it was believed at the time, made some money from their writings; Scott, Byron, and Moore made fortunes; and a few others lived comfortably on their earnings, although much of it came from journalism.[74] Most of the thousands of others either received nothing, paid for the privilege of seeing their works in print, or had the costs paid by patrons, and such readerships as they had were largely confined to friends and family.[75]

During the same period, the number of novels published was almost as large as for verse, with about 3,000 new prose fiction titles known to have

---

[71] John Sutherland, 'The Book Trade Crash of 1826' in *The Library* (1987). The number of titles published in 1830 was about 60 per cent above its 1800 level which itself was far higher than pre-1774 levels. See Eliot.

[72] Figures quoted by Lord John Russell who had made a direct inquiry, quoted in *Monthly Magazine* (1822), 58.

[73] The first comprehensive survey of volumes of verse printed during the romantic period was prepared by J. R. de J. Jackson in *Annals of English Verse, A Preliminary Survey 1770–1835* (Garland, New York 1985). This showed that the number of new titles published in Great Britain, and to a lesser extent, in Ireland, was vastly greater than had previously been appreciated. Jackson's excellent *Romantic Poetry by Women, A Bibliography, 1770–1835* (Oxford 1993) added many other titles, and by implication, this evidence suggested that the number of verse books written by men was even larger then *Annals* implies. C. R. Johnson's *Provincial Poetry, 1789–1839* (1992), which includes many titles which were not included in Jackson's books, reveals how pervasive the culture of writing, printing and publishing books of verse was throughout Great Britain, showing that they were far more numerous, their places of publication far more geographically spread, and their authors far more socially diffused than had previously been appreciated. Other unrecorded titles, and editions of all kinds are still constantly being found. I am grateful to Professor Jackson for giving me his personal (1995) estimate of living poets 'between two and three thousand'. His *Romantic Poetry by Women* lists about 900 female poets between 1770 and 1835, and suggests the ratio of men to women was 5 or 6 to 1.

[74] Estimate of James Montgomery, *Lectures on Poetry* (1833) 378. Examples of huge figures obtained for the sale of copyright are given in *Books and Authors*. The information is said to have come from Thomas Tegg, the remainder bookseller, who was in a position to know. They seem to have been taken from figures used in the parliamentary and pamphlet debates about lengthening the copyright.

[75] Books described as 'printed for the author' were printed at the author's expense. Others known to have been published on commission give no indication on the title page that they were financed in this way.

been published between 1790 and 1830, with many reprints both of new and of older titles.[76] Publishing novels seems to have been almost always a commercial enterprise, with both authors and publishers making some money, however small, on every book, and only a few published at the author's expense on commission.[77] In the 1760s, when circulating libraries first became common, the going rate for the outright sale of a manuscript of a novel with its copyright was very low. Lowndes, for example, is known to have paid the authors of novels between £5 and £10 a title, depending on length.[78] By the turn of the eighteenth century the going rate was a little higher – an archive of copyright contracts of George Robinson shows an average payment to authors of about £25 in a wide range.[79] The £250 paid to Fanny Burney for *Cecilia* in 1795 was highly exceptional. By the middle of the romantic period, however, the prices paid to writers of novels was rising sharply. By 1824 even a relatively little-known author as 'the author of Marriage' (Susan Ferrier) was able to obtain £1,000 for the copyright of *The Inheritance*, to be published anonymously.[80] Godwin, a named author with an established reputation, was able to sell the copyright of his weak *Cloudesley*, written in old age, for £5,000, equivalent to about one pound to the author on every copy produced.[81] But if writers of novels were receiving larger financial rewards, they were still more like piece workers than independent 'authors', and most novels of the period were still published, as had been a custom in the eighteenth century, without the author even being named.[82] A few, including Edgeworth, Godwin, and Amelia Opie saw their names on the title pages of their later works, but anonymity seems to have been normal, particularly for first books. Throughout the romantic period, all novels, whether anonymous or not, were normally classified

---

[76] Figures from Garside, Raven, and Schöwerling in appendix 7, 563–4.

[77] Examples in appendix 5, 508.

[78] 1764   A. Woodfin was paid 5 guineas (105 shillings) by Lowndes for *Marian Middleton*, to be received in books at the accustomed booksellers' price. Upcott collection i, 212.

  1764   Another novel by A. Woodfin, *Sir John Cobler*, five guineas. Upcott i, 212.

  1767   *Woman of Fashion* by Arabella Smith, Lowndes, four guineas (84 shillings) for half the copyright. Upcott iii, 199.

  1767   *Major Bromley*, 2 vols. Lowndes.

  1767   £11 (220 shillings) for half the copyright, Upcott iii, 199.

  1768   *Happy Discovery*, Lowndes, five guineas for half the copyright. Upcott iii, 199.

  I do not know if all or any of these works were in fact printed under these or other titles.

[79] Bentley, 'Copyright Documents'.

[80] Feldman from William Blackwood archives.

[81] Richard Bentley archives, BL add. mss. 46,560. Novelists as much as poets were at the mercy of the type of contract and the extent to which the publisher was truthful about his actual costs and sales.

[82] I mention other fictional prose writings so as to include De Quincey, Lamb, and others who were not strictly novelists but whose prose works were published anonymously or pseudonymously.

in booksellers' lists and in circulating library catalogues, alphabetically by title, not under the name of the author. Although a high proportion of the novelists of the romantic period were women, therefore, this was not obvious or known to readers at the time.

Successful anonymous novelists seldom kept their secret for long, but it was one thing for family and friends to know, another for potential customers ordering from bookshop and library catalogues in the provinces.[83] (Austen's) *Sense and Sensibility* (1811) was attributed on the title page to 'a Lady', *Pride and Prejudice* (1813) was by 'the author of Sense and Sensibility', *Mansfield Park* (1814) by 'the author of *Pride and Prejudice*', as was *Emma* (1816). During the romantic period one could not go to a circulating library and ask for works by Miss Austen. The guesses as to who was the author of her works made during Austen's lifetime were usually wide of the mark, including the comment that they were far too good to have been written by a woman.[84] Austen is not even mentioned in the voluminous *Biographical Dictionary of the Living Authors of Great Britain and Ireland* (1816), although that book revealed the identity of other anonymous writers. Even her tombstone in Winchester Cathedral makes no mention of her writings, and she was not publicly named until some years after her death.

Most other novelists had to wait until *Bentley's Standard Novels* reprint series in the 1830s for their names to be printed in their books.[85] Throughout the romantic period, with the possible exception of 'The Author of Waverley', there is little evidence that readers cared much about the identity or gender of the writers of the novels they read. Why there should have been a tendency towards greater anonymity, at the time when the rhetoric of romanticism strove to celebrate artists and writers as unique and independent creative geniuses, needs an explanation.

One factor was that anonymity protected publishers and printers from the law of libel. Hazlitt's book of contemporary portraits, *The Spirit of the Age* (1825) was anonymous, as was Byron's *Don Juan* (1819–1824) which mocked many identifiable living people. Many novels satirised the manners of high society with characters drawn from real life. Anonymity thus not only encouraged *romans à clef*, but helped members of novel-reading coteries to feel, rightly or wrongly, that they were in the know. Part of the

---

[83] Fanny Burney early in her career complained that her publisher Lowndes implied that she was the author of *The Sylphs* by advertising it in the same sentence as the famous but anonymous *Evelina*. Joyce Hemlow *et al.*, eds. *The Journal and Letters of Fanny Burney (Madams d'Arblay)* (Oxford 1972–) iii, 233. When she was famous, her novel, *The Wanderer* (1814) was attributed on the title page to 'the author of *Evelina, Cecilia*, and *Camilla*'. Godwin too, who had been known as a named novelist since 1794, had his weak late novel *Cloudesley* attributed to 'The author of *Caleb Williams*'.

[84] Contemporary comments are usefully summarised by Gilson.   [85] See also chapters 18 and 21.

success of (Thomas Hope's) *Anastasius, or Memoirs of a Greek* (1819) was due to the rumour that it was written by Lord Byron. He 'wept when he read the book', Byron is said to have told a visitor, 'and for two reasons, first that *he* had not written it and secondly that *Hope* had'.[86] Anonymity also reduced the risk of being called out to fight a duel, a form of literary criticism which killed more than one writer of the romantic period. If a nobleman or gentleman had been publicly insulted by someone of comparable rank, he might feel it his duty to challenge, but there was no duty in the code of honour to seek out a cowardly, skulking, anonymous, insulter, even when his name was known, or to pay attention to the insults of non-gentlemen.[87] But the main driving force towards the anonymisation of fiction was probably the ongoing attempt by the publishers and the circulating libraries to impose greater similarity, regularity, and predictability, on the nature and habit of novel-reading, in other words to turn novels into uniform and mutually substitutable commodities, and the renting and reading of them into a regular habit. After 1814, one name dominated the age, 'the author of Waverley', not publicly acknowledged to be Sir Walter Scott, the famous poet, until the 1820s.[88]

Because so many thousands of books of verse are known to have been printed during the romantic period, it is sometimes assumed that verse was the preferred reading of the age, and that at the end of the romantic period, there was a shift in public taste in which the reading of 'poetry' gave way to the less demanding reading of novels.[89] However, the fact of a book's having been noted in a bibliography as having been printed is no guarantee that it was produced in more than a tiny edition, let alone that it was widely sold, circulated, or read. When quantified, the apparent shift from verse to prose does not appear nearly so sharp as traditional parade models of literary history imply.[90] Seen in a longer time horizon, verse and prose publication were proceeding in opposite directions. The authors of verse still came from the aristocracy or gentry, were proud to be named, and wanted to reproduce copies for friends at their own expense, either in manuscript or with the help of print. With novel publishing, by contrast, previously anonymous, genderless, low-skilled, low-paid, piece-workers were successfully claiming

---

[86] *Conversations of Lord Byron with the Countess of Blessington* (1834) 74.
[87] See Patrick O' Leary, *Regency Editor, Life of John Scott* (1983).   [88] Discussed in chapter 12.
[89] For example Lee Erickson, *The Economy of Literary Form* (1996). and William G. Rowland Jr, *Literature and the Marketplace: Romantic Writers and their Audiences in Great Britain and the United States* (Lincoln, Nebr. 1997).
[90] Discussed further in chapter 21.

a more explicit acknowledgement of their role in the production process, and a greater financial share in the rewards from the market. The poetry of the romantic period was supply-pushed by authors and patrons. Novels were demand-led by book purchasers, by commercial borrowers, and by readers. Poetry was moving socially and materially downwards, reducing from quarto to octavo and then to duodecimo. The novel was moving upwards from duodecimo to octavo. Poetry publishing saw the expiry of the traditions of the guild and the early modern periods. The publishing of novels was a fully commercial enterprise.

Manufacturing

The main manufacturing centres for the books of the romantic period were London and Edinburgh. The printers, who were legally liable for the lawfulness of the texts to be printed, sometimes asked for changes to be made to the manuscript fair-copies. It was the printer, for example, not the publisher, who told Shelley that he must make large-scale revisions to *Laon and Cythna* in order to avoid prosecution for blasphemous libel.[1] The printers were also the final authority on spelling and punctuation, and often made changes without the author's consent.[2] William Godwin, noted for the punctiliousness of his punctuation, was still complaining that his wishes were not respected fifty years after he wrote his first book.[3] Capitalisation too was often a cause of dispute.[4] Coleridge, for example, had difficulty in persuading printers to use initial capitals for his abstract nouns, such as Hope, a point which affected the meanings he wished to convey.[5]

When a book was to consist of more than one volume, the printing was frequently contracted out simultaneously to more than one firm. The three volumes of *Glenarvon* (1816), an anonymous *roman à clef* by Lady Caroline Lamb, for example, were each printed by different printers.[6] Splitting the printing saved time and provided some protection against proofs being stolen and sold to pirate publishers abroad.[7] When the printing of some of Austen's novels was divided, the different printers used different type fonts, a matter of little importance for books intended primarily for commercial renting, in which each volume was out to a different borrower.[8] Ballantyne of Edinburgh, and Bulmer, Davison, Whittingham, Caslon, and others

---

[1] See *SC* v, 160.   [2] Discussed by Timperley. Examples in *SC* v, 157.
[3] Godwin's letters to Bentley in the 1830s, mostly unpublished, Pforzheimer collection, NYPL.
[4] The third edition of Mary and Charles Lamb's *Tales from Shakespear*, printed by Davison, 1816, for example, prints 'Gods.' The fourth printed by McMillan, 1822, changed this to 'gods.'
[5] Discussed by Morton Paley, *Coleridge's Later Poetry* (1996).   [6] Evidence of surviving copies, Ac.
[7] For the French offshore pirate Galignani's success in obtaining stolen proofs see chapter 15.
[8] Note by Nicolas Barker in Gilson.

in London, developed typefaces of a higher quality than had previously been seen. The Scottish print founder Miller invented a specially durable metal. Thomas Davison had a secret process to produce high-definition ink.[9] The more expensive books were now 'hot-pressed' to smooth the paper. However, in essentials, the technology of text copying by print was largely unchanged since the fifteenth century. Moveable metal type, each piece made individually by hand by a skilled craftsman, was set by hand by skilled printers who copied by eye. After the setting of the print, came the inking, the drying, and the pressing of the sheets, and then the folding, the stitching, and the binding.

The paper was made by hand, sheet by sheet. The battlefields of Europe were picked over before the blood was dry for every scrap of cloth that could be sold in the rag fairs and on to the international markets. The cast-off smocks of Hungarian shepherds, the shirts of Italian sailors, and the bonnets of Irish ladies all made their way to the booming British paper mills which were springing up along many British rivers.[10] Boiled, bleached, and smoothed, the paper from which most English books of the romantic period were made remains white and spotless after two hundred years, shaming all subsequent books. Paper was expensive and heavily taxed. Under an Act of Parliament of 1794, if paper was to qualify for the tax rebate on exports, it had to bear a dated watermark.[11] Many books of the romantic period therefore reveal their date of manufacture to within a few months. The books in which most of the texts written in the romantic period were inscribed were manufactured entirely by hand, with the use of hand-held tools, by skilled men who had served a long apprenticeship in their trade. The types, the paper, the ink, the press, the binding were all manufactured without the aid of machinery or of mechanical power. The books of the romantic period were products of the pre-industrial age.

The taxation rules prevented paper being supplied in quantities of less than half a ream, that is 250 sheets. The main printing firms insisted on paper for 250 copies of a book even if fewer were ordered, the rest of the paper being embezzled, and the main London publishers, who had their own paper scams to preserve, were unable to break this ancient trade practice.[12] Edition sizes of new books published by the regular publishers

---

[9] Timperley 919.   [10] Knight, *Old Printer* 254.

[11] According to a modern survey the average interval between the manufacture of the paper, as dated, and its use in a book was not quite three years, although it was often less and occasionally books were made from paper watermarked with the following year's date brought hurriedly from the mill to meet a sudden brisk demand. See Hilton Kelliher, 'Early Dated Watermarks in English Papers' in Stephen Spector, ed., *Essays in Paper Analysis* (1987).

[12] See the answers given by members of the trade in *Select Committee*.

in London and Edinburgh were therefore normally in multiples of 250. A ream consisted of 516 sheets rather than 500, so as to allow for wastage, and the extra paper was often used to run off unofficial extra copies, known as 'overcopies', which did not always find their way into the accounts. Since the publishers had to estimate the amount of paper needed for an edition to the nearest half ream, they sometimes asked authors to lengthen or shorten the text, or to add smaller pieces to bulk out a volume, as late as the proof stage.[13] With shorter books, the text had to be made to fit the format from the beginning. Chapbooks and ballads, for example, still had normally to fit on half a sheet, one sheet, or two sheets folded.

When time was short, the writing, the printing, and the proof- correcting often proceeded simultaneously. Wollstonecraft's *A Vindication of the Rights of Woman*, for example, was sent to be printed sheet by sheet as it was being written, a fact which helps to account for the repetitiousness and lack of order in the argument.[14] Even when the manuscript of a whole work was available, the proofs seem usually to have been sent for correction as the printing proceeded, and it was easy for inconsistencies to remain unspotted. One reason why some of Scott's Waverley novels were weak in artistic unity and contained many minor inconsistencies is that they were sent to be printed in sections as they were written.[15]

With moveable type it was possible to make corrections and changes during all the stages of the manufacturing. Many books reveal by their physical make-up that new amended pages, 'cancels', were inserted after the printing was well advanced, and Hazlitt, for one, seems frequently to have made changes very late.[16] Since the publishers and booksellers continued to sell whatever they had until the reprinted sheets arrived, there are often minor textual variations among books which appear to be from the same edition. The early editions of Byron and Scott, which were usually produced against the clock, contain many corrections, new errors, and some substantial variations, introduced at different times during the course of the manufacture. With Byron's *Marino Faliero*, for example, some copies contain a long passage not present in others. The printer's archives note the printing of 500 half sheet cancels for Wordsworth's *Lyrical Ballads* for

---

[13] *Ibid.*

[14] For the publication of this work and how it should be situated in both material and cultural terms see chapter 14.

[15] Described by Lockhart, Edgar Johnson, *Sir Walter Scott, The Great Unknown* (1970) and in detail by John Sutherland, *The Life of Walter Scott* (1995). Scott was sending the manuscript to be printed as it was being written as early as *The Antiquary*, the third of the Waverley novels, published in 1815. Johnson 517.

[16] See Geoffrey Keynes, *Bibliography of William Hazlitt* (second edition 1981) xiv.

Longman on 30 March 1801, so there are probably two versions, which a scrutiny of surviving copies may one day bring to light.[17]

Edition sizes varied widely, but despite the rapid expansion of the total market, there was little upward shift in the average. Some of the romantic poems of Walter Scott were produced in first editions of several thousands, and the first print runs for Waverley novels were often 6,000 to 10,000. The first edition of Byron's *Childe Harold's Pilgrimage, Canto the Fourth* (1818) consisted of 10,000 copies, enough, as matters turned out, to satisfy the market, including a remainder market, for many years. But long print runs were highly unusual. Apart from standard works such as school textbooks and the cheaper old-canon reprints, it was usual for the publishers to order editions with print runs of 250, 500, 750, 1,000, or occasionally 1,500, or 2,000, and to order a reprint, much the same range as in earlier centuries when the market was a fraction of the size.

If a work was to be reprinted for a second or a subsequent edition, the author was encouraged to correct, revise, and add to the previous text, usually by marking up a copy of the previous printed version. A second or subsequent edition might then be noted on its title page as 'revised' or 'corrected', but often there was no overt indication that textual changes had been made. With some books there could, therefore, be a succession of differing texts. For the first edition of *The Giaour* (1813), for example, Byron provided 685 lines; for the second he extended the poem to 816 lines; for the third to 950; for the fourth to 1,048; and finally for the fifth to 1,215, all written and published within a few months in 1813.[18] Wordsworth's poems were compulsively revised so often for successive editions through a long life that the printed versions have been described as staging posts in a continuous process of composition and amendment.[19]

The textual differences between editions were intrinsic to the technology of manufacture by moveable type. Since every edition was a new investment, with opportunities for corrections, additions, revisions, and new paratexts, moveable type encouraged instability between editions. Authors often wished to revise their texts and publishers encouraged amendments and additions as a means of maintaining or renewing interest. In 1811 Scott's publishers were advertising that *The Lady of the Lake* was in its ninth edition, *The Lay of the Last Minstrel* in its twelfth, and *Marmion* in its seventh.[20]

[17] Charles Whittingham and Co., archives, 41,902.
[18] Discussed by Jerome McGann in Byron, *Poetical Works*.
[19] Stephen Gill, *William Wordsworth, A Life* (1989) 191.
[20] Advertisement in copy of *Don Roderick* (second edition 1811), Ac.

Murray too liked to give the public the impression that no sooner was a new book by Byron put on sale, than the edition was sold out. In April 1814, *Childe Harold's Pilgrimage, A Romaunt,* was already in its eighth edition, *The Giaour* in its eleventh, *The Bride of Abydos* in its seventh. On examination, however, the later editions turn out to have been made, wholly or in part, from unsold sheets of earlier printings, dinner left overs re-heated for next day's lunch, made more appetising by a few fresh garnishings, an added poem, a new preface, or new notes, but sometimes with nothing but the title page changed to a new date. *Paradise Lost* had needed five title pages before the first edition was sold out.[21] In many cases, the publishers pretended to editions which had never actually existed. With Byron's *Lara,* for example, there is a first edition and a fourth, but nobody has found a copy of the second or the third. With Hannah More's conduct novel *Coelebs in Search of a Wife,* the publishers numbered the editions, third, fifth, seventh and ninth, etc., without printing the even numbers.[22] These ancient selling practices, to be found throughout the era of moveable type, were known as 'lifting a book'.[23]

Some time about 1816, Murray and the other leading publishers stopped advertising in this way. One explanation may have been that other publishers began to mock them. William Hone's edition of Byron's *Poems on his Domestic Circumstances* (1816), for example, a collection of shorter pieces, some not by Byron, on which no copyright was enforceable, reached a so-numbered twenty-third edition.[24] In 1831 Stockdale, another outsider, produced a so-called thirty-fifth edition of the *Memoirs of Harriette Wilson,* mainly made from old unsold sheets, but by now the trick had been exposed.[25] The leading publishers went to the other extreme. Murray's records show that in 1816 he ordered and produced two editions each of *Childe Harold's Pilgrimage, Canto the Third,* and of *The Prisoner of Chillon,* but these are not distinguished as such on the title page.[26] Literary works, especially in verse, it was now implied, came perfect from the press and did not need to be revised or corrected. Whereas, in the case of a historical or scientific book, readers might welcome updates and corrections as making the book more truthful, with works of 'literature', the aesthetics of romanticism increasingly required that the poet should no longer

[21] Curwen 25.   [22] See 'Hannah More', appendix 9, 621.
[23] Ruff 109, quoting several printed and manuscript sources.
[24] Some are genuine editions, others are old sheets reissued with a new title page.
[25] Noted by counsel in the case of Blore *v.* Stockdale in Harriette Wilson iv, 57.
[26] John Murray archives.

be regarded as a craftsman constantly revising and improving his or her work, but as a unique creative genius driven by occasional bursts of intense inspiration.

There were other, longer-term, benefits to the publishers from revision. As had been noticed after 1774, if a text were revised sufficiently, it could qualify as a new intellectual property and command a higher pricing profile. In the late 1820s, Walter Scott set out to revise and add to all his published works in verse and prose with the deliberate intention of being able to claim a new copyright, and two different versions were simultaneously on sale for most of the remainder of the century.[27] Wordsworth's heirs were able to assert a new copyright over his works in 1855 by giving the publisher some sundry notes which Wordsworth had dictated in 1843.[28]

The literary works of the romantic period were not, for the most part, works of individual creation, but socially produced by authors, family, friends, advisers, publishers, editors, printers, and others, in a collective commercial enterprise. Nor were they held fixed at the moment of composition. As far as readers were concerned, the printed texts to which they had access often differed from the texts which the authors first wrote, from the texts which other contemporary readers were reading, and from the texts which present-day readers find in modern editions.[29]

By the 1810s, a new form of text copying began to be applied to the manufacture of reprints. Stereotype plates were made after the text of a book had been set up in moveable type and the proofs corrected. By taking a plaster mould of the type into which molten metal was then poured, it was possible to make a durable metal plate, in effect a duplicate of each sheet of moveable type. After a number of copies had been printed from the first edition made by moveable type, and the types put back in the cases for use on the next order, as many copies as were required could be run off from the plates. The plates could then be put in store, to be brought out and used for making reprints. In the Netherlands a form of stereotyping was in use before 1700.[30] In 1797 the French firm of Firmin Didot patented a method which produced a beautifully clear printed page.[31] But in England during the high monopoly period, attempts to develop it had been resisted, and occasionally sabotaged, by the printers and print typefounders. Stereotyping was only adopted in the mainstream book industry in London after the process

---

[27] Described by Jane Millgate, *Scott's Last Edition* (1987).
[28] See Stephen Gill, 'Copyright and the Publishing of Wordsworth' in Jordan and Patten 79.
[29] For a discussion, see Jerome J. McGann, *A Critique of Modern Textual Criticism* (1983).
[30] McKitterick ii, 176.   [31] Timperley 795.

Figure 6. A stereotype foundry of 1829. From George A. Kluber, *A New History of Stereotyping* (New York 1941).

had been pioneered and introduced by firms from outside the London syndicates.[32]

In 1807, it was said that the cost of commissioning a set of stereotype plates was the equivalent of printing an extra 750 copies of the first edition by traditional moveable type methods.[33] At that time, it was suggested, only about twenty or thirty titles could justify the investment. The first titles to be selected for the technology in the 1810s were those for which a continuing large demand was expected at that time, reference works and dictionaries, and the bestselling anthologies and abridgements of the old canon, including school textbooks, and the archival record tends to confirm that they turned out to have a long life with many reimpressions over many years.[34] Both Enfield's *Speaker* and Murray's *Reader*, which had brought

---

[32] For the earlier history of stereotyping in Scotland, including the sabotaging, see John Carter, 'William Ged and the Invention of Stereotype' in *The Library*, 15 (1960), and 'A Postscript' in *The Library*, 16 (1961). For the slow commercial development in the romantic period, see Michael L. Turner, 'Andrew Wilson: Lord Stanhope's Stereotype Printer, A Preliminary Report' in *Journal of the Printing Historical Society*, 1975.

[33] *Monthly Magazine*, April 1807, quoted by Kubler 65. [34] Examples in appendices 5 and 6.

English literature of the old canon to schools in the late eighteenth century were stereotyped early and the plates kept regularly at work into the second half of the nineteenth century.[35]

In the early decades of the new text-copying process in England, the plaster stuck to the plates, the plates needed frequent repairs, and the resulting printed pages sometimes looked spotty. 'No printer should stereotype who wishes his type to be a credit to his house', wrote the printer Hansard in 1825, although to a modern eye the best stereotyped books of the time are sometimes difficult to distinguish from books made direct from moveable type.[36] But the technological problems were soon solved. By 1839 it was said that 100,000 impressions could be taken from one set of plates, and with care a million, and the invention of paper moulds and electrotypes soon afterwards raised the potential output figures even higher.[37]

As had been the case with the shift from manuscript to moveable print, the new copying technology had effects on reading patterns which went far beyond the reductions in the unit cost of manufacturing extra copies of particular texts. With moveable type, the industry was normally obliged to utilise the expensive hand-made type as frequently as possible, seldom keeping type standing for more than a few days or weeks, before it had to be put back in the cases for use in printing other orders. With stereotyping, although the initial costs of setting up a text remained the same, and the cost of making the plates was extra, once the plates were made, the moveable type was not needed again. Since the melt-down value of the plates as scrap was low, they could be kept in store until it was certain that they would never be needed again. For the first time in history, a publisher could plausibly promise never to let a title go out of print.[38]

The new technology altered the balance of economic incentives between publishing new titles and reprinting existing titles. For any level of printing/reprinting output, therefore, stereotyping enabled the printer to operate with less of the most expensive component of his fixed capital, namely the hand-made types. Furthermore, since reimpressions could be manufactured quickly without the need for new editing, type-setting, and proof-reading, the working capital required in making reprints was lower than in the

---

[35] See appendix 6.

[36] Quoted by Kubler 65. Thomson's *Seasons*, stereotyped by A. Walker in 1809, is as clear and as readable as books made from moveable type.

[37] See 'The Printer's Devil' in *Quarterly Review*, December 1839. To avoid unnecessary repetition I use the term 'stereotype' to include 'electrotypes'.

[38] See, for example, the note in *The Vocal Library* (1824). 'This volume, being printed in Stereotype, will never, like its predecessors, become out of print, but may constantly be had of all Booksellers. Additions will, however, be made from time to time.'

days of moveable type, as were the risks to unsold stocks from fire and water.

Text copying by moveable type had tended to stabilise texts within editions, but promote instability between editions. Stereotyping ensured that texts were also stable from edition to edition. Authors were still permitted, and sometimes encouraged, to add a new preface, which could be added to the previous version, and publishers frequently changed the title pages and sometimes the illustrations. But as far as the main text was concerned, gone were the days when authors could rewrite from edition to edition. As far as readers were concerned, printed texts came increasingly in one version only, fixed once and for ever, not at the moment when the author or editor laid aside his or her pen, but when the production manager in the printing shop passed the proofs as fit for stereotyping. Although corrections and additions to the plates could be made, some plates carried their errors for the remainder of their material lives, which could be half a century or more.[39]

The arrival of stereotyping was to have greater effects on the whole system of texts, books, and reading than any change since the arrival of print. The authors of the romantic period were to be among the greatest beneficiaries but not until after most of them were dead.[40]

---

[39] See chapter 16 for the fifty-year lives of the stereotypes of Byron's *Don Juan* and Shelley's *Queen Mab*. For the destruction of plates in 1914–18, see chapter 21.
[40] See chapter 21.

CHAPTER 11

Selling, prices, and access

After the manufacturing came the selling. The publishers of new titles were able, by going to a single agent, to place simultaneous advertisements in all the best-known English national and provincial newspapers. Another agent offered the same service in Scotland. Advertising, always in the romantic period highly taxed, and one of the highest components of the costs of publishing a new title, was essential if it was to be successfully sold.[1] 'Published this Day', the heading under which the latest books were announced, and which was often reinserted in the same newspapers over a period of weeks or months, was not to be read literally.

As important as the advertising were notices in the literary reviews, of which there were many. Some production statistics, which show the huge increase that occurred in the romantic period, are given in appendix 8. The two leaders, the *Edinburgh Review* on the more liberal side of politics, and the *Quarterly Review*, its London rival, which was more conservative, circulated nationally throughout the United Kingdom and beyond, as did their many rivals. The literary reviews were expensive, more books than newspapers, and runs were often bound, catalogued, and carefully kept, both by individuals and by libraries, with volumes being reprinted, sometimes long after they were first published, in order to enable newcomers to make up sets. By dividing their notices of recent books in accordance with the categories used in booksellers' and library catalogues (divinity, philosophy, travel, science, polite literature, etc.), they helped to entrench the ways into which knowledge, as well as texts, was divided and presented.[2]

The eighteenth-century literary reviews, some of which still continued, saw their main role as providing summaries of new books and often included

---

[1] See the figures offered by the publishers for the costs of publishing a new title summarised in appendix 5, 506.

[2] Discussed by Jon Klancher, *The Making of English Reading Audiences, 1790–1832* (Madison, Wis. 1987).

substantial extracts. In 1797, quotations took up over half of the articles.[3] In 1817 Anne Lister read to her aunt the extracts from Moore's *Lalla Rookh* quoted in a review.[4] But this loophole was closing. The advancing intellectual property law and custom not only forbade anthologies and abridgements but quotations in reviews that were thought long enough to undermine sales. As was argued by counsel in a trial in 1825, 'Even extracts, in the case of reviews, have been declared to be infringements of the author's rights, if they were calculated to satisfy the reader's curiosity, and so prevent their purchase of the original.'[5]

Some literary reviews guarded their independence. Although most accepted free copies of books from the publishers, the *Monthly* would only take them as a loan.[6] Increasingly however, the literary reviews of the romantic period no longer saw themselves as a means of providing information to readers, but as offering hard-hitting essays and political comment which aimed to be influential, instructive, and entertaining. In its attempt to increase sales by personal attacks, *Blackwood's Magazine*, the main challenger to the *Edinburgh* and *Quarterly Reviews*, paid out large sums in libel damages in its first five years.[7] However, if one looked only at their textual content, it would be easy to misjudge the extent to which they were genuinely fearless. The three main reviews, each of which was owned by book publishers, were an integral part of the horizontal and vertical network of ownership whose main business was the production, selling, and renting of books. To judge from such little archival evidence as can be found for a murky area, the owners seldom suffered romantic agonies about protecting the creative liberty and artistic integrity of their well-paid editors and contributors. Most literary reviews seem to have unashamedly puffed the books published by the publishing houses who owned them, even when these were out of line with their normal political stance. *Blackwood's Magazine*, for example, published some of the few favourable notices which Shelley was ever to receive in his lifetime, mainly because Blackwood was the Edinburgh agent of Shelley's London publisher, Ollier.[8] By contrast, the London publisher Phillips believed that the *Edinburgh Review* had a policy of ignoring his publications altogether, although this was denied.[9]

---

[3] Estimated from figures given by Derek Roper, *Reviewing before the* Edinburgh (1978) 42.
[4] Lister 12.   [5] Harriette Wilson v, 134.
[6] This emerges from an 1818 letter of Murray quoted by Antonia Forster in 'Review Journals' in Isabel Rivers, ed., *Books and Readers in Eighteenth-Century England: New Essays* (Leicester 2001) 177.
[7] According to Lockhart, £8,300 exclusive of legal fees. See Strout 36,
[8] See Robinson.
[9] Constable ii, 264. For other examples of exchanging favours, see Blackwood, e.g., i, 399.

Like the rest of the printed-book industry, the literary reviews, rivals in some ways, cooperated in others. The publisher Cadell told Blackwood that the anonymous *Amarythus the Nympholept* was written by Mrs Cadell's youngest brother, the rich and well-connected Horace Smith, and asked him to try 'to have the censure dealt out with a sparing hand'.[10] Sometimes, to make the inclusion of a favourable review as easy as possible, the book publishers offered review articles that were already written. Longman, who had a share in the *Edinburgh Review*, for example, engaged Reverend W. Shepherd, a Longman author, to prepare a review of Moore's *Lalla Rookh* so that it could be offered free to the *Quarterly Review*.[11] Shelley, independent thinker in many ways, wrote anonymous puffing reviews of books by his wife, Mary Shelley, his father-in-law Godwin, and his close friend Peacock, in hopes of placing them in *The Examiner*, which was owned by his friend Leigh Hunt.[12] Blackwood too, although his magazine prided itself on the fearlessness of its comments, was open to inducements. When in 1819, the editor of the *Literary Review* asked for and obtained a favourable review for one of his friends in *Blackwood's*, his promise to provide reciprocal arrangements was accepted.[13] Southey believed that half of his sales were attributable to puffs. As he wrote to his friend, 'Puff me, Coleridge! if you love me, puff me! Puff a couple of hundreds into my pocket.'[14] The commonly held belief that literary journals could be bribed was, according to Hazlitt, himself both a reviewer and an author much sneered at by reviewers, quite untrue – a favourable notice, he says, could be obtained 'through interest or to oblige a friend, but it must invariably be done for love, not money'.[15] By the 1830s, the stench of publishers' puffery had become as inescapable as that of London's river, and it required the efforts of the new generation of Victorians to clean it up.[16]

At a time when many books bought individually were collectively read within the family, any books which the reviews declared unsuitable for ladies were commercially sunk. As Hazlitt discovered, a damning review could sometimes halt the sale of a successful book almost immediately.[17] Particularly vicious attacks might have a perverse effect, some authors hoped, by precipitating a *succès de scandale*. The only effect of Southey's spiteful

---

[10] Printed in Besterman 62. The book contains other examples.
[11] Quoted in 'The three main romantic period literary reviews', appendix 8, 573.
[12] See chapter 18. They were not all published at the time.   [13] Quoted in appendix 8, 574.
[14] Southey, *Life* iii, 134.
[15] Hazlitt, 'On Patronage and Puffing' in *Table Talk* (second edition 1824) ii, 311.
[16] Discussed with many examples, by Leslie A. Marchand in *The Athenaeum, A Mirror of Victorian Culture* (Chapel Hill 1941).
[17] See 'William Hazlitt', appendix 9, 604.

personal attack on Shelley in the *Quarterly Review*, Byron told Murray, had been to sell an edition of *The Revolt of Islam* which otherwise nobody would have thought of reading.[18] Quantification, however, destroys a good story – the record shows that Shelley's sales remained minuscule.[19]

The literary reviews were generally believed to be influential, both on opinion and on sales. There are stories of men and women reluctant to venture an opinion until they knew which way the wind was blowing, and of others who bluffed their way socially by reading reviews rather than books.[20] When members of libraries proposed titles for purchase they often quoted reviews in support of their suggestions.[21]

In general, however, the influence of the reviews appears to have been greatly exaggerated both at the time and by subsequent writers. Given the time differences between the publication, selling, and reading of a book and the appearance and circulation of the review notices in the literary reviews, it would be misleading to regard them as normally intermediating in the market like the book pages of modern newspapers. During the romantic period many newly published books were bought, read, and opinions formed on them weeks before the literary reviews appeared. The success of Byron's *Childe Harold's Pilgrimage, A Romaunt*, owed little or nothing to reviews. Scott's *Marmion*, one of the most-loved, most admired, and most widely read, literary works of the nineteenth century, was dismissed by the *Edinburgh Review* when it first came out. The huge success of *Waverley* caught the publishers by surprise and there were plenty of much-praised works which failed to sell. I can discern no correlation between reviews, reputations, and sales, or between contemporary and later reputations. Although it has been the custom to treat published reviews as 'reception', they turn out to be a poor indicator both of commercial sales and of the reactions of readers.[22]

Advertising and review notices were aimed not only at potential readers but at the bookshops and circulating libraries. The romantic period sees the arrival of another professional intermediary between author and reader, the publishers' sales representatives, who toured the retail and renting outlets, with their printed catalogues, selected quotations from reviews, and order books. By the middle of the period every substantial town in Great Britain had at least one shop which sold books, and most had several, far more than in the high monopoly period. In Norwich, a city of about 40,000

---

[18] Byron to Murray, 24 November 1818, Byron, *Letters and Journals* vi, 83.
[19] See 'Percy Bysshe Shelley', appendix 9, 649.   [20] Some examples in Clive 181–97.
[21] See an example relating to Coleridge in 'Bristol Library Society', appendix 10, 670.
[22] For the usefulness of reviews in establishing the 'horizons of expectations' see chapter 14.

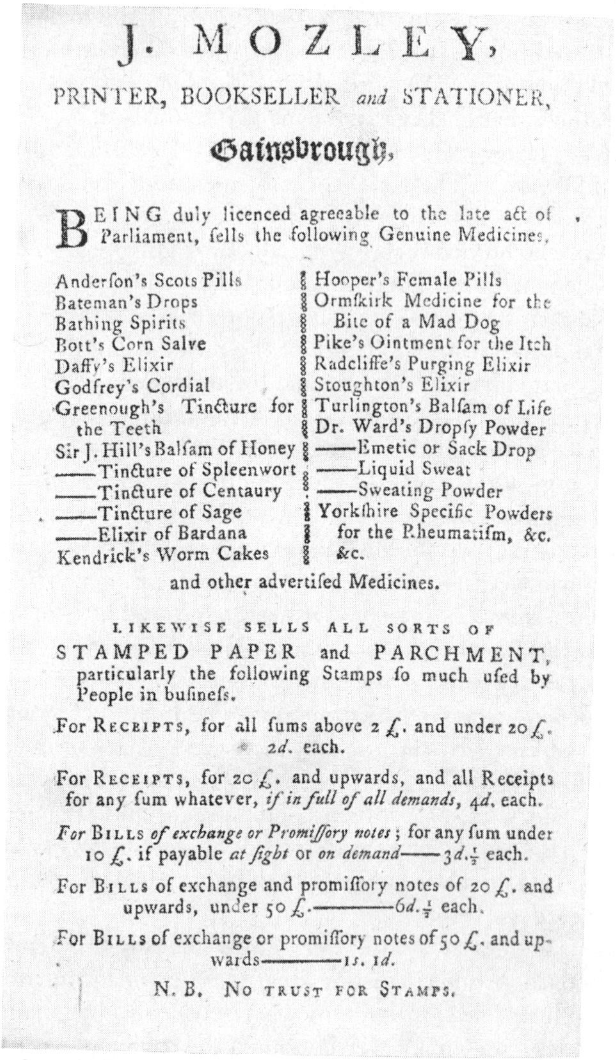

J. MOZLEY,

PRINTER, BOOKSELLER *and* STATIONER,

Gainsbrough,

BEING duly licenced agreeable to the late act of Parliament, sells the following Genuine Medicines,

Anderson's Scots Pills	Hooper's Female Pills
Bateman's Drops	Ormskirk Medicine for the
Bathing Spirits	Bite of a Mad Dog
Bott's Corn Salve	Pike's Ointment for the Itch
Daffy's Elixir	Radcliffe's Purging Elixir
Godfrey's Cordial	Stoughton's Elixir
Greenough's Tincture for	Turlington's Balsam of Life
the Teeth	Dr. Ward's Dropsy Powder
Sir J. Hill's Balsam of Honey	——Emetic or Sack Drop
——Tincture of Spleenwort	——Liquid Sweat
——Tincture of Centaury	——Sweating Powder
——Tincture of Sage	Yorkshire Specific Powders
——Elixir of Bardana	for the Rheumatism, &c.
Kendrick's Worm Cakes	&c.

and other advertised Medicines.

LIKEWISE SELLS ALL SORTS OF

STAMPED PAPER and PARCHMENT, particularly the following Stamps so much used by People in business.

For RECEIPTS, for all sums above 2 £. and under 20 £. 2d. each.

For RECEIPTS, for 20 £. and upwards, and all Receipts for any sum whatever, *if in full of all demands*, 4d. each.

For BILLS *of exchange or Promissory notes*; for any sum under 10 £. if payable *at sight* or *on demand*——3d.½ each.

For BILLS of exchange and promissory notes of 20 £. and upwards, under 50 £.————6d.½ each.

For BILLS of exchange or promissory notes of 50 £. and upwards————1s. 1d.

N. B. NO TRUST FOR STAMPS.

Figure 7. Advertisement of a provincial bookseller, late eighteenth century, showing the close links between the printed book and pharmaceutical industries. Pasted in a copy of Eliza Heywood's *Epistles for Ladies*, property of Lloyd and Dennis's Circulating Library, Thetford.

inhabitants, there are records of seventeen shops selling books at different times over the romantic period.[23] In Edinburgh, a city of about 150,000 inhabitants, there were said to be 105 booksellers in 1836.[24] Almost all of the shops seem only to have sold books as part of a wider business including stationery, patent medicines and perfumery.[25]

A credit-worthy country bookseller or individual, by sending a single letter to one of the leading London or Edinburgh publishers could order all the books he wanted from the whole British book trade. It was part of the training of apprentice booksellers in London and Edinburgh to carry their bag from publisher to publisher, making up town and country orders, new and second hand.[26] Carried by water in coastal, river, and canal vessels, and by land in horse-drawn carts, stage coaches, and by personal messengers, copies of books could reach the city and provincial bookshops and commercial lending libraries in England, Wales, and Scotland within a few days or weeks at most.[27] In Ireland, outside Dublin and a few other towns, there were fewer bookshops and credit was less reliable. The Irish market for books remained small in relation to its population. Of the initial huge editions of the Waverley novels at the height of their popularity, for example, about 6,000 copies were shipped to London for retail booksellers in London and the south, about 2,000 served Scotland and England north of York, but only 100 copies were sent to Dublin.[28]

In their evidence to the 1818 Parliamentary Select Committee the representatives of the London publishers described the main features of their publishing, pricing, and selling practices. If a new book was expected to sell at least 250 copies, they said, it could be manufactured and issued in quarto format. If a sale of more than 500 was expected, the book was normally published in octavo, and books published as quartos were normally tranched down to octavo after an interval if they sold adequately at the higher price. During the period, some publishers started to manufacture and advertise books in 'foolscap octavo', 'post octavo', 'royal octavo', 'crown octavo', and other previously unfamiliar formats which few readers outside the paper business are likely to have understood. In terms of readability, these 'octavos' were more like duodecimos than normal octavos, as may have been the intention.[29] One outsider publisher, Daly, advertised his

---

[23] Trevor Faucett, 'Some Aspects of the Norfolk Book Trade 1800–1824' in *Transactions of the Cambridge Bibliographical Society*, 1968.
[24] Discussed by Thin.   [25] See chapters 2, 13, and 22.
[26] For a detailed description see Thin, who started in 1836.
[27] An example of cost from Leith to London in 'Internal transport', appendix 5, 517. The Halifax Circulating Library archives note that they received a book by Walter Scott by sea.
[28] See the example of *Kenilworth* in 'Walter Scott', appendix 9, 638.   [29] Noted by Wheatley 99.

books as printed in 'imperial folio', but the large sheets were folded into tiny, fat, uncomfortable-to-read, pocket volumes.[30] On the whole however, the catalogues still used the ancient manufacturing terms of folio, quarto, octavo, and duodecimo, to signal to their customers what they might expect.

The books of the romantic period, whether newly published titles or reprints, normally reached the public in paper wrappers stitched with thread or temporarily bound in cardboard covered with blue or grey sugar paper. Although the pages of the text were normally cut, so that it was unnecessary for the British reader to carry a knife or letter-opener, as was the custom in France, the rough deckle edge made it difficult to turn over the pages or to find the place. Wrappers quickly curled and boards fell off. Many of the books which survive in this state were presentation copies, given free by authors to friends or colleagues who decided not to have them bound.[31] Others were remainders dumped on the market long after the initial interest had passed. The books 'perfect, as issued, in original boards' that have been specially prized by book collectors, as part of the romantic quest to approach as near as possible to the act of literary creation, are usually those that were unsold, unread, and therefore inert, when they were first offered. Shelley's *Prometheus Unbound* told its own story. Who would bother to have it bound?[32]

The first thing most buyers in the romantic period did, before they even took a new book home, was to place an order to have it rebound in leather (morocco, full calf, or half calf), pressed again, its pages trimmed smooth, and gilded, sometimes adding their personal crest and bookplate. Binding, like all aspects of book manufacture, was a hand craft, with machines scarcely used before the 1830s.[33] Lewis, Hering, and other famous London binders of the romantic period made Regency book binding one of the fine arts, but every city and large town had a local binder who would make a book serviceable, durable, and elegant within a few days. When on 3 August 1817, Shelley asked for the octavo of Moore's *Lalla Rookh* to be bound, he expected it to be ready by the 8th.[34] It was low tone for a gentleman to have unbound books on his shelves – like putting milk bottles on the breakfast table. With their fine printing, wire-woven hot-pressed paper, and fine morocco or half-calf gilded bindings, the books of the romantic period

---

[30] Advertisements in copies, Ac.   [31] Identified by manuscript inscriptions.
[32] Examples in Sylva Norman, *The Flight of the Skylark* (1954) 50. See also W. Roberts, *The Bookhunter in London* (1895) 296.
[33] See Potter.   [34] Shelley, *Letters* i, 549, 552.

emitted an air of luxury, to the extent that 'hot pressed' became a term of derision.[35]

Expensive bindings are to be found on books of philosophy, travel, antiquities, sermons, poetry, and conduct, but only occasionally on novels.[36] Many of such works carry armorial book plates, ownership and presentation inscriptions, and other confirmation that they were bought and owned by members of the aristocracy, the gentry, and the richer classes of society. Some may have been bought and not read, 'furniture books' as the publishers called them, in order to display and to impress, and other books were produced as gifts and may not have been much read. However, in an age when many of the higher income classes had ample leisure, we can probably take it that most new books were, if not read through word by word, at least actively perused.

Retail prices, which were fixed by the publishers under resale price maintenance, were usually printed on the labels of the books before they were bound, and disappeared in the rebinding as did the advertisements, publishers' price lists, and other reminders that books were objects of commerce. The literary journals too, maintaining the fiction that reading was still for men and women who did not need to worry about money, seldom mentioned prices. Table 11.1 shows some typical retail prices for books newly published in the romantic period either for the first time or as reprinted editions.[37]

To understand these prices, and the potential customers they imply, we need to devise a contemporaneous standard of the value of money. Converting to present day money terms understates the huge divergencies that have occurred in relative as well as in absolute prices and incomes. It also ignores the changes in what constituted the cost of living that have occurred since the romantic period, an age still largely dependent on human and animal power. A preferable approach is to construct a standard which reflects the social and economic structures and expectations of the time, including the income and wealth distribution within society, and the prices of other goods which made up the cost of living. In constructing such a standard we have a reliable foundation in the parsimony of the British Treasury.

In 1815 the long war with France at last came to a decisive end. It had been going on almost continuously for twenty-two years, and many men who had served in the army and the navy knew no other occupation.

---

[35] See, for example (T. J. Mathias) *The Pursuits of Literature, The Seventh Edition, Revised* (1798) 75.
[36] Examples of binding prices in appendix 5.   [37] Many other examples in appendices 7 and 9.

Table 11.1 Representative book prices, 1810s, 1820s, retail (shillings, before and after estimated binding costs)

	Unbound		Bound	
	4to	8vo	4to	8vo
VERSE				
Scott's *Marmion*	31.5	14	37	17.5
Byron's *Childe Harold's Pilgrimage*				
A Romaunt	30	12	36.5	15.5
The Giaour, The Bride, The Corsair		5.5 (each)		20 (together)
Moore's *Lalla Rookh*	42	14	48.5	17.5
Campbell's *Poetical Works* two volumes		15		22
Rogers's *Italy*		7.5		11
Deluxe				63
Wordsworth's *The Excursion*	42	10.5	48.5	14

	Unbound	Bound
NOVELS		
(Austen's) *Sense and Sensibility*, three volumes, 1811	15	22.5
(Austen's) *Pride and Prejudice*, three volumes, 1813	18	25.5
(Scott's) *Ivanhoe*, three volumes, 1820	30	37.5
(Scott's) *Kenilworth*, three volumes, 1821	31.5	39
(Peacock's) *Headlong Hall*, one volume, 1816	6	7.5
NON-FICTION		
Boswell's *Life of Johnson*		
four volumes, 8vo	36	48
five volumes, 12mo	25	35
Bruce's *Travels to Discover the Source of the Nile*		
seven volumes, 8vo, and plates, 4to	126	195
Schlegel's *Lectures on Literature*, two volumes	21	27
John Scott's *Visit to Paris*	12	15.5
Adam Smith's *Wealth of Nations*	27	36

In 1816, when many prices and wage rates had stabilised back to pre-war levels after the war-time inflation, the British government set new rates of pensions and half-pay to reflect peacetime conditions, and they remained in force for many years, generally accepted as fair.[38] From these, and other such indicators we can suggest a standard of £5 (100 shillings) a week. That would be the typical income of a senior retired commander in the Royal Navy with some independent income, a reasonable but not extravagant income for members of the upper- or upper-middle classes.[39] Isabella Bridgewater, the widow of a wealthy barrister, to whom Hazlitt was briefly married and

---

[38] *Navy Lists* for 1816 and later.   [39] Some figures in appendix 1.

whose money transformed Hazlitt's life by allowing him and his wife to go on a tour to France and Italy, had 'an independence of nearly £300 a year', near to my suggested standard.[40] Letitia Landon, one of the most famous and prolific authors of the later romantic period, lived on £120 a year, less than £2 10s (50 shillings) a week.[41]

Against the standard of 100 shillings a week, we can regard the prices of books expressed in shillings as percentages.[42] Thus, at the time it was first published in 1812, a bound copy of *Childe Harold's Pilgrimage, A Romaunt* in quarto cost about half the weekly income of a gentleman. A collection of Byron's tales, a few evenings' reading at most, when bound in one volume, was the equivalent of about 20 per cent. We can interpolate for younger sons, clergymen, officers, doctors, merchants, widowed ladies on annuities, journalists, university students and the large constituency of potential readers whose income lay between 100 and, say, 50 shillings (£5 and £2 10s). Buying a new book of poetry or novel would be a high, in many cases prohibitive, slice of their weekly budget. As for those lower down the social scale, the highest-paid skilled workers in the country, the printers, were paid about 36 shillings (£1 16s) a week from 1810.[43] Carpenters were paid about 25 shillings (£1 5s). *Childe Harold's Pilgrimage, A Romaunt*, even in octavo, was far out of reach for them, as a third or a half of a week's income. Lawyer's clerks in London were paid about 10.5 shillings (10s 6d), from which they might occasionally afford 0.5 shillings (sixpence) towards the price of a book.[44] Bookseller's apprentices, young men of ability and ambition who hoped after five years to become partners or to start their own businesses, were paid 4 shillings a week in 1814. For the price of 1.5 shillings (1s 6d) a week a bookseller's apprentice in Edinburgh could have a shared bedroom, a landlady to do the cooking, and the right to sit by the fire. His food could cost as little as 0.25 shillings (threepence) a day.[45] For such men there could be no question of buying the newly published literature, although they might have chances to read in the shop.

As for journeymen, tradesmen, farm workers, factory workers, domestic servants, and the rest of the employed population who had to provide for families as well as for themselves, only a few earned as much as 10 shillings

[40] Letter of John Hunt of 31 August 1824 quoted in *The Letters of William Hazlitt* edited by Hershel Moreland Sykes and others (1978) 336, no source given.

[41] Jerdan iii, 185.

[42] Some adjustment for wartime inflation is needed in estimating real prices during the inflation of the 1790s and 1800s.

[43] See Ellic Howe, *The London Compositor, Documents relating to the Wages, Working Conditions, and Customs of the London Printing Trade, 1785–1900* (1947).

[44] Mentioned in William Hazlitt's 'On Londoners and Country People' in *The Plain Speaker* (1826).

[45] Chambers 88, describing his own experience.

a week. In the late 1790s the wages in rural Somerset were a shilling a day for those who could get the work.[46] The Scottish poet William Thom says that during his seventeen years as a handloom weaver in Aberdeen the average wage for first class hands was 6 to 9 shillings and for second-class hands 3 to 5 shillings before deductions and fines.[47] Thomas Kelly, later a highly successful publisher, when he served as a shopman in a London publisher's printing house, was paid 4 shillings a week.[48] James Watson, a radical bookseller, gives a breakdown of the pay and deductions of an average journeyman framework knitter in Leicester in 1833. Gross pay 9 shillings for a seventeen hour, six day, week, net take-home pay 5 shillings.[49] A pint of wine in a provincial hotel cost about 6 or 6.5 shillings (6s 6d), the equivalent of three weeks' wages of the maid who served it.[50] A copy of *Childe Harold's Pilgrimage a Romaunt*, even in the cheaper octavo version, would have cost her six weeks' income, seven weeks if she had the book rebound.

Whichever measures of comparison we use, they reassert and reconfirm the same conclusion. In the romantic period the new books of the time were expensive luxuries which could be bought, if at all, only by the richest groups in society. Constable, the publisher who made his first fortune by selling Walter Scott's books at high prices, calculated that he could make a second fortune by reducing prices and selling more copies. A half penny (0.04 shillings) of profit per book, would, he declared from his studies of the national tax returns, 'make me richer than the possession of all the copyrights of all the quartos that ever were, or will be, hot-pressed'.[51] The figures bear him out. A parliamentary inquiry of 1818 reported that books were more expensive at that time than they had ever been in the history of British books.[52]

In the second decade of the nineteenth century, all over the northern hemisphere the winters started earlier, ended later, and were more severe than any time for over a century. In the Alps the glaciers of Switzerland advanced down the valleys. In Scotland the sea froze.[53] In 1814 there was an ice-fair on the Thames. The harsh weather brought poor harvests. Potatoes rotted before they could be harvested. The price of cereals soared and,

---

[46] Hannah More's figure in *The Shepherd of Salisbury Plain*. See chapter 17.
[47] William Thom, *Rhymes and Recollections of a Handloom Weaver* (1880 edition) 3.
[48] See Fell's *Kelly* 43. He served his time with Hogg, one of the old canon publishers whose list is described in appendix 6.
[49] Linton 8. The compulsory deductions were for rent of the frame, materials, candles and coals, and master's charge of 3s 10d (3.9 shillings).
[50] Lister 23, 353.   [51] Lockhart 548.   [52] *Select Committee.*
[53] See H. H. Lamb, *Climate, History and the Modern World* (1982).

Figure 8. Lackington's 'Temple of the Muses', Finsbury Square, London.
Part of an engraving by Thomas Tagg, c. 1810. The inscription above the door
reads 'Cheapest Bookseller in the WORLD. The dark strip above, contains densely
written advertisements for the half million volumes said to be always available.
From *Jones's Classical Family Library* (1830).

Table 11.2 An indication of the shape of the demand curves, copyrighted books, romantic period. Sales of Moore's 'Lalla Rookh'

	Prices in shillings, unbound	Copies printed
1817, 4to	42	2,500
1817 to 1827, 8vo	14	18,000
1829 to 1835, 12mo	5	4,500

with it, the price of bread. In 1816 the price of a quartern loaf was at its highest level ever in real terms in the history of British bread.[54] Gangs of discharged soldiers and sailors joined by immigrants from Scotland and Ireland added to the unemployed. But not everyone suffered and some benefited. With the high cereal prices, agricultural rents were increased and there was another spate of private enclosure of previously common land. The income of landowners rose as that of others fell. Books for most people, whether rich or poor, are discretionary and marginal purchases, to be made, if at all, from what remains after more pressing needs have been met. Although books were expensive for everyone, for those who lived on income from rents from land, they were tending to fall as a proportion of their incomes.

Not only were initial prices high, tranching down was slow. The steepness of the demand curve, and the concentration of demand at the higher price levels, can be seen in the case of Thomas Moore's famous romantic poem *Lalla Rookh* (1817).[55] See Table 11.2.

In the case of Wordsworth's *The White Doe of Rylstone* (1815) it was part of the contract that no new edition would be published until all 750 copies of the expensive quarto were sold, and that had not happened by 1831.[56]

Since many books were sold by publishers to other publishers who sold them retail to the public and wholesale to others within the industry, the selling out, or 'exhausting', of an edition did not mean that all the copies printed had reached retail buyers or readers. One method of shifting slow-moving books was for the publishers to sell them by auction at the special restricted entry trade sales, so enabling other members of the industry to

---

[54] Prices are conveniently given in the *Annual Register*.

[55] For more details on Moore see 'Thomas Moore', appendix 9, 619. For the effects when prices fell see chapter 16.

[56] Longman to Wordsworth, 28 January 1815. Longman archives. See also 'William Wordsworth.'

buy them at larger than normal discounts. Other books were remaindered, although seldom soon.[57] The last thirty-eight copies of Wordsworth's *The Excursion* (1814) in quarto were not remaindered until 1834, less than one copy a year having been sold for ten years.[58] Copies of many of Byron's books published in the early 1820s are found in remainder bindings of the 1830s.[59]

As long as books were valued above their alternative use as waste paper, they could continue to be read. Lackington, Tegg, and the other dealers in remainders, the funeral undertakers of literature, stood ready to take away the unwanted dead, like corpses, in their sheets. Lackington's 'Temple of the Muses', the biggest second-hand and remainder bookshop in the world, contained half-a-million volumes immediately available to be sent by catalogue mail order all over the country and abroad.[60] Tegg seems normally to have bound a proportion to sell in Ireland, in the poorer districts of northern England, and later in Australia, and other places to which the normal channels of the mainstream industry did not flow, and although his prices were often not much below the full price, he was so successful at finding markets that he commissioned a large amount of reprinting on his own account.[61] Books unsellable at London prices could also sometimes be sold to booksellers in the United States, another way of removing them from the British market without much risk of their returning, but only if the price was lower than the cost of local manufacture, which was very low.[62] But, as in the high monopoly period, copies of some books were destroyed in order to protect prices of the most expensive editions. In 1817 Longman 'wasted' 1,500 out of the 3,000 copies of Burney's *The Wanderer*.[63]

The boom in the long historical verse romance began with the publication of Walter Scott's *The Lay of the Last Minstrel* in quarto in 1805. Building on the success of *The Minstrelsy of the Scottish Border*, a scholarly work for which a grand format was normal, Scott's publishers persuaded their

[57] See, in particular, the heavy remaindering of travel books noted in appendix 7.
[58] See also the publishing history in 'William Wordsworth', appendix 9, 661.
[59] E.g. *Marino Faliero*, &c.
[60] Some figures relating to Lackington's business in James Raven, 'Selling One's Life, James Lackington, Eighteenth Century Booksellers, and the Design of Autobiography' in Brack 3.
[61] See James Grant, *The Great Metropolis, by the Author of 'Random Recollections of the Lords and Commons' Second Series (1837)* ii, 35 for an estimate of the numbers sold. The title pages of Tegg's books from about 1840 mention partners, all called Tegg, presumably family members, in Dublin and Sydney. For selling in Ireland see Bloomfield.
[62] See, for example, the letters of John Taylor and of John Hunt to an American bookseller about (Byron's) *The Liberal* quoted in chapter 20.
[63] Longman to Madame D' Arblay, 4 September 1817, Longman archives i, 100, 133.

Table 11.3 Rising retail price of the long romantic poem
(boards, before rebinding)

		Shillings
4to		
1805	Scott's *The Lay of Last Minstrel*	25
1805	Southey's *Madoc*	42
1808	Scott's *Marmion*	31.5
1809	Margaret Holford's *Wallace*	25
1810	Scott's *Lady of the Lake*	42
1810	Southey's *The Curse of Kehama*	31.5
1810	Campbell's *Gertrude of Wyoming* [a slim volume]	25
1812	Byron's *Childe Harold's Pilgrimage, A Romaunt*	30
1813	Scott's *Rokeby*	42
1814	Wordsworth's *The Excursion*	42
1815	Wordsworth's *The White Doe of Rylstone* [a slim volume]	21
1815	Scott's *The Lord of the Isles*	42
8vo		
1805	Scott's *The Lay of Last Minstrel*	10.5
1808	Scott's *Marmion*	12
1810	Scott's *The Lady of The Lake*	12
1812	Byron's *Childe Harold's Pilgrimage, A Romaunt*	12
1813	Hogg's *The Queen's Wake*	12
1813	Scott's *Rokeby*	14
1815	Scott's *The Lord of the Isles*	14
1818	Byron's *Childe Harold's Pilgrimage, Canto the Fourth*	12
1820	Wordsworth's *The Excursion*	14
1824	Hogg's *Queen Hynde*	14

customers that fictional works on similar topics deserved a similar respect. After the success of *The Lay*, Scott wrote four other long verse romances set in Scotland or in the Borders, all of them commercially highly successful, and other poets soon copied or adapted the formula. As table 11.3 shows, the three market leaders, Longman, Murray, and Constable, raised the prices of long verse narratives, both for quartos and the follow-up octavos, until they reached a plateau with Scott's *Lady of the Lake* (1810) and Wordsworth's *The Excursion* (1814).

Southey, a professional author, understood the commercial strategy that underlay these prices. 'I am startled at the price of Madoc', he wrote in 1805, 'not that it is dear compared with other books, but it is too much money; and I vehemently suspect that in consequence, the sale will be just sufficient for the publisher not to lose anything, and for me not to gain anything.'[64]

---

[64] Southey, *Life* ii, 322.

Readers too offered occasional cries of resistance. 'I have not read the *Lady of the Lake*', wrote Lord Dudley in 1810, 'two guineas is too much for six cantos, and I shall therefore wait patiently for the 8vo.'[65] 'I had ordered my bookseller to send me Rokeby as soon as it might be had for twelve shillings', wrote Hannah More in February 1813, 'but my kind Lady Olivia Sparrow sent me the costly quarto. Two guineas for four hours reading!'[66] 'You have probably seen Walter Scott's poem already', Lord Dudley complained in 1812 about *The Lord of the Isles*. 'I never buy those fine wire-wove quartos, so that as far as I am concerned, it will be unpublished till the 8vo, price 18 shillings, comes out.'[67] 'Oh – and I must tell you', wrote Lady Spencer to her friend in 1810, 'as the *Lady of the Lake* is not yet published in octavo, Mama sends you [Porter's novel] *The Scottish Chiefs*.'[68] When the Duchess of Devonshire declared in 1812 that *Childe Harold's Pilgrimage* was 'on every table', she meant on the tables of the aristocratic families who could afford about 50 shillings (£2 10s) to buy a copy of an edition of 500 copies.[69]

In a letter of 1802, Wordsworth described the readers of quartos and octavos as 'gentleman, persons of fortune, professional men, ladies, persons who can afford to buy, or can easily procure, books of half-a-guinea [10.5 shillings] price, hot-pressed and printed on super fine paper'.[70] Such readers were not, he protested with some disdain, the best judges of human nature or of literature. However, a few years later, in hopes of matching the money which Scott and Byron were making, Wordsworth agreed with Longman to finance two-thirds of the costs of his next poems in exchange for two-thirds of the net profits, becoming, in effect, a high price publisher himself. The publisher's ledger shows the initials 'W.W.' written in against the accounts, implying that Wordsworth personally inspected and approved them on a visit to London.[71] At 42 shillings (£2 2s) before binding, over 45 shillings (£2 5s) bound, *The Excursion* in quarto was, for its length, perhaps the most expensive work of literature ever published in England, and Wordsworth had to wait six years for most of the 500 copies to be sold before the book was reprinted in octavo.[72] Wordsworth may have believed that the rural poor were more sensitive to literature than gentlemen, but he did not

---

[65] S. H. Romilly, ed., *Letters to 'Ivy' from the First Earl of Dudley* (1905) 104.
[66] Roberts iii, 271.   [67] Romilly, ed., *Letters to Ivy* 173.
[68] Mrs Hugh Wyndham ed., *Correspondence of Sarah Spencer Lady Lyttleton, 1787–1870* (1912) 105.
[69] Vere Foster, ed., *The Two Duchesses* (1898) 376. The letter, as transcribed, is undated. If it was sent later in 1812 it may refer to a time when the octavo version was also available. A total of 6,500 copies were manufactured in 1812. See Table 9 'Lord Byron.'
[70] *The Early Letters of William and Dorothy Wordsworth (1787–1805)* arranged and edited by Ernest de Selincourt (Oxford 1935) 295.
[71] Longman archives.   [72] Details in 'William Wordsworth', appendix 9.

number many leech gatherers among his readers. For the price of one copy of *The Excursion* in quarto, a reader in Salisbury could have bought over a hundred fat pigs.[73] Wordsworth's own income from his writing was below 100 shillings (£5) a week for most of his life, and he could not easily have afforded to buy his own books. Even gentlemen with incomes well above the gentility standard did not like his prices. In 1833, when Wordsworth was the grand old man of English literature, he learned that not a single copy of his *Poetical Works* had been sold in his native Cumberland.[74] None of this prevented the poet's son from putting about the story that Wordsworth wrote 'of & for, the poor'.[75]

But if the price rise for long verse narratives was substantial, that for novels was enormous. As table 11.4 shows, in the publication of the three-decker novel, the publishers of the romantic period raised the prices by 300 per cent.

It was a source of particular satisfaction to Constable, the previous price leader, that it was Murray, not himself, who made the final increase to 31.5 shillings (£1 11s 6d), 'If the Booksellers take a Novel from Albemarle Street [i.e. from the publisher John Murray] in 3 vols at 31/6 [31.5 s]', he wrote, 'the public will not think itself imposed upon with a new work from the Author of Waverley like Ivanhoe at £1/10 [30 shillings].'[76] Newly published novels remained priced at 31.5 shillings until the end of the nineteenth century despite a drastic reduction in the manufacturing costs of books and a rise in the purchasing power of money, that is a further large increase in price in real terms.[77]

Meanwhile, alongside the small sales/high price monopoly publishing of new titles, a quite different form of publishing was also prospering. As far as the older out-of-copyright authors were concerned, all could be legally reprinted by any publisher willing to take the commercial risk. Many were available in a wide variety of formats at widely differing prices. Expensive versions were on sale, but also cheaper versions with small type and utility bindings. Some were designed to be sold at the lowest profitable price and were then made even more easily accessible by being sold in parts. In the

[73] 7.5 shillings (7s 6d) a score. William Cobbett, *Rural Rides* (Nelson Classics edition) 11.
[74] See the extract from his letter to Moxon quoted in 'William Wordsworth', appendix 9.
[75] Quoted by Stephen Gill, 'Copyright and the Publishing of Wordsworth' in Jordan and Patten 78. The letter is undated. The words can conceivably be stretched to mean that Wordsworth believed that the lot of the poor can only be improved if the richer classes were persuaded by reading to adopt a new sensibility in their attitudes.
[76] Constable to Hurst Robinson his London agent, 10 December 1819. Archibald Constable archives.
[77] See chapter 21.

Table 11.4 Steeply rising retail price of the
three-volume novel (boards, before rebinding)

		Shillings
1790 to 1800, average		about 9
1801	novels published by Lowndes[a]	9
1800 to 1810, average[b]		about 12
1811	(Austen's) *Sense and Sensibility*	15
1813	(Austen's) *Sense and Sensibility, Second edition*	18
	(Austen's) *Pride and Prejudice*	18
1814	(Scott's) *Waverley*	21
	(Austen's) *Mansfield Park*	18
1815	(Scott's) *Guy Mannering*	21
1816	(Scott's) *The Antiquary*	24
	(Austen's) *Emma*	21
	(Lady Caroline Lamb's) *Glenarvon*	24
1817	Godwin's *Mandeville*	21
1818	(Mary Shelley's) *Frankenstein*	16.5
	(Peacock's) *Melincourt*	18
	(Scott's) *Rob Roy*	24
1819	(Hope's) *Anastasius*	31.5
1820	(Scott's) *Ivanhoe*	30
	(Scott's) *The Monastery*	24
1821	(Scott's) *Kenilworth*	31.5
All subsequent Waverley novels in three volumes		31.5
1830	Godwin's *Cloudesley*	31.5
1840	51 out of 58 new novels published[c]	31.5

[a] Advertisement in a copy of [Burney's] *Evelina* (1801) ac. Lowndes's
novels are all listed as 3s a volume.
[b] Summarised from figures quoted by Blakey.
[c] Altick 263.

out-of-copyright sector of the book industry some of the general restrictive practices were present, notably resale and retail price maintenance, and much of the reprint sector was fully integrated into the main industry, but the prices were far lower, as table 11.5 shows.

Many titles which passed through the brief copyright window, were available at a quarter of the price of Scott and Byron. In terms of a unit of reading material, the differential is even wider. Because the older authors were printed far more tightly and in smaller formats than the new, you could buy many more hours of reading for your shilling. In table 11.6 I compare a typical basket of favourite older authors, with a basket of roughly the same length of reading material from the moderns.

With novels, the price differences were, by the middle of the romantic period, even wider, as is shown by table 11.7.

Table 11.5 Illustrative prices of out-of copyright poets, 1810s and 1820s (boards, before rebinding, shillings)

	luxury	octavo	Sharpe	Jones	Dove	parts
Cowper's *Works*	52	42	4	5	5	1
Thomson's *Seasons*	84	13	2	1.5	2.5	0.5
Young's *Night Thoughts*	33.5	15	2	3.5	3	0.5

Table 11.6 Prices of comparable baskets of verse reading, c. 1820, at cheapest new retail prices (boards)

	Shillings
OLDER OUT-OF-COPYRIGHT	
Collins, Gray, Beattie, Thomson, Young	9
NEW COPYRIGHTED AUTHORS	
Scott's *The Lay of the Last Minstrel, Marmion,* and *The Lady of the Lake*; Byron's *Childe Harold's Pilgrimage, A Romaunt*; Campbell's *The Pleasures of Hope,* and *Gertrude of Wyoming*; Rogers's *Italy*	95.5

Table 11.7 Prices of a comparable quantity of novel reading, c. 1820, at cheapest new retail prices (boards, shillings)

	Roscoe	Cooke	Limberd	parts
Defoe's *Robinson Crusoe*	na	5	na	0.5
Goldsmith's *The Vicar of Wakefield*	5	2	1	0.5
Smollett's *Roderick Random*	5	3.5	na	0.5

For six shillings you could buy an evening with Peacock's *Headlong Hall* or a month with Richardson's *Clarissa*.

The pleasant small-sized series of *Walker's English Classics*, was profitably published in editions of many thousands of copies at prices of about one or two shillings.[78] The retail price of Longman's handsome stereotyped edition of Thomson's *Seasons*, a book always in demand, was only 2 shillings, produced in an edition of 6,000 copies.[79] By positioning themselves lower down the demand curve, achieving more sales at lower prices, the profits were lower in absolute terms, but the rates of return on capital employed may have been comparable.

[78] See appendix 5.   [79] Longman archives.

The new books of the romantic period were too big and too valuable to be taken outside. Apart from a few multi-volume 'library editions', by contrast, the old-canon reprints were of 'cabinet' or pocket size, a new name for the revived duodecimo. As the publishers' advertisements emphasised, the handy format and easy mobility were attractive to men and women who had to snatch their reading moments. Since they could also be read more easily in private, the small format was an advantage to women and young people whose normal reading took place in the supervised space of the drawing room or the school room.

Even at a tenth or twentieth of the price of newly published copyrighted books, however, the cheapest out-of-copyright books were too expensive for the majority of the population. Here too, in the competitive sector, the book industry responded as modern models of economic competition would have predicted. During the romantic period the publishers seem to have refused to allow anyone to sell copyrighted books in parts, or instalments, known as 'numbers', although Constable was forced to sell off stocks of Waverley novels in this way during the cash flow crisis of 1826.[80] In the competitive sector, however, many books were sold at 0.5 shillings (sixpence) a part, as a form of consumer credit. Sometimes the books were simply broken up into several parts and sold with new wrappers, but with others the format of the book was designed from the beginning with serialisation into parts in mind.[81] By the beginning of the romantic period there appears to have been a substantial 'numbers' industry with its own distinctive force of salesmen or 'numbersmen' travelling round the country. 'I doted on their type, on their ornaments, on their wrappers containing lists of other poets, and on the engravings', Leigh Hunt wrote about his early reading, confirming the importance of the illustrations to new readers, 'When the master tormented me – when I used to hate and loathe the sight of Homer, and Demosthenes, and Cicero – I would comfort myself with thinking of the sixpence in my pocket, with which I should go out to Paternoster Row, when school was over, and buy another number of an English poet.'[82] Thomas Kelly, who from his childhood years as a shepherd's son in Kent was aware of the huge unmet demand for reading, made his first fortune by buying remaindered out-of-copyright books and splitting them to sell in paper wrappers as numbers.[83] They were sold by door-to-door 'canvassers'

---

[80] E.g. Constable discussed the possibility of selling the Waverley novels in this way with Hurst Robinson. They were also sold in this way later. See chapter 21.

[81] See Bew's list summarised in appendix 7. 'Numbers' appear to have been regarded as different from 'parts', although Hazlitt seems to have used the terms interchangeably.

[82] *The Autobiography of Leigh Hunt* (1860 edition) 76.   [83] See Fell's *Kelly* 64.

and 'deliverers' paid on commission in proportion to their sales.[84] Soon Kelly started producing books specially designed to be sold in numbers, and in 1814, having been refused cooperation by the moveable-type printers, he built a stereotype foundry under his own control.

For the numbers trade, we see the figure of sixpence (0.5 shillings) or occasionally threepence (0.25 shillings) becoming established as the maximum expenditure which new entrants to the reading nation could be expected to pay.[85] Anyone who, like Limberd in the mid 1820s, took the price lower than that figure was frozen out from the normal distribution channels.[86] Sixpence was just about affordable by families with incomes of 10 shillings or £1 (20 shillings) a week, the revival of selling in numbers probably helped to bring many groups into the reading nation. But, in absolute terms, the books for the poor were not cheap. When, in the 1830s, the price of numbers of a wide range of literary, educational, and practical texts had been forced down to a penny (0.08 shillings) a week, it would have taken over a year to accumulate the complete works of Shakespeare.[87] Kelly's *Family Bible*, which was sold in 173 numbers at eight pence (0.66 shillings) a number, cost its patient purchasers a total of £5 15s 4d (115.3 shillings), several times more than the price of the same books bought outright.[88] Throughout the romantic period those book buyers who had no savings and no access to other forms of credit paid an extremely high premium in their occasional purchases. The books sold in 'numbers' were, according to Charles Knight, the publisher, 'the dearest books that came from the press, even in the palmy days of expensive luxuries', and the archival record bears him out.[89]

In the debates leading up to the Copyright Act of 1842, it was argued by authors and publishers, that over time, a long copyright period was 'good for literature' for, without the income which a long period of copyright protection conferred, authors would not bother to write. However recent experience offered little support to that opinion. All the great writers of the romantic period had emerged under a short copyright regime, and a

[84] See *ibid.* 68.
[85] For stereotyping see Andrew Wilson's open *Letter to the Public* dated 1 January 1819, printed as a prospectus, copy in Reading University Library. Some figures of books sold in numbers are given in appendix 7, 568. Kelly made a fortune and became lord mayor of London in 1836. Curwen 370.
[86] See appendix 6.
[87] Notably the publications of the *Penny National Library*, of which some copies, with advertisements for the changing terms, survive in the BL. A fuller list of books in the series available is advertised in *The Tourist, or Sketch Book of the Times*, 8 October 1832, Ac.
[88] Publishers' and Booksellers' ephemeral print, papers of Gillyat Sumner, Bodleian.
[89] Knight, *Passages* i, 227.

few, such as Scott and Byron, had achieved fortune as well as fame. The stance of those commercially unsuccessful authors such as Wordsworth who felt inadequately rewarded – to blame the public for not buying their books while at the same time wanting to make it even more expensive for them to do so – was not that of an economist, nor even of an author who hoped to reach more than a small number of readers. Some of those who had a surer understanding also favoured a lengthening of copyright monopoly, but for other reasons. Southey and Coleridge, for example, had little but contempt for the new growing reading public, and had no wish to encourage it to grow.[90] A parliamentary bill of 1836 proposing to give sixty years was only killed off when printers and educationalists from all over the country petitioned parliament. They knew that a long copyright period meant higher book prices, slower tranching down, a smaller book industry, a loss of job opportunities, and a less-well educated population.[91]

The effects of the changing regime on prices, on access, and therefore on readerships can be seen by comparing the effects on different authors. William Cowper, who died in 1800, stood nearest to the cross-over point. In 1812, with only two years of copyright to run on all the poems published in Cowper's lifetime, the owners were able to float a share to other publishers for a large sum.[92] Whether they made a good bargain is not known, but in 1814 most of Cowper's works went out of copyright, the prices plummeted, sales soared, and his works reached the large and growing readership which cheapness helped to create. Cowper was soon up with Thomson as the most commonly read poet of the romantic period. Forty editions are known to have been issued between 1817 and 1825, with at least another one a year until 1840. Relative to the size of the reading public, Cowper was probably the most popular and most read modern poet that had ever lived.[93] We can calculate that if Cowper had managed to hang on to life for just a few months longer, his works would have remained expensive all through the romantic period and beyond. As it was, the arrival of Cowper's rural religious verse was the cultural equivalent of Blücher's army at Waterloo, late reinforcements in support of the values of old regimes.

---

[90] For Southey's attitude, in addition to the well-known altercation with Byron, see, for example, his essay in *The Doctor*, edited and abridged by Maurice H. Fitzgerald (1930) 34. See Coleridge's contempt for the reading public as expressed in lectures, letters, and published works as collected by Lucy Newlyn, 'Coleridge and the Anxiety of Influence' in *Romanticism* 12 (1995).

[91] The lists of petitioning printers, recorded in the *Commons Journals*, volume 93, 1838, include many metropolitan printing offices as well as others in towns and cities all over the United Kingdom. See also Feather, *Publishing*, although he takes the publishers' arguments at face value.

[92] £6,764. Goodhugh 297.

[93] See Norma Russell, *A Bibliography of William Cowper to 1837* (Oxford Bibliographical Society 1963) 163.

The works of Byron, most of which were published after the law changed in 1808, were in copyright for twenty-eight years, with some later works qualifying for the extension granted by the 1842 Act. The eastern tales, on which his reputation as a romantic poet had been built, mostly went out of copyright and fell drastically in price in the early 1840s.[94] As for *Childe Harold's Pilgrimage*, the first two cantos went out of copyright in 1840; the third not until 1858; and the fourth not until 1860, so holding back the benefits of cheap reprinting and widening readership until after that date.

Of the six novels of Jane Austen, all of which were first published between 1811 and 1818, *Sense and Sensibility, Pride and Prejudice*, and *Mansfield Park* were in copyright for twenty-eight years, until 1839, 1841, and 1842, but *Emma, Northanger Abbey*, and *Persuasion*, which qualified for the 1842 extension, remained privately owned until 1857 and 1860. Coleridge, whose first poems were published before the end of the eighteenth century, died before the 1842 Act, but the several *Poetical Works of Coleridge* which were published cheaply in the 1830s and 1840s, doomed their readers to disappointment for some of the most famous works, were not included.[95] Wordsworth, who had argued for a long posthumous copyright, lived long enough for all of his printed writings to qualify under the 1808, the 1814, and the 1842 Acts, so prolonging the regime of high prices, small sales, and modest readerships far into Victorian times. Since, over a long career, Wordsworth's compositions had appeared in successively revised versions, the effect of the dribbling out of copyright was that, when at last, in Victorian times, Wordsworth began to achieve the large readership for which he had craved, the texts which most of his readers read were a muddle of differently dated versions.[96]

Scott's verse romances, mostly published before 1810, went out of copyright, in their unrevised versions, at various dates in the mid 1830s.[97] By 1835, the first to enter the public domain, *The Lay of the Last Minstrel*, for

[94] See appendix 13 and chapter 21.
[95] For example, *The Poetical and Dramatic Works of Samuel Taylor Coleridge, With a Life of the Author* (John Thomas Cox 1836); *The Poetical and Dramatic Works of Samuel Taylor Coleridge, With a Life of the Author* (Allman 1837); *The Poetical Works of Samuel Taylor Coleridge, With Life of the Author* (Daly n.d., c. 1839); *The Poetical and Dramatic Works of Samuel Taylor Coleridge* (John James Chidley 1847); *The Poetical and Dramatic Works of Samuel Taylor Coleridge, New Edition* (Daly n.d.). Some contain versions of *The Rime of the Ancient Mariner*, first published in 1798, but the cheap editions mainly consisted of *Poems* (1796), occasional poems which had first appeared in newspapers and whose position under copyright law was uncertain, and some of the plays. The official *Poetical Works* first published in 1828 was sold at high prices in modest print runs until the copyrights expired late in the nineteenth century.
[96] See Stephen Gill, 'Copyright and the Publishing of Wordsworth, 1850–1900' in Jordan and Patten.
[97] Except for the weak *The Lord of the Isles*.

which the minimum price, even after drastic tranching down, had previously been 5 shillings, was immediately made available already bound,
in an attractive format, complete with engraved illustrations, from several
publishers, at half that price.[98] By 1839 you could buy *The Lay of the Last
Minstrel, Marmion*, and *The Lady of the Lake* for less than one shilling
each.[99] The readership of Scott's poems, which was already huge among
the upper- and middle-income groups, soared even higher and they were
amongst the favourite reading of the whole nation throughout the nineteenth century.[100] With Scott's novels, on the other hand, the intellectual
property wheel of fortune favoured the producer interest. The 1842 Act
came into effect on 1 July, just six days short of twenty-eight years from the
date when the first copies of *Waverley* had been put on sale in 1814. As the
then three owners looked at their records, they were delighted to discover
that the last-minute delays which had caused annoyance in 1814 gave them
a windfall bonanza in 1842. When the Stationers' Company registry opened
its doors for business in London on 1 July 1842, the owners were the first in
the door, and they registered not only *Waverley* and all the Waverley novels but virtually all Scott's prose writings and a corpus of revised 'author's
versions' of the poems.[101] The period of monopoly for the Waverley novels
was prolonged at least until 1856, or in the case of Scott's revised editions,
until 1871 and in some cases until 1871 or 1876.[102]

Similarly haphazard patterns of texts, prices, and access, depending upon
the date of first publication, the date of death of the author, and the effects
on each printed text of the changes of 1808, 1812, and 1842, can be seen
across all the new writings of the romantic period. In every case I have
looked at I find the same direct correlation between intellectual property,
price, and access, and the same rapid sensitivity of the price mechanism.
As far as readers were concerned, it was not until late-Victorian times that
the effects worked their way through the system.[103]

---

[98] For example in the editions of Spettigue, price 2.5 shillings (2s 6d) and Daly.

[99] Chambers' Peoples Edition advertised in *Publishers' Circular*, December 1839, *Lay of the Last Minstrel* 0.55 shillings (6¹/₂d), *Marmion* 0.9 shillings (10¹/₂d), *Lady of the Lake* 0.75 shillings (9d).

[100] Some figures for the Chambers editions are given in appendix 5, 516.

[101] The owners were Walter Scott's son, young Sir Walter, his publisher Cadell, and his son-in-law and executor Lockhart. Stationers' Company registers, Copy 3/1. Public Record Office, Kew.

[102] For details see appendix 9, 643 and discussion in chapter 21.

[103] See chapter 21 for a discussion of the effects.

CHAPTER 12

Romance

Which literary authors of the romantic period were most respected at the time? Reputation is not the same as readership or influence, but it affects both, and may be a starting point from which to discern patterns. The men and women of the period knew that they were living in a rich period for English literature and there were many discussions about the relative merits of the leading authors. In retrieving opinion we are, of course, limited to the comments of those who left a written record. However, as far as writing in verse is concerned, then the most highly respected and probably most often read, literary form, there was almost complete agreement about which authors were the best. The same eight names, those of Byron, Campbell, Coleridge, Moore, Rogers, Scott, Southey, and Wordsworth, occur again and again as the consensus choice of a broad range of opinion for half a century.[1] Shelley and Keats, who would appear in most modern canons, were not picked out from twenty or thirty poets who were assigned to a lower rank. Until the late nineteenth century, Blake was scarcely known or mentioned outside tiny coteries.[2]

---

[1] The printed sources I have used include Byron's Parnassus, Byron's *Letters and Journals* iii, 220. Leigh Hunt's much revised poem, *The Feast of the Poets* (1811, 1815, 1832, 1860). Talfourd's *An Address to Estimate the Poetical Talent of the Present Age* (1815); Moore's speech given in 1818, reported in J. W. Lake, *A Biographical and Critical Sketch of Thomas Moore, Esq.* included in Galignani editions of Moore's works (1829); Hazlitt's *On the Living Poets* (1819). John Wilson [Christopher North] in an anonymous article, *Blackwood's Magazine*, May 1820; James Montgomery's *Lectures on Poetry at the Royal Institution, 1823* (1831); (P. G. Patmore) Victoire, Count de Soligny, *Letters on England* (1823) ii, 1; Dibdin 740; T. A. M. in *The Literary Magnet*, August 1824; Hazlitt's *Spirit of the Age* (1825), 'Modern Poets of Great Britain' selected for reprinting by Galignani, 1826 to the 1840s. D. Carey, 'Introductory View of Contemporary Poets' in *Beauties of Modern Poets* (1826); Bulwer Lytton's *England and the English* (1833); Henry Reed's *Lectures on the British Poets* (1857); Revd W. M. Hetherington's *Lectures on the Moral Influence of Modern Poetical Literature* (1842); D. M. Moir (Delta), *Lectures on the Poetical Literature of the Last Half Century*, delivered 1850/1 (1856); Russell's *Moore*, preface; J. C. Sharp, *Studies in Poetry and Philosophy* (1868) 3.

[2] Notably that of Isaac D'Israeli. See Dibdin 742.

Contemporaries tended to take 'the Living Poets' as their category and to choose a starting date around 1800. There was no inclination to include Cowper, who died in 1800, and the Living Poets continued as a literary category until about 1830 even although some of them were dead. The canon was established early – none of the hundreds who began their careers after 1812 was admitted – and it remained essentially unchanged, with some additions, both as a canon of reputation and as a formal publishing canon, until the First World War.[3] Only one writer of the time, John Wilson, suggested that the poets shared a common outlook which transcended their differences.[4] The feature most often noticed was the sharp opposition between those writers who were broadly conservative in their religious and political opinions, such as Coleridge, Scott, Southey, and Wordsworth, and those such as Byron and Shelley, who disliked what they saw and worked for change.

Not only was there little conception of some unifying 'romanticism', but the word 'romance' had a precise application. *The Rime of the Ancyent Marinere*, published in the anonymous *Lyrical Ballads* (1798), was probably the first poem of the time to be described as 'romantic' by its author, although Coleridge did not use the word until later.[5] The first poem to be called romantic in its title was Southey's *Thalaba, A Rhythmical Romance* (1801). He had written in an irregular metre, Southey explained in his preface, in an attempt to recapture something of the original Arabian version. Scott's *Minstrelsy of the Scottish Border* (1802) consisted of 'Historical and romantic ballads' which Scott had collected from local traditions. In *The Lay of the Last Minstrel* (1805), the author explained that he had adopted the conventions of 'the ancient metrical romance' in order to capture something of 'the rude spirit of chivalry'. In the preface to *Marmion, A Tale of Flodden Field, A Romance in Six Cantos* (1808), he explained that he called his poems 'romantic' to pre-empt any suggestion that he was writing 'epic', a word used at the time, without embarrassment, by the untalented Poet Laureate Pye.[6] Southey's *Joan of Arc, An Epic Poem* (1799) would be read, Byron declared, 'when Homer and Virgil are forgotten, but – *not till then*'.[7]

---

[3] For the change in the formal canon in mid-Victorian times see chapter 21.
[4] 'This age has unquestionably produced a noble band of British Poets . . . all of them bound together (however little some of themselves suspect it) by rich participation in the stirring and exalted spirit of the age.'
[5] In *Biographia Literaria* (1817) after the term was well established and recognised. For the effects of Percy's *Reliques* on spelling see chapter 17.
[6] E.g. Cottle.   [7] In the notes to *English Bards and Scotch Reviewers*.

In 1812 Byron called *Childe Harold's Pilgrimage* a 'Romaunt'.[8] Moore's *Lalla Rookh* (1817) was 'An Oriental Romance', Keats's *Endymion* (1818) 'A Poetic Romance'. The more modest word 'tale', which also provided protection against ridicule, appears to have been used synonymously with 'romance'. Byron's *The Giaour* (1814) was 'A Fragment of a Turkish Tale'; *The Bride of Abydos* (1814) was 'A Turkish Tale'; *The Corsair* (1814) 'A Tale'. Campbell's *Gertrude of Wyoming* (1809) was 'A Pennsylvanian Tale'. When Scott turned from verse to prose, his *Ivanhoe* (1819) was 'a Romance'. The first collected edition of the Waverley novels was 'Romances by the author of Waverley'. John Foster, who wrote an essay on the word 'romantic' in 1805, said that it was generally used as a term of contempt, but like 'puritan' and 'methodist' was being adopted as a badge of honour.[9]

No one at the time regarded Wordsworth, whose only attempt at the genre was *The White Doe of Rylstone* (1814), as a 'romantic poet'. That was a Victorian innovation which can be pinpointed to the 1870s.[10] As the reviewers noted, in his sentiments and subject matter, Wordsworth

---

[8] The secondary title, *A Romaunt*, was used in all the early editions of the first two cantos of the poem which, as far as readers before 1816 were concerned, was the complete work. The secondary title was dropped from *Childe Harold's Pilgrimage, Canto the Third* in 1816, and *Childe Harold's Pilgrimage, Canto the Fourth* in 1818, but was revived in the first edition of the whole poem in 1819. Murray, and some pirates, continued to use the secondary title, but it disappeared quickly.

[9] John Foster, 'On the Epithet Romantic' in *Essays in Series of Letters to a Friend* (1806) ii, 1.

[10] I draw this conclusion from the following books, encyclopaedias, and textbooks, some frequently reprinted over long period, good sources for the norms being taught at schools, universities, and elsewhere. Not all publication dates refer to the first edition. William Hazlitt, *Lectures on the English Poets* (1819); James Montgomery, *Lectures on Poetry* (1830); Robert Chambers, *History of the English Language and Literature* (1837); *Chambers' Cyclopaedia of English Literature* (1843); Thomas Shaw, *Outlines of English Literature* (1849); Mrs Foster, *A Handbook of Modern European Literature* (1849); D. M. Moir, *Poetical Literature of the Past Half-Century* (1856); David Masson, *Essays, Biographical and Critical: Chiefly on English Poets* (1856); Henry Reed, *Lectures on the British Poets* (1857) and *Introduction to English Literature* (1860); (Simpkin and Marshall's) *Guide to English Literature* (1860s and 1870s); Thomas Arnold, *A Manual of English Literature* (1862); Joseph Angus, *The Handbook of English Literature* (c. 1865); William Spalding, *The History of English Literature* (1870s); J. Devey, *A Comparative Estimate of Modern English Poets* (1873); He distinguishes 'Lake school' of Wordsworth, Coleridge, Southey, from 'Classical school' of Rogers and Campbell; 'Romantic school' of Byron, Scott, and Moore; and 'Alexandrine school' of Shelley and Keats; H. A. Dobson, *The Civil Service Handbook of English Literature* (1874); H. A. Taine, *History of English Literature* (1875), translated from the French: 'The romantic school . . . started by Southey, Coleridge, Wordsworth.' This appears to be the first mention. Stopford A. Brooke, *English Literature from A.D. 670 to A.D. 1832* (1876); George L. Craik, *A Compendious History of English Literature* (1875), entries arranged chronologically by groups of authors. The editor describes the turn of the century in 1800 as 'an awakening and fructifying power upon literary genius in these islands', but the word 'romantic' is not used. William Francis Collier, LLD, *A History of English Literature* (1882), the word 'romantic' is still used of Scott and Byron. Wordsworth scorned 'the used up subjects of the Romancists'. Blake is not mentioned among the 700 authors discussed. William John Coulthorpe, *The Liberal Movement in English Literature* (1885): 'The Revival of Romance. Scott, Byron, Shelley'. Mrs Oliphant, *The Literary History of England In the End of the Eighteenth and Beginning of Nineteenth Century* (1886), entries arranged mainly by author, beginning with Cowper. On the year 1800: 'face of English literature changed . . . old follies put to

was much nearer to the rural, religious, old-canon poets of the previous century than to Scott or Byron. As Macaulay said, he repeated 'the old flimsy philosophy about the effect of scenery on the mind'.[11]

After the success of Scott's long narrative verse romances, the word was applied to an easily recognisable and much admired type of writing. As Longman advised Margaret Holford, who was contemplating a successor to *Wallace, or The Fight at Falkirk*, a historical verse narrative in the style of Scott, 'The success of a volume of small poems is more doubtful & rarely so extensive as that of an interesting single poem on an interesting subject.'[12] A romantic poem was set in the past, or in some imaginary age which mixed past and present, often divided into 'books' or 'cantos'. Many of the books have their title pages printed in the old English black letter, obsolete except in ballads since the seventeenth century, so taking the reader at once into a past world.[13] As was explained in innumerable introductions, the authors of verse romances wished to revive the apparent simplicity of the old English and Scottish narrative ballads.[14]

---

flight and the new life brought in, with a tremulous ecstasy and universal quiver of emotion and movement . . . new flood of genius'. The word 'romantic' is not used, but all the poets are described as 'The New Brotherhood'. J. Logie Robertson, *A History of English Literature* (1894); Professor William Minto, edited by Professor William Knight, *The Literature of the Georgian Era* (1894); R. McWilliam, Inspector to the School Board for London, *Longman's Handbook of English Literature* (1896), entries chronologically by author: Scott and Byron, 'rivals in the fields of romance'. George Saintsbury, *A History of Nineteenth Century Literature* (1896), arranged mainly by groups of authors, beginning with Cowper. Word 'romantic' is not used, but all the poets after 1800 are described as 'The New Poetry'. Blake discussed, almost for the first time in such literary histories. Henry Morley, *A First Sketch of English Literature* (1896); Anna Buckland, *The Story of English Literature* (1896), word 'romantic' not used except of Scott. Frederick A. Laing, *A History of English Literature* (late 1890s); Edmund Gosse: *A Short History of Modern English Literature* (1897), arranged by key authors: 'The Age of Wordsworth', 'The Age of Byron', 'The revival of romanticism'. Johanna Siedler, *History of English Literature for the Use of Ladies' Schools and Seminaries* (1900): distinguishes 'Lake School' from 'Romantic School' of Scott, Moore, Byron, and Shelley. J. M. D. Meiklejohn, *The English Language, Its Grammar, History, and Literature* (1901); Charles Edwyn Vaughan, *Periods of European Literature. The Romantic Revolt* (1907); Arthur Symons, *The Romantic Movement in English Poetry* (1909): the author says that he does not wish his title to be taken 'in too exclusive a sense'. Andrew Lang, *History of English Literature* (1913): 'The so-called Romantic movement'. W. J. Courthorpe, *A History of English Poetry* (1913): 'Romantic' used as a defining category. Crabbe 'anti-romantic'. E. M. Tappan, *A Brief History of English Literature* (1914): 'Romanticism' discussed. *The Cambridge History of English Literature* (1915): 'The Romantic Period'. *The Oxford Book of Regency Verse* (1928): renamed in the second edition (1935): *The Oxford Book of Romantic Verse*; Stuart Curran, *Cambridge Companion to British Romanticism* (1993): 'A crucial transition between an Enlightenment world view and the values of a modern industrial society'. Jerome J. McGann, *The New Oxford Book of Romantic Verse* (1993): 'Romanticism . . . at its epipsychic core [is] . . . a quest for desire itself.'

[11] G. O. Trevelyan, *Life and Letters of Lord Macaulay* (1878) iv, 45.

[12] Letter of 28 April 1811, Longman archives i, 97, 48. *Wallace* had been first published in quarto in 1809.

[13] For the 'romantic revival' see chapter 17.

[14] Notably in Scott's introduction to the 1830 edition of *The Lay of the Last Minstrel*.

Romantic poems often contained explanatory and historical prose notes. In *Childe Harold's Pilgrimage, A Romaunt*, Byron's prose offers a perspective on contemporary Greece entirely different from that of the verse, so that, when read as a whole, the book offered an intellectual as well as an emotional view on the situation facing the Greeks.[15] The division between poetry and prose, and between 'literature' and other writing was less sharp than it has since become. The notion that 'poetry' is a uniquely dense and complex type of writing, mainly concerned with inner feelings, and is necessarily obscure and inaccessible except to those who have a specially trained sensibility, still lay largely in the post-romantic Victorian and modernist future. To the men, women, and children of the romantic period, verse was not difficult or strange, but normal mainstream reading. The Victorian and modern editors of Byron and Shelley who omitted the prose notes, or who treated them as mere paratexts, have made it harder for modern readers to understand the reading experiences of the first readers.[16]

Many dozens of romantic poems were published in the romantic period.[17] Their authors took inspiration from Scotland, Wales, and Ireland, but mostly they looked abroad. Among the European literatures on which they drew for material were French, German, Italian, Spanish, Dutch, Portuguese, Norwegian, Danish, Icelandic, Russian, Polish, Serbian, and Hungarian. The romantic poets wrote about the ancient Jews, Babylonians, Greeks, Romans, Goths, Ancient Britons, Knights, Crusaders, Spanish Conquerors, explorers and voyagers, and military heroes of all nations. They loved verse descriptions of foreign places and exotic names, real or invented. Many poems were concerned with war and violence, victory and conquest. 'Stick to the east', Byron advised Moore as early as 1813, '. . . the North, South, and West, have all been exhausted.'[18] Moore, negotiating like an imperialist, offered Byron a free hand in Turkey if he would keep out of Persia.[19] But soon the east too was overrun, Albania, Greece, Turkey,

---

[15] See William St Clair, 'Literature and Politics, the Case of Byron and Greece' in *Essays by Divers Hands*, Royal Society of Literature (1980) and *Lord Elgin and the Marbles* (third edition 1998).

[16] As far as Byron is concerned, some late-Victorian editions abbreviated or omitted the notes. In the current standard edition, *The Complete Poetical Works of Lord Byron* edited by Jerome J. McGann (1980–93), the editor has interspersed his own comments with those of Byron. As far as Shelley is concerned, the first official edition to drop the prose notes was published in 1852.

[17] Titles in J. R. de J. Jackson, *Annals of English Verse. A Preliminary Survey, 1770–1835* (Garland, New York 1985).

[18] Byron *Letters and Journals* v, 101.

[19] Moore extracted a promise from Byron that he would not write about 'peris', that is Persian girls, without prior discussion. He also withdrew from writing a story set in Turkey which appeared to be too similar to *The Bride of Abydos*, despite Byron's assurance that *The Bride* did not 'trench upon your kingdom in the least'. Byron *Letters and Journals* iii, 184.

Palestine, Syria, Egypt, Arabia, the area of present day Iraq, then into Persia and India. During the romantic period, every place in a long, broad, coastal strip from the Mediterranean to India was explored and exploited in a scramble for poetic exoticism as keen as the later scramble for colonies and oil. Other poets ventured to Africa, to North America, the West Indies, and then to South America, the Pacific Ocean and Australia. Southey took Paraguay; James Montgomery took Greenland; Bishop Heber was left with the North Pole. Apart from Byron, few of the poets who wrote about these exotic places had travelled outside Europe, but they had read the travel books. The single most striking common feature about the romantic poets, taking them as a whole, major and minor, and using the word romantic as it was used at the time, is that they seldom wrote about England and they seldom wrote about the present day. To contemporary readers the great poems of the romantic age were not those that feature in modern university courses but *The Lay of the Last Minstrel, Marmion, The Lady of the Lake, Childe Harold's Pilgrimage, The Giaour, The Bride of Abydos, The Corsair, Manfred, The Pleasures of Hope*, and *Lalla Rookh*.

Collections of short poems were associated with the occasional verses written by amateurs, by women, and by provincial poets published on commission. Measured by numbers of titles, the majority of the poets of the romantic age wrote short works in the traditional style on traditional topics. Like their old-canon predecessors, they described religious feelings, the hand of God in sublime Nature, youth and age, love and family affections, parting, death and grief. Uncounted poets, men and women, attempted poetic descriptions of their local scenery, a verdant hill, a fertile valley, a ruined castle. They celebrated the flowers and the trees, the sounds of the birds, the passing of the seasons, the rhythms of the rural economy, and they linked their feelings to a sense of awe at the divine. Of the many hundreds of books of verse by men and women published on commission, and printed and distributed in the provinces, there was scarcely a romantic poem among them.[20]

In terms of authors, there was a clear gender division. Of the hundreds of women whose poems were printed during the romantic period, most wrote in the non-romantic tradition in celebration of the private sphere of home, family, and local neighbourhood, sometimes explaining that such writing was best suited to their experience, to their sensibility, and to their essential nature as women.[21] To write about war, history, and voyages to remote lands,

[20] My conclusion from the descriptions in Johnson.
[21] See the bibliographies by Jackson, *Annals*, and *Romantic Poetry by Women, A Bibliography, 1770–1835* (Oxford 1993).

was to venture into the masculine public sphere about which they could be expected to know little. Only a handful of women, notably Hemans and Holford and, to a lesser extent Landon, attempted the long historical verse narrative with prose notes, and their romances are not distinctively feminine in any obvious sense. These female romantic poets celebrated death in battle – like that of Casabianca, the boy who refused to leave the burning deck of a doomed warship. They bore witness to the shame of families of soldiers shot for desertion and the misery of the lonely end which awaited religious sceptics.[22] In their celebration of official religious and military values the women romantic poets were more unyielding than the men.

The contemporaneous canon was a judgement of literary value, not a list of bestselling authors.[23] As every author knows, reputation does not mean readers, and print runs are not sales. However, when the differences are as great as the archival record reveals, further refinement does not much alter the main patterns which emerge.[24] Since almost all copies manufactured appear eventually to have been sold, we can take the production statistics as broadly the same as the sales. As table 12.1 shows, in terms of copies of books manufactured for sale during the romantic period, the differences among the eight canonical authors were huge.

The author whose verse works were sold in the largest numbers during the romantic period was, by far, Walter Scott. By 1836, four years after Scott's death, at least 180,000 copies of his long romantic poems had been printed, more than 200,000 counting the less famous works, and they were still being reprinted in ever larger print runs. After Scott, the poet whose works were produced in the largest numbers was Byron. Before *Don Juan*, the biggest seller of all, *The Corsair*, at 25,000 copies was commercially the most successful, but at least three of Scott's poems were printed in more copies over a comparable period.[25] Thomas Campbell and Thomas Moore too both enjoyed long print runs as well as high reputations, but did not match Scott and Byron. As for the other poets of the contemporaneous canon, the poems of Rogers and of Southey were printed in far larger

---

[22] Many examples in the works of Hemans. For Landon, see, for example, 'The Deserter' in *Poetical Works of Letitia Elizabeth Landon* (1853) ii, 183.

[23] It excludes, for example, Bloomfield, Pollok (appendix 9, 582 and 629), and Robert Montgomery, all of whom had huge sales.

[24] For more detailed information, see appendices 5 and 9.

[25] For *Don Juan* see chapter 16.

Table 12.1 Printed verse of the romantic period. Records and estimates of total book production during the period[a]

	000s of copies
CANONICAL EIGHT	
Scott, *Lay of Last Minstrel, Marmion, Lady of the Lake, Rokeby, Lord of the Isles, Field of Waterloo*	117
Byron, *Childe Harold's Pilgrimage, A Romaunt,* and tales	100
Others, excluding *Don Juan*[b]	100
Moore, *Lalla Rookh* and *Loves of the Angels*	28
Others, more than	30
Campbell, *Pleasures of Hope* and *Gertrude of Wyoming*	45
Rogers, all	45
Southey, all except *Wat Tyler*[c]	33
Wordsworth, all	13
Coleridge, all the verse writing, including the plays	7
OTHERS WHOSE WORKS SOLD WELL	
Robert Bloomfield	100
James Montgomery	38
Crabbe	35
Kirke White[d]	21
Hemans	18
Milman	15 to 20
Pollok	15
Robert Montgomery[e]	10
Hogg	10
Clare	8
OTHERS	
Shelley, total for eight poems	3
of which sold at unremaindered prices	1.5
Keats, all	1.5
of which sold at unremaindered prices	0.5
Blake, all	0.2

[a] Records or estimates. Fuller information for most of the authors in appendix 9.
[b] For *Don Juan* see chapter 16.
[c] For *Wat Tyler* see chapter 16.
[d] Broad estimate. White died young, his poems went out of copyright early, and, without ever quite being accepted into the old canon, they were reprinted in cheap as well as expensive editions.
[e] Broad estimate from numbers of editions.

Table 12.2 Individual long romantic poems. Production during the romantic period

Excluding collected editions, imports and piracies.[a] For Byron's *Don Juan* and Shelley's *Queen Mab* see chapter 16

	000s of copies (estimated)
Scott's *The Lady of the Lake* (1810)	32.25
Scott's *Marmion* (1808)	31.5
Scott's *The Lay of the Last Minstrel* (1805)	30
Byron's *The Corsair* (1814)	25
Moore's *Lalla Rookh* (1817)	25.25
Rogers's *The Pleasures of Memory* (1793)	22
Campbell's *The Pleasures of Hope* (1799)	?20
Pollok's *The Course of Time* (1827)	15
Scott's *The Lord of the Isles* (1815)	13.75
Byron's *Childe Harold's Pilgrimage, A Romaunt* (1812)	13.75
Campbell's *Gertrude of Wyoming* (1810)	?13
Byron's *The Giaour* (1813)	12.5
Byron's *The Bride of Abydos* (1813)	12.5
Byron's *Childe Harold's Pilgrimage, Canto the Third* (1816)	12
Montgomery's *West Indies* (1810)	10.5
Byron's *Siege of Corinth* (1816)	10.5
Byron's *Childe Harold's Pilgrimage, Canto the Fourth* (1818)	10
Montgomery's *The World before the Flood* (1813)	10
Scott's *The Field of Waterloo* (1815)	10
Scott's *Rokeby* (1812)	9
Byron's *Lara* (1814)	9
Byron's *Prisoner of Chillon* (1816)	9
Montgomery's *The Wanderer in Switzerland* (1805)	7.5
Montgomery's *The West Indies* (1810)	7.5
Milman's *Fall of Jerusalem* (1810)	7.25
Moore's *The Loves of the Angels* (1823)	7
Crabbe's *Tales of the Hall* (1812)	7.5
Southey's *Roderick* (1814)	7
Southey's *Madoc* (1805)	4.75
Hogg's *Queen's Wake* (1813)	4
Montgomery's *Greenland* (1819)	3.75
Hemans's *The Forest Sanctuary* (1825)	3.75
Southey's *The Curse of Kehama* (1810)	3
Southey's *The Poet's Pilgrimage to Waterloo* (1815)	3
Montgomery's *Pelican Island* (1827)	3
Southey's *Joan of Arc* (1798)	2.25
Wordsworth's *The Excursion* (1814)	2
***	
Keats's *Lamia* (1820)	1
Wordsworth's *The White Doe of Rylstone* (1814)	0.75
Shelley's *The Revolt of Islam* (1818)	0.75
(Coleridge's) *The Rime of the Ancyent Marinere*, printed in *Lyrical Ballads* (1798)	0.5
Shelley's *Prometheus Unbound* (1820)	0.5
Keats's *Endymion* (1818)	0.25
Blake's *Jerusalem* (1804)	0.006
Blake's *Milton* (1804)	0.004

[a] Summarised from appendix 9.

numbers than those of Wordsworth, let alone of Coleridge, about half of whose modest total are the verse plays.[26]

Other verse writers were commercially far more successful than most of the canonical eight. James Montgomery pursued a long and successful career in what may be called the 'religious romantic', long poems with prose notes, drawing on biblical themes and celebrating missionary enterprises abroad. He was such a consistently reliable favourite that Longman suggested that, if properly advised, he could join the select group whose long romantic verse narratives were initially published in expensive quarto.[27] Robert Bloomfield's *The Farmer's Boy*, a successor to Thomson's *The Seasons*, was probably the poem which sold most copies and which circulated most widely. George Crabbe too, another poet who celebrated rural life, saw his works produced in many more copies than the Lake poets. Robert Pollok's *The Course of Time*, a long poem written in reply to what the author saw as the irreligious despair of Byron, became one of the most reprinted poems of the nineteenth century. John Keble's collection of religious verse, *The Christian Year* (1827) sold in large numbers for most of the century.[28] Robert Montgomery, no relation of James, also achieved both fame and sales, although not for long.[29]

Keats and Shelley were both published with short print runs, tiny sales, their books difficult to shift even as remainders with many copies wasted. The Victorian book collector, Harry Buxton Forman, who searched without success for lost works of Shelley, begged readers to examine the linings of their old trunks.[30] Scott and Byron sold more poems in a normal afternoon than Shelley and Keats did during the whole of their lives. As for William Blake, whose books were mostly sold on individual order as expensive art books, he is believed to have produced only a couple of hundred copies during his lifetime, and many copies remained unsold at his death. In whatever way we arrange and interrogate the record, it is clear that the modern canon cannot be the starting point for any investigation of historic readerships in the early nineteenth century.

As far as the prose fiction of the romantic period is concerned, there was no recognised contemporaneous canon. Indeed, the whole notion of a canon

---

[26] For the two parts of *Wallenstein*, Coleridge was paid a fee as translator not as author, Longman archives.
[27] Longman to Montgomery, 1 February 1815. Longman archives i, 99, 65.
[28] See 'John Keble', appendix 9, 613.
[29] See Thomas Lord Macaulay's review essay, published among his *Literary Essays* (1905).
[30] Harry Buxton Forman, *The Shelley Library* (1886) 17.

made little sense when most novels were published anonymously. One writer dominated the age, 'the author of Waverley', not publicly acknowledged to be the famous poet Sir Walter Scott until the mid 1820s. The Waverley novels, with their many imitators and successors, like the romantic verse narratives to which they were direct successors, also took all European history and geography as their world – the Scottish Highlands, Elizabethan England, Mediaeval France, the crusades – in an easy transition from verse to prose. Only once, among some twenty-five full-length works did the author of Waverley write about contemporary life, but *St Ronan's Well* was not regarded as worth repeating.[31] More ancient chivalry, more romance, that was what the public wanted, as Scott's editor constantly advised.

The long romantic historical prose narrative, as perfected by Scott, like the verse romance, mixed imaginative writing with historical fact. In reconstructing real past events and characters Scott was concerned to be as accurate as he could. In both his verse and his prose writings Scott supplied from his imagination the aspects of real life that traditional political and military history left out, social and personal relationships, manners and mores, costumes and customs, and the individual lives of ordinary people. Romance, to Scott and his readers, was a new, fuller, and therefore in some ways a more truthful way, of imagining the past. With prose fiction, as with verse, a broad division can be seen between domestic novels of the kind written by 'a Lady' most notably of the kind written by Austen, seen as predominantly a women's genre, and historical romances of the kind popularised by 'the author of Waverley', which were rightly assumed to have been mainly written by men.

With prose fiction, as with poems, when we compile quantified lists and estimates of the numbers of books by the main contemporary authors manufactured and sold until the 1830s, the differences again turn out to be huge as is shown by table 12.3.

In 1828 the then owners sharply reduced the price of Waverley novels, bringing about a further huge increase in sales.[32] It was partly this success which persuaded the publisher Richard Bentley to begin his innovative series of *Bentley's Standard Novels* which over the next few years made available many other recent novels at a similar price of 6 shillings, a fraction of three-decker prices and with far longer print runs.[33] With all the main novels of the romantic period there is, therefore, both a clear starting point,

---

[31] For Ballantyne's insistence on a rewriting to avoid offending readers see chapter 9.
[32] See chapter 21.   [33] Discussed further in chapter 18.

Table 12.3 Novels of the romantic period. Estimated total
book production during the period and later[a]

	ooos of copies
(Austen) six novels to 1830s	10 to 12
(Scott) Twenty-five Waverley novels to 1829	500
Austen's six novels to about 1860	40
Scott's twenty-five Waverley novels to 1860s	? 2, 000 to 3,000

[a] Summarised from appendix 9.

the date of first publication, and an easily recognisable publishing break
point in the 1830s, within which to make comparisons. On one side are
each and all of the Waverley novels whose immediate sale was often in the
range 6,000 to 10,000 for every title. On the opposite side are all the other
novels, whose sale in the period was usually in the range of 500 to 1,500.
With novels as with poems, by sales as well as by reputation, the dominant
author of the romantic period, and indeed of the Victorian period which
followed, was Walter Scott. During the romantic period, the 'Author of
Waverley' sold more novels than all the other novelists of the time put
together. Even by about 1850, as table 12.4 shows, no novel by any other
recent novelist, including Austen, had achieved cumulative sales of 8,000,
a number which several Waverley novels reached in the first week.

The discouragement of anthologies and abridgements continued to be
an intrinsic part of the regime. The law was unclear on how far it was
legal for others to reprint texts which had appeared in print in newspapers,
sometimes as part of the publishers' marketing, or as an extended quotation
in a review, and some fringe publishers claimed a right to sell anthologies
drawn from quotations in periodicals.[34] But, as Longman discovered, by
running off a few copies of an apparently 'special' edition, and depositing
a copy at Stationers' Hall, he could claim to have 'published' the book
and so obtain injunctions against unauthorised anthologising.[35] The luxurious 'large paper' copies that Scott and Wordsworth liked to present to
patrons, a revival of the aristocratic traditions of earlier centuries, now had
a commercial purpose.

---

[34] Among the apparent and unexplained exceptions which I have come across are F. Campbell, editor,
Beauties of the British Poets (printed by Richard Edwards 1824), James Ely Taylor, editor, *Beauties of
the Poets, Lyric and Elegaic* (1824); and Herbert Barton, *The Mirror of Poesy* (1826).
[35] The device is described by Longman to Ballantyne on 30 April 1811, Longman archives i, 97, 64.

Table 12.4 Individual new novels and romances. Estimated sales during the romantic period. Excluding collected editions, exports, imports and piracies

	000s of copies
(Scott's) *Waverley* (1814), sales to 1836	40
(Scott's) *Guy Mannering* (1815), sales to 1836	50
(Scott's) *Rob Roy* (1818), sales to 1836	40
About twenty other novels by 'the author of *Waverley*'	10 to 30 each
(Burney's) *Camilla* (1795)	4
Individual novels by Burney, Galt, Godwin, Edgeworth, Ferrier, Opie, and probably others	low to mid thousands
(Burney's) *The Wanderer* (1814) Most copies were wasted	3.5
(Austen's) *Pride and Prejudice* (1813), sales before mid 1830s	2 to 3
(Austen's) *Emma* (1815), sales before mid 1830s	2
Of which sold at unremaindered prices	1.5
(Peacock's) *Headlong Hall* (1815), sales before mid 1830s	1 to 3
(Austen's) *Sense and Sensibility* (1811), sales before mid 1830s	1.5 to 2
(Austen's) *Mansfield Park* (1814), sales before mid 1830s	1 to 2
(Austen's) *Northanger Abbey* and *Persuasion* (1818), sales before mid 1830s	1.75
(Mary Shelley's) *Frankenstein* (1818), sales to 1831	1
(Hogg's) *Justified Sinner* (1824)	1
Most new novels published by Colburn, Longman, and others during the romantic period	0.5 or 0.75

The archives contain many examples of the measures taken to prevent unauthorised anthologies.[36] A telling episode occurred in 1824 when William Hazlitt edited a large new anthology that he had selected from the whole of English poetry. About two-thirds was taken from out-of-copyright older writers, but the final third consisted of extracts from contemporary poets on whom Hazlitt had recently delivered public lectures. The publication, whose title, *New Elegant Extracts*, was a direct challenge to the main

---

[36] For example a letter from Longman to Reverend John Bullar, the editor of *Selections from the British Poets* (Southampton 1822), dated 19 September 1822, demands that the copyrighted pieces he had included be omitted in any future edition, Longman archives i, 101, 315. Longman reminds him that Cottle's *Selection* 'was stopped in sale' by Joseph Johnson, the publisher of Cowper and of Barbauld, and that Power, who owned the copyright of Moore's *Melodies* had successfully 'prosecuted two or three persons for introducing into Selections some of his songs, & recovered heavy damages'. The Johnson letter book shows that in 1805 Johnson wanted Cottle to cancel the offending pages, but he offered to accept the remaining 967 copies of the edition at cost price and sell it himself. The letter book also shows him suppressing a piracy printed in Perth.

Figure 9. 'Four specimens
of the reading public'.
By A. Crowquill.
Published by Fairburn,
7 August 1826.

old-canon anthology, *Elegant Extracts*, was suppressed by court order.[37] It was not until the 1850s and 1860s, when the poets of the romantic period began to dribble out of copyright, that printed anthologies which included substantial extracts from the romantic period poets, became available.[38] As had been the case since around 1600, the effect was to intensify the tendency to restrict access to newly published texts to the upper reaches of the income scale and to confine those lower down the scale to the increasingly obsolete literature of the old canon.

But if there were almost no printed anthologies of contemporary literature, readers who had some access to the primary texts could make their own. During the romantic period there was a revival of a literary form of the early modern period, the manuscript miscellany or commonplace book, a form of writing and reading which has been largely forgotten.[39] The revival may be connected with the eighteenth-century custom of educating young ladies in feminine accomplishments, but price was also a factor. The commonplace book kept by Emma Garland in the 1820s, for example, was entitled: 'A collection of pieces made at various periods (chiefly modern) from writers of acknowledged excellence, but whose books are diffuse and expensive.'[40]

The manuscript commonplace books, later often called albums, could be bought ready for use, normally in quarto format, often made of fine paper of different pale colours and bound in fine morocco. Many have the owner's name specially stamped on the cover in gold letters. The owners inserted original drawings and water colours, cuttings from newspapers, epitaphs collected in churchyards, and occasional prose, but in the romantic period they mainly filled them with poetry. In some towns professional poets took commissions from the public, professional scribes offered manuscript copies already written out, and professional artists could also provide drawings. Harriet Elliott Cowell included 'Lines composed by a corporal in a

---

[37] One copy survives in the BL, another in the Bodleian. Another anthology of the 'Living Poets', in manuscript and evidently offered for publication but not published, is among the Blackwood archives. For the large continuing sales and readerships of *Elegant Extracts*, and the derisive comments of Coleridge and others, see appendix 6. When the updated edition appeared in the same year of 1824, it was much the same as the original version in 1788, with only about ten pages of Scott and Byron out of a total of 788, and no extracts from Wordsworth or Coleridge or other recent writers.

[38] Noted by Sabine Haas, 'Victorian Poetry Anthologies' in *Publishing History* (1985) without connecting the high prices to the copyright regime.

[39] My remarks are based on an examination of over a hundred such books in my collection, others seen in the BL, NLS, Keats House, Hampstead, Gennadios Library, Athens, Newstead Abbey, Nottingham, and other libraries as well as innumerable others seen in bookshops or described in booksellers' catalogues.

[40] The book, purchased in Hull, was presented by her father, c. 1825, Ac.

Highland regiment and sung to us in a wild recitative by a fellow soldier, our guide from Dalmally to Inverary in 1825.'[41]

Although they were compiled and used by both sexes, those kept by men are often more in the form of notebooks of useful information, often with more prose than verse, aids to memory and intensive educational reading. One careful reader, for example, made an impressive compilation of writings on the Elgin Marbles printed in the press, as well as of the poems of the then virtually unknown poet, Keats, printed in *The Examiner*.[42] Poems cut from the magazines, recorded Benjamin Gregory, recalling his boyhood as a methodist preacher's son in Yorkshire in the 1820s, were 'not read and cast aside, but re-read, conversed upon, and kept as household treasures'.[43] The majority of the literary commonplace books that survive, apart from some large collections taken on voyages by naval officers, appear to have been kept by women, mainly young women from the upper income groups. They were added to over many years and then passed down through the family across the generations.

Some were on public display, with poems, riddles, acrostics, conundrums, and other light amusements to beguile away a rainy day, and visitors were often asked to contribute. Repeating the same metaphors that had been used in antiquity and the Renaissance, many include an invitation to offer an original composition or a favourite piece of poetry:

> My album is a Garden Plot
> Here all my friends may sow
> Where Thorns and Thistles flourish not
> But Flowers alone may grow.[44]

Soon they had created their own genre, 'verses written in a lady's album'. All the major poets, Wordsworth, Coleridge, Byron, Campbell, and others, not only copied extracts from their own famous works into such commonplace books on request, but composed occasional pieces.[45] Southey was so plagued by requests that he suggested to Wordsworth that they 'should institute a society for the suppression of albums'.[46] Charles Lamb published a whole volume called *Album Verses*.

---

[41] Ac.

[42] A scrap of a letter addressed to 'Chadwick, Praerogative court, Doctors Comns' may indicate the owner, Ac.

[43] Benjamin Gregory, *Autobiographical Recollections* (1903). This book contains an account of the books that Gregory read during childhood and youth.

[44] Jane Cox, begun 1829, Ac. Also written in is 'I hope you'll pay for peeping'.

[45] For a comment by Southey, see *Life* v, 302.

[46] *Selections from the Letters of Robert Southey, edited by his son-in-law John Wood Warter* (1856) iii, 284. For an example of a lady sending her album to Wordsworth and Southey, see v, 302.

Most commonplace books appear to have been mainly compiled by the owners and their friends for their own use.[47] Some, with the extracts written entirely by their owners, were evidently always intended to be private. Some have locks and keys to keep out peepers, self-made books, containing reading material to be returned to and perused alone. Anne Lister's diary of 1820, for example, shows her struggling to keep some order in her four volumes of copied 'Extracts' by compiling indexes.'[48]

The writers of the commonplace books of the romantic period not only revived the use of manuscript as a form of text copying and scribal publication alongside print, but they repeated many of the features of the manuscript miscellanies of the sixteenth and seventeenth centuries. They drew on both printed and unprinted verses, and almost all the pieces they transcribed were modern at the time – there is, for example, almost no Shakespeare. Many contain conduct advice and *sententiae*. One owned by Eliza Bonniwell, which contains many contributions by churchmen in Lincolnshire, contains a motto written in by the visiting Dean Farrar 'What care I for the albums of this world, there is one above.'[49] We find verses by a man about his ideal wife being replied to by a woman, as a kind of courtly wooing. This performative function of the commonplace book, reminiscent of the sonnet sequences of Elizabethan times, was caught in Austen's *Emma*, in which Harriet Smith, the condescended-to 'natural daughter of somebody', kept a manuscript album. 'The only mental provision she was making for the evening of life', the narrator of *Emma* declares, was the collecting and transcribing of riddles of every sort that she could meet with, into a thin quarto of hot pressed paper.'[50] And when Mr Elton was asked to compose a verse acrostic for the album, he chose the intimate word 'courtship', an episode round which the novel pivots.

As for what the women miscellanists chose to include, many copied out Scott's description of his exemplary heroine Elizabeth Vernon, spirited but traditional in her unquestioning loyalty. They often copied the famous lines in which Scott celebrated an ideal of womanhood which combined the traditional virtues with just a little, well controlled, skittishness:

[47] Chambers 153. Although most of the drawings in albums appear to be of good amateur quality, others by named professional artists appear to be original and not just copies. Surviving commonplace books have often had their drawings removed by the antiques trade, so destroying much of their original appearance as cultural artefacts. I have seen a reference to a receipt by Landseer which appears to be a paid commission for providing a drawing.

[48] Lister 124.   [49] Ac.

[50] *The Novels of Jane Austen*, edited by R. W. Chapman (1923) iv, 23, 69. For another example see [Susan Ferrier] *Inheritance* (1824) i, 285.

O Woman! in our hours of ease,
Uncertain, coy, and hard to please,
And variable as the shade
By the light quivering aspen made;
When pain and anguish wring the brow
A ministering angel thou![51]

But they also transcribed the same passages on war and patriotism as appealed to men, notably Scott's lines from *The Lay of the Last Minstrel*, 'Breathes there the man, with soul so dead', Campbell's *Battle of Hohenlinden*, and *The Mariners of England*. Many excerpted the last words of Marmion at the battle of Flodden 'Charge Chester charge! On Stanley on!'[52] Almost every commonplace book that I have seen transcribed a version of 'The Burial of Sir John Moore at Corunna', which must in many cases have come from having heard it read or recited, for the poem was not easily available in printed book form.[53] The same is true of what is the probably most frequently transcribed poem of all, 'Forget Me Not' which exists in many variants.

Byron's works – including *Don Juan* that many women were prevented from reading – were amongst the most frequently quoted, and many compilers also copied Byron's portrait or clipped an engraving. We find a good deal of Rogers and Moore, notably Moore's song 'Tis the Last Rose of Summer', Montgomery's 'The Negro's Vigil', and Pollok, but very little Wordsworth or Coleridge, and only occasionally Shelley or Keats. Quotations from women authors are plentiful, especially Hemans and Landon, but they are not picked out for special treatment. Women's reading, at any rate women's reading of the upper-income groups, the commonplace books suggest, was by no means limited to writings regarded as suitable for women.

The first short poem in Byron's *Childe Harold's Pilgrimage, A Romaunt*, 1812, entitled 'Written in an Album', which exists in many manuscript versions, and was probably amongst the most read verses of the romantic period, caught the spirit of the commonplace books of the romantic period:

---

[51] From *Marmion* 6, xxx echoing *Hamlet* v, 1, 260.   [52] From Scott's *Marmion* 6, xxxii.
[53] The poem, by Reverend Charles Wolfe, first appeared in an Irish newspaper without the author's permission and was later reprinted in many London newspapers. It was much admired by Byron, to whom it was often attributed, and he kept a copy of the magazine in which he had read it. See Reverend John A. Bushell, *Remains of the late Rev. Charles Wolfe, A. B.* (third edition 1827) 27.

> As o'er the cold sepulchral stone
>   Some name arrests the passer-by;
> Thus when thou view'st this page alone
>   may mine attract thy pensive eye!
>
> And when by thee that name is read,
>   Perchance in some succeeding year,
> Reflect on me as on the dead,
>   And think my heart is buried here.[54]

The leaves of flowers inserted in many of the books to dry and wither are laid beside pieces of painted silk brought by menfolk returning from China and India and soon to be off again. A sonnet by L. J. A. called 'She is Far from the Land where her Young Hero sleeps', jostles with 'Lines on Leaving Skye' and verses on Chittagong. Byron's *Fare Thee Well* was more often transcribed than any of his other shorter pieces, along with the other Thyrza poems which were included in the early editions of Byron's *Childe Harold's Pilgrimage*. A passage called 'Night at Sea', which is seldom selected in modern anthologies, was the most frequently copied passage from the main work.

> 'Tis night when Meditation bids us feel
> We once have lov'd, though love is at an end:
> The heart, lone mourner of its baffled zeal,
> Though friendless now, will dream it had a friend.
> Who with the weight of years would wish to bend,
> When Youth itself survives young Love and Joy?
> Alas! When mingling souls forget to blend,
> Death hath but little left him to destroy!
> Ah! Happy years! Once more who would not be a boy?[55]

The verses of the women's commonplace books emit a sense of loss, of parting, of wasted youth, of hopeless love, death of friends. Separation, loneliness, and loss were the real experiences of many women, whether unmarried, married, or widows, in an age when many men were at the wars in the army or navy or building the empire overseas in other ways. When Samuel Rogers reports stories of ladies in Buckinghamshire weeping over *Childe Harold*, this was, I would suggest, the aspect which touched them.[56] In commonplace books, as in life, the men left home, many never to return, the women stayed behind, to remember, to endure, and to grieve.

---

[54] Byron *Poetical Works* i, 273. For Byron's autograph writing in commonplace books, see Christopher Fletcher, 'Lord Byron – Unrecorded Autograph Poems' in *Notes and Queries*, December 1996, 425.
[55] *Childe Harold's Pilgrimage*, canto 2, stanza 23.
[56] Revd Alexander Dyce, ed., *Recollections of the Table Talk of Samuel Rogers* (1856) 231.

Although these books cannot give us a window into the minds of the compilers, and they too are written in accordance with generic conventions, they do offer a more personal glimpse into the literary reading that occurred, both self-selected and prescribed, public and private, than most documents. On the whole they suggest that the patterns of reading for women of the upper-income groups was much the same as that of men, and that it was much the same across the whole country, with some local additions in Scotland and Wales. The patterns of copying follow the patterns of the production of books, with the most frequently printed providing most of the source materials. They reinforce earlier conclusions about the reading of romance.[57]

I do not know if a time came when fathers, husbands, brothers or the printed-book industry began consciously to discourage women from keeping private manuscript commonplace books. But in the 1820s, we see the arrival of a new type of printed book which coexisted and competed with the them. The printed 'albums', 'gift books', and 'annuals', sold every Christmas ready-bound in silk, soft morocco, or decorated leather, contained ready-selected collections of poems, stories, and engravings such as a woman might wish to have copied into her manuscript book.[58] By 1829 they were a substantial sector of the book market, and the boom lasted for another ten years. We find examples of intermediate stages between self-selected manuscript and editorially selected print, books, for example which are mainly blank but with printed advice on how to make selections, or blank pages interspersed with pages containing printed pictures and verses. In their final form, however, the printed books left nothing for the owner to write in except her name, and she was even given a place in which to do that. The privacy of a manuscript gave way to the openness of the printed book. For the readerly freedom to control the texts to be reread in accordance with individual preference was substituted the confinement of receiving a commercially produced gift whose texts had already been pre-selected and pre-censored by others in accordance with the mainstream official ideology and within the tight constraints of intellectual property.

Among many dozens of titles, the best known were *The Keepsake, Forget-Me-Not, Literary Souvenir, The Book of Beauty, Friendship's Offering*, and the *Drawing Room Scrap Book*, but by the mid 1830s the producers were running out of titles: *Affection's Gift, Affection's Keepsake, Affection's Offering,*

---

[57] In chapter 11.
[58] See especially Andrew Boyle, *An Index to the Annuals* (Worcester 1967), Frederick W. Foxon, *Literary Annuals and Gift Books* (1973), Ralph Thompson, *American Literary Annuals and Gift Books* (New York 1936), Anne Renier, *Friendship's Offering* (Private Libraries Association 1964).

Album Wreath, Amaranth, Amethyst, Amulet, Anniversary, Annual Souvenir, Annual Token, Apollo's Gift, Biblical Keepsake, Bijou, Book of Beauty, Book of Gems, Book of Royalty, Bouquet are the names of those beginning with A and B published in England. *The Keepsake* alone, at its peak, sold 15,000 copies every Christmas in the early 1830s, and there was a market for 'super-annuated' annuals even after the year to which they allegedly related had passed.[59] All the printed albums proclaimed their suitability for women, many were edited by women, including some titled ladies, and women provided the majority of the contributions. The annuals paid their contributors well. The canonical authors despised them, but took the money.[60] Wordsworth, accepting a large fee for writing a single poem, excused himself by saying that the annuals would pay for his losses from the French pirates, and he was tempted by the fees offered to venture again into the modern genre of oriental romance.[61] Scott was paid £2,500 for two weak prose pieces.[62] Moore refused an offer of 600 guineas from Heath, the publisher, to fill a single issue. Who was the more mad, their friends wondered, Heath for offering or Moore for refusing?[63] By contrast, Letitia Landon (LEL) received only £2 2s (42 shillings) each for her many poems and only £100 a year for writing the whole text, both the verse and prose, of *Fisher's Drawing Room Scrap Book* (1832–8).[64]

Superficially, the albums look like printed versions of the manuscript commonplace books, and many of the verses to be found in the manuscripts were evidently copied from them. Many, including those of the two most famous romantic poetesses, Felicia Hemans and LEL, were also concerned with parting, loss, and grief, but most of what gave vigour to the manuscript commonplace books was lost. There were virtually no extracts from Byron, except the favourite extract from *Childe Harold's Pilgrimage, A Romaunt* known as 'Night at Sea', for which the editors may have paid a permission fee, no favourites from Scott or Moore.

In material terms, the printed albums were specific to the conditions of the 1830s. The pale silk in which many were covered was a response to the severe depression in the Spitalfields silk industry aimed at relieving

---

[59] See appendix 7 for some statistics.

[60] Scott, despite his desperate need for money, refused the editorship of *The Keepsake*, but he provided verses in return for a generous payment.

[61] In *The Egyptian Maid*. See Peter J. Manning, 'Wordsworth in the *Keepsake*' in Jordan and Patten 61. For the French offshore piracies, see chapter 15.

[62] Shaylor 43.

[63] The offer is recorded by Moore in his diary, Russell's *Moore* 562. Quoted by Peter Manning in 'Copyright and the Publishing of Wordsworth' in Jordan and Patten. The joke is noted in a letter quoted by Jerdan iv, 102.

[64] Jerdan iii, 185. See also F. J. Sypher, ed., *Letters of Letitia Landon* (Delmar NJ 2001) 72.

unemployment. Also specific to the decade was the marriage of literary text and engraved image. With copper engraving, 4,000 impressions was usually the maximum before the plates became too worn, a figure not out of line with the edition sizes of the printed books.[65] By the 1830s, however, with the development of woodcut and steel engraving from which many more impressions could be taken, the makers of plates could supply publishers with tens of thousands of more copies of engraved works of art at falling prices. The result of this technological, economic, and intellectual property conjuncture was that in the annuals of the 1830s, the engravings originally made to illustrate the masculine romances of Scott, Byron, and Moore were recycled to illustrate the newly composed bland, tearful, often simpering, romance intended for ladies.

How, if at all, were these books actually read? Men mostly despised them. As the author of the satire, *The Age Reviewed*, sneered in 1828:

> Sweet Album hail! – morocco, green or jet
> The puny minstrel's scrawl-devouring pet;
> Well-pawed preserver of pellucid trash,
> On thy smooth leaves, what tinkling phrenzies flash!
> Or thumb'd by blues or filled by Lady Lamb
> A rhyme-stuffed bundle of pedantic sham.[66]

There are however also plenty of approving examples in the historical record.[67] Clarissa Trant, a conventional lady, was worried that the description of feelings in her 1837 *Keepsake* was 'too glowing for public exhibition'.[68] Charlotte Brontë, starved of pictures of any kind in Haworth, treasured a few annuals, copying out the pictures, including a portrait of Byron.[69] There are also many examples in fiction.[70] Becky Sharp in Thackeray's *Vanity Fair* has a lavish supply of annuals in her drawing room in Mayfair, all given by admirers.[71] When Ned Plymdale comes to court Rosie in *Middlemarch* he brings the latest *Keepsake*, sure he has found a winner.[72] When Lydgate arrives, he defends himself against his contempt. 'There are a great

---

[65] Geoffrey Wakeman, *Victorian Book Illustrations* (1973) 33.

[66] Robert Montgomery [attrib.] *The Age Reviewed* (second edition 1828) 127.

[67] Many usefully collected by Cruse, *Englishman* 276.   [68] Quoted by Cruse, *Englishman* 282.

[69] See Christine Alexander and Jane Sellars, *The Art of the Brontës* (Cambridge 1995) to which I conrtibuted some identifications.

[70] For the distinctiveness of fictional records see chapter 20.

[71] William Makepeace Thackeray, *Vanity Fair*, edited by Geoffrey and Kathleen Tillotson (1963) 527. When the crash comes and the bailiffs arrive, her maid makes off with six *Keepsakes* and *Books of Beauty*.

[72] George Eliot, *Middlemarch*, edited by David Carroll (Oxford 1986) 263.

many celebrated people writing in the *Keepsake* . . . This is the first time I have heard it called silly.'[73]

One of the most illuminating imagined descriptions of women's reading in the romantic period is in Eliot's *The Mill on the Floss*. Maggie Tulliver was disgusted with the books she was given at school, and when she tried Tom's school books for boys, they were only a little better.

The days of chivalry are not gone . . . Bob . . . had as respectful adoration for this dark-eyed maiden as if he had been a knight in armour calling aloud her name . . . Sometimes Maggie thought she could have been contented with absorbing fancies: if she could have all Scott's novels and Byron's poems! then perhaps she might have found happiness enough to dull her sensibility to her actual daily life. And yet . . . they were hardly what she wanted. She could make dream-worlds of her own, but no dream world would satisfy her now . . . She wanted some key that would enable her to understand, and in understanding, endure, the heavy weight that had fallen on her young heart . . . If she had been taught 'real learning and wisdom such as great men knew', she thought she should have held the secrets of life; if she had only books that she might learn for herself what wise men knew! [74]

Bob, knowing of her longing for books, has been to the bookstall, and has bought a collection, selected by the bookseller, which he brings as a gift, tied in a red handkerchief. In the course of the chapter the titles of these books are mentioned: a superannuated *Keepsake*, some *Portrait Galleries*, *Beauties of the Spectator*, Johnson's *Rasselas*, *The Economy of Human Life*, Gregory's *Letters* (two conduct books), Keble's *Christian Year*, and Thomas à Kempis, a roll-call of the books regarded as most suitable for women's reading.[75]

During the long wars from 1793 to 1815 British navies and armies were deployed to many places round the globe. The war was fought on the continent of Europe, in the Mediterranean, in the East and West Indies, and in the Far East, and the effects were felt in areas far beyond the fighting. Military men on reconnaissance, naval men on patrol, scientific explorers, industrial exporters, travelling gentlemen, and Christian missionaries penetrated to ever more remote, previously unvisited, lands, bringing home shiploads of art and antiquities, plant and animal specimens, and diaries

---

[73] *Ibid.* 265.

[74] George Eliot, *The Mill on the Floss*, edited by A. S. Byatt (1979) 378.

[75] *Ibid.* 382 and 681. The allusion is probably to John Gregory's *Father's Legacy* (I suggest Byatt is mistaken in reading this as a reference to the letters of Pope Gregory). For the large sales of Gregory see appendix 9. Byatt has also failed to recognise Dodsley's *Oeconomy of Human Life*, another conduct book which was produced in vast numbers over many decades in the eighteenth and nineteenth centuries.

which told of their adventures and their discoveries. During the romantic period, besides the literary writing in verse and prose, there was a rapid expansion of new writing on foreign travel, voyages, exploration, politics, military history, customs of the people, and the whole field of what is now anthropology. Month after month new books poured from the presses, on France, Italy, Germany, Spain, Russia, India, Egypt, Ottoman Turkey, Africa, China, and there seemed no limit to the number of books which could be successfully published. In 1800, for example, a British traveller about to go to Greece would normally have relied on Wheler's *Description of a Journey into Greece*, first published in 1682 and never reprinted. By 1820 another twenty or thirty books and translations had appeared, many full of careful observation and excellent research, and the number was continuing to grow.[76]

Romantic poetry and modern travel writing went together. John Cam Hobhouse, for example, who accompanied Byron to Albania and Greece, wrote a long detailed prose travel book which serves as a counterpoint to *Childe Harold's Pilgrimage, A Romaunt.*[77] Later he wrote a prose book about Italy to accompany *Childe Harold's Pilgrimage, Canto the Fourth.* But the marriage usually took place within the sheets of the books. In prose notes, the writers of verse romances acknowledged their debts to the prose writers who, unlike themselves, had actually experienced the storms at sea, the heat of the desert, the shade of the palms, the frozen seas, and who had observed with their own eyes the mosques, the pagodas, the fierce animals, and the strange customs of the exotic east. Quotations and learned historical and geographical notes were as much part of the book as the verse.

By the 1820s there was scarcely a place in the world, however remote, which had not recently had a book written about it – Iceland, Lapland, the Crimea, Afghanistan, Korea, Tonga, description, history, adventures, antiquities. The print runs were short, often only 500 copies in expensive quarto, but the books were widely noticed in the literary reviews.[78] For each man who participated directly in this new age of war and exploration, there was now a constituency at home who followed the story of every new discovery. During the romantic period, in both their verse and in their prose reading, the reading elites of Britain, both men and women, took all geography and all history into their consciousness. They appropriated the whole civilised and uncivilised world, and all past and present time, recorded and unrecorded. There was no territory too remote or too barren,

---

[76] See William St Clair, *Lord Elgin and the Marbles* (third edition Oxford 1998) bibliography.
[77] Noted in appendix 9, 608: 'John Cam Hobhouse'.
[78] Examples in table 7. For travel books in the book clubs see chapter 13.

no period of the past too obscure, but it was of interest to the travellers, the historians, the archaeologists, the poets, and the readers of Great Britain. There was nothing in the world which the British did not feel was partly their own.

What could not have been foreseen at the time of the various changes in the intellectual property regime, was that the large and widening price differential between the newly published romantic literature and the old canon should coincide so exactly with the cultural differential. Among the expensive new authors there were many locally English, rural, religious poets, Crabbe, Wordsworth, Clare, and the majority of the scarcely read others. On the cheap side of the price divide, however, there was no corresponding symmetry. At the time when Great Britain was rapidly becoming the most urbanised, most industrialised, and most international and imperial nation that had hitherto existed, the imaginations of one part of the reading nation flew with Byron, Scott, Moore, and their imitators to the ruins of Greece and Rome, to the wild and lawless Scottish Highlands, to Arabia, Persia, and India. They marched to the crusades, charged with their lances at gorgeous medieval tournaments, and relived episode after episode in the violent history of every nation of Europe. But most readers lived in another past, making an occasional voyage with *Robinson Crusoe* and Falconer's *Shipwreck*, but mainly staying at home with Thomson, Young, and Cowper, *Elegant Extracts*, Enfield's *Speaker*, Murray's *Reader*, *The Spectator*, *The Vicar of Wakefield*, and *Meditations among the Tombs*.

CHAPTER 13

Reading constituencies

Since books can be read and reread by many people over long periods, statistics of titles of books printed or sold cannot be adequate surrogates for numbers of acts of reading. If we are to recover the history of reading, we need to develop an understanding of how many persons may have read each copy, a multiplier that is unlikely to be constant from title to title. The *Edinburgh Review* believed that the average multiplier for a new title in the romantic period was about one to four.[1] The households the writer probably had in mind were typically a gentleman, his wife, and sons and daughters, and often included unmarried sisters, widowed sisters, and governesses who might be present as books were read aloud, besides servants who might have some access. An average multiplier of four might imply a wide range.

Since, if a book was bought for a library, the multiplier could be much larger, any attempt to estimate readerships must give them particular attention. Since libraries differed widely in their economic and social characteristics, in the type of texts they made available, and in the constituencies they served, they need to be considered separately. From the names alone, 'circulating libraries', 'proprietary libraries', 'subscription libraries', 'public libraries', 'book societies', 'reading societies', 'book clubs', 'literary societies', and others, it is not possible to categorise them.[2] 'Public libraries'

---

[1] See appendix 5.

[2] Some statistics in appendix 11, but these are incomplete. Kaufman is still useful for his archival work. The Bodleian has a collection of circulating library labels, together with a card index of notes by the bibliographer A. N. L. Munby. Although the representative quality of this collection cannot be assumed, when taken with other evidence about the earlier period, it tends to confirm not only that the first surge was reversed, but was followed by another much stronger surge after the 1750s. The Library History Database compiled by Robin Alston, and available free online, lists over 3,000 libraries of all types founded between 1700 and 1799. Statistics of start-ups, or of references to circulating libraries having existed, which do not take account of the libraries which went out of business or were taken over by new owners under different names, do not, however, yet enable a quantified estimate to be made of the net growth.

were only public in the sense that they were open to all customers able and willing to pay.

Under various statutes, the British Museum in London, and a changing list of university and other libraries in England, Scotland, and Ireland, were entitled to claim one copy of every book published. This levy was intended to preserve the nation's scholarly and scientific texts for the use of professionals and researchers, but it was not universally applied. At Cambridge, for example, well into the nineteenth century, the librarians were under standing instructions to exclude all novels, unless an exception was authorised. One such exception was *The Antiquary* (1815), the third of the Waverley novels, another example of the immediate and pervasive influence of Scott. Until mid-Victorian times, although one of the duties of the Stationers' Company was to prepare lists of recent publications from which the copyright libraries could make their claims, the industry seldom cooperated wholeheartedly. Only those books which had been entered in the Stationers' Register could be demanded, and after a 1768 decision that registration was not necessary to secure copyright, most titles were not registered.[3] In 1803 and 1804, of nearly 800 books published in London, the Cambridge University Library obtained fewer than fifty.[4] Among the books offered but not accepted, from 1814 to 1817, were [Austen's] *Emma*, [Byron's] *The Siege of Corinth*, [Peacock's] *Headlong Hall*, Shelley's *Alastor*, and Wordsworth's *Thanksgiving Ode*.[5] During its whole period of entitlement between 1710 and 1836, the University of St Andrews received fewer than 20,000 titles.[6]

In the eighteenth century, Edward Gibbon complained that 'for the want of a good public library, he was often obliged to send for books from abroad; sometimes large and expensive works, in order to verify a single citation'.[7] Adam Smith, in Edinburgh, made an arrangement for the bookseller to buy back the books as soon as he had read them.[8] In the romantic period things were little better. As the author of a guide to London complained in 1804, 'It is a disgrace to the metropolis that it contains no Public

[3] In 1768 a court upheld a copyright although the title had not been entered in the register. Timperley 718. That registration was optional was confirmed in another ruling in 1798. Timperley 798.
[4] Basil Montagu, *Enquiries and Observations respecting the University Library* (Cambridge 1805) 11, with a list which shows a number of novels.
[5] Listed in appendix to *Select Committee*. A copy of Byron's *Mazeppa* (1819) Ac, belonging to the 'Brasen Nose College Book Club, Oxford', suggests that literary works were not then regarded as suitable for college libraries.
[6] D. W. Doughty, *The Tullis Press, Cupar 1803–1849* (Dundee 1967) 10.   [7] Quoted by Minto 50.
[8] The Bell and Bradfute archives show Smith obtaining Burney's *History of Music* on these terms. Unfortunately the archives only cover the last years of Smith's life.

Subscription Library, on a liberal and extensive plan, similar to those which exist at Liverpool, Bristol, Birmingham, and other places . . . Those paltry establishments which now assume the name of Public Libraries . . . are wretchedly contemptible, and unworthy even of the small degree of patronage which they meet with.'[9] Visitors from abroad too were amazed that Great Britain, rich in so many respects, was so neglectful. As Augustus Gottlieb Goede noted, 'It will scarcely appear credible, that there does not exist in the United Kingdom a single public library, stored with the most important works in the various departments of literature.'[10]

Cathedral libraries held a range of books which were available free, or for a small fee, to those who could secure an introduction – Coleridge used the Cathedral Library at Carlisle – but a survey of the holdings and borrowing records reveals modest holdings, a preponderance of older texts, scarcely any imaginative literature, and low borrowing rates.[11] Some noblemen and gentlemen allowed their private libraries to be used but access was difficult even for the favoured few. The Dissenters, who were excluded from the English universities, had their own libraries, as did various professional and learned societies. On the whole, however, scholarly libraries were, as Thomas Campbell said of angels' visits, few and far between.

For some types of books, readers could turn to the commercial renting sector. By 1801, there were believed to be about 1,000 circulating libraries in Great Britain, often attached to bookshops so that customers had the choice between buying and renting, and their numbers had grown to about 1,500 in 1821, with many more established later. In London a few catered for the wealthy, with prices to match.[12] The best known, and probably the largest, the Minerva, had tens of thousands of volumes, constantly changing, and offered to set up new circulating libraries anywhere in the country on any scale between 100 and 10,000 volumes. In Norwich, between 1800 and 1824, there are references to about twenty, but some were small and there was a rapid turnover.[13] To judge from surviving catalogues, a typical circulating library in 1820 carried a few thousand books for a membership of about seventy, but there was a wide range.[14] Mrs Crew's Library in Liverpool had only about 1,000 volumes, the Knaresborough only 300.[15]

---

[9] Quoted by Kaufman 18 from Feltham's *Picture of London* (1804).
[10] Augustus Gottlieb Goede, *Memorials of Nature and Art Collected on a Journey in Great Britain during the Years 1802 and 1803* (1808) iii, 36.
[11] Kaufman 76.   [12] Examples in appendix 10.
[13] *Monthly Magazine*, April 1801; Stewart-Murphy 15.
[14] The estimate of the traveller, *Monthly Magazine*, June 1821.   [15] John Johnson.

Figure 10. 'The Library'. Coloured aquatint by Ackermann, 1813.

Commercial borrowing of books was well established by the seventeenth century. 'If any Gentlemen repair to my House aforesaid', declares an advertisement in a playbook printed in 1661, 'they may be furnished with all manner of English or French Histories, Romances, or Poetry, which are sold, or read, for reasonable considerations.'[16] 'All sorts of Histories to buy, or let out to read by the week', proclaims an advertisement of 1674. The hero of *The English Rogue* (1668) declares 'I likewise hired several books of a stationer, for which I gave him so much a week – These being chiefly knight-errantry and romances, I took much pleasure therein.'[17] From the seventeenth century, coffee shops as well as bookshops seem frequently to have carried books and newspapers for their customers to borrow and read on and off the premises. In 1694, for example, we hear that 'the Coffee-man against Cree-Church in Leaden-Hall Street keeps a Library in his Coffee-Room for his Customers to read'.[18] By early in the high monopoly period, however, a change had occurred. In 1725 when Benjamin Franklin lived in London, there were no book-renting facilities of any kind.[19] In Lichfield where Samuel Johnson's father was a bookseller, there is no trace of a lending library.[20] As the London publishers admitted to a parliamentary inquiry in 1818, their predecessors had tried to prevent bookshops and coffee shops from renting books off the premises.[21] In 1742, they protested at 'the scandalous and Low Custom that has lately prevail'd among those who keep *Coffee-Houses*, of buying one of any new Book . . . and lending it by Turns to such Gentlemen to read as frequent their Coffee-House'.[22]

At some time not long after that date, the London book industry suddenly reversed its policy. During the later eighteenth century we have records of circulating libraries being successfully started in many cities and towns all over Great Britain and, to a lesser extent, in Ireland and in the American and other overseas settlements, with the full cooperation of the

[16] Quoted by Hilda Hamlyn, 'Eighteenth Century Circulating Libraries' in *The Library*, 1946/47. The play, *The Thracian Wonder*, is not by Webster and Rowley as was then thought. Other references to early borrowing in Kaufman 188.

[17] Quoted by Stewart-Murphy.   [18] Quoted by Kaufman 115.

[19] Of six booksellers in a corner of the City of London in 1748, none is known to have offered renting facilities. Kaufman, 'Community Library' 10. The first circulating library in London was thought to have been Wright's, founded in 1740. By 1770 there were thought to be still only four in London and the immediate neighbourhood. Timperley 664, 771.

[20] Paul Kaufman, 'Reading in Eighteenth Century Lichfield' in *The Library*, 1973.

[21] Lackington says that the London booksellers took the view that circulating libraries, would damage sales, Lackington 262. See also Knight, *Old Printer*, 229 and the London publishers' evidence in *Select Committee*. This shift was particularly damaging to readers of plays, including Shakespeare plays. Indeed it may have been the very success of Francis Kirkman's playtext-renting business which brought about the reversal.

[22] Quoted by Kaufman 116.

London publishers.[23] Contrary to what has often been assumed in narratives about 'the growth of the reading public', there was no steady growth of circulating libraries during the eighteenth century. The pattern is of some commercial renting in the seventeenth century, a successful attempt to reverse its growth, and then, a generation later, a sharp change in policy followed by a boom.

Why did the change occur when it did? The London industry may have decided to follow the success of lending libraries in Germany. Part of the explanation may be, however, that the industry solved the problem of how to prevent the growth of an effective second-hand market. If there had been a free market after the books from libraries had completed their initial circulation, the library owners might have wanted to sell them off. I cannot, however, find any references to reading from second-hand circulating library copies in the historical record. Some ex-circulating copies have survived from the romantic period, but only a tiny number of Minerva Press books.[24] It is sometimes suggested that such books were so badly damaged by the time they had done their rounds that they had no financial value and were thrown away. However, such books had strong leather-backed bindings designed for heavy usage, and are far less likely to have fallen to pieces than many other books which have survived in large numbers. At a time when a single volume of one new novel would have cost more than a week's income for most of the population, when the print runs were seldom above 500, and when there was a market even for single, damaged, and incomplete books of other kinds, it is hard to believe that second-hand copies of new novels would have had no value.[25]

What we may be seeing are the results of restraints on resale, a restrictive trade practice, whereby the producers make it a condition of giving trade discounts that the goods must be sold back in part exchange or that they should not be resold until after a certain period of time has passed. I

[23] Surviving catalogues often quote the price of a book for sale as well as the title and shelf reference number for borrowing.

[24] Of novels known to have been published between 1770 and 1799, about 10 per cent are entirely lost, and many others exist only in single copies. See Raven in Garside, Raven, and Schöwerling i, 20. Many are only known from the collection in Corvey in Germany where a noble family bought English novels as they were published.

[25] The catalogues of Hodgsons, a wholesale book dealer, held in the British Library, show sales of circulating library stocks but mainly, it would appear, from firms going out of business, and unsold publishers' stocks put on the market some time after publication when regular sales had dried up. The printed catalogues of Lackington show no evidence of a turnover in discarded circulating library copies.

know of no documentary evidence for the existence of this business practice in the romantic period, but it is plentiful for the Victorian. Mudie's Select Library, founded in 1842 and 50 per cent owned by a consortium of London publishers, by monopolising the novel-renting market for the rest of the century, decisively influenced the conditions in which new English novels were written, the textual limits, the degree of access, and the social composition of readerships. Mudie's practice was to sell off a selection of circulated books, after an interval, at prices which were always kept high enough to avoid undermining the price of one volume reprints which in Victorian times followed three deckers, after an interval. Other novels were sent to be shredded and spread on the fields along with the 'night soil' of the cities, a fitting end, many believed, for such filth. But Mudie kept most of the books which had done their rounds in huge 'catacombs' for decades or longer. It was, the historian of Mudies has suggested, the sheer impossibility of storage which led to the firm's eventual collapse.[26]

Whatever the resale conditions in the romantic period, if they existed, the circulating libraries should be regarded as an emanation of the high monopoly period, not as an exception. Their sudden growth preceded 1774, and although they contributed to the growth of reading by widening the amount of reading among the upper-income groups, they did little to deepen it down the socio-economic scale. Although, in England, commercial circulating libraries were the main source of reading for nearly a century, membership never widened beyond the aristocratic, professional, and business classes. Although they maintained a nationwide network, they never reached more than about 1 per cent of the population.[27] It was only when the commercial market had manifestly failed to raise educational standards that parliament was persuaded to set up free public libraries.[28]

In Scotland, with its good primary education, local libraries open to the public free of charge were occasionally to be found; circulating libraries seem to have been less directly under the control of the publishers; and there are examples of libraries which rented cheaper, usually old-canon books, to a socially diverse membership. William Chambers, the founder

---

[26] Griest 31.
[27] See Nicholas Hiley, "'Can't you find me something nasty?' Circulating Libraries and Literary Censorship in Britain from the 1890s to the 1910s' in Myers and Harris, *Spreading* 125.
[28] Among the few surviving lists, I have examined the unpublished subscription book of Wright's Royal Colonnade Library, Brighton, that begins in 1821, Brighton Public Library. See also the fictitious list in Austen's *Sanditon*. For the reasons for establishing free public libraries, see Minto.

of a publishing house dedicated to bringing cheaper books to wider readerships, remembered his boyhood in Peebles, in the Scottish borders, in the
first years of the nineteenth century. At that time, apart from three or four
newspapers which were passed from hand to hand until they crumbled,
there were scarcely any books other than chapbooks. A copy of *The Works
of Josephus* (1720) was read aloud, instalment by instalment, house to house,
every year.

'Weel, Tam, what's the news the nicht?' would old Geordie Murray say, as Tam
entered with his Josephus under his arm, and seated himself at the family fireside.
'Bad news, bad news', replied Tam, 'Titus has begun to besiege Jerusalem.'

When, in about 1800, a local farmer started a bookshop and circulating
library in the shed where he kept his cows, the main stock was Bibles, catechisms, and chapbooks, but Chambers 'read a considerable number of the
classics of English literature, or heard our father read them'. He mentions
Gulliver's Travels, Don Quixote, Peregrine Pickle, Pope, and Goldsmith, all
older titles books that had recently fallen in price.[29] But such arrangements
were exceptional even in Scotland. Walter Scott told his publisher in 1816
that in the Scottish borders there were many lairds with handsome homes
and expensive carriages, but he doubted whether any of them spent ten
pounds (200 shillings) a year on books, apart from a subscription to a
circulating library.[30]

From the 1750s until late-Victorian times when circulating libraries flourished, almost every writer who mentioned them made two comments – that
women, especially impressionable young ladies, were their main customers,
and that they only supplied sensational modern novels. Neither claim is
fully borne out by the surviving records. The few membership lists so far
found suggest that, in England, membership was divided roughly half and
half between men and women, sometimes with members of the same family
having separate memberships, but books taken home by members could,
of course, be read by others in the family.[31] According to Clara Reeve,
herself a novelist, writing in 1785, women read novels and romances more
than men.[32] Lackington, the remainder bookseller, thought the same.[33] The

[29] Chambers 52.   [30] Lockhart, quoted by Altick 268.
[31] An example from Bath in Kaufman 227. The same pattern can be seen in the subscription book
   of Wright's Royal Colonnade Library, Brighton, although that too, as a subscription library for
   visiting royalty, aristocracy, and the fashionable, may be untypical. For the mid-eighteenth century,
   see Jan Fergus, 'Women Readers: a Case Study' in Vivian Jones, ed., *Women and Literature in Britain
   1700–1800* (Cambridge 2000) 155. Fergus uses the Timothy Stevens archives and also those of Samuel
   Clay's Circulating Library described in her article in *Papers of the Bibliographical Society of America*,
   1984.
[32] [Clara Reeve] *The Progress of Romance . . . by C. R.* (1785).   [33] Lackington 266.

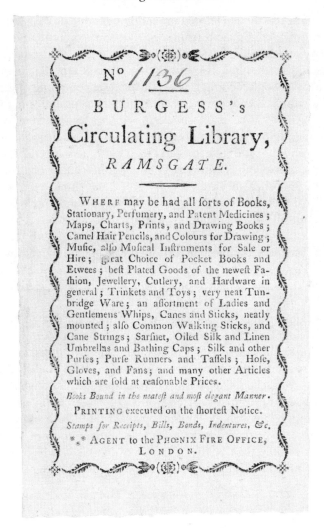

Figure 11. A label of Burgess's Circulating Library, Ramsgate. Pasted in a copy of *Letters of Abelard and Heloise* (1785).

fact that women were able to become members was itself an innovation. As Fanny Price, a character in Austen's *Mansfield Park*, noted, she was 'amazed at being anything *in propria re* [in her own right], amazed at her own doings in every way; to be a renter, a chuser of books!'[34]

[34] Jane Austen, *Mansfield Park*, edited by R. W. Chapman (1923) 398.

Circulating libraries were predominantly feminine in the nature of the texts they provided. By the romantic period, books other than novels may have been as much as half the total holdings, but only in the larger libraries.[35] The business of most English circulating libraries was not to provide a comprehensive book-lending facility for the local community, but to rent out the latest novels and romances when they first appeared, and to replace them frequently.[36] The main circulating-library owners were also book publishers, and from the beginning the close interdependence between the producing and the renting sectors and their customers affected the texts.[37] During the 1790s, Lane's Minerva Press published about one-third of all the novels published in London.[38] By 1791 Lane employed a workforce of thirty and had four printing presses. In the romantic period, as many as a third of all novels, including the first published novel by Austen, claimed to have been written 'by a Lady'.[39] Most were formulaic gothic 'German' romances, produced in editions of 500 or 750 and never reprinted. 'Minerva Press' novel became a common term to describe a particular type of light society romance or thriller, much condemned in conduct literature.[40]

In the eighteenth century, novels were normally published in as many volumes as it took to print the text in comfortable reading size, Richardson's *Clarissa*, for example, being first published in nine volumes. By the middle of the romantic period, however, most novels were published in three volumes, 'three deckers' like Nelson's battleships, even although this meant that some had to be printed with few words to the line, few lines to the page, and few pages to the volume, and others padded out with short stories to make them fit the required format.[41] It was common to print more copies of the first volume than of the others, knowing that readers who rented the first volume might not bother with the second. We see the producers

---

[35] Some proportions of actual holdings in Paul Kaufman 'The Community Library, A Chapter in English Social History' in *Proceedings of the American Philosophical Society*, 1967.

[36] See also Knight, *Passages* i, 278.

[37] From the 1770s title pages of novels commonly declare that the book had been 'printed for [Bell, Jones, Lowndes, Noble, Vernor, Hall, Cawthorn, &] at his circulating library'. Many examples of this formulation are given in Garside, Raven, and Schöwerling. William Lane, owner of the Minerva Press, also manufactured his books on the premises in his own print shop, so making himself even more independent of his colleagues.

[38] Raven in Garside, Raven, and Schöwerling i, 79.

[39] *Ibid.* 42. See Austen *Sense and Sensibility* and the changes in the way in which Austen was referred to in appendix 9, 578.

[40] See chapter 14.

[41] For the case of *Frankenstein*, see chapter 18. Other examples are given in Garside, Raven, and Schöwerling.

trying to commodify the texts textually as well as materially by implying that they were broadly similar, within quite narrow limits, both in subject matter and in the ideologies they advocated.

With print runs short, and over a thousand circulating libraries, we cannot assume, at least, until the 1830s, that holdings were much the same round the country. Nor can we assume that, even in London, Edinburgh, and the larger towns, there was easy access to the novels of the writers of the time who are now best known, even when customers knew the names to ask for. In the case of Austen, for example, a census of surviving copies suggests that, from the early editions, about half the copies were bought by members of the titled classes and gentry of the kind she wrote about, the others probably going to circulating libraries.[42] Hazlitt, who wrote and lectured professionally on contemporary literature, never mentions any book by Austen.

After 1814, what subscribers to circulating libraries read most were Waverley novels. After the runaway success of *Waverley*, the sales of prose romances by 'the author of Waverley' were enormous.[43] At the height of the boom, which lasted for nearly ten years, the initial print runs for each new title, extremely expensive though they were, rose to about 10,000 copies, more than most authors sold in a lifetime. When a ship bringing the first copies of the latest Waverley novel from Edinburgh docked in London, the books would be distributed by noon the next day, even breaking the rules against working on the Sabbath. Scott's publisher Constable, who came from Edinburgh on board the ship bringing *The Fortunes of Nigel*, told Scott that he saw men chuckling in the streets of London.[44] Macaulay, then a student at Cambridge, tells how he used to walk out along the London road to meet the coach that was bringing the first copies of the next Waverley novel.[45] Some London circulating libraries, it was said in 1826, were 'obliged to have from fifty to seventy copies of each novel when it comes out'.[46] The demand for borrowing so outran supply that we hear of circulating libraries splitting volumes in half, to make six volumes per title instead of three.[47] Shops which never previously handled books went into commercial book lending exclusively to hire out Waverley

---

[42] In Gilson.   [43] See 'Sir Walter Scott', appendix 9, 638.
[44] Quotation in appendix 6, 638.   [45] Cruse, *Englishman* 230.
[46] *Rejected Articles* (second edition 1826) 201. The anonymous author, to judge from the detail in his appreciative parody of Hazlitt, was a literary insider.
[47] [James Thin] *Reminiscences of Booksellers and Bookselling in Edinburgh in the Time of William IV. An Address to a Meeting of Booksellers' Assistants* (privately printed, Edinburgh 1905).

novels. Not every reader who handled a volume, we can be sure, read it through or went on to the next volume, but few men and women who read any new books at all did not read Waverley novels at least in part, and many read every title as it came out. It was a publishers' joke that a man had been discovered at a London party who had not read the Scotch novels.[48]

The larger the sales, the record shows, the more frequently a book was also rented. The bigger the sales, therefore, the bigger the multiplier needed to convert to readership. This is such a strong pattern that we can use it as a model. We can, for example, take the information on print runs for individual literary authors, and estimate both absolute levels of reading and the relativities between different texts.[49] The predominance of Scott and Byron over all the other modern literary authors turns out to be many times greater than we might have estimated from the production and sales figures, huge though these are.

Another response was for a group of friends or colleagues to form a cir-culating library of their own, buying the books and passing them round to be read in turn.[50] The first reading society of this kind in England was believed to have been formed by the Dissenters of Leicester in about 1740, and the Dissenters were prominent in many other societies founded later.[51] The tradition was older in Scotland and much of the impetus for establish-ing reading societies in northern England, and perhaps in London, appears to have come from expatriate Scots.[52] Like circulating libraries, reading societies predated the abolition of perpetual copyright in 1774, and should be regarded as an intrinsic part of a high-price regime not as a departure from it.

In many provincial cities, the founders intended, from the first, to establish a permanent library, with an increasing membership. Elsewhere, book clubs with a small self-electing membership of between a dozen and two dozen individuals, bought a succession of new books to be read by each member and then disposed of. Like circulating libraries, subscription libraries and books clubs, 'reading societies', were an innovation introduced

---

[48] James Grant, *The Great Metropolis* (1837) i, 134.   [49] Some figures in appendices 5 and 6.

[50] For example a copy of Cesare, Marchese de Beccaria's *Essay on Crimes and Punishments* (1785) contains an inserted manuscript list of the names of the twenty-one members of 'Innes's Circulating Library' who passed the book to the next member on the list every eight days. Ac.

[51] The opinion of the traveller, *Monthly Magazine*, June 1821. The members of the first reading society included Dr Pulteney and Reverend Mr Aikin, father of Dr Aikin and Mrs Barbauld.

[52] See, for example, the notes on the Bolton Caledonian Book Club in appendix 10, 669.

at a specific historical moment. Like the circulating libraries, they enjoyed discounts and may have been subject to resale conditions.[53] But in their aims, in their financing, in their membership, and in the nature of the books which they bought, they were very different. The members, instead of paying to read texts selected by others, themselves chose what to read. In the case of reading societies which accumulated their books, the members owned a valuable growing resource, and their shares could usually be sold or inherited subject to pre-emption provisions. In book clubs, the books which had done their rounds were sometimes sold back to the club's bookseller, adding the receipts to their revolving capital fund for purchases, but whether the booksellers kept them off the market is not known. In other book clubs, the member who proposed the book was obliged to buy it at half the purchase price, or the books were sold to members at special auctions. In the Bedale, it was decided in 1817 that every member should pay 10s 6d (10.5 shillings) and take all the books he had ordered at a quarter of the price.[54] As with circulating libraries, all these provisions had the effect of widening the amount of reading among the upper social groups, but they did little to deepen it downwards.

The 1790s saw an upsurge of new reading societies all over Great Britain and elsewhere in the English-speaking world, but as the dates of foundation show, the trend had started some years before and cannot be directly related to anxieties about the implications of the French Revolution. By 1800, besides many in London, reading societies had been established in all major and many minor towns in Yorkshire and, in a separate diffusionary wave, across the Pennines in Lancashire and the north-west of England. In the south of England the surge came later, independently of what was happening in the north. Most clubs were locally based, the Cheadle Book Society, the Clapham Book Society, the Newmarket Book Society, the Ovingham Book Society, the South Shields Subscription Library, the Thaxted Book Society. Their printed labels proudly proclaim the date of foundation, the year when serious modern reading reached their town: 'The Chichester Library Society Established 1794', 'The Kenilworth Book Club, 1795', 'The Masham Book Society, Established 9 August 1814', 'The Guthlaxton Book

---

[53] As late as 1794 we find the Liverpool book retailers complaining about the discounts given to the Liverpool Athenaeum. See the letters quoted in Besterman 142–4. A letter of 1812 from Gale and Curtis, booksellers to the Eclectic Book Society, announces that, 'in consequence of certain regulations adopted by the trade', they could no longer sell at the trade price. Instead they would give 12.5 per cent if settled half yearly and 15 per cent if settled quarterly. Eclectic Society Minute Book, Guildhall Library, London, mss. 988A.

[54] *The Diary of Benjamin Newton, Rector of Wath, 1816–1818*, edited by C. P. Ferdall and E. A. Crutchley (Cambridge 1933).

Figure 12. Printed bookplate of Worcester Library. In *The Exodiad* (1808).

Society, Instituted September 1822'. Some appear to be named after their founder or their bookseller, for example 'Mr Ridge's Book Society'. The St Thomas's Southwark Book Society was probably connected with the London hospital. 'The New Vizagapatam Book Club' sounds like a group of friends who had been in India or one operating among the expatriate British community there.

The aims were grand and defiantly non-commercial. 'Here we are humanized without suffering', declared the Gentlemen's Library at Wigton in 1806, with only a touch of irony, 'acquire a fine polish without travelling; and without the trouble of study, imbibe the most pleasing, most useful lessons.'[55] The Greenock Society had formed their library, the members bluntly declared, 'to save themselves the expense of purchasing many books, and to avert the fatal effects which are sometimes occasioned by circulating libraries'.[56] The gentlemen who founded the Lewes Literary Society in 1786, were 'disgusted at the usual trash of the circulating libraries'.[57] Within eight years the membership had grown to sixty, including eleven women. In 1794, apparently unaware that Lewes was far from the first, the members of the society wrote a letter to the *Gentleman's Magazine* recommending other towns to follow their example.[58]

Some societies deliberately kept themselves expensive, small, and exclusive. Others, often set up later and in opposition, kept the entry fees and subscriptions low, welcomed a growing membership, and opened their premises to the local community. Thomas Cooper, a shoemaker in Gainsborough in Lincolnshire, secretly paid the bookseller to be allowed to read the books of the local book club when they were not out to members.[59] In England, however, there does not appear to have been much dissemination down the income scale. The terms of membership were simply too expensive even if there had been no other barriers and biases. The penalties for holding up a book beyond the allowed date were very high.[60] Failing to write in the date in ink, or allowing a book to be damaged, could incur a heavy fine.[61] The books were jealously guarded, every smudge, burn, and candlewax blot carefully recorded and charged for. The worst sin was to lend the book outside the membership. The Minchinhampton, for example, levied a fine of 10s 6d (10.5 shillings), the Oswestry, 10 shillings. 'Any subscriber lending a Book', declares the label of an unknown book society, 'will be charged D O U B L E their original subscription', implying a fine of at least two guineas (42 shillings).[62] The staff too were tightly bound by the financial regime. In the Halifax Subscription Library, however, the librarian

---

[55] Quoted by Kaufman 159, from a contemporary catalogue.

[56] Quoted by Frank Beckwith 'The Eighteenth-Century Proprietary Library in England' in *Journal of Documentation* (1947) 89, from the *Statistical Account of Scotland*.

[57] In the introduction to the long celebratory poem, John Button, *The Lewes Literary Society* (1804).

[58] *Gentleman's Magazine*, January 1794.

[59] See *The Life of Thomas Cooper Written by Himself* (1869), which contains a great deal of information about his reading at all stages of his life.

[60] For example, the Biggleswade Book Society charged sixpence (0.5 shillings) for each day a book was retained beyond the time allowed. Label in Bodleian copy of [Byron's] *Letter to **** *****) (1821) Dunstan B421.

[61] For example, 5 shillings at the Minchinhampton Reading Society.   [62] John Johnson.

was liable to a fine of 10s 6d if he lent a book out of hours. Since his salary was only £9 (180 shillings) a year that was a substantial deterrent, but at least one subscriber successfully bribed him. The Clapham took no risks, every book had to be returned to the Reverend Mr Sharpe 'by whom it will be forwarded to other members in succession to prevent the loss and detention of books'.[63]

The city subscription libraries typically had several hundred members and the smaller towns a hundred or so. In Liverpool in 1760 the members were mainly businessmen: a silk merchant, a pipe merchant, a sugar merchant, an iron merchant, forty-seven who called themselves simply merchants, brewers, drapers, a hosier, a chandler, a grocer, a sail maker, a rope maker, a cooper, a cabinet maker, a painter, a druggist, a mercer, six surgeons, two doctors, four attorneys, a customs officer, a teacher, a schoolmaster, a lady innkeeper, an esquire, four gentlemen and only two clergymen. The same social pattern, and almost total absence of women, is to be found in the other lists that have been found. Many of the members of such institutions were probably the first generation in their families to have had regular access to newly published books, new entrants to the reading nation who had probably read nothing except old-canon authors and school books before they joined.

English book clubs appear usually to have had from a dozen to two dozen members. On the lists of the country clubs it is common to see the names of 'Sir George' this or 'Lady' that. Clergymen were among the most common members, often several in one club. The Woodstock Book Club included amongst its twenty members the Duke of Marlborough, the Earl of Normanton, two titled ladies, and other members of the nobility.[64] The Hay Book Club had twenty-five members, including one viscount, six clergymen, and one colonel.[65] The Deritend and Bordesley Book Club consisted in 1827 of twenty-four members of whom two were women. The Clapham Book Society consisted of eighteen members of whom three were married women. The Biggleswade in 1821 had ten members of whom four were clergymen, and two women, including one titled.[66] The Luddenden Reading Society in Yorkshire appears to have consisted only of men, although widows were permitted to inherit their husbands' rights.[67] Of the Oswestry

---

[63] Halifax Subscription Library details quoted by Beckwith, 'The Eighteenth-Century Proprietary Library' 91. Details of the Clapham Book Club and Mr Sharpe are from David H. Knott, 'An Eighteenth Century Book Club at Clapham' in *The Library* (1969) 243.
[64] Label in Hazlitt's *Spirit of the Age*, John Johnson.   [65] John Johnson.
[66] Knott, 'An Eighteenth Century Book Club at Clapham'.   [67] See appendix 10.

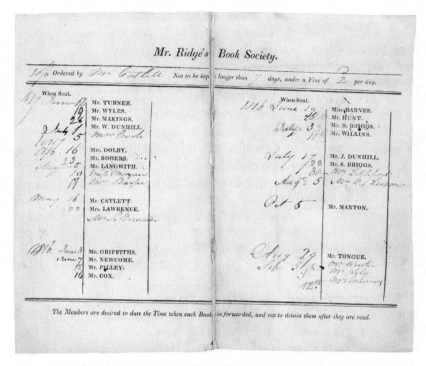

Figure 13. Printed label of Mr Ridge's Book Society, 1817. Probably Newark. In a copy of Southey's *The Poet's Pilgrimage to Waterloo* (1816).

Book Society's thirty-four members, on the other hand, twenty-two were women, including two with titles.[68]

In Scotland, membership was more socially mixed and reached further down the income scale. The Wigton Subscription Library consisted of the Earl of Galloway, two other titled land owners and their factors, the Sheriff Clerk of Wigtonshire and his Depute, the Collector of Customs, eight ministers of religion, and two dozen local professional and business men.[69] In the Ayr Library Society the members were ministers of the Scottish church, doctors, writers (lawyers), and schoolmasters, but also merchants, a baker, a cabinet maker, and a watchmaker. At Innerpeffray in Perthshire there was one esquire, the others being a barber, a bookseller, an army captain, a cooper, a dyer, a dyer's apprentice, a factor, a farmer, a flax

[68] John Johnson.
[69] Archives of the Wigton Subscription Library, archives, Hornell Museum, Kirkcudbright.

dresser, a gardener, a glover, a mason, a merchant, a miller, a minister, a quarrier, a schoolmaster, a servant, a student, a smith, a surgeon, a surgeon's apprentice, a tailor, a watchmaker, a weaver, and a wright.

Many book clubs, which in their early days disposed of the books after they had done their rounds, later decided to keep them. They began with a cupboard, then a room. Soon they needed a paid part-time librarian, and then specially designed premises. A book club could over time transform itself into a permanent library, opening its facilities to increasing numbers of partners able to pass their shares to their children. Soon the libraries and clubs began to erect purpose-built buildings, proclaiming the march of civilisation, behind impressive Grecian columns. From Stirling to Bury many a town had its Athenaeum, often with a statue of the goddess of wisdom standing above the door to welcome those entering her sacred temple. Unlike the churches whose gothic they challenged in the high streets, such libraries asserted the civic and educational values of the Enlightenment. Liverpool boasted an Athenaeum and a Lyceum. Leamington, at one time, had an Athenaeum, a Lyceum, and a Parthenon.

In a few clubs women constituted a high proportion of the membership, often being members in their own right, and there were some women-only clubs. In general, however, the reading societies, like the circulating libraries, were strongly gendered. If the mainly feminine circulating libraries concentrated on novels, the mainly masculine reading societies read the non-fiction texts of the public sphere. The registers of the bookseller to three book clubs in Gloucestershire in the 1790s show him supplying history, sermons, and pamphlets, but scarcely any imaginative literature.[70] 'Beware of indulging the imagination and enfeebling the understanding by books of mere amusement', advised the author of 'Hints for a plan for a Book Club' in 1799.[71]

In the 1810s, of the books purchased by the Eclectic Book Society, a club of gentlemen of the City of London, the biggest category was religion. The society also took many books on travel and exploration, especially those relating to India, antiquities and archaeology at home and abroad, military history, trade and finance. Literature in both verse and prose was bought frequently and regularly but represented only a small proportion of the

---

[70] Kaufman 65.
[71] *The Oeconomist or Englishman's Magazine* (1799). This article was first used by Frank Beckwith in 'The Eighteenth Century Proprietory Library in England' in *Journal of Documentation* 3, 1949. By 'book club' the author here meant subscription library.

purchases. As the society's poet declared at the annual dinner in 1818 when the previous year's books were divided out among the members:

> Who has not travelled sitting safe at home,
> O'er the wild Steppes where vagrant Tartars roam?
> Or glow'd beneath the Arabs' scorching Sky,
> While heavy snow clouds formed his Canopy?
> What Bosom, Manfred! has not sigh'd to see
> So much of Hell's Divinity in thee?
> Or with an elevated ardour thrilled
> As mighty Chatham's Eloquence distilled?
> Like Warriors now we rest retir'd from toil,
> T'enjoy the Victory and divide the Spoil.[72]

At the Bristol Library Society a member presented a set of Bell's *British Poets*, but the library did not buy much imaginative literature before the 1800s. By the 1810s they were buying theology, classics, history, economics, some science, and more poetry.[73] The overwhelming interest after religion, in Bristol as in the Eclectic, was foreign travel, exploration, and antiquities. Again, it would be a mistake to assume that the members of reading societies round the country read the same texts. With most travel books, for example, which were normally published in editions of 500 or 750, the reading societies were only able to take a selection. In Hampshire, a county with strong connections with the navy, where Jane Austen was a member of a book club, the subjects covered all parts of the world.[74] But in other parts of the country one society might take their members to Tartary, another to Iceland.[75]

The more evidence about the reading societies that is brought to light, the more it confirms that the same pattern was repeated throughout the country. At the end of the eighteenth century, when they were first established, they concentrated on books on religion, classics, history, and on political pamphlets.[76] They took the works of the Enlightenment, Smith's *Wealth of Nations*, Gibbon's *Decline and Fall of the Roman Empire*, and the long histories of England, Scotland, America, and India, by Hume, Smollett, and Robertson.[77] Indeed, if, in terms of a parade or parliament model, the Enlightenment was an eighteenth-century event, in terms of readers,

---

[72] Guildhall Library, London, mss. 988A. Byron's *Manfred* had recently been published.
[73] Listed in appendix 10.   [74] See the quotations in appendix 10.
[75] Appendix 10 brings together scattered information about the stocks in various reading institutions for which records survive.
[76] For Blair see chapter 14 and appendix 9, 580.
[77] Figures for Smith and Gibbon in appendix 9, 651 and 597.

it occurred mainly in the next generation, being read simultaneously with works by Gisborne, Hannah More, and Paley who constituted a Counter-Enlightenment.[78]

By the early years of the nineteenth century, imaginative literature, especially novels, was still rarely taken. In the years around 1805, however, we see a change. For many book societies, the decision to buy *The Lay of the Last Minstrel, Marmion*, or *The Lady of the Lake*, marked their first venture into modern literature. After Scott they bought Byron, although often refusing *Don Juan*. And it is clear from the few borrowing records which survive that, among the books which were bought, the national bestsellers were borrowed more frequently than the others. The registers of the Bristol Subscription Library, for example, for which a unique set of borrowing records survive, show even the weakest of Scott's romances out on loan year after year in multiple copies. For years after the arrival in the library in 1812 of Byron's *Childe Harold's Pilgrimage, A Romaunt*, there was scarcely a gap between its return from its fortnight with one member and its leaving with another, yet more evidence that the bigger the sales, the bigger the multiplier needed to estimate readerships.

With the coming of *Waverley* in 1814, there was another change. Members began to demand every novel by 'the author of Waverley' as soon as it appeared, and were willing to do without other books in order to have them. Within a year or two almost every reading society, like every circulating library, began to take each new Waverley novel as soon as it came out, although sometimes only after protests at the abandonment of the original aims. Deep into Victorian times, the Waverley novels remained the only modern works of prose fiction to be admissible within the new temples of knowledge and wisdom.

In past centuries, the elites outside London had kept themselves up to date by making occasional visits to the capital, and discussing the latest news on their return. By their reading of the *Monthly Magazine* and the *Critical*, and later the *Edinburgh Review* and the *Quarterly Review*, the members of the reading societies could feel themselves part of a national as well as of a local reading community, with the smaller book clubs setting aside time to talk about the books. Indeed talk sometimes came first. The Mauchline of Ayr, to which Robert Burns belonged, had begun as a conversation and drinking club and then decided to buy books financed from fines. *The Country Book Club*, a poem of 1788, describes the squire, the vicar, the draper, the surgeon,

---

[78] For Gisborne and More see chapter 14 and appendix 9, 599 and 621.

and the barber, sitting down to a good gossip, a good argument, and a good deal of drink.[79] In the Eclectic in the City of London, the twelve members met once a month in rotation over dinner – one member who resigned just before his turn came round to supply dinner was reprimanded in the minutes. Other clubs that were more abstemious were just as sociable. The Clapham Book Society, for example, home of the so-called Clapham sect of Christian evangelicals, met monthly for tea.

When decisions are taken collectively, minorities as well as majorities have an effective veto. Purchasing policy was often controversial. Some societies banned religion, others novels. A suggestion that the Hull Society might buy chapbooks was regarded as a contemptuous joke.[80] Some members voted against any book which was politically dangerous, but for others these were the very books they wanted to read. In some towns there were rival clubs with different outlooks. Southey complained that his books were rejected by book clubs on political grounds, even though he was a staunch advocate of the government's authoritarian policies and of censorship.[81] We see members trying to slip new policies past the purchasing committees by offering to accept cheaper second-hand copies. From time to time there would be purges of books regarded as irreligious, seditious, or improper. But the collectivisation which is such a strong feature of the reading of the romantic period may have helped to forge and maintain a developing unity among elites across the nation. If every member had a say in choosing the books, he or she was also more or less obliged to read the books proposed by others, particularly in clubs which debated the books as well as reading them. The book club at High Wycombe was said to have helped to break down local prejudices 'imbibed either on political or religious principles' in the years after the French Revolution.[82] In the Eclectic those members who wanted most to read, say, the romances of Scott and Moore also found themselves reading and discussing the latest prose histories of Scotland and Persia. The financiers read philosophy as well as finance; the art lovers and antiquarians were kept up to date on military and naval history; and admirers of Byron were subjected to regular sermons on the serious risks they were running.

The book clubs took many political pamphlets, another means by which members could not only keep themselves reasonably up to date on national and international events but also participate in current debates, in the consolidation of consensuses, and in the formation of attitudes and policies.

---

[79] [Charles Shillito] *The Country Book Club, A Poem* (1788).   [80] See appendix 10.
[81] See *The Doctor* edited and abridged by Maurice H. Fitzgerald (1930) 325.
[82] Gomme, *Literary Curiosities* 147 quoting *Gentleman's Magazine*, 1800. Knight, *Old Printer* 235.

In the years that followed the French Revolution, an array of pamphlets was printed, in which some of the most vital issues in modern history were debated in a continuous procession of claims, replies, and counter replies. The debate widened from the significance of the French Revolution itself, and the immediate question of peace or war, to explore deeper philosophical notions concerning the natural rights of man, the legitimacy of the state and of the church, and the rights of women. Although most of the pamphlets were printed in London in modest editions, many apparently at the expense of their authors, and copies were often presented free to members of the government and other politically influential figures, they circulated nationally through the subscription libraries and book clubs.[83] 'I have many pamphlets to finish before I close my eyes', says General Tilney, a character in Austen's *Northanger Abbey*, as he shoos the young women off to bed, 'and perhaps may be poring over the affairs of the nation for hours after you are asleep'.[84] 'I cannot in decency', he remarks on another occasion, 'fail attending the club.'[85]

In the 1790s, when the crisis of political legitimacy struck England, a few years after it struck in France, the key text was Tom Paine's pamphlet, *The Rights of Man*. When, in 1791, the first copies arrived in Windsor where Charles Knight was the local bookseller, King George III, on his early morning stroll to the bookshop saw the parcel being opened, read the book for half an hour, but he made no comment and continued to visit.[86] In three book clubs in Gloucestershire of which we have a record for the 1790s, *The Rights of Man* was the most common pamphlet.[87] But when Paine reduced the price from 3s 6d (3.5 shillings), already a low price for pamphlets, to just sixpence, and arranged for several editions to be sent to be distributed among the working men of the manufacturing cities, he caused a scare throughout the government. At sixpence, *The Rights of Man* could be bought, read by, and read aloud to groups who normally had no access to pamphlets. By refusing a personal fortune – he was offered a thousand guineas (£1, 050) for the intellectual property rights – he had broken through the censorship of price.[88] Paine himself was hurriedly convicted of seditious libel in his absence, a number of booksellers went to prison for continuing

---

[83] To judge from a few records in the Whittingham archives, 750 appears to have been a common size for a print run.

[84] Jane Austen, *Northanger Abbey*, edited by Marilyn Butler (1995) 163. [85] *Ibid.* 182.

[86] Story told about Knight's father in Knight, *Passages* i, 37. [87] Kaufman 72.

[88] This offer, which would have confined discussion of Paine's ideas to elites was reliably reported by the printer of part of the *Rights of Man* at Paine's trial. See *The Whole Proceedings on the Trial of an Information Exhibited ex officio by the King's Attorney-General against Thomas Paine: for a libel upon the Revolution and settlement of the Crown and regal government as by law established* (1793) 83.

to sell copies, and the book ceased to be available. A pamphleteer of 1794 claimed gleefully that all copies had been expelled from all the book clubs and circulating libraries in Somerset.[89]

The Rights of Man was probably among the most influential of all texts printed in Britain during the romantic period, but the extent of its actual circulation within the reading nation appears to have been much exaggerated both at the time and by subsequent historians. Some of the claims and estimates made at the time and repeated since, such as the 'many hundreds of thousands' of copies said to have been 'rapidly sold' after 1792, the 200,000 copies sold in the first year, and the 'hundreds of thousands of copies' which made Paine's writings known 'in every village on the globe where the English language is spoken' defy credibility when we put such claims against what can be recovered from archival sources.[90]

Many hundreds of political pamphlets were printed in Great Britain in the years after 1789. A parade or parliament model of literary or cultural history arranges them in chronological order of first publication, noting how the texts engage with one another. In terms of readers, however, a different pattern emerges. Burke's pamphlet *Reflections*, with the possible exception of Paine's *Rights of Man*, was printed in far larger numbers than any of the others – 20,000 during its first fifteen years, compared with 500 or 750 each for most of the others. When *The Rights of Man* was outlawed and withdrawn, *Reflections* was left triumphant in the field as the main political text of the time, becoming more widely available at ever cheaper prices and reaching virtually every reading society. It seems likely that the many tens of thousands of influential readers who discussed the implications of the French Revolution did so on the basis of having read Burke's *Reflections* and of no other pamphlet.

When a political pamphlet did reach a mass readership, the results could be direct, dramatic, and reasonably rapid. During the eighteenth century, although the Atlantic slave trade was increasingly concentrated in British hands, and many stable commodities such as sugar were produced by slave labour in British colonies, most of the British public were not much aware either of the scale or of the cruelty. Even in the late 1780s when calls were made for a boycott of West Indian sugar, the impact of the abolitionist campaigners was limited, as the publication figures for their print show, and no action resulted.[91] By the early 1790s however, when one large slaving

---

[89] *A Country Carpenter's Confession of Faith, with a few Plain Remarks on the Age of Reason in a letter from Will Chip the Carpenter in Somersetshire to Thomas Pain Stay-Maker in Paris* (1794). Price 2½d (0.24 shillings) or twenty-five copies for 3 shillings. Bodleian.

[90] Discussed in appendix 9.

[91] For the publication figures for 1788, see appendix 7, 'Anti-slavery campaign'.

vessel was leaving a British port for Africa every other day, the campaigners were able, with the help of a far heavier distribution of print, to mobilise a huge constituency of support that included groups who had hitherto scarcely participated in politics.[92]

An Address to the People of Great Britain, on the propriety of abstaining from West India Sugar and Rum written by William Fox, Baptist minister and founder of the Sunday-School Society, first printed in 1791, and extensively reprinted for free distribution, was one of the most immediately influential pieces of print hitherto published in the English-speaking world. In 1792 over 500 petitions demanding the abolition of the slave trade were delivered to parliament with over 700,000 signatures. In Manchester alone 20,000 names from a population of 60,000 were attached. Faced with such an unprecedented display of public feeling, by 1807 parliament had agreed to abolish the British slave trade, and by the end of the romantic period, faced with an even greater demonstration of opinion mobilised with the help of public meetings, and vast distributions of free print, had decided to abolish slavery itself. Here too, we not only see the potential power of reading to influence minds and events, but the limitations of the parade and parliament models. When, in 1823, Sir George Rose gave his countrymen his views on the slave trade, he produced a pamphlet of 500 copies, of which a proportion was circulated and even fewer read.[93] In the same year the Anti-Slavery Society were circulating over 200,000 pamphlets a year, a figure soon to rise to half a million a year.[94]

The members of the reading societies were the leaders of local life, a social, economic, and intellectual elite.[95] The societies were a flowering of intellectual confidence, a boom in serious reading to match the boom in serious writing, the embodiment of local and civic as well as national pride, a celebration of the power of books to make mankind wiser and better. It was from these men, many people hoped, that civilisation would spread to England's backward and still largely illiterate rural poor, into Ireland where the levels of education were even lower, and perhaps even to the teeming frightening masses in the new industrial cities. They were, to use a word coined by Coleridge, the 'clerisies' who would gradually take over

[92] See James Walvin, 'The Public Campaign in England against Slavery, 1787–1834', in David Eltis and James Walvin, eds., *The Abolition of the Atlantic Slave Trade* (Madison 1981). For a summary of the surprising results that have resulted from initial work on the Du Bois database of 27,000 slave voyages, produced by Du Bois Institute, Harvard University, see Bernard Bailyn, 'Considering the Slave Trade: History and Memory', in *William and Mary Quarterly*, 57 (January 2001).
[93] See appendix 7, "Pamphlets".   [94] 'See appendix 7, "Anti-Slavery Society"'.
[95] This was, for example, the view of the book-trade traveller of 1821, 'A Traveller' in *Monthly Magazine*, June 1821.

the intellectual, educational, and socially progressive role which in earlier centuries had been the province of the Christian churches.

However, although the reading societies were a manifestation of the Enlightenment and progressive in the sense that their members wanted to be up to date with the latest ideas, it would be a mistake to believe that the members were liberals. In 1798 the members of the Shrewsbury Library voted to expel the books whose sentiments they did not like, including philosophical works and novels by Rousseau, Godwin, Mackintosh, Holcroft, Wakefield, and Wollstonecraft's *A Vindication of the Rights of Woman*, as well as the *New Monthly* and the *Analytical*, in effect rejecting the radical canon of the age.[96] The fines which the book clubs imposed on members for lending outside the membership were not only economic deterrents against free riders, but part of an array of instruments which ensured exclusivity of access. One of the post-war measures which aimed at restricting political participation was the imposition of a heavy stamp duty on pamphlets.[97] Members of book clubs were the same men who, as members of the House of Commons and House of Lords, were passing new laws, year after year, extending the death penalty to ever more trivial offences and who, as judges, thought themselves dangerously soft if they commuted death sentences to transportation to Australia. The number of capital crimes grew to over 200, and more men and women were hanged as a proportion of the population than at any time before or since. Byron's *The Prisoner of Chillon*, with its invocation of the 'Eternal spirit of the chainless mind', is often regarded as an example of the free spirit of romanticism, and we know much about the attitudes of those readers, real and fictional, who learned the poem by heart.[98] Most contemporary readers were, however, probably more in sympathy with the prison authorities of Chillon than with the undefeated Bonnivard, and the book sold badly.[99] The Tory *Quarterly Review* said that the poem showed that the English death penalty was superior to the long prison sentences common on the continent. In the romantic period a man could be hanged or sent to Botany Bay for stealing a copy of *The Excursion* or of *Lalla Rookh*, although there is no record of anyone taking the risk.

What cannot easily be established is how far the same families belonged both to circulating libraries and to reading societies, the women taking the novels from the circulating libraries, the men the non-fiction and pamphlets

---

[96] See Heather Jackson, *Marginalia, Readers Writing in Books* (Yale 2001) 78.
[97] See chapter 16.   [98] See chapter 20.
[99] The production run of the first and only edition was 6,000, and the book was still available as a remainder eight years after publication.

from the subscription libraries and the book clubs. But if there were an overlap between the female private and the male public sphere within families, it was probably limited and unusual. Austen, who exceptionally belonged to a book club as well as to a circulating library, read the books of both, but if her representation of the family of General Tilney can be regarded as more typical, the two reading spheres were separate even within the walls of the same household.

Towards the end of the romantic period, a number of libraries specially designed for mechanics, that is the skilled and literate upper-working classes, were created by the Society for the Diffusion of Useful Knowledge. By 1825, mechanics institutes had been established in many cities and towns all over Great Britain, and had attracted many hundreds of members, more proportionally in the small towns than in the large industrial cities, but well spread across the nation in the rural as well as in the urban areas, with a disproportionately large number in Scotland. The organisers believed that by educating the aristocrats of labour, the natural leaders of the emerging urban working classes, and by giving them a share of the national reading from which they had been excluded, they would raise the moral level, as well as the economic efficiency, of the nation. In their design and constitution the institutes closely resembled book clubs, and membership was exclusively male. Mechanics paid an annual subscription which allowed them to borrow from the library, to attend lectures, to participate in debates. But the subscriptions were heavily subsidised by patrons and by employers who became members at a much higher rate.[100] Although in form the institutes were, like the book clubs, under the control of their members, in practice they remained under the control of the employers.

But if there was an element of paternalism in the whole notion of mechanics institutes, there was nothing patronising about the books they offered. The libraries generally contained a wide selection of books on science and technology, some simplified, but by no means all were educational or vocational. Many mechanics institutes libraries had copies of Smith's *Wealth of Nations*, Gibbon's *Rome*, and the expensive books of modern travel, some donated, but most bought with institute funds, and many mechanics had better access to modern thought than their economic and social superiors. Nor did the books lie unread on the shelves. When the central organisers of the movement made a structured inquiry about the state of progress round

[100] Examples in appendix 10.

the country, most institutes reported that the books were heavily borrowed, out week after week to a wide circulation among members. What mechanics did not have access to in their libraries were works of the modern imaginative writers. In none of the catalogues of even the most progressive of the libraries in 1826 is there a trace of Byron or Scott, let alone of any other modern poets or novelists. Although the members of the book clubs had usually relaxed their own rules by about 1820, it was to be another decade before they let the same books be read by mechanics. When they did, in the end, decide that fiction might be bought, in mechanics institutes as in other libraries, the breakthrough occurred with the Waverley novels and the line held there for some time.

Like the reading societies, the mechanics institutes brought a new tranche of society into the reading nation. But again it would be unwise to exaggerate the liberalism. In some cities, particularly in the industrial areas, employers kept aloof, afraid that providing mechanics with a meeting place would encourage trade unionism. And even those employers who gave them active support had an agenda beyond the encouragement of reading for its own sake. The mechanics institutes movement, its founders believed, would help to avert the threat of violent revolution by coopting the potential leaders of the workers into the most advanced constituencies of the reading nation, by sharing most modern thinking with them, and by giving them the best that they had. As Sir J. F. W. Herschell declared in a speech to the Windsor and Eton Public Library in 1833, in English literature 'you possess all you require to strike your grappling iron into their souls, and chain them, willing followers, to the car of advancing civilization'.[101] Lord Carlisle, a tireless advocate of liberal causes, constantly reiterated his belief that, with the help of mechanics institutes, 'the different classes of society [would] be bound together in mutual good will, and the whole mass leavened with knowledge, virtue, and religion'.[102]

In addition to, and in opposition to, this Enlightenment agenda for coopting the working classes, we also see what can be described as Counter-Enlightenment libraries being established, particularly in the rural areas. On the whole these libraries appear to have been small, a few dozen books at most, often donated. The texts thus made available were overwhelmingly educational and didactic: history, geography, conduct books. If literature was admitted, it was usually Young, Thomson, Cowper, and the other

---

[101] *The Importance of Literature to Men of Business: A Series of Addresses Delivered at Various Popular Institutions* (1852) 44.
[102] Earl of Carlisle, *Lectures and Addresses* (1852) iv. This book contains several lectures delivered to mechanics institutes in the 1840s.

old-canon favourites who reinforced mainstream religious, political, and social ideologies, and there were few if any novels.[103] How far such libraries can be regarded as creating reading constituencies is doubtful, but they provided some focus for the older culture which clustered round the old canon which was now beginning to overlap with the long-frozen popular reading of Bible, almanac, ballad, and chapbook.[104]

The large differences between the main types of collective-reading institutions and their reading constituencies can be summarised as in table 13.1.

The rapid growth of collective-reading institutions in Great Britain coincided with the industrial revolution in manufacturing, the biggest change that had occurred for many centuries. Although industrialisation was a technological revolution, the adoption of mechanisation in many industries was only made possible by the simultaneous invention and application of new financial and organisational structures (for example the discountable commercial bill, the joint-stock company, limited liability), which developed uniquely in Great Britain and spread round the world. As far as printed books were concerned, although there was little change in manufacturing methods until the 1820s, here too we see spectacular changes in the methods by which reading was financed, most of which predated the industrialisation of book manufacture. The commercial circulating libraries depended for their success on a complex set of mutually supporting restrictive trade practices. The member-owned reading societies, including the mechanics institutes, could not have succeeded if they had not been able, with the cooperation of the publishers and the retail booksellers, to invent and adapt ever more imaginative new financial instruments. The returnable entry fees, the revolving capital funds, the heritable (but often not saleable) partnership shares, the differential scales of fines and incentives, and the complex and carefully regulated disposal arrangements, were as delicate a set of interlocking mechanisms as the gears and levers of the new steam-driven machines which so impressed foreigners with Britain's industrial inventiveness.

None of these changes flowed inevitably from the logic of earlier developments. It is hard, for example, to relate the growth of libraries and collective reading directly to the emergence of a northern European bourgeois ethic, influential although such general factors may have been. Nor can they be easily related to the emergence of a more open market-oriented economy – on the contrary their success was dependent on the continuation

---

[103] Examples in appendix 10.   [104] Discussed in chapter 17.

Table 13.1 Characteristics of collective reading institutions

Circulating libraries
Commercially owned
Much used by women of upper income groups
Associated with the selling of feminine products
Mostly deal in new novels, especially love in high society and gothic romance
Many libraries also take poetry by Scott and Byron, and the later Waverley novels
Choice of books supply-pushed by book industry
Most of the stocks quickly turned over
Believed by many to encourage immorality in behaviour as well as in thought and desire
Widely despised as damaging the values both of the old canon and of the Enlightenment.

Book clubs and subscription libraries
Owned by the members
Membership almost exclusively men
Associated with male pursuits, e.g. dining, drinking, and debating
Mainly politics, religion, war, history, travel, antiquities, plus many books of the
    eighteenth-century Enlightenment
Then Scott, Byron, and Waverley novels
Many pamphlets on contemporary political issues, with a few such as Burke, far more
    widely available than the others
Choice of books demand-led by members
Stocks accumulated
A national elite conscious of their leadership role

Mechanics institutes libraries
Owned by the members who included industrialists as well as mechanics
Almost exclusively men
Strongly utilitarian, with a heavy bias against all imaginative literature especially novels,
    but also many serious up-to-date books on history, travel, antiquities, and many books
    of the eighteenth-century Enlightenment
Choice of books demand-led by members
Stocks accumulated
A nationwide attempt to educate and coopt the topmost tranche of the urban working
    classes

Parish libraries
Books donated by local leaders
Used by women as well as by men
Strong religious bias, conduct books, old-canon authors, school books, and almost
    nothing contemporary
Stocks largely static except for occasional donations
The older intensive reading, rural, religious culture

of restrictive mechanisms associated with guilds. Nor is there any neatly fitting historical explanations of why the different new ways of financing the collective reading should have been invented when they were and not earlier or later, why they co-existed, and why they should have coincided so exactly with cultural and gender categories. One conclusion however seems clear. The huge changes in book production and book reading which followed the invention of circulating libraries in the 1750s, the abolition of perpetual copyright in 1774, the start up of many book clubs in the 1770s and later, and the consequent collectivisation of the reading of newly written books were as much driven by publishers and local enthusiasts as by authors or by readers. If we are to develop an understanding of texts, books, and reading as a system, we need to take account of these entrepreneurs.[105]

In a speech to the House of Commons in 1822, Lord John Russell offered an estimate of the number of collective-reading institutions in the country:[106] A more detailed estimate is given in a letter from a commercial traveller for one of the London publishers. The information is consolidated in table 13.2.[107]

One thousand of the voluntary societies were said to have been formed within the previous three years. The small libraries run by church and chapel vestries, by schools, and by proselytising bodies, which the traveller believed were not much used and had little influence, were omitted from his estimate, as were the mechanics institutes that came later.[108] From the traveller's figures it is also possible to deduce the relative intensity of collective-reading institutions in the different countries of the United Kingdom. As table 13.3 shows, they illustrate a continuing high penetration in Scotland, and the low penetration of reading societies in Ireland.[109]

In 1838, William Howitt confirmed the contrast between England, where book clubs were largely confined to the towns and to the middle classes, and Scotland where they reached a wider range.[110] 'Why cannot England

---

[105] The implications are discussed further in chapter 22.

[106] Quoted in *Monthly Magazine*, 1822, 58.

[107] *Monthly Magazine*, June 1821, in a letter signed 'A Traveller': 'My opportunities for collecting the information . . . are peculiar and personal, and though I may be considered as a very humble pioneer of literature, yet it is obvious that no other person could have had the same opportunities of collecting the information, however learned or dignified . . . In three several journies, in connection with books, booksellers, and lovers of books, I have sedulously directed my enquiries . . . and have systemized my information.' Dibdin, xxii, writing in 1824, says that the number 'of travellers dispersed all over the country from the great houses of Paternoster Row is nearly doubled'.

[108] See a comment on one in Berwickshire in appendix 10, 674.

[109] Indeed the proportion for Ireland looks too high when compared with the number of societies actually identified by name.

[110] Quoted in appendix 10, 674.

Table 13.2 Collective reading institutions

	Numbers		
Lord John Russell's estimate, 1822			
Circulating libraries	1,000		
(of which in London 100)			
Book clubs	1,500 to 2,000		

The Commercial traveller's estimate

	Numbers	Borrowers	Average membership
Commercial circulating libraries	1,500	100,000	70
Plus occasionally	100,000		

Voluntary societies under the control of members

	Numbers	Families
Book clubs[a]	600	14,000
Permanent libraries	260	8,000
Magazine societies	750	9,000
Totals rounded	1,500	30,000
Newspaper societies	5,000	50,000
Totals	6,500	80,000

[a] The traveller says 'there are not less than', but later in the article he uses a figure of 600.

Table 13.3 Reading societies, 1821, geographical spread

	Population (million)	% of UK	Reading societies %
England	11	50	59
Scotland	3	14	24
Ireland	6	27	12
Wales	2	9	6
Total	22	100	100 (rounded)

have book societies in the country districts', Howitt asks, 'as well as in the towns?' The authors he recommends are the safe religious and rural authors, Milton, Thomson, Cowper, 'the pious and tender Montgomery', and Bloomfield.[III]

From the estimates of families served it is possible to deduce the multipliers which he had in mind when he made his estimates of readerships, as shown in table 13.4.

[III] William Howitt, *The Rural Life of England* (1971 edition) 205.

Table 13.4 Implied multipliers, 1821

	Regular individual borrowers	Readers
Circulating libraries	70	n a
	families	readers ($\times$4)
Book clubs	25	100
Permanent libraries	30	120
Magazine societies	12	48

Broad estimates for the size of the population of the United Kingdom as used by the book trade in 1821 were given in the traveller's table. We also have more exact, carefully constructed, recent estimates for the size and growth of the population of England (though not for Scotland, Ireland, and Wales) during the nineteenth century.[112] As a broad-brush estimate, taking into account the special position of Dublin and of the other English-speaking cities and towns of Ireland, the national English-speaking population of the United Kingdom in the romantic period was of the order of fifteen million, and rising fast. We also have various estimates for literacy although there are difficulties in choosing definitions which are suitable for purposes of comparison. Literacy rates evidently differed greatly through the United Kingdom, both geographically and by social class, and there appear to have been many men and women who were able to read without necessarily being able to write. Many occupations increasingly demanded an ability to read and probably also increasingly to write as well. It seems likely that, by the middle of the romantic period more than half the adult population had the ability to read, some quite well, and in some areas such as London and lowland Scotland a higher proportion. Even if we include a generous allowance for multipliers, from what we know of the numbers of copies produced, there is no arithmetical way that the readerships even of authors who were well known at the time, can turn out to be more than a small fraction of the reading nation and a tiny fraction of the nation as a whole. The same is true of most of the books of history, travel, exploration, and antiquities whose production base was extremely small. There must have been many men and women who, if they read any new literature at all, read only Scott and Byron.

It seems certain too that in the romantic period there was still a large gap between the nation as a whole and the literate nation, and another gap

---

[112] See appendix 1.

between the literate nation and the reading nation. With such small figures, and making an allowance for voluntary abstainers such as Sir Walter Elliot, a character in Austen's *Persuasion* who opened no book but the Baronetage, it makes little sense to classify the readerships by such broad social or economic categories as aristocracy or middle class. On the other hand, the reading nation was not so much a scatter of individuals reading this and that, but a group of reading constituencies, with cohorts joining and leaving, a reading class which was geographically well spread and which was not commensurate with social class, income, gender, or with age, and which only in part coincided with the economic and social elites.

CHAPTER 14

Horizons of expectations

Implicit in the notion of literary influence is that the reading of the texts influenced the minds, and therefore, the behaviour, of the readers. Some reading by some readers of some texts may have helped to bring about changes, other reading may have consolidated existing mentalities, and there are innumerable variations in between. If mentalities were influenced by reading, even if only temporarily, they developed along a trajectory which was different from the counterfactual trajectory which would otherwise have occurred. If we follow the parade or parliament conventions, we can try to trace influence by comparing the printed texts in which we are most interested with others published later, a methodology which risks falling into simplistic *post hoc ergo propter hoc* modes of arguing. If, however, we regard the writing, publishing, and subsequent reading of a text as an intervention into a large and complex existing dynamic system with many active agents, then the methodology of the comparison needs to include readers. Indeed, since texts remain inert until they are read, the site where influence occurred, if it occurred at all, has to be primarily located in the minds of readers. How to assess influence is among the most difficult of all the methodological challenges that historians face in attempting to understand the diffusionary rise and fall of ideas. Although it may be impossible to attempt grand counter-factual history, such as asking what would have happened if Napoleon had won the battle of Waterloo, the implicit counter-factual in all judgements of influence cannot be wished away. In attempting histories of reading and of its influence, we need a better comparator which is methodologically more secure than the modern researcher's chosen standpoint.

Can we draw on the experience of other disciplines, such as policy evaluation, that have developed their own solutions?[1] Earlier I used a figure of

---

[1] See (W. L. St Clair) *Policy Evaluation. A Guide for Managers* (1988).

£5 (100 shillings) a week, a typical income of a gentleman of the romantic period, as a standard against which to judge economic information, such as the impact of book prices on access.[2] Can we find some standard against which texts and mentalities can be judged? What I propose is to take the concept of 'horizons of expectations', a theory used to connote the state of mind in which the reader approaches the act of reading, to widen it from the individual reader to the constituency, and from single texts to groups of texts, and to attempt to retrieve the main historical elements of some of the actual horizons that were present in the romantic period.[3] This does not produce a dynamic base case against which change can be assessed, but it does provides a denominator against which not only textual content, but the responses to the reading of texts, and wider outcomes, can all be situated. Any procedure which enables us to relate changing mentalities to a reasonably fixed point is likely to be an improvement on those which leave the concept of influence unexamined or unexplicit. In navigating across the uncharted oceans of historical mentalities, a few bearings on lighthouses that are clearly marked on our charts are more useful than any number of sightings of other moving ships.

The candidate for a reasonably fixed cultural comparator that I have selected is the official mainstream ideology as it stood during the romantic period. In making this suggestion, I do not wish to imply that there necessarily ever was a single ideology, let alone that it was always assented to or practised even by those to whom it most appealed. My suggested standard, like the notion of ideology itself, can never be more than a constructed simplification of a range of changing mental states among innumerable participants, too complex to be fully comprehended, described, or abstracted in language. But, as it happens, during the romantic period, the country's political, ecclesiastical, and educational leaders devoted a good deal of effort to identifying, devising, and describing a culture which they believed was appropriate to the times, and which they wished to see diffused and applied through the nation's political, religious, judicial, educational, and other opinion-forming institutions. The texts in which that ideal culture was described, which were simultaneously an emanation of official ideology, a means by which that ideology was constituted and affirmed in language, and an instrument of persuasion, can provide a few fixed lighthouses which may help us to plot the position of ideas.

[2] In chapter 11.
[3] For reader response theory, of which 'horizons of expectations' is a key concept, see the summary in chapter 1.

The foundation text of the English, Scottish, and later of the British state, was the version of the English-language Bible first published in 1611. During the romantic period, huge efforts were made by various private societies to take this Bible to constituencies who had not had much personal access. In addition, commercial publishers, such as Kelly sold millions of copies of other, usually annotated, English-language Bibles both as complete books and in cheap numbered parts to the lowest tranches of the book market. Although successive governments since the Reformation had attempted to make the English-language Bible available, the pricing structures associated with the franchising of the text to commercial organisations who had to pay the state for their franchise had always been a barrier, and it was only in the romantic period that English-language Bibles came within the range of the whole reading nation.[4] More copies were produced, distributed, and read, than in all the previous centuries put together.[5]

The large and miscellaneous nature of the biblical texts, and the heavy historical overlay of selection and controversy to which they had been subjected, make it hard to identify a consistency of interpretation within the romantic period other than in general terms. However, we have a more focused statement in three other much printed texts of the time, each of which were not only accorded the highest authority but were sold in large quantities. Blair's *Sermons*, Buchan's *Domestic Medicine*, and Burn's *Justice*, were the three standard textbooks of the three main learned professions, the church, medicine, and the law. A copy of each was needed in every town, if not quite in every parish, in the country. Taken together the three Bs, to whom a toast was drunk at the book industry's annual dinner, laid down all that was required to run a well-ordered civil society.[6]

Of the three, the *Sermons* of Hugh Blair, a minister of the Church of Scotland and professor of rhetoric and belles-lettres in the University of Edinburgh, are the most useful for the purpose of identifying an official ideology. King George III is said to have expressed the wish that every youth in the kingdom might possess a copy of the Bible and of Blair. He included Blair's *Sermons* in his travelling library of essential books, and Blair was given a royal pension.[7] Blair's *Sermons* were officially recommended as a source from which all those in authority could safely draw in giving their own advice. They could be used by clergymen in preparing sermons, in speeches by officers to soldiers and seamen, in addresses to school children, and on all other occasions when the reading met the non-reading nation.

---

[4] See chapter 4.   [5] See 'The official supernatural, primary texts', appendix 7, 551–2.
[6] The fourth B was Blackstone's *Commentaries on the Law of England*. Rees and Britton 130.
[7] Dibdin vii.

Figure 14. A Scottish child being taught to read from the family Bible.
From Mrs Marshall, *A Sketch of My Friend's Family* (1818).

The *Sermons* were published in five successive volumes, the first in 1778, the fifth in 1800, with each set being printed and reprinted in large editions. By 1815, the archival record shows that nearly a quarter of a million copies of the various volumes had been sold.[8] Since Blair died in 1800, the earlier volumes slipped through the brief copyright window, and became part of the old canon. Blair's *Sermons* were, as a result, frequently anthologised,

[8] For the huge sales see 'Hugh Blair', appendix 9, 581–2.

abridged, and included in school textbooks, reaching virtually the whole reading nation, men, women, and children. So wholesome was the name of 'Blair' that Phillips the publisher invented a Reverend David Blair, so that the huge corpus of school books which he had run up as 'Blair's' catechisms, classbooks, readers, and science textbooks, would be wrongly assumed to be the work of the Reverend Hugh.[9] Blair's *Sermons* can be regarded as the romantic period equivalent of the homilies, catechisms, mandatory prayers, and other compulsory and semi-compulsory texts with which the English state and church had earlier attempted to impose a degree of uniformity on the mentalities, moralities, and conduct of the people. They can, I suggest, be used as a reliable summary of the core official ideology, supernatural, political, and social, that was administered to the nation day by day, Sunday after Sunday, all over Great Britain.

How far Blair's *Sermons* were in practice effective in influencing mentalities and behaviour cannot be easily judged. As Miss Crawford, a character in Austen's *Mansfield Park*, remarks doubtingly to Edmund Bertram when he tells her he is considering a career in the church for 'the guardianship of religion and morals'

How can two sermons a week, even supposing them worth hearing, supposing the preacher to have the sense to prefer Blair's to his own, do all that you speak of?[10]

For the purpose of establishing a reasonably fixed standard, however, no judgement on whether Blair's *Sermons* were effective or not is needed. And since they were amongst the most admired, printed, and performed texts of the romantic period, with stronger claims to be a representative emanation of the mentalities of the romantic period than many literary texts, it would be unwise to dismiss them out of hand.

A friend and neighbour of Adam Smith, Blair is sometimes classed among the philosophers of the Scottish Enlightenment, but he was not an innovative thinker. As Leslie Stephen remarked in his *History of English Thought in the Eighteenth Century*, Blair was:

A facile and dexterous declaimer whose rhetoric glides over the surface of things without biting into their substance . . . For unction there was mere mouthing; instead of the solid common sense of earlier writers, an infinite capacity for repeating the feeblest of platitudes . . . The morality can scarcely be dignified by the name of prudential, unless all prudence be summed up in the great commandment, be

---

[9] See William E. A. Axon, *Stray Chapters in Literature, Folk-Lore, and Archaeology* (Manchester 1888) 257. Phillips also invented a Reverend J. Goldsmith so that his textbooks on history and geography would be wrongly assumed to be by the famous Oliver.

[10] Jane Austen, *Mansfield Park*, edited by R. W. Chapman (1923) 92.

respectable; the theology is retained rather to give a faint seasoning to the general insipidity of moral commonplace than seriously to influence the thought . . . Blair is . . . a mere washed out retailer of second-hand commonplaces.[11]

But what Stephen saw as Blair's weakness was the essence of the appeal. It was because he replayed the commonplaces and *sententiae* of the culture of his day that he was, and is, so useful.[12] He is in favour of honesty, kindness, truthfulness, modesty, patriotism, and of many of the other traditional virtues associated with the teachings, though not the practice, of the Christian tradition. He recommends what can be described as the puritan (later 'bourgeois'), values of thrift, enterprise, and self-reliance. But, as Stephen noticed, his *Sermons* contain little that is specifically Christian. Indeed, they scarcely mention religion at all. Although a minister of the Presbyterian Church of Scotland, Blair's prescriptions were consistent with the doctrines and teachings of the Episcopalian Church of England, and indeed with those of most other Christian religious groups, an idea that would have been unthinkable in the seventeenth century. Many of the propositions which had been at or near the centre of the English and Scottish official supernaturals in earlier times, such as repentance, atonement, and salvation, are absent. Unlike his many predecessors, the authority which Blair claims as a Christian minister is not based on the ancient biblical and patristic texts.

But, although, in Stephen's terms, Blair was not an Enlightenment author, he was a product of the Enlightenment. He perches somewhere between the old world of Christian belief and an emerging secularism. In Blair, the organised religion of official Christianity, with its dogmas, its doctrines, its liturgies and its ceremonies, that he appears to find embarrassing, is not commended because it is true, but because it is politically and socially useful. If the people felt no fear of God and of his punishments, and there were no ecclesiastical institutions to promote such beliefs, he implies, why should anyone obey the secular laws? To judge from Blair, the official supernatural that the British state and its churches recommended at the end of the eighteenth century was more deist than Christian, more a useful instrument of cultural, and therefore of political, governance than a set of propositions and ideas believed to be true.

In addition to Blair, we have the writings of William Paley, a more intellectual writer, whose works were also reprinted and circulated in large numbers during the romantic period, and who, because he wrote mainly during the brief copyright window, also entered the old-canon lists, with

---

[11] First published 1876. Quotations from x, 89, and xii, 20.   [12] For commonplaces see chapter 4.

extracts and abridgements.[13] In his *Natural Theology, or Evidences of the Existence and Attributes of the Deity* (1802), Paley offered one of the most vivid statements of the argument from design, the key concept of deist natural religion, whose rhetorical power is still evident today:

In crossing a heath, suppose I pitched my foot against a *stone*, and were asked how the stone came to be there, I might possibly answer, that, for anything I knew to the contrary, it had lain there for ever; nor would it, perhaps, be very easy to show the absurdity of this answer. But suppose I had found a *watch* upon the ground . . . the inference, we think, is inevitable, the watch must have had a maker.[14]

But far more widely circulated was his *Principles of Moral and Political Philosophy*, in form a textbook of philosophy but essentially a conduct book, which, like Blair's *Sermons*, qualified under the brief copyright window, and was extensively reprinted, abridged, and anthologised.[15] Often overlooked are the 1817 *Sermons*, known as *Astronomical Discourses*, by Thomas Chalmers of Glasgow, another defence of natural religion and of the historical evidences of Christianity, which sold 20,000 copies in 1817 alone.[16] According to Hazlitt, Chalmers's books 'ran like wild-fire through the country, were darlings of the watering places, were laid in the windows of inns, and were met with in all places of public resort'.[17] 'The tartan beats us all', George Canning remarked, commenting on the huge crowds which Chalmers attracted when he preached in London.[18]

If we can take Blair and these others as the cultural equivalent of my economic standard of £5 (100 shillings) a week, we can then place other printed texts of the time in relation to it. We can, for example, connect the Blair standard directly with the huge upsurge in the reading of the old-canon rural religious literature which occurred at the same time and was entrenched into school teaching. As far as readers were concerned, Blair and old-canon classics reinforced one another, not only in the sentiments inscribed in the texts but by being materially bound together in the many books, abridgements, and anthologies, in which the official ideology was disseminated. Blair was also largely consistent with moral essays, such as *The Spectator*, being reprinted in large numbers for the rapidly growing reading nation, and especially for young women. We can see that the movement led by Hannah More to try to reform the morals of the poor by giving

---

[13] See appendix 9.
[14] William Paley, *Natural Theology, or Evidences of the Existence and Attributes of the Deity* (1802). Opening words of chapter 1.
[15] Some figures in 'William Paley', appendix 9, 626–7.
[16] Some figures in 'Thomas Chalmers', appendix 9, 591.   [17] Quoted by Keir 31.   [18] Ibid.

them short printed tracts was not primarily Christian, or even religious, but was a mainstream effort to influence conduct, Blair ladled out in spoonfuls as a kind of literary soup kitchen for those who had few other sources of nourishment.[19] Lord Chancellor Eldon, the man who, when he was Attorney-General Scott, had threatened to prosecute the authors of pamphlets which were priced too low, judged that to cast doubt on the doctrines of fall and atonement was blasphemous, that Trinitarianism was the essence of Christianity, and that Unitarianism was illegal under English common law.[20] Measured against the Blair standard, however, such attempts to use the law to enforce belief in the official supernatural can be seen as part of a reactionary political movement aimed at winning back ideological ground which had, intellectually, already largely been lost.

Another source for establishing official horizons is to be found in conduct literature. During the romantic period, there was a boom in the publishing both of conduct books which made clear what their purpose was in their titles and didactic texts which were infiltrated into circulating libraries and school rooms disguised as novels, romances, and tales for children.[21] Many titles were newly written. But the archives also show extraordinarily long print runs for reprints of such older titles as Lady Pennington's *Mother's Advice to her Absent Daughters*, Gregory's *Father's Legacy*, Fordyce's *Sermons for Young Women*, and Chapone's *Letters on the Improvement of the Mind*, texts written and published before the French Revolution and reissued later to meet a new demand for older certainties. There were dozens of other titles, too numerous to list, which were published in single editions or reprinted once or twice only. Conduct books were among the first printed books to be stereotyped, an indication of the industry's confidence that they would sell well over the medium term, and there is plenty of evidence that copies were actually read, sometimes by many people over generations. Conduct books define and prescribe what it is to be a prince, a princess, a lord, a gentleman, a lady, a Christian, a good wife, a responsible parent, a worthy citizen, a good employer, a trusted servant. Some are concerned with conduct in a narrow sense, teaching courtesy and etiquette more than morality, exterior manners rather than interior virtue, but in the romantic period the books invariably advise that genuinely good conduct must always derive from a pure heart, a sound understanding, and a respect for religion. They too are attempts to formulate in language the complex aspirations

---

[19] Discussed in chapter 17.   [20] Paul M. Zoll, 'Lord Eldon's Censorship' in *PMLA* (1953) 440.
[21] For an indication of the scale, see appendix 9 under 'Hester Chapone', 'Thomas Gisborne', George Gregory', 'Hannah More', 'Taylor family', and 'Jane West'.

about how a society should operate in an ideal world.[22] Like Blair's *Sermons*, they constitute a body of texts which, if we are to be fair to the mentalities of the romantic period, deserve our attention.

Conduct books appear to have been given and received throughout the reading population, not just among 'evangelicals', as later writers have tended to assume.[23] Indeed, like Blair's *Sermons*, although many are written by ministers of religion, they say little about religion, except as a kind of accomplishment, mainly suitable for ladies. As Kitty's aunt declares, in Austen's *Catharine*, when listing the many benefits she has conferred on her niece, 'I bought you Blair's Sermons and Coelebs in Search of a Wife.'[24] Irony lurks in many of such literary references, but the documentary record shows that conduct books were often taken entirely seriously. Goodhugh's 1827 recommendations for a gentleman's library, for example, include a section on 'Practical Piety' which includes the standard conduct books.[25] The Eclectic Book Society, the club of City of London merchants who read the latest Byron, the economic theories of Ricardo, and works on trade possibilities in China, also spent their closely rationed purchase money on *Coelebs*, on *Hints to Young Females*, and on *Maternal Solicitude*.

Daniel Macmillan, founder of the publishing company, records that, as young men, he and his friends wished that they had access to such books, and noted that the large number of young men who arrived in London fresh from the country had an especial need of printed guidance.[26] A copy of Cobbett's *Advice to Young Men* contains an inscription by its owner. 'This volume was one of the Factors in my success in life.'[27] In a scene in Austen's *Pride and Prejudice*, the Reverend Mr Collins is invited to read aloud to the Bennet family. They offer him a book from a circulating library, but he is horrified. Mr Collins chooses instead Fordyce's *Sermons for Young Women* and proceeds to read several pages before Lydia interrupts him. 'I have observed', Mr Collins declares when the family make their apologies, 'how little young ladies are interested by books of a serious stamp, though

---

[22] For a full discussion on the types of information about a society that can be obtained from conduct literature and how it can be used to assess changing ideologies, see the introductions to William St Clair and Irmgard Maassen, editors, *Conduct Literature for Women, 1500–1640* (2000), and *Conduct Literature for Women, 1640–1710* (2002).

[23] Examples in Cruse, *Englishman* 76.

[24] *The Novels of Jane Austen*, edited by R. W. Chapman (1954), *Minor Works*, 232. The piece, which was unpublished in Austen's lifetime, was written in 1792, but the substitution in the manuscript of *Coelebs* for Seccar's *Explanation of the Cathechism* cannot have been made earlier than 1810.

[25] Goodhugh 16–19. Information on the sales of the following authors of conduct books is given in appendix 9: Hugh Blair, Hester Chapone, Thomas Gisborne, Hannah More, William Paley, the Taylor family, Jane West.

[26] Hughes 118.   [27] Ac.

written solely for their benefit.'[28] But, like the attempt of Mrs Morland, a character in *Northanger Abbey*, to alleviate her daughter's unhappiness by commending 'a very clever Essay in one of the books upstairs upon much such as a subject, about young girls that have been spoilt for home by great acquaintance – "The Mirror" I think', the many literary references tend also to show that many readers sincerely believed, at least to some extent, in their efficacy.[29]

The huge numbers of conduct books produced during the period, can, I have suggested elsewhere, be linked to the anxieties among the governing élites at the assaults on the existing religious, political, and social order that occurred during the period, anxieties whose changing intensity can be measured in the price of British Government gilt-edged stocks.[30] Much of the prose literature of the romantic period can be read against the foil of the conduct books, a presence always felt even when not referred to explicitly. But we can also use them, as I suggest we use Blair, to build a picture of the mainstream ideology that was perceived as being under threat. Indeed there are so many conduct texts, and they are so similar in their advice, that it is possible to construct a weighted statement, distinguishing the central agreed core from the outliers on either side.

I offer one example of how my suggested approach can be applied. Mary Wollstonecraft's *A Vindication of the Rights of Woman* (1792), which sought to explain how and why women had allowed themselves to become the inferiors of men, and to suggest remedies, was undoubtedly an innovative printed text, an intervention in a long-established system, and an unfailable candidate to be included in any parade or parliament model of intellectual or cultural history. *The Rights of Woman* is often said to have been immediately influential and to have continued to be so.[31] When situated in its material and cultural context, however, a different pattern emerges.

At the time it was published, the *Vindication* was not so much a book as a long pamphlet, one of the many replies to Burke which were circulated

---

[28] Jane Austen, *Pride and Prejudice*, edited by R. W. Chapman (1932) 69. The book concerned is James Fordyce's *Sermons to Young Women* (1766 and later editions). For a discussion of how conduct-book language permeated the speech of Mr Collins, and of other characters in the novels of Austen and Burney, see Joyce Hemslow, 'Fanny Burney and Courtesy Books' *PMLA* (1950) 732.

[29] Jane Austen, *Northanger Abbey*, edited by Marilyn Butler (1995) 210.

[30] See also St Clair, *Godwins and Shelleys*, appendix 3. Since that book was written, I have found more information both about titles and print runs but have not yet made the needed recalculation.

[31] See, for example, Robert Woof, Stephen Hebron, and Claire Tomalin, editors, *Hyenas in Petticoats, Mary Wollstonecraft and Mary Shelley* (1997), the catalogue of the anniversary exhibition in the National Portrait Gallery, which talks of the *Vindication* 'being read and discussed all over Europe and North America' and 'having been steadily reprinted ever since'.

among the mainly masculine book clubs as part of the political debate about the implications of recent events in France. Written in an essentially ephemeral type of print, the book had disappeared from the catalogues of such circulating libraries as had taken it before the turn of the century. Although the likely total print run of its three early editions may have been 1,500 or 2,000 copies or more, on such a small material base, even with the large multipliers associated with pamphlets, the number of readers cannot have been high.[32] It was nearly fifty years before the book was again made available in print. A few copies of a cheap, paper-covered, 'third edition' have been found, published by a radical publisher of the 1840s, at the time of the Chartist agitation, but the *Vindication* did not join the radical canon of Paine, Godwin, Volney's *Ruins*, Byron's *Don Juan* and Shelley's *Queen Mab*, and the other books which helped to shape the emerging new urban culture in the 1820s, 1830s, and 1840s.[33] Nor was the lack of reprints due to intellectual property considerations.[34] Another half century passed until two celebratory editions were produced in 1892 to mark the centenary of first publication. The book then went out of print until the later twentieth century after which its circulation in book form and its cultural influence are clear. With only a few thousand copies of the book manufactured during the whole of the first century after first publication, a figure often surpassed by Scott and Byron on the day of publication, it would have been difficult, and unusual, for anyone, woman or man, to find and read the book.[35]

Compared with the *Vindication*, the material production of conduct books for women was enormous. While we cannot measure influence by the weight of print of competing texts, for every family that had access to the *Vindication* there were probably fifty or a hundred which owned a book which advised against Wollstonecraft's ideas. Only a handful mention her by name and they almost all misspell it, a sign that their authors were not familiar with her book.

---

[32] Such details as I have found are in 'Mary Wollstonecraft', appendix 9, 658–60.

[33] See chapter 16. Noticed also by Barbara Taylor, *Eve and the New Jerusalem* (1983).

[34] The text on publication would have qualified for a copyright period of fourteen years, with an extension of another fourteen if the author was alive at the end of the period. Since the author died in 1797, there was no scope for a fourteen-year extension, and the work probably became free of all legal and customary restrictions as soon as the 1799 edition went out of print. Indeed it was only because the text was by that time free of copyright restrictions that the lone 1840s Chartist edition was possible.

[35] Some examples of women trying to keep the reading of Wollstonecraft alive are noted by F. B. Smith, *Radical Artisan, William James Linton, 1812–97* (Manchester 1973) 14. Others are noted by Pam Hirsch, 'Mary Wollstonecraft, A Problematic Legacy' in Clarissa Campbell Orr, ed., *Wollstonecraft's Daughters* (Manchester 1996).

Joseph Dacre Carlyle, in a book published in 1805 by subscription among the aristocracy, included a poem, *The Salted Cherry*, 'To be written in Mrs Woolstencroft's Rights of Women', about a lady who bids adieu to frowns and folios, resumes her lute, and is married within a month.[36] At the end of the romantic period, Mrs John Sandford, warned that:

it must be allowed that literary ladies have not been always very prepossessing. The disciple of Woolstonecraft [sic] threw off her hat, and called for a boot-jack; and imagined that by affecting the manners of the other sex, she should best assert her equality with them. The female pedant appears in a disordered dress, and with inky fingers; and fancies that the further she is removed from feminine grace, the nearer she approaches to manly vigour.[37]

What also emerges is that many of the apparently anti-Wollstonecraft warnings to be found in conduct literature had been written long before the *Vindication* was published. Fordyce's *Sermons to Young Women*, for example, the book from which Mr Collins read to the Bennet sisters in Austen's *Pride and Prejudice*, declares that:

War, commerce, politics, exercises of strength and dexterity, abstract philosophy, and all the abstruser sciences, are most properly the province of men. I am sure those masculine women that would plead for your sharing any part of this province equally with us, do not understand your true interests.[38]

The fact that Wollstonecraft dashed off the *Vindication* so quickly may suggest that she was already familiar with the arguments which had perhaps been the subject of a hundred conversations.[39] In this individual case, and without lapsing into exaggerations about the power of great books, we can, I suggest, read Wollstonecraft's *Vindication* as representative of a broader consciousness which, because of her unusual talents and opportunities, she was able uniquely to turn into print. In terms of impact, however, from what we know of the constructions of ideal femininity prevalent from the eighteenth century until the suffragist movements at the end of the nineteenth, Wollstonecraft's book made little or no difference to general attitudes to women and scarcely dented the mainstream ideology of femininity prevalent through most of society. It was simply overwhelmed.

[36] Joseph Dacre Carlyle, *Poems* (1805). Published by subscription. For Carlyle see William St Clair, *Lord Elgin and the Marbles* (third edition, revised, Oxford 1998) *passim*.

[37] *Woman in her Social and Domestic Character* (fourth edition 1834) 24. This book, first published in 1830 can be regarded as the last of the romantic period conduct books for women. After Mrs Sandford fewer were published and many, such as those by the bestselling Victorian conduct-book writer Mrs Ellis, concentrated on women as mothers.

[38] James Fordyce, *Sermons for Young Women* (third edition 1766) 272.

[39] For an example of such conversations see the description of John Henry Price's aunt, quoted in 'Mary Wollstonecraft', appendix 9, 660.

We can use printed sources to retrieve mainstream contemporary horizons of expectations towards the nature of literature, that is to reconstruct the official ideology of reading itself. Blair's *Lectures on Literature and Belles Lettres* (1783), for example, were as frequently endorsed by those in authority as his *Sermons*, and also sold in large numbers.[40] To Blair can be added Burke's *A Philosophical Enquiry into the Sublime and Beautiful* (1757), another much endorsed and much reprinted text.[41] Extracts and adaptations of both are to be found in conduct literature, school anthologies, and the other print by which the ideology was disseminated.

In these texts, reading itself, especially reading by young people and women, is seen primarily not as a means to knowledge but as an aspect of conduct that needs to be regulated. Hester Chapone's *Letters on the Improvement of the Mind*, for example, first published in 1770, at the time when circulating libraries were expanding fast, and kept in print until Victorian times, devotes about a third of the book to advice on reading. Chapone advises against studying 'the learned languages' (Latin and Greek) and against books on religion other than 'practical divinity' (i.e. conduct). She recommends especially the reading of history, ancient and modern, moral essays, such as *The Spectator*, are said to be particularly useful. 'I do not mean to confine you solely to that kind of reading – on the contrary, I wish you frequently to relax with poetry or some other amusement.' Poetry, 'if applied to its true ends, adds a thousand charms to those sentiments of religion, virtue, generosity, and delicate tenderness by which the human heart is exalted and refined'. Chapone recommends Shakespeare and Milton, translations of the Greek and Latin classics, some science, philosophy, and history particularly of the ancient world. She warns against reading novels which raise expectations of extraordinary adventures and cause readers to admire extravagant passions, and lead to unacceptable conduct. Young women should only read novels under supervision. 'I am persuaded that the indiscriminate reading of such kind of books corrupts more female hearts than any other cause whatsoever.'

During the romantic period we also see books solely devoted to advice on reading, seen as one of the biggest threats to the existing social structures.[42] Some distrust almost all reading. Others urge their readers, especially women and young people, to be moderate in the amount of reading

---

[40] See 'Hugh Blair', appendix 9, 581.   [41] See 'Edmund Burke', appendix 9, 582–3.

[42] Conduct books which contain much advice on reading include, besides those already mentioned, *Advice from a Lady to her Grand-Daughters, in a Series of Familiar Letters* (1808); Elizabeth Appleton, *Private Education; or A Practical Plan for the Study of Young Ladies* (third edition c. 1816): J. Aikin, MD, *Letters from a Father to his Son on Various Topics Relative to Literature and the Conduct of Life Written in the Years 1792 and 1793* (1796), and *Letters to a Young Lady on a Course of English Poetry*

they indulge in, choose carefully what to read, make their choices under guidance from the church, from parents, from teachers, to keep common-place books of *sententiae*, and to avoid desultory browsing. Reading should be undertaken in moderation and under supervision. Women were at risk of liking reading too much. It was too exciting, too distracting, and it inflamed the imagination. Women were liable to become literature abusers, with dis-astrous consequences for themselves, their families, and society at large.

The effects of reading poetry and novels were particularly feared. As the medical doctor, Aikin, wrote in one of two books devoted to advice on reading:

Congratulations on receiving the 'elegant present of a set of the English Poets' . . . 'I shall take it for granted that you are already well grounded in the principles of morality, and therefore may be trusted to extract what is most valuable from a set of authors who, in general, are friends to virtue and decorum, while you pass lightly and unhurt over the dubious matters which may be mingled with the rest.'[43]

According to Elizabeth Appleton, author of a book on female education, 'A book may be the ruin of innocence; the prop of virtue; the comfort of the weak, the terror of the strong; the polisher of a mind, or the depraver of a heart.'[44] 'The recollection of passages of polite literature, wrote the Rev-erend Thomas Broadhurst, with an Aeolian harp in mind, 'may cause your hearts to vibrate with the purest pleasure, and communicate a warmth and vigour of sentiment that may operate with the happiest effects upon the moral frame'.[45] 'Poetry affords a rich source of improvement, interest, and amusement'; wrote another respected churchman, 'but it must be of that kind which elevates the thoughts, ameliorates the heart, kindling benevo-lence by pathetic narrative or description, and presenting vivid pictures of

---

(1804), Thomas Broadhurst, *Advice to Young Ladies on the Improvement of the Mind, and the Conduct of Life* (second edition 1810); Mrs Child, *The Mother's Book* (n.d. many editions). A. S. Hunter (a woman), *Miscellanies, Designed chiefly for the benefit of Female Readers* (1810); John Angell James, *The Christian Father's Present to his Children* (first published 1824 shortly before the news of the death of Byron and had reached a fourteenth edition by 1844); Edward Mangin, *An Essay on Light Reading, As it May be Supposed to Influence Moral Conduct and Literary Taste* (1808); Hannah More, *Hints Towards Forming the Character of a Young Princess* (1805) and her other works; *Several Observations on Authors and Books in the English and Foreign Languages . . . necessary for the Formation of a Select and Small Library* (1813); J. Thornton, *Counsels and Cautions for Youth. In a Series of Letters from a Father to his Son* (1829); Anna Williams, *Hints From an Invalid Mother to her Daughter, on Subjects Connected with Moral and Religious Improvement in the Conduct of Life* (1825); *The Young Man's Own Book: A Manual of Politeness, Intellectual Improvement and Moral Deportment* (1830s) (American but also circulated in Britain). The debate on reading, particularly the reading of novels, is discussed in many modern works, from the time of Leavis, including Houston, and James Raven, *Judging New Wealth, Popular Publishing and Responses to Commerce in England, 1750–1800* (1992).
[43] Aikin, *Letters to a Young Lady*.   [44] Appleton, *Private Education* 240.
[45] Broadhurst, *Advice to Young Ladies* 52.

what is grand and beautiful in nature, or good and fair in morals.'[46] The mind refined, the conduct literature advises, is a more moral mind. Good poetry makes men and women kinder, more sensitive, more generous, more charitable. Cumulatively this refinement is civilisation, a countless number of instances of finer feelings leading to better actions. Literature, in most conduct literature, is the intellectual ally and the emotional support of the official supernatural. In the mainstream ideology of the romantic period, as in the old canon, the only literature that could be good was one that harnessed the aesthetic to social morality.

If, as innumerable introductions to old-canon anthologies proclaimed, the mind can be made virtuous by reading correct literature, it can be corrupted by incorrect. 'Poetry is bewitching', advises one churchman, 'and if not of a strictly moral character, a dangerous species of writing.'[47] In making his selection, wrote one poetry anthologist, his policy had been 'to guard against every sentiment or expression, however much soever recommended by poetic gracefulness, that would give the mind an improper bias, or tend, even remotely, to corrupt the heart'.[48] 'A passion for poetry is dangerous to a woman', writes John Bennett, author of several books on education. 'It heightens her natural sensibility to an extravagant degree, and frequently inspires such a romantic turn of mind as is utterly inconsistent with all the solid duties and proprieties of life.'[49] The authors who are recommended for women and young people to read far into the nineteenth century are primarily old canon, religious authors, above all Milton, Young, Thomson, and Cowper.[50] Walter Scott and Wordsworth were later regarded as permissible, preferably under supervision. 'Beware too much poetry', declares Tegg's *Present for an Apprentice*, a book given to real apprentices by their employers in the London livery companies. 'Facts are the solid treasure of the mind.'[51]

Reading was also feared because it took the imaginations of women and young people from the social control of families. No book, the conduct books advised, should be read in private which could not, with propriety, be read aloud among the whole family. The reading of novels in private,

[46] (Mary Ann Hodge) *Affection's Gift to a Beloved God-Child* (1819) 34.
[47] James, *The Christian Father's Present* ii, 8.
[48] (John Bullar) *Selections from the British Poets, Commencing with Spenser, and Including the Latest Writers* (Southampton 1822).
[49] John Bennett, *Letters to a Young Lady* (third edition 1803) i, 204.
[50] For example, Benjamin Frankland, *Outlines of Literary Culture from the Christian Standpoint* (1845) and Charlotte M. Mason, *Home Education: A Course of Lectures to Ladies* (1886).
[51] *A Present for an Apprentice. To which is Added, Franklin's Way to Wealth. by the late Thomas Tegg, Esq* (second edition 1848) 109.

Figure 15. 'Tales of Wonder'. A satirical print by Gilray on the effects of reading on
impressionable ladies. Undated. From Amy Cruse, *The Englishman and his
Books in the Early Nineteenth Century* (1930).

Hannah More advised, had much the same effect on women as drunken-
ness had on men – it made them morally unfit for their duties. Women,
she advised, should not read novels. 'The imagination, that notorious cor-
ruptor of the heart . . . by indulgence of seducing images . . . prepares
for surrender of virtue.' 'The circulating library is no unfrequent road to
Doctors' Commons' (the criminal divorce court).[52] Novels are addictive,
declared Gisborne, 'the appetite becomes too keen to be denied, and . . . the
heart is secretly corrupted'. The harm which circulating libraries caused,
was, he advised 'extreme and its worst effects are on the female mind'.[53]

The 'imagination', a key concept of later constructions of romanticism,
was seldom approved of by those who believed that reading had lasting
effects.[54] According to Henry Belfrage, a writer at the more authoritarian

---

[52] Hannah More *Moral Sketches of Prevailing Opinions and Manners, Foreign and Domestic* (1819) 247.
[53] Thomas Gisborne, *An Enquiry into the Duties of the Female Sex* (1797) 119.
[54] Notably in the works of Hannah More, and Emma Parker, *Important Trifles: Chiefly Appropriate to Females on their Entrance into Society* (1817).

Christian end of the range, the 'romantic imagination' aroused by reading was pernicious. 'The pleasure which is felt in these imaginations renders the humbler joys of real life insipid . . . It would be easy to state numerous instances in which . . . qualities which might have blessed society have withered under peevish repining and gloomy seclusion.'[55] 'Allow me to lift up a loud voice against the ravings of the imagination', writes the Reverend John Todd, author of *The Students Manual*, 'by which the mind is at once enfeebled, and the heart and feelings debased and polluted.' He is referring to the dangers of reading the poetry of Moore and Byron. Todd's book was highly respected during the nineteenth century, frequently reprinted, at various prices for all pockets. Unlike Belfrage, it was a mainstream book, revised and commended by a Canon of St Paul's Cathedral. It was given as prizes to noblemen at famous public schools, and sold as a suitable birthday present until the end of the nineteenth century.[56] One version goes into a paragraph of discreet Latin to explain the dangers of imagination to anyone who has not caught the meaning. Imagination leads to fantasising which leads to masturbation which leads to physical weakness, insanity, and an early death – as the example of Byron was thought to prove.[57]

Another source for building our understanding of horizons of expectations are the printed reviews in literary journals such as the *Edinburgh Review* and the *Quarterly Review* which, like conduct books, were to be found all over the country, often standing on the same shelves as Blair, Buchan, and Burn, in towns where few other substantial books were to be seen. One procedure for assessing influence has been to collect the contemporary printed review notices, especially of those authors today regarded as canonical.[58] Efforts are made to break the anonymity of the writers of these reviews – Jeffrey, Lockhart, Croker, Barrow – so that in addition to the romantic poets we have the romantic reviewers. However there are questionable assumptions about the nature of authorship lurking in this traditional procedure for assessing 'reception'. When reviewers employed the royal 'we', they were implying that their views were those of the institution for which they were writing and of a constituency of the reading nation whom they claimed to represent, not just their own views. They were not only part of the printed-book industry's commercial arrangements for helping to sell books, liable to

[55] Henry Belfrage, *Practical Discourses, Intended to Promote the Improvement and Happiness of the Young, by Henry Belfrage, Minister of the Gospel, Falkirk* (Edinburgh 1817) 252.
[56] Advertisement in 'People's Byron'. See also chapter 21.
[57] See, for example, the long chapter, 'Physiological argument', with its phrase about 'prodigally spending vital force' in Harriet Beecher Stowe's *The Byron Controversy* (1870) 247.
[58] In such volumes as the *Romantics Reviewed* or the *Critical Heritage* series.

be manipulated by their owners, by the state, and by powerful individuals, but they usually saw themselves as appointed to judge new texts against existing standards.[59] It is not necessary to go all the way with John Stuart Mill who believed that periodical writing, since it has to make its impact on an immediate reading, simply catches and reinforces the opinions already held by its readers.[60] But, by making a sample selection of articles in the mainstream literary reviews, we can draw out the implied preconceptions which the owners, editors and reviewers brought to their role. Reviews are, therefore, valuable sources for reconstructing the historical horizons of expectations against which newly printed texts were perceived.

Many literary reviews, for example, seem to have shared the assumption that the main criterion against which a work of literature should be judged was its effect on the minds and morals of readers. Provided that a text was safe, that is, if its reading seemed unlikely to subvert the mainstream values, then it was often appraised in terms of whether it was likely to be rhetorically successful in creating a sense of the sublime, which they believed both proved and promoted the truth of natural religion. Many sentiments about 'Nature' to be found in Thomson and other old-canon poets, and which have later been attributed to Wordsworth as if they were new and original, were the clichés of the day.[61] It was, for example, high praise to compare a modern poet with the masters of the old canon. Wordsworth, according to Hazlitt, one of his warmest admirers, was 'little inferior to . . . Akenside'.[62] At his best, according to other reviewers, he was 'unequalled by Collins', although 'not to be compared with Cowper'.[63] In such sentiments the reviews were reflecting attitudes made more explicitly in the conduct literature. Gisborne, for example, advised that poetry should be committed to memory, but only poetry which:

elevates the heart with the ardour of devotion; adds energy and grace to precepts of morality; kindles benevolence by pathetic narrative and reflection; enters with accurate and lively description into the varieties of character; or presents vivid pictures of the grand and beautiful features which characterise the scenery of nature. Such in general are the works of Milton, of Thomson, of Gray, of Mason, of Beattie, and of Cowper . . . It is thus that taste will be called forth, exercised and corrected. It is thus that judgment will be strengthened, virtuous emotions cherished, piety animated and exalted.[64]

---

[59] For their place in the selling structures see chapter 11.   [60] Quoted by Clive 184.
[61] This was often pointed out by reviewers. See chapter 7.
[62] See Hazlitt 'On Mr Wordsworth's "Excursion"' in (Hazlitt and Leigh Hunt) *The Round Table* (1817).
[63] For example *London Magazine*, 1820. *Monthly Review* review of *The Excursion*, 1815.
[64] For the large sales of Gisborne's works, see 'Thomas Gisborne', appendix 9, 599–600.

When they discuss the newly written romantic works of the day, such as those of Scott and Byron, the mainstream printed reviews delight in the exotic, and in 'beauties', candidates for copying into commonplace books. Much of the comment is about literary matters in a narrow sense, the appropriateness of differing verse genres, the extent to which irregularity of rhythm and rhyme is admissible, whether images drawn from Latin and Greek authors are still effective.

Printed reviews in the liberal and radical press, by contrast, perhaps reflecting the emerging romantic aesthetic more quickly than their rivals, preferred literature to be original, not simply celebratory of existing values. They too wanted literature to be effective in influencing states of mind, and therefore conduct, but as encouragement to social and political change. As many of the pirated editions of Byron and Shelley proclaim in their prefaces, literature could be a means of liberating minds from inherited conventions, of throwing off the mind-formed manacles, of raising expectations of what is possible. Literature to them was a source of information, a critique of society's values, a weapon in the struggle against the kingdom of cant, and an engine of improvement.[65]

Another rich source for reconstructing ideologies is the Bowles controversy about 'correctness' in poetry, which took place in 1821 and 1822, an example of how the reading elites of the country, although thinly spread and geographically widely separated, but potentially unified by their collective reading of pamphlets in book clubs, were able to address a particular issue of the day, and, if not always to achieve a consensus, at least to articulate and to settle the limits of the question.[66] Bowles, a clergyman of the Church of England, was a well-known and successful poet who had revived the sonnet form in English. The Bowles explanation of poetry, by which he meant literature and art more generally, is an update of theories that go back to Longinus, which were adopted in the eighteenth century, and repeated, though seldom so fully or so explicitly, in innumerable contemporary books and lectures; in literary manifestos; in educational books; and in sermons. It is found in speeches by politicians, businessmen, and other non-literary men of influence, notably in addresses to reading societies, local athenaeums, and mechanics institutes. It too can be regarded as part of the mainstream official ideology.

What is poetry, Bowles asks? A mountain is poetic, a forest is poetic, a field of corn is poetic. The word poetic is used as an aesthetic term to describe the sublime scene which produces the observer's response of wonderment and

---

[65] See chapter 16.   [66] Byron, *Prose Works* 120 and 399.

admiration. It is the external reality which is poetic not the words of the text. Indeed sublime scenes do not necessarily require the intermediation of the poet. Some contemporary writers, such as Byron's friend Dallas, aware of the scope for confusion, proposed to call the induced feeling 'poetry' and the writing about it 'poesy', as we may distinguish history from historiography, but this suggestion was not taken up.[67] Art, the theory ran, linking it firmly to natural religion and notions of the sublime, is the work of Man and Nature is the work of God. Much of the debate was about the extent to which the intrusion of Art makes Nature more or less poetic. The ocean is poetic – is it made more so by having a full-rigged ship sailing on its waves? The mountains and skies of Greece are poetic – do they become more so by the presence of the ancient ruins on the Acropolis of Athens? A correct poet is one who correctly judges the balance between Art and Nature. Since the poet is describing a real experience in literary terms, the risk is that his efforts will be too literary, that he will draw on memory or tradition or on the words of other authors instead of capturing the experience direct. Such poetry is untrue to nature, such poetry is incorrect.

Another 'poetic' spectacle, according to Bowles, was an army ready for battle or a fleet of warships. The men and women of the romantic period found sublimity in war. War was honourable, often glorious. War was romantic, and the long romantic poem as practised by Scott, Byron, Southey, and many others, was violent. Every modern victory produced its poetic celebrations, which could now draw on the older romantic traditions of earlier wars. And, as the manuscript commonplace books show, women were expected to share in the romance of national war as much as men.[68] Weeping widows, and hungry orphans, soldiers and sailors mutilated by war but content with their chew of tobacco, all had their allotted place in the scheme of things alongside the beggars, celebrated in innumerable works of literature and conduct books as fitting objects of sympathetic sensibility. During the long wars with France between 1793 and 1815, most writers, including the famous women poets, celebrated patriotic war which was always assumed to be honourable.[69] When we understand that almost nothing which questioned or undermined the institutions of the nation

[67] See David Masson, *Essays, Biographical and Critical: Chiefly on English Poets* (1856). When Byron and Hobhouse wrote to one another about 'poesy' or 'poeshie', they were probably simply mocking John Murray's Scottish accent.

[68] See chapter 12.

[69] See *British War Poetry in the Age of Romanticism: 1793–1815*, compiled and edited by Betty T. Bennett (New York 1976). An exception is Southey's *Battle of Blenheim*, first published in 1798 during Southey's radical phase. '"But what good came of it at last?" / Quoth little Peterkin. / "Why that I cannot tell," said he / but t'was a famous victory.'

state at war was published in the mainstream literature of the romantic period, we can more easily appreciate the virulence of the reaction to Byron and Shelley.[70]

By reconstructing the mainstream horizons which readers, and reading constituencies, may have themselves brought to the act of reading, or which, even if they did not share in them, they were well aware of, we can begin to answer some questions which ought to concern students of the romantic period. How, for example, can we account for the overwhelming and continuing popularity of the Waverley novels? Why were they sold, from the beginning, in huge quantities despite being extremely expensive? Why were they accepted into reading constituencies, such as book clubs and mechanics institutes' libraries, from which all novels had hitherto been excluded? Part of the answer is that their formula of violent romance, neo-chivalric femininity, and political and social harmony based on mutual respect between the rich and the poor, did not offend in the slightest degree against the official and mainstream ideologies. In the Waverley novels, the feedback loop which connected the author to his readers was particularly strong, and every turn round the circuit tended to reinforce its power.

Against our constructed standard, we can, I suggest, better understand the distrust accorded to the romantic tales of Byron. One of the charges was that Byron had made crime exciting. He had glamorized violence outside the permitted limits of honourable war, but he had also made violence disgusting, as in his descriptions of dogs eating human corpses in *The Giaour*. In *Don Juan* he had made war seem pointless, casual, and essentially ridiculous. More generally, Byron undermined the mainstream view of the very nature of literature. 'We hear passages, not the most pure in point of delicacy', Hannah More wrote, 'repeated with enthusiasm by young ladies, from the works of a noble, but profligate and infidel poet, a poet rich in abused genius, and abounding in talents . . . But from the same lips hear little of Milton, and of Spenser, of Cowper, and of Young, of Thomson and of Goldsmith, of Gray and of Beattie, names once dear to every lover of enchanting song.'[71] Southey wrote a satire on Byron as 'Miss Anne Thrope'.[72]

Even the most mainstream and conservative of the new poets, such as Scott and Southey, had, it was increasingly seen, damaged the old nexus between poetry and piety. Their poetry – their sublimity – was set in the

---

[70] For the radical canon, see chapter 16.
[71] She is referring to works published before *Don Juan*.
[72] Jerdan ii, 40. Not included in the Southey canon.

olden days when honourable knights clashed with infidel Saracens. The authors of romantic poems had exported poetry and hence sublimity from the here and now. If they wrote about the present day it was about the bandits of Albania, the fire worshippers of Khoristan, or the noble forest savages of Wyoming, Pennsylvania. Samuel Rogers was among many who tried to bring it back. His tale of English village life was, he claimed in his 1812 poem, *Human Life*, as strange:

> As any that the wandering tribes require,
> Stretched in the desert round their evening fire;
> Or any sung of old in hall or bower
> To minstrel harps at midnight's witching hour.[73]

A question which ought to puzzle literary historians is why *Childe Harold's Pilgrimage, A Romaunt*, caused such a stir among the aristocracy when it was first published in 1812. To the modern reader, cantos 1 and 2, the only parts to appear at that time, are by no means as affecting as 3 and 4 which came out later, and it is easy to see why Byron could not find a publisher. Seen against the contemporary conventions and expectations, however, the puzzle begins to be resolved. Childe Harold looks upon some of the most poetic sights in the world, the mountains of Albania, the ruins of Athens, the Seraglio of Constantinople, the battlefield of Actium where Antony and Cleopatra lost an empire, but he remains – not so much misanthropic, the word used at the time – as unimpressed.

For readers a secret was out. Looking at the wonders of nature and art did not always lift the spirits, induce a sense of the sublime, or instil religious feelings. If even Lord Byron with all his wealth and opportunities had difficulty mustering the right responses, who could blame a bored English lady whose main opportunity for poetic sublimity was a muddy walk in the woods or across the fields to visit a neighbouring lady, with the occasional frisson of getting her feet wet and having to stay over. As Byron wrote in a hurried preface which he added to the third edition when the first reactions were coming in, even he, at this early stage of his career, believed still that poetry ought to be morally improving and that his invented character of Childe Harold was abnormal.

[Childe Harold] was never intended as an example, further than to shew that the beauties of nature and the stimulus of travel . . . are lost on a soul so constituted, or rather misdirected.

---

[73] *The Poetical Works of Samuel Rogers*, edited by Edward Bell (1892) 109. The poem was first published in 1819.

At the time, reactions to beauty were discussed in terms of truthfulness or sincerity. Bowles referred to the 'invariable principles of poetry'. 'Poetry has this much, at least, in common with religion', the *Edinburgh Review* declared, repeating the same conventional sentiments, 'that its standards were fixed long ago by certain inspired writers, whose authority it is no longer lawful to call in question.'[74] In our post-romantic culture it is hard to conceive of literature being subject to fixed moral standards or to fixed standards of taste – we normally expect writers to have an individual outlook, a unique voice, not just to reaffirm and remobilise the old ideas and values.

The theory of correctness in literature defined as unrefined everyone who did not admit to having the correct feelings. As the *Edinburgh Review* author wrote in the same article,

The love, or grief, or indignation of an enlightened and refined character is not only expressed in a different language, but is in itself a different emotion from the love, or grief, or anger of a clown, a tradesman, or a market wench.

Like modern political correctness, the ideology carried a hint of menace and it encouraged pretence. But there is no need to accuse Mary Russell Mitford of insincerity when she described her disgust at *Childe Harold*. 'Not but there are very many fine stanzas and powerful descriptions; but the sentiment is so strange, so gloomy, so heartless, that it is impossible not to feel a mixture of pity and disgust.'[75] When Thomas Grenville declares that the poem 'is written in a deadly spirit of scorn and hate which curdles the blood and chills every kindly feeling instead of cheering and promoting them', he may be insincere but is also merely repeating the cultural conventions in which he and most of his contemporaries were educated.[76] When Wordsworth wrote of Byron, 'What a monster is a Man of Genius whose heart is perverted', he may not be so much hypocritical or jealous but simply unable or unwilling to alter his horizons of expectations of the nature, purpose, and potentialities of literature.[77]

The most sublime – the most poetic – sight in all Europe was Mont Blanc, known to innumerable members of the British aristocracy and gentry as part of the education of the grand tour, and read about by many others.

---

[74] Unsigned review by Francis Jeffrey, October 1802. Quoted by Lionel Madden, *Robert Southey, The Critical Heritage* (1972) 68.

[75] A. G. L'Estrange, *The Life of Mary Russell Mitford* (1870) i, 193.

[76] Grenville to Samuel Rogers, 1812, quoted by P. W. Clayden, *Rogers and His Contemporaries* (1889) i, 89.

[77] Quoted by Andrew Rutherford in *Byron, The Critical Heritage* (1970) 267.

The hotels at Chamonix had visitors' books in which it was customary to record the feelings of religious awe which the mighty mountain inspired. In the years after Waterloo many British people whose horizons of expectations had been formed by the mainstream ideology, looked on the mountain with their own eyes and, according to their accounts, experienced the correct feelings. The grandeur of the scene reinforced their belief in the existence of a benevolent God and a well-designed and well-ordered universe.

Coleridge's *Hymn before Sun-Rise in the Vale of Chamouny* is full of the exotic imagery associated with romanticism.

> Ye Ice-Falls! ye that from the Mountain's brow
> Adown enormous Ravines slope amain
> Torrents, methinks, that heard a mighty Voice,
> And stopped at once amid their maddest plunge!
> Motionless torrents! Silent Cataracts!
> Who made you glorious as the Gates of Heaven
> Beneath the keen full Moon?

It is at the same time entirely correct.

> Thou dread Ambassador from Earth to Heaven,
> Great Hierarch! tell thou the silent Sky
> And tell the Stars and tell the rising Sun,
> Earth, with her thousand voices, praises GOD.

Wordsworth too, when he described his experiences in the Alps in *The Prelude*, is entirely conventional in the conclusions he draws, insisting that whatever wonders he saw and experienced 'were all like workings of one mind, the features of the same face, blossoms upon one tree'.[78]

Shelley, perhaps more than any writer of the period, tried to break the links which had been assumed to connect literature, sublimity, correct feelings, the doctrines of benevolent natural religion, and virtuous conduct. His poem, *Mont Blanc*, which not many of his contemporaries had the chance to read, captures the sublimity of the mountain as vividly as Coleridge or Wordsworth. But he made connections to which most others had been blind. The same severe winters which made the mountain such a sublime sight had caused the glaciers to smash their way into the Swiss valleys, destroying innumerable homes, and reducing the local population to misery and beggary. How could the destructive Mont Blanc represent an ordered divine benevolence? On the contrary:

[78] *The Prelude*, book 6, line 637.

> Thou hast a voice, great Mountain, to repeal
> Large codes of fraud and woe; not understood
> By all, but which the wise, and great and good
> Interpret, or make felt, or deeply feel.

If Blair and the old canon had enabled religion to continue to thrive by quietly substituting natural religion for historical and scriptural Christianity, Shelley's readers, few of whom would ever have the opportunity to look upon the great mountain, could see that one person's natural religion was another's natural atheism. One of Shelley's readers was so incensed at what he saw as the poet's blasphemous response to the mountain that he published a pamphlet on the point at his own expense.[79]

---

[79] Samuel Glover, *Chamouni; or, A Sketch from Nature* (third edition 1828). 'Printed for the Author', Ac. The title page which quotes the *Quarterly Review* of 1818 makes clear that it is Shelley who is attacked. The prefatory poem, is 'Dedicated (without permission) to a Celebrated Atheist'. Shelley would scarcely have merited a rejoinder so long after the article if his views were not spreading rapidly in the 1820s as a result of pirate publishing. See chapter 16.

CHAPTER 15

'Those vile french Piracies'

After 1774, with the equalisation of intellectual property law and practice across Great Britain, the Scottish book industry became part of a national British industry. Following the 1801 Act of Union between Ireland and Great Britain, the Irish book industry too was brought within the same statutory regime as the rest of the now-enlarged United Kingdom and, for the first time, the book industries of the three kingdoms were subject to the same textual controls, the same intellectual property regime, and the same restrictions and taxes at the borders. However, with the loss of its offshore status, the Irish industry was no longer able to operate at the same level of business. Shortly after the union, many of its members migrated to the recently independent United States, taking with them both their professional skills and their capital stock of types and presses, and thereby helped to build a new reprint industry in a rapidly expanding new English-speaking market.[1]

Some offshore publication of English-language texts occurred in Switzerland, in some of the German states, in the Netherlands, and elsewhere in continental Europe.[2] After the end of the war in 1815, however, the main centre was Paris. Galignani's 'French, English, Italian, German and Spanish Library' was a home from home for the thousands of British who flocked to the continent as soon as it was reopened to private travel. Galignani provided a *poste restante* service, and maintained a visitors' book which kept visiting expatriates informed on who was in town. The English newspapers arrived every morning, and there was a comfortable reading room and circulating library.[3] Galignani's own printed guidebook offered a pleasing picture of the attractions:

---

[1] Discussed further in chapter 19.   [2] Until 1830 the Netherlands included what is now Belgium.
[3] Giles Barber, 'Galignani's and the Publication of English Books in France from 1800 to 1832' in *The Library* (1961); and James J. Barnes, 'Galignani and the publication of English Books in France: A Postscript' in *The Library* (1970).

... subscribers can walk or sit and read, the victims of ennui, the lovers of sentiment, admirers of poetry, the readers of research; in short all who prefer occasionally a book to a ball-room, even in the gay capital of Paris, may supply their different literary tastes.[4]

Giovanni Antonio Galignani, whose family had been printers in Italy since the sixteenth century, established his foreign-language bookshop in Paris in 1798. In 1818, he reprinted Byron's *English Bards and Scotch Reviewers* and *The Curse of Minerva*, two poems which Byron had suppressed and which were difficult to buy in Britain.[5] Soon he was reprinting each of Byron's new poems as they came out, then his earlier poems, then favourites by Scott and Moore.[6] The Galignani reprints were only a few francs each, a fraction of British prices at current rates of exchange.[7] Almost immediately, another Paris publisher, Baudry, started reprinting his own English editions, and within a year, the idea had been take up by printer/publishers in other continental cities.[8]

Because, in Britain, the ownership of texts was sometimes split among several publishers, each of whom had stocks of books waiting to be sold, editions of 'collected works' tended to be incomplete. The ownership of Scott, for example, both the poems and the novels, was not only spread but divided into shares, and it was only the forced sales which followed the crash of 1826 that enabled all the intellectual property rights to be brought together. The copyrights of Byron were also split, some being owned by Byron, others by Murray and his partners, and there were works whose status was uncertain.[9] The British editions of *The Works of Lord Byron* published by Murray during the romantic period excluded some of Byron's longest and most famous works.[10] Galignani, however, and other continental publishers who were not bound by British intellectual property laws, were soon producing attractive multi-volume editions which were not only cheaper but textually more complete than anything available at home.

---

[4] *Galignani's Paris Guide*, reprinted frequently during much of the early nineteenth century.
[5] For the huge demand for *English Bards*, met and unmet, and the effects on prices and supply, see chapter 9.
[6] See 'Offshore publication of English language texts', appendix 5, 520–4.
[7] Under the gold standard the rate was stable at 25 francs to £1 (20 shillings).
[8] *The Works of the Right Honourable Lord Byron, in Seven Volumes* (Brussels 1819). Some of the poems are paginated so that they could be sold individually. *The Works of the Right Honourable Lord Byron, in Five* [later more] *Volumes* (Zwickau 1819). Printed for the Brothers Schumann in small square Tauchnitz style, with illustrations, some apparently original, others copied from Stodhart as published by Murray in their 'Pocket Library of English Classics'.
[9] For example poems, such as *Fare Thee Well*, whose first printing was in newspapers.
[10] Murray's first collected edition to include *Don Juan* was published in 1831. See 'Lord Byron', appendix 9, 590.

In 1826 Galignani made another breakthrough. Besides continuing with his single works and multi-volume editions, he offered the *Complete Works of Lord Byron* in a single large volume, a format convenient for visitors and for families often on the move. Since Byron was now dead, Galignani's edition was able to contain everything which the poet had written that had been printed in any form. The one-volume Byron was such a success that Galignani decided to reprint the works of other favourite modern poets in the same format. Baudry immediately printed his own rival one-volume Byron soon after, to be followed by other pirates in Brussels, Leipzig, and now Frankfurt, who all adopted the same format.[11] Galignani also brought together the works of authors such as Coleridge, Shelley, and Keats who had been published by a variety of publishers, which had often been remaindered or sent to the trunk-makers and pastry-cooks, and which were hard to find in Britain in any form.

Galignani's editions were tightly but clearly printed, with scarcely a misprint. They were manufactured by stereotype plates, or as the French called them, clichés. Galignani was therefore able to supply his markets at reducing prices or wider margins.[12] Those volumes which included the works of more than one author were printed and paginated so that they could be sold by individual author.[13] They all had an engraved title page, a portrait, a life of the author, with critical remarks, and other attractive features, including a specimen of the author's handwriting engraved in facsimile intended to emphasise the individual romantic genius of the author. Galignani employed competent British editors, who drew heavily on Hazlitt's 1819 lectures, and added much commendatory writing.[14]

[11] I have been unable to ascertain whether Galignani was quite the first. Broenner of Frankfurt and Fleischer of Leipzig also published one-volume editions of British poets in 1826, the year the new format began, and it is possible that they may have anticipated Galignani by a few months.

[12] French printers had introduced stereotyping earlier than in Britain, even for foreign-language books. A copy of *The Vicar of Wakefield* published by Didot in the 'Seventh Year of the French Republick' (1799) is called 'Stereotype edition' on the title page, Ac. The printing of some successive Galignani editions of Byron and Moore, to which later poems were added, is identical, except for the placing of the printers' key signatures on the page which I take to be a sign that they were made from separate impressions from the same plates. For the most-demanded authors there appear to be have been new impressions even within apparently identical editions, for example copies of Byron, 1826, are found with the key signatures in different places. In some British books the key signatures were part of the text which was stereotyped, but in others they appear to have been added with each new impression. I have been unable to discover what was the standard practice in France, Germany, or the United States, or if practice was indeed standard.

[13] Only a few copies of individual authors taken from the composite volumes have survived, probably because booksellers have subsequently regarded them as incomplete. It seems likely that Galignani and Baudry may have offered even shorter portions, for example the 'Life of Byron' by Lake prefixed to the volume may have been available separately. An example in Ac.

[14] For the modest sales of Hazlitt's book see 'William Hazlitt', appendix 9, 605.

As texts, the Galignani editions were in the tradition that, in England, stretched back to the Jonson and Shakespeare first folios, of presenting the author as an acknowledged classic, canonised and memorialised in a splendid single large volume. In some editions, the portrait of Byron shows him wearing a laurel wreath. As had happened with the old canon, the first canonising series of the romantic poets was produced outside England.

After the one-volume poets came the one-volume novelists. At first Galignani copied the three-volume format in which most new British novels were being published. Soon, in association with Baudry, he produced single-volume editions, already bound, which were even better value. Charles Manby Smith, a printer who went to Paris in 1826 in search of work, remembered the first books Galignani gave him to reprint: the third volume of the most recent Waverley novel, *Woodstock*, James Fenimore Cooper's *Last of the Mohicans*, and a pocket edition of Byron. The *Woodstock*, Smith's eye could see, was the corrected second proofs, complete with the famous nameless author's manuscript corrections transcribed. It was a copy of corrected proofs obtained surreptitiously from the printing shop.[15] In the previous century the Irish offshore pirates had boasted that they could obtain a copy of the printed text of any book before it was even published in London. Galignani could do the same. By the late 1820s, every new British novel was on sale in Paris within three days of its publication in London, in a beautiful, well printed, convenient, cloth bound, single-volume edition, at a quarter of the British price.

Byron, Moore, and Scott, and their publishers, realising that Galignani would reprint their works anyway, gave him formal permission, provided he undertook only to sell the books on the continent. By doing so they gained some control over the texts and a modest fee.[16] Galignani's editions were, in the eyes of the French law, not piracies, and they therefore qualified for copyright protection in France. Galignani, who warned in his advertisements against buying inferior Belgian or German versions, was thus able to take legal measures against French publishers who pirated his piracies. Within a few years Galignani, Baudry, and a few others had established an offshore pirate syndicate, sharing printing and distribution facilities, and combining to crush other offshore pirates. By the 1830s they were able to offer a full range of recent English literature in a wide variety of formats. Baudry's catalogue of 1841, for example, included modern poetry, modern novels, a range of English old-canon classics, including Shakespeare, selections from favourite authors, anthologies in verse and prose, books

[15] Manby Smith 59.   [16] £100 in the case of Byron. Smiles ii, 117.

for children, and school textbooks, but with only a few exceptions, no non fiction.[17] By 1850 the Baudry/Galignani one-volume series contained all the Waverley novels and about 450 other titles, almost all recent British novels, including those of Dickens. A single company offered English literature for all ages at highly attractive prices.

Galignani's Messenger, an English-language newspaper which circulated all over the continent, kept the expatriates informed of the political news from home. *Galignani's Weekly Repertory and Literary Gazette* pirated and summarised the best articles from the literary reviews. British expatriates in France and Italy could, if they chose, share in the literary life of their country more easily and more cheaply than many of their friends at home. In the absence of restrictions on excerpting, abridging, and adapting, excellent anthologies of the modern British poets were available at reasonable prices abroad long before they appeared in Britain.[18] School children in France, Germany, and the United States were reading Scott and Byron in cheap, specially prepared, editions when British children were still largely confined to Thomson, Young, and Cowper, to Enfield's *Speaker* and Murray's *Reader*.

Despite the strict textual controls in force in Britain during the romantic period and later, the French offshore industry was entirely a commercial enterprise concerned with evading the effects of private intellectual property. It did not, as did other offshore book industries, serve as a means of by-passing state censorship. In the eighteenth century, it had been offshore French publishing in Switzerland and the Netherlands which enabled many texts which undermined the legitimacy of the regime to be circulated and read.[19] In Germany too, as the publisher Friedrich Perthes noted in 1814, in practice there was freedom of the press because what could not be published in Prussia could be published in Württemberg and what was forbidden in Hamburg could be printed ten paces away in Danish-controlled Altona.[20]

The English-language books produced by the offshore pirates were sold in all the places in mainland Europe where the overseas British were to be found, the French channel towns, Paris, Brussels, Geneva, Florence, Rome, and other cities along the route of the grand tour. In Florence alone there were 200 English families in 1825.[21] The books were sold to British tourists, to officers and families of the British army and navy, to members of the

---

[17] There is a full list in a copy of *The Poetical Works of Scott* (1841), Ac. Such exceptions as there were tended to be associated with the main authors, for example, Scott's *Life of Bonaparte* and biographies of Byron.

[18] Examples in appendix 5.   [19] See Darnton, *Forbidden*.

[20] Quoted in translation by Blanning 140.   [21] Leigh Hunt, *Autobiography* (new edition 1840) 368.

colonial administrations in the Mediterranean and elsewhere, and to the many British expatriates who had settled abroad to take advantage of the favourable rate of exchange – officers on half-pay (normally a good deal less than half), widows on annuities, invalids in search of sunshine, and many others on incomes well below £5 (100 shillings) a week. All over the continent there were British men and women who had fled abroad to escape arrest for debt, because their personal partnerships were irregular, or simply to escape the oppressive laws and heavy taxes of post-war England. William Hazlitt, no lover of country or provincial life, described the habits of the English he met on his continental tour: the daily walks, the visits to other expatriates, and the endless reading of the Scotch novels – 'to be had of every library on the Continent in English, French, German, or Italian, as the reader chooses'.[22] Whatever the reasons that took the British to their dull lives, they could all enjoy a cheap scud up the Mediterranean with Conrad the Corsair, a chase across the Trossachs with the Lady of the Lake, a feast among the clashing knights at a mediaeval tournament, or a glimpse of Good Queen Bess and the Merry England of Kenilworth Castle as imagined by the author of Waverley.

The continental offshore editions were much read by those to whom English was not their first language, indeed may have contributed to its spread. The King of Portugal had a Galignani Byron in his library.[23] Byron, Scott, and Moore, in particular, appear to have been widely read in France, Germany, Italy, and elsewhere in western Europe, in their original language, translated, illustrated, adapted for the opera, and otherwise mutated and appropriated into local cultures. The German pirates took them on to Poland and Russia, with effects on the literature of those countries too. An advertisement leaf in Broenner's Frankfurt edition of *The Poetical Works of Scott*, for example, lists the names of booksellers who sold his English-language books in Amsterdam, Brussels, Copenhagen, Leyden, Milan, Moscow, Paris, St Petersburg, Philadelphia, and Venice.[24] Like the publishers of Latin books in the early modern period, the French, German, and Dutch offshore publishers supplied the most famous texts in all the main European languages to a thinly spread but influential group of readers all over the continent and into the new world. If the romanticism of the 1820s and later was a European-wide phenomenon, with Scott and Byron among the leaders, then the offshore reprinters, which made access to new

[22] W. Hazlitt. *Notes of a Journey through France and Italy* (1826) 386.
[23] Copy with the royal librarian's stamp seen in a Lisbon bookshop, 1994.
[24] Printed advertisement in *The Poetical Works of Walter Scott Complete in One Volume* (Francfort O. M. Printed by and for H. L. Broenner (1826), Ac.

foreign-language texts cheaper than to new local-language books in almost every country, helped to bring it about.

The importation of offshore reprints into the United Kingdom was forbidden by law if they were intended for resale, but books owned by individuals and intended for their personal use could be brought in provided excise duty was paid.[25] As the London publishers had warned, with the street price of Byron in London six times the street price in Paris, it was impossible to keep the pirates out. Even if Galignani had honestly tried to restrict the sales of his books to continental markets, a differential of that size was unsustainable. From the mid 1820s Galignani's books poured across the channel. The Galignani family were professed anglophiles – one of the sons was awarded a medal for his generosity to British charities in France. But the London literary establishment hated the French pirate and all his works. To Wordsworth and Southey, he caused only annoyance when he sent each of them a complimentary copy of his edition of their poetical works, specially printed on 'vellum paper'.[26]

In 1829, with measures reminiscent of those taken against Scottish books in the mid eighteenth century, the London publishers decided to tighten their cartel. They set out the 'permitted' terms of prices and discounts in 'Regulations' and established a permanent committee to enforce them. By denying the normal credit facilities to publishers who remained outside the cartel and refusing to handle their books, they forced them to conform. 'Underselling', that is breaches of resale price agreements, was condemned and public campaigns mounted to persuade parliament and the public that high book prices were, in the long term, in the public interest. The main new focus of their attention was, however, as it had been in the high monopoly period, on the tying-in arrangements. By requiring that their books could only be sold from designated bookshops, the publishers tried to drive. out of business any traders whose premises were not open to inspection by the officers of the cartel. The stated objective was to make bookshops more attractive, but the real purpose was to deny the offshore pirates access to retail outlets. The publishers also tried to erect new entry barriers. The minimum capital requirements, for example, would have precluded men such as Lackington and Tegg who had started with no capital apart from a few books on a stall.

However, although the publishers sent inspectors round the bookshops and circulating libraries, and publicly blacklisted any found to be handling

---

[25] See Giles Barber, 'Treuttel and Wurtz: Some Aspects of the Importation of Books from France, c. 1825' in *The Library* (1968), 139. The scale of excise duties is noted in appendix 5.

[26] Southey, *Life* vi, 89.

imported piracies, they had only partial success.[27] By the late 1830s, as they noted in a formal protest to the government, they had lost their markets on the continent, the Channel Islands, in America, and in all the colonies. 'All the circulating libraries upon the coast', they declared in one submission, 'and for nearly forty miles inland, together with a great number of the small libraries around London, are supplied entirely from these pirated editions.'[28] Since most of the imports were clearly illegal, the government agreed to take action. Excise officers were instructed to rummage travellers' luggage to make sure that any books imported were for personal use and not for resale. To meet this test, it was enough for a traveller to write his name on the title page. Many surviving Galignani books as a result provide rich direct information about their first owners.

The effect was however to inconvenience law-abiding travellers without stopping the main trade. An invoice of 1839, discovered during a search by excisemen, shows John Bushell of Dover supplying Galignani's reprints to a circulating library at Bolton in Lancashire, fetching them from across the channel in his own boat.[29] His son, an employee of Galignani, arranged regular supply to Galignani's agents in the French channel ports. The Bushells were not casual or opportunistic smugglers, but were running a profitable, sophisticated small business. In 1840 the bookseller A. D. English of Hull offered an imported edition of Byron's *Collected Works* in one volume, at 18 shillings compared with Murray's lowest price of £2 2s (42 shillings).[30] Individual customers could order direct from Paris, and after paying all customs and freight costs, still save 50 per cent on price. Wordsworth told his publisher how he went anonymously into a bookshop in Piccadilly and asked if he could buy a copy of the Galignani edition of Wordsworth's *Complete Works*: 'Yes.' 'Could I have five.' 'Yes.' 'Ten.' 'Yes.' When Wordsworth asked about ordering 500, the shop assistant said 'give me only time'.[31]

In 1842 the London publishers persuaded the British government that such imports were theft, and deserved to be destroyed even if they were bought abroad for personal use abroad. What were expatriates to do when they returned home, Lord Mahon asked in the House of Lords, throw their libraries into the sea? The official answer was yes. In 1843 a certain Colonel Clavering returned to England after long military service abroad. Among his luggage the excise officials discovered copies of the works of Byron and Scott which he had bought years before and on which he had paid import

[27] James J. Barnes, *Free Trade in Books* (1964) 26.
[28] Quoted in James J. Barnes, *Authors, Publishers, and Politicians, The Quest for an Anglo-American Copyright Agreement 1815–1854* (1974) 96.
[29] Noted in appendix 5.   [30] Gillyat Sumner papers, Bodleian.   [31] Wordsworth, *Letters* vii, 328.

duty. The books were seized and destroyed. A proposal from the publishers that the excisemen should raid circulating libraries and burn any imported books they found there too, was, however, not proceeded with.

Instead the government began to build an international copyright convention and the publishers began to create an international market-sharing agreement which would protect them in the future. In 1837, according to a Galignani advertisement of that date, all the poets in the original 1829 list were still available, and the trade continued through the 1840s.[32] In 1850, however, with the coming into force of the Anglo-French copyright convention, the French pirates were obliged to sell all the unauthorised books which they held in stock at that time, in the biggest literary-distress sale of the century.[33] Almost all of the books Galignani and Baudry ever produced were still available, their price reduced to a twelfth of London prices.[34] A unique episode in the history of the offshore printing of books was finally over, and another stage reached in the globalisation of intellectual property.

There are no known archival records of Galignani's costs, production or sales. Byron, who made inquiries, was told that in Paris an edition of 400 was enough to pay all its expenses, only a little less than the British rule of thumb but at a lower price level.[35] Wordsworth heard from a Galignani employee that the firm had printed 3,000 copies of his collected poems, a figure which, if broadly correct, was equivalent to about a quarter of all his regular sales achieved till that time.[36] Murray believed in 1828 that at least 15,000 copies of Byron piracies had been imported from France by that date alone.[37] Whatever the actual levels, the offshore production of the romantic period, like the Irish offshore publication of the eighteenth century, was no mere skimming of the surface, but a substantial addition to the number of printed texts in circulation both in the United Kingdom and elsewhere.

Who were the readers? Despite attempts to shame them into buying British – 'No one need condescend to purchase foreign editions', Murray declared in his advertisements – the British public did not refuse to pay the lower prices. To judge from ownership inscriptions, armorial bookplates, and library catalogues, many of Galignani's customers were members of the same upper- and middle-income groups who bought new books at the

---

[32] Copy among the Blackwood archives.
[33] William B. Todd and Ann Bowden, *Tauchnitz International, Editions in English 1841–1955* (1988).
[34] Advertisements in the 1853 edition of *Galignani's Paris Guide*, Bodleian.
[35] Byron, *Letters and Journals* x, 134.   [36] Wordsworth, *Letters* vi, 384.
[37] Smiles ii, 305. The date of Murray's quoted letter is not given.

full price and who joined book clubs and subscription libraries. But the less than rich could also buy: half pay officers, poorer clergymen, students, higher-paid artisans, and others previously excluded or deterred by the high prices. The young Tennyson owned a Galignani Byron.[38] William Godwin, always on the brink of financial disaster, owned a one-volume German offshore piracy of Byron which was even cheaper.[39] John Clare, the Northamptonshire poet, who came to believe that he himself was Byron, owned a Galignani edition.[40] Richard Brinsley Sheridan, the playright's grandson, owned a copy of the Galignani *Coleridge, Shelley and Keats* volume, as did the young William Gladstone.[41] John Ruskin, recalling his boyhood education, remembered the 'large octavo containing the works of Coleridge, Shelley and Keats which so often lay on my niche table'.[42] The copy of Byron from which his father read to Ruskin was probably also a Galignani. And although Wordsworth complained about Galignani's piracy of his own work, he too had the Galignani *Coleridge, Shelley and Keats* in his library, a gift from his brother.[43] Since the foreign pirated books were frequently bought by book clubs and circulating and subscription libraries as well as by individuals, there is a high multiplier. The Nottingham Mechanics Institute bought a Baudry piracy of their local poet, Byron.[44] A label of Pike's Book Society of 1846 shows twenty-five members passing the Baudry *Complete Works of Lord Byron with Notes*, a volume of nearly 1,000 pages, to the next member every fortnight.[45]

A member of the public wrote to Wordsworth, whose writings were among the most expensive books in the history of British literature, to tell him that, out of loyalty to British writers, he had refused to buy the Galignani edition. If the price of the regular edition had also been below £1 (20 shillings instead of 42), he had been told by his bookseller, he would have sold ten times the number of copies.[46] Wordsworth discussed the point with Longman but was persuaded that high book prices were good for authors as well as for publishers. 'If it were not for those vile french Piracies', Wordsworth commented in 1835, 'we should do well.'[47] Wordsworth longed for a wider readership and he envied contemporaries whose books sold well,

[38] Seen in the Tennyson collection, Lincoln Public Library.

[39] A. N. L. Munby, general ed., *Sales Catalogues of Libraries of Eminent Persons* 8 (1973) 286.

[40] A copy of the 1828 version was presented to him in 1831. Clare's library, Northampton Central Library. See also Anne Barton, 'John Clare Reads Byron' in *Romanticism*, 2.2 (1996).

[41] Copy with Gladstone's bookplate seen at a book fair in June 1994.

[42] Sheridan's copy seen in Blackwell's bookshop, 1994. For Ruskin, see *The Complete Works of Ruskin*, edited by E. T. Cook and Alexander Wedderburn (1903–12) xxxv, 274.

[43] A. N. L. Munby, general ed., *Sale Catalogues of Libraries of Eminent Persons* 9 (1974) 57.

[44] Ac.   [45] Ac.   [46] Wordsworth, *Letters* v, 225, 261.   [47] Wordsworth, *Letters* vi, 93.

despising them for pleasing the present when his only hope was to please posterity. He later liked to claim that he had created his own public by the sheer force of his genius. The pick-up in his sales and income began in 1827, the year of his *Poetical Works* in five volumes, which sold 254 copies before May 1828, a figure which would scarcely have been noticed by Scott or Byron, but which for Wordsworth was an unprecedented commercial success. Although the Galignani piracy of the same year has been seen as a confirmation of the growing interest in Wordsworth among the reading public, it was probably as much the cause as the result.[48] The same may be true of Coleridge and Keats, and, to some extent, of Shelley.

Of the 2,000 or so 'Living Poets' whose works were printed in Great Britain in the romantic period, the European offshore publishers pirated nineteen. Of that nineteen, only four, Scott, Byron, Moore, and Campbell, were sufficiently in demand to be pirated by more than one European pirate. The German pirates only reprinted Scott, Byron and Moore, the 'three great stars', as one German publisher described them, 'who eclipsed the rest of the new constellation'.[49] On the other side of the cut-off line, the writers who did not quite achieve the distinction of a Galignani piracy, were included in another form of text which could only be produced offshore, the large anthology of contemporary writing.[50]

The author of a conduct book for ladies, writing in the late 1830s, complained that the French pirates published the wrong texts.

In advertisements and catalogues . . . Byron and Moore have always a conspicuous place, while Southey and Campbell are seldom seen, and Milton and Cowper never . . . [M. Galignani] told the writer that for every copy of *Paradise Lost* he had sold more than two hundred of *Childe Harold* and *Don Juan*, and while an edition of Southey's poems he had published would occasion considerable loss, one to the same extent and expense of the poems of Moore would yield him a very large profit.

This was proof, the lady concluded that British expatriates were 'people of the least purity of taste or that their taste had become vitiated by a continental residence'.[51] And there were other effects of which she would

---

[48] E.g. Thomas M. Raynor, 'The Establishment of Wordsworth's Reputation' in *Journal of English and Germanic Philology* (1955). For the high prices of Wordsworth see chapter 11 and appendix 9.

[49] Preface to H. L. Broenner's edition of *The British Poets* (Francfort o.M 1828).

[50] For example *The Living Poets of England. Specimens of the Living British Poets, with Biographical and Critical Notices, and an Essay on English Poetry* (Paris Baudry and others) (1827), which Galignani and Baudry sold in partnership, and *British Poets*.

[51] Author of *The Lady's Keepsake; and Maternal Monitor* (no date, late 1830s) 312. Since no other continental publisher reprinted Southey, we can be almost sure that Galignani is the bookseller referred to.

have disapproved. Before Galignani, the buying or renting of an expensive book was, for many families, a collective decision, and also one which enabled the reading of the family to be rationed, monitored, and conducted mainly in public. But now women whose families borrowed or hired the Galignani Byron to read *Childe Harold's Pilgrimage* could peep at *Don Juan* if they dared. If a parson ordered Galignani's Coleridge, a poet known to favour a strong state religion and tight controls on reading, the atheist Shelley came in the same parcel.

When, in the 1840s, the offshore pirates were finally driven out of the British market, the way was open for the British publishers to produce books in any way that suited the needs of the new public that Galignani and his rivals had helped to bring into being. When Murray resumed his monopoly of Byron, his first action was to publish his own unwieldy edition of the collected works in one large stereotyped volume. Like the Galignani version which he had so long hated, Murray's volume was printed tightly in double columns. The poems were arranged chronologically by date of first publication, with preface, notes, portrait, and a specimen of the poet's handwriting engraved in facsimile. Murray's memorialising of his most famous author, a clone of the defeated offshore pirates in every particular, was published in an initial print run of 10,000 and was kept in print for thirty or forty years, with many reimpressions which were usually for only 250 each.[52] Every few years the reimpressions were supplied with a newly dated title page, not real 'new editions' but marketing break points in an almost continuous production.[53] Soon the London and Edinburgh publishers were producing one-volume stereotyped editions of Crabbe, Scott, Southey, Moore, Wordsworth, Shelley, and Hemans. Shakespeare, Milton, Burns, Longfellow and other Victorian favourites followed, some in books almost too heavy to lift. The great verse romances which had carried the imaginations of their first readers to the highland glens of Scotland, the deserts of the Middle East, the mountains of Greece, and the ruins of Rome, were now, as Shakespeare had been in 1623, put under house arrest by the sheer size and inconvenience of the books.

Successful offshore piracy relied on speed in being able to identify changing opportunities and taking advantage of them. Whereas the British publishers were defending an entrenched monopoly position, Galignani and the foreign pirates were venture capitalists, operating at the leading edge of production and marketing, changing their products and practices whenever

---

[52] See 'Lord Byron', appendix 9, 590.   [53] For the effects of stereotyping see also chapters 9 and 21.

they sensed a shift in customer mood. The offshore pirate lists, created in a crucible which burned away many of the non-literary structural, institutional, and financial barriers which normally separated writers from readers, may, therefore, give a measure of the relative intensity of demand, including unmet demand. They are indicators of changes in preferences among the large constituency of influential readers who coincided to a large extent with those who founded and supported the subscription libraries, the book clubs, and the mechanics institute libraries.

Of the 2,000 or 3,000 or so poets who had tried their art and their luck during the age of Scott and Byron, only about twenty or thirty were ever later reprinted in Great Britain.[54] With the exception of Blake, the others disappeared, like Lucifer, never to hope again. For the most part the survivors were those identified by Galignani in the late 1820s. His list was therefore, in practice, not only a canonisation but a harbinger of things to come. The same pattern emerges, although less clearly, with regard to novels, Baudry's offshore, numbered and author-classified series, *Collection of Ancient and Modern British Authors*, anticipates the onshore canonisation of *Bentley's Standard Novels* which adopted many of the same characteristics a few years later.[55] The single book of poetry which was added to both the French and the American offshore lists after 1829, Hemans's *Poetical Works*, published ten years later, lies far outside the normal pattern.[56] It looks like a harbinger of the popularity which Hemans, the champion of the domestic affections, was shortly to enjoy in Victorian times, in Britain and the United States. Just as, in the eighteenth century, the *British Poets* prepared by Bell in Edinburgh was the start of a long procession of similar works in England, so the continental offshore reprints of the romantic-period poets anticipated what was later to happen in Britain.

One puzzle remains. Why, we may also ask, did Galignani and the other European offshore pirates reprint only poetry and novels? Why, as economic agents, did they not claim a share of the monopoly market on the many books of history, travel, exploration, antiquities, and other non-fiction which were also being published in Britain at high prices during

---

[54] The other poets of the romantic period frequently reprinted after their deaths included Crabbe, Hemans, Hood, Leigh Hunt, James Montgomery, and Pollok, but few others.

[55] See chapter 18.

[56] *The Poetical Works of Mrs Felicia Hemans: Complete in One Volume. With a Critical Preface* (Paris: Galignani 1836). This book appears to be identical with a locally edited and stereotyped cloned edition published in Philadelphia in the same year, *The Poetical Works of Mrs Felicia Hemans: Complete in One Volume. With a Critical Preface* (Philadelphia 1836): 'Published by Thomas T. Ash, Chesnut Street. Stereotyped by John Fagan, Philadelphia'. The Paris edition was either manufactured from imported sheets or, possibly, a set of stereotype plates was shipped to America.

the years of the offshore pirates' greatest success? The Scottish offshore printers reprinted only two literary works of the English Elizabethan age, Sidney's *Arcadia* and Shakespeare's *Venus and Adonis*, an indication of the special popularity of those texts. The Dutch offshore printers of the seventeenth century had concentrated on English-language Bibles and devotional books, such as Lewis Bayley's *Practice of Piety*.[57] Later, at the time of the Restoration, their main business was plays, including Shakespeare. The Irish pirates of the eighteenth century had reprinted anything they thought would sell, including all the great eighteenth-century works of literature, history, philosophy, political economy, and travel. At the turn of the century the Swiss firm of Tourneisen concentrated on the multi-volume philosophical and historical works of the Scottish and English Enlightenment.[58] As late as 1818, when the London publishers appeared before a Select Committee, the examples they gave of offshore piracy were almost all of non-fiction. Why, in the 1820s and 1830s, we have to ask, did no publisher on the continent reprint at least some of the many expensive quartos of travel and exploration that are such a feature of the printed literature of the romantic period in Britain and which were being produced in editions of about 500?

There may be specific explanations which further research could uncover. It is possible, however, that such apparent exceptions were showing the reliability of offshore pirate publishing as a leading indicator of future trends. The romantic period was the last time when a man or woman of general education, could, by reading a range of modern books available through a subscription library or book club, keep reasonably well informed and up to date on all the latest discoveries in the arts and sciences. By Victorian times, both writing and reading were increasingly specialised among professionals and experts. Galignani may have foreshadowed the impending triumph first of 'literature', then of 'the novel' as the only medium which gave unity and shared values to an increasingly differentiated society of Victorian Britain.

[57] First published in 1637, and reprinted over fifty times, one of the biggest sellers of the seventeenth century.
[58] See appendix 5. Examples with prices are quoted in *Select Committee*.

CHAPTER 16

'Preparatory schools for the brothel and the gallows'

Everyone knew that money could be made by reprinting privately owned texts for sale at lower prices. If a case was brought, the courts gave injunctions, the stocks were condemned to be burned, and the pirates punished, although not with death, the normal penalty for theft at this time.[1] However, in an age when most of the population were cut off from reading, the pirate publishers did not regard themselves as thieves. On the contrary, they presented themselves as the advance guard of a new political consciousness among the excluded. Why were modern books so luxurious? Why should the paper be as white, as expensive, and as smoothly pressed as Beau Brummel's shirts? The gilded leather in which every new volume was dressed could cost more than a pair of shoes. Why should printed books, the main medium of all civilisation, be regarded by the law as manufactured goods to be bought and sold in a rigged monopoly market?

Why, they asked, should the grand national aims proclaimed by a thousand reading societies apply only to the topmost income groups and to a few co-optees in the mechanics institutes? Why should the spread of knowledge of the recent discoveries of philosophers, historians, scientists, and political economists be restricted by price? Why should most of the reading nation be condemned to the print of the old canon, a locally English, rural, religious literature written before the French Revolution, that became less relevant to the lives of urban-industrial Britain with every passing year? The reading of good literature, the pirates declared, repeating the clichés, could benefit society by elevating the moral sense of the population. The declared aim of William Benbow, one of the most persistent pirates, was simply to print cheap books for the poor.[2] By showing that a book priced

---

[1] William Benbow, who reprinted Moore's *Irish Melodies* in 1823, was fined £20 reduced to £10 when he agreed to discontinue publication. Quoted by Charles Henry Taylor, *The Early Collected Editions of Shelley's Poems* (Yale 1958) 140, from a report in *The Examiner*.

[2] E.g. in *Scourge for the Laureate* (1825), quoted by Samuel C. Chew, *Byron in England, His Fame and After-Fame* (1924) 126.

Figure 16. The government's attempts to prevent freedom-loving Britannia from reading. From *The Man in the Moon* (William Hone, second edition 1820). The figures wielding the noose, axe, dagger, and chains are Wellington, Castlereagh, and Canning.

at £2 (40 shillings) could be profitably sold at 4 shillings, he declared, he was combating a hypocritical abuse, 'the cupidity of the monopolising booksellers'.[3]

The pirate publishers were also fighting a more general battle. It was not only the private intellectual property regime which kept prices high, but government policy backed by the criminal and civil law. Many in authority feared the growth of reading as such, irrespective of textual content.[4] The romantic period in Great Britain saw political and economic upheaval, teeming new industrial cities, widespread social unrest, unemployment, and riots. Harvests were catastrophic, grain prices rose sharply, and so did the price of bread. It was also a time of severely repressive legislation. More people were hanged, in proportion to the population, than at any other time in recent centuries. Reading, the authorities feared, would cause a resurgence of the political philosophies and egalitarian ideals that had inspired the revolution in France. In the decades after Waterloo, the British government, in close association with its ally, the Church of England,

---

[3] Benbow in *The Rambler* quoted by McCalman 159.   [4] See chapter 4.

reverted to a system of state controls similar in their comprehensiveness to those applied during the seventeenth century. As the Bishop of London told the clergy of his diocese, he lamented the lack of 'humble docility and prostration of the understanding' which had previously made it easier to control the opinions of the common people.[5] During the romantic period and later, the British state mounted the last sustained attempt in the country's history to control the minds of citizens by controlling their access to print.

The first instrument was price, one of the best means of restricting access, as the government knew. William Godwin's *Political Justice* (1793) as radical as Tom Paine and a favourite among the book clubs, escaped prosecution because it was published in expensive quarto and then tranched down to slightly less expensive octavo.[6] As the prime minister, William Pitt, advised his colleagues, 'a three guinea book could never do much harm among those who had not three shillings to spare'.[7] The attorney general applied an explicit policy of restricting access by price. As he wrote to an author in 1793:

Continue if you please to publish your reply to Mr Burke in an octavo form, so as to confine it probably to that class of readers who may consider it coolly: so soon as it is published cheaply for dissemination among the populace it will be my duty to prosecute.[8]

The heavy taxes on paper and advertisements were progressive, in the sense that the bigger the book, the bigger the tax, and those members of the aristocracy and gentry who bought the quartos and octavos helped to pay the interest on the national debt of which they themselves were the main holders.[9] The stamp duties on pamphlets and newspapers, on the other hand, were flat rate and regressive, not so much means of raising revenue as targeted attacks on the reading matter which the state most feared. All books below a certain size were taxed at the flat rate of 3 shillings per copy, equivalent to a third of the weekly wage of a working man. By taxing pamphlets, the government taxed political participation, confining readerships to the upper-income groups and the members of book clubs. Byron's *Ode to Napoleon Buonaparte,* when first published in 1814, consisted of fifteen stanzas printed on fourteen pages. When Murray realised that, at that size,

---

[5] Quoted in *Black Book* 336.   [6] Figures for Godwin in appendix 9, 600.
[7] St Clair, *Godwins and Shelleys* 85.
[8] Quoted by Gerald P. Tyson, *Joseph Johnson, A Liberal Publisher* (Iowa City 1979) 124.
[9] Examples in appendix 5.

the book was liable to be taxed as a pamphlet, he asked Byron to write another stanza and reissued the poem a page longer so that it became a 'book' and escaped the pamphlet tax.[10] The stamp duty on newspapers at the flat rate of four pence a copy, equivalent in some cases to several hundred per cent, taxed the dissemination of information as such. A newspaper that was commercially viable if sold at sixpence was difficult to sell at ten, but those which were sold at one or two pence to readers who had recently joined the reading nation could not stay in business if compelled to charge five or six. Although the newspaper industry continued to grow, the rate was held back by taxation – by the 1830s the United States had almost twice as many newspapers for a population of similar size.[11]

Then there was the window tax. Every house was entitled to six small windows tax free, but a tax was levied on every window of one square foot or more above the limit. Between 1808 and 1823, when the window tax was at its highest, landlords all over the country bricked up every non-essential aperture to bring their properties below the limit, so consigning innumerable families to smoke, smells, and darkness. During the first half of the nineteenth century the population of Great Britain doubled but glass production scarcely increased. The window tax was, according to Charles Dickens, the most effective of all the taxes on knowledge.[12]

The taxes were enforced with great severity. In the 1820s and 1830s over 500 men went to prison for selling unstamped newspapers.[13] But the law was only enforced against print whose textual content the state and its church disliked. James Watson, imprisoned for failing to pay a fine of £20 for selling *The Poor Man's Guardian* unstamped, petitioned parliament in 1833. At his shop, he declared, he had on sale twenty penny periodicals, including *The Penny Magazine, The Penny Cyclopaedia, The Christian's Magazine,* and others published by educational and religious organisations. The tax authorities, he claimed, never interfered with any of these, although they too were legally liable to the stamp duty.[14] Since the apparatus of taxation required an official presence in every town, the stamp duties provided opportunities for patronage, one of the main means by which a deeply disliked regime maintained itself in power.[15] When Wordsworth accepted the office of Distributor of Stamps in Westmorland, he became a

---

[10] Thomas J. Wise, *A Bibliography of. . . Byron* (1933) i, 99. Print runs in 'Lord Byron', appendix 9, 587.
[11] Noted by Frederick von Raumer, *England in 1835* (1836) iii, 57.
[12] Altick 92. See also Vincent 122, quoting an official report.   [13] Linton 33.
[14] *Ibid.* 2.   [15] For these sinecures see *Black Book* 5.

direct personal beneficiary of an abuse of state power aimed at discouraging reading.[16]

In addition to these fiscal disincentives against all reading, the textual controls were tighter than they had been since the seventeenth century. The Seditious Societies Act of 1799, introduced at the height of the anti-Jacobin scare, and reasserted in 1811, was designed to prevent the circulation of 'cheap publications adapted to influence and pervert the public mind'.[17] Under the act, all printing presses had to be registered with the authorities. All printers were required to keep a register of their clients, and to record their imprint (that is, their own name and address) on every piece of printed matter they produced, however short. Any book, pamphlet, newspaper, printed ballad, or poster, could, so it was intended, be traceable back to its author or originator. The law prescribed crushing penalties on printers who printed leaflets and pamphlets without an identifying imprint, even if they were textually entirely lawful, and members of the public could claim rewards by reporting infractions.[18] When the nineteen-year-old Shelley asked his servant Healey to paste up a few political posters in Barnstaple in 1812, Healey was fined £20 on each of ten counts, equivalent to several years' income. Healey spent six months in prison after defaulting on the fines which Shelley declined to pay.[19] In addition to the criminal law, the Society for the Suppression of Vice, a well-financed organisation of ecclesiastical and aristocratic notables, with the Duke of Wellington at its head, established a fund from which to pay bounties to private snoopers who nosed out unlawful cheap publications, often by entrapment.[20] The Society for the Suppression of Vice, declared Sidney Smith, was 'The Society for the Suppressing of the Vices of Persons whose Income does not Exceed £500 per annum.'[21]

A pirate bookseller, as the word had been used earlier, was one who infringed private intellectual property rights. But in the early nineteenth

---

[16] The value of the official appointment, which Wordsworth held from 1813 until near the end of his life, was thought initially to be about £400 a year, gross, about half of that net after paying others to do most of the work. Although Wordsworth is recorded as taking his duties seriously, the post paid far more than was needed in order to collect the duties, and was to a large extent a sinecure, and he was in perpetual fear that the patronage system would be reformed. See Mary Moorman, *William Wordsworth, A Biography, The Later Years 1803–1850* (1965) 244. Wordsworth's name appears among the pensioners and placemen listed in the *Black Book*.

[17] Todd, preface.   [18] *Ibid.*   [19] White i, 248, 280.

[20] When the Bishop of Clogher was discovered undressed with a guardsman in the back room of a public house, it emerged that he was a prominent member of the society and that he had allowed another man to be falsely convicted (believed put to death) as part of an earlier cover-up. McCalman 206. The incident is alluded to in Byron's *Don Juan* viii, 388 'taken by the tail – a taking / Fatal to bishops as to soldiers'.

[21] Quoted by Hugh J. Luke Jr, 'The Publishing of Byron's *Don Juan*' in *PMLA*, 80 (1965).

century only the most legalistically minded could have easily distinguished among those printers and publishers who committed a civil offence by reprinting texts without the owner's permission, those who committed a criminal offence by defying the imprint and registration laws, those whose books were liable to criminal prosecution as seditious, blasphemous, or obscene libel, those whom the state decided not to prosecute but who were privately prosecuted and harassed by the Society of the Suppression of Vice, and the large unrespectable publishing, bookselling, and print-selling industry which operated outside the main stream.

In the struggle for the allegiance of minds which took place after the end of the war in 1815, the power was, however, not all on one side. In 1817, William Hone won a notable victory when a jury acquitted him of charges of blasphemous libel for publishing a series of parodies in ecclesiastical language. The list of people who contributed financially to the costs of his defence is a roll call of the liberal conscience of the nation, from the Duke of Bedford who sent a hundred guineas, to the unknown Mr Shelley of Marlow who sent £5.[22] Nor, outside the mainstream industry, was printing expensive. The taxes on newspapers put many printers out of work, and men who had learned without a formal apprenticeship were willing to undercut the normal rates even further. Nor was the equipment expensive. In 1820 a new state-of-the-art iron printing press, a Columbia or a Stanhope, could be bought for £60 or £70. In 1808 new wooden presses were being advertised for as low as £21.[23] In the late 1820s William Chambers started his business with a second-hand press bought for £3, much the same price as a copy of Wordsworth's *Excursion* bound in quarto.[24]

Many men who had started in other trades took up printing in order to promote their reformist politics. William Benbow had been a soldier and a shoemaker, John Cleave a seaman, James Watson a drysalter's warehouse-man. When the right to trial (habeas corpus) was suspended in 1817, they were among the first to be arrested and the last to be released. Benbow was imprisoned several times for alleged political and publishing offences, though never charged. Besides philosophy, politics, and literature, his shop offered expensive, illustrated, erotic, French novels.[25] These, he claimed, were sold only to the rich, a claim which his published prices tends to confirm.[26] William Dugdale, another pirate, sold pornographic books and prints for much of the nineteenth century, eventually dying in prison in 1867.[27] In his prime, so it was said, he never served his sentences in full.

[22] Subscription list included in *The Proceedings at the Public Meetings . . . for William Hone* (1818).
[23] James Moran, *Printing Presses* (1973) 52.   [24] Chambers 157.   [25] Summarised in appendix II.
[26] Examples in appendix II.   [27] Summarised in appendix II.

Friends in high places were always able to get him released when he put on a show of being ill.[28] As the British state faced what many of its political and ecclesiastical leaders saw as a pre-revolutionary situation, it was remembered that when France had faced its test in 1789, few came forward in defence of the *status quo*. As Robert Darnton has convincingly shown, one factor in the sudden and unexpected collapse of the *ancien régime* in France was that, for decades before, the authority of the monarchy and of church had been sapped by an insistent flow of scandalous, often pornographic, publications smuggled from Switzerland.[29] Stories of financial sleaze and sexual scandal at Versailles had done as much to undermine the structures of power in France as the philosophical writings of Voltaire and Rousseau.

Richard Carlile was a very different pirate. Fashionable, even foppish, in his dress, he was a familiar figure as he strode along Fleet Street between his two shops. Although there was no pornography for sale in either, nor even novels, he sold printed advice on effective female contraception, a subject which was almost as scandalous.[30] Among his other publications was *The Principles of Nature*, by the Reverend Elihu Palmer, which drew attention to seldom-read passages in the Bible, such as the command by the victorious Moses to put to death all the people of conquered Palestine except virgin girls. When in 1819 Carlile was sentenced to three years in prison and fined £1,500 for publishing this 'blasphemous libel', Mrs Carlile took over the business. When she went to prison for continuing to sell the book, her sister took over, until she was imprisoned, and then Carlile's son.[31] Richard Carlile the elder spent nineteen years in prison.

To guard against spies, the Carlile family installed a device to prevent the customers seeing the shopmen. A dial showed the names of the books for sale. The customer turned the hands to point to the title of the book he wanted which was then delivered from a hole in the ceiling, tied up in a parcel. The customer left his money and took the parcel without a word being spoken. Despite such precautions, the snoopers of the Society for the Suppression of Vice managed to gather evidence against the shopmen and bring them before the courts in private prosecutions. Humphrey Boyle was sentenced to eighteen months for selling Palmer's book. Charles Trust, another of Carlile's shopmen, said in his defence that he had not read the book, was a firm Christian, and had resigned from Carlile's employment, but was sentenced to six months, fined £20, and required to find sureties of £100 for five years for himself and £40 from two others. Since these

---

[28] Thomas Frost, *Reminiscences of a Country Journalist* (1886) 54.   [29] See Darnton, *Forbidden*.
[30] For the description and other details, see Vizitelly.   [31] Linton 12.

amounts were equivalent to several years income, there was no possibility of their being paid except from subscriptions collected from sympathisers. The effect was to impose a continuing heavy levy on the government's opponents, to give the authorities power to seize stocks of books and other assets as part payment, and to enable them to rearrest defaulters whenever they chose. A colleague who knew Carlile suggested that he 'was not averse to being prosecuted' because of the publicity and the money, but if this was true, it did not apply to the procession of shopmen who came forward to take their places in his shops.[32] 'I am so extremely poor that prison will be a home to me', Robert Wedderburn, a black man, told the judge when sentenced to two years for writing a freethinking pamphlet, 'and as I am so advanced in life I shall esteem it an honour to die immured in a dungeon for advocating the cause of truth'.[33]

James Watson, Carlile's disciple, opened a bookshop in a street along-side Bunhill Fields, the Dissenters' graveyard where Bunyan lay buried. A fellow-printer who met Watson in 1835 described him as 'a thin, haggard, thoughtful man with a grave but gentle manner', much weakened by his three spells in prison.[34] Watson was determined to break the sneer of 'cheap and nasty' which was easily transferred from the books to the publishers and the readers. Watson, it was said:

Cared . . . for the correctness and decent appearance of his books, even the cheapest. They were his children . . . he would have them well-dressed and fit to be admitted anywhere . . . Good matter, carefully edited, on fair paper, cleanly printed, squarely folded, thoroughly stitched, in plain but always neat binding or wrapper: you could not but see that it was done by a conscientious worker, gifted with a keen sense of fitness and propriety.[35]

Benbow had worked for Cobbett. Dugdale learned the pornography business by working for Benbow. Watson, Clarke, and others had worked for Carlile who had worked for Eaton, veteran printer of radical pamphlets in the 1790s who, when convicted in 1812 for publishing part III of Paine's *The Age of Reason*, was sentenced to stand in the stocks. And behind the leaders stood a changing army of volunteers. A young man would arrive in London determined to play a part in the struggle for reform. He might join one of the many debating societies or freethinking chapels, serve as a shopman in a bookshop or as pressman in a printing shop, and go to prison for a time. Some branched into business on their own, and for a few, the pornography which had at first been a sideline became the main business.

---

[32] Vizitelly i, 74.   [33] Quoted by McCalman 160.   [34] Linton 59.   [35] *Ibid.* 28.

The law required the printer's imprint on the first and the last pages of every book. Printers responded by providing extra pages carrying nothing but the legal imprint so that they could be torn out without damaging the text. Another trick was to print the imprint so low down the page that it was cut off in the trimming when a book was bound.[36] Some books appear to have been routinely mutilated as a precaution even if they were lawful.[37] Another evasion was to pretend that illegal books were foreign imports. Benbow's edition of Shelley's *Queen Mab* claims on the title page to have been published in New York. An 1822 Erasmus Perkins piracy of Moore's *Irish and National Songs* purports to have been printed by 'Erasmo Perchino' at Pisa, then the centre of what Southey called the 'Satanic School of Poetry'. Although the law laid heavy responsibilities on printers, it said nothing about the publishers, mysterious figures whose motives are not always clear. Numerous books of doubtful legal status claim to be 'Printed for the Booksellers', who remain unnamed. Thomas Dolby, a gentleman's servant, established his successful theatrical, radical, and pornographic bookshop with the help of a loan from his employer.[38] Some of the men whose names appear on the title page as 'printers' are otherwise unknown. Others were shopmen or pressmen accepting the risk on behalf of their employers. A number of Benbow's piracies, for example, claim on their title pages to have been printed by Dickinson, his next-door neighbour, whose name appears in the official registers of printers but who is not otherwise known. Other Benbow books purport to have been printed by Jack Mitford, a pornographer, who is unlikely to have done more than hire out his worthless name.[39]

Most illegally printed books that survive carry the imprint required by law, and despite the registers, the inspectors, and the snoopers, the printers were difficult to catch. In the 1820s, in central London alone, there were several thousand registered printing presses. Over a hundred in the Strand area alone, another hundred in Fleet Street, and fifty or more round St Paul's and Paternoster Row. In London there were sixty or seventy new registrations every year.[40] The printers constantly changed their business addresses up and down Fleet Street and the Strand, where nearly every close had at least one press and some had half-a-dozen.[41] Ownership could be transferred over a handshake. A journalist who worked in Dugdale's printing

---

[36] Attributed by Todd to the printer McMillan.
[37] A copy of Godwin's *History of Greece* (1822) has the title page removed and McMillan's name stabbed out, Ac.
[38] £40 (800 shillings). McCalman 158.   [39] See, for example, 'Harriette Wilson', appendix 9, 657.
[40] Estimates from Todd.   [41] This can be seen from the lists in Todd.

shop briefly in the 1830s described him as a stout, sensual, semi-intoxicated man, operating from a dirty cobwebbed room where seven or eight compositors printed his books.[42] Dugdale frequently moved his address in the course of his long career, as did his colleagues in the pornography business. In Holywell, at the edge of the theatre district with its prostitutes and its drugshops, the poor met the rich, the unrespectable provided services to the respectable. It was mainly because ladies had to pass through in their carriages that some of the last remaining Elizabethan houses in London were pulled down.

While expensive books were sold in ones and twos through a network of respectable retail bookshops in the main towns, unrespectable books were diffused across the country through channels which nobody in authority could understand or control. Pornographers, it was said, threw books over the walls into girls' boarding schools in order both to stimulate and to satisfy demand.[43] Many towns had a shop like Dirty Kay's in Edinburgh which sold 'Freethinking or Atheistical books' and the books, which were mostly easily portable, made their way to the villages through the chapman network.[44] A tinker in one of Bulwer Lytton's novels offers *Paradise Lost* and religious tracts, but also Paine's *The Age of Reason* and Owen's *Principles of Socialism*.[45]

The most decisive single event in shaping the reading of the romantic period occurred in 1817. In that year the publisher Sherwood put on sale printed copies of the manuscript of *Wat Tyler*, a verse drama by Southey, the poet laureate, which had been written in the 1790s when Southey was, briefly, a republican radical. Southey had given his manuscript to a friend to arrange publication, but it was not printed and the manuscript was not returned. Sherwood published it without Southey's knowledge or permission, with the deliberate intention of embarrassing him. *Wat Tyler's* ridicule of royal extravagance, oppressive taxes, aggressive wars, and cynical bloated churchmen was a change from the laureate's recent celebrations of the royal family. But Southey had changed his opinions. *Wat Tyler*, he declared, would help to encourage popular unrest and revolution, and the attorney general should not only correct the blatant theft but prosecute the publisher for sedition.[46] The fact that the piece was written in verse made it all the more dangerous. 'If there be any evil connected with poetry',

[42] The same had been said of John Bell and the other Scottish interlopers who had threatened the London business two generations before.
[43] Quoted by McCalman 213.   [44] Thin 24.   [45] Edward Bulwer Lytton, *My Novel* (1852) i, 225.
[46] Southey, *Life* iv, 239.

he wrote to a friend, 'it is that it tends to make us too little masters of ourselves, and counteracts that stoicism, or necessary self-control, of which all of us must sometimes stand in need.'[47]

Southey applied for an injunction and damages for breach of copyright under the civil law. As the author of a work who had not ceded his intellectual property rights to a printer or publisher, he was the undoubted owner, as the court readily agreed. However, as Lord Chancellor Eldon declared, the prior point at issue was whether the text was lawful. Southey's lawyer had spoken of the 'wickedness' of the piece and his client's 'shame' at seeing it printed. But the more the lawyers apologised, the more they weakened their case in law. For if a book was 'injurious', its intellectual property could not be protected by the courts. 'I cannot grant him injunction', Eldon concluded, 'until after Mr Southey shall have established his right to the property by action.' This would have meant Southey himself precipitating a trial of the printer or publisher for seditious libel before an unpredictable jury, an unattractive option with an uncertain outcome.[48]

If *Wat Tyler* had been published in the regular way, it would probably have been priced at 10s 6d (10.5 shillings), with half the stock remaindered. But with no risk from the law on intellectual property, the pirates seized the moment, and Sherwood's piracy was quickly copied by half-a-dozen other pirates.[49] Carlile is said to have financed his expanding publishing business from the profits.[50] But, as table 16.1 shows, the price soon fell drastically to a tenth and then a hundredth of the normal price. The total immediate sale was believed by Southey's son to have been about 60,000 copies, twice as many copies as even the most popular works of Walter Scott. The piece which Southey later refused to reprint among his *Collected Works* sold twice or three times as many copies as all his other works put together. And the readership spanned the whole nation. The Eclectic Book Society chose it as one of their selection for 1817, but we also hear of *Wat Tyler* being read aloud in crowded theatres.[51] Nor was it just a book of the day. *Wat Tyler* was still in print and easily available for twopence decades later.

After *Wat Tyler*, came Shelley's *Queen Mab, A Philosophical Poem*, written when still in his teens. His theme, he told his friends, was the past, the present, and the future. Queen Mab takes her readers on a ride into the heavens to reveal the world as it is and give them a vision of what it

---

[47] *Ibid.* 242.
[48] The episode and the legal arguments are described by Paul M. Zall, 'Lord Eldon's Censorship' in *PMLA* (1953) 436–42.
[49] I have seen the editions by Bailey, Fairburn, Hone, Sherwin, Sherwood, and Watson.
[50] Linton 12.   [51] *Ibid.*

Table 16.1 Southey's 'Wat Tyler', all pirated

		Price (shillings)	Production
1817	Normal price of a new book of this length	10.5	500 or 1,000
1817	Sherwood's editions	2	na
1817	Hone's editions, with explanatory notes	1	na
1817	Fairburn's edition	1	na
1817	Bailey's edition	1	na
1817	Carlile's edition[a]	na	20,000 sold
1817	Sherwin's edition	0.25	na
Another Sherwin edition		0.16	na
Total immediate sale[b]		believed to be about 60,000	
c. 1817	Fordyce of Newcastle's edition	na	na
1830s	Watson's edition[c]	0.18	na
1830s	Cousins's edition	0.16 post free	na
1840s	Cleave's edition	0.16	na
1850s	Sales in Manchester[d]		450 a week

[a] *Isis*, 7 July 1832.
[b] Southey, *Life* iv, 237.
[c] Advertisements for Watson's list 1830s and perhaps later, Ac.
[d] Quoted by Altick 352.

might be. The verse is reinforced by a long selection of prose notes, mainly quotations from sceptical ancient and modern philosophers. In *Queen Mab* the prose was for understanding, the verse for creating sympathetic involvement, in line with Shelley's theory that reading could help to change the world. In 1813 Shelley had had 250 copies printed at his own expense. The book was dangerously illegal, not only because some passages of the verse and of the prose notes offended against the blasphemy and sedition laws, but because the book contained a false imprint. To give an appearance of legality Shelley asked the printer to print the name and temporary address of P. B. Shelley as the publisher and the printer, but there is no record of his having taken out a printing licence. Who the actual printer was has not been discovered – he was someone who knew his craft for the book is beautifully and accurately produced even to the long quotations in Greek.

Shelley seems to have sent many copies of the book to friends and to prominent men whom he admired but did not know, including Byron. He usually clipped the pages which contained the illegal imprint, so increasing the book's aura of danger,[52] but, as far as is recorded, none of the early

[52] E.g. in the copy he gave to Mary Godwin. See St Clair, *Godwins and Shelleys* 358.

readers took much notice and, as with most privately printed books, most copies stayed in the warehouse. Soon Shelley's mind turned to other things. He was content to let lie *Queen Mab* as a composition of his youth before the mature work of his mid-twenties. In 1817, however, the year of *Wat Tyler*, *Queen Mab* returned to haunt him. In a lawsuit concerning the custody of his two children, the court decided that a man who had written *Queen Mab* could not be a suitable father, and Shelley was warned that he was liable to be prosecuted for blasphemous libel. The court ordered that the children should be brought up by foster parents, with restricted paternal access, and Shelley never saw them again. A copy of the book found its way into the hands of 'Erasmus Perkins', the associate of Benbow, and knowledge of it began to spread. In 1819 Carlile asked Shelley's permission to bring out a reprint but was refused, but in 1821 two separate pirate editions were put on sale without Shelley's permission.[53] The government decided not to prosecute, but a private action for blasphemous libel was brought by the Society for the Suppression of Vice.

When the case came to court in 1822 Clarke, the nominal printer/publisher, was sent to prison.[54] The court ordered the unsold stocks to be destroyed, and some were handed over for burning, but Carlile found a way of taking over the unsold sheets and reissued the book with a new title page. A new version was also prepared which omitted or bowdlerised some of the passages which fell foul of the law, but the full, uncensored, version was also still available to customers who knew what to ask for. Carlile then produced a cheaper version and then another even cheaper, and other pirates followed.[55] Secret signs mark who the real investors were.[56] 'TM' is Thomas Moses, a printer, who financed some of Carlile's publications when Carlile was in prison. The 'ep' in Greek letters which appeared on the title page of *Queen Mab* are the initials of Erasmus Perkins, the real publisher. They also stand for 'epea pteroenta', Homer's winged words.[57]

As had happened with *Wat Tyler*, the price of *Queen Mab* plummeted and, despite police seizures, sales soared.[58] As with *Wat Tyler*, the contradictions between the criminal law and the intellectual property law had brought about the very effects they were intended to prevent. After 1821 *Queen Mab*

---

[53] For a summary of the publishing history see appendix 11.
[54] The real investor appears to have been the printer Thomas Moses. See St Clair, *Godwins and Shelleys*, appendix 3.
[55] Among the eight titles published in the first year of the Joint Stock Book Company.
[56] See St Clair, *Godwins and Shelleys*, appendix 3, 'Shelley and the Pirates'.
[57] Erasmus Perkins signed some of his anonymous writings with the printer's mark '¶'.
[58] Reported in Carlile's publications.

flew as free as the fairy queen. By the 1830s the poem was stereotyped, available at one shilling, soon to be reduced to sixpence, affordable by the very groups from whom the authorities wished to keep it. The book was never again out of print, being reprinted separately in cheap editions right through the nineteenth century. *Queen Mab* was, by far, Shelley's most easily available, most frequently printed, cheapest, and most widely read book.

Shelley's other books had, by the time of the poet's death, ceased to be available at all. Most of them, whose first and only editions had consisted of 750 copies or less, had lain in the warehouse, been remaindered, or sent for trunk lining.[59] In the 1820s, however, stimulated by the interest in *Queen Mab*, pirate editions of the rest of his works began to appear at cheap prices. In 1834 a publisher called John Ascham, otherwise known only as a pornographer, produced the first *Collected Works*, to be sold in a dozen monthly parts at a shilling each.[60] That was followed by a stereotyped edition in one fat little volume by another hitherto unknown pirate called Charles Daly. Henry Vizitelly, a journalist who served his apprenticeship in Fleet Street in the 1830s, recalled in his autobiography that 'forbidden books, furtively obtained' were eagerly read and discussed by the apprentices during the working hours. 'The book that of all others had the greatest fascination . . .', he wrote, 'was Shelley's *Queen Mab* in which ardent liberals found the expression of their aspiration.'[61] '*Queen Mab* is clandestinely sold and scarce', wrote the editor of a French pirate anthology in 1827, offering a summary as well as a condemnation, and the whole poem including the notes was reprinted in the offshore Galignani edition of 1830.[62]

When in November 1829 Arthur Hallam and Alfred Tennyson, then undergraduates at Cambridge University, challenged a team from Oxford to debate the question 'whether the poems of Shelley had an immoral

---

[59] Edward John Trelawny records that, in visiting Ollier's shop in 1821, he had to satisfy Ollier that he was a friend of the poet before Ollier would agree to sell him copies of Shelley's published poems. *Letters of Edward John Trelawny* edited by H. B. Forman (Oxford 1910) 272. Since only *Queen Mab* was at risk from the law, this was a strange response from a commercial bookseller unless he was deliberately holding back sales of books sold on commission. See chapter 9 and William St Clair, 'Trelawny's Lost Years' in *SC* viii, 611.

[60] Ascham may have been a front man for 'Erasmus Perkins'. See St Clair, *Godwins and Shelleys*, appendix 3.

[61] Vizitelly i, 121. He also mentions Paine's *Rights of Man*, and *Age of Reason*, Southey's *Wat Tyler*, Byron's *Vision of Judgment*, and a report of the trial of Thomas Muir.

[62] *The Living Poets of England: Specimens of the Living British Poets, with Biographical and Critical Notices, and an Essay on English Poetry* (Paris Baudry and others (1827) 369. The 'Literary Memoir' is initialled 'A.P.'.

tendency', they could only have read his works from pirated copies.[63] John Clare, Robert Browning, and Algernon Swinburne all owned copies of Benbow's pirated edition of Shelley. Thomas Moore owned a Carlile piracy. Aubrey de Vere, the Victorian poet, tells how in the 1830s his friends read Shelley from an anthology, *Beauties of Shelley*, a type of publication which would not have been allowed if normal intellectual property restrictions had applied. The book was now affordable by, and accessible to, new classes of readers who had previously been cut off from all new books: clerks, artisans, shop workers, indeed to anyone who was literate. As the letters from James Watson's Belfast agent confirm, Shelley's poems, now inextricably associated with other radical works, were making their way to the furthest borders of the reading nation.

In addition to our regular booksellers, two cheap *Number* booksellers have established themselves in High Street and Castle Place within the last 12 months. One of them, a Scotchman procured for me some of Owen's Tracts from Glasgow, & exposes Shelley's Works (Daly's) in his window & other cheap works. A more adventurous person, such as an Englishman, might proceed farther & by degrees accustom us to the sight even of Paine and Mirabaud. I know many in the country around who eagerly desire such works.[64]

Thomas Cooper, the Chartist leader who, while in prison successfully went on hunger strike for the right to read, remembered that among the books which his friends sent in was 'Shelley (the small pirated edition)' as well as Gibbon.[65]

Printed on poor quality paper, folded into 12 mo, 18 mo, 24 mo, 32 mo, and even 64 mo, sold with paper covers in tiny volumes, most editions were designed to be cheap. Some editions have such tiny type that the modern eye marvels at the skill of the printers in setting them. Some can scarcely be read by the naked eye except in the brightest of daylight, and some need a magnifying glass. Yet the surviving copies with their underlinings, their marginal comments, and their presentation inscriptions as they were passed from friend to friend, generation to generation, confirm that they were not only read but read intensively. As George Bernard Shaw remarked when he was shown a collection, and is confirmed by surviving copies, the books were 'blackened with the finger marks of many heavy handed trades'.[66] We hear of Shelley's works being read at rallies and quoted on banners. Some were turned into songs, reprinted in editions with sales

---

[63] The Galignani edition was not yet available.
[64] Letters of E. Burns to Watson, BL add. mss. 46,345.   [65] Cooper 252.
[66] *The Works of George Bernard Shaw* (1931) xxix, 257.

totalling hundreds of thousands of copies.[67] Some readers may not have read any other modern author.

In 1825 another subversive text poured through the *Wat Tyler* gap. The *Memoirs of Harriette Wilson*, semi-fictitious accounts by a society courtesan of her encounters with some of the most famous men of the time, was originally intended for sale only in expensive parts to the richest members of society. Those who were named as about to be exposed in forthcoming parts could buy themselves out.[68] But when Onwhyn, the man who had first pirated *Don Juan*, put on sale a pirated edition at a quarter of the price, the courts declared that no intellectual property rights in such an immoral book could be enforced. The way was again opened for piracies of all kinds, falling prices, and widening readership. Once more the attempts to clamp down on the texts which the leaders of society most feared brought about the opposite of what they intended. As in France before the Revolution, the pretence that the country's rulers were as noble in their behaviour as in their titles was seriously undermined.

Meanwhile for Byron too, the interaction of the intellectual property and the criminal law produced results contrary to the intentions of both. In 1820 and 1821, Benbow and Dugdale started to offer cheap reprints of the books whose copyrights were not owned by Murray and whose copyright status was doubtful.[69] When Dugdale was in court, Byron's lawyer was instructed not to press the full rigour of law – Dugdale was a poor man, he said, with a family to support – he should not be driven out of business. A nod was as good as a wink. In the mid 1820s, Benbow, Dugdale, and others reprinted almost all of the works of Byron in small paper-covered pocket editions at a tenth of the official price, and although Murray pursued them they continued to do so.[70]

It was only two years since the *Wat Tyler* case when Byron sent the manuscript of the first two cantos of *Don Juan* to Murray. It was a very different work from the romantic verse tales that, five or six years previously, had made Byron the most adored and bestselling author after Scott, and had built the Murray fortune. Although the earlier poems had caused some offence by what critics at the time called Byron's misanthropy, *Don Juan* was outrageous. It parodied the ten commandments for which William Hone

---

[67] Freethought Publishing Company. See appendix 11.
[68] See Frances Wilson, *The Courtesan's Revenge, The Woman Who Blackmailed the King* (2003). Publication figures in 'Harriette Wilson', appendix 9.
[69] Notably his youthful works *English Bards and Scotch Reviewers* and *Hours of Idleness*.
[70] See titles and editions in appendix 11.

had been unsuccessfully prosecuted in 1817. It poured scorn on admirals, generals, politicians, and fellow writers. Later cantos were to subvert the neo-chivalric ideologies of war and honour, now being given new vitality by the Waverley novels. Byron was publicly frank about his estranged wife, a serious breach of the code of nobility, and subverted the whole construction of women as set out in the conduct literature. In *Don Juan* the women are not chaste, silent or obedient, and it is they who are the seducers. At the same time the poem contained episodes of beauty, humanity, pathos and tenderness unmatched by any contemporary. Not so much satire as epic, *Don Juan* offered a view of life as essentially arbitrary and contingent, and by its very form it struck at the notion of a well-ordered, divinely guided universe. If *Don Juan* was, by far, the most original work of literature produced in Great Britain during the age of romanticism, it was also, as Southey declared, reflecting the mainstream notion of what literature should be, an act of high treason against English poetry.[71]

After the scandals which caused Byron to leave England in 1816, his commercial appeal had declined.[72] Although the sales of his recent books were still huge, they were well down on those of the romantic tales which had made him famous in earlier years. As the publisher of the *Quarterly Review*, Murray knew the constituency of men and women who had adored *Childe Harold* and *The Corsair*. They were rich and mostly members of the landed classes. They were in favour of strong government, the royal family, high grain prices, and established religion. They were against democracy, rights of women, reform of parliament, reform in general. The first two cantos of *Don Juan* came into the world in expensive quarto format, £1 11s 6d (31.5 shillings) in boards, about £1 15s to £2 (35 to 40 shillings) when bound, finely printed with broad margins, with a Latin quotation from Horace on the title page.[73] Although short, this was a book in rich dress presenting itself to Byron's previous readership. But in other ways it looked like a gutter satire. Some stanzas and lines are blanked out with asterisks, making them appear more shocking than they are. No author's name is given on the title page, although internal evidence makes clear that the poem is by Byron. Most unusual of all, the title page does not even carry the name of the publisher, and Murray denied that he had been responsible.[74] Instead there is only the name of the printer, Thomas Davison, as required

---

[71] Quoted in Andrew Rutherford, *Byron, The Critical Heritage* (1970) 179.
[72] See the production figures for the poems published after 1816 in appendix 9.
[73] Details of publication history are given in appendix 8. This modifies the account given in St Clair, *Byron*.
[74] Byron, *Letters and Journals* ix, 84.

by law. Puzzled readers, as they turned over the white hot-pressed pages, were inclined to see the poem as a brilliant piece of play, an in-joke for society London. To the pirate publishers, however, these features carried another signal. Murray, this book proclaimed, was ashamed of the book; he was timid and self-censoring; he feared the public reaction; he was worried about libel; and he was uncertain whether intellectual property rights could be enforced.

Almost at once a pirate publisher produced a reprint at 4 shillings, an eighth of the official price, to be followed by another soon after. A court injunction to stop them was granted, but other pirates came forward to take their place, offering the text at even cheaper prices. It was clear that if Murray was going to protect his investment he would have to prosecute, but after *Wat Tyler* and *Queen Mab*, it was doubtful whether he could win. His worry was not wholly commercial. As his lawyer advised him: 'The evil, if not stopped, will be great. It [*Don Juan*] will circulate in a cheap form very extensively, injuring society wherever it spreads.'[75] A writer in the *Quarterly Review*, believed to be Southey, publicly warned of the effects if the reading of the book was not stopped.

But no sooner was it whispered that there was no property in 'Don Juan' than ten presses were at work, some publishing it with obscene engravings, others in weekly numbers, and all in a shape that brought it within the reach of purchasers on whom its poison would operate without mitigation – who would search its pages for images to pamper a depraved imagination, and for a sanction for the insensibility to the sufferings of others . . . without the power of comprehending what it contains of good. 'Don Juan' in quarto and on hot-pressed paper would have been almost innocent – in a whity-brown duodecimo, it was one of the worst of the mischievous publications that have made the press a snare.[76]

Byron offered to refund his fee. But he knew that if *Don Juan* was pronounced 'injurious', the law might try to deprive him of his rights as a father, as it had done in Shelley's case.[77]

In 1823 *Don Juan* came to court again, this time at the instigation not of Murray but of Dugdale, pirate and pornographer. As a man often in trouble with the law, Dugdale was used to pleading that his publications did no harm. But he too knew the implications of the *Wat Tyler* decision. It was *not* true, he told the court, that *Don Juan* was harmless. On the contrary, some scenes in the book were:

[75] Smiles i, 406.
[76] (Robert, Southey), 'Cases of Walcot v. Walker; Southey v. Sherwood; Murray v. Benbow, and Lawrence v. Smith.' in *Quarterly Review*, 27 (1822) 128.
[77] Byron, *Letters and Journals* vi, 252.

immoral, and licentious, and calculated to produce the worst effect on the minds of those inexperienced persons who read it, and destructive of the moral feeling of the community . . . scenes so warm, so highly coloured, so licentious, that no father of a family would permit the book to be seen in his house.[78]

If such writings were widely read, he went on:

the demoralising principle would go on increasing, until at last we should behold a revolution, as great, as awful, and as dangerous as the French Revolution, and which might like that end in a despotic usurpation of which the author of Don Juan might take advantage to raise himself to sovereign power.

The Lord Chancellor squirmed but the legal point could not be denied. If *Don Juan* was 'injurious', as the pornographer argued, it could not be accorded intellectual property protection. The injunctions were lifted. Anyone who wished could now reprint *Don Juan* without fear of the law. Dugdale immediately put on sale a cheap version of all the cantos that had so far appeared, and he was quickly followed by half a dozen others. The price fell rapidly. *Don Juan*, like *Queen Mab*, was now affordable by clerks, artisans, shopkeepers, and higher-paid manual workers. Once more the law had brought about the very effect it was designed to prevent, and this time with the most famous author of the age and with what was fast becoming his most famous poem.

In 1823, with several more cantos already written and ready to be published, Byron broke with Murray who had been his publisher since he woke and found himself famous with *Childe Harold's Pilgrimage, A Romaunt*, in 1812. He had never been sympathetic to Murray's policy of high prices which cut him off from most of his potential audience. With his large readerships in Europe and America, he cared little for the opinion of the small group of deeply conservative English readers in whose custom Murray seemed exclusively interested. Byron wanted to keep his intellectual property rights, and he was willing to make textual changes to ensure that the remainder of the poem was not 'injurious' in the eyes of the law. And he believed he could still make money. As he wrote to his agent in London during the negotiations with Murray,

don't you be talked over by the fellow – He will prate of piracy – but recollect that he might neutralize this in a great measure by publishing *very cheap*, small editions *of the same type with former piracies* – at the same time – reserve his *smooth* octavos – for former publishers [? mistake for 'purchasers'] of the same more expensive Calibre.[79]

---

[78] Reported in *The Examiner* (1822) 522. A slightly different version is quoted by Zall, 'Lord Eldon's Censorship' 440.

[79] Byron, *Letters and Journals* ix, 207. See also ix, 187.

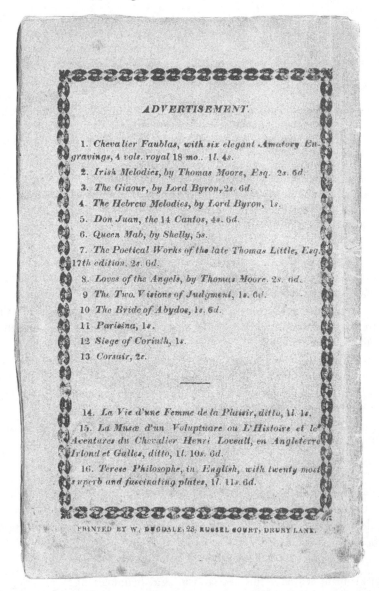

Figure 17. Advertised publications of the pirate publisher William Dugdale (1824), showing that Byron's *Don Juan* and Shelley's *Queen Mab* were sold cheaply alongside expensive pornography. Printed on covers of Byron's *The Prisoner of Chillon*, pirated in 1822.

Table 16.2 'Don Juan', early cantos. Prices and production

	Price (shillings)	Production
Murray, 1 and 2, 4to, 1819	31.5	1,350
Murray, 1 and 2, 8vo, 1819	9.5	3,750
Onwhyn (pirate) 1 and 2, 1819	4	na
Sherwin (pirate) 1 and 2, 1819	4	na
Murray, 1 and 2, 'small paper', 1820	5	na
Murray, 3, 4, and 5, 8vo, 1821	9.5	1,500
Murray, 3, 4, and 5, 'small paper', 1821	5	4,500
Onwhyn (pirate) 3, 4, and 5, 1819	4	na
Sherwin (pirate) 3, 4, and 5, 1819	4	na
Hunt, 6, 7, and 8, 8vo, 1823	9.5	1,500
Hunt, 6, 7, and 8, 'small paper', 1823	7	3,000
Hunt, 6, 7, and 8, 'common', 1823	1	17,000

In 1823, after unsuccessfully trying various other respectable publishers, including Constable, Byron agreed with John Hunt, Leigh Hunt's brother, for a new type of publishing. The remaining cantos of *Don Juan* were to be published in succession as they were ready, simultaneously in three different formats. First, a traditional octavo like Murray's with which it could be bound to make up a set – this was the edition for the traditional book-buying classes. Secondly, a smaller cheaper 'small paper' version which could also be bound up with Murray's editions – this was also intended mainly for middling income customers. Thirdly a 'common' edition available for one shilling – intended for the huge new readership identified by the pirates. For the first time in English literary history, as table 16.2 shows, a great new work of literature was designed, manufactured, and priced so as to be able to address the whole reading nation simultaneously.[80]

Although there was nothing illegal in the later cantos, it seems to have been assumed that if copyright was not enforceable in cantos 1 and 2, it could not be enforced on the rest. Hunt's official editions had many pirate rivals, although none, it seems, were able at that time to offer a lower price than one shilling. But the poem was excerpted in twopenny magazines, and sold in parts and numbers. Already by 1823 the minimum cost of reading large passages of *Don Juan* had fallen below the level of most newspapers. In 1826 it was reported that the price had fallen to a half-penny (presumably for one of the parts second-hand).[81]

---

[80] See summary of fall in prices in appendix II.   [81] *Memoirs of Harriette Wilson* (1831 edition) v, 8.

When Byron died in 1824 and there could be no more cantos apart from a spate of fakes, a new problem arose. Readers wanted to read the whole poem, but it was only available officially in volumes published by two different publishers. The copyright of cantos 1 to 5 was owned by Murray, that of cantos 6 to 16, by Byron's heirs. Both Murray and Hunt also had large unsold stocks of the more expensive editions. The situation was a pirates' charter. A huge supply came forward to satisfy a huge demand. In the twenty years after *Don Juan* first appeared at least thirty pirate publishers produced editions, many of them more than one. Most were printed in London, but the book was also republished in Edinburgh, Glasgow, Manchester, and perhaps elsewhere. Some piracies are fine octavos scarcely distinguishable from Murray's regular editions, and were sold to the customers he had lost. Others captured the intermediate market. *Don Juan* could be bought in avant-garde reform bookshops alongside their radical political tracts and in the pornography shops of Holywell. In 1822 Benbow hung a picture outside his bookshop and called it 'The Byron's Head', as if it was a tavern, partly as a way of putting the name of Lord Byron on the title page – 'Published at the Lord Byron's Head' – without endangering his position at law if he publicly named the author.[82] It was Benbow's shop that Southey had in mind when he wrote about the pirate bookshops:

It might have been thought that Lord Byron had attained the last degree of disgrace when his head was set up for a sign at one of those preparatory schools for the brothel and the gallows, where obscenity, sedition, and blasphemy are retailed in drams for the vulgar.[83]

Freed from every consideration beyond conveying the printed text to the maximum number of readers at the lowest possible price, the pirate publishers of *Don Juan* pushed at the extremes of book production, folding the paper sheets to ever smaller formats, using poorer and poorer quality paper, printing in ever smaller type, and cramming ever more words on the page. In the previous century Sheridan had likened a poem in a quarto to 'a rivulet of text meandering through wide meadows of margin'.[84] *Don Juan* in the original luxurious quarto had contained sixteen stanzas to the

---

[82] Many bookshops in London had, in earlier times, hung an image of a famous writer outside: Homer's Head, the Shakespeare Head, the Dryden Head. The bookshop in Edinburgh where Constable began had a signboard with the head of Thomson. Constable i, 9.

[83] From a published letter to the Editor of *The Courier* dated 8 December 1824, quoted in Southey, *Life* v, 361, and Rowland E. Prothero, *The Works of Lord Byron. A New, Revised and Enlarged Edition* (1898–1904) vi, 389. See also other similar remarks in Andrew Rutherford, ed., *Byron The Critical Heritage* (1970).

[84] In act I, Scene I of *The School for Scandal* (1777).

sheet. By the time of Hunt's common edition of 1823 the number had risen to forty-eight, near the limit for reading with the naked eye. By the later 1820s, the number of stanzas per sheet was usually eighty and Dove managed to squeeze in a hundred, and Mayhew and Isaac reached one hundred and forty four. Tiny print, with scarcely a gap between stanzas, every corner of the page crammed, and numbered stanzas – for without numbered stanzas the reader would never have been able to find the place – *Don Juan* increasingly resembled a miniature pocket Bible, and by some readers it was so regarded.[85]

Small size is not a disadvantage to the reader of a disreputable book. According to one writer, 'Every body pored over the wicked smiling face of Don Juan – pirated duo-decimo competing it all over the island with furtive quarto.'[86] Some pirated versions have their covers disguised to look as if they were a volume of old-canon poems or plays, but *Don Juan* could be slipped into a pocket or a handbag without the need for explanation or permission.[87] The text of the whole poem was stereotyped by more than one pirate publisher in the 1820s. Once set in metal, the marginal cost of manufacturing and therefore of pricing fell further. A visitor to the printing shop of Clowes in the 1830s saw a set of *Don Juan* plates awaiting their regular call-out, stored alongside those of the conduct books against which it posed such a threat.[88] One set of plates was sent to Manchester and another to Glasgow for editions to be manufactured there in the 1840s and 1850s. Another set manufactured in the late 1820s was still being taken out, repaired, and used to make a new edition as late as 1875, and was still in existence in 1906.[89]

As table 16.3 shows, within twenty years the minimum price had fallen to ten per cent of that at first publication and it was continuing to fall rapidly until by the 1870s it was down to one per cent.

The text of *Don Juan* which almost all readers read was not the text Byron wrote, but the self-censored version put out by his publisher Murray. Some pirate editions were further bowdlerised, omitting stanzas and phrases that even Murray had permitted. Those produced by the publishers of satirical prints have naughty illustrations, some coloured. The prefaces to some editions proclaim their radicalism. Others are shamefaced and apologetic. One has a preface by a clergyman. It was a publisher's joke that an editor

---

[85] See the examples caricatured by Dickens in chapter 20.   [86] Strout 83.
[87] Copy in Ac. For example Hester in Eliot's *Felix Holt*, see chapter 20.
[88] 'Next to "Doddridge's Works" lie the plates of "Don Juan": close to "Hervey's Meditations" lie "The Lives of the Highwaymen." 'The Printer's Devil' in *Quarterly Review*, December 1839.
[89] See the editions of Morris (1829) and Chatto (1875) in appendix 11, 689 and 691.

Table 16.3 'Don Juan', whole poem, falling prices

	Year	Shillings
Murray and Hunt, made-up set, octavo, regular	1824	57
Murray and Hunt, made-up set, 'small paper', regular	1824	38
Benbow and Hunt, made-up set, 'common', part pirate part regular	1824	6.5
Benbow, two volumes in one'[a]		7
Jones, pirate, one volume	1825	6.5
Benbow, made-up set	1825	5
Dove, pirate	1828	6
Smith, pirate, 12mo	1828	5
Smith, pirate, 24mo	1828	3.5
Morris, pirate	1829	2.5
Murray, official, with additions which allowed him to claim a new copyright	1837	5
Cornish, pirate late	1830s	1.5
Daly, pirate	1840s	2.5
Love, pirate	1840s	2
Milner, pirate	1850s and later	1
Dicks	1870s and later	0.5

[a] Advertisement list in *The Poetical Works of Thomas Little* (1825), Ac. Perhaps the same as the previous item.

was offering a *Family Don Juan* expurgated like Dr Bowdler's *Family Shakespeare*.[90] In 1828 Cawthorn, who had published *English Bards*, produced an anthology volume of *Beauties of Don Juan*, like the *Beauties of Shelley*, a type of publication which was only possible because of the absence of enforceable intellectual property rights. 'No', the editor proclaims, struggling to preserve the old links between literature, awe, and virtue, 'Lord Byron had not a perverted moral sense. Nature, as Sir Walter Scott beautifully expressed it, was incapable of paying so bad a compliment to genius.'[91] But the work cannot be disassembled into correct and incorrect passages. It was impossible to preserve the sublime from the deflation, to save the pathos from the bathos.[92]

'It is consoling to think', wrote Thomas Dibdin when in 1824 he contemplated the many cheap reprints of old-canon poetry available on the

[90] *Quarterly Review*, August 1834.
[91] *The Beauties of Don Juan: Including those passages only which are calculated to extend the real fame of Lord Byron* (1828). The preface dated June 1828, and various notes, are written by someone who never actually met Byron, but who implies a connection, perhaps Cawthorn himself.
[92] See (Charles Caleb Calton), *Remarks Critical and Moral on the Talents of Lord Byron, and the Tendencies of Don Juan* (1819).

market, 'that such numerous and useful works keep down the blasphemy and absurdity which finds refuge only in the premises of Mr Carlile.'[93] But Dibdin was premature as well as complacent. Within a year, *Don Juan* had been adopted among the 'British Classics' of more than one publisher, the first work to be admitted since the brief copyright window had closed.[94] By the 1830s and throughout the Victorian period it was on the lists of several publishers who specialised in selling religious conduct books to the urban and rural poor. Byron would have enjoyed being among the English poets a year after his death. But would not this sturdy cuckoo squeeze out the legitimate weaklings? The first version to be published among the formal old canon was further bowdlerised.[95] Many readers probably went straight from Thomson and Young to *Don Juan*, and liked what they found. The Reverend Robert Brown of Douglas, Isle of Man, for example, would not allow any novels into his house, not even Waverley novels, but because poetry was traditionally regarded as morally improving, he read and reread *Don Juan*.[96] Ben Brierley, a Lancashire weaver, wrote that his 'soul was not much lifted' by the poetry books which were all that were within his reach when he was young. 'It was not until I joined the companionship of Burns and Byron [in the 1830s] that I felt the god within me.'[97]

One of the features which distinguished the old-canon books was that they were normally illustrated with an engraved frontispiece and a portrait of the author. In the years when Byron's romantic poems were read in the drawing rooms of the octavo-buying public, Murray had put on sale sets of engravings for binding into his books. A portrait of Byron led the series, and Childe Harold, the Corsair, Lara, and the other Byronic heroes were drawn to look exactly like him. The image of the poet, hair curly and slightly receding, his face and hands sensitive and feminine, and his shirt extravagantly open at the neck, became part of the reading experience of a few readers at the topmost end of the market. But now the portrait of Byron was as important as the title page. Since the pirates were afraid of weakening their case at law by naming the author of a work which was formally anonymous, almost every pirate edition carried an engraved frontispiece and a portrait of Byron. The portrait by Thomas Phillips, round which Murray had built the legend of Byron as the romantic hero of his own

---

[93] Dibdin xv.
[94] Notably Dove, the main old-canon reprinter of the time but also Allman, Jones, and Scott and Webster (see appendix 6), and later Milner.
[95] Dove's edition of 1826 see appendix 11, 687.   [96] Quoted by Cruse, *Victorians* 68.
[97] Quoted by David Vincent, *Bread, Knowledge and Freedom. A Study of Nineteenth-Century Working Class Autobiography* (1981) 155.

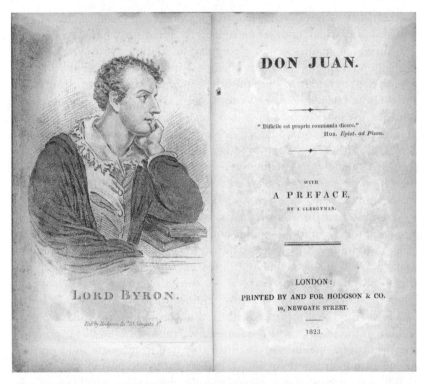

Figure 18. Byron's *Don Juan*. Title page and portrait frontispiece of a pirate edition. The author identified by the excessively Byronic portrait, reversed from an original by Harlowe.

poems, and the sketch by George Harlowe which caught something of the poet's air of haughty disdain, were copyrighted. It was important therefore not to run risks by copying too closely. Byron in life had complained that his official portraitists made him too Byronic. After his death the same handful of images were copied, recopied, reversed, exaggerated, and added to by unnumbered, mostly unskilled, pirate engravers, becoming ever more Byronic with every re-engraving.[98] An air of melancholy or of contempt hung round the lips of the great poet who had died before his time. Lightning flashed round his head. Grecian columns lurked in the background along with exotic pashas and camels: Byron, the genius of his age, the hater of cant, the teller of truth, the champion of the oppressed, who had dreamed of freedom and foreseen a brighter future.[99]

[98] For the low costs of setting up as an engraver see appendix 5, 513.
[99] In some of the pirated editions of *Queen Mab*, Shelley was also shown as extravagantly open necked. As his portrait was engraved and re-engraved for later editions, he too became ever more Byronic.

And if Byron was Childe Harold, he was also Don Juan. The Don who was found naked on the shores of a Greek island by the beautiful and sensuous Haidee, was unmistakeably Byronic. It was a Don looking just like Byron who was seduced by the grand ladies of Europe. If Byron's oriental tales helped to spread an orientalist fantasy, he was himself in the picture. As early as 1829 Byron, his poems, his life, his reputation, his portrait, and his image had together created Byronism, a celebrity different in scale from anything that had gone before. A fashion writer, who in 1828 published a book on *The Art of Tying the Cravat*, included a plate to illustrate the 'cravat à la Byron'.[100]

Of regular editions of *Don Juan*, over 100,000 copies of the different editions are known to have been produced in the poet's lifetime, all of which were eventually sold, some cheaply as remainders. *Don Juan*, even in its official form, was by far the biggest seller of any contemporary literary work during the romantic period. As for the pirate editions, Benbow claimed as early as 1822 that the pirated *Don Juan*, had sold 'thousands' which was many times the total number of regular copies printed at that time, and he, as the chief pirate, knew better than anyone. The later cheaper pirates probably had larger sales, but it is difficult to make an estimate. Half-a-dozen editions of *Don Juan* are only known from the survival of single copies, which suggests that other editions have vanished altogether. If we estimate, say, 200,000 copies of *Don Juan*, official and pirated before 1840, multipliers imply a readership of part at least of the poem in a range which might be as wide as half a million to a million and a half. But whatever assumptions we postulate for building an estimate, the conclusion is inescapable – *Don Juan* was read by more people in its first twenty years than any previous work of English literature.

Don Juan reached the reading nation unmediated by the normal institutional, publishing, and price conventions. It penetrated more deeply and more widely within the reading nation, although not uniformly, and it continued to be feared, reprinted in large numbers, and widely read as a separate book right through the Victorian period. Few books reveal more vividly the differences between quantified histories of reading and traditional literary and cultural history seen as a parade or parliament of texts. As an example of literary diffusion, *Don Juan* is unique, an episode in which all the normal activities of authors, publishers, editors, printers, illustrators, reviewers, book buyers, and readers can be seen accelerated and intensified. It repays detailed study not only in its own right, but as a case study from which other more general lessons about the system of texts, books, reading,

---

[100] H. Blanc, *The Art of Tying the Cravat* (1828).

and cultural formation can be taken. *Don Juan* is the Galapagos Islands of literature.

With the continuing fall in price of *Don Juan*, the fashion spread ever deeper down the social and income scale. 'Each beardless bardling, whether baker's, butcher's, or barber's apprentice', declared D. M. Moir, a Scottish poet who hated *Don Juan*, 'had his hair cut and his shirt-collar turned down à la Byron.'[101] Thomas Frost, the Chartist, recalled James Emslie Duncan, editor of the *Rising Star*, arrested in 1848: 'a young man of ardent temperament and greater aptitude for the poetic than the practical side of the Utopia idea . . . long fair hair, parted like a woman, and shirt collar à la Byron.'[102]

The more popular *Don Juan* became, and the more extensive its readership, the more hateful the book became to a large section of the octavo-buying public, and we hear again the old metaphors that had been used to condemn texts since time immemorial. In the view of Allan Cunningham, 'under seemingly playful covering are hidden words more poisonous than the tongues of serpents'.[103] Byron's works 'are enough to corrupt the morals of a nation', advised the author of a standard conduct book, 'Young people should understand that to touch his volumes is like embracing a beautiful woman infected with the plague.'[104] 'Books contain a deadly and secret poison', warned another conduct-book writer, Joel Hawes, 'Many a young man has been destroyed by reading a single volume' – although evidently not Hawes himself.[105] 'The blast of the desert, at once breathing pestilence into the hearts, and scorching with a fatal death-blight, the minds of myriads', declared a Scottish minister in a lecture to young men in Glasgow on the moral influence of modern poets. 'Fatal, unutterably fatal has been the influence of . . . Byron to many thousands of youthful readers.'[106]

From the beginning the readership diverged. The records of the Bristol Library Society, a subscription library, show that *Don Juan Cantos 1 and 2* was approved for purchase in 1819 when it first came out, but since it does not appear in the lending registers or in the catalogue of 1824, the approval seems to have been quickly withdrawn. At the Newcastle Literary and Philosophical Society, *Don Juan* was ordered by the committee by a

---

[101] D. M. Moir, *Sketches of the Poetical Literature of the Past Half-Century* (1851) 161.
[102] Frost 49 and 57.
[103] From the 'Life' in Daly's edition of *Don Juan* noted in appendix 11.
[104] J. A. James, *The Christian Father's Present to his Children* (fourteenth edition 1844) 190.
[105] Joel Hawes, *Lectures to Young Men, on the Formation of Character . . . with an Additional Lecture on Reading* (1829) 156.
[106] *A Course of Lectures to Young Men: Science Literature, and Religion: Delivered in Glasgow, By Ministers of Various Denominations. Second Series* (Glasgow 1842) 342.

majority of six to five, but there were so many protests that another meeting was called at which the majority of the sixteen or seventeen committee members present voted against the decision. Since the committee did not have power to remove a book once a purchase had been decided, the matter had to be put to the full membership. On that occasion some 300 members decided to eject the book by a ratio of twenty to one.[107] Even the commercial circulating libraries had trouble. The Greer Circulating Library, Newry, Northern Ireland, for example, published (c. 1835) a list of books for sale or rent including '– –, *Hours of Idleness and English Bards and Scotch Reviewers*, 6s 6d'. This refers to Dove's pirate edition of *Don Juan*. The entry appears in its correct alphabetical place under D so if one knew what to ask for one could get it.[108]

The book was regarded as especially dangerous for women. As Elizabeth Barrett told Mary Russell Mitford, 'Papa . . . has very strict ideas about women and about what they should read . . . I heard him say once that he could not think highly of the modesty of any woman who could read Don Juan!! He used to keep a Canto locked up from wandering eyes.'[109] Even the pirates thought so, or at least some pretended to. 'No modest woman will confess to have read *Don Juan*', wrote the editor of Daly's edition, 'and for those of any other description, it matters very little what they read.'[110] Respectable women did not frequent the shops which sold sedition, atheism, and pornography. Nor did respectable women buy their books from chapmen and numbersmen. But few appear to have had difficulty in finding a copy to read if they wanted to. According to one scandalised male writer, a titled lady 'on being reproved . . . for having *Don Juan* in her library, replied "Oh but you don't see in what good company I have placed him" . . . it was found that her Ladyship had put the volume between Young and Cowper.'[111]

The polarisation of response was met by a polarisation of supply. There are at least eight nineteenth-century editions of Byron's 'poetical works' which omit *Don Juan* altogether or which confine themselves to a few safe extracts.[112] The lives of Byron which accompany these editions hurry

---

[107] T. S. Dorch, 'An Amateur's Appraisal: James Losh and Byron' in *Byron Journal*, 18 (1990).

[108] Gillyat Sumner Collection, Bodleian.

[109] *The Letters of Elizabeth Barrett Browning to Mary Russell Mitford 1836–1854*, edited and introduced by Meredith B. Raymond and Mary Rose Sullivan (Waco 1983) ii, 462.

[110] *Lord Byron's Poetical Works: With Life and Notes by Allan Cunningham, Esq. Illustrated. Family Edition* (no date, early and mid Victorian).

[111] Colton, *Remarks on Don Juan* 2.

[112] For example by the following publishers: Daly, Gall and Inglis, Nimmo, Lofts, Walker, Bohn, Milner, Routledge.

past *Don Juan* in one sentence or, in some cases, omit all mention of the fact that he had written the most widely read long poem of the century. Textbooks and histories of English literature by Victorian professors and educationalists contort their sentences to avoid even naming the book, afraid that even the words 'Don Juan' on a printed page would drive their readers into the arms of perdition.[113]

What part did the reading of pirated texts play in the competition for the allegiance of minds? On one side of the struggle was ranged the power, wealth, and prestige of the pre-industrial political, economic, and ecclesiastical establishment, on the other side a variety of ideas about the rights of man, the possibility of economic and social progress and of justice, a scepticism about the received values, a growing understanding of the hypocrisies of the ruling classes, and a determination not to be manipulated and controlled. By the 1820s there was already a radical canon of printed books in which the ideas were set out, composed, as table 16.4 shows, to a large extent of books on which, for a variety of reasons, no intellectual property could be enforced and which were therefore cheap.

Many readers claimed that their eyes had been opened. Thomas Cooper, records that, when he was a young man, three unlawful books, Palmer's *The Principles of Nature*, Volney's *The Ruins of Empires*, and Voltaire's *Philosophical Dictionary* were offered to his working men's book club 'by a travelling bookseller, very pressingly, and at low prices'.[114] The members of the club were not convinced by Palmer's arguments, but they stopped going to church. Cooper later became a leader of the reform movement. It was the reading of *Queen Mab*, William Linton, another Chartist leader, wrote, 'that roused his passion for reform'.[115] *Queen Mab*, it was said, was the Chartists' Bible, by far the most quoted literary work in the reformist radical press.[116]

If the older rural tradition of respect had been reinforced by the literature of the old canon, a new urban class of society now had its own literature and its own pamphlets, its philosophers, its poets, its songs, its epigrams, and its epics. There was no violent revolution in Britain, such as occurred in

---

[113] For example, the Victorian textbooks by Mrs Foster, Moir; Reed, and Simpkin and Marshall's *Guide*. Also: Arnold; Angus; Spalding; Stopford A. Brooke, Collier, Craik, Oliphant, Minto, Morley, Laing, Siedler, Meiklejohn. For titles see chapter 12, 212. The same suppression can be seen in popular biographies such as *Lives of the British Poets: with specimens of their writings*, published by Nimmo in Edinburgh 1873.

[114] Cooper 49.

[115] F. B. Smith, *Radical Artisan, William James Linton, 1812–97* (Manchester 1973) 9.

[116] See Bouthaina Shaaban, 'Shelley in the Chartist Press' in *Keats Shelley Memorial Bulletin*, 1983.

Table 16.4 The radical canon, 1820s onwards

Volney's *Ruins*
Paine's *Rights of Man*
Other works by Paine
Owen's *New View of Society*
Southey's *Wat Tyler*
Shelley's *Queen Mab*
Other works by Shelley
Songs by Shelley, especially 'Men of England'
Works by Robert Dale Owen, many of which use biblical scholarship to undermine belief
    in the official supernatural and ecclesiastical institutions
Pamphlets giving practical advice on birth control
Byron's *Don Juan*
Palmer's *The Principles of Nature*
Godwin's *Political Justice*
Surgeon Lawrence's *Lectures on Anatomy* (which denied the existence of 'souls')
Byron's *The Vision of Judgment*, with Southey's *The Vision of Judgment*
Pamphlets on Chartism, other current political questions, sceptical biblical scholarship,
    and recent discoveries of science

Often available from the same shops
Pornography
After 1825. *Memoirs of Harriette Wilson*

Not included
Wollstonecraft's *Vindication of the Rights of Woman*
Other specifically feminist writings.[a]

[a] See also chapter 14 and appendix 9.

many European countries. But those who declared that Byron and Shelley would be fatal to the nation were, in their own terms, proved right. The culture which they represented and which they struggled to uphold did not fall, but it did lose its previous dominance, although not immediately and not entirely. In 1850, Southey's son, the Reverend Cuthbert Southey, broke into his narrative of his father's life to comment on the effects of the events of thirty years before when his father had called Byron and Shelley the 'Satanic School of poetry':

What method more subtle or more certain could the Enemy of Mankind use to enlarge the limits of his empire than to destroy all belief in the reality of virtue, to convince men that all that is good, noble, virtuous, or sacred is to be laughed at, disbelieved in, and despised? . . . the clergyman who finds cheap editions of *Don Juan*, and Shelley's *Queen Mab* lying in the cottages of his rural flock, who knows that they are sold by every hawker of books throughout the country and that they are handed about from one to the other by schoolboys and artisans to supply shafts for the quiver of ribald wit and scoffing, blasphemy . . . [Can see how right his father had been.][117]

Frederick Engels writing in 1848, recalling his experiences in Manchester in 1845, made the same observation from the other end of the political spectrum:

It is the workers who are more familiar with the poetry of Shelley and Byron . . . Shelley's prophetic genius has caught their imagination, while Byron attracts their sympathy by his sensuous fire and by the virulence of his satire against the existing social order. The middle classes, on the other hand, have on their shelves only ruthlessly expurgated 'family' editions of these writers.[118]

In 1839, after forty years, the laws requiring registration of printing presses were repealed. The last bounties were paid, the last spies and snoopers were retired, the last sustained attempt to control the mentalities of the people by controlling their access to reading had proved not only ineffective, but perverse. The might of the roaring machinery, declared Frederick von Raumer, a visitor from Germany, 'should convince censors and the secret police of their impotency'.[119] A new urban culture was emerging, no longer deferential, impatient of hereditary landed authority, insistent on the need and possibility of political and economic reform, agnostic towards religion and distrustful of ecclesiastical institutions, but with a strong, often deist, moral idealism. Raumer's conclusion was premature, not least in his own country, but in Britain the poets and the pirates had helped to bring about a shift that remains, for the most part, unreversed.

---

[117] Southey, *Life* v, 75.
[118] Frederick Engels, *On the Condition of the Working Classes in England* (1848), writing of his experiences in Manchester in 1845. For some 'family' editions see appendix 13. For Bowdler's family Shakespeare see appendix 12, 712.
[119] Quoted by William Louis James, *Fiction for the Working Man* (Oxford 1963) 10, from F. von Raumer, *England in 1841* (1842) 317.

CHAPTER 17

At the boundaries of the reading nation

When John Clare was a boy in Northamptonshire at the beginning of the nineteenth century, the printed texts to which he and his friends had easy access had changed little during the previous 200 years. The King James version of the English-language Bible was read in church and at home, and there were plentiful almanacs, many with astrological and magical prognostications.[1] The ballads and chapbooks sold at fairs and from house to house by chapmen contained many titles which predated the 1600 clamp-down.[2] Other books were occasionally to be found, notably the ancient and misleading guide to sex, *Aristotle's Compleat Masterpiece* and the standard school book, Dyche's *Guide to the English Tongue*. Clare tells how he walked six miles to the nearest town to try to buy a copy of Thomson's *Seasons* which he had heard was for sale cheaply.[3] With agricultural wages around a shilling a day, even Thomson's *Seasons* was beyond the reach of most families.[4]

Nor does Clare's experience appear to have been different from that of many boys. The same ballads and chapbooks were part of the childhood of Edmund Burke, Thomas Holcroft, William Godwin, Francis Place, Samuel Taylor Coleridge, Thomas Carter, George Crabbe, William Hazlitt, William Wordsworth, and Walter Scott.[5] Hugh Miller who grew up in the far north of Scotland and Samuel Bamford in industrial Manchester knew many of the same titles, and reading in rural Ireland was little different.

[1] See almanacs in appendices 1 and 7.
[2] See chapter 2 for the economic and physical constraints, chapter 4 for the freeze.
[3] Clare's childhood reading can be reconstructed from the many references in 'Sketches of the Life of John Clare, written by Himself . . . March 1821' in Clare's *Autobiographical Writings*. See also *John Clare by Himself* edited by Eric Robinson and David Powell (1996).
[4] Hannah More's figure put in the mouth of a character in her tract *The Shepherd of Salisbury Plain* (n.d. 1790s). Reprinted in *The Miscellaneous Works of Hannah More* (1840) i, 130.
[5] Examples in appendix 5. Others, with quotations from original sources, in Collins, *Profession of Letters* 32, 51, 53. Burke and others are mentioned in Spufford 74. Coleridge's recollections are quoted by Nick Groom, *The Making of Percy's* Reliques (Oxford 1999) 238. Bamford's reading is discussed by Vincent 61.

Two wholesale trade catalogues prepared in 1754 and 1764 at the height of the high monopoly period list the extensive stocks which were then available through the chapman networks of England and America.[6] Although only a few copies of the materials that were advertised have survived, the catalogues enable us to reconstruct the whole culture of print, both literary and visual, that was consistently available to a large constituency of the English-speaking reading nation across many generations.

   Chapbooks consisted of twelve or twenty-four pages made from one or two sheets, folded and unstitched. Ballads were printed on one sheet or half a sheet. The length of the texts was, to a large extent, determined by what could be comfortably included in multiples of a half sheet. In many cases there were both chapbook and ballad versions of the same story, and some longer stories were divided into parts which could be bought and read independently or in series. Almost invariably, they were illustrated with at least one woodcut from a store of blocks, many of which were also very ancient. Manufacturing on the eve of the romantic period had scarcely changed since the sixteenth century. The minimum print run was a ream, or a half ream, equivalent to editions of 1,000 or 2,000 for chapbooks, or 2,000 or 4,000 for ballads, but, when we find that, as early as 1736 a single Irish chapman had more than 2,000 copies of some titles in stock, it seems likely that the normal print run was longer than the minimum.[7] According to Thomas Gent, a printer writing in the early eighteenth century, the apprentices and journeymen who made the ballads worked from five in the morning until midnight.[8]

   During most of the eighteenth century, the centre of manufacturing was Aldermary Churchyard in London with stocks held in the Ballad Warehouse nearby. From there the chapbooks and ballads were sold retail to individuals and wholesale to chapmen serving a wide radius round the

---

[6] Titles in 'Book trade catalogues. Popular literature', bibliography, 730. The title pages of these catalogues, in addition to the royal arms, reproduce the device of a royal patent, affirming the claim to the exclusive rights to print classes of works, such as the ABCs, catechisms, and maps, for which letters patent had been granted in earlier centuries. The Bodleian copy, which belonged to Percy, includes his annotations of other titles he found in the Ballad Warehouse. The whole stock is transcribed by Thomson 288. The 1764 catalogue was known to Charles Gerring who quoted from it in *Notes on Printers and Booksellers with a Chapter on Chap Books* (1900), but was unsuccessfully searched for by Victor E. Neuburg, 'The Diceys and the Chapbook Trade' in *The Library* (1969). Many of the titles are noted in Ashton 483.

[7] Some figures from seventeenth-century inventories are given in Spufford 93. For the 1736 Irish inventory, see Newcomb 253 and M. Pollard, *Dublin's Trade in Books, 1550–1800* (1989) 219. Other figures in C. R. Cheney, 'Early Banbury Chap-Books and Broadsides' in *The Library*, 1936.

[8] Thomson 84, quoting Gent.

capital which seems to have been roughly the extreme reach of a man walking. The owners had agents in a nationwide network of English provincial centres, all easily reached by water, where other stocks were held. During the 1720s, newspapers published in provincial towns began to advertise the routes which their chapmen would take round the villages.[9] By the high monopoly period, the popular print sector had become almost completely monopolised in the hands of a single London firm of Dicey, which held the intellectual properties, the unsold stocks, and the manufacturing plant, in all the favourite titles.[10] The Victorian antiquary John Ashton, who made a collection of eighteenth-century chapbooks printed in Newcastle, noticed that many were almost exactly the same as those produced in London, even to the woodcut illustrations. Although these books may have been copied, without permission, from the London originals, as is commonly assumed, they may be evidence of the licensing of manufacturing in the north of England.[11]

The London publishers continued to use the old black-letter fonts for nearly a century after they had ceased to be used in mainstream print. The same woodblocks, some registered as intellectual properties as early as the sixteenth century, were reused again and again until they became so badly worn as to be scarcely recognisable.[12] The same woodcuts were used to illustrate a wide range of texts, that of the Virgin Queen Elizabeth doing equally well for *The Wanton Wife of Bath*. Until the 1580s it had been common for mainstream books, including histories and English-language Bibles, to consist both of printed texts and of engraved illustrations. But suddenly after that date, most newly published books consisted only of print. Some historians have linked the change to an increasing aversion to images as relics of the old Roman Catholic religion. In the popular balled and chapbook sector, however, illustrations continued to be an intrinsic part of the book all through the whole period of the freeze. This suggests that, as with other sudden shifts in publishing practice, we should be looking for explanations based on changes in the governing structures, perhaps some

---

[9] Myers and Harris *Spreading* 68.

[10] See chapter 4. Dicey seems to have been the manager and part owner.

[11] See Frances M. Thomson, *Newcastle Chapbooks* (1969). The Newcastle list, besides all the old favourites, includes the same handful of modern authored works as are found in Dicey's catalogue and no others. Like the London chapbooks the Newcastle chapbooks are undated, but of the long list of chapbook publishers known to have been in business in Newcastle, there is only one who was undoubtedly operating before 1774.

[12] Many examples in the Harvard collection. See Charles Welsh and William H. Tillinghast eds., *Catalogue of English and American Chapbooks and Broadside Ballads in Harvard College Library* (1961)

stricter demarcation between printers and engravers, or some agreement when the popular sector divided from the mainstream, rather than assuming that they reflected changes in readerly taste.[13]

Some editions have silly printing errors even on the title pages, *Tom Stitch the vaylor* (instead of 'taylor') *Sir Bevis, a most nodle* [for 'noble'] *Knight*, signs of haste in manufacturing and the carelessness of a monopolist.[14] Titles were frequently reregistered, and seldom came on the market. Although they looked primitive and provincial, features which have fostered the fallacy that they are emanations of 'the folk', they were actually produced by rich owners who were as much part of the central management of the London book industry as the franchisees of the English-language Bible and the proprietors of Shakespeare.[15] At least one was knighted.[16]

Most chapbooks and ballads, even those abridged from longer works by famous authors, were printed without any author being named, and most were undated. Many had a continuous history back to the age of manuscript, having become private intellectual properties in the earliest days of print.[17] Others were the work of Thomas Deloney, Richard Johnson, and other abridgers, adapters and balladeers of the Elizabethan age. The 1596 anthology of pre-clamp-down ballad versions of longer works, *The Garland of Good Will* was still available in the romantic period, having apparently been continuously available for over two hundred years.[18] Innumerable thousands read the romance of *Argalus and Parthenia* who had never heard of Sidney's *Arcadia* from which it had long ago been abridged. *Dorastus and Fawnia*, an abridgement of Robert Greene's *Pandosto* (1592) was still being reprinted every few years.[19] And although Shakespeare's plays had long since disappeared from popular reading, the ballads of *Sir Lancelot du Lac* and *The Constancy of Susanna* which Sir John Falstaff and Sir Toby Belch sang in 2 *Henry IV*, and *Twelfth Night* respectively, and of which only snatches were given in the printed Shakespearian texts, were still well

[13] James Knapp, *Illustrating the Past in Early Modern England* (2003) 2.
[14] Harvard, no. 1847, Bodleian Douce PP 178, Harvard, no. 569. Some of the Pepys books have obvious errors, e.g. 'Pinted' for 'Printed'. See list in Thompson.
[15] The late Victor Neuburg, who did much to advance understanding of English popular culture, seems never to have realised that until 1774 popular print was as much part of the intellectual property regime as other printed texts.
[16] Sir James Hodges. See Timperley 733.   [17] For example *The Gospel of Nicodemus*.
[18] See 'Anthologies. The pre-1600 flurry of printed literary anthologies. Poetry miscellanies', appendix 3, 490.
[19] See 'Abridged "ballad versions" of longer literary works common before 1600, but only a few later', appendix 3, 496.

known across England.[20] According to John Clare the people had heard of Shakespeare but only from playbills.[21]

The stories, verses, and woodcuts were formulaic and predictable, textually as well as materially. Besides their array of kings, queens, and ladies, real and mythical, the residue of mediaeval and renaissance romance, the stories were filled with stock characters, the lusty miller, the shrewish wife, the cheating townsman, the stupid Welshman. The picture of life they offer is harsh and violent, full of unexpected tragedies, murders, seizures of women, tricks, knaveries, and luck. They tell tales of chance encounters with princes, poor men becoming rich – *Fortunatus* has a purse which refills whenever it is empty and a wishing cap which can whisk him to wherever he desires to be. Few of the old stories suggested that a man could raise himself by merit and hard work rather than by drawing a winning ticket in the lottery of life.

The woodcuts, that were sold in black and white but could be coloured in watercolours, had much in common with the printed texts. Hung on walls or pinned to a bench at the work place, many had the same verses as the ballads. Many a cottage and inn at the end of the eighteenth century was decorated with 'a pretty slight drollery, or the story of the Prodigal, or the German hunting in waterwork', the cheap art which Sir John Falstaff recommended to Mistress Quickly.[22] The images appear to have been more strictly religious than the written texts, with innumerable Bible stories from the New as well as the Old Testament, and only a few of the non-canonical biblical myths or the illegitimate supernatural. Although the literary texts of the popular canon are often frozen from pre-Reformation times, the images appear to have been continually added to. It is as if, at some date, ecclesiastical inspectors had brought the popular images into line with the official post-Reformation supernatural while still allowing pre-Reformation popular literary texts to be printed.[23]

Amongst the largest constituencies for chapbooks and ballads during the whole print era were adults in the country areas, and young people in both the town and the country. It would be a mistake, therefore, to regard the ancient popular print as confined to those whose education fitted them for nothing longer or textually more difficult. Many readers, whether adults or children, lived at the boundary between the reading and the non-reading

---

[20] Both are in the trade catalogues.
[21] For Clare's remark see Richard Terry, *Poetry and the Making of the English Literary Past* (Oxford 2001) 177. Both ballads are listed in the 1764 catalogue.
[22] *2 Henry IV, ii*, 1, 141.   [23] For a discussion of how this may have come about see chapter 4.

nations. They were the marginal reading constituency whose numbers fell when prices rose and rose when prices fell. Both groups of readers often felt apologetic, or were made to feel guilty, for enjoying this form of reading. Richard Baxter, for example, the seventeenth-century author of religious books which entered the old canon, confessed to reading chapbooks rather as he might have confessed to stealing apples.[24] Samuel Johnson regretted the hours he wasted reading romances in his father's bookshop.[25] To judge from the many warnings against the reading of romance to be found in conduct books, women were among the readerships from the earliest times.

Many of those who read these stories, or who read them aloud to their friends or to their children, had probably heard them from parents, friends, or – a constant worry among the upper-income groups – from house-servants. The printed text and engraved pictures were, we may guess, used more as aids to a performance, with plenty of acting, invention, ritual repetition, and interruptions – just as the chapmen at the fairs told the stories and sang the ballads they had for sale – rather than read, word for word, alone, and in silence.[26] The readership was therefore probably a large multiple of the numbers of copies manufactured and sold, and the tradition was so long lived that it served to set the horizons of expectations of each succeeding cohort of readers and viewers. On the eve of the romantic period, a large constituency of English-speaking readers continued a tradition which went back to the performers, writers, abridgers, and woodcut artists of the English renaissance.

In much modern writing on 'the romantic revival', the editors of the eighteenth-century printed collections of old ballads, Percy, Ritson, Evans, and others, have been presented as intrepid tireless explorers whose anti-quarian efforts recovered an ancient popular culture, surviving in remote and threatened rural habitats. From Thomas Percy's *Reliques of Ancient English Poetry* (1765) to Cecil Sharp and the English Folksong Society, many collectors have thought that they were only just in time to capture the last remains of a rapidly disappearing oral culture. Almost all silently subscribed to a hierarchy of authenticity which put country over town, oral performance over manuscript, and manuscript over print.[27] It was a

---

[24] Quoted by Spufford 74.   [25] Spufford 75.

[26] There are many accounts of story-telling as the main entertainment in the country, some quoted in Collins, *Profession of Letters* 34.

[27] Well analysed by Thomson, who discusses the 'folksong' collectors, but similar attitudes are to be found in recent books. Groom, for example, assumes there was a 'genuine' oral tradition which was later recovered by Child and others which was separate from the 'antiquarian' printed versions he

disappointment for some who did research in the field to find that many of the old songs turned out to have existed in printed versions.

The hero of the 'romantic revival' narrative is the unnamed editor of *A Collection of Old Ballads* (1723–5), seen as the first mainstream printing of the ancient texts. Since there are similarities with the ballads published from Aldermary Churchyard in the mid-eighteenth century, it has also been thought that the firm of Dicey 'pirated' from the printed book. These accounts, however, depend upon a misunderstanding of the conditions under which popular print was published. The *Collection of Old Ballads* was not a collection put together by an assiduous antiquarian researcher from higher literary culture, but a reprint commissioned by the then intellectual property owners made from printed versions held in their Ballad Warehouse. They had a strong commercial reason for publishing the book when they did. Published during the transitional period before the terms of the 1710 Act came into force, the *Collection of Old Ballads* could claim a new copyright, just as Rowe's edition created a new intellectual property in Shakespeare.[28]

The collection made by Thomas Percy, also produced under the private intellectual property regime of the high monopoly period, was intended by the then owners as a successor to *A Collection of Old Ballads* in the same way that Pope and Theobald succeeded Rowe.[29] When Percy visited the Ballad Warehouse in 1761 he was given copies of 'above four score' of old printed ballads he had never seen.[30] In the end, Percy's book was much more than a reprint collection. Having rescued a manuscript book from a housemaid who was about to use it to light a fire, Percy claimed that his edition was drawn not from printed versions but from the more authentic text of the manuscript. Although his unwillingness to allow others to see the manuscript encouraged the belief that, like the 'manuscripts' of Macpherson's Ossian and Rowley's Shakespeare, it did not exist, the story was more complex. Percy's manuscript did exist – it was a late-seventeenth-century miscellany which, like many such compilations, drew on both printed and performed versions.[31] However, on the basis that he had access to ancient sources unavailable to others, Percy made drastic changes to the received printed versions on which he mainly drew, adding his own conjectures and inventions, introducing 'olde Englishe' spelling for which

---

associates with *A Collection* and with Percy. He talks, on page 25, about Percy 'fixing' the ballads on the printed page.

[28] See 'High monopoly period.', appendix 4, 501.   [29] Groom 136.

[30] From an original letter quoted by Leslie Shephard, *John Pitts, Ballad Printer* (1969) 28.

[31] BL add. mss. 27,879.

he had no authority. More knowledgeable antiquarians saw at once that, even if a manuscript did exist, Percy had, under the guise of 'editing', faked up a good deal of the text to make it fit his theory of old English minstrelsy.[32]

It is often assumed that the ballads which only survive from the seventeenth- and eighteenth-century printed versions have been textually so much altered in transition compared with their lost predecessors that they cannot be relied upon to give us more than a general impression. Popular print, being oral and performative, it is assumed, is by its nature textually unstable, and when the printed versions are put alongside the manuscript versions found in miscellanies, there are indeed many differences. However, in the cases where I have checked the succession of editions from the 1600 clamp-down to the ending of perpetual copyright in 1774, the printed texts did not change much, other than in typography and spelling.[33] What was recovered by the 'romantic revival' was not an oral and performative popular tradition stretching back into the mists of time, but a continuous privately owned print tradition that had never been interrupted. Indeed, if we use *A Collection of Old Ballads*, and disregard Percy, our knowledge of the printed ballad literature of the Elizabethan age is both full and reliable.

Wordsworth was among the many authors of the romantic period who looked back nostalgically to the reading of their youth that was fast disappearing. As he wrote in *The Prelude* (1850):

> Oh! Give us once again the wishing cap
> Of Fortunatus, and the invisible coat
> Of Jack the Giant Killer, Robin Hood
> And Sabra in the forest with St George!
> The child, whose love is here, at least doth reap
> One precious gain, that he forgets himself.[34]

Other authors too made a conscious attempt to regain something of the spirit of wonderment which they remembered from a world that had been lost. William Godwin at the opposite end of the political spectrum from Wordsworth, praised the power of the ancient chapbooks to stimulate the

---

[32] Notably Joseph Ritson, another editor of ballads. His dispute with Percy is discussed in Bertrand H. Bronson, *Joseph Ritson, Scholar at Arms* (Berkeley 1938).

[33] The text of the ballad version of *Titus Andronicus* which has a long recorded textual history was stable. See also another worked example in '*The Duchess of Suffolk's Calamity*', appendix 4, 502.

[34] In *The Prelude* (1850). St George and Sabra is from Richard Johnson's *Seven Champions* or an abridgement.

imagination of children.[35] For Scott, the chapbooks provided a model for the meeting of real historical figures with imagined characters from low life which he exploited in the Waverley novels. The old ballads and chapbooks, many writers believed, had a directness, an absence of cant, a humanity, and a magical quality which had largely disappeared from the classicising mainstream literature of the eighteenth century, and it is easy for readers of the present day to share such feelings. However, the question which the historian of reading needs to address is why an ancient tradition that had seemed secure and timeless less than a generation before should suddenly lose its readerly appeal around 1800. And, for the sudden unfreezing of the tradition, as for the freezing, an intellectual property model provides a more precise and convincing explanation than speculations about changing readerly tastes. What we see, in material terms between 1774 and the end of the romantic period, is the effect on books and reading of the ending of the monopoly in the supply of popular print.

The first effect of the abolition of intellectual property, as we would expect, was the reprinting by newcomers of the old favourites for sale at lower prices, and as with other books, the first breaks occurred in Scotland. It is clear from remarks in Boswell's diary, for example, that the chapbooks which he read in Edinburgh in the 1740s had come from London.[36] By the middle of the century, however, there were thriving chapbook industries in Edinburgh and Glasgow, producing both new titles by modern writers such as Dougal Graham, and reprinting older titles over which the London industry claimed perpetual copyright.[37] As with other books, the commercial contest between the English and Scottish systems appears to have been most keen in the north of England. 'The Wanderer', the hero of the first book of Wordworth's *The Excursion*, who teaches the poet his sense of natural piety, was a former Scottish chapman who had settled in northern England.

Since the manufacturing costs of popular literature were low relative to the distribution costs, the best way to take advantage of the new economic conditions after 1774 was to manufacture nearer to the final markets. We duly find the presses in the provincial towns that had previously been part of the supply network being used to start local chapbook industries

[35] Writing under the pseudonym William Scolfield, in preface to *Bible Stories* (1802). See William St Clair, 'William Godwin as Children's Bookseller' in Gillian Avery and Julia Briggs, eds., *Children and their Books* (Oxford 1989). The text is reprinted in *Political and Philosophical Writings of William Godwin* (1993), v, 312.

[36] *Boswell's London Journal 1762–1763* edited by Frederick A. Pottle (1950) 299. Boswell's collection, with others collected later, is in the Child Memorial, Harvard University.

[37] See Graham.

supplying local chapmen. During the romantic period at least seventy-four towns published chapbooks.[38] As with other print, many of these reprinting centres are near the Scottish border. We also find economic competition. In many towns previously supplied from London too, we suddenly find records of three or four different publishers competing for the chapmen's business, some claiming to offer the lowest prices in the country.[39] In the romantic period in Newcastle, a key distribution centre reached by sea as easily from Edinburgh as from London, there are records of about a dozen publishers producing chapbooks and ballads, and even in a small town like Whitehaven there were half a dozen. By the 1820s many chapbooks and ballads were being printed from stereotypes, sometimes from foundries built in small towns. A stereotype foundry was built in the tiny northern English town of Alnwick as early as 1812, at a time when there was still scarcely any stereotyping in London.[40] Another was in Falkirk, an iron-founding town in the Scottish Lowlands. When the chapbook industry adopted printing by cylinder, enabling chapbooks and ballads to be manufactured and sold in rolls by the yard, prices fell even more drastically than in other sectors.

In much modern writing, it has been assumed that the ballad chapbook industry of the romantic period was a relic of pre-industrial Britain, an older form of print culture lingering in the more rural areas but retreating rapidly towards an inexorable extinction before the forces of modernity.[41] But quantification produces a different picture. During the romantic period there was no decline in chapbook production – on the contrary – more chapbook titles, both old and new, were published, in larger numbers, and in many more towns, than at any previous time. Far from being an industry on the verge of extinction, the chapbook industry of the romantic period formed part of the explosion of reading which began in the late eighteenth century. The boom seems to have continued at least until the 1840s when the arrival of the railways enabled longer printed texts to reach remoter areas previously supplied by water and by animal power. What happened in the romantic period was not that chapbooks and ballads as such ceased to be produced and sold, but that the traditional titles were replaced by more recently composed texts.

---

[38] Webb 30, from the Harvard collection.
[39] Shown, for example, by the advertisements on surviving copies: 'These are to give Notice that Chapmen, Travellers, and others may be supply'd with the best sorts of small Histories, Godly Books, Old Ballads, Garlands, Broadsheets & as cheap as at any Place in England' in *David's Repentance*, Wilson of Bristol and Cook of Gloucester, n.d. probably, late eighteenth or early nineteenth century, Lauriston Castle chapbooks, NLS.
[40] See Peter Isaac, *William Davison's New Specimen of Cast-Metal Ornaments and Wood Types* (1990).
[41] See chapter 4.

After 1774 the huge corpus of authored literature printed before the middle of the eighteenth century became available not only to be reprinted but to be abridged, excerpted, and adapted. By the end of the century many old-canon novels, books of history, travel, and exploration, had been abridged from texts which were no longer in private ownership. By the 1810s we see the rapid growth of what we might call chapbook gothic, stories of horror, of seduction, of elopements, of Italian castles and German nuns, many of which appear to be abridged adaptations of Minerva Press titles which were coming out of copyright at that time. The children's book industry boomed. We see new versions of *Robinson Crusoe* and *Gulliver's Travels*, some of which take the stories far from the original.[42] We see a proliferation of poetry anthologies for children, of 'Lilliputian Libraries', of abridgements and adaptations of histories and books of travel, of chapbook versions of the beasts, the birds, and the fishes taken from the *Natural History* of Buffon,[43] and much other printed material which would not previously have been permissible.

As with larger books, the ending of monopoly meant a transfer of income from profits to readers. After 1774, furthermore, the prices of old-canon books fell so far that some of those who previously could only have afforded ballads and chapbooks could now buy old canon. The chapmen who had previously taken ballads and chapbooks to the villages now took the old canon, both as small-format books and as parts and numbers.[44] The long separation between modern authored literature and the reading of the economically less well off, that had opened up around 1600 now began to close. From 1798 Cooke's English poets, novels, and classics were circulating across the country at sixpence a part, not far from the price of a traditional chapbook. By 1823, Limberd's *British Novelists* offered old-canon novels at sixpence a title or two pence in numbers of sixteen pages.[45] At these prices, many constituencies of readers whose reading had previously been largely confined to the Bible, almanac, and ballad culture of King James were able to make a leap, not into modernity, but into the less obsolete printed literature of the eighteenth century.

---

[42] For a text-based discussion see 'Rethinking Folklore, Rethinking Literature: Looking at *Robinson Crusoe* and *Gulliver's Travels* as Folktales, A Chapbook-Inspired Inquiry' in Cathy Lynn Preston and Michael J. Preston eds. *The Other Print Tradition, Essays on Chapbooks, Broadsides, and Related Ephemera* (New York 1995).

[43] *Histoire naturelle, générale et particulière* by Georges Louis Leclerc, comte de Buffon (Paris 1769), an English translation of which was published in 1775, for many decades the standard work on natural history and the main source of secondary writings across Europe.

[44] See, for example, Bew's list in appendix 4, 503.

[45] See Figure 3, chapter 7, and appendix 6.

Within a generation of 1774, many titles, such as *Robin Hood*, when adapted, passed into the burgeoning children's book industry. But many dozens of other titles, even although they were for a time offered at a fraction of previous prices, soon ceased to be demanded altogether and were never again reprinted. Some of the ancient stories which we might have expected to survive as children's books, such as *Fortunatus*, quickly died out. With Shakespeare himself now available cheaply, both in full and in adapted, abridged, and children's versions, no one now wanted the ballad versions of *Titus Andronicus* and *King Leir and his Three Daughters*, the nearest to the real thing which had been available to those at the boundaries of the reading nation since the 1590s, and they disappeared without a tear even from Wordsworth. The biggest casualties were the old romances of Christian knights and fighting heroes. In a single generation, *Guy of Warwick* and *Bevis of Hampton*, two of the most famous and most ancient stories of all, which had been read in England by every generation for at least 500 years across the oral, the manuscript, and the print era, died out, like the dinosaurs, as part of a sudden mass extinction.

The history of the chapbook and ballad sector of the English book industry offers general lessons about the nature of the links between books, reading, cultural formation and outcomes which go far beyond a particular episode in the long story. If we consider the industry simply as an economic supplier of material goods, we have one of the few examples in economic history where we can trace the effects of an unregulated private monopoly from the first invention of a new product in the sixteenth century, through increasing cartelisation, to near total monopoly. We then see a prolonged period of equilibrium and stagnation, which was followed by an immediate and drastic change as soon as the monopoly was brought to an end. We have, therefore, in this industrial sector, a well-documented historical example of the long-run obsoletising effects of private economic monopoly as such. When, however, we consider the sector as a supplier of literary and visual texts carried by the materiality of print, then another conclusion seems inescapable. It cannot be enough to say that the only or main reason why the ancient print lasted as long as it did is that the texts reflected, in some special way, the mentalities of the readers, or catered for their needs and aspirations.[46] We have to conclude instead that it was only because, in their economic and cultural circumstances, the readers at the boundaries had no alternatives that they kept the tradition going, and that the moment

---

[46] For a discussion of the mentalities of the population in the rural areas see, among many others, Vincent 156.

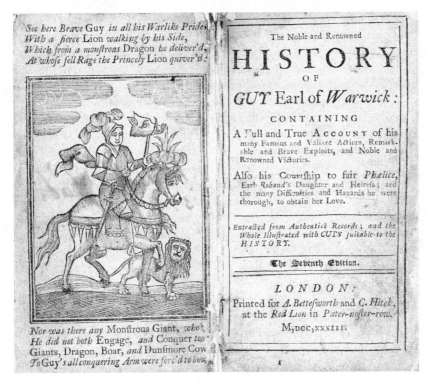

See here Brave Guy *in all his* Warlike Pride,
With a *fierce* Lion *walking by his* Side,
Which *from a* monſtrous Dragon *he deliver'd*,
At *whoſe fell* Rage *the* Princely Lion quiver'd:

The Noble and Renowned

HISTORY
OF
GUY Earl of *Warwick*:
CONTAINING

A Full and True Account of his
many Famous and Valiant Actions, Remark-
able and Brave Exploits, and Noble and
Renowned Victories.

Also his Courtſhip to fair *Phælice*,
Earl *Roband's* Daughter and Heireſs; and
the many Difficulties and Hazards he went
thorough, to obtain her Love.

*Extracted from Authentick Records; and the
Whole Illuſtrated with CUTS ſuitable to the
HISTORY.*

The Seventh Edition.

LONDON:
Printed for *A.* Betteſworth and *C. Hitch*,
at the Red Lion in Pater-noſter-row.
M,DCC,XXXIII.

Nor *was there any* Monſtrous Giant, *who*
He *did not both* Engage, *and* Conquer *too*
Giants, Dragon, Boar, *and* Dunſmore Cow
To Guy's *all conquering* Arm *were* forc'd *to bow*,

Figure 19. Title page and illustration of *Guy of Warwick*, a mediaeval romance read mainly in abridged versions until the mass extinction in the romantic period.

they had a wider choice, they jettisoned it without regret. In terms of the dynamics of cultural formation, we have an example here of how intellectual property combined with commercial monopoly kept a large constituency of marginal readers in ancient ignorance.

The biggest effect of the breakdown of the monopoly was felt in London. The firm at Aldermary Churchyard was so well established and enjoyed so many advantages that, with some adaptation, it ought to have been able to withstand the abolition of perpetual copyright, or at least to preserve a large part of its business in the south. But in the event it seems quickly to have lost its dominance. Perhaps, like many long-established monopolies, the firm had lost the skills to market and sell its products in conditions of competition, but in any case, in an era of water transport and animal power, London was not a suitable centre from which to run a national chapbook industry. It was in these circumstances, when their business was in decline, that the then owners of the now broken monopoly accepted what was in effect a take-over bid from Hannah More and the Cheap Repository Tract Society, not for the titles or for the plant but for the asset which was now of most value, the chapman distribution network.

If some visitors to popular print, such as Wordsworth, were inclined to nostalgia, others took a different view. Hannah More and her sister were horrified to discover that the actual rural England they found when they set up a school in Somerset was not at all like the picture of harmonious simple life presented in the English georgics of Oliver Goldsmith's *Deserted Village*, James Thomson's *Seasons*, or William Cowper's *The Task*. Literacy levels were low, schools thinly spread and of poor quality, and what they found most disturbing of all, much of England was only in name a Christian country.[47] The mentalities, beliefs, and 'folk' superstitions of the agricultural workers and rural poor, with their astrological prognostications, their fighting champions, their giants, fairies, witches, and enchantments of all kinds were not all that different from the mentalities which had horrified the reformers at the time of the English Reformation. And now, in the 1790s, there was a more frightening prospect. When the news of the French Revolution arrived in the farthest corners of Europe, many of the British elites suddenly realised that if the writings of Voltaire and Rousseau had precipitated such a social and political upset in France, the pamphlets of Tom Paine, and later *Queen Mab*, *Don Juan*, and the other printed texts of the radical canon, could do the same in England. As Hannah More wrote to Zachary Macaulay in 1796, 'Vulgar and indecent penny books were always common, but speculative infidelity, brought down to the pockets and capacities of the poor, forms a new era in our history.'[48] 'To teach the poor to read without providing them with safe books', she wrote on another occasion, 'has always appeared to me to be an improper measure.'[49] What More and her financial backers hoped to do in taking over the chapman network was to use it to distribute a type of print, mainly newly composed by herself, which would drive out both the old chapbooks and the radical pamphlets. In the struggle to shape the mentalities of the people by controlling their access to print, the tract movement dovetailed neatly into the gap created by tight textual controls and heavy taxes.[50]

At first sight, Hannah More's cheap repository tracts looked almost identical with the print she hoped to displace. But from both an economic and

---

[47] A point Hannah More also made in describing the views of the rest of society in *Thoughts on the Importance of the Manners of the Great to General Society* (1809).
[48] Spinney 296, from Roberts ii, 461.   [49] Spinney 298.   [50] See chapter 16.

a cultural point of view, they were different. The old ballad and chapbook industry, though a monopoly, was a wholly commercial operation with the final buyers/readers paying for all the costs of production and distribution. The cheap repository tracts were financed not by readers but by subscriptions from members of the wealthier classes of society, the same ecclesiastical and political constituency that financed the Society for the Suppression of Vice. Since it was thought that the final customers at whom the tracts were aimed would be less suspicious, maybe more appreciative, if they had to pay at least a nominal amount, the tracts were, according to the initial plan, to be sold at a price which undercut the commercial chapbooks and ballads.[51] The older print was to be driven out by predatory pricing.

As far as the texts were concerned, although they were written as part of a Christian agenda, they contained, like the sermons of Blair, a minimum of formal Christianity. As with Blair, the religion is downplayed in favour of social cohesion and concord between the haves and the have nots. Many of the tracts were essentially conduct books for the poor, infiltrated into the normal reading channels just as Hannah More and her allies also infiltrated conduct novels into the circulating libraries. In the old chapbooks, the local miller was a well-known character. Sometimes he had the luck to meet the king in the street and his fortune was transformed, but usually the miller's role was to seduce the local wives. In Hannah More's adaptation, when winter is harsh, the river freezes, and there is only one mill in the district which is able to operate, the miller invites all the local millers to use his mill without charge, and despite the shortage, not a single one of them puts up his prices during the emergency.[52] In *The Shepherd of Salisbury Plain*, a gentleman is riding across the plain, contemplating the splendour of God in creation, when he meets a poor shepherd, who knows his Bible well, who persuades the gentleman that his life style on a shilling a day is not only morally superior to that of the gentleman but brings greater happiness. Because of his attitude, the shepherd is given money by the gentleman which enables him to buy medicine for his sick wife and move to a new house. On the wall of the shepherd's house, incidentally, where previously there might have been an old ballad, hangs one of the Cheap Repository Tracts.

The key to the success of More's plan was the attitude of the sales force, that is the chapmen. From the start, they agreed to distribute the tracts

[51] See the summary of the financing in appendix 5.
[52] *The Honest Miller of Gloucestershire, A True Ballad* (n.d. 1790s). Reprinted in *The Miscellaneous Works of Hannah More* (1840) ii, 253.

but only if they were guaranteed their incomes, even if they sold nothing, a condition the promoters accepted. Before long, the promoters turned to completely free distribution. The men and women whose subscriptions paid for tracts to be produced, bought them themselves, usually in bulk batches of a hundred at a time, and sent them to be distributed in hospitals, workhouses, prisons, and among members of the armed forces. The chapmens' insistence from the start that the tracts should be printed on soft paper, rather than the smoother book paper favoured by the promoters, suggests that they were well aware of the ignoble fate to which they would soon be consigned.[53]

Many millions of tracts produced by various societies at the expense of their members were printed during the romantic period, along with many hundreds of thousands of Bibles bought and distributed at heavily subsidised prices.[54] How far the books were actually read, and with what effect, is hard to gauge. The experience of William Cameron, a Scottish chapman in Dunfermline in 1820, may have been typical:

When I got to the lodgings, I unharnessed myself, and went to a bookseller's named Miller, for ballads or histories, but he had nothing but tracts. These were *a bad fit* but the drink being in the garrett I took four dozen of them, went into the street, and began a long story. I soon gathered an audience who relished the story and many bought . . . One of the buyers called me an impostor, saying I had given him John Covy [a tract] in place of what I called.[55]

However, to the American Samuel Goodrich, Hannah More's tracts were the first books he read with enthusiasm, as he recalled later the ecstasy he felt at being able to visit the places where *The Shepherd of Salisbury Plain* was set, and he himself later set up as a producer of improving literature for children.[56] By 1820 some thought that the social benefits of promoting the reading of such 'cheap publications' could be detected in the behaviour of working people. In the past, it was said, it was impossible for a hundred men to gather without turning into a riotous mob, but now crowds of up to 100,000 would assemble, listen to speeches, make petitions, and disperse peaceably.[57]

---

[53] For the differing quality of paper see Spinney 303 although he did not realise why soft paper books sold extremely cheaply, or given away gratis, could find takers even if they were never read.
[54] Some figures in appendix 5.
[55] John Strathesk, ed., *Hawkie, The Autobiography of a Gangrel* (William Cameron, a Scottish chapman) (1888) 57.
[56] Goodrich 172.   [57] *Black Book* 335.

With popular print, as with the rest of the book industry, the sudden thaw of 1774 was followed by a slow renewal of the freeze, as the brief copyright window was closed. By the 1840s it was possible, using newspaper technology, to produce printed texts of many pages for profitable sale at two pence and the price of access to the cheapest forms of print continued to fall.[58] But the intellectual property regime now again stood in the way of anthologies, abridgements, adaptations, or chapbook versions from mainstream literature. There were no abridgements of the Waverley novels or of Byron.[59]

Denied permission to reprint good modern English literature, the cheap fiction publishers turned to novels first published in the United States, France and Germany which, in the absence of international copyright, could be freely reprinted, translated, abridged, and adapted. As one overseas source after another was closed off, the publishers of cheap fiction increasingly employed hack writers to produce the hack stories needed to fill their columns. As one retail outlet after another was denied them, they were increasingly obliged to bypass the regular bookshops.[60]

By the 1840s, the mechanics institute libraries which had begun as a resource for skilled manual workers had been largely taken over by the middle classes.[61] By the mid nineteenth century the literature and the reading of the working and clerical classes was already largely separated both textually and materially from the literature of the higher-income groups, so reinforcing the other barriers which divided the social classes. We see a continuing proliferation of the illegitimate supernatural, old astrology but now also palmistry, fortune telling from playing cards, and sensationalist 'penny dreadfuls' and 'bloods'. As Wilkie Collins noted in 1858, there was an 'Unknown Public', three million readers 'right out of the pale of literary civilization', a huge constituency of the still-expanding reading nation about which the elites knew little.[62]

The decision of 1774 transferred a huge quantum of purchasing power from book publishers to book buyers, leading to an explosion of reading in the romantic period, a growth in the size of the reading nation, and a sharp rise in the quality of the national literature to which there was now cheaper and more plentiful access. The 1842 Copyright Act produced a reciprocal effect. A wide range of literary texts which were just about to

---

[58] For example the *Romancist Library* see chapter 19.
[59] See the discussion of *Frankenstein* in chapter 18.   [60] See also chapter 18 for the American reprints.
[61] Minto 52, quoting evidence to the *Select Committee on Public Libraries, Reports* (1849–52).
[62] Quoted by Martyn Lyons, 'New Readers in the Nineteenth Century' in Cavallo and Chartier 315.

enter the public domain were converted into valuable windfall assets from which the lucky owners could take a rent for many more years. The change kept the prices of the reasonably modern English books higher than would otherwise have been the case, and held back most of the nation's access to recent good literature for another generation. Victorian moralists often complained that their less well-off countrymen read mostly rubbish, and they were right. The intellectual property regime which they established in 1842 was among the main causes.

CHAPTER 18

Frankenstein

Of all the literary works written during the romantic period, *Frankenstein* is the one whose continuing presence is most obvious. The idea arose one evening in 1816 when Byron, Percy Bysshe Shelley, Mary Godwin, and Byron's doctor, Polidori, who were living by the Lake of Geneva, agreed that each would write a ghost story. The outline of Shelley's story has been preserved, and Polidori's *The Vampyre* was later published and frequently reprinted, partly because it was falsely attributed to Byron.[1] But only Mary Godwin, or Mary Shelley as she later became, composed a full scale work.[2] She was aged eighteen when she wrote the first words which she put into the mouth of Victor Frankenstein, 'It was on a dreary night of November that I beheld the accomplishment of my toils. With an anxiety that almost amounted to agony, I collected the instruments of life around me, that I might infuse a spark of being into the lifeless thing that lay at my feet.' In the months that followed, Mary completed the story, with collaborative help from Shelley who added to and sharpened the draft.[3]

Without implying that texts should be judged solely in terms of authorial intentions, it is legitimate to consider what the author and her collaborator were aiming to achieve. From the plentiful biographical sources, we know a great deal about their opinions, values, and aspirations, and how they attempted to steer the expectations of readers. The preface, for example, drafted by Percy Bysshe Shelley, explains that the story was not 'a mere tale

---

[1] For the publication of *The Vampyre* see *SC* vi, 777–81. Despite public denials by Byron, Galignani continued to include the piece among Byron's works, although with a disclaimer. In the 1880s and 90s, when *Frankenstein* first reached its mass popular readership, *The Vampyre* was also on sale as one of Dicks's cheap paperback editions, still falsely attributed to Byron.

[2] From a reference in Shelley, *Letters* i, 561 it seems certain that Claire Clairmont also wrote a book which was turned down by Lackington, and Taylor and Hessey.

[3] See E. B. Murray, 'Shelley's Contribution to Mary's *Frankenstein*' in *Keats Shelley Memorial Bulletin* (1978). Shelley contributed about a fortieth in terms of words. Not all of his suggestions were accepted into the final printed version.

of spectres or enchantment', but 'a point of view to the imagination for the delineating of human passions more comprehensive and commanding than any which the ordinary relations of existing events can yield'. The book was dedicated to Mary Shelley's father, William Godwin, an indication that it was written by someone sympathetic to Godwinian ideas.[4] *Frankenstein* was a serious book with a reformist purpose.

There is another source of unique value for determining authorial intentions. Nowadays it is unprofessional for authors to review books written by their friends or relatives. In the romantic period, however, when reviews were invariably anonymous, publishers sometimes supped review editors with review articles.[5] The three reviews which Shelley prepared in 1818, including one of *Frankenstein*, were discovered among a publisher's archives, but their exact status and provenance have never been established. A passage from the review of *Frankenstein*, although not published at the time, can be taken as an authoritative statement of what he and Mary Shelley regarded as the meaning and message of the work.

In this the direct moral of the book consists; and it is perhaps the most important, and of the most universal application of any moral that can be enforced by example. Treat a person ill, and he will become wicked. Requite affection with scorn; let one being be selected, for whatever cause, as the refuse of his kind – divide him, a social being, from society, and you impose upon him the irresistible obligations – malevolence and selfishness. It is thus that, too often in society, those who are best qualified to be its benefactors and its ornaments, are branded by some accident with scorn, and changed, by neglect and solitude of heart, into a scourge and a curse.[6]

Like all the books written by members of the Godwin and Shelley families, *Frankenstein* had a political and ethical purpose. In accordance with the Godwinian theory of progress, *Frankenstein* would, they hoped, help to change the perceptions, the knowledge, the understanding, and therefore the behaviour, of those who read or otherwise encountered it. The reading of the book would, they hoped, contribute, in its small way, to the general intellectual and moral improvement of society in its slow, much interrupted, progress towards perfection.[7]

---

[4] It may have been because this feature would have made it harder to find a publisher that the dedication leaf was not inserted until a late stage of the production of the book.

[5] Discussed in chapter 11.

[6] The piece was first published by T. Medwin in *The Athenaeum* (1832), and *The Shelley Papers* (1833).

[7] See, for example, St Clair, *Godwins and Shelleys* 434–9.

Shelley told publishers that he was acting for a friend abroad, a pretence which authors often adopt to protect themselves from disappointment. A phrase in the preface implied that the author was a man.[8] But if publishers thought that Shelley was himself the author, that was no advantage in the negotiations. Both *Queen Mab* and *Alastor* had been printed 'on commission', and the same was to be true of *Laon and Cythna* which was being turned down when Shelley was negotiating for *Frankenstein*. Until the pirate reprinting of *Queen Mab* in 1821, Shelley was just one of the many scarcely known and commercially unsuccessful authors whose books could only be published at his own expense, if at all.[9] *Frankenstein* was rejected by the leading publishers.[10] Ollier, Shelley's publisher, took only three days to say 'no'. The reason why *Frankenstein* was turned down so decisively was probably more to do with self-censoring doubts about its subject matter than with any fears about its innovative literary quality or its commercial prospects. Publishers and circulating-library owners were well aware that the narrow constituency of readers upon whom their livelihoods depended was, for the most part, conservative, indeed reactionary, in its political and religious opinions.

Shelley then turned to the outsider firm of Lackington, and in August they contracted to publish an edition of 500 copies, dividing the net profits, one third to the author, two thirds to the publisher. *Frankenstein, or, The Modern Prometheus*, went on sale later in the year. Like most novels of the time it was anonymous, in three volumes, and expensive, a book intended to be sold primarily to commercial circulating libraries, with perhaps less than half the edition expected to go to individual buyers.[11] *Frankenstein* was only stretched to three volumes by printing few words to the line, few lines to the page, and few pages to the volume.

Lackington specialised in magic, the illegitimate supernatural, and horror, a fact emphasised by advertisements.[12] For many readers therefore Lackington's printed advertisements tipped into the book acted as an optional

[8] 'his labours.' In the usage of the time the phrase might also be read as gender neutral.
[9] See Robinson 183.
[10] See the remark and editor's note in Shelley *Letters*, i, 551. Another candidate for the third publisher known to have said 'no' is Hookham who published Thomas Love Peacock's novels.
[11] The book is dated 1818 on the title page, but most copies appear to have been already sold to the retail distributors late in 1817.
[12] The copy in the Codrington Library, All Souls College, Oxford, carries a long advertisement description of Lackington's other publications in the associated genres, including *The Magus or Celestial Intelligencer*, *Lives of the Alchemystical Philosophers*, *Apparitions, or The Mysteries of Ghosts, Hobgoblins, and Haunted Houses*, *The Life, Prophecies and Predictions of Merlin Interpreted*, Toland's *Critical History of the Celtic Religion*, *Tales of the Dead*.

disposable extra paratext whose effect was to offset the authorial paratext, and the plea for the book to be taken seriously was largely ignored when the book was reviewed in the literary press.[13] The notion that the dead could be made to live again by manmade agency was, it was suggested, atheistical and blasphemous, a secret attack on a central tenet of Christianity. 'These volumes have neither principle, object, nor moral', thundered the *British Critic*. 'The horror which abounds in them is too grotesque and *bizarre* ever to approach the sublime.' The young Thomas Carlyle, who had only read a review, reported that 'Frankenstein, by Godwin's son in law, seems to be another unnatural disgusting fiction.'[14] According to William Beckford, *Frankenstein* was 'perhaps the foulest Toadstool that has yet sprung from the reeking dunghill of present times'.[15]

The whole edition of 500 copies was sold to the retail booksellers as soon as the copies were printed, so passing all the remaining sales risks to them, and the book reached its initial readers over the following months and years.[16] The net profit declared to the author was more than the total cost of manufacturing, advertising, and selling the book. In 1818 Mary Shelley, with her third share, was commercially a far more successful author than Shelley. The first edition of *Frankenstein* outsold all the works of her husband put together. It made more money than all Shelley's works were to fetch in his lifetime. The gross rate of return to the publisher cannot have been less than about 300 per cent at an annual rate. With such high and immediate profits on small sales, and with plenty of publicity already obtained, it might have been expected that the publisher would have wanted to build on his success, especially as the possibility of a second edition had been discussed. But for Lackington, the selling out of the first edition was the end of the matter. In making that decision Lackington was following the usual practice. Publishers' archives record the publication of dozens of novels in three volumes in editions of 500 or 750, many without a spark of originality.[17]

In 1823, five years after the first publication, Godwin wrote to tell his daughter that he had heard that a stage version was to be produced.[18]

---

[13] The reviews, from which the quotations are taken, are noted and summarised in W. H. Lyles, *Mary Shelley, An Annotated Bibliography* (New York 1975) 168.

[14] *The Collected Letters of Thomas and Jane Welsh Carlyle* (Durham, NC 1970) i, 124, 30 April 1818.

[15] Forry ix.

[16] The account is transcribed in *SC* v, 397, from the manuscript in the Bodleian, and in appendix 5, 509.

[17] See appendix 7.

[18] Godwin to Mary Shelley, 22 July 1823. Quoted by Forry 3, from an unpublished letter in the Huntington Library, California.

Godwin was able to negotiate for a second edition from another publisher which included some textual changes, this time in two volumes, still in a lavish format, and still at a high retail price. Perhaps in an attempt to exploit the notoriety of the name that had now been publicly revealed, the second edition was advertised as by Mary Wollstonecraft Shelley.[19] Copies were still available at full price in the 1830s and probably later.[20] In 1831, however, again as a result of the interest caused by stage versions, Mary Shelley was able to sell the copyright to Richard Bentley for inclusion in *Bentley's Standard Novels* for £30, the last financial benefit she or her family was ever to receive.[21]

In the late 1820s, Richard Bentley, like the publishers of the Waverley novels, had understood the implications of the sharp increase in the price of three-decker novels brought about in the previous decade. Bentley realised that, if he could buy the tail-ends of copyrights of out-of-print novels cheaply, he could start a uniform series which would take a second tranche from libraries and individuals who had not bought first time round. *Bentley's Standard Novels*, which began in the 1830s, included works by many excellent recent authors whose works had then become unavailable: Austen, Beckford, Burney, Edgeworth, Ferrier, Galt, Godwin, Peacock, and others. With the exception of the Waverley novels, Bentley made himself the owner of almost all the best fiction of the romantic period and later of the 1830s. With a new title coming out every few weeks, *Bentley's Standard Novels* provided several years' worth of continuous serial reading, a delayed, carefully selected, series of most of the best fictional writing of recent times. Since Bentley arranged the series by name of the author, for the first time, the names of Jane Austen, Susan Ferrier, John Galt, and others appeared on the title pages. Bentley did for romantic-period novels what the editors of the initial old-canon series had done at the end of the previous century. Novels such as Hogg's *Justified Sinner* and Godwin's *Mandeville*, which failed to be selected, disappeared from public attention until the twentieth century.

Bentley insisted that the author should correct errors and supply new material either in the text or as a paratextual preface or notes. Even if the changes were minimal, the revisions allowed him to claim a new copyright which, if not valid in law, would normally be respected within the industry. If authors were reluctant to revise their texts, Bentley would provide

---

[19] *Morning Post*, 23 August 1823, quoted by Forry 37.
[20] Still advertised in the *London Catalogue* (1835).
[21] Bentley archives, BL. See also Gettman, although some of the figures he offers are not borne out by the archival record.

a professional reviser to do the work.[22] If, as in the case of Austen, the author was dead, Bentley asked a member of the family to write a memoir. In accepting Bentley's offer to republish *Frankenstein*, Mary Shelley was happy to comply with his conditions. She made changes to the text, some substantial, and added an autobiographical introduction, explaining how and when the book came to be written. The new introduction, which was printed alongside the original 1817 preface, emphasised that in essentials, the story was unchanged and that the composition had been written in collaboration with Shelley, but it said little further about the book's political and moral purpose. *Frankenstein*, like many books in the series, was described as 'Revised, Corrected, and Illustrated, with a New Introduction by the Author'.

The books were tightly printed in one volume, and sold already bound in cloth, so saving customers the usual further cost of rebinding, and they each included an engraved frontispiece. The texts of some titles had to be cut back in order to fit the one-volume format.[23] Almost all were stereotyped. Although, over time, the plates became worn and the books became harder to read, the plates could occasionally be repaired to prolong their useful life.[24] The *Bentley's Standard Novels Frankenstein* is found with four different title pages, dated 1831, 1832, 1839, and 1849. But, the archives show, this does not mean that there were four editions or four printings from the stereotype plates, as has been assumed in bibliographies. With *Frankenstein*, as with the other books in the series, Bentley's decisions on when to create a new title page were not timed to the selling out of previously printed stocks, but to his policies for occasionally reannouncing and repricing the series as a whole.[25] Although, at an initial price of 6 shillings, *Bentley's Standard Novels* were less than a fifth of the price of new novels, they were not cheap by absolute terms. In the 1830s, a single *Bentley's Standard Novel* cost about half the weekly wage of a clerk or skilled manual worker. Bentley's novels

---

[22] As he told Fanny Burney, some of whose works had already come out of copyright and been reprinted in cheap editions, he had to insist. See his letter of 12 October 1835 quoted in Joyce Hemlow, general ed., *The Journals and Letters of Fanny Burney* (Oxford 1984) xii, 879.

[23] Examples in Gettman.

[24] In the case of *Frankenstein*, a repair, effected by soldering in a plug which is not quite aligned, can be seen on page 35, where, in the 1849 reimpression, the word MODERN in the running title has been replaced. This appears to have been an error on the part of the repairer for it is the word PROMETHEUS which had become worn. The engraved title page was also dropped in the later reimpressions, perhaps because the plates had become too worn.

[25] For prices see Gettman 51, and Michael Sadleir, *Nineteenth-Century Fiction, A Bibliographical Record* (1951) ii, 97. The prices noted in these books are however mainly for new volumes appearing in the series for the first time. The dates when the prices of existing titles such as *Frankenstein* were reduced are not all known.

were more expensive than Waverley novels whose sales were far higher.[26] They were twice as expensive as reprints of out-of-copyright novels of similar length.[27] Within his chosen market, Bentley positioned himself as far upmarket as he could go.

When he bought *Frankenstein*, Bentley could, as the law stood at the time, have expected to keep his monopoly until 1846, and, if the revised version was respected within the book industry, until 1859.[28] If the old pre-1842 regime had continued, Bentley could have extended his list almost indefinitely, adding say, Dickens, Trollope, Thackeray, and the other mid-Victorian novelists to his list as their works went out of copyright. But after the ending of the brief copyright window in 1842, he was boxed in. With the new longer copyright regime, publishers were no longer willing to let him have copyrights cheap – they wanted to exploit them themselves. The supply of tail-end copyrights fell to a trickle and the latter titles of *Bentley's Standard Novels* were less distinguished than their predecessors. At the same time, as events turned out, Mary Shelley and other authors were still alive at the time of the Copyright Act of 1842. Bentley and his heirs thus found themselves windfall owners of a copyright in *Frankenstein* which they could enjoy at least until 1866 and with luck until 1879. Bentley was the monopoly owner of a range of excellent, but increasingly obsolete, intellectual properties and also of the increasingly obsolescent plant from which copies could be manufactured.

In 1838, before the copyright change, William Hazlitt Junior, the essayist's son, asked Mary Shelley's permission to include *Frankenstein* in his series, *The Romancist and Novelist's Library, The Best Works by the Best Authors*. By this time, as a result of mechanisation of manufacturing methods and reductions in the taxed price of paper, a new branch of the book industry had grown up, able to use newspaper manufacturing technologies to offer fiction at prices far lower than anything that had been possible even a few years before. *The Romancist* was cheap not only in relation to new, three volume, novels and to Bentley's reprints, but in absolute terms in relation to incomes. 'It is astonishing to me how much can be got for 2d [two pence].' Mary Shelley replied to Hazlitt. 'I must have every Wednesday enlivened by your sheet.'[29] But, having sold the copyright, it was not Mary

---

[26] The Waverley novels, sold to the trade at 3s 10d (3.8 shillings) for retailing at 5 shillings were often 'undersold' at 4 shillings. James J. Barnes, *Free Trade in Books* (Oxford 1964) 6.

[27] See for example the English Classics produced by Dove, Scott and Webster, and other publishers at this time, noted in appendix 6.

[28] As I calculate, twenty-eight years from 1818, or twenty-eight years from 1831.

[29] Mary Shelley, *Letters* ii, 299.

Shelley's decision. The owners, protecting their high prices, said 'no', and they apparently refused permission for any of the titles in *Bentley's Standard Novels* to be reprinted.[30] Other publishers of other copyrighted novels seem to have done the same. The sharp fall in the price of recently published books which, before the copyright change of 1842, would have occurred in the 1840s was postponed for a generation.

Most of *Bentley's Standard Novels* were kept continuously in print for twenty years, with supply kept closely in line with demand. Bentley and his successors brought the price down from 6 shillings to 3s 6d to 2s 6d (3.5 to 2.5 shillings), but then stopped. Why they did not tranche down further, as the publishers of the Waverley novels did with success, is not known, but the effects of this single publishing decision on the reading of the novels of the romantic period were enormous. Whereas, in the case of the Waverley novels, the further lowering of price took the texts to a reading nation of several millions, in the case of the other novels of the period, readerships remained confined to the upper tranches.[31] Cumulative production, even of Austen, never reached more than about 8,000 per title over the twenty years before the plates were melted, a sales figure reached by several of Scott's novels in the first month.[32] By the mid 1850s, when the price of *Frankenstein* was down to 2s 6d, demand had fallen to a trickle and the series was allowed to die. Some time before 1861, by which time most of the copyrights were expiring, all the stereotype plates from the series, other than those of Austen and Ferrier, were melted as scrap.[33] After that, with only a few exceptions, little of the prose fiction of the romantic period other than Waverley novels was selected to be reprinted in the vast late-Victorian sixpenny-fiction paperback market.[34]

With one exception, for most of the 1850s, 1860s, and 1870s, *Frankenstein* was out of print. It had also disappeared from the circulating libraries.[35] As a novel, as a text, as a piece of writing in fixed form in which a property right had been established by law, *Frankenstein* was condemned to a long period of catalepsy, neither quite dead nor quite alive. Unable to think of a

---

[30] The Hodgson Parlour Library edition is a possible exception. I have found no record among the Bentley archives either of permission having been given or of a complaint of piracy. Since Hodgson's edition is taken from the 1831 version, it would have been hard for him to claim that he was not infringing copyright.

[31] For the Waverley novels see chapter 21.

[32] I exclude the sea stories of Marryat which were first published after the end of the romantic period and sold more. See appendix 7.

[33] Inventory of stereotypes 1861, Bentley archives.

[34] See the lists of reprint collections in the *English Catalogue of Books, 1881–1889* (1891).

[35] It does not appear, for example, in the *Catalogue of W. H. Smith's Subscription Library* (1872). John Johnson collection, Bodleian.

way of enjoying the intellectual property themselves, the then owners were determined, like a dog in the manger, to deny others the opportunity. While in copyright, *Frankenstein* was never issued as a yellow back, as a shilling shocker, never abridged, turned into a chapbook, or otherwise adapted for the lower-income readers who were joining the reading nation in the middle nineteenth century.

For the first fourteen years of its life in print *Frankenstein* existed in about a thousand copies, fewer than most of the works of Byron and Scott sold on publication day.[36] During its first forty years, a total of between 7,000 and 8,000 copies were printed and sold, still fewer than Byron and Scott commonly sold in the first week. Although copies were frequently bought by circulating libraries, the total readership cannot have been large on such a small base.[37] Nor was *Frankenstein* unusual in this regard. The figures for Austen show a similarly modest success. The cumulative sales over half a century of none of the other novels of the romantic period reached the readership levels of half-a-dozen Waverley novels in their first week. During the first fifty years of *Frankenstein*'s existence, the readership was largely confined to a narrow constituency of men and women at the topmost end of the income scale.

The main change occurred in late-Victorian times. As soon as *Frankenstein* came incontrovertibly out of all copyright restrictions and trade courtesies in about 1880, the reprinting began. The demand that had been held back after 1842 could at last be satisfied. The price plummeted and the print runs soared. In its first year the first reprint of *Frankenstein* sold more copies than all of the previous editions put together. By the end of the century *Frankenstein* was available in a range of editions adapted to different groups of book buyers. You could buy it, in full, with illustrations, at one per cent of the original price, and there were abridgements and books in parts, as well as a few more expensive versions. At the turn of the nineteenth century, eighty years after its first appearance, *Frankenstein* at last became accessible to the whole reading nation.

---

[36] See 'Mary Shelley', appendix 9, 644. Many currently available editions still spread the error that the book sold well from the beginning. 'The novel was an instant success', Mary Wollstonecraft Shelley, *Frankenstein, The Original 1818 Text*, edited by James Rieger (New York 1974) xx. '*Frankenstein* became an immediate best-seller', Mary Shelley, *Frankenstein*, edited with an introduction by Maurice Hindle (London 1985) 8. 'Immediately became a best seller', Mary Shelley, *Frankenstein, Or, The Modern Prometheus*, Modern Library (New York 1993) ix. '. . . enjoyed enormous success'. Mary Wollstonecraft Shelley, *Frankenstein, The Original 1818 Text*, edited by D. L. Macdonald and Kathleen Scherf (Peterborough, Ontario 1994) 35.

[37] From a sample of circulating-library catalogues in the Bodleian Library.

Some of the late-nineteenth-century reprints were intended for the poor and the poorly educated, offered with well intentioned condescension to men and women who had previously lived largely without books. *Routledge's World Library*, a paperback series, set out the publisher's aims of the series, and described the implied and expected readership, in a printed paratextual advertisement:

When I think of the long, gossiping, yawning, gambling hours of grooms, valets, coachmen, and cabmen; the railway stations conveniently provided with book-stalls, and crowded every morning and evening with workmen's trains – the winter evenings in thousands of villages, wayside cottages, and scattered hamlets – the brief, but not always well spent leisure of factory hands in the north – the armies of commercial and uncommercial travellers with spare half hours – the shop assistants – the city offices with their hangers on – the Board Schools – the village libraries – the Army and Navy – the barrack or the dockyard – again the vision of Routledge's World Library rises before me, and I say, 'This, if not a complete cure for indolence and vice, may at least prove a powerful counter charm.'[38]

'I issue "Frankenstein" with some degree of hesitation', the editor confessed, 'The subject is somewhat revolting, the treatment of it is somewhat hideous.' *Frankenstein* remained morally (and perhaps politically) suspect, and even after the texts passed out of private ownership, it was seldom reprinted for a middle-class readership. The late nineteenth-century campaigners for women's suffrage, who wanted to promote Mary Shelley as a woman of achievement in her own right, found her book an embarrassment. 'Everyone now knows the story of "The Modern Prometheus", wrote Mrs Marshall in her biography in 1889, but she appears ashamed to admit that Mary Shelley wrote 'the ghastly but powerful allegorical romance'.[39] Richard Church, who wrote the Mary Shelley volume for the *Representative Women* series, blames Shelley for not discouraging Mary's 'girlish romanticism' and so allowing the book to be 'marred very seriously by a certain haste, an indolence, a vagueness of construction'. 'Mary Shelley', he remarks, picking up the ancient warnings to be found in conduct literature, 'suffered from an overtrained intellectual conscience.'[40]

These attitudes seem to have continued for most of the first half of the twentieth century. Although, with this period too, it is frequently assumed that the book sold well, the archival record shows a different picture. At a time when the United Kingdom had a population of about fifty million,

[38] Advertisement by the editor, the Reverend H. R. Haweis, MA, in copies of books published in *Routledge's World Library*.
[39] Mrs Julian Marshall, *The Life and Letters of Mary Wollstonecraft Shelley* (1889) i, 139, 143.
[40] Richard Church, *Mary Shelley* (n.d. c. 1895) 52.

was fully literate, and reading was the main entertainment, the total annual sales of the main edition, that of *Everyman's Library*, to the whole British market, which included India, Australia, South Africa, New Zealand, and other English-speaking countries overseas other than North America, were only rarely above 500 a year.

During most of the nineteenth century, it was not the reading of the text of the book, but seeing adaptations of the story on the stage which kept *Frankenstein* alive in the culture, and here we have another example of how the nature of cultural production and reception was decisively influenced by the regulatory regime of intellectual property and textual controls. Since 1737, only two theatres in London, Covent Garden and Drury Lane, and a few in other cities, were licensed to perform plays, whether they were newly written pieces, old favourites, or Shakespeare. The consolidation of a state-enforced monopoly in theatrical performance, from which the state benefited through the capitalised fee for the patent, ensured that admission prices remained higher than they would otherwise have been, and during the seventeenth century the size of the theatre audience, like the size of the reading nation, may have fallen relative to the size of the population.

During the eighteenth century the regulatory regime also seems to have brought about many of the same effects as we see in the case of printed books, rising financial returns to the producers (playwrights, theatrical owners, and perhaps other workers in the industry), but also a tendency to entrench the obsolete, as producers preferred to recycle older, well-tried, theatrical texts for which the capital costs had been amortised, rather than to invest in new compositions.[41] In other respects, the eighteenth-century London theatre continued the regime of the state licensing period of the late seventeenth century as it had been applied to printed books, a limit on the absolute size of the industry, access to the cultural production restricted to elites, and pre-censorship controls on textual content. In these respects the determinants of theatrical production in the eighteenth century were very different from those governing the production of printed books.

In the romantic period, every stage performance was individually licensed by the Lord Chamberlain, the state censor. Besides controlling the patented theatres, the censor was empowered to grant licences for performances such as opera, pantomime, and other spectacles which were less likely than straight plays to contain material which the state found ideologically

---

[41] See Judith Milhous and Robert D. Hume, 'Playwrights', Remuneration in Eighteenth-Century London', in *Harvard Library Bulletin*, vol. 10 (1999 but actually 2001).

threatening, and since 1788 a large theatre/entertainment industry supplying such performances had grown up in London and elsewhere. All performances in such theatres also needed a licence from the Lord Chamberlain which would not be granted if the submitted texts offended against certain criteria. The adaptations of *Frankenstein*, like those of most adaptations, were, we can say, officially pre-censored not only to check that they were ideologically acceptable to the political and religious authorities but to ensure that they were not legitimate drama.

Although the direct textual controls were tighter than for printed texts, there was no regime of intellectual property. Until the Dramatic Copyright Act of 1833 a theatre wishing to put on a commercial production did not need to obtain the permission of the holder of the copyright in a printed play. In 1822, for example, Murray brought an action against the Theatre Royal, Drury Lane, for putting on a performance of Byron's recently published play, *Marino Faliero*, abridged and adapted, without permission. In the contract Byron had sold Murray 'the tragedy and poem and copyright thereof, and the exclusive right of printing and publishing, and all benefit and advantage thereof', an indisputable assignment of all his intellectual property rights as the author. However, the court confirmed that no intellectual property rights had been infringed. The Copyright Acts, the court decided, protected only the printing of a text, they did not prevent a printed text from being performed.[42] At the time when *Frankenstein* was first adapted for the stage, theatres were also able to make adaptations of printed texts without the need for permission either from the author or the owner of the intellectual property. However, all such adaptations had to include a good deal of music to pretend to be operas or pantomimes, not straight plays.

In the novel the being created by Frankenstein comes into the world full of natural human sympathy which is refined by his education, including his reading of one of the works of the radical canon, Volney's *The Ruins of Empires*.[43] It is only when he is misjudged and mistreated by unfair, unenlightened, human beings that he is corrupted into violence. Treat other people as you would like them to treat you is the explicit message, a Christian as well as a humanist sentiment. The many stage versions which were put on after 1823 are also scarcely subversive – if they had been, they would not have been licensed. The first, as its title, *Presumption, or the*

---

[42] Gavin McFarlane, *Copyright: the Development and Exercise of the Performing Right* (1980) 37.
[43] In volume ii, chapter 5 of the 1818 version. For the radical canon see chapter 16.

Fate of Frankenstein, emphasised, saw the story as a warning against human pride. But, as had happened with the reviewers of the book, others feared something more sinister. The *Morning Post* led the attack:

To Lord Byron, the late Mr Shelley, and philosophers of that stamp, it might appear a very fine thing to attack the Christian religion . . . and burlesque the resurrection of the dead . . . but we would prefer the comparatively noble assaults of VOLNEY, VOLTAIRE and PAINE.[44]

Other reviews of the play linked it with the hated names of the two authors whose books, *Queen Mab* and *Don Juan*, were at that very time becoming available to the same literate urban clerical and working classes whom conservatives most feared.[45] The play, according to *John Bull*, was taken from the novel by 'one of the coterie of that self-acknowledged Atheist Percy B. Shelley'.[46] By the time *Presumption, or the Fate of Frankenstein* reached Birmingham in 1824, it had become part of the surrounding ritual of the performance that warning posters were circulated by local upholders of public morality, denials were issued by the theatre, and threats of legal action thrown about by both sides.

The English Opera House, where *Presumption* opened in 1823, was able to hold about 1,500 persons.[47] The Coburg Theatre, where *Frankenstein or the Demon of Switzerland* opened shortly afterwards, held over 3,800.[48] Admission to the English Opera House cost 5 shillings for a box, 3 for the pit, 2 for the gallery, and 1 shilling for the upper gallery, and, if the house was not full, the prices were reduced.[49] Midweek was for 'the better classes', Monday for 'the higher working classes'.[50] Every single night when one of the *Frankenstein* plays was performed brought a version of the story of the manmade monster to more men and women than the book did in ten or twenty years.

Some managers asked authors to write their own adaptations, and Scott, most of whose works were dramatised, for one, cooperated. On the whole, however, stage versions were prepared by professional adapters. When in 1833 the law was changed to grant an exclusive right to publishers to put

---

[44] Quoted by Forry 5.   [45] For the mass reading of *Don Juan*, see chapter 16.
[46] For 29 July 1823, quoted by Forry 5.
[47] I have been unable to find a more exact figure. Capacity at the time was normally measured in money terms, gross nightly takings. It is however clear from figures given by witnesses to the House of Commons *Report of the Select Committee on Dramatic Literature* (1832) that the English Opera House was comparable in size to the Haymarket which held between 1,600 and 1,700.
[48] The boxes held 1,230 persons, the pit 1,090, and the galleries 1,512.
[49] 'Second prices': boxes 3 shillings; pit 1s 6d (1.5); lower gallery 1 shilling. Information from a playbill for a performance on 27 August 1828.
[50] Evidence by the theatre managers to the Select Committee on Dramatic Literature 1832.

on performances of plays that they had printed, there was still no provision for an author or text owner to claim an intellectual property right over performed adaptations.[51] If anything, the new regime encouraged a widening of the gap between original text and the theatrical adaptation, for the further the adapter departed from the original, the more free the theatre was from any intellectual property claim. The theatrical versions are, therefore, not so much attempts to turn a good printed text into dramatic form, but misshapen creatures designed to fit into the complex regulatory regime. In the adaptations of *Frankenstein* the location was moved to wicked Venice, to icy Swiss forests, or to burning Sicilian mountains. Names, such as Manfred, were taken from more familiar stories, and Ratzbaen, Tiddliwincz, and Captain Risotto invented for laughs. Fritz, the hunchback, who is not in the book, stole the show so often that he became indispensable.[52] Turbans, veils, and turned-up slippers gave a hint of the east, and there were plenty of Italian banditti. Early in its stage life *Frankenstein* frequently amalgamated with *The Vampyre*, not because that piece had been written on the same occasion in 1816, but as part of a general muddling of gothic, of horror, and of laughs. From the start, the stage *Frankensteins* mocked themselves. They are full of topical allusions and jokes, mostly probably now irretrievable. In the late-Victorian version, for example, the Monster wore a hat which, copying Gilbert and Sullivan in *Patience*, brought a laugh at the expense of Oscar Wilde. The story was cut, added to, transformed into pantomime or farce, amalgamated with other stories, parodied, burlesqued, and reduced to cliché, tag, and catchphrase.

The playbills of the first 1823 version advertised *Presumption*, a new romance, with no mention of Frankenstein in the title.[53] But the name itself was soon a magic word, a vital part of the appeal. In both favourite early stage versions, the primary and secondary titles were soon reversed. *Presumption, or the Fate of Frankenstein* became *Frankenstein, or, The Danger of Presumption*. *The Man and the Monster* became *Frankenstein, or, The Monster*. By 1824 it was already common for the unnamed monster to be called 'Frankenstein' instead of the scientist who constructed him, a confusion put about by the actors. By the end of the century the reversal of the names had become so common that Fowler's *Modern English Usage* felt able to call it 'a blunder almost, but surely not quite, sanctioned by custom'. Comparing the dates of the printed books and the main stage and

[51] McFarlane, *Copyright* 51.
[52] In film versions he was renamed Egor and made famous by Marty Feldman.
[53] E.g. in *The Theatrical Observer* for 2 August 1823.

film adaptations, we can see how they interacted.[54] In 1823, and again in 1831, the printed novel was revived by the stage versions. The stage versions of the 1850s were stimulated by the Hodgson edition. In the 1880s the large-scale reprinting of the novel when the copyright expired led to the putting on of a new play version, which in its turn stimulated more reprints.[55] *Frankenstein* did not become part of popular culture with the cinema: the film industry picked it up from the stage where it was already vigorous. There is an episode in the 1931 classic where the as yet uncorrupted creature, acted by Boris Karloff, plays happily with the innocent little girl. But such survivals of the original moral purpose are rare. The *Frankenstein* films in both Britain and the United States are as unstable as the stage versions. Continuing the tradition of their stage predecessors they laughed at themselves and chased every passing fashion.[56] Far into the twentieth century Frankenstein and his monster continued to live largely independently of books. In so far as they had a printed or material existence at all, it was in films, posters, comics, and funny masks of Boris Karloff.

Almost every book published in early nineteenth-century London which achieved any kind of popularity as a book was adapted and transformed for the stage. Every Waverley novel was followed by at least one stage version, often by several.[57] Byron was often adapted and performed in versions such as *The Corsair, The Corsair's Son, The Corsair's Bride*. On the early nineteenth-century stage the romance of Scott's Scotland might be conjured up by a glimpse of tartan, the spirit of Byron by an extravagant open necked shirt, and the oriental fantasies of Moore by a whirl of silk over pointed slippers. The stage versions lived (and mostly soon died) alongside the printed texts of the original works, which continued to be readily available and to be widely read. The mutating stage versions came and went, collectively influential and infiltrating themselves in innumerable irrecoverable ways into popular oral culture, memory, and myth.

Charles Dickens, who hated to see his work mangled, realised that stage adaptation was an intrinsic part of the reception of his books. He invented a conversation between Nicholas Nickleby, the aspiring author, and an adapter for the stage who is modelled on R. B. Peake and H. M. Milner who had each adapted *Frankenstein*.

---

[54] See the list in appendix 9.
[55] Summarised in 'Mary Shelley', appendix 9, 644–6.   [56] See the list in appendix 9, 647.
[57] See Richard Ford, *Dramatisations of Scott's novels: A Catalogue* (Oxford 1979), and H. Philip Bolton, *Scott Dramatised* (1992).

. . . there was a literary gentleman present who had dramatised in his time two hundred and forty seven novels as fast as they came out – some of them faster than they had come out – and who *was* a literary gentleman in consequence.[58]

Since, in most cases, the printed texts were easily available to readers and audiences, any new mutated stage version had to compete anew with a knowledge of the original printed text. The printed texts stood like fixed beacons, circumscribing the limits to the range of possible mutation, and ready at all times to draw audiences and new adapters back to the originals. In the case of *Frankenstein*, on the other hand, with long periods with no easily accessible printed version, new stage versions tended to mutate from other earlier mutations rather than directly from the original. Parodies parodied parodies, moving in any direction that the moment made promising. Refused a life in the reasonably stable culture of print and reading, *Frankenstein* survived in a free-floating popular oral and visual culture, with only the central episode of the making of the creature holding it tenuously to its original.

In Victorian times, even when *Frankenstein* was not in print and when there was no play on the stage, the story was alive in the nation's memory. All through the nineteenth century we find allusions in literature, journalism, and politics.[59] Scholarly books have used hermeneutic and psychoanalytical techniques to explore the Frankenstein monsters lurking in the Victorian mind.[60] Such allusions are, it is suggested, the occasional visible manifestations of deeper myths. No doubt the Victorians suffered from monsters like everybody else. But such claims rest on assumptions that the novel was being read, or that its text had somehow emanated from or infiltrated into the collective subconscious and had stayed there, and that the collective unconscious can be recovered by modern critical reading of texts. In fact, most of those who used, heard, and understood Frankenstein expressions in Victorian times are unlikely to have read the book, and if they saw a stage version, they could have had only the sketchiest idea of the rich layers of meaning of the book.

The word 'Frankenstein' in Victorian culture is a cliché, a convenient tag for those who fear change.[61] If you free the slaves, reform parliament, give votes to the working class or independence to the Irish, you will create a Frankenstein monster which will destroy you. Already by 1824, within a year of the first stage version, that had become the single, simple, unvaried meaning. By the end of the century, the simplicities of the stage versions

---

[58] *Nicholas Nickleby*, chapter 48, quoted by Altick 456.   [59] See 'Mary Shelley', appendix 9.
[60] Notably Baldick.   [61] The full list of examples in appendix 9.

had decisively defeated the complexities of the literary text. Anyone who took a different meaning was reading against the grain and against the norm. So universal was the accepted meaning that the editor of the Penny Novels abridgement dropped the author's preface, and provided a preface of his own to ram home the perverse interpretation.[62]

Frankenstein thus stands in contrast to Shelley's *Queen Mab* and Byron's *Don Juan*. In the 1820s, 1830s, and for many years later, there was a clear demand for access to all three books particularly by readers for whom all books were expensive and largely inaccessible, but who often went to the theatre. But whereas, owing to quirks in the copyright law, *Queen Mab* and *Don Juan* were freed from private ownership, their price plummeted, their readerships soared, and the cultural influence of both was enormous, the original *Frankenstein*, as a result of other quirks, was held back from most of its potential readers. A gripping tale with a reformist moral message, the book might have taken its place alongside other famous works of the radical canon which helped to shape a new sceptical, reformist, urban culture. As events turned out, the Frankenstein story, for most of those who encountered it, conveyed a message which was contrary to the plain meaning of the original text. The impact has been, for the most part, the opposite of what the author and her collaborator had hoped for and intended.

[62] Quoted in appendix 9.

CHAPTER 19

North America

Historians of American literature have usually followed the parade of canonical authors convention. The older literary histories hurried through the texts printed in the English (after 1707 British) North American colonies, mainly almanacs, devotional manuals, sermons, school textbooks, books of verse, provincial histories, and pamphlets on local topics, and only began their main narratives when they reached Washington Irving, James Fenimore Cooper, and William Cullen Bryant, post-Independence American-born and American-published authors.[1] Concentrating on the northern colonies where most local printing occurred, these histories offered a story of a plain, pioneering, religious people, and of an unfolding wider destiny. Like Macaulay, who performed a similar myth-making role for England, they exaggerated the earlier backwardness in order to emphasise the later achievement. Charles Angoff, in his *Literary History of the American People,* for example, wrote of the colonial period:

It is therefore only by politeness that we can speak of literature in the first one hundred and fifty years of the United States. We really had no literature then.[2]

Recently, with increasing distrust of the assumptions behind canonicity, more attention has been paid to the printed writings of the colonial period. The 1994 *Cambridge History of American Literature,* for example, not only devotes almost the whole of one of its three volumes to these texts, but uses them to make broad claims about the mentalities of the colonists – on the grounds that 'literary forms plot their home cultures'.[3] Modern literary histories, like their predecessors, however, still usually

---

[1] For example, Charles Angoff, *A Literary History of the American People* (New York 1935); Robert E. Spillar, Willard Thorp, *et al. The Literary History of the United States* (New York 1948); and Marcus Cunliffe, *The Literature of the United States* (1954).
[2] Charles Angoff, *Literary History of the American People* (1935) 6.
[3] Sacvan Bercovitch, general ed., *The Cambridge History of American Literature* (Cambridge 1994) i, 26.

regard as truly 'American' only those texts which were written and physically printed in the mainland settlements which later became the United States.

A history of reading offers a quite different picture. The records of the book holdings of American colonial libraries, local booksellers' advertisements, customs statistics of book exports from Britain, archives of booksellers and book clubs, and personal documents, show that 'American literature', so conceived, was in most cases a tiny proportion of the texts that were read.[4] Those literary histories which try to derive American colonial mentalities from 'American' literature are therefore not only methodologically questionable, but are unfair to the colonists. Benjamin Franklin and Thomas Jefferson would not have become figures of the Enlightenment if their minds had been formed by reading books composed and manufactured in North America.[5] From the time of the earliest European settlements, the English-speaking colonies were part of a wider world within which texts and books circulated between the countries of Europe and European communities elsewhere. Indeed, the customs records show that between 1701 and 1780, the export of books to the British West Indies, was, by weight, greater than to the whole of New England.[6] The first volume of the recent *History of the Book in America,* recognising the danger of seeing the culture of the past in terms of national boundaries, is perceptively called *The Colonial Book in the Atlantic World.*

However, although recent history is widening the perception of American literary and cultural history, there has been little attempt made to identify the economic/intellectual property structures which determined or constrained the nature of the printed texts made available to different constituencies of readers at different times. Book history in the United States, as elsewhere, has tended to centre on authorial copyright, which was adopted into post-independence law, on the model of the 1710 British Act, rather than on the customs and practices of the book industry. Indeed, because there are no overt references to copyright in colonial laws, it has generally been assumed that, with some exceptions, printers in American colonial cities could print or reprint whichever texts they chose, constrained only by the censoring power of the local colonial governor and the undeveloped

---

[4] See, for example, the archives transcribed by Ford; Raven, *London Booksellers*; Edwin Wolf, *The Book Culture of a Colonial American City* (Oxford 1988); some of the essays in Davidson; and Raven, *Export.* Many individual examples are mentioned by Richard D. Brown, *Knowledge is Power, The Diffusion of Information in Early America, 1700–1865* (Oxford 1989).

[5] For a useful summary see, for example, Douglas L. Wilson, *Jefferson's Books* (Monticello, Va. 1996).

[6] See Raven, *Export.*

state of the local market for books. One of the general editors of *The Colonial Book in the Atlantic World*, for example, declares that 'There was no colonial copyright.'[7] However, to regard absence of an explicit local legal framework as implying the absence of an intellectual property regime may be to misread the situation.[8] What has not, I believe, been given sufficient weight is that the English royal charters which conveyed legislative powers to colonial assemblies usually contained the explicit proviso that any local laws should be in agreement with, or 'not be repugnant with', the laws of England.[9] Some charters, such as those of Maryland and Carolina, referred also to the 'customs' of England. In hearing appeals from colonial governments, the authorities in London always assumed that the English common law applied.[10]

As far as printed books were concerned, the English laws and customs which were thus transferred to the English colonies included the whole changing panoply of instruments by which the English book industry was regulated and managed within England itself, including textual controls, intellectual property, privileged franchises, price controls, customary trade practices, limitations on numbers of presses and foundries, and the regulation of apprenticeships. Some English decrees declare specifically that they apply to other territories under English jurisdiction. As in England, textual controls and intellectual property went together, and both were integrated into the structures of colonial government. *The Oath of a Free-Man* of Massachusetts Bay Colony, a broadsheet of 1639, the first piece of local American colonial print, and a text easy to misinterpret as an early manifestation of a distinctively American democratic spirit, commits the swearer to maintain not only the liberties, laws, orders etc. of the colony but also the established 'privileges'.[11]

---

[7] Hugh Amory in *CBAW* 326. See also James N. Green, 'English Book Trade' in *CBAW* 296: 'Since there was no copyright law in America'. James Gilreath, 'American Literature, Public Policy and the Copyright Laws before 1800' in *Wills* xv: 'Before 1770 there was little activity relating to copyright in the colonies. Cultural conditions and attitudes about the relationship among writers, publishers, and the state hindered any legal agreement.' As an earlier example, John Tebbel, *A History of Book Publishing in the United States, The Creation of an Industry, 1630–1865* (1972) i, 44.

[8] See appendix 2, 487.

[9] For example, those of Massachusetts Bay and Connecticut.

[10] Joseph Henry Smith, *Appeals to the Privy Council from the American Plantations* (New York 1950) 465. I have found no record of an appeal to London involving printing, censorship, or copyright, but this is not surprising since it was the colonial governments who made such appeals not aggrieved citizens. There are, however, a few examples of appeals to the local colonial governments against excessive book prices.

[11] Evans i, 1.

The changing English governing structures permitted and encouraged a certain amount of local publishing and reprinting.[12] Almanacs, which in North America, as in Europe, provided the information on which the working of the economy depended, were locally produced in huge numbers 'by authority', which I take to mean as an explicitly allowed exception to the Stationers' Company monopoly. There was much local printing of primers, psalters, catechisms, and other educational books. Fisher's *American Instructor*, published in Philadelphia in 1748, is, for example, described on the title page as 'The Ninth Edition Revised and Corrected', although it is the first American printing of a book hitherto printed only in England.[13] Many texts written by residents of the colonies, including Jonathan Edwards, members of the Mather family, and Franklin, were published in London in the normal way, just as an author from Norwich or Bristol would prefer his work to be published in London rather than in his local city.[14] As late as 1775, on the eve of the American Revolution, Franklin was having his pamphlets printed in London, so ensuring that they would be available across the whole English-speaking world, including the residents of other colonies.[15] Some titles first printed in the colonies were entered in the Stationers' Company registers as a record of ownership just like texts first produced in England.[16] Some London publications included a large component specially for the American colonies. For example George Whitefield, proposing a volume of sermons in 1741 intended 2,000 copies

[12] For American imprints see Evans. Most of the surviving American archival evidence which I know of, such as Knox, relates to the latter years of the colonial period. There is much information in the William Strahan papers about the publishing of books by American authors, including Benjamin Franklin, and of the export of books. For the immediate post-independence period I have made use of the records of Evert Duyckinck, bookseller, printer, and publisher in New York, day books (i.e. records of orders discharged, including records of his own publications) from 1795 until the 1820s, NYPL; and the records of Joseph Johnson, publisher, letter book 1795–1806, Pforzheimer collection, NYPL; the Bell and Bradfute ledgers, and other primary sources. Remer has drawn on a large number of early American archival sources relating to publishing in Philadelphia. Some recorded colonial print runs are given in appendix 1.

[13] A. S. W. Rosenbach, *Early American Children's Books* (1933) 17.

[14] For example Cotton Mather, *Ecclesiastical History of New England* (London 1702), Lowndes vi, 1512. Other examples are noted in R. C. Simmons, *British Imprints relating to North America, 1621–1760, A Checklist* (1996).

[15] William Strahan papers.

[16] For example, *Wonder Working Providence . . . being a History of New England* is entered in the Stationers' Register for 1 September 1653 as 'by Edward Nash of New England, gent.', Arber, *Transcript* i, 427. Mather's *Brief History of the War with the Indians*, was described in the Stationers' Register, Arber, *Transcript* 3, 30, as 'by Increase Mather, Teacher of a Church of Christ in Boston in New England'. *New England Primer, or Milk for Babes* (1683), Arber, Transcript iii, 199. *Psalms, Hymns, and Spiritual songs . . . For the Edification of the Saints in Public and Private, and more especially in New England* (1712), Curwen 83. Some early registrations are transcribed by Ford.

for England and 1,000 for America.[17] As the population grew, an increasing proportion of home production went to America. In the 1760s, for example, Strahan was exporting between £2,000 and £3,000 worth of books every year to Hall of Philadelphia.[18]

Some texts travelled in the other direction. The *Bay Psalm Book* (1640) was reprinted at least eighteen times in England and twenty-two in Scotland.[19] Franklin's *The Way to Wealth*, *sententiae* which captured the Protestant ethic of early rising, honesty, thrift, and saving, was to be found for many decades all over the English-speaking world, not only as a much-reprinted old-canon classic, but as a source for mottos on engraved pictures.[20]

Like English provincial printer/publishers until 1774, American printer/publishers were caught in a cycle of low levels of activity and inadequate physical plant, with most of their business consisting of local commercial and official printing and latterly of newspapers, of which the rapid growth in the colonies in the eighteenth century seems to have matched the growth in England.[21] In book publishing, as in other matters, the towns of colonial North America were more like English provincial and university towns which happened to be located thousands of miles away, and were accorded a measure of local autonomy, than metropolitan centres of different jurisdictions.

Without knowing the circumstances of each American colonial reprint of a text first printed in Great Britain, which in the absence of archival records is impossible, it is difficult to judge whether it would have been reprinted with the consent of the intellectual property owners in London.[22] After the British Act of Parliament of 1710, although it did not apply specifically to territories outside Great Britain, the presence in the American colonies of many Scottish booksellers selling Scottish books, seems to have encouraged some American printer/publishers to claim their statutory rights under English law. There are, however, some texts, such as reprints of Samuel Richardson and Laurence Sterne which would undoubtedly have been illegal in England if they had been reprinted without the permission of the English owners. Given the length of the communication lines, some

---

[17] Strahan papers.   [18] *Ibid.*   [19] Noted by Gohdes 14.
[20] Timperley 646. The maxims had first been printed in Franklin's *Poor Richard's Almanac*, begun in Philadelphia in 1732.
[21] See, for example, the long extract from Franklin and Hall's work book for 1765 transcribed by Wroth 218.
[22] Some examples of texts being reprinted without permission in both directions can be found in the Strahan papers, some quoted by Cochrane.

piracy or anticipation of owner approval is to be expected. It would be easy to conclude that all exceptions can be explained, if we only knew what the explanations were.

The same conclusions about the nature of the colonial intellectual property regime emerge when we examine the many incidents of dogs in the night which did not bark. Throughout the colonial period, for example, all English-language Bibles, by far the largest component of American colonial reading, were imported and the absence of reprints cannot be wholly attributed to lack of local resources.[23] Hornbooks too, the simplest printed teaching texts, which required scarcely any printing skill or plant, were all imported.[24] Before independence, there were no reprints, anthologies, or abridgements of the literary texts most frequently read in England. If the colonists had been free to ignore intellectual property considerations, they would surely have reprinted, or at least abridged, the texts which were held in especial regard, Milton's *Paradise Lost,* Young's *Night Thoughts,* Thomson's *The Seasons,* and Defoe's *Robinson Crusoe.* But all printed copies of these texts appear to have been supplied exclusively from London, with some legal Scottish and some illegal Irish imports in the last decades before the Revolution.

The same pattern emerges in popular literature. To judge from early records of reading in New England found by C. A. Herrick, ballads and chapbooks were amongst the commonest types of reading in the colonies, as in England, at that time.[25] Many of the old favourites appear on Benjamin Franklin's list of books for sale in his shop in the 1740s.[26] Victor Neuburg who examined the printed catalogues of chapmens' books available in colonial Philadelphia, Boston, and New York noted that they were almost identical with those of Dicey of London.[27] The colonists developed a distinctively American variant, the Indian captivity narrative, of which many were locally composed and printed and sometimes reprinted in London. However, as far as I can judge from the extensive collections of surviving chapbooks in the libraries at Harvard and New York, not a single one of the old favourites was

---

[23] As early as 1661–3 the Bible was translated into the Massachusetts language, a huge investment, both in intellectual and manufacturing terms, undertaken by a small expatriate population on the very edge of the Europeanised world. For some colonial print runs, including the Indian Bible see appendix 1.

[24] See E. Jennifer Monaghan, 'Literacy, Instruction, and Gender in Colonial New England' in Davidson 55.

[25] See C. A. Herrick, 'The Early New Englanders, What did they Read?' in *The Library* (1918).

[26] Quoted by Edwin Wolf, *The Book Culture of a Colonial American City* (Oxford 1988) 65.

[27] Victor Neuburg, 'Chapbooks in America' in Davidson.

reprinted in America before the ending of perpetual property in England in 1774.[28]

Herrick suggested that the absence of local reprints of the old favourites was due to the laziness of the local booksellers who preferred to import. But such explanations are unconvincing, especially for print which required minimal capital stock and little human skill. What is more likely is that these valuable intellectual properties were as secure from piracy in the American colonies as they were in central London. As in England, as soon as the controlling structures broke down, among the first titles to be reprinted in America were old ballads and chapbooks that had previously been imported. *The Children in the Woods*, for example, the ownership of which was first entered in the Stationers' Company registers in 1595, and kept in print in London ever since, was reprinted in Boston in the mid-1770s.[29] *A Chrystal Glass for Christian Women*, by Philip Stubbes, a Puritan conduct book for women first printed in England in 1591 and kept continuously in print at least until 1764, was reprinted in Albany in 1781, and there was another American reprint in 1793.[30] This evidence suggests that the Bible, almanac, and ballad culture recorded by John Clare and others at the end of the eighteenth century had been as frozen in rural North America as it had been in rural England.[31] Indeed, as later collectors of 'folksong' were to find, the freeze may have been deeper and more persistent in the remoter communities in America than it had been at home. The British colonies in the West Indies and Canada show a similar pattern of locally printed almanacs, sermons, newspapers, and official documents, with reliance on imports from Britain for other types of print.[32]

As in England, the key was pricing. Some colonial American booksellers emphasised in their advertisements that the books they offered were available 'at the very same price they are sold in London'.[33] Small orders to 'gentlemen', that is to credit-worthy individuals, were charged at London

---

[28] I draw this conclusion from the extensive lists in H. B. Weiss, *A Catalogue of Chapbooks, and Broadside Ballads in New York Public Public Library* (New York 1936), and Charles Welsh and William H. Tillinghast eds., *Catalogue of English and American Chapbooks and Broadside Ballads in Harvard College Library* (1961).

[29] A. S. W. Rosenbach, *Early American Children's Books* (1933) 30. *The King and the Cobbler*, another ancient text, was reprinted by the same publisher at the same time.

[30] Usually known as *Katherine Stubbs,* in which the account of her successful struggle with the devil at the moment of her death sets out the essentials of the ideal of femininity to which her cult aspired. Reprinted in facsimile, with explanatory headnote, by William St Clair and Irmgard Maassen, eds., *Conduct Literature for Women, 1500–1640* (2000) iii, 1.

[31] For the freezing see chapters 4 and 17.

[32] Marie Tremaine, *A Bibliography of Canadian Imprints 1751–1800* (Toronto 1952) xviii. For Jamaica, see Roderic Cave, 'Printing in 18th Century Jamaica' in *The Library* (1978).

[33] Quoted by Neuburg, 'Chapbooks in America' 86.

retail prices, plus the cost of shipping with twelve months credit. Since shipping costs were often as low as 2 per cent of the value of a consignment, and uncertain sailing times meant that it took a minimum of six months to obtain an ordered book, this arrangement was little different, apart from the longer delay, than that operating in the English provinces.[34] Even in times of war, when the cost of insurance cover was heaviest, the elaborate system of credit, prices, and discounts ensured that London books could be sent to Boston, New York, Philadelphia, Baltimore, Charleston, and thence up the great rivers to the remotest English-speaking settlements while still leaving an adequate profit margin at each step of the distribution.[35]

The revolutionary war which began in 1776 interrupted the import of books from Britain. However, as soon as independence was formally recognised, an accounting reconciliation of outstanding claims and counterclaims took place, with the London booksellers claiming interest on unmet payments for seven, eight, and nine years.[36] After that, book exports from Britain resumed strongly. A glance at the long list of books advertised for sale by James White of Boston c. 1787, for example, shows how similar his stock was to that which might have been expected in a large English city at that time.[37] From independence until the 1790s, a time of rapidly rising population in America, the importation of books from Britain boomed. Irish imports too grew strongly after independence made them legal.[38] Nor does the boom seem to have been much interrupted by the outbreak in 1793 of the European wars, although insurance costs rose. In 1803, a bookseller in Charleston, South Carolina, imported 50,000 volumes in a single consignment, the largest importation hitherto made to the United States.[39]

As Thomas Dibdin observed about Suttaby's old-canon reprint list in 1824:

Thousands of copies are circulated abroad, especially in America. Within these last twenty years SEVEN HUNDRED THOUSAND volumes of the whole, collectively have been dispersed at home and abroad, averaging 35,000 copies per annum. Upon such a vast scale does knowledge, of every kind, travel.'[40]

---

[34] See Hernlund 84. Part of the reason why Rivington was forced into bankruptcy by his book-trade colleagues was that he sold at a discount both wholesale and retail.

[35] An example from the Bell and Brafute archives is given in appendix 5.

[36] These transactions can be seen, for example, in a long account dated March 1787 in the Duyckinck archives, box 60. When the United States adopted the dollar, sterling was converted in New York at the rate of £1=$2.5.

[37] Reproduced in facsimile in *CBAW*, 49.

[38] Between 1782 and 1799 Irish imports were worth £10,000. See Raven in *CBAW* 185.

[39] Raven, *London Booksellers* 204.   [40] Dibdin xiv.

Although the evidence is scattered, and still largely unquantified, it seems likely that in English-speaking America, as in England, the 1780s marked a steep change in the growth rate of books and reading, and that the accelerated trend continued, matching, and then outpacing, the increase in population all through the nineteenth century.[41] And as in England, many of the texts which fuelled the initial explosion were the lower priced reprints of seventeenth and early eighteenth-century literature.

One of the earliest results of the success of the American Revolution was the tearing down of the intellectual property structures which had favoured the London and Edinburgh industries. Beginning in 1787, the individual states, and soon the federal government, erected a specifically American intellectual property regime modelled on the British Act of 1710, that is an authorial copyright which could be assigned to a publisher for fourteen years, in some circumstances for twenty-eight, before entering the public domain. They also adopted the price control provisions of that act, although these do not appear to have been used. What was most innovative, indeed the single most important determinant of the reading of the new republic for nearly a century, is that the new American regime gave copyright protection only to the works of local American authors. Indeed it specifically excluded texts initially printed outside the United States. As the 1790 Federal Act declared:

Nothing in this act shall be construed to extend to prohibit the importation or vending, reprinting or publishing within the United States, of any map, chart, book, or books, written, printed, or published by any party not a citizen of the United States, in foreign parts.[42]

By this protectionist legislation the previous restrictions on intellectual property, whatever they had been, were swept away. All the printed writings in English that had originated in Great Britain, old and new, were now available to be reprinted in the United States, as well as all the printed texts printed in any language in the rest of the world. The way was thus opened to a huge expansion of local printing. Carey, an Irish printer who emigrated to America in 1784, was given a loan by La Fayette to set up his press in Philadelphia, the then federal capital.[43] Many other Irish printers arrived after 1801 when the union deprived Ireland of its offshore status.[44] Between 1790 and 1805, the number of printers in Philadelphia rose from

---

[41] For binding for the American trade see Potter 262.
[42] For the early copyright law immediately after independence see Wills, and Lehmann-Haupt 103.
[43] The loan was $400. Davidson in Davidson 159.   [44] See chapters 6 and 15.

twenty-six to fifty-one.[45] The number of titles printed in the United States, which in 1778 totalled less than 500, had by 1798, risen to over 1,800, the majority of them local reprints of texts written and published in Britain.[46] Between 1790 and 1800, over 15,000 American imprints are recorded, about the same as for the whole colonial period, a boom greater than in Britain.[47] By 1820 the volume of book production in the United States was valued at $2.5 million.[48]

By the beginning of the nineteenth century, the United States was producing its own English-language Bibles, old-canon classics, and school anthologies. Despite the attempts to develop a distinctively American literature, the reading of the citizens of the early republic still coincided, to a large extent, with that of Britain. Indeed the regime which enabled intellectual property from Britain to be imported free helped to continue the dominance of English-language texts first written in Britain. Virtually every mainstream book on every subject published in Britain during the romantic period was reprinted at once in the United States. Some of the most valuable intellectual properties in the world, such as Enfield's *Speaker* and Murray's *Reader,* were reprinted in numerous large editions, with other local adaptations, such as Webster's *American Preceptor,* given a national American veneer. As in England, anthologies of old-canon rural religious writers replaced the catechetic Dyche and Dilworth in schools, helping to entrench the old pre-industrial and pre-Enlightenment culture in the minds of successive generations of American children.[49] In 1793 alone, the main old-canon British authors such as Addison, Swift, Thomson, Blair, Cowper, Dodsley, Goldsmith, Pope and Sterne were all reprinted in America.[50] They were all out of copyright in Britain, but the works of Byron, Scott, Moore, Wordsworth, Southey, Austen, and hundreds of other contemporary texts were also now free for the taking. And, in sharp contrast with the situation in Britain, there was scarcely any price differential between the old and the new.

At first, the American reprint business seems to have been mainly an offshore manufacturing operation with the books intended for local sale. Despite the war which broke out between the two countries in 1812 and which lasted for several years, some of Byron's poems were printed by

---

[45] Remer 1.   [46] Noted by Lehmann-Haupt 122.
[47] Wills ix.   [48] Silver 141 from Goodrich ii, 380.
[49] For some American print runs of these books, see appendix 7. Linley Murray, whose family were American loyalists who moved to England before the Revolution, had spent his early years in America. The stabilisation of the old-canon culture is well attested by the statistics collected for the Windsor district by Gilmore 64.
[50] Wills xxiv.

different publishers simultaneously in Boston, Philadelphia, and New York, copying from one another as well as from copies brought by ship from England. The error which one printer made in the title of *The Prisoners* [sic] *of Chillon*, was, for example, repeated in other editions.[51] Carey of Philadelphia would sometimes hire all the seats on the mail stage coach to be sure that copies of his reprints would reach New York before they could be reprinted there.[52] It was some time, however, before the full implications of the American law were realised in practice. Under the federal law of 1790, the monopoly right to take a rent from each new title published in Britain was, in effect, being given away free to the first American publisher who could print it. Just as European-Americans could take lands beyond the frontier into their private possession simply by settling on it and registering a private property claim with the appropriate authorities, so the intellectual property in texts imported from Britain could be taken into private American ownership by those printer/publishers who were quickest off the mark.

As with the Stationers' Company registers in England, only a proportion of titles, normally the most valuable, were registered. In 1790, for example, a copyright was accorded to *The Book of Common Prayer* and the *Psalter* of the American episcopal church, more valuable intellectual properties than many real properties taken over from the previous colonial owners.[53] In New Jersey in 1811, a partnership of printer/publishers in New Brunswick, New York, Philadelphia, and Boston, successfully claimed intellectual property rights in the *Nautical Almanac*, a publication of the British Board of Longitude published annually in London.[54] In the case of Byron, by 1816 Moses Thomas of Philadelphia had gone into partnership with printer/publishers in the three main east-coast cities to share production costs and to divide out the market. At the same time, Thomas registered his private ownership of the intellectual property rights of all the many works of Byron which had hitherto been printed in the United States, including the paratextual locally written life, and the locally re-engraved copies of the British illustrations.[55] Thomas claimed to have included some works of Byron hitherto

---

[51] The 1817 Boston and the New York editions both call the poem *The Prisoners of Chillon*, an error unlikely to be coincidental. *Poems by Lord Byron* (1817) is described as 'New York, published by Thomas Kirk and Thomas B. Mercein, Moses Thomas, M. Carey and son, Philadelphia; Wells and Lilley, Boston; and Coale and Maxwell, Baltimore', Ac. See also Accardo 42, 43.

[52] Noted by Bradsher 18.

[53] Wills 2.

[54] See Joseph J. Felcone, *New Jersey Copyrights, 1791–1845* (Worcester, Mass. 1994) 67.

[55] For example, *The Works of Lord Byron including Several Poems now first collected. Together with An Original Biography. Embellished with a portrait, title-page, and six other engravings. Vol.1 [2] [3]*

unpublished either in Britain or the United States which he had taken direct from manuscripts, texts may have been forged for the occasion, so as to make it more difficult for his ownership of the rest of Byron's works to be contested.[56]

I cannot judge to what extent the taking of British texts into private American ownership enabled the owners to move to a higher point on the demand curve, but, at any rate during the romantic period, the price of access to imported texts remained cheaper than comparable locally produced texts on which an American copyright applied from the beginning.[57] By the 1820s, in the larger cities, the publisher had separated from the printer, and the printing was sent to the suburbs and then to out-of-state locations where manufacturing and storage costs were cheaper. As in Europe in previous centuries, the sharing of the costs of manufacturing, the exchanging of long lines of credit, and paying in kind rather than in money, quickly brought about a large measure of syndication and cartelisation. By 1830, the date of publication of Moore's sure-fire *Letters and Journals of Lord Byron*, the list of partners who took a share in the stereotype included virtually all the leading printer/publishers in the country, including sixteen in New York.[58] The period during which there was genuine price competition in the United States was quite short.

The American reprints were tightly printed by hand from moveable type, manufactured in small format on poor quality paper, and sold at less than half the British prices. Some texts were adapted to fit the smaller format. Waverley novels, for example, which had been padded out to fit the British three-volume convention, were depadded into two volumes.[59]

Biography, Poems, Childe Harold (Philadelphia 1816). 'Published by Moses Thomas, J. Maxwell printer' notes in its printed paratext that it had been registered for federal copyright in 1816 in the District of Pennsylvania 'on the 8th day of August in the fortieth year of the Independence of the United States', Ac. As far as I can judge, from that date, the sheets of works of Byron printed in the United States were probably manufactured centrally, and sold locally by each partner who supplied his own title page.

[56] Translations from classical authors allegedly made by Byron while at Harrow. As far as I know, the status of these pieces has not yet been fully investigated. They are not included among the genuine works by McGann, the editor of Byron, *Poetical Works*.

[57] In 1824 Charles Wiley of New York, advertised recent novels by Cooper at $2 which appears to be slightly higher than the usual $1.75 for Waverley novels. Cover of *Don Juan Cantos* 12, 13, 14 (1824), Ac. An advertisement leaf of publications of Wells and Lilly of Boston inserted in a copy of J. W. Cunningham's *Sancho the Proverbialist* (1817), notes several other reprints of British three deckers on sale at $2.

[58] Accardo 50.

[59] The differences between price, print run, and degree of market penetration are illustrated in appendix 5, 522: 'American offshore reprinting of a British bestseller. [Scott's] *Woodstock*, 1826'. For the pruning see Remer 90. For prices, see Remer 139. This price is confirmed by advertisements on covers of Byron's *Marino Faliero* (Philadelphia 1821), Ac.

Byron's works, some of which had been published in London in volumes containing two or three pieces, were all available individually.[60] Byron's *Don Juan* appears to have been available by the canto.[61] What is most striking, when we quantify, is that although the population of the United States in 1820 was less than half that of Britain, the initial print runs of the American printer/publishers were usually either much the same length or longer.[62] Whereas the British publishers started at the top of the perceived demand curve and slowly tranched down, the American reprint printer/publishers positioned themselves far lower down the demand curve than most British books reached for many decades. In the case of Scott's eagerly awaited *Life of Napoleon Buonaparte*, for example, published in 1827 at the height of Scott's fame, the first two British printings totalled 8,000 copies. The first American edition, produced simultaneously, by arrangement, totalled 12,500 copies.[63] Often there was over-production but trade sales and remaindering took the texts even lower down the curve. In terms of their reading, the Americans of the romantic period had easier access to the literature being written in Great Britain than most of their contemporaries across the ocean.

For titles for which a long life was expected, the American printer/publishers were quick to adopt stereotyping. Most of the Greek and Latin Delphin classics, one of the most valuable properties of the London syndicates until 1774 had been stereotyped by 1823.[64] Shakespeare, first reprinted in 1795, was stereotyped in 1823 in a tightly printed edition, with no pages left blank or unfilled, and the plates kept in use for decades producing many impressions of unknown cumulative length.[65] In the late 1820s, with the appearance of Galignani's editions in Paris, the American printer/publishers were offered the choice between reprinting from the original London or from the offshore French editions. Since the French editions were at that time textually superior they chose the French. The Galignani single-volume editions of the poets were cloned line for line, with lives of the authors, prefaces, and the rest of the paratext, complete and unaltered, and then stereotyped. Some of the illustrations were re-engraved so accurately that

---

[60] See Accardo 4.
[61] This appears to have been the case with *The Works of the Rt. Hon. Lord Byron In Eight Volumes. – Vol. VIII* (1824 Philadelphia; B. W. Pomeroy). Each canto is paginated separately, and the printers' key signatures start with each canto. Copy with pages uncut, Ac.
[62] Population figures are given in appendix 1.
[63] Figures for Scott's British publication are given in appendix 9 'Walter Scott'. Some American printing figures are in appendix 5.
[64] See the letter quoted by Bradsher 36.
[65] As late as 1851 the plates were sold for $1,400 (£280) a figure which implies that, even at that time, they were still expected to yield many more copies which could be profitably sold. Remer 98, 115.

they can only be distinguished from the originals with the help of a magnifying glass.[66] The cloned plates were then reused over many decades. The three poets whom it was most difficult to buy from mainstream bookshops in Britain, Coleridge, Shelley, and Keats, were available to mainstream readerships in the United States a generation before they reached such audiences in Britain.[67] The American publishers also frequently copied and cloned engraved illustrations, with the result that American readers had access to the visual orientalism of Byron and Moore before such images became available to most readers in Britain.

There are records of about a hundred early American editions of Byron, published in eight cities, but since the number made from shared sheets has not yet been established, it is difficult to estimate the total print runs.[68] Captain Marryat, a British author much interested in copyright, was later given an American estimate of the effects of the regime.

I applied to the largest publishers in New York and Philadelphia, to ascertain if I could, how many copies of Byron had been published. The reply was that it was impossible to say exactly, but they considered that from *one hundred and fifty to two hundred thousand* copies must have been sold![69]

When in 1815 an American visitor to London presented Byron with a copy of an American reprint of his works in two volumes, Byron:

. . . expressed his satisfaction at seeing it in a small form because in that way, he said, nobody would be prevented from purchasing it. It was in boards, and he said he would not have it bound, for he should prefer to keep it in the same state in which it came from America.[70]

When in Italy in 1822 Byron was invited on board an American warship, the captain showed him an American edition of his collected works carried on board ship, which pleased Byron as another sign of the extent of his readership.[71] However, British authors who were more dependent on

---

[66] MacGillivray.

[67] See the history of the stereotype plates of this volume summarised in appendix 5.

[68] Price 37.5 cents to 50 cents for a longer work.

[69] Frederick Marryat in *A Diary in America* (1839) ii, 206, quoted by Accardo 493. Marryat was amazed to find complete editions of Byron even in the log houses of the fur trappers in the far north west, and noted that in the southern states 'Byron' and 'Ada' were names commonly given to slaves. Marryat, *Diary* 175, 191.

[70] *Life, Letters, and Journals of George Ticknor* (Boston, 1876) i, 62. Byron later gave the volumes to his friend Scrope Davies who had to leave England in a hurry shortly afterwards overwhelmed by his debts. See Ernest Hartley Coleridge, ed., *The Works of Lord Byron* (1905) vii, 90.

[71] See Ernest J. Lovell Jr, ed., *His Very Self and Voice* (New York 1954) 290, and Byron's *Letters and Journals*, volume 9, 168.

their pens took a different view. In 1836 Wordsworth and Southey held a conversation about the American reprints of their works.

Wordsworth said it was wonderful what an interest they took in our literature – 'it was the yearning of the child for the parent'. While Southey remarked, with a smile – 'Rather the yearning of the robber for his booty.'[72]

The biggest literary export was the Waverley novels. When in 1832, shortly after the death of Scott, the British publishers appealed to the United States Senate to agree to international copyright, they drew a picture of the cruel treatment which the Americans had inflicted on the greatest author of the age in his hour of need.

That while the works of this author, dear alike to your country and to ours, were read from Maine to Georgia, from the Atlantic to the Mississippi, he received no remuneration from the American public for his labours; that an equitable remuneration might have saved his life, and would, at least, have relieved its closing years from the burden of debts and destructive toils.[73]

However, although it was true that British authors had not benefited directly from American reprints, British publishers had. Aware that the ability to confer on an American publisher the gift of priority was itself an asset which had a monetary value, from 1817 onwards Scott's British publishers began to accept payment for sending proofs to the American offshore publisher of their choice in sealed packages sent in at least two fast vessels.[74] In 1820 boats were sent to sea to meet the British ship that was carrying the first copy of *Rob Roy*.[75] For the four volumes of *The Fortunes of Nigel*, nine printing shops were put simultaneously to work and the reprints were ready for sale in three days.[76]

It seems likely, from studies of numbers of editions and of library-borrowing records which have already been made, that the Waverley novels, by far the most read literary texts in Britain in the romantic period and later, were also pervasively read in the United States.[77] In histories of American literature, Scott usually features only as a footnoted influence on James Fenimore Cooper. In histories of American reading, or in any attempt

---

[72] Southey, *Life* vi, 301. Wordsworth is referring to three-decker novels.
[73] Quoted by Mumby, *Routledge* 41.
[74] After Constable's bankruptcy, the American fee of £295 for advance copies of *The Life of Napoleon* was paid direct to Scott. See Todd and Bowden 452, 611. Constable took £50 for each novel, later £75. See also Bradsher 131.
[75] From a contemporary source quoted by Bradsher 81.   [76] Noted by Bradsher 87.
[77] See Emily B. Todd, 'Walter Scott and the Nineteenth-Century American Literary Marketplace' in *Papers of the Bibliographical Society of America*, 93, 4 (1999). Scott, and to much lesser extent, Byron, feature in the statistics collected for the Windsor district by Gilmore 64.

to assess how far cultural formation and mentalities were influenced by reading, he must be regarded as one of the most influential authors.

Nor was it only literary works which were locally reprinted, but virtually all mainstream British publications in all fields, of politics, travel, economics, science, agriculture, and medicine, including school books, maps, music, practical guides, conduct books, and encyclopaedias. Before 1790 there were reprints of Blackstone, Adam Smith, and Robertson, and before 1800 of most works in English, old and recent, which were still read in Britain. It was open to the American printer/publishers to abridge them, to anthologise them, and to appropriate them in any way they chose.[78] The *Analectic Review*, for example, which started in Philadelphia in 1813, drew on articles in the *Edinburgh* and *Quarterly Reviews*. Texts, such as pamphlets, travel books, and essays on political economy such as Wollstonecraft's *Rights of Woman* and Babbage's *On the Economy of Machinery and Manufactures*, which in Britain were produced in small expensive editions mainly for the male members of book clubs were available to a wider readership, including American book clubs. During the first half of the nineteenth century all the most important texts produced in Europe on all subjects became available to be read in the United States at a fraction of European prices.

Although British texts would undoubtedly have reached the United States even if international copyright had existed, what seems to have occurred is that, because of the unequal protectionist intellectual property regime, that lasted over a century, enabled the United States to receive a far larger inflow of ideas of British origin, and to diffuse them more widely and deeply through the American reading nation, than would otherwise have been possible. According to Bryce writing in the 1880s, America was 'the land of the general reader . . . Nowhere in the world is there growing up such a vast multitude of intelligent, cultivated and curious readers'.[79] In economic terms, the 1790 protectionist regime brought about a huge free transfer of intellectual property in the formal sense from British publishers to American publishers, and thence, through lower prices, to American book buyers and American readers. In intellectual terms in a wider sense, it provided an opportunity for American readers to read the most up-to-date European writings on all subjects at prices which were determined by manufacturing costs rather than by private intellectual property ownership.

[78] Titles noted by Bradsher 31.
[79] Quoted in 'The Reading Public in England and America in 1900' in Altick, *Writers*.

In the British system, the extent of readerly access to modern information, ideas, and literature, was directly related to the socio-economic class of readers, with the least well off having to wait for years, sometimes for ever, for prices to fall to levels they could afford. By contrast, the American system of the time was open and classless, with the price of access to all texts, new and old, more or less the same. In Britain, because of these governing structures, only a handful of texts, notably Byron's *Don Juan*, were read by the whole reading nation shortly after they were written. In America, all recent British writing came quickly and it came cheap. In Britain there emerged a distinctive urban working-class culture, with its own texts and canons, committed to radical reform of the governmental and economic structures. In the United States the reform movement, being less differentiated by its reading, was both less radical and socially more broadly based. The post-independence intellectual property regime helped the United States to become one of the most modern countries in the world.

But the flow of ideas was not always as intellectually and morally progressive in its effects as Thomas Jefferson assumed. According to Mark Twain, the states of the American South stood to gain immeasurably from the example of the French Revolution, and from the 'great and permanent services to liberty, humanity, and progress' brought about by the European enlightenment. But

> then comes Sir Walter Scott with his enchantments, and by his single might checks this wave of progress, and even turns it back; sets the world in love with dreams and phantoms; with decayed and swinish forms of religion, with decayed and degraded systems of government; with the silliness and emptinesses, sham grandeurs, sham gauds, and sham chivalries of a brainless and worthless long-vanished society. He did measureless harm; more real and lasting harm, perhaps, than any other individual that ever wrote.[80]

Scott, Twain insisted, 'had so large a hand in making Southern character, as it existed before the [American Civil] war, that he is in great measure responsible for the war'.[81] Scott's writings were having a similar effect at home.[82]

The transatlantic textual transfers were not all in one direction. Many copies of American reprints of British texts made their way to Britain in the cabins of sea captains and in the kit-bags of soldiers returning from Canada. Surviving copies carry inscriptions by British owners or show

---

[80] Quoted by Forrest G. Robinson, *The Cambridge Companion to Mark Twain* (Cambridge 1995) 40.
[81] *Ibid*. 81 from *Life on the Mississippi*.   [82] Discussed in chapter 21.

other evidence, for example in their bindings, of having been taken to Britain. There is also evidence of some being specially produced for export to Britain, or repackaged for sale in Britain, having, for example, prices printed in shillings and pence. Some pirate editions printed in Britain, notably Shelley's *Queen Mab*, masqueraded as imports from America, a ruse which would not have succeeded if American books had not been a common sight.[83] However, despite the large price differential, for reasons which I have not been able to discover, the importation of American offshore reprints never appears to have become commercially organised as the French, nor to have attracted so much attention from British publishers.

More significant than books were texts. If the United States was an offshore publisher of British titles, Britain was an offshore publisher of American titles. The London and Edinburgh publishers seem mostly to have chosen not to weaken their demand for international copyright by unauthorised reprinting of texts first published in the United States, and they too resorted to various devices, in association with American partners, to try to secure simultaneous legal copyright protection in both countries. A book first published in Britain was entitled to full copyright protection, and even when, in 1868, the House of Lords declared that the author had to be living in the British Empire at the time of publication, a successful American author could make a trip across the Atlantic or up to Canada.[84] But, during the romantic period and for long after, many British publishers took advantage of their freedom. Tegg's cheap *Gems from American Poets* offered selections from Bryant, Halleck and other American imitators of Scott and Byron to British readers who could not afford the real thing. From the 1840s there was a huge British readership for Longfellow, destined to become, by far, the most popular poet of the British Victorians, selling in hundreds of thousands of copies over many decades.[85] If the slavery of the American South was buttressed by cheap offshore copies of the Waverley novels, a huge British readership was influenced to a different perception by cheap offshore copies of *Uncle Tom's Cabin*, of which more than a million-and-a-half copies are believed to have been sold in Britain within a few years of first publication.[86]

The main inward effect of the American regime in Britain was, however, on popular reading. After 1842, with the final closing of the brief copyright window in Britain, American books and magazines were among the few

---

[83] For example Daly's edition of *Childe Harold's Pilgrimage*, Ac. For *Queen Mab* see chapter 16.
[84] Noted by Gohdes 17.   [85] Some statistics given in appendix 13.
[86] For the vast sales of this title see the figures in appendix 5, some of which I have been able to confirm from publishers' archives.

sources of texts which could be printed to be sold cheaply in Britain. With the novels of the old canon already available at extremely low prices, and all newly written British novels subject to high prices, long copyright protection, restrictions on abridgements, and, as happened in the case of *Frankenstein*, a dog-in-the manger refusal to allow cheap reprints even when a text was out of print, there was a dearth of local reading material with which to supply the rapidly expanding British reading nation.[87]

By the 1840s, it was economically feasible, because of changes in manufacturing technology and reduced taxes on paper, to print and sell novels in full or abridged versions in much the same format and at much the same price as newspapers, and a large industry grew up which was, to a large extent, separate, both in text and price, from mainstream publishing. As William Hazlitt, Junior, editor of the *Romancist and Novelist's Library,* boasted in 1840, in three years he had published, at a cost to the buyer of only 13 shillings, no fewer than 121 works, totalling 3,572,400 words and 17,862,000 pieces of moveable type, equivalent to sixty-five volumes sold at the normal price of a guinea and a half (31.5 shillings).[88] Hazlitt's publication sold for two pence a part. The *Novel Newspaper,* published at about the same time, offered the equivalent of three-decker novels, printed in type so small as to be scarcely readable, but at sixpence. A high proportion of the texts included in both these series were from the United States, France, and Germany, including the works of Fenimore Cooper, a special favourite.[89] The shops which sprang up near the new railway stations, it was noticed, were filled with offshore piracies of American books, 'cheap French novels of the shadiest class', and other 'positively injurious aliment for the hungry minds that sought refreshment on their feverish way', including the ubiquitous *Don Juan*.[90] The 400 titles of Routledge's 'Railway Library' contained a high proportion of works of American origin.[91]

Although, in Britain, most of the political discussion about international copyright concerned the economic losses which the American regime

---

[87] For the then owners' refusal to allow *Frankenstein* to be reprinted see chapter 18.

[88] Preface printed in *Romancist* iii, Ac. See list of titles from Michael Sadleir, *Nineteenth-Century Fiction, A Bibliographical Record* (1951) ii,164.

[89] See also the lists in William Louis James, *Fiction for the Working Man* (Oxford 1963) 212. For the *Novel Newspaper's* defence against the charge that it was unfair to Cooper to publish his works so cheaply, i.e. that they were only doing what Americans did to British authors, see Sadleir, *Nineteenth-Century Fiction* ii, 145.

[90] Sir Herbert Maxwell, *Life and Times of . . . William Henry Smith* (1893) especially i, 49–58. Noted, for example, by Charles Knight in *Passages of a Working Life* (1865) iii, 17, referring to an observation made in 1851. The other collections of cheap novels in series, *The Parlour Library,* and *The Novelist, A Collection of Standard Novels,* like *The Romancist,* also contained many foreign titles.

[91] Noted by Gohdes 21.

imposed on the British book industry, there were also fears for the effects on British mentalities of the American inflows. Walter Scott was simply amused that the episode he remembered from his boyhood in which John Paul Jones had sailed up the Firth of Forth, and which posed not the slightest danger to Edinburgh, had been transformed by Fenimore Cooper into an American myth of anti-British heroism.[92] Many readers in Britain, including young people, were given so many stories of American patriots and mercenary British redcoats, of intrepid frontiersmen and noble redskins, that some adults feared that their own national identity was being undermined.

In 1891, after nearly a century of Anglo-American dispute, the United States, having by this time built up a strong local publishing as well as printing industry, and having become a net exporter of the potential intellectual property implicit in printed texts, joined the international copyright treaties.[93] Since that time American governments have pressed other countries to join in a global intellectual property regime, and adherence to the regime has become a condition of countries participating in the world's trade and financial institutions. Indeed intellectual property has become one of the main instruments by which the United States dominates the modern world.

---

[92] Lockhart 521. The book was *The Pilot*.
[93] See James J. Barnes, *Authors, Publishers, and Politicians, The Quest for an Anglo-American Copyright Agreement 1815–1854* (1974).

CHAPTER 20

Reading, reception, and dissemination

How did the reading of books lead to change? Is it possible to take the analysis forward from acts of reading to cultural formation and changes in mentalities? If we are to do this, we need to move from the macro approach adopted so far, and look also at the micro evidence for the reading behaviour of individuals. The starting point is to historicise the actual reading practice of the romantic period.[1]

Much reading nowadays is done indoors, sitting on a chair. In the romantic period it was common to read outdoors while walking. We hear of groups of men meeting to read in parks in order to escape the dark and smells of windowless houses.[2] Thomas Carter, a tailor, sat on his heels.[3] To save on the costs of borrowing, the Chambers brothers sat together outside, one holding the book, the other turning over the pages.[4] To minimise on wax candles, which were expensive, and of rushes dipped in animal fat which dripped and stank, many readers read by firelight, stretched on the floor, their hair sizzling with constant singeing, sparks exploding and shadows dancing on the walls.[5] *Frankenstein* by firelight is a different reading experience from *Frankenstein* in a university library. Reading nowadays is mainly a solitary activity conducted by individuals who have personally chosen the text they read. In the romantic period the selection of the books, the reading, and the subsequent discussion, were often collectively decided through book clubs, but every reading family was, to an extent, a reading society subject to pressures from its members. In many houses, the ladies and gentlemen spent time sitting in the parlour sewing, reading or listening to a book being read aloud. Besides the many books of advice on what to read, there were others

---

[1] See Alan Richardson, *Literature, Education, and Romanticism: Reading as Social Practice, 1780–1832* (Cambridge 1994).
[2] William Thom, *Rhymes and Recollections of a Hand-Loom Weaver* (1844).
[3] (Thomas Carter), *Memoirs of a Working Man* (1845).   [4] Chambers 56.
[5] See Vincent, and Chambers, 130. Abraham Lincoln famously read by firelight.

on how to read.[6] If a visitor made a social call when the family was at home, the book was the natural starting point for conversation, and it had to be selected with that purpose in mind.[7] Nor was reading aloud confined to the better-off. We hear of children who had learned to read reading aloud to parents who had not.[8] 'The evenings I usually spent with another fellow prisoner', wrote James Watson, the radical bookseller, of one of his periods in prison, 'For three or four hours after dark we read to each other.'[9]

In the romantic period, although there may have been a move from intensive to extensive reading, the same texts were still read many times over.[10] Sometimes the books were re-read because nothing different was available, but for many readers, frequent re-reading was a conscious choice. As Hazlitt noted in a modern-sounding phrase as he contemplated his little library of frequently read, old-canon books, they were 'standard productions . . . links in the chain of our conscious being [which] bind together the different scattered divisions of our personal identity'.[11]

Then there was memory, another huge difference between the mental world of the romantic period and that of our own times. Ruskin could recite at least two of Scott's long poems by heart. Macaulay, always precocious, could recite *The Lay of the Last Minstrel* at the age of eight after a single reading – he also knew the whole of *Paradise Lost*.[12] Marie Corelli is said as a girl to have 'read her favourite poets, Shakespeare, Keats, Shelley, and Byron by the hour, and . . . learned much of them by heart.'[13] Committing long passages of text to memory was additional to, and to an extent substitutable for, the reading of printed books. Indeed the less access that particular groups had to books, the more they had to rely on memory. The printer Charles Manby Smith, asked by a prospective employer to supply a specimen of his handwriting, 'occupied himself for four hours in spoiling a quire of paper with extracts from Milton, Shakespeare, and Byron, transcribed from memory', with no suggestion that he thought he was unusual in being able to do so.[14] Some of those who, like Frances Kemble, could entertain friends with a recitation of Byron's *The Prisoner of Chillon* did not possess a copy of the book.[15] Among the reasons why, in the romantic

---

[6] Notably Thomas Sheridan, *Lectures on the Art of Reading* (1775 and much reprinted) which discusses both prose and verse reading.

[7] A point made by Harriet Martineau. See Cruse *Englishman* 15.   [8] Lackington 257.

[9] Watson, *Memoirs* 20.   [10] For the examples of Mill, Ruskin, and Stephen see chapter 21.

[11] 'On Reading Old Books' in *The Plain Speaker* (1826).

[12] Cruse, *Englishman* 277, and A. N. L. Munby, *Essays and Papers* (1977) 122, drawing on Trevelyan's *Life*.

[13] Bertha Vyver, *Memoirs of Marie Corelli* (1930) 13.   [14] Manby Smith 50.

[15] Examples in Cruse, *Victorians* 175.

Figure 20. Reading aloud to the family by candlelight. From *A Course of Lectures for Sunday Evenings* (1783).

period, verse was preferred to prose, was that it was literally more memorable, more easily appropriated into the mind of the reader, more accessible
again later, and more social.

Who were the readers? Information is plentiful. In surviving books we
often find ownership and presentation inscriptions, bookplates, booksellers'
labels, and marks of having been owned by book clubs. We have catalogues
of the libraries of individuals and of institutions and sales catalogues when
libraries were dispersed. We have the membership lists of libraries and book
clubs, and a few lending records. There are numerous references to books
and reading in contemporary diaries, in letters, in notes of conversations and
table talk, and in autobiographies and biographies. Some readers, such as
Godwin and Gladstone, made lists of all the books they read during their
adult lives. The reading lists of Mary Russell Mitford show that she read
about twenty-four novels a month.[16]

The evidence is particularly plentiful for two groups, members of the
governing elites, and men and women who were themselves authors or
reviewers. Lords, gentlemen, professional men and their ladies, when not
in London, spent much of the time in the country, reading, conversing, and
writing to their friends. Members of the Houses of Lords and Common
used their free postage privileges to send books round the country.[17] As for
writers, there were enough poets and novelists reading each others' works to
sustain a sizeable book industry on their own. As influencers of opinion, the
aristocracy and the literary are, no doubt, among the more important. But
direct evidence for the reading of others is also plentiful. There are dozens
of autobiographies, memoirs, diaries, and letters, of politicians, businessmen, clergymen, artisans, and other working men, many of whom describe
their education and their reading, including reading in childhood. William
Linton, the Chartist, recalled how, as a boy, he read the verse romances of
Scott from the quartos used to prop up his seat in the schoolroom.[18] Harry
Burton, son of a house-painter, recalled that there were few books in his
family's house, but when he was about eleven he came across *Don Juan*, full
of words he did not understand but 'leaving vaguely pleasing sensations.'[19]
It would need only time and patience to compile a database of named
readers of named printed books of the romantic period, and to build an

---

[16] Cruse, *Englishman* 98.
[17] E.g. S. H. Romilly, ed., *Letters to 'Ivy' From the First Earl of Dudley* (1905); Vere Foster, ed, *The Two
Duchesses . . . Family Correspondence* (1898) 361.
[18] Linton, *Memories* 24.
[19] Quoted by Jonathan Rose, *The Intellectual Life of the British Working Class* (Yale 2001) 374.

increasingly reliable picture of the reading nation arranged by texts, time, age, gender, and socio-economic class.[20]

That reading had effects was seldom doubted. Autobiographies teem with examples of lives shaped or changed by reading. Cobbett, for example, was 'propelled headlong into republicanism and democracy' by reading Paine's *Rights of Man* in 1791.[21] H. M. Swanwick became a champion of women's rights from reading Shelley and Mill.[22] Whether circulating libraries caused an increase in seduction, adultery, and suicide cannot be statistically established, but many people at the time saw a connection. Also hard to establish is how far an accumulation of reading experiences shaped personal character, but contemporaries saw innumerable examples. As was said of Anna Aikin, she 'read and re-read the books to which she had access with that concentrated attention which assimilated their contents with the mind; they shaped her principles of action, and tinctured for ever the warp and woof of thoughts and feelings.'[23] 'Ought I to be very much pleased with *Marmion*?', asks Jane Austen. 'As yet I am not. – James reads it aloud in the Eveng – the short Eveng – beginning about 10, & broken by supper.'[24] 'The description of Love almost makes *me* in love', writes Lady Melbourne in 1813 on reading Byron's *Giaour*. 'Certainly he excels in the language of Passion, whilst the power of delineating inanimate nature appears more copiously bestowed on other poets.'[25] 'Do not be angry with me for beginning another letter to you', Austen writes to her sister Cassandra in March 1814. 'I have read The Corsair, mended my petticoat, & have nothing else to do.'[26] 'Did you ever read anything so exquisite as the new Canto of Childe Harold', writes Ferrier in 1816 when the third canto was published. 'It is enough to make a woman fly into the arms of a *tiger*.'[27] Trollope recalled in his autobiography that his mother had 'raved' about Byron and read Scott avidly, and that he himself, as a young man, had read Shakespeare 'out of a bicolumned edition.'[28] John Nicol, later one of the first professors of English literature, recalled how when he was a boy his father read aloud to the family from Scott's *The Lady of the Lake* and Byron's *The Island*. His mother, he also remembered, read aloud from Wordsworth. 'I remember my delight on hearing the *Blind Highland Boy*, and how I almost tired her

[20] See also chapter 22.
[21] Ian Dyck, *William Cobbett and Rural Popular Culture* (Cambridge 1992) 17.
[22] Noted by Kate Flint, *The Woman Reader 1837–1914* (Oxford 1993) 245.
[23] Williams 283.   [24] Austen, *Letters* 131.
[25] Mabell, Countess of Airlie, ed., *In Whig Society, 1775–1818* (1921) 161.
[26] Austen, *Letters*, 257.
[27] *Memoir and correspondence of Susan Ferrier, 1782–1854*, edited by J. A. Doyle, *et al.* (1898) 131.
[28] *Anthony Trollope, An Autobiography* (1883, edited by John Sutherland 1999) 14, 6.

by my constant requests to hear it read over . . . Moore's *Lalla Rookh* was to me perfect.'[29]

We have records of collective reading through circulating libraries and book clubs. Benjamin Newton, a Yorkshire clergyman, who belonged to both the Bedale Book Society and the Ripon Book Society, records an impressive range of reading in religion, history, current affairs, art, science, Scott and Byron, and travel.[30] A good deal is recorded about the reading of Austen, who belonged both to circulating libraries and to book clubs.[31] There are occasional references to authors whose works circulated only among tiny constituencies. Henry Crabb Robinson, for example, an indefatigable collector and recorder of literary gossip, noted a conversation which took place during a walk with Wordsworth on 24 May 1812, a couple of months after *Childe Harold* had made Byron instantly famous. 'Rose late; at half past ten joined Wordsworth in Oxford Road, and we then got into the fields and walked to Hampstead. We talked of Lord Byron. Of his moral qualities we think the same. He adds that there is insanity in Byron's family, and he believes Lord Byron to be somewhat cracked. I read Wordsworth some of Blake's poems. He was pleased with some of them, and considered Blake as having the elements of poetry a thousand times more than either Byron or Scott.'[32] There are many references too to the reading of works which seldom appear in literary history. In her letters, the poet Lucy Aikin writes enthusiastically about Milman's *Fazio*, 'brilliant with poetry . . . a rising star, destined to blaze far and wide'. She is excited at being able to propose James Montgomery's new poem for her book club.[33] 'I should be chargeable with gross ingratitude', wrote Benjamin Gregory about his early days in Yorkshire in the 1820s, 'if I could forget the chief agents of the evoking of my sensibilities and faculties . . . Robert Bloomfield . . . Bernard Barton, the delicate subtle thoughtfulness of Wiffen, Whittier, William and Mary Howitt . . . the tender humanising hallowing strains of Mrs Hemans . . . Heber, Milman, Bowring, Montgomery.'[34]

The old-canon authors, too, are well represented in the anecdotal record. Leigh Hunt writes about his schooldays at the beginning of the century, when Cooke's *British Poets* first became available. 'I had got an odd volume

[29] William A. Knight, *Memoir of John Nichol* (Glasgow 1896) 42.

[30] *The Diary of Benjamin Newton, Rector of Wath, 1816–1818*, edited by C. P. Ferdall and E. A. Crutchley Cambridge (1933).

[31] See Margaret Anne Doody, 'Jane Austen's Reading' in J. David Gray, ed., *The Jane Austen Handbook* (1986). Her remarks on book clubs are quoted in appendix 10, 669.

[32] Quoted by Andrew Rutherford, *Byron, The Critical Heritage* (1970) 37.

[33] *Memoirs, Miscellanies and Letters of the late Lucy Aikin*, edited by P. H. Le Breton (1864) 104, 150.

[34] Gregory contains an account of the books he read during childhood and youth.

of Spenser; and I fell passionately in love with Collins and Gray.'[35] Anne Lister seeks consolation in Young's *Night Thoughts*.[36] And we can pile up examples which describe the reading of other types of texts, old and new. During the childhood of Letitia Landon, for example, her brother recollected that 'he and his sister read together not less than a hundred and fifty volumes of Cooke's *Poets and Novelists*, besides other books of the same sort, a proof of negligent oversight in the governess, and of habitual deceptiveness in the pupil.'[37]

The micro evidence is consistent with what the study has concluded about print runs, prices, access, and reading constituencies. But we can also see the limitations of the anecdotal approach. They are so plentiful that, without the corrective of the quantified macro evidence, we might easily have fallen into the false assumption that they make a representative sample. Indeed, without the macro evidence, the piling up of printed reviews and anecdotes in diaries can given a misleading picture, as has happened, for example, in the case of Wollstonecraft's *Vindication of the Rights of Woman* and Mary Shelley's *Frankenstein*.[38] In other respects too, as a means of assessing reception, diffusion, impact, and influence, records of individual acts of reading are less useful than they may at first appear. Once a mental experience has been put into a text, even as simple a text as a note in a diary, it requires historical and critical interpretation. Why were certain reactions to reading recorded and not others? Who were the implied readers for these texts and what did the writer hope to achieve? What horizons of expectations did the authors bring to their reading and writing?[39] The words themselves need to be historicised. In describing the effects of their reading, the readers describe, recommend, and condemn. The words they use, 'affecting', 'poetic', 'sublime', 'passionate', 'truthful', 'incorrect', 'tedious', 'pathetic', are amongst the most imprecise and most fluid in the language. 'Moral' has narrowed to mean ethical. 'Elegant', Hazlitt noticed, had been a sincere compliment when applied to the works of Rogers before 1800, but by the time he wrote in 1819 the word was turning into a sneer. As used in advertisements for the old-canon classics, 'elegant' meant safe for women.[40] 'Powerful' was used to describe literature for the first time by Wordsworth in 1798, but by the early 1820s it was 'a regular slang term in London conversation', overused by Hazlitt.[41] 'Talented' was

---

[35] *Autobiography of Leigh Hunt*, edited by Roger Ingpen (1903) i, 86.
[36] Lister 349.   [37] Williams 496.   [38] See chapters 14 and 18.
[39] *Memoirs, Miscellanies . . . Lucy Aikin* 66.
[40] 'On Criticism' in *Table Talk* (1824). For the use of 'elegant' to describe various old-canon editions in series see appendix 6.
[41] *London Magazine*, March 1823.

another innovation. Traditionalists such as Coleridge hated these coinages, although he made many of his own.[42] But even if we retrieve a better understanding of the meanings of the terms commonly used, the problem of how to assess actual reception is only partly lessened. Since every act of reading is unique, we cannot assume a consistency between the changes in states of mind which occur, say, when a reader is young or when he or she is older. And the problem of assessing the representative equality of the micro evidence remains.

At this point we may be near the end of the progression of the inquiry which has taken us from the writing of texts through the materiality of print to acts of reading. Should we simply leave matters here, and rely on more impressionistic historical approaches to link the recovered reading patterns with perceived wider outcomes observed later, as the study has already done in some cases?[43] Or are there other ways by which we can increase our understanding of the processes at work. As inheritors of the romantic notion of seeing works of literature as autonomous, and of hermeneutic traditions of drawing out precise meanings from critical reading of texts, we may be at risk of expecting more than can ever reasonably be demanded. Given the infinitude of interrelated transactions which occurs in any cultural diffusion, it may be that all we can reasonably hope for is to recover the main patterns. Of one thing we can be certain. We cannot recover the effects on readers by ever more careful study of the texts being read, that is attempting to find the outputs of the system from the inputs. Looser models of reading, reception, and dissemination can not only avoid circularity, but may produce a more truthful understanding of what happened.

The romantic writers themselves offer models of reading which involve readers as well as writers. Scott, for example, compared the reading of a long romantic poem to the experience of a passenger going on a journey in a coach. When the passengers look out of the window they all see the same main features, the mountains, the fields, the towns, but they see them at different angles and with individual expectations. The carriage from which they see the view is moving all the time, and, with it their mental states.[44] The effect of the scenery is different if it is winter or summer, morning or evening, if the passengers are hungry or tired or have had a glass of wine, if the company is congenial or boring. Some of the time the passengers absorb the regarded scenery in silence; sometimes they talk about it, pointing out

---

[42] *Memories, Miscellanies . . . Lucy Aikin* 66.   [43] Notably in chapter 16.
[44] I have forgotten in which of his many works Scott offers the carriage metaphor of reading.

this or that feature, willing to be persuaded to new opinions, and always liable to be interrupted or side-tracked into new thoughts. Scott's reception model does not displace the 'implied reader' nor the 'critical reader', and accepts, indeed requires, 'interpretative communities' who share common 'horizons of expectations' from within the coach. Scott's model does grant autonomy to readers.

For dissemination too, as for reception, one way of loosening the grip of input-based studies may be to return to models offered by the romantics themselves. The favourite metaphor of the mind in the romantic period was that of the Aeolian harp or Aeolian lyre, or rather the music made by the lyre, references to which whistle through the works of every poet of the period. Left in an open window, the harp played its music as the breezes touched its strings. Like mental states, Aeolian harp music consists of an unending succession of unique conjunctures, irreversible, irrecoverable, and whose patterns are not immediately discernible. In Shelley's *Ode to the West Wind*, the poet who has made his intervention, longs to become an Aeolian lyre.

> Make me thy lyre, even as the forest is:
> What if my leaves are falling like its own?
> The tumult of thy mighty harmonies
>
> Will take from both a deep autumnal tone,
> Sweet though in sadness. Be Thou, Spirit fierce,
> My spirit! Be thou me, impetuous one!

The poet imagines the reception and dissemination of his words in a rush of metaphors:

> Drive my dead thoughts over the universe,
> Like wither'd leaves, to quicken a new birth;
> And, by the incantation of this verse,
>
> Scatter, as from an unextinguish'd hearth
> Ashes and sparks, my words among mankind!
> Be through my lips to unawaken'd earth
>
> The trumpet of a prophecy! O Wind,
> If Winter comes, can Spring be far behind!

The images jostle together – the minds of readers receiving and reacting to the unique winds of experiences, including their experiences of reading; the new seeds he has scattered combining with the dead leaves – almost literally the paper leaves of his books – to make a new birth, the unextinguished hearth scattering ashes and sparks which start new fires here and there in unpredictable places. Like Scott's reception model, Shelley's dissemination models acknowledge that the spread of ideas is not uniform, but scattered, lagged, and unpredictable, sometimes even apparently random, and they acknowledge the autonomy of readers within the limitations of their circumstances and their contexts. By allowing for the associations of the thoughts which occur in reading and in conversation, they loosen the grip of strong biographical narratives of the unified self.[45]

There is one other resource, already used from time to time in this study.[46] The imaginative writers of the romantic period and later were much interested in the effects of reading. They were nearer in time than we are to the events they wrote about, had better opportunities to observe reading and its effects, and in many cases they were interested in the wider changes which they perceived as occurring. Furthermore, in some respects, the representations of reading which imaginative writers offer are rhetorically different from those in documentary records. The readers who wrote of their reading experiences in letters, diaries, etc., were composing private texts, often in manuscript, to be read by readers whom they knew personally, including themselves. In a sense all such texts can be regarded as forms of 'scribal publication'.[47] The imaginative writers, and especially the novelists, were writing public texts, to be diffused in print, to be read by a wide constituency of readers unknown to them personally and about whose horizons of expectations they only knew from their own experience. The rhetorical stance of the imaginative writer in relation to the implied or intended reader was different from that of a private writer, and a different range of literary skills was needed if the texts were to achieve their effects. The fictional characters whom the novelists invented and depicted may appear to be unique, but they are also usually representative in some way, sometimes of types, sometimes of classes of society, of movements, of feelings, opinions, of everything dynamic in the culture, often exaggerated. Indeed if the characters in a fiction were not, in some way, recognisable as believable representations, then the rhetoric of the fiction failed. The characters who are described as readers of books are, therefore, to an extent, constructed according to criteria which we can understand and, if necessary offset, including the horizons of expectations operating at the time. Many are not only shaped by their reading but also defined by it.

---

[45] For some discussion of these issues see the essays in Peter France and William St Clair, eds., *Mapping Lives, The Uses of Biography* (Oxford 2002).
[46] For example in describing the effects of romance in chapter 12.
[47] Discussed in chapter 3.

Figure 21. 'Sketches from a Fashionable Conversazione'. 'Sentimental, Narcissical, Byronical, Ironical'. From a cartoon by 'Shortshanks' (1828).

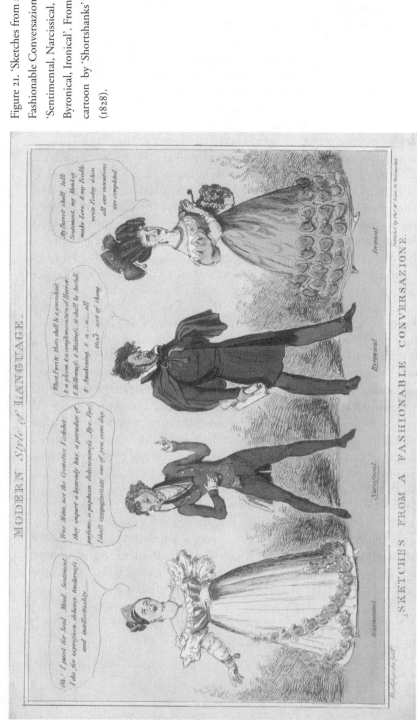

Julia Dawkins, a character in Helen Brunton's novel *Self Control*, personifies the frivolity that novel reading might induce, for 'having no character of her own, this young lady was always as nearly as she was able, the heroine whom the last read novel inclined her to personate. When *Camilla* was the model for the day she became insufferably rattling, infantile, and thoughtless.'[48] Mr Graham, in Anne Brontë's *The Tenant of Wildfell Hall* who never went anywhere, outside or in, without 'a pocket edition of some classic author in his hand', is a typical gentlemen who maintained the values which the reading of the old canon represented.[49] Lord Erpingham, a man of the 1830s invented by Bulwer Lytton, 'was generally considered a sensible man. He had read Blackstone, Montesquieu, Cowper's Poems, and *The Rambler*, and was always heard with great attention in the House of Lords.'[50] Colonel Newcome, the Victorian Indian army officer in Thackeray's *The Newcomes*, when overseas, read Boswell's *Johnson*, Caesar, Tacitus, *The Spectator*, *Don Quixote*, and *Sir Charles Grandison*. 'I read these, sir', he explains, 'because I like to be in the company of gentlemen.'[51] Squire Thorne in Trollope's *Barchester Towers*, who liked nothing later than *The Idler*, *The Spectator*, *The Tatler*, *The Guardian*, and *The Rambler*, offers a glimpse of another reader who, by his reading, kept his states of mind well behind the times. His sister was familiar with names as late as Dryden, but regarded the works of Spenser as the purest poetry her country had ever produced.[52] Gertrude, in Ferrier's *Inheritance*, was an inert product of Blair's sermons, women's conduct books, and poetry anthologies, 'religious – what mind of any excellence is not? but hers was the religion of poetry – of taste – of feeling – of impulse – of any thing but Christianity'.[53]

Mr Martin, in Austen's *Emma*, is also a man of the older culture, which in this case also marks his lesser social status, but one willing to extend his reading. He:

. . . has read a great deal – but not what you would think anything of. He reads the Agricultural Reports and some other books, that lay on the window seats – but he reads all *them* to himself. But sometimes of an evening, before we went to cards, he would read something aloud out of the *Elegant Extracts* – very entertaining. And I know he has read the *Vicar of Wakefield*.[54]

---

[48] Quoted by Cruse, *Englishman* 35.
[49] Anne Brontë, *The Tenant of Wildfell Hall*, edited by Herbert Rosengarten (Oxford 1992) 67.
[50] In Bulwer Lytton's *Godolphin*, quoted by Cruse, *Englishman* 14.
[51] Quoted by Cruse, *Victorians* 213.   [52] Quoted by Cruse, *Victorians* 207.
[53] (Susan Ferrier) *Inheritance* (1824) ii, 8.
[54] *The Novels of Jane Austen*, *Emma*, edited by R. W. Chapman (1923) iv, 29. For the pervasiveness of *Elegant Extracts* see chapter 6 and appendix 6.

Sir Edward Denham in Austen's *Sanditon*, liked the correctness that was
debated in the Bowles controversy at its most commonplace and conventional. He gives us a glimpse of conventional mainstream horizons of
expectations in practice.

He began, in a tone of great Taste & Feeling, to talk of the Sea & the Sea shore – &
ran with Energy through all the usual Phrases employed in praise of their Sublimity,
& descriptive of the *undescribable* Emotions they excite in the Mind of Sensibility. –
The terrific Grandeur of the Ocean in a Storm, its glassy surface in a calm, it's
Gulls & its Samphire, & the deep fathoms of it's Abysses, it's quick vicissitudes,
its direful Deceptions, its Mariners tempting it in Sunshine & overwhelmed by
the sudden Tempest, All were eagerly & fluently touched; – rather commonplace
perhaps – but doing very well from the Lips of a handsome Sir Edward, – and she
could not but think him a Man of Feeling – till he began to stagger her by the
number of his Quotations, & the bewilderment of some of his sentences. – 'Do
you remember, said he, Scott's beautiful Lines on the Sea? – Oh! what a description
they convey! – They are never out of my Thoughts when I walk here. – That Man
who can read them unmoved must have the nerves of an Assassin! – Heaven defend
me from meeting such a Man un-armed.'[55]

'Shakespeare,' declares Mr Lyndsay in Susan Ferrier's *Inheritance*, mixing
romanticism with Dr Bowdler, is

indeed a poet of Nature's own creating; but the dross of his compositions is daily
draining off in improved editions . . . The profane and licentious works of Lord
B[yron] . . . while all that is fine in his words will be culled by the lovers of virtue,
as the bee gathers honey . . . so shall it be with Burns – so shall it be with Moore.[56]

Miss Douglas, a character in the same novel, on the other hand, 'prefers
the lofty strains of the mighty Minstrel of the Mountains to the more pol-
ished periods of the Poet of the Transatlantic Plain' (i.e. Scott to Campbell).
    When Lord Cumnor in Elizabeth Gaskell's *Wives and Daughters* quotes
the famous phrase '[butchered] to make a Roman holiday', his wife, sensing
looming incorrectness, immediately interjects that 'I'm surprised at your
lordship's quoting Byron, – he was a very immoral poet.'[57] If we think
we know Fanny Price in *Mansfield Park*, we believe we know the kind of
reader who responded to Crabbe. 'Are you an admirer of Crabbe's Tales?'
Miss Graves is asked in Susan Ferrier's *Marriage*. 'I don't think ever I tasted
them – Indeed I don't think our crabs have tales', a neat illustration of the
anarchy of actual reception.[58]

---

[55] Jane Austen, *Sanditon* (1817).   [56] (Ferrier) *Inheritance* ii, 114.
[57] Elizabeth Gaskell, *Wives and Daughters*, edited by Angus Easson (1987) 143.
[58] (Susan Ferrier) *Marriage* (Edinburgh 1818) iii, ch. 18.

Mr Benwick in Austen's *Persuasion* had his mind changed by his reading of the most famous and most widely read romantic poets.

For, though shy, he did not seem reserved; it had rather the appearance of feelings glad to burst their usual restraints; and having talked of poetry, the richness of the present age, and gone through a brief comparison of opinion as to the first-rate poets, trying to ascertain whether *Marmion* or *The Lady of the Lake* were to be preferred, and how ranked the *Giaour* and *The Bride of Abydos*; and moreover, how the *Giaour* was to be pronounced, he shewed himself so intimately acquainted with all the tenderest songs of the one poet, and all the impassioned descriptions of hopeless agony of the other; he repeated, with such tremulous feeling, the various lines which imaged a broken heart, or a mind destroyed by wretchedness, and looked so entirely as if he meant to be understood, that she ventured to hope he did not always read only poetry; and to say, that she thought it was the misfortune of poetry, to be seldom safely enjoyed by those who enjoyed it completely; and that the strong feelings which alone could estimate it truly, were the very feelings which ought to taste it but sparingly.[59]

In *Adam Bede*, which is set in 1799, there is a conversation about a book that has recently arrived in a parcel from London. 'I know you are fond of queer wizard like stories. It's a volume of poems, *Lyrical Ballads*. Most of them seem to be twaddling stuff, but the first is in a different style *The Ancient Mariner*.'[60] Given the small numbers of copies of *Lyrical Ballads* available to be read at the time implied, the story is historically unbelievable, but the myth may have been convincing to Eliot's late-Victorian readership. Again, when in *Daniel Deronda* Eliot mentions the precocious poet 'who wrote *Queen Mab* at nineteen', there was no need, by 1876, to give his name.[61]

Mrs Transome, in Eliot's *Felix Holt*, had been thought:

wonderfully clever and accomplished, and had been rather ambitious of intellectual superiority – had secretly picked out for private reading the lighter parts of dangerous French authors – and in company had been able to talk of Mr Burke's style, or of Chateaubriand's eloquence – had laughed at the *Lyrical Ballads* and admired Mr Southey's *Thalaba*.[62]

In the original version, which would have been historically more likely, Eliot wrote that Mrs Transome had compared 'the poetical merits of Mr Southey and Mr Walter Scott'.

[59] *The Novels of Jane Austen, Persuasion* v, 100.
[60] George Eliot, *Adam Bede*, edited by Valentine Cunningham (1996) 66.
[61] George Eliot, *Daniel Deronda*, edited by Graham Handley (1984) 152.
[62] George Eliot, *Felix Holt, the Radical*, edited by Fred C. Thomson (1980) 27.

In *Revolution in Tanner's Lane*, Mark Rutherford imagines a young clerk, who is later to become a great reformer, stuck to his desk in a dreary office, carried to the exotic east on the viewless wings of Byron's poesy.

Zachariah found in the *Corsair* exactly what answered to his own inmost self, down to its every depths. The lofty style, the scorn of what is mean and base, the courage, – root of all virtue – that dares and evermore dares in the very last extremity, the love of the illimitable, of freedom, and the cadences like the fall of waves on a sea-shore were attractive to him beyond measure.[63]

For another constituency, Rutherford gives a description of 'Cowfold', a country town fifty miles from London in the 1840s. The town is full of competing churches and chapels, peopled by brutish men and women. Only the local ironmonger and his family are able to escape from the grinding gloom by reading Byron and Scott, and they are under suspicion for reading anything at all.[64]

There are many ladies in Victorian fiction who, like Lady Eustace in *The Eustace Diamonds*, wished that English men were more like Corsairs. And there were numerous gentlemen who wished that English women were more like the black-eyed peris of *Lalla Rookh*. 'Know that I doat on Corsairs', declares Miss Ingram when she flirtatiously asks Rochester to sing an adaptation of Byron, as Jane Eyre sits silently in another corner of the room.[65] In *Middlemarch*, the worthy Mr Lydgate had learned Scott's poems by heart. Rosie, who preferred excitement, and in whose conception of romance 'it was not necessary to imagine much about the inward life of a hero', also knew much poetry by heart – her favourite was *Lalla Rookh*.[66]

When the shy Mr Rivers calls on the lonely Jane Eyre in an imagined slightly telescoped time about 1810 when the romantic verse narratives of Scott and Byron were both new, he brings a book 'for evening solace'.

And he laid on the table a new publication – a poem: one of those genuine productions so often vouchsafed to the fortunate public of those days – the golden age of modern literature.

The book is *Marmion*, and Jane 'glances eagerly at the bright pages'.[67] For Jane Eyre, it is implied, the white hot-pressed paper helped to confirm her imagination in the world of romance which was to determine her life.

---

[63] Quoted by Cruse, *Englishman* 161.   [64] Cruse, *Victorians* 75.

[65] Charlotte Brontë, *Jane Eyre*, edited by Jane Jack and Margaret Smith (Oxford 1969) 225.

[66] George Eliot, *Middlemarch*, edited by David Carroll (Oxford 1986) 265, 163. For other references to the reading which defines Lydgate see 140.

[67] Charlotte Brontë, *Jane Eyre* 473.

In the key incident in Anne Brontë's *Tenant of Wildfell Hall*, set in 1828, Gilbert Markham has made frequent visits to Mrs Graham at the hall. They have talked about painting, poetry, and music, theology, geology, and philosophy – all of them subjects of a typical book club from which women were usually excluded. They have lent one another books and discussed the poetry of Scott. But when Markham gives her a copy of 'an elegant and portable edition of *Marmion*' which he has ordered from London:

A momentary flush suffused her face . . . She gravely examined the volume on both sides; then silently turned over the leaves, knitting her brows the while in silent cogitation; then closed the book, and turning to me, quietly asked the price of it. – I felt the hot blood rush to my face. 'I'm sorry to offend you, Mr. Markham', said she 'but unless I pay for the book, I cannot take it.' And she laid it on the table.[68]

Margaret's father in *North and South*, a clergyman, shows his essentially liberal attitudes by delivering lectures to working people 'at a neighbouring Lycaeum' – although, we note, the subject he chooses, 'ecclesiastical architecture', is of more interest to him than to his audience.[69] Arthur Pendennis, another supporter of book-club reading, enjoys meeting with:

Mr Simcoe, the opposition preacher, and with the two partners of the cloth factory at Chatteris, and with the Independent preacher there, all of whom he met at the Clavering Athenaeum which the Liberal party had set up in accordance with the advanced spirit of the age, and perhaps in opposition to the aristocratic old reading room, into which the 'Edinburgh Review' had once scarcely got an admission, and where no tradesmen were allowed an entrance.[70]

There is scarcely a constituency of readers of whom fictional examples cannot be found. Uncle Toby in Sterne's *Tristram Shandy* recalls his chapbook reading of the 1720s, but he does not get the names quite right:

When *Guy, Earl of Warwick*, and *Parismus* and *Parismenus*, and *Valentine and Orson*, and *The Seven Champions of England* were handed around the school, – were they not all purchased with my own pocket money?[71]

Wordsworth's Wanderer remembered the easy mingling of the traditions of the official and illegitimate supernaturals which marked the mentalities of the rural poor:

[68] Anne Brontë, *The Tenant of Wildfell Hall* 71.
[69] Elizabeth Gaskell, *North and South*, edited by Esther Alice Chadwick (1914) 135.
[70] *The Works of W. M. Thackeray, The History of Pendennis* (1871) ii, 641.
[71] Quoted by Harvey Darton, *Children's Books in England* (Cambridge 1932) 81.

> A straggling volume, torn and incomplete,
> That left half told the preternatural tale,
> Romance of giants, chronicle of fiends,
> Profuse in garniture of wooden cuts
> Strange and uncouth; dire faces, figures dire,
> Sharp-kneed, sharp-elbowed, and lean ankled to,
> with long and ghostly shanks.[72]

Victorian novelists picked up that the texts of the radical canon were read by men and women from outside the normal reading constituencies. Dickens has a waiter 'obsessed by Shelley' who would not have been able to afford to read him except in a cheap pirated edition. The copy of *Queen Mab* which Lady Eustace in Trollope's *The Eustace Diamonds* reads by the sea in Scotland in order to maximise its sublimity is also 'a little volume', and she carries it hidden in her pocket. 'She had often talked of it and perhaps thought she had read it.' But she could quote passages by heart.

Neither Dickens nor Thackeray liked the social upstart attitudes which the reading of *Don Juan* had encouraged, but that does not lessen the value of their writings for our understanding of the dynamic processes at work. Thackeray's Waggle, for example, is:

of the middle classes . . . He has been abroad where he gives you to understand that his success among the German countesses and Italian princesses, whom he met at the *tables-d'hôte*, was perfectly terrific . . . He passes his mornings in a fine dressing gown, burning pastilles, and reading 'Don Juan' and French novels. . . . He has twopenny-halfpenny French prints of women with languishing eyes, dressed in dominoes – guitars, gondolas and so forth – and tells you stories about them . . . His friend was writing a continuation of *Don Juan*, _ 'superior to Byron, Sir, superior to Byron.'[73]

Another Thackeray character, Pogson, 'is a city man, who travels in drugs for a couple of the best London houses, blows the flute, has an album, drives his own gig, and is considered, both on the road and in the metropolis, a remarkably nice, intelligent, thriving young man. Pogson's only fault is too great an attachment to the fair: – 'the sex', as he says often, 'will be his ruin': the fact is, that Pog never travels without a 'Don Juan' under his driving-cushion. Pogson tries to seduce a *baronne*, wonders if she is connected with 'The author of Don Juan, Child 'Arold, and Cain, a Mystery'. He only did so 'because he was given to understand by Lord Byron's *Don Juan* that making love was a very correct healthy thing'.[74]

[72] *The Excursion*, i, lines 177ff.
[73] *The Works of W. M. Thackeray, The Book of Snobs* (1872) ix, 141.   [74] *Ibid.* vii, 11.

Mr Septimus Hicks, in Dickens's *Sketches By Boz*, another *Don Juan* reader who leaves his wife, is:

... a tallish, white-faced young man, with spectacles, and a black ribbon round his neck instead of a neckerchief – a most interesting person; a poetical walker of the hospitals; [medical student] and a 'very talented young man'. He was fond of 'lugging' into conversation all sorts of quotations from *Don Juan* ... He was quite sure of his author, because he had never read any other.[75]

The works of the Victorian women novelists, such as Mary Elizabeth Braddon, Charlotte Yonge, and Ouida, abound with dashing young men who adored *Don Juan* and women who liked them better for it, confirming that the diffusion of that book was not only widespread but long lasting.[76] 'Who do you think is the greatest poet?' Stephen Daedalus is asked in *Portrait of The Artist as a Young Man*, recalling his time at school in Ireland at the end of the century. 'Byron of course'. His poetically correct schoolmates all burst out laughing. 'Byron the greatest poet! He's only a poet for uneducated people.' Stephen gets beaten up.[77]

The young Marie Corelli who provocatively quoted *Don Juan* to her governess believed that by shocking her in this way she was among the advance guard of a coming cultural change in the role of women.[78] She was a late-nineteenth-century suffragist. Even a few words can sometimes speak volumes. 'The house seemed to possess every requisite for a "genteel" family, as auctioneers advertise', wrote Surtees in *Hillingdon Hall* half a century earlier, when introducing and defining a woman who scarcely says a word during the whole book.

Mrs Jobson was basking in an arbour on the west side, in an elegant morning dishabille – white muslim with lavender-coloured ribbons – reading a pocket edition of *Don Juan*.[79]

In a crucial incident in George Eliot's *Felix Holt*, a novel set in 1831, published 1866, Felix accidentally knocks over Esther's work basket. Among the things which fall out is a book.

... a duodecimo volume which fell close to him between the table and the fender ...
   'Byron's Poems' he said, in a tone of disgust ... 'The Dream' – 'He'd better have been asleep and snoring. What! do you stuff your memory with Byron, Miss Lyon?'

[75] Charles Dickens, *Sketches by Boz* edited by Thea Holme (Oxford 1957) 278.
[76] Cruse, *Victorians* 175.   [77] James Joyce, *Portrait of the Artist as a Young Man* (1916) 91.
[78] Vyver, *Memoirs of Marie Corelli* 19.   [79] R. S. Surtees, *Hillingdon Hall* (1844) chapter 12.

Felix on his side, was led at last to look straight at Esther, but it was with a strong denunciatory and pedagogic intention. Of course he saw more clearly than ever that she was a fine lady.

She reddened, drew up her long neck, and said as she retreated to her chair again –

'I have a great admiration for Byron.'[80]

What a rich cargo of meanings is carried by the word 'duodecimo'. Esther is reading Byron in a pirated edition. She is caught in an action of defiance and of concealment, possibly of immorality. For if Esther is buying Byron, what else may she have bought and read? *Queen Mab?* Tom Paine? Pornography? Advice on birth control? When we have reconstructed the production, access, sales, and readerships of the materiality of books, when we have identified reading constituencies, collected the historical evidence of recorded individual reading, constructed horizons of expectations, when we have drawn all we can from the macro and the micro empirical approaches, but not till then, our best resource for understanding the impact of the reading of the literature of the romantic period may be literature itself.

---

[80] George Eliot, *Felix Holt, the Radical* 61.

CHAPTER 21

The romantic poets in the Victorian age

It would overextend the scope of the inquiry to try to trace the effects of all of the writings of the romantic period into the Victorian age. I propose however briefly to consider one group of texts, the works of the romantic poets and novelists. The Victorian age was when these authors reached their largest readerships, when they were most actively admired, promoted, and made available across the nation, and when we would expect the effects of reading to have worked through the system and for any resulting outcomes in terms of mentalities to have become most visible.

When Queen Victoria came to the British throne in 1837, it was already clear that an unusual period in the history of English literature was at an end. Scott, Byron, Coleridge, Crabbe, Hemans, Keats, and Shelley were dead. Campbell, Rogers, Southey, and Wordsworth had largely stopped writing. The only new books written in verse which the main London publishers would consider were those financed by authors 'on commission', fillers to keep the manufacturing side of the book industry in work.[1] Murray, whose fortune had been built on publishing Scott and Byron, declined even to read offered manuscripts, and Longman, who had published Bloomfield, Campbell, James Montgomery, Moore, Southey, and Wordsworth, withdrew from literary publishing.[2] There had, as one commentator noted, been too many poor imitations of the violent *Marmion* and the brooding *Childe Harold*, too many sonnets to the moon, elegies on a dead sparrow, odes to a drowning kitten, stanzas to pathetic old women in red cloaks, effusions on a withered rose, and thoughts on storms at sea.[3] During the 1830s new verse had become a ladies' genre, confined within the silk covers of the annuals. Poetry seemed suddenly to have lost its long primacy as the most highly regarded literary genre and as the form most favoured by

---

[1] Examples of commercial failure are noted by (James Grant's) *The Great Metropolis Second Series* (1837).
[2] See Merriam v; and Smiles, ii, 374.
[3] A.S. Hunter, *Miscellanies, Designed Chiefly for the Benefit of Female Readers* (1810).

readers. New writers, sensing the new status of the novel brought about by the success of the Waverley novels, now preferred to write long prose fiction, often serialised in the booming periodical press.

The long romantic historical verse narrative was not dead. Barham's *Ingoldsby Legends*, which first appeared in 1840, and Macaulay's *Lays of Ancient Rome* (1842), each sold far more copies than Byron and Scott had done over a comparable period, and Tennyson was soon to do the same.[4] Longfellow was the bestselling author of verse in the Victorian period in Britain.[5] And, of course, the Victorians did not only read Victorian literature. The verse works of Scott, Byron, Moore, Wordsworth, Coleridge, and others continued to be reprinted for mainstream reading.[6] If the 1830s marks a change in the nature of English literature when arranged as a parade of authors, as far as readers were concerned, the change was far less noticeable.

The reputation of the eight 'living poets' of the romantic period which had been established around 1812, remained firm right through the century.[7] The Victorian critics promoted the reputation of Wordsworth, mainly for his reassertion of natural religion.[8] They sharply downgraded Byron, most of them wishing that *Don Juan* had never been written.[9] Critics were ambiguous towards Shelley, adoring his poetic power, but shut their ears to his main message. On the eve of the First World War, however, the grand canonising series, *The Oxford Standard Poets*, included Byron, Campbell, Coleridge, Hemans, Keats, Moore, Scott, Shelley, Southey, and Wordsworth, not far different from the canon of reputation constructed a hundred years earlier.

The determining structures within which reprints were produced in Victorian times differed from those which had existed as recently as the 1820s. As far as intellectual property is concerned, with the closing of the brief copyright window in 1842, the period of time before a printed text came out of private ownership, that had been around one generation in the romantic period, was now equivalent to two or three generations. The other main change was in the technology of book manufacturing. By mid century stereotyping was the normal means of manufacturing for all texts for which a continuing demand was expected after the printing of a first small high-priced edition made from moveable type. Copper engraving gave way to steel engraving which produced more durable plates from which many more impressions could be taken, paper manufacture was mechanised,

---

[4] Altick 387, gives some production figures.
[5] Some statistics are given in appendix 13.   [6] Some figures shown in appendix 9.
[7] For the canon of reputation established around 1812 see chapter 12.
[8] See Stephen Gill, *Wordsworth and the Victorians* (1998).   [9] See chapter 16.

pressing was powered by steam machinery, and books were now sold in ready-made bindings. The taxes on knowledge were abolished or reduced. Without the fall in prices made possible by these falls in manufacturing and selling costs, it is hard to see how the growth of reading which began in the late eighteenth century could have been sustained until it reached near universality a hundred years later. But, as after 1774, the fall did not occur across the full range of print. On the contrary, the divergence between the privately owned monopoly sector and the public competitive sector continued to widen. The ratio of the minimum price of buying a newly published novel compared with that of buying an out-of-copyright novel of comparable length, which had been about ten to one in the romantic period, widened to about sixty to one in the 1880s.

Some of the first publishers to use stereotypes, following the tradition of moveable type, made no overt distinction between capital and current costs, and used the new technology to make large initial print runs, to be followed by a succession of reimpressions of more modest length, some tiny.[10] To judge from surviving financial accounts, it was probably Routledge in the 1860s who first fully understood that, even more than moveable type, stereotype plates were, in economic terms, fixed capital, or 'plant' as he called them, seeing the direct analogy with other forms of factory production. Routledge realised that, provided continuing sales of a title were likely, he did not have to recoup all his capital costs from the first edition, but could amortise them over a number of impressions. By spreading the attributed capital costs of stereotype plates over four expected editions, and in this way bringing his costing and pricing policies more nearly into line with the underlying economics, Routledge proved commercially more successful than his competitors, and pointed the way for others to follow.[11]

When reprinting from moveable type was the only manufacturing option, a publisher who had choice at the margin between publishing a new work or reprinting an old title faced much the same manufacturing costs. For a publisher who owned stereotype plates, on the other hand, provided there was expected demand, the cost of reprinting an old title was lower, and therefore other things being equal, carried relatively less risk. The text-copying technology of the Victorian age therefore changed the balance of economic incentive towards reprinting.[12] Even when a text passed out

---

[10] For example Bentley in the 1830s, and Gall and Inglis who reprinted the romantic poets in the 1850s.
[11] See the example of *Frankenstein* in appendix 5, 515–16.
[12] Compare the example of the long reluctance of French farmers to adopt tractors instead of animal power which can be explained in similar terms, discussed by Paul A. David, 'The Landscape and the Machine', in *Technical Choice, Innovation, and Economic Growth* (1975).

of private ownership, the owners of plates were at an advantage compared with any competitor thinking of entering the market who would have to make a capital investment in type-setting and plates and to set the prices at levels which would recoup this investment. At the same time, owners of plates would be reluctant to invest in newly set editions of the works concerned, that is reluctant to compete with themselves, but would be under continuing economic pressure to maintain operation of their old plant until it deteriorated beyond repair or sales fell to near zero. As in the high monopoly period, the Victorian book regime tended to confine the reading of newly written texts to economic elites; to stratify the book-reading nation into socio-economic constituencies marked by a lengthening degree of obsolescence of the texts to which they had access; to privilege a number of out-of-copyright canonical texts; and to concentrate the reading prescribed to the non-elites, including children, on these texts. Only with the advent of free public libraries in the latter part of the century were the obsoletising tendencies of these structures offset.

By Victorian times, routine novels which in the era of the moveable type period would have had a single edition and been sold out over a year or two, were kept in print for twenty or thirty years. An immense children's literature, some dating back many decades and constantly reprinted, reinforced the cultural expectations and horizons of those entering the reading nation. By 1839, one of the sights of London was a warehouse built like a Greek temple in which the printing firm of Clowes stored half a million stereotype plates on behalf of many publishers. But, with the development soon afterwards of cheap nationwide postal and railway services, the publishing and manufacturing branches of the book industry became geographically separable.[13] Since the texts of their back lists were fixed in metal, and no proof-reading was required, all that the London or Edinburgh publishers needed to have under their personal eyes was a ledger of their intellectual properties and an address book of the firms where the plant was stored. Soon the plates both of texts and illustrations, were being sent to locations outside London, for example, Bungay in Suffolk and Perth in Scotland where storage and reprinting costs were cheap.[14] By the latter part of the century, publishers could arrange to have their reprinting done anywhere in the country, largely in accordance with cost, and could switch whenever they wished.

---

[13] For the importance of cheap postage in encouraging literacy, see Vincent.

[14] For example the plates of the text of Byron were kept by Clay of Bungay but those of Shakespeare by Morrison and Gibb in Edinburgh. The plates of the illustrations were held elsewhere. Frederick Warne and Co. archives.

Longman, the biggest firm of the romantic period, may have with-drawn from new publishing, but he could still enjoy his large portfolio of stereotyped textbooks. By 1831, he was still each year reprinting 5,000 copies of what he called the 374th edition of Mavor's *Spelling*.[15] Murray too, with his stereotypes of Byron turning out low risk reprints for decade after decade, also altered the balance of the business.[16] The two sets of plates of Murray's *Reader*, which belonged to Longman and to Murray, seem to have been almost continuously at work, producing several hundreds of thousands of copies, and helping to entrench the old canon in the reading of the nation's youth during the first half of the nineteenth century.[17]

Stereotype plates could be duplicated, and sold or hired to other publish-ers. Even when a firm failed, the plates could be taken over by a successor, and the text reissued under a new title page.[18] Stereotyping also made it easier to sell texts to publishers in the United States, and to export books to protected markets in India and the Australasian colonies. We see the emer-gence of specific 'colonial' editions, books which, although made from the same plates and textually identical with the metropolitan editions in every particular, were designed to be sold at lower prices. By enabling different prices to be in force in many markets simultaneously, the Victorian method of text copying contributed to a globalisation of printed texts in the English-speaking world, with the two main producing countries agreeing to divide the market between them.

Now that production could be closely and quickly geared to market changes, the whole concept of an 'edition', an invention of the moveable type era, loses much of its meaning. The Warne archives record some books which had initial impressions of 24,000 still being kept going several decades later with re-impressions of different lengths, some as large as 6,000 and others as small as 500.[19] Nor can the listing of a title as being available in the London book trade's official catalogues be taken as evidence of demand. The cumulative production of some of Routledge's *British Poets* was well over 100,000, but others less than 10,000.[20] Some of Warne's *Poets* show the same wide range, *The Poetical Works of Dryden*, for example, although advertised and available to be bought in the same series over

[15] Charles Whittingham and Co. archives. Vincent 68 notes a 322nd edition in 1826.
[16] See the example of the one-volume Byron quoted in chapter 15.
[17] Longman archives i, 99, 221.
[18] As happened when Moxon's stock was taken over by Ward Lock. See appendix 13.
[19] Byron Chandos classics. The reimpressions of the more expensive Warne versions were sometimes as low as 250. Warne archives.
[20] See appendix 13.

the same long timescale, sold only 4,000.[21] With differences as wide as these, it is impossible, and often misleading, to estimate the numbers of copies produced by traditional methods of edition counting, as revealed by differences in title pages.[22] Stereotyping has, therefore, many implications for our ways of estimating the number of copies produced, a problem which lies at the heart of any attempt to write histories of reading. Although, in some ways we know far more about book production in the Victorian period than in the age of exclusively moveable type, estimating the scale of production, and therefore of readerships, except where archives survive, is much more difficult.[23]

The continuous production methods also affected the nature of readerly reception. Since, in order to facilitate continuous production and selling, publishers now routinely omitted all dates from the title page and the paratext, readers of books made from stereotypes had few ways of knowing when the text they were reading had first been written. Indeed, the frequent changing of illustrations, and binding styles, intended to offset readerly resistance to perceived obsolescence, tended to imply that texts were more recent than they were. A late-Victorian purchaser of the Warne edition of '*The Beauties of Shakespeare* selected by the Rev. William Dodd LLD', for example, had no means of knowing from the book itself that the selection had been made over a century before.[24] Across the whole reading nation, the long-run effect of the adoption of stereotyping for text-copying was to slow the movement down the demand curve, and to entrench the obsolete, particularly at the lower tranches of the book market, including school books.

With Scott's Waverley novels, which had, by a stroke of good fortune for the owners, qualified for a longer copyright under the 1842 Act, we see a pricing pattern carefully designed to take maximum advantage both of the changing intellectual property regime and of the Victorian technologies of book manufacturing. In the late 1820s the then owners made stereotypes of the whole series, sharply reduced the prices, issued the titles in weekly parts, and were rewarded with a huge surge in sales.[25] Before 1850 over seven million copies of weekly numbers had been sold, but the demand continued

---

[21] Warne archives. See appendix 5.
[22] For example in the *Cambridge Bibliography of English Literature*.
[23] One promising technique is to try to count the differing impressions by comparing the placing of printers' key signatures and assessing cumulative usage of plates by the degree of wear and tear and the extent of repairs.
[24] A copy in the author's collection has an ownership inscription of 1878.
[25] See 'Walter Scott', appendix 9, 642.

unabated. In 1852, the then owners, having retooled their manufacturing plant, embarked on a long, stepped, move down the demand curve, taking one tranche after another throughout the remaining copyright period. In the 1850s when the price was reduced to 2 shillings, sales approached a quarter of a million; in the early 1860s, when the price was reduced to a shilling, sales reached a million; and when in 1866 the price was taken down to sixpence the total reached two millions within two years. Scott was by that time, by several orders of magnitude, the author whose works had sold the largest number of copies in the English-speaking world. No comprehensive figures are available for the period after 1868, but it is striking that when the copyrights eventually expired in the 1880s, other publishers who entered the market at that time were able to halve the price yet again, selling Waverley novels profitably at three pence, and abridgements even more cheaply.[26]

As far as Scott's verse romances were concerned, since they were published during the brief copyright window and Scott died in 1832, the regime under which they were produced differed from that of the novels. They entered the public domain in the 1830s, when they were immediately reprinted in cheaper editions by many publishers. Already by the mid 1830s the minimum price of *Marmion* and *The Lady of the Lake* had fallen to a shilling, a tenth of the previous minimum price, and it continued to fall.[27] They were sold competitively in single works and in collected editions, illustrated or plain, some lavishly produced, others squashed into double columns, sold in parts, extensively anthologised, and included in school textbooks.

As the reading nation expanded steadily during the Victorian age, Sir Walter was always the first modern author to welcome the new arrivals, men, women, and children, as they crossed the boundary. As John Campbell Shairp, professor of poetry at Oxford University, declared in 1880, Scott's poetry was so familiar to all men from their childhood as to merge into their childhood memories.[28] Nor was Scott regarded as light reading suitable only for children or for the less than fully educated. During the Victorian period, Scott was almost universally regarded by the leading critics of all classes of society as one of the greatest writers the world had ever known, his achievement compared with that of Homer.[29] Leslie Stephen read all thirty-two volumes of the Waverley novels aloud to his large family, and then started again.[30] Ruskin, who had read them so often that he complained that

[26] See Dicks's list in appendix 13, 721.   [27] See the list of falling prices in appendix 5, 516.
[28] J. C. Shairp, *Aspects of Poetry, Lectures Delivered at Oxford* (1881) 377.   [29] *Ibid.*
[30] Hermione Lee, *Virginia Woolf* (1996) 112. See also Noel Annan, *Leslie Stephen* (1984) 332.

he knew them too well, frequently proclaimed that reading the Waverley novels would encourage correct moral judgement, and therefore virtuous conduct, in their readers.[31] One of the griefs of his old age, he wrote, was that he knew Scott by heart.[32] As Ethel May, a character in Charlotte Yonge's *The Trial* (1864) declares to a relative, picking up the way in which the Victorians passed on their values to their children. 'You who taught us to love our Sir Walter next to our *Christian Year* and who gave us half crowns for rehearsing him.'[33]

It is hard to believe that all the millions of Victorian readers who read Scott from childhood till old age were not mentally influenced. Scott is as much an emanation of Victorian culture as of the romantic period, as much of a formative influence on Victorian readers as say, Dickens, Eliot, or Thackeray. Whatever our modern views about his literary merits or readerly appeal, any study of the impact of the literature of the romantic period has to take account of the overwhelming amount of reading of these texts that occurred among so many constituencies over a hundred years. If there are links between texts, books, reading, cultural formation, and mentalities, then Scott is the author to whom, above all, we should look.

As far as the other poets of the romantic period are concerned, we again see the effects of the intellectual property and manufacturing structures. By the late 1850s, virtually all of the writings of the canonical eight which had been published during their lifetimes were either in the public domain or were about to become so, and the way was at last open for the literature of the romantic period to be reprinted in a uniform formal canonising series. The first publisher off the mark was the Edinburgh firm of Gall and Inglis with their *Family* [i.e. expurgated] *Edition of the Poets*, but within a few years half a dozen firms in Edinburgh and London were producing their own lists in series, and they continued to do so until the end of the century or later.[34] As after 1774, the publishers copied one anothers' list, using one anothers' books as copytexts, there is a large measure of overlap.[35] Between 1860 and the end of the century we find an outpouring of different series of the collected works of the poets, with each author's works crammed into one volume with illustrations, as competitive market mechanisms were brought to bear on the supply of texts which had hitherto been privately

---

[31] References too numerous to list here in *The Complete Works of Ruskin* (1903–12) of which volume xxxix provides an excellent index, e.g. see xviii, 115; xxxiv, 283; 588; xxxvii 493.

[32] *Ibid.* xxxiv, 606.   [33] Quoted by Cruse, *Victorians* 49.   [34] See appendix 13.

[35] I owe this point to Professor Mark Reed who has made a textual stemma based on a detailed collation of the Victorian reprints of Wordsworth.

owned monopolies.[36] The formal Victorian canon did not, with only a few exceptions such as Shakespeare, Milton, Burns, and Cowper, merge with the old canon but helped to bring the earlier canon to a sudden end, with some authors who had previously been amongst the most highly prized, such as Dryden, Young, and Thomson scarcely figuring in the new lists, and selling poorly when they did.[37]

We can reconstruct the shape of the demand curve, author by author, an indication of their relative commercial popularity in the Victorian market. We can also trace the diffusion of the texts, tranche by tranche, down through the expanding reading nation, and follow the cycle of lower prices leading to higher sales and growing readerships which, even before the advent of universal primary education and free public libraries, had already made Great Britain a reading nation. Although I have only been able to recover sales figures for a few of the dozen or so firms which competed in this market, they show enough similarity for them to be taken as representative of the whole. The advice of the Victorian critics and professors seems to have had little effect on production, sales, or reading patterns. The sales of Wordsworth, Shelley, and Keats rose, but never approached the figures for Scott and Byron who remained as dominant in Victorian times as they had been in their own.

In the eighteenth century, books of verse had been dedicated to members of the aristocracy whose names appeared on the printed dedication pages before the title, a continuation of the days when a single manuscript copy might have been physically presented. Byron, Scott, Rogers, and Moore had begun the practice of dedicating to one another, asserting themselves as a new literary aristocracy, which drew its power direct from the book-buying and reading public, without any need for patronly favours.[38] The publishers of the old-canon formal series, conscious that they were giving the nation texts which had previously been privately owned, had played variations on 'British Poets' and 'English Classics'.[39] The publishers of the new Victorian canon, however, gave their series names such as the 'Lansdowne Poets', the 'Chandos Poets', the 'Grosvenor Poets', the 'Arundel Poets', the 'Cavendish Classics', the 'Burlington Library', the 'Tavistock Library'. It was not that the dukes had returned: the Victorian publishers named their series from the names of the streets in central London where their imposing corporate headquarters were situated.

---

[36] See chapter 8.   [37] See appendix 13.
[38] A point noted by Macaulay in his 1830 review of Robert Mongomery's *Omnipresence of the Deity* reprinted in *Critical and Historical Essays, Everyman edition* (1907) ii, 645.
[39] The last was *Bell's English Poets* for which see appendix 6, 549.

The poets selected for Warne's 'Imperial Poets', produced at the time of Queen Victoria's jubilee, and whose volumes were illustrated with the new technological medium of photography, consisted not only of Shakespeare and Milton, Byron and Wordsworth, but also Burns and Scott, Scotsmen, Moore an Irishman, and Longfellow an American. One woman was included: Mrs Hemans, who celebrated the Christian domestic affections at home and the military virtues overseas, and one secular radical, Shelley coopted, after the sting had been taken out. The Crown Poets, the Albion Poets, and the Globe Edition, for sale to the middle classes, asserted the claim of the national poets of the United Kingdom to stand at the heart of a great world-wide cultural empire, more extensive in its reach even than the political or the commercial.[40] The clerical class and the educated workers were offered their 'National Poets', 'Standard Poets', 'Popular Poets', and 'People's Editions'. The rural and urban poor had their *Cottage Library* produced by Milner in six factories in Halifax.[41]

The books of the Victorian formal poetry canon were illustrated in the contemporary Victorian style, so repeating the chronological mismatch between text and image which had marked the old-canon reprint series in the romantic period. For many Victorian readers, Scott, Byron, Moore, and the other romantics now came with engravings of deserts and mountains, ruins of ancient civilisations, views of picturesque foreign cities, battle scenes of long ago involving armoured knights and flashing swords, inscrutable and cruel eastern potentates, and the teasing semi-nudity of lethargic oriental women. The home poets such as Wordsworth and Hemans lived among flowers, birds, and butterflies. Keats, scarcely read in the first half of the century, looked a thoroughly Victorian author among engravings of the pre-Raphaelite painters who had rediscovered him. Shelley too seemed even more of 'a beautiful and in ineffectual angel, beating in the void his luminous wings in vain', as Matthew Arnold mistakenly called him, when surrounded by engravings of swirling spirits in the style of Blake, another romantic-period author rediscovered by the pre-Raphaelites.[42]

---

[40] The reprint houses had a large export business. See, for example, 'Routledge's Sales Extract for 1898', appendix 13.

[41] Working-class readers were the main buyers of the Staffordshire ornaments for the mantlepiece which were sold in millions at a penny or twopence each. Most of the characters portrayed in these ornaments are of characters from the Bible, kings and queens, nineteenth-century politicians, admirals, and generals, and some literary favourites such as Little Red Riding Hood and Uncle Tom. The only writers to be honoured as Staffordshire figures were Shakespeare, Milton, Burns, and Byron.

[42] For the comments by Matthew Arnold and other Victorian commentators see White ii, 412.

Compared with the days of moveable type, stereotype publishers had greater freedom to choose when and at what price to tranche down, but they now had a problem of how to signal their position in the market. In the days of quarto, octavo, and duodecimo, the declining price was made immediately apparent by the physical size of the book. Several publishers printed some editions on a larger paper size, with a red border round the outer edge. These 'red-line' or 'red-rule' books, which offered an illusion of easier legibility, commanded a premium over the normal plain editions. Books containing identical stereotyped texts were now also differentiated by their bindings, now an intrinsic part of the book as sold to the final buyer.[43] The publishers, dissatisfied with the range which the existing, largely utilitarian, binding industry could provide, established their own specialised artistic binderies under their own control.[44] For a set of titles, they now offered a range of half-a-dozen binding covers in different colours of cloth, as well as in different qualities of leather, at a wide range of prices. The bindings were frequently changed, moving from Puginesque gothic to understated *art nouveau*, and special mock-up displays of the current range of available bindings were now carried by the commercial travellers on their rounds of the bookshops.[45] In the age of stereotype, the external packaging which could give an old text a superficially modern appearance, became, for the first time in the history of printed books, an essential aspect of the situating of texts in the market. For customers at the top of the market, the bindings were made from gilded leather or even vellum, a reminder of, and an imitation of, the days when books were individually bound for gentlemen. For those in the middle ranks, the favoured bindings were strong cloth or buckram, designed to withstand long and hard wear, like their clothes. For those at the lowest end of the reading nation, however, there was only paper.

In the books sold at the top of the market, prices were never mentioned either inside or out, as befitted objects still purportedly intended for the nobility and the gentry. The books for middling ranks, whose province was commerce, normally contained long lists of the other books available from the same publisher, and whose now inescapable integration into the book itself caused some offence.[46] As for the paperback editions, every spare space inside and out was taken up with advertisements for other products. Most were for the heavily branded and patented products of the

---

[43] Examples in appendix 13.
[44] For example, Ward and Lock. Liveling 53.   [45] Copies among Warne archives.
[46] For example, James Spedding, *Publishers and Authors* (privately printed 1867), a book which he had been unable to have regularly published.

pharmaceutical industry, the book industry's traditional partner. With their unignorable exhortations to buy Lamplough's Pyretic Saline (for 'headache, sea or bilious sickness, constipation, indigestion, lassitude, heartburn, and feverish colds . . . typhus, scarlet, and other fevers, smallpox, measles, and eruptive, or skin complaints, and various other altered conditions of the blood'), and Beecham's Pills ('For females of all ages . . . a few doses of them carry off all gross humours, open all obstructions, and bring about all that is required'), Victorian paperbacks never allowed their readers to forget the undignified fate for which they were soon destined.[47] If, at the top of the market for romantic poetry, readers were offered the illusion that texts were autonomous and ethereal, those at the lowest tranches could not escape insistent reminders of the disasters, perils, unpleasantness, and banality of everyday life.

As had happened after 1774, one of the biggest effects of the release from intellectual property restrictions on the romantic-period authors was an outpouring of anthologies and abridgements. By the 1880s, in another rerun of the changes after 1774, the English literature of the period which entered the public domain at that time became an established school subject. Chambers of Edinburgh, the Clarendon Press, and many others began to offer the poets in textbooks edited with explanatory notes. School editions emphasised the direct lessons which children should draw. By the 1890s, as part of the effort towards universal education, the romantic poets were made available, in abridged form, throughout the country at one penny each, less than the price of a loaf of bread or a pint of beer. Among the readers was Wilfred Owen, whose copies of the *Penny Poets* have been preserved.[48] By the end of the nineteenth century one could buy the complete poetical works for sixpence. It was possible to buy *Lalla Rookh* for three pence, *Marmion* for two pence, *The Corsair* for a penny. These were probably the lowest real prices ever achieved for printed literary works.

It is now time to return to the question with which this inquiry began. What, we can now ask, would be the likely result of steeping the mind of a nation in the old-canon texts, in the long romantic verse narratives of Scott, Byron, Moore, and the others, in the range of more specialised print normally found in the book clubs and subscription libraries, and above all, in the Waverley novels? We might, I suggest, expect to see a culture self-confident and used to success, international in its outlook with

---

[47] Examples from copies of Dicks's editions, Ac. The advertisements in the Ward Lock paperbacks seem to have been much the same, Ac.
[48] In the English Faculty Library, Oxford University.

a particular fascination with the exotic east, a culture which celebrates and admires war, conquest, patriotic death in battle, and military values generally, a culture which, in the tradition of revived romance, admires honour and respect from equals rather than virtue as such. It would be a culture deeply imbued with what today is called 'heritage', inventing imaginary pasts and semi-fictional history, fascinated by ruined castles, suits of armour, stained-glass windows, battles long ago, and medievalism of all kinds. Although enterprising and adventurous, many of the participants in this culture would be only intermittently interested in the changes brought about by industrialisation, urbanisation, and population growth which were happening under their eyes in their own country in their own times.

In this culture, strong passions would occur abroad, mainly in hot countries, as do wars. Emotions at home are mild, unthreatening, and mostly under control. It would be a religious culture, but among the intellectual elites more deist than literally Christian, although with some groups sending out missionary expeditions as part of the colonial enterprise. It would be masculine, neo-chivalric in its attitudes to women, attitudes in which most of the women themselves shared, although they mainly participated in a clearly defined, domestic, private sphere, with special responsibility to educate the male children in national values. And all this would be superimposed upon an English pastoral/bucolic myth, continuously repeated in the childhood reading of each successive generation and uninterruptedly repeated during adulthood, a myth derived from the Augustan eighteenth century and the classical Alexandrian and Roman poets, which sees country life as more authentic than town life, and dreams of a harmonious, social order, in which all groups from the lord to the leech-gatherer are content with their divinely appointed lot. As the children sang in one of the nation's favourite hymns, 'The rich man in his castle, the poor man at his gate, God made them high or lowly, and ordered their estate.'[49]

Looked at this way, there seems to be quite a good overlap between the historic patterns of reading of the elites of the romantic period and how we might characterise the mentalities of their Victorian successors.

More specifically, we may be able to discern the influence of the reading of Walter Scott on attitudes to Scotland both within Great Britain and elsewhere. The religious and ethnic quarrels of a past which was still recent in the romantic period were turned into a harmless tartan tourist industry, irrelevant to modern life. To some extent the same process of mythologising that Scott performed for Scotland can be seen to have been performed by

---

[49] From 'All things bright and beautiful', written by Mrs C. F. Alexander, 1818–95.

Figure 22. 'Catherine Macaulay in her Father's Library' from *Clever Girls* (Victorian n.d.).

Moore for Ireland and for India, and Byron for Greece and Turkey.[50] It may be possible to trace the effects of the reading of Scott and Byron on the local literatures of non-English-speaking countries, including France and Russia, and the attitudes to individual freedom, nationalism, and other qualities which romantic Byronism, although not the Byron of *Don Juan*, both represented and promoted.

It might be possible too, more speculatively, to link Victorian reading to the erosion of British industrial supremacy. Generations of inventors, innovators, and entrepreneurs gave up inventing and working to become country gentlemen living on investment incomes. Was the decline of the British economy relative to other industrialised countries partly the result of so much childhood reading of Thomson, Cowper, and Walter Scott? Paul Fussell has convincingly linked the reading of the poetry of the romantic period to the attitudes of the young officers who went to their deaths in the First World War – the persistence of notions of chivalry and honour, the tendency to see war and weapons in obsolete romantic terms, knightly foemen, battlements, swift arrows and trusty swords, not rat-infested trenches, barbed wire, machine guns, bombs, and poison gas.[51] Lord Ernle, a minister during the war, noted that he had read all the Waverley novels many times before he was ten.[52] According to John Maynard Keynes, writing in the early twentieth century, the bankers and industrialists of his day who believed themselves to be entirely free of any intellectual influence were the unwitting slaves of some defunct economist.[53] The men and women of that time, it emerges, were also the slaves of defunct romantic poets.

The advance of the poets, we can also note, coincided with one of the biggest changes to occur in the nineteenth century, the abandonment of Christian belief by most of the country's intellectuals. In a long passage in his autobiography, John Stuart Mill, a man whose education was prodigious, described how he searched the literature of his country for some comfort from the confusion of his beliefs. Byron, he found, was too cynical and sneering, even if truthful in his observations, and only Wordsworth gave him what he most desired, some sense of transcendence.[54] But as the century progressed, natural religion too came increasingly to seem no more than a staging stop on a long intellectual march from belief to scepticism

[50] For Greece see William St Clair, *That Greece Might Still Be Free* (Oxford 1972) and David Roessel, *In Byron's Shadow. Modern Greece in the English and American Literary Imagination* (New York 2002).
[51] Paul Fussell, *The Great War and Modern Memory* (New York 1975).
[52] Lord Ernle, *The Light Reading of Our Ancestors* (n.d. c. 1927) vii.
[53] In the 'Concluding Notes' to *The General Theory of Money, Interest, and Employment* (1936).
[54] John Jacob Coss, ed., *Autobiography of John Stuart Mill, published . . . from the original manuscript* (New York 1924) 103.

which had started at the end of the seventeenth century and progressed, with only a few setbacks, through to their own day. It was a march being joined by an ever widening proportion of the population, and although the churches frequently tried to regroup under a reconstituted set of supernatural propositions, their credibility continued to decline.

By the middle of the Victorian period Shelley and Wordsworth had become the most esteemed authors of the liberal intellectual and scientific aristocracy, the dynasties of Stephen, Sidgwick, Darwin, Keynes, Russell and others, as well as of writers such as Robert Browning and Thomas Hardy. This was a time when, with reluctance, many of the country's intellectual leaders finally decided that the explanatory claims of Christianity and of natural religion could no longer be accepted. They made the change slowly and with reluctance, conscious that they were abandoning what had been the central feature of European civilisation for 1,500 years, but in the light of the accumulating discoveries of geology, of biology, of archaeology, of history, and of biblical scholarship, they knew that, if they were to be honest with themselves, they no longer had a choice. Among the factors which encouraged them to make the final reluctant break was their hope that they could reject both the supernatural and the historical claims of religion without at the same time opening the way to moral chaos or to an entirely materialist alternative world view. Wordsworth and Coleridge, and above all Shelley, seemed to offer a way through. Of Henry Sidgwick for example, the philosopher of ethics who, along with Leslie Stephen, refused an academic career because he declined to submit to the religious tests, it was said that 'Of poetry he had powers of intense enjoyment, and a prodigious memory for it which he never lost.'[55] The romantic poets offered them reassurance that a secular culture need not lack beauty, or moral idealism, or a strong ethical basis.

In the old canon, the link between literature, sublimity, feeling, and morality had been constantly emphasised, and any hint of irreligion condemned and excluded. In this new Victorian canon the morally improving power of literature was still emphasised, but except in expurgated 'family' editions, *Queen Mab* and *Don Juan* were readily accessible. Wordsworth, the theist, shared the glory with Byron who, in *Cain*, had put convincing arguments in the mouth of Lucifer. As literature and art began to supply some of the psychological needs previously offered by religion, the Victorian canon of poets, both as texts and as books, increasingly acquired

---

[55] See D. G. James, *Henry Sidgwick. Science and Faith in Victorian England* (1970). The lines are from Shelley's translation of the Homeric 'Hymn to Apollo.'

the traditions previously accorded to religious and ancient classical texts, concordances, commentaries, hermeneutic studies, lives of great authors published in series, shrines for pilgrimages. Like the religious texts they were superseding, the works of the great English poets were to be read intensively. At the same time, some of the worship that previous generations had accorded to saints and heroes was transferred to artists and poets. William Michael Rossetti's comments on Blake, an author/artist that the Pre-Raphaelites regarded, along with Keats, as their own discovery, is an example of this romantic ideology at its most extreme.

'An amazing genius', 'a glorious luminary', 'the intrinsic greatness of the man and of his work . . . patent and irrefutable'. 'He transcended other men.' 'By some unknown process he had soared to the top of a cloud-capped Alp while they were crouching in the valley', 'to his own ideal, his own inspiration . . . loyal beyond praise and beyond words . . . to aught else . . . impenetrable and contumacious'. 'Rapt in a passionate yearning, he realized, even on this earth and in his mortal body a species of nirvana: his whole faculty, his whole personality, the very essence of his mind and mould, attained to absorption into his ideal ultimate.'[56]

In some cases, the change was part of an explicit secularising agenda. As Frederic Harrison, one of the leading liberals of the time, suggested in 1891 in a book which recommended the 'Best cheap editions' then available:

The immortal and universal poets of our race are to be read and re-read till their music and their spirit are a part of our nature; they are to be thought over and digested till we live in the world they created for us; they are to be read devoutly, as devout men read their Bible and fortify their hearts with psalms.[57]

Whereas, in the romantic period, the educated working classes were encouraged to read the weightiest contemporary works of history and political economy, and discouraged from reading poetry, novels, and plays, their Victorian successors were given the very literature which had earlier been discouraged. Scott, Byron, Wordsworth, Shelley and the now universal Shakespeare would not supplant the English-language Bible as the defining texts of the nation, but would be elevated to a near equal status in official esteem. Some of the cheapest series which aimed to make the best literature available for a few pence, such as 'Cassell's National Library', and the 'Masterpiece Library', had a humanist faith that 'literature', almost irrespective of textual content, would bring about a more moral world. It was from an old religious mystery play, that 'Everyman's Library' took some lines for

---

[56] William Michael Rossetti, ed., *Poetical Works of William Blake*, introduction to the New Aldine Edition (c. 1870).
[57] Frederic Harrison, quoted by Arthur Acland MP, in *A Guide to the Choice of Books* (1891) 60.

its secular agenda. 'Everyman, I will go with thee and be thy guide. In thy most need to go by thy side.'[58]

If the texts in this secular Pantheon were not religious, the books were. An air of churchiness hangs over the appearance of many of the middle-class editions of the romantic poets, by late-Victorian times routinely sold in limp leather or padded bindings, invariably red or black, previously the distinguishing clerical dress of Bibles, prayer books, and hymn books. Some editions, with their scarlet and gold bindings, bejewelled and cameoed, are like gorgeous reliquaries, splendid boxes seldom to be opened, whose contents were certain to disappoint. The Shelley family in Victorian times, alert to the religious aura which increasingly surrounded their wayward and much hated relative, prepared a special volume of his works with fragments of his charred bones windowed in the cover.[59] The books in which the secular religious texts were unreadably inscribed were sacred objects, with their own associated rituals, gifts for godchildren at christenings, wedding presents, and prizes at school.[60] As the books became externally more enticing, inside, the tiny type, often badly printed in the first place, became increasingly worn, smudged, spotted, and illegible. By late-Victorian times the covers were carefully protected by a Victorian invention, the dust jacket, invariably a plain pure white sheet, an outer veil which was removed in the shop when the book was bought to reveal the splendour of the inner gilded binding, but not the (now often almost unreadable) text which lay within.[61]

As in the high monopoly period, the Victorian system of writing, books, reading, horizons of expectations, and mentalities, contained so many stabilising structural features, both material and cultural, that only a strong external shock could break its self-reinforcing tendencies. One of the effects of the First World War that, as far as I know, has not been noticed, was the destruction of the material plant from which the printed texts of the Victorian era were manufactured. From the moment hostilities began in 1914, the call went out to save shipping space by melting scrap metal, especially metal containing copper and zinc, and some publishers sent many stereotype plates to be melted as early as 24 August 1914.[62] The Warne archives report the sending for melting during 1914 of innumerable plates, mainly of titles first published many years before for which prewar demand had been low and intermittent. As the war progressed, however, the calls for

---

[58] See Ernest Rhys, *Everyman Remembers* (1931) 239.
[59] In BL.   [60] As the publishers' advertisements often emphasise.
[61] Examples of surviving Victorian white dust jackets are among the Warne archives.
[62] Mould and plate book, Richard Clay archives.

metal, like the calls for men, grew ever more insistent. Soon the government refused to release the metal needed for new printing except in exchange for a compensating amount of scrap, and the numbers of plates sent for destruction rose inexorably. With each call for metal, a large swathe was cut from the national stock of stereotypes, and every year the texts that were sacrificed became younger. The Reverend Legh Richmond's *The Dairyman's Daughter*, of which at least a million and a half copies had been circulated to innumerable children, went to be melted early in the war, as did Godwin's *Caleb Williams*, a text that had been continuously in print since the eighteenth century.[63] Warne's editions of Campbell, Hemans, and Longfellow, were sent to the furnaces in 1915. In 1916, the year of the Somme, Routledge sent their plates of all the Waverley novels, together with the novels of Marryat, Ainsworth, Lytton, Dumas, and other historical romances of bygone days.[64] Longman's archives show a similar pattern.

In 1918, Winston Churchill, then the Minister of Munitions, made a specific appeal, which was reported throughout the printing and publishing industry trade press.

THE WAR
How Printers can Help to Win it.

Go over your store rooms and cellars, bring out all type, furniture, stereos, electros, and all the hundred things which contain 'non-ferrous metals', and pass on all that can by any sacrifice be spared to the big metal merchants who are producing Munitions. Do it now and Win the War! and Win for the Great Craft the honour of having Done their Bit.[65]

By the end of the war, the material base of much of the late-Victorian and Edwardian reading nation had been destroyed, and with it the opportunity to produce books at low marginal cost. With the coming of peace, the choice at the margin between reprinting old texts and investing in new titles was more nearly neutral. Famous texts could be, and were, reprinted, and old pictures re-engraved, but the routine children's books, textbooks, conduct literature, romantic novels, and adventure stories on which the mentalities of pre-war reading generations had been nourished from cradle to grave were gone for ever.[66] And more destruction was soon to follow. The plates of Macmillan's *Poetical Works of Sir Walter Scott*, having done

---

[63] Warne archives. See also Mumby, *Routledge* 140.

[64] Although I have found no inventory of Routlege plates as such, the stock book shows these titles, along with others, ceasing to be produced in 1916/17.

[65] 'Members Circular of the Federation of Master Printers' January 1918. St Bride's Printing Library, London.

[66] Longman's register of stereotypes, 288.

sterling service since the 1860s, were melted in 1935.[67] The plates of Warne's *Poetical Works of Lord Byron* that had produced 169,000 copies between 1868 and 1893 and an unknown number later, had also survived the First World War, but were melted in 1937 in the rearmament drive which preceded the Second.[68] In the wars of the twentieth century, the romantic poets provided some of the ammunition.

[67] Total impressions before 1935 quoted by Simon Eliot, 'To You in Your Business' in Elizabeth James, ed., *Macmillan: A Publishing Tradition* (2002) 25 from archival records.
[68] Warne archives.

CHAPTER 22

The political economy of reading

The study concludes that there is indeed a recognisable correspondence between historic reading patterns and consequent mentalities. The correlation is far from exact, but over the whole print era, the links, both general and particular, between texts, books, reading, and wider consequences appear to be secure. For example, the persistence of rural and religious constructions of Englishness far into the urbanised industrialised age was greatly assisted by the entrenchment of the reading of seventeenth- and eighteenth-century literary texts in school books.[1] The development of a distinctive, reformist working-class culture could not have occurred, at any rate to the same extent, if the price of access to certain texts had not been unusually low and the resulting readerships unusually wide.[2] There is a perceptible fit too between the immersion of the reading nation over nearly a century in the writings of Walter Scott, the values of Victorian Britain, and the states of mind that led to the American Civil War and the First World War.

The inquiry has helped to explain why, during most of the eighteenth century, reading in the English-speaking world was concentrated in the upper-income groups, and why after 1774 the reading nation grew rapidly until near universality was reached by the end of the nineteenth. It has discovered patterns and elucidated answers to some questions that have rarely been asked, for example, why printed literary anthologies which drew on earlier print suddenly ceased around 1600 and reappeared in huge numbers around 1780, why Shakespeare disappeared from popular reading, in chapbook versions, from 1594, and why a body of texts of mediaeval romance that had been continuously favoured for many centuries should suddenly lose all appeal around 1800.[3]

Taking a long view, we can see that, although new texts were being written, circulated, and read during all periods of the past, most of the

---

[1] Discussed in chapter 7. [2] Discussed in chapter 16. [3] Discussed in chapters 4 and 17.

reading that has historically occurred has been of older texts that were accorded value after they were first written and that continued to be copied for new readers by whatever technology was available. We can however see too that the balance of production, of reading, and therefore, potentially, of effects on mentalities, between the new and the old has not been constant, but has been subject to sudden drastic shifts. In the manuscript era, the copying technology tended to encourage the production of more copies of the existing body of texts rather than new texts. By contrast, the copying technology of moveable type, dominant from the sixteenth to the early nineteenth centuries, shifted the balance towards producing new texts, most of which circulated in small numbers among elites. But then, in the era of copying by stereotype and electrotype, that lasted for nearly a century and a half from the 1830s, the balance shifted back towards producing more copies of existing texts. In the present era of text copying by electronic media, both new and old texts can potentially be produced and circulated at infinitesimal cost, but non-technological factors, notably private intellectual property, have replicated some of the inhibiting effects on prices, access, and reading that were previously due to the technology as such.

In some ways the general result is both unsurprising and reassuring. Surely, my patient reader may say, nobody has ever seriously doubted that reading influences attitudes, opinions, states of mind, and ultimately behaviour? The historical reconstruction offered by the study, that patient reader might go on to say, adds to our knowledge of the links between texts, books, reading, consequent mentalities, and even behaviour, but all that the study has done has been to fill out a messy process which everyone has always correctly assumed was occurring. Although there may be discoverable correspondences, some of these can be explained, at least in part, by the feedback loops between writers and readers, as the study acknowledges.

However, once it is accepted that the study has shown the existence of a perceptible system, and not a chronological procession of events, then the conclusions are neither obvious nor reassuring. For if the study has found systemic correspondences between historic reading and historic mentalities, it has disconnected them from many of the traditional ways by which the world of past mentalities has been conceptualised and presented. Parade-of-author literary histories, which mostly take the form of celebratory annals of the cultural production of elites, being almost exclusively concerned with authorial inputs rather than readerly outputs, cannot tell much about impacts and influence. They also tend to be circular. Trapped in the endless tautology that the culture which produced the texts was also the culture which was produced by them, and yet aware that mentalities are always changing, the literary annalist can only escape by postulating changes in readerly taste.

The convention of presenting the processes of cultural formation as a parliament of printed texts also places the main site of change in the writing of the texts rather than in the reading of the books. As much as the parade model, it cannot adequately cope with the fact that readers did not always, or even normally, accept meanings that were offered by authors, that only a few readers had access to the full range of contemporaneous new texts, and that some ideas were much more frequently encountered than others. By excluding the reading of older texts, and therefore ignoring most of the reading which historically occurred, the convention disenfranchises most citizens from having influenced the development of their nation's culture.[4] At the same time, by concentrating on contemporaneous texts and contemporaneous debates, the parliament convention risks giving disproportionate attention to those voices which were recorded in print, exaggerating the influence of authors, including writers of pamphlets, who could afford to pay for their texts to be printed.[5] The parliament convention is, therefore, for the most part, also more concerned with authorly inputs than with readerly outputs and mental outcomes.

Parade and parliament histories present the culture of a society in terms of trajectories of development and change, even if the trajectories are not straight. A history of reading reveals constituencies of readers of widely different ages, experiences, and horizons of expectations interacting with texts of widely differing degrees of obsolescence. The periodicity of reading, with its changing patterns of stacked chronological layers, is so different from the periodicity of writing that it cannot be adequately captured by traditional linear narrative. When examined in this way, many common assumptions are undermined or invalidated. The study, for example, offers little support to the view that canons of reputation have provided a stable or a developing foundation for enabling us to understand the changing mentalities of the past. The formal old canon of English literature established around 1780 can only be adequately explained within the context of the break-down of the previous intellectual property regime, and the establishment of the formal Victorian canon, which replaced it in the 1860s, is also related to the vagaries of copyright legislation.[6] Nor does the study

---

[4] Discussed in chapter 1.
[5] For example the pamphlets discussed in chapter 12, and 'on commission' literature discussed in chapter 8.
[6] Discussed in chapters 7 and 20.

suggest that knowledge of useful discoveries or of new ideas always, or even usually, soon trickled down from the reading elites to the rest of society. On the contrary, anthologies, abridgements, and adaptations, the main print media for trickle down, with some important exceptions, ceased to perform that function around 1600, and even after the changes of 1774, it was mainly obsolete texts which were anthologised and abridged.[7] None of these findings can be adequately explained by postulating feedback loops between writers and readers.

As is the case with many complex systems, we see long periods of stability punctuated by sharp changes of direction as a result of particular events. Indeed there is little evidence that, as far as readers were concerned, the system for those outside the elites offered much progressivity, except over such long time spans as to render the word inappropriate. Sometimes large changes turned on particular events. For example, the establishing, and widespread reading, of the old canon was a direct result of the decisions of the courts in 1774, and the subsequent lock-in can be shown to be related to the intellectual property legislation in 1808, 1814, and 1842.[8] Many of the consequences of 1774 were unforeseen, notably the entry of English literature to the school room, a shift from a catechetic to a critical form of teaching, and the entrenchment of the rural religious values of the pre-industrial world into perceptions of essential Englishness.[9] The 1774 decision which effectively forbade the practice of perpetual copyright, one of the most momentous events in the long history of reading in the English-speaking world, can be linked to the advance of Enlightenment ideas about the disbenefits of monopoly formulated by Adam Smith and already known to opinion formers. In systems terms, it can be seen as emergent from a larger hierarchical system. Other events which had momentous consequences on reading, however, such as Lord Chancellor Eldon's decisions not to accord intellectual property privileges to *Queen Mab* and *Don Juan*, can only be adequately explained within quite narrowly limited historical, legal, and even biographical contexts.[10]

As the example of popular print between 1600 and 1780 shows, large reading constituencies were sometimes held for long periods in an unsatisfactory equilibrium marked by the increasing obsolescence of the main printed texts to which they had access. This episode offers what is probably the most illuminating case that is likely to be found of the long-term consequences of an unregulated private commercial monopoly on the nature of

---

[7] Discussed in chapters 4 and 7.   [8] Discussed in chapters 3 and 6.
[9] Discussed in chapter 7.   [10] Discussed in chapter 16.

texts, books, prices, access, reading, and resultant mentalities. It is unlikely, for example, that those who around 1600 were caught in the pre-scientific world of the English-language Bible, the ballad, the chapbook, and the astrological almanac, actively rejected modernity for the next two hundred years, or preferred that the medical and birth control advice which they received in print should be out-of-date and ineffective.

If the inquiry has disconnected outcomes from traditional text- and author-centred approaches, it has at the same time connected them to other ways of understanding complexity. If my patient reader still doubts whether it is useful to regard the relationships between texts, books, reading, and mentalities as a system, such scepticism about the value of the approach looks less reasonable, when applied to the materiality of texts. One striking conclusion is the extent to which simple, well-understood, and empirically well-tested economic models, such as price and quantity, monopoly and competition, have been able to account for the behaviour of the printed-book industry, and therefore also the patterns of readerly access, during all the centuries when print was the paramount medium. The study has shown that the tendency of monopolistic industries to pay most attention to the topmost tranches of the market, to move slowly down the demand curve, to ration supply to the market in order to protect the market value of their properties, to neglect large constituencies of the market altogether or to supply them with obsolete and often shoddy goods, can be observed in the monopolies and cartels operated by the printed-book industry through the institutions of private intellectual property. Basic economic theory can, therefore, help to explain how the reading nation came to be divided into overlapping layers of readers, differentiated not only by income, by socio-economic class, and by educational attainment, but by the degree of obsolescence of the print to which each layer had access. To have linked mentalities to historical reading is, therefore, to have linked them to the economics of the production and marketing of texts in the age of print.

It has seldom been doubted that during the sixteenth and seventeenth centuries, the English and Scottish governments and churches, by promoting the mandatory reading of Bibles, catechisms, homilies and other texts of their respective official religions, in close financial alliance with the industrialists who were franchised to manufacture and supply the print, greatly influenced the beliefs of the people. In the case of astrological almanacs, however, another monopolised sector of the book market in which, in England, the same industrialists were closely allied with the state, we can also trace the effects through to the mentalities, and in some cases to the behaviours, of large sections of the less-well educated population. In the case of both the official and the tolerated unofficial supernaturals, price was used simultaneously as a form of private commercial monopoly rent-taking, as a tax, and as a reasonably successful instrument of cultural governance. Indeed, in the case of the astrological almanacs, it is striking that, when private commercial and state fiscal considerations came into conflict with the official religion, it was the former which were given preference, with the result that, for over 200 years, astrological almanacs continued to be produced in huge quantities, under the royal arms, with all the apparent authority of the English state.

In general, it emerges that the development of virtually all aspects of texts, books, and reading, including the English-language Bible and Shakespeare, have been influenced by the three main governing structures of the print era, private intellectual property in the hands of the text-copying industry, cartelisation within the industry, and a close alliance between the state and the industry in which the industry delivered textual policing and self-censorship in exchange for economic privileges. It emerges too that the governing structures of private intellectual property enforced and guaranteed by the state, which, in England, were first put in place in the early sixteenth century and, although constantly undermined by manuscript, pirate, and offshore publication, had a large measure of success in achieving their aims. Even when, as in the case of *Don Juan*, a text slipped through the normal constraints, the self censorship of publishers offset some of the potential effects on readers.[11] If the findings of my inquiry are confirmed, then it follows that these governing structures helped to determine society itself, affecting every stage of cultural formation from textual production, through the choice, production, and distribution of print, to readerly access, readerly horizons, choice of reading, reception, and consequent mentalities.

There have, of course, been many writers who have perceived or postulated links between the institutions of property and the mentalities of the society within which economic power is exercised. Cultural consciousness, according to the tradition of cultural materialism, is the superstructure which rests upon society's economic base. According to such theories, high literary texts, as the most complex symbolic system which society produces, can therefore be historically analysed to illuminate the nature of the society which produced them. The difficulty has been that it has proved impossible,

---

[11] For the so-called 'family editions' see chapter 16.

other than in terms which strain the key Marxist concepts beyond their normal limits, to relate literary texts directly to the economic base. It is easy, in the case of, say, Hannah More's 'Cheap Repository Tracts', to discern an overlap between the interests of the groups who financed and distributed them and the morality, economic behaviour, and personal conduct which the texts recommend to their readers. Tracts were, however, unusually crude and transparent in their propaganda aims, as readers usually saw. It is much more difficult to relate, say the works of Shakespeare to some notion of a hegemonic system of class exploitation operating in Elizabethan England or at the many later times when Shakespeare was read. As for Byron's *Don Juan*, it can only with extreme contortions be fitted into any Marxist theory of texts, and when the price of access fell and the work was widely read, its main effect was to undermine and destabilise the very social and political structures of which Marxist theory requires it to be an emanation.[12] Attempts to equate literary texts with ideology have also proved unfruitful, 'banging one inadequate category against another', as Raymond Williams remarked.[13]

However, by attempting to apply the theory of economic base and cultural superstructure to 'literature', cultural materialists, like other literary and cultural historians, being more concerned with authors and texts than with books and readers, may have placed the main site of change in the wrong place. By applying an existing theory top-down, cultural materialists have unduly neglected the economic processes which put certain texts in the hands of certain readers. By contrast, the conclusions of the present inquiry have emerged, bottom-up, from the observed patterns in material production, including the governing economic and intellectual property structures, financing, manufacturing, prices, access, and actual reading, quantified in many cases. Although my conclusions do not, therefore, arise from any direct attempt to address the question on which Marx wished to overturn Hegel, namely whether cultural consciousness determines the way human life is lived or whether it is the lived life as part of economic production which determines cultural consciousness, they are highly relevant to any discussion of that question. Marxist theory, the results of the study suggest, can link books and reading to consciousness far more convincingly than it can literary texts and ideologies. Indeed, with the help of the findings of the present study, many parts of Marxist theory could, like the dismembered body parts which Victor Frankenstein assembled from the charnel houses of Ingolstadt, be put together to make a new living creature, and one

---

[12] Discussed in chapter 17.   [13] Raymond Williams, *Marxism and Literature* (1977) 52.

which, according to the original Frankenstein story, would be essentially benign.

There is, however, no need to invoke the ghost of Marx. Literary and cultural historians of all kinds, not just cultural materialists, the study suggests, have tended to ignore, or severely to underestimate, the effects of such economic processes as the turning of texts into material books, the price of access to readers, the development of vested economic interests in prolonging the obsolete, and the cumulative effects of such processes on the minds of readers acting within their readerly horizons of expectations and personal economic constraints. Cultural production, the study suggests, whether in a guild or a commercial system, whether in a monopoly or in an open competitive market, has been an integral part of economic production, subject to many of the same economic forces and governing structures as other forms of production, and explainable in similar terms. If the study has linked mentalities with reading it has therefore linked them directly to the exercise of economic and political power.

In the centuries of the print era in the English-speaking world, during which the paramountcy of printed books was unchallenged, we have examples of many types of governing regimes, and can assess their effects, both in economic terms, and in terms of the texts they made available. At one end of the spectrum we have a regime marked by an almost complete absence of intellectual property rights. In eighteenth-century Ireland, the book industry developed into a vigorous offshore centre, reprinting texts originating in Great Britain, producing books mainly for export. Although this regime produced local economic benefits, for example in employment, and conferred price and cultural benefits on the local English-speaking population who were able to buy and read many modern texts at a fraction of the prices operating in Great Britain, where the texts originated, it discouraged the publication of new texts locally, and so may have helped to reinforce English-speaking Ireland's status as a reader of texts produced in metropolitan centres elsewhere. When, in 1801, Ireland was fully integrated into the commercial system of the rest of the British Isles, Ireland too adopted an intellectual property regime, and Irish authors and readers were put on a par with their British compatriots.

At the opposite end, we have the example of a regime of the complete private and perpetual monopoly ownership of all printed texts, closely owned within self-perpetuating syndicates and cartels, as in England until 1774. This regime, as it was operated at its peak in the mid-eighteenth century, produced a stable and prosperous industry, in which authors, publishers, and printers were all well rewarded, and it enabled many long and substantial new works of lasting value in history, philosophy, political economy, science, and literature to be carried into print. But it concentrated the benefits on the upper ranks of society, tended to delay and restrict access for the majority of readers, and it excluded some of the largest reading constituencies altogether. Indeed it was only when the monopoly ownership of texts was drastically reformed in 1774 that the long period during which only a minority of readers had access to reasonably modern texts was brought to an end, the previous century having, if anything, shown a tendency for the reading nation to contract.

Between these extremes, we have the example of the intellectual property regime of the newly independent United States in which, after 1787, copyright protection was accorded to locally produced American texts but not to texts originating elsewhere. This regime, as in eighteenth-century Ireland, enabled a profitable printed-book industry to develop. It also produced an immense benefit to local readers and to the general development of the United States by encouraging an inflow of modern knowledge from the intellectual centres in Europe. At the same time by making the price of access to texts of British origin cheaper than access to those produced locally, it tended for a time to reinforce the intellectual hegemony of Britain which the colonists had hoped to throw off. Seen from the other side of the Atlantic, the regime encouraged an outflow of American texts to Great Britain, particularly at the popular end of the market, which disbenefited both the American authors and publishers who received no financial remuneration and the British authors, publishers, and moralists who felt that their superior local print culture was being swamped by cheap foreign trash. This asymmetrical protectionist regime too proved unsustainable as the United States became more fully integrated into global commercial structures, and developed a growing commercial interest in asserting and protecting the intellectual property in texts of American origin.

For another example of a mixed system, we can turn to Scotland from 1710 to 1774 where a regime of short statutory copyright was operated. This enabled a thriving book industry to develop, producing both new copyright-protected titles and cheap reprints of out-of-copyright titles. During this period, which coincided with the Scottish Enlightenment, the size of the reading nation in Scotland expanded rapidly. After 1774, Great Britain as a whole experienced a short copyright equivalent to about one generation, but since 1842 the country has operated under a long copyright of two, three, or more generations. The brief copyright window of the romantic period coincided with one of the most dynamic periods of British history in terms of texts, books, readers, and education, during which England was able, to a large extent, to catch up with Scotland. Since the United States joined the international copyright conventions in the late nineteenth century, the intellectual property regime has become increasingly uniform across the English-speaking world and beyond, with a marked tendency for virtually every change to advance the producer interest of authors and publishers against the consumer interest of buyers and readers.

We also have the experience of the different intellectual property regimes operated in countries outside the English-speaking world, although in the general absence of quantification except by title, these must be regarded as provisional. Studies of eighteenth-century France, for example, show that the highly controlled monopolistic regime of the *ancien régime* tended to cause a stagnation, with heavy reproduction of the texts of the previous century, alleviated by a vigorous offshore publishing industry.[14] Although, by the eighteenth century, the practice of renewable privileges brought about virtual perpetual intellectual property in all modern French texts for which there was demand, the French booksellers, unlike their English colleagues, never succeeded in taking into their private ownership the huge body of texts produced before the advent of printing.[15] Whether this asymmetrical intellectual property regime, which enabled classical and patristic texts and the huge body of mediaeval romance to be reprinted in the provinces, brought about a price differential in favour of the long obsolete, and so helped to consolidate obsolete mentalities outside the elites, would be worth investigating.

When set against French experience, the British book industry of the eighteenth century can be seen to have some of the characteristics of an *ancien régime*, although at a much lighter level of textual control. When the French Revolution abolished all intellectual property in 1793, the result was an explosion of printed material, mainly of short periodical texts, to be followed by a steady increase in the publication of longer works when intellectual property was reintroduced. Historically in many jurisdictions, at all periods, from the arrival of print to Victorian times, we see that offshore and pirate publishing has been a vital factor in offsetting both the power of states to control the circulation of ideas within their jurisdictions and the tendencies of private intellectual property regimes to restrict access to new texts to the topmost tranches of society. Indeed it may not be too

---

[14] Carla Hesse, 'Economic Upheavals in Publishing' in Darnton and Roche 83. See also Darnton, *Forbidden* which draw on the archives of the Société Typographique de Neuchâtel.

[15] For the complex history of intellectual property in *ancien régime* France I have relied on Pottinger, especially 210–34.

large a claim to suggest that some of the biggest shifts in mentalities that have occurred in recent centuries, including the German and later European Reformation, the collapse of the authority of the *ancien régime* in France, and the slow but relentless withdrawal of belief in Christianity, were not only assisted by pirate and offshore publication, but were only made possible because the local governing structures were successfully circumvented.

In some ways, therefore, historical experience seems to suggest a bleak choice between a monopoly regime which, as in the eighteenth century English-speaking world, favours excellence and innovation but restricts the benefits to the few, with delayed and uncertain trickle down of the benefits to wider constituencies, and a market unrestricted by private intellectual property which, unless offset by deliberately non-commercial institutions, supplies only short-term news and comment, and recycled, and increasingly obsolete, trash. Whatever our judgement about the implied trade-off, however, the conclusion of the study is that each of the differing regimes shows a clear consequential link between the governing intellectual property structures on the one hand and the provision of texts, the supply of books, prices, access, and reading on the other. We have moved the analysis of the historic processes of the supply of texts from events to structures, from individual agency to corporate economic behaviour, from historically specific anecdote to explanatory model. That conclusion by itself is enough to encourage us, as participating members of a society, to pay close attention to the nature of the regime within which texts are produced. If we accept the conclusion of the study that there are identifiable correspondences between reading and mentalities, then the public interest in the nature of the governing structures that should be put in place becomes a vital matter of democratic self-government.

What are the implications for improving our understanding of these processes in which we ourselves participate, of which our present mentalities are among the current outcomes, and which we must expect will continue to change in the future? If we accept the need to integrate material and economic factors more fully into our investigations, and to regard the history of books as an indispensable component of the study of texts and of culture broadly defined, what future lines of research are needed? First, as I suggested in chapter 1, such constructs as 'readers' and our notions of 'impact' and 'influence' need to be more closely related to empirically observed behaviours and emerging patterns, just as 'the investor', a theoretical construct in an analogous discipline, is both carefully theorised and based on quantified empirical studies of observed investment behaviours.

If this is to be done, then a prerequisite is to improve the available factual basis of empirical data on which all such studies are, or should be, dependent. Until recently, for example, most author bibliographies were largely descriptions of books, offering no information on contracts, prices, print runs, reprints, or readerships, even when this was recoverable. Bibliography as a whole has been itself largely a parade of texts, participating in the hierarchical assumptions of the parent discipline of literary criticism, which long regarded anything to do with money with fastidious disdain. Even modern 'book history' tends to centre round the material artefact, rather than treating the recovery of the history of books as a first step towards recovering reading, itself a step in trying to improve our understanding of communication, cultural formation, and the construction of mentalities.

If we are to develop a fuller understanding of the links, we need to compile a cumulative, accurate, database of actual recorded costs, prices, print runs, method of manufacture, and sales of books, including imports, reprints, adaptations, and abridgements. The production information can be supplemented with reports of actual reading and fictional representations. Since, as far as Great Britain is concerned, the majority of the archival records which would enable a comprehensive catalogue to be compiled have already been lost, even for the nineteenth century, this is not as gigantic an enterprise as may at first appear. However, although still being eroded at an alarming rate, enough information can be recovered, as the study has shown, even for the early centuries of print, to enable the main features to be reconstructed.[16] Since some of the systemic characteristics are already understood even a fragmentary archival record can provide a framework within which gaps can be more reliably estimated by interpolation. Since

---

[16] Among the losses are those of Woodfall, known in the nineteenth century but since disappeared. See *Notes and Queries*, first series, xi (1855) 377–8, 418–20. Marston, Septimus Rivington, *The Publishing Family of Rivington* (1919), Shaylor, and other secondary authors quote from sources now lost. The records of the Tonsons appear to have survived, unresearched, until sent for 'salvage' in the Second World War. See Kathleen M. Lynch, *Jacob Tonson, Kit-Cat Publisher* (University of Tennessee 1971) 208. The ledgers containing the incoming letters to Chatto and Windus, including those of the older firms which had been taken over were sent for 'salvage' during the First World War. See Michael Bott, 'The Archive of British Publishers at Reading University Library' in *Leipziger Jahrbuch zur Buchgeschichte* (1992) 442. The archives of Ward Lock were destroyed in a fire in 1911, to be followed by the loss of the file copies in the bombing in 1940. See Liveling, ii, 98. The archives of the king's printer were lost with those of Eyre and Spottiswoode in 1940. See Harlan 132. Those of Cassell were destroyed by bombing in 1941. See Simon Nowell-Smith, *The House of Cassell, 1848–1958* (1958) publisher's note. Many records of Clowes the printer were also lost to bombing. Galignani seem to have destroyed their records in the 1970s, after removing the literary items such as letters from Byron. Most of the archives of Warne were dispersed as recently as 1995 although I managed to retrieve a substantial quantity. I have also obtained the impression books of the Edinburgh firm of Gall and Inglis. The surviving records for the early United States appears to be more complete, although so far not much studied.

the history of books is the history of an industry, we also need to carry the economic analysis forward. We need, for example, to develop such essential informational tools as a long-run index of book prices, denominated in real and in nominal terms, in accordance with a range of criteria other than manufacturing format, and a readily available reference source for the changing textual control and intellectual property regimes, more comprehensive than I have been able to offer. With time, it would be methodologically simple to compile the basic data which are demanded and taken for granted in many other disciplines, as the foundation for investigation into more complex questions.

We should be able to improve our understanding of the origins and characteristics of the knowledge-based modern economy within which the people of Great Britain have lived for the last two centuries and take more reliably informed decisions about how the public benefits can be maintained and improved. The advent of printing had permitted useful knowledge about science, medicine, and technology to be more securely stored and more widely disseminated.[17] But the extent to which such useful knowledge could be adopted in practice was limited by the academic and social institutions by which knowledge and industry were organised, including the secrecy implicit in the guild system, the barriers to access, and the high price of the printed texts themselves.[18] When, from the eighteenth century, certain countries led by Scotland and England learned to apply useful knowledge to the solution of real world problems of manufacturing, the change, as Joel Mokyr has remarked, 'affected the world more than all other social and political changes put together'.[19] The conjuncture of conditions that brought about that change, the start of which Mokyr puts conventionally at 1750, are not yet fully understood, but it seems likely that among the contributing factors was the fall in the price of access to the print that carried recent useful knowledge brought about by 1774, and the accompanying surge of abridgements, anthologies, children's books, and school textbooks that made it available to the whole nation.

We may also be able to improve our understanding of the political economy of books and reading, and of cultural production more generally, by making comparisons with industries with similar economic characteristics, especially with pharmaceuticals, with which the book industry was closely associated throughout the print era. Like the book industry, the pharmaceutical industry dealt in small volume/high value patented goods, which were produced and manufactured in metropolitan centres. It too depended

[17] Mokyr 8. [18] *Ibid.* [19] *Ibid.* 297.

upon advertising, retail price maintenance, regular physical communications both with the shops in the towns and with the fairs in the villages, and especially on intellectual property. There are many direct comparisons besides the sharing of distribution and advertising. The taking into private ownership of the ancient English oral ballad popular tradition, for example, can be compared with the present day patenting of useful knowledge of herbal properties available in some developing countries.[20] The impoverished mental and physical life historically suffered by constituencies of low-income readers whose access to modern knowledge was limited by price, can be compared with the poor levels of health suffered by those who were, and are, unable to afford the prices of drugs which are set far above the costs of manufacture. Comparing the two industries would enable the general discourses of invention, investment, freedom, markets, and property, within which their practices are usually discussed, to be augmented by a greater knowledge of the actual measured effects on prices, access, and outcomes. There are also many direct parallels with the intellectual property practices of the information technology industries.

Of course the collecting of data would be of little value in itself unless it were integrated into some provisional models of how authors, texts, books, reading and cultural outcomes are related. At least two such models, those of Robert Darnton and of Adams and Barker, have been proposed.[21] Both offer diagrammatical representations of how the production of printed texts requires the participation of many agents besides authors, how books not only derive from, but at the same time impact upon, wider societal factors, and how the whole system is criss-crossed with feedback loops. However these models, simplifications though they are, require more data than can ever, under any reasonable expectation, be empirically retrieved, and cannot be run so as to yield new results which are more than illustrations of the general descriptive validity of the model. Both the Darnton and the Adams/Barker models emphasise the circular nature of the processes which connect authors with readers, and vice-versa, 'communications circuits', and it is true that authors have a prior idea of the mentalities of the readers whom, they expect, will encounter the texts which they write. However, in all cases, when authors are not just writing for themselves but attempt

---

[20] See *Integrating Intellectual Property Rights and Development Policy, Report of the Commission on Intellectual Property Rights* (2002).

[21] Robert Darnton, 'What is the History of Books' in *Daedalus*, 1982; in Cathy N. Davidson, ed., *Reading in America* (Baltimore 1989); in Robert Darnton, *The Kiss of Lamourette* (1990); and in Finkelstein and McCleery 12. Thomas Adams and Nicolas Barker, 'A New Model for the Study of the Book' in Nicolas Barker, ed., *A Potencie of Life* (1993).

Table 22.1 Author-led model

1. Authors and editors write texts.
2. Publishers and booksellers print and sell these texts in the form of books and other print.
3. Readers buy, borrow, hire, and read the books or acquire knowledge of the texts in other ways.
4. Readers and other recipients experience a change in their knowledge, their values, opinions, and attitudes, or they are confirmed in their previous mentalities.
5. Readers and others change their behaviour, or their behaviour remains much the same.

to anticipate the effects on their readers, the readers who are anticipated are always different from the past readers of past texts on whose reactions the author's anticipatory judgement has been based. Even in a fast-moving world of commodified texts being produced to satisfy consumerist markets identified by market research, the actual readers can never be culturally, or even physically, identical with the readers whom the author had in mind in the writing of the text. Furthermore, postulating a feedback between readers and authors can only be useful if we stay with annalistic parade conventions which exclude all but initial readers. Postulating a strong feedback loop between authors and readers makes little sense, for example, in the case of most readers of the English-language Bible or of Shakespeare.

In order to develop usable models in which the empirical can actively interact with the theoretical, it would defeat the purpose to start with too much complexity. In the literary/cultural economy, there are simply too many interactions for us to have any hope of tracing, let alone of connecting, them all. Something simpler, which gives primacy to the most powerful links, may however still be able to yield good results. For this purpose, chronological models, which are bound to have some strongly linear features, are likely to be the best starting points. Table 22.1 is probably an adequate simplification of many common assumptions.

The author-led model distinguishes between texts and books, but without making the latter a central part of the process. The model is chronologically linear with some feed-back loops, of unknown varying influence connecting the participants which are not shown. Although it is at its most plausible when applied to newly written texts, it can accommodate later reprinting.

We can also postulate a reader-led model as in table 22.2. Indeed, since most of the study has been concerned with texts which could be successfully sold in markets which were limited by the incomes and other circumstances

Table 22.2 Reader-led model

1. Members of a society, at any historical moment, being the outcome of past events, including past reading, have a shared basis of language, knowledge, value, genre, and the many of the other characteristics which enable them to be regarded as a culture ('horizons of expectations'). They also have unfulfilled needs, aspirations, or desires which may or may not differ from those within their current horizons.
2. Readers seek to read texts which they hope will satisfy these needs and aspirations, within the limits of their economic circumstances and of their cultural horizons.
3. Publishers seek to identify such texts from what is available from living authors and from already printed texts, and to supply them in the form of printed books which they believe readers will buy.
4. A number of such books are read by readers who take and make meanings from them.
5. The horizons, needs, aspirations, and behaviour of the readers either change or remain much the same.

of buyers, and there were innumerable texts and books which were not favoured by buyers, this is probably a better starting point than the author-led model. It too is chronological and therefore linear and need not be confined to initial publication.

This model too distinguishes between the immaterial states of mind of participants and the material print by the reading of which minds were constituted and influenced. The two models are not mutually exclusive. On the contrary, the author-led and reader-led models follow chronologically, the one after the other, in a continuous progression. Taken together, they enable the historical data, macro and micro, quantified and anecdotal, to be put into a provisional theoretical context, and so may enable some of the clearest underlying patterns to emerge. In running both models with actual texts, the changing historical environment, including the prevailing economic, regulatory, and intellectual property regimes, can be factored in.

It is plain, however, that many changes in the system occurred which these models do not easily accommodate. They do not answer such questions as why collective reading institutions were invented, took root, and flourished in Great Britain when they did and not at some earlier or later time, or why the two different newly invented ways of financing collective reading, commercial renting and member-owned co-operatives, should have co-existed and should have coincided so exactly with cultural and gender divisions.[22] Both the author- and the reader-led models need to include provision for other active agents besides authors and readers, especially

---

[22] Discussed in chapter 13.

Table 22.3 Commercial and political model

1. Entrepreneurs, mostly publishers but also political, ecclesiastical, and commercial interest groups, perceive that there are unmet needs or aspirations which can be profitably met by supplying material print for reading at appropriate prices, or that they may be able to advance their interests by supplying such print.
2. These entrepreneurs devise, or acquire from others, packages of financing, manufacturing, and marketing such as enable the selected texts to be successfully advertised, sold, and distributed to readers.
3. Certain authors and editors take advantage of the opportunities offered by the entrepreneurs to provide them with the requisite texts.
4. The entrepreneurs supply the texts to the market at prices which conform to their commercial and ideological interests.
5. Certain readers acquire the books and read the texts.
6. The horizons, needs, and aspirations of the readers then either change or they remain much the same.

for independent agency in the material book part of the system as it was exercised within the governing structures. We need therefore, what I will call a commercial and political model, as noted in table 22.3.

The commercial and political model can easily accommodate the many cases in which the same entrepreneurs sold antithetical texts, as, for example, in the European Reformation, some printer/publishers printed both orthodox and heretical pamphlets, or in the British romantic period, when the publisher Cadell simultaneously supplied the main texts of the Counter-Enlightenment and of the Enlightenment. The commercial and political model can also easily accommodate practices which restrict, rather than facilitate, reading, such as textual controls, the clamp-down on abridgements and anthologies, the discouragement of lending libraries during the first decades of the high monopoly period, and all the pressures to self censorship at all stages of the process which tend to stabilise horizons of expectations at levels which match the perceived needs of the producer interest. As simple representations of a highly complex human system, the explanatory power of these models is not undermined by acknowledging that many of the agents were themselves part of the system. Some printers, for example, were part of the constituencies whose ideas they wished to promote. Publishers were themselves readers with their own horizons, needs, and aspirations which they brought to their role as commercial agents.

In recent times, private ownership has been widened to include virtually any text, however short, literary, visual, or performed. It now includes not only texts but scientific and other discoveries. The period of state-enforced and state-guaranteed intellectual property monopoly has been successively lengthened, and there are almost no external regulation, price controls, or codes of conduct, such as modern societies increasingly apply to other monopolies, including real property. Although the notion of a shared national or international culture is essentially public, social, interactive, cumulative, and cross-generational, the texts in which culture is inscribed are divided into ever smaller privately owned parcels. Such historical studies as have been done suggest that the links between science, technological progress, industrial innovation, and patents, if they exist at all, are obscure and debatable.[23] Indeed, as far as scientific research is concerned, there is growing evidence that the disincentives to intellectual enquiry and exchange brought about by private intellectual property are now having deleterious effects on the progress and application of scientific knowledge and therefore on human health and welfare broadly defined.[24]

In 1813, Thomas Jefferson, one of the founding fathers of the United States, offered a manifesto of Enlightenment, which pointed up one of the essential differences between real property and intellectual property:

That ideas should freely spread from one to another over the globe for the moral and mutual instruction of man and improvement of his condition, seems to have been peculiarly and benevolently designed by nature when she made them like fire, expansible over all space, without lessening their density in any point, and like the air in which we breathe, move, and have our physical being, incapable of confinement or exclusive appropriation.[25]

Jefferson might have added that ideas of any length or complexity could not, in his day, be transferred unless they were carried by the material vehicle of print, and that the price of access to that print was set in conditions set by the public through their democratic institutions. In 2003, the Supreme Court of the United States disallowed an appeal against a further, and in some cases retroactive, lengthening of the period of private monopoly, rejecting the argument that the Jeffersonian ideal of a well-informed and participative citizenry was being put at risk.[26]

Across the English-speaking world we are moving towards a realisation of the nightmare of Ms Mei-Mei Wu described in a recent book.

[23] Mokyr 295.

[24] See, for example, *Keeping Science Open: the effects of intellectual property policy on the conduct of science* (London: Royal Society 2003).

[25] Quoted by David, *Intellectual Property* 10, from *The Life and Selected Writings of Thomas Jefferson*, edited by Adrienne Koch and William Peden (New York 1972) 629.

[26] In the case of Eric Eldred, *et al.*, Petitioners *v.* John D. Ashcroft, Attorney General. Decided 15 January 2003.

Every descriptive word in the English language has been registered as a trademark and cannot be used by anyone else and every merely descriptive term has acquired a secondary meaning as a trademark, so I decide to use ordinary words but to convey different meanings, and find that they have all been registered as arbitrary trademarks. In desperation, I make up new words from the letters of the alphabet, but find that they too have already been registered as coined or fanciful trademarks.[27]

The argument that intellectual property is a privilege granted for a limited period in order to reward and encourage innovation that is valuable to the society that grants it is as valid today as it was in Adam Smith's time. The conditions within which the privilege should be granted are therefore an issue of public policy, which ought to be decided, not in accordance with dogmas about the rights of property, but with eyes open to the public interest in the likely consequences. When, for the first time in history, copies of texts of all kinds can be reproduced and circulated instantaneously in limitless numbers at infinitesimal unit cost, it is perverse that much of the technological and business effort of the text-copying industries is devoted to preventing copying and to keeping up the price of access.

To develop a political economy of texts, books, reading, and mentalities would not meet the high aspiration of the Enlightenment to write a history of the progress of the human mind. Such an enterprise could, however, contribute to answering some of the most vital, as well as most difficult, of all human questions. How did it come about that we of the present generation think the way we do? How can we, as a help towards making more informed societal as well as personal choices, build a fuller, more scientific, more theoretical, and more critical understanding of the governing structures within which cultural texts are produced, the forces that shape both the inputs and the outcomes, including cost, price, access, and degree of obsolescence? And how can we, when equipped with such knowledge, appreciate the essentials of the relationship between the representations made available to society and the opinions, beliefs, attitudes, and behaviours that may derive from the consumption of such representations? In such an ambitious undertaking, studies of the 400 years during which the printed book was supreme and unchallenged offer many lessons of continuing validity.

[27] Quoted by Loewenstein 25.

Appendices

In accordance with convention, I have abbreviated the format sizes of quarto, octavo, duodecimo, sextodecimo, vicesimoquarto, and trigesimosecundo, as 4to, 8vo, 12mo, 16mo, 24mo, and 32mo.

Prices are normally given in shillings before binding.

Appendix 1 Markets, book production, prices, and print runs

MARKETS

The English-speaking world

England[1]   *Estimates of population, millions*

1551	3
1601	4.1
1651	5.2
1701	5.1
1751	5.9
1761	6.3
1771	6.6
1781	7.2
1791	7.8
1801	8.6
1811	9.8
1821	11.4
1831	13.2
1841	14.9
1851	16.7

[1] Rounded from the table in E. A. Wrigley, R. S. Davies, J. E. Oeppen, R. S. Schofield, *English Population History from Family Reconstitution* (Cambridge 1997) 532.

Appendix 1 (*cont.*)

Scotland[2]

1600	less than 1

Of which about half lived in the mainly Gaelic-speaking
areas north of the Tay

1700	1
1750	1.2
1800	1.6
1850	2.5

Ireland[3]

1600	1
1712	2.8
1767	3.5
1791	4.8
1800	5

Of whom probably about half did not normally speak English[4]
Early nineteenth century. Rapid population growth, with many people living at near
subsistence levels

1845. The peak of population before the Great Famine[5]	8.5

English-speaking North America

Mainland colonies which became the United States[6]

1650	0.050
1700	0.25
1750	0.9
1760	1.6
1780	2.8

United States

1790	3.9
1800	5.2
1810	7.2
1820	9.6
1830	12.9
1840	17

---

[2] John Cannon, *The Oxford Companion to British History* (1997) 763.   [3] *Ibid.* 763.
[4] T. W. Moody and W. E. Vaughan, *A New History of Ireland* (Oxford 1986) iv, 161 and 383.
[5] *A New History of Ireland* (Oxford 1989) v, 108.
[6] Extracted from *Historical Statistics of the United States, Bicentennial Edition* (Washington 1975).

Other English-speaking book-buying communities

West Indies, Canada, South Africa, Australia, New Zealand, India, and elsewhere, naval bases and military garrisons, and expatriate families living in continental European countries. The size of these markets is difficult to estimate, but they were significant from the late-eighteenth century onwards.

Estimated annual growth in economic output, England, per cent[7]

1700–60	0.7
1760–80	0.6
1780–1801	1.4
1801–1831	1.9

Estimated annual growth in income per head, England, per cent[8]

1700-until second quarter of nineteenth century	0.3

BOOK PRODUCTION

England

Indicators of London book production, estimated average annual output of books by title[9]

1630s	600
1640s	1,600
1650s	1,200
1660s	800
1670s	1,000
1680s	1,500
1690s	1,400

The following series, not compiled on the same basis as the one above, is drawn from the London book industry's trade catalogues, which excluded pamphlets and publications by publishers operating outside the mainstream industry. The estimates probably also exclude publications published at the authors' expense. Although it cannot be directly compared with the previous series, it gives some measure of the growth of output.

1700–50[10]	500
1750–89	600

---

[7] Nick Crafts, 'The Industrial Revolution' in Floud and McCloskey i, 47.   [8] *Ibid.*

[9] Summarised from Maureen Bell and John Barnard, 'Provisional Count of *Wing* Titles 1641–1700' in *Publishing History*, 24 (1998). See also D. F. McKenzie, 'The Economies of Print, 1550–1750', 390, in *Produzione e Commercio della Carta e del Libro secc. XIII–XVIII*. Istituto Internazionale di Storia Economica (1992).

[10] Information from Maxted, whose statistics of titles are based primarily on the London book industry's own estimates from trade publications, as advertised in the periodical press, a measure which excludes pamphlets, publications of the fringe industry, and ephemeral print. A graph in James Raven, *Judging*

Appendix 1 (*cont.*)

1790–1800	800
1800–1810	800
By 1827[11]	1,000, rising fast

London edition sizes, high monopoly period, from the ledgers of Strahan, printer and publisher, 1738–85[12]

Edition size	Orders	Per cent of total
250	37	7
500	175	34
750	77	15
1,000	139	27
1,500	43	8
2,000	28	5
3,000	15	3

Expansion of printing capacity in London, numbers of master printers[13]

1724	75
1785	124
1808	216
1824	306
1855	368

Much of this capacity was used for printing newspapers and commercial documents.

New Wealth, Popular Publishing and Responses to Commerce in England, 1750–1800 (1992) 32, based on titles in the *Eighteenth Century Short Century Catalogue*, BL Microfiche 1982–1990, includes many forms of ephemeral print besides books (for example, sale catalogues and legal documents) but not newspapers. This table shows a sharp rise beginning in the 1770s, and therefore tends to confirm the general picture shown by the figures on the more limited basis used by Maxted. C. J. Mitchell, who also made some detailed calculations based on the *ESTC* information, seems to have come to the conclusion that there was an absolute fall in titles printed in mid-century in both France and England (not simply a fall relative to the size of the population or of the economy). See 'The Spread and Fluctuations of Eighteenth century Printing' in *Studies on Voltaire and the Eighteenth Century* (1985), quoted by Alvin Kernan, *Printing Technology, Letters, and Samuel Johnson* (Princeton 1987) 60. Kernan's suggestion, much repeated in other works, that England at last became a 'print culture' in the mid eighteenth century is hard to reconcile with the production information, unless the term 'print culture' is used to mean principally newspapers and commercial print. According to Floud and McCloskey, average real incomes rose steadily over the period, and income distribution appears to have been static. Some authors, such as Feather, *Publishing* 76, who note 'a rapid growth in the [book] trade in the eighteenth century', have tended to assume, from the large change from 1700 to 1800 that the growth was steady during the century.

[11] Goodhugh 82.
[12] Quoted from Patricia Hernlund, 'William Strahan's Ledgers and Standard Charges for Printing, 1738–85' in *Studies in Bibliography* (1958).
[13] McKitterick ii, 4.

Appendix 1 *(cont.)*

Expansion of book-binding production in London, a more precise measure of the growth of book production than printing capacity[14]

1794. Master binders	69
Journeymen	165
1808. Master binders	121
1813. Master binders	151

The number of journeymen per master was also rising

Production in 1803

'It is computed, that upward of eight hundred new publications are annually ushered into the world from the London shops, the value of which, it is estimated, upon an average, at half a million sterling.'[15]

CURRENCY UNITS

Until 1972 England (and later Great Britain and the United Kingdom of Great Britain and Ireland), had an official currency system of pounds, shillings and pence. There were 20 shillings (s) in a pound sterling (£) and 12 pence (d) in a shilling. A guinea was 21 shillings, a crown 5 shillings, a farthing a quarter of a penny. Occasionally other denominations were used, such as the noble (three to the pound), the mark (13.3 shillings), the groat (four pence), and the florin (two shillings). Until the union of 1707 Scottish prices were denominated in Scottish currency which from 1603 was a twelfth of the sterling equivalent. The Irish currency was separate until 1800, and the currencies in use in the American colonies also varied. In order to allow comparisons to be made, I have converted most small figures for costs and prices into English sterling shillings, a denominator which has the advantage of being no longer familiar. Some indicators against which the impact of prices can be compared, ways of understanding 'real' prices, are given below. For a discussion of the value of the shilling relative to income and wealth distribution in the romantic period, see chapter 11.

PRICE CONTROLS

England

1534. 'High and unreasonable' book prices are specifically outlawed. Institutions are set up to deal with complaints, with provision for redress and penalties.[16]

1583. A Commission on Privileges finds 'no cause of complaint', endorses the existing system of price controls, but recommends uniform prices.[17]

---

[14] Quoted by Potter 162.
[15] Augustus Gottlieb Goede, *Memorials of Nature and Art Collected on a Journey in Great Britain during the Years 1802 and 1803* (1808) iii, 56.
[16] *CHBB* iii, 610, from A. Luders *et al.*, *Statutes of the Realm* (1810–28) iii, 456.
[17] Greg, *Companion* 33.

Appendix 1 *(cont.)*

Various decrees of the 1580s require that those books produced under Letters Patent be 'reasonably' priced and sold at the same price to rich and poor alike.[18]

1598. Maximum prices for all newly published titles laid down by the Stationers' Company. They are calculated in accordance with maximum prices per sheet of print of various sizes, that is in accordance with the costs of manufacturing, with no allowance for the possible costs of buying manuscripts or intellectual property rights.[19] Why reprints were excluded is not known. This exception was closed by decree in 1637 and by law in 1643.

1603. A publisher fined for breaching the price controls.[20]

1604. The margin between the production cost and the maximum permitted final retail price of the *Ten Commandments*, a broadsheet which all parish churches were obliged to purchase, seems to have been far higher than any effective price-control system would have allowed.[21]

1622. Bacon's *History of Henry the Seventh*. Price reduction ordered.[22]

Great Britain

1710. The Act provides for redress against excessive prices and profits. No evidence found that the provisions were ever applied.

1739. Act of Parliament. All legal safeguards against excessive prices abolished without replacement.

BOOK PRICES

England. Guild and early monopoly periods. Scattered records and indicators. (For Shakespeare see appendix 12.)

Compulsory books, *Book of Common Prayer*	*Shillings*
1549. Unbound[23]	2.2
1552. Maximum permitted prices, as printed in the book[24]	
In quires, i.e. unbound for sale within the book industry	2.5
Bound in parchment	3.3
Bound in leather	4

---

[18] See documents on price controls printed in Greg's *Companion*, especially that on page 124.

[19] The maximum figures are quoted by Francis R. Johnson 84, from Greg and Boswell 58. Reprinted with modernised spelling by Bennett, 1558–1603, 299. Some figures on maximum print runs, 1635, quoted by Plant 93, from primary records.

[20] Jackson 2.

[21] Cost about a penny (1d) maximum price 15d. See Edwin E. Willoughby, *A Printer of Shakespeare* (1934) 66 from public records.

[22] Jackson 149. For another case in which a complaint about excessive prices was rejected, 1615, see Greg and Boswell, *Records* 352.

[23] *CHBB* iii, 600. [24] Gomme, *Bibliographical Notes* 277.

The second impression, leaving out the forms of consecration of priests and other materials	
In quires	2
Bound in parchment	2.5
Bound in leather	3.3

Compulsory books, *Homilies*

Prices recorded as having been paid by parishes, from churchwardens' accounts, spelling modernised[25]

1549. Leverton, Lincs	
Second book and tome of homilies	4.7
1556/7. St Michael's Cornhill, London[26]	
Two bookes called the homilies	1.4
1563. Wing, Bucks.	
The Homily book	4
1564. Minchinhampton, Glos	
Second book of Homilies	3.5
and first book of Homilies	1.4
1569. Eltham Kent	
A book called the Homilies and the charges to buy it	12.5

Other compulsory books

1544. Six books of the Litany in English	1.5
1548. 'The half part' of *Paraphrases of Erasmus*	5
1549. Two new Psalters	10
1549. *The Second Tome of Homilies*	4.66
1549. *Paraphrases of Erasmus*	7
A chain to secure the book	0.33
1551. Eight Psalters in English	13.3
1559. Four song books and a Psalter[27]	6.6
1570. Jewell's *Apology*	10
1581. An abridgement of the Statutes, to remain in the church	9

Non-compulsory books

1498. (Voragine's) *Golden Legende*, lives of the saints with woodcuts, printed by Caxton, folio, 1483[28]	6.66 and 5.66

---

[25] Except where shown, from records in *Archaeologia* 36, 21, 35, 409, and 34, 58, and Gomme, *Bibliographical Notes* 277, 169, 172.
[26] Plant 240.   [27] Timperley 413 quoting church records of St Helen, Abingdon, Berks.
[28] Gomme, *Literary Curiosities and Notes* 21 from St Margaret's Westminster parish records. The lower price is thought to be a trade price.

Appendix 1 (*cont.*)

1509. Two parchment processioners printed by Pynson, for a chapel[29]	2.66 the pair
1510. Five books printed by Caxton[30]	6.66
1514. A processioner for a chapel[31]	1
1555. 'Payde for a legend' [presumably Caxton's][32]	5
1592. Greene's *Groatsworth of Wit* Shakespeare (see appendix 12)	presumably 0.33
1600. *Godfrey of Bulloigne, done into verse by E. Fairefax*, folio[33]	5.5
1602. Chaucer, *Complete Works*, large folio[34]	21
1621. Bacon's *Henry VII*[35]	7
1624. Purchas's *Pilgrims*, 4 volumes	66.6
1635. Bacon's *Sylva Sylvarum*, small folio of about 280 pages[36]	4.6
1638. Sandys's *Journey*[37]	7
1673. Sir William Davenant's *Works* (plays in folio)[38]	24 bound

Print runs, early modern period, examples recorded in archives from elsewhere in Europe[39]

	Print-run
Plantin of Antwerp	100 to 5,000
Paris	250 to 2,600
Wolrab of Leipzig	1,000 to 1,500
German cities, editions recorded of	4,000, 3,000, 1,500, 800, 500
Netherlands, sixteenth century	2,500, 2000, 1,000, 500, 100

Transport costs, early modern period, an archival example from Italy[40]

1550. A consignment of books, to be sent from Rome to Lyon by pack animal	scudi 18
The same consignment by water transport	scudi 4

---

[29] *STC* 16232. Christianson 17, noting how much cheaper these books were than their manuscript predecessors.
[30] Wheatley 194.   [31] Christianson 17.
[32] Timperley 413, quoting church records of St Helen, Abingdon, Berks.
[33] See T. W. Baldwin, *Shakspere's Love's Labours Won, New Evidence from the Account Books of an Elizabethan Bookseller* (Carbondale, Ill. 1957) 23.
[34] Price noted on title page of a copy done before contemporary binding, Ac.
[35] And following item. Wheatley 94.
[36] Contemporary inscription on title page of a copy, Ac. Possibly a price after binding.
[37] Mary Elizabeth Bohannon, 'A London Bookseller's Bill, 1635–1639' in *The Library* (1938), 442.
[38] Catalogue of John Starkey bound in a copy.
[39] Quoted by contributors to Gilmont 19, 44, 165.   [40] Noted by Richardson 37.

Appendix 1 *(cont.)*

Raising the price of English-language Bibles, early modern period, prices on first publication, with a few recorded print runs

	Shillings	*Print run*
1531. Tyndall's New Testament and Pentateuch[41]	7	3,000
Offshore Dutch 12mo. A reprint of the English language New Testament[42]	1.1	
1539. Matthew's Bible[43]	na	1,500
1541. Coverdale's 'Great Bible'[44]	10 unbound, 12 bound	2,500
Three other editions in 1541[45] A compulsory book, the cost of purchase to be met by local priests and their parishioners. Parishes found to be without the book to pay a fine of 40 shillings a month[46]		
1551. Day's Bible, sold in four parts to enable wider access, 'yt they whiche ar not able to bie ye hole, may bie a part'[47]		
1559. A Bible and a Paraphrase'[48]	16	
1562. Geneva Bible[49]	10	
1568. 'Bishops' Bible[50]	24 bound, 20 unbound	
1611. The newly published authorised 'King James' version bought at Worcester	58	
1612. Another copy bought at Lynn[51] These were presumably copies of the folio black letter version, reissued in 1613, using old sheets	53.3	
1612. tranched down to 4to and 8v	na	
1617. Tranched down to 12mo	na	
1620. Tranched down to 24mo	na	
1641, Edition sizes.[52] Folio		1,500 and 3,000
Quarto		3,000
Octavo		6,000 and 10,000

[41] Noted by Townley 179.   [42] Townley 179. Print run from Moulton 50.
[43] Print run from Moulton 123. Further details quoted by John J. Lowndes, *An Historical Sketch of the Law of Copyright* (1840) 7.
[44] Quoted by Altick 21.   [45] Print run from Moulton 143.   [46] Noted by Townley 185.
[47] Quoted by Charles C. Butterworth, *The Literary Lineage of the King James Bible 1340–1611* (Philadelphia 1941) 151.
[48] Gomme, *Literary Curiosities and Notes* 172 from parish records.
[49] Timperley 414 quoting church records of St Helen, Abingdon, Berks.   [50] Arber ii, 749.
[51] A. S. Herbert, *Historical Catalogue of Printed English Bibles 1525–1961* (1968) 133.
[52] Ian Green, *Print and Protestantism in Early Modern England* (Oxford 2000) 52, from Sparke's *Scintilla*.

Appendix 1 *(cont.)*

BIBLES, SCOTLAND

1572. Folio, Bassandyne/Arbuthnet, price set by Privy   £Scots 5
Council[53]

1610. Geneva Bible, a recorded price[54]   £Scots 6

1640s. Folio[55]   £Scots 12

Octavo Bibles, the commonest size used, followed the same pattern at levels 25 per cent lower. The Scots pound which stood at 4:1 in the 1560s in relation to sterling had fallen to 12:1 in 1603, at which rate it was effectively tied until the union of 1707.

Print runs

Information on the size of English editions in the early modern period is rare, and since most records relate to printed texts which were commercially the most important, its representative quality is difficult to gauge.

	Price (shillings)	Print run
1493. Pynson. *Dives and Lazarus*[56]	Wholesale 4	600
1493. Church service book[57]	Wholesale 2	1,000
1493. Boccaccio's *Fall of Princes*	Wholesale 4	600
1499. Abridgement of Statutes 409 unsold copies in existence in 1553[58]		?1,000
1538. English language Bible printed in Paris[59]		2,500
1540s. Acts of Parliament[60]		mostly 500
1558. Official proclamation of the death of Queen Mary and accession of Queen Elizabeth, one leaf[61] unit cost to the state	0.05	500
1558. Official proclamation on licensing of preachers, one leaf unit cost to the state	0.08	106
1576. More's *In Praise of Folly*[62]		limited to 1,500 per edition
1560s. Official decrees[63]		from 20 to 700, mainly at lower end

[53] Mann 202, 211.   [54] *Ibid.* 203.   [55] And following item. Mann 211.

[56] H. R. Plomer, 'The Lawsuits of Richard Pynson' in *The Library* (1909) 115. I give the date of the contract to supply. Some of the titles had been printed earlier.

[57] And following item. Plomer, 'Lawsuits' 115.

[58] Quoted by *CHBB* iii, 427 from an inventory made for a lawsuit.

[59] Noted by Townley 184.   [60] Arber ii, 54.

[61] This and following two items calculated from accounts transcribed in Arber i, 564, from a manuscript in BL, add. mss. 5756.

[62] Arber ii, 307.   [63] Arber i, 570, 576.

Appendix 1 (*cont.*)

	Print run
1577. John Dee's *General and rare memorials pertaining to the art of navigation*[64]	100
1582. Robinson's *Harmony of King David's Harp*[65]	100
before 1583. 'Birdes and Tallis musicke'[66]	more than 717
1583. *Thee first foure bookes of Virgil, his Aeneis*	more than 928
1587. Grammar and Accidence (school book), Bible in 8vo, Psalms, proclamations, statutes, and almanacs, a maximum of four impressions of 2,500 are permitted in any year, thereafter maximum impressions[67]	1,250
1581. *ABC* and Catechism – an edition printed in defiance of the privilege, what would later be called a pirated edition[68]	600
1587. A reprint of *Bullinger's Decades* (sermons) Of which about half seem to have been sold by 1594.[69] A compulsory book	1,250
1593. Official Catechisms[70]	3 reams

Compulsory or semi-compulsory

1595. Foxe's *Martyrs*[71] Semi-compulsory	1,200 to 1,350
1599. Hayward's *Henry IIII*, second edition with revised text The edition was destroyed and the printer imprisoned[72]	1,500
1598. *A Plain and Ready Form to Teach Children to Read in a Short Time.* Maximum print run permitted[73]	500
1606. Lambert's *Eirenarche* (law book)[74]	1,250
c. 1602. Ascham's *English Schoolmaster* Another edition[75]	500 / 1,500
1603. An unauthorised edition of *Basilikon Doron* (King James VI and I's advice to his son)[76]	500
1606. An edition of a book of canon law[77]	850
1614. Appendix to a book setting out the common law[78]	1,500 maximum
1615. Dent's *Sermons*, an edition to be surrendered to the owner of the copy[79]	700

[64] Quoted by Plant 93. No source given. Perhaps from Lowndes ii, 610.
[65] See George McGill Vogt, 'Richard Robinson's *Eupolia* (1603)' 635, in *Studies in Philology* (1924).
[66] And following item. Number of copies recorded as unsold in an inventory. See John Barnard and Maureen Bell, 'The Inventory of Henry Bynneman (1583) A Preliminary Survey' in *Publishing History* (1991) 35.
[67] Greg and Boswell 25.   [68] Judge 46.
[69] Greg and Boswell 22.   [70] Arber i, 566.   [71] Greg and Boswell 51.
[72] Clegg 203. See W. W. Greg, 'Samuel Harsnett and Hayward's Henry IV' in *The Library* (1956).
[73] Arber iii, 116. Not identified in *STC*.   [74] Jackson 22.   [75] Greg and Boswell, 88.
[76] Arber ii, 836.   [77] Jackson 24.   [78] Arber iii, 554.   [79] Jackson 81.

Appendix 1 (*cont.*)

	Print run
1619. John Taylor, the Water Poet, *Pennilesse Pilgrimage*[80]	500
1619. Brooke's *Catalogue and Accession of Kings, Princes* folio[81]	500
1620s to 1652. Sparke's *Crums of Comfort*, total sales[82]	60,000
1624. Gee's *The foote out of the Snare*, three editions	4,500
1627. May's English translation of Lucan's *Pharsalia*[83]	
1630. Hayward's *Life and Raigne of . . . Henry IV*	1,000 or more
1631. An edition of French and German versions of the Psalms	1,000

The compiler ordered to bear all costs, to be given a quarter of the copies printed, and all subsequent rights to revert to the Stationers' Company[84]

1635. The restrictions on the maximum edition sizes raised to 1,500 or 2,000 for ordinary books, and to 3,000 and 5,000 for those printed in the smaller type fonts[85]

1638. An edition of Josephus[86]	1,250

1641. Lilly's *Grammar* (1540) price recently raised from 0.33 to 0.66 in quires[87]

	annual print run
	20,000

Scotland

1577. Works of Sir David Lindsay, copies unsold in an inventory[88]	505
1599. Sidney's *Arcadia*, printed offshore for an English bookseller[89]	500
1591. *Sacrifice of a Christian soule*[90]	more than 600

England. Civil War and Commonwealth

Most printing presses are used for newsbooks, official documents, pamphlets

---

[80] His own figure. See Watt 291.
[81] Mentioned in Jaggard's 'The Printer' in Vincent's *Discoverie of Errours* (1619), *STC* 24756.
[82] Ian Green, *Print and Protestantism in Early Modern England* (Oxford 2000) 386, and following item 174.
[83] Arber iv, 174.   [84] Jackson 231.
[85] W. W. Greg, *Some Aspects and Problems of London Publishing between 1550 and 1650* (Oxford 1956) 16.
[86] Jackson 313.   [87] Sparke in Arber iv, 37.
[88] Robert Dickson and John Philip Edmond, *Annals of Scottish Printing* (1890) 290.
[89] For the record of the punishment of the bookseller by the Stationers' Company, which mentions the print run, see Greg and Boswell 82. The title is Aldis no. 321. See also C. J. Sisson, *Lost Plays of Shakespeare's Age* (Cambridge 1936) who used previously unpublished court records.
[90] Quoted from an original record relating a to a seizure, by F. S. Ferguson, 'Relations between London and Edinburgh Printers and Stationers (–1640)' in *The Library* (1927), 154.

Appendix 1 *(cont.)*

		Print run
Titles printed in 1640s and 1650s[91]		23,000

In 1652, the printer responsible for John Fry's *The Accuser Shunn'd*,
  and *The Clergy in their Colours*, both 1649, told Parliament he
  had printed 1,000 copies, 'the ordinary number of such things'.[92]

England. State licensing period and post-1695 hiatus

Apart from the compulsory and semi-compulsory texts published
  by the Stationers' Company, information on print runs is still
  rare

1666 (reprinting after the fire of London)[93]

ABCS		20 reams
Old primers		12,000
Latin school books, such as Aesop		3,000
Classical texts in Latin, each author		1,500
?1679. (Henry Care), *English Liberties*		5,000

The publisher Harrison was arrested for publishing this pamphlet[94]

1679. *The Protestant Tutor for Children*		500
1686. Rawlet's *Christian Monitor*, copies sold in nineteen editions by 1697[95]		95,000
Many romances and plays, old and new[96]	1	na
1697. Remainder price for some romances[97]	6 for 12	na
(1680s) Keach's *Travels of True Godliness*[98]		10,000 sold
(1680s) Shirley's *Lord Jeffrey's Life*[99]		6,000 sold
1685. *Fifteen Comforts of Matrimony* (chapman's book)[100]		1,000
1691. Bate's *Pharmacopea* (medical)[101]		1,500
1694. Holder's *Treatise on Harmony* (music)[102]		500

1695. John Locke, *The Reasonableness of Christianity*
Locke agreed to be paid 10s a sheet, the first impression not to
  exceed 1,500 copies, and no later impressions to exceed 1,000[103]

---

[91] Feather, *Publishing* 45, quoting a number of Thomason tracts.

[92] H. John McLachlan, in a letter to *The Times Literary Supplement*, 7 March 1952, quoting *Commons Journals* vi, 536.

[93] Blagdon 186.

[94] This and the following item from a printed petition reproduced by Ford opposite 88.

[95] Quoted by D. F. McKenzie, 'The Economies of Print, 1550–1750,' 390

[96] Altick 22. Hunt, Mandlebrote, and Shell 57.   [97] *Ibid.* 59.   [98] Dunton 177.

[99] *Ibid.* 184. Not identified from the description.

[100] In an original document quoted by Don-John Dugas, 'The London Book Trade in 1709' in *Papers of the Bibliographical Society of America* 95. 2 (2001).

[101] Blagden and Hodgson 211.   [102] *Ibid.* 211.

[103] Photostat of the contract document, Reading University Library. The terms closely follow those for the contract dated 13 January 1693, for *An Essay Concerning Humane Understanding*, of which a photostat is also in the Reading University Library, from the original in the Bodleian. Partly printed by Maurice Cranston, *John Locke, A Biography* (1959) 318.

Appendix 1 *(cont.)*

	Print run
1699. *Tablet of Cebes*	750
1699. Howell's *Medulla Historiae Anglicanae*[104]	1,250
1701. An edition of Bunyan's *Pilgrim's Progress*, part I[105]	8,000
1701. An edition of Bunyan's *Pilgrim's Progress*, part II[106]	5,000
1701. Horace (in Latin)	2,000
1702. Catullus, Tibullus, and Propertius (in Latin)	750
1702. Stillingfleet, *Natural and Revealed Religion,* seventh edition	1,500 planned, about 1,100 printed
1702. Bennett's *Discourse of Schism*, second edition	1,000
1704. Third edition	750
1705. Schrevelius's *Lexicon*	4,000
1705. Clarendon's History, small paper edition[107]	2,000
1705. Dumont's *Voyage to the Levant*[108]	1,000
1708. Whiston's *New Theory of the Earth*, second edition	500
before 1710. *The Judgment of Whole Kingdoms and Nations* Discounts for multiple orders, an abridged version available to be distributed free. The book may also be borrowed free[109]	8,000 in 3 impressions
1711. Bentley's *Horace* (in Latin)	1,025

Scotland

1707. Ruddiman's *Volusenus*[110]	1,200

Official supernatural, production, 1766 to 1795, Cambridge University Press alone[111]

Bibles	460,000
New Testaments	350,000
Prayer books	over 500,000

Tolerated illegitimate supernatural. Almanacs

1508. First evidence of almanacs being printed in England[112]

1520. A reference to almanacs and prognostications being sold for 1 to 6 pence[113]

---

[104] Quoted from a contemporary document by Stoker 66.
[105] Stoker 68.   [106] *Ibid*. 68.   [107] Bennett and Clements 209–211.
[108] Closed trade sale catalogue, 9 Feb 1743/4. This was a second edition.
[109] Printed note inserted in copy of the fifth edition. Ac.   [110] *Typographia* i, 195.
[111] McKitterick ii, 226 from the archives of Cambridge University Press.
[112] Gomme, *Bibliographical Notes* 120.   [113] Dorne 79.

Appendix 1 (*cont.*)

		Print run
1547. Almanacs and prognostications included in the letters patent (monopoly) given to the king's printer, and then to the Stationers' Company.[114]		
Examples of production runs		
1660s in England, total sold annually[115]		about 400,000
1761, annual sales of some individual titles[116]		
Vox Stellarum, '*Old Moore*' (prophecies, nationalistic, anti-Catholic)		82,000
Rider's (prophecies)		24,000
Ladies' Diary (essays, advice, poems, riddles)		15,000
Partridge's (prophecies, nationalistic, anti-Catholic)		8,000
Poor Robin's (jokes, bawdy, and riddles)		11,000
Wing's		7,000
Four others, each		2,500 to 3000

England. Examples of recorded edition sizes, high monopoly period[117]

early 1700s. Sermons printed in Cambridge[118]		400 to 1,150
1711. Aesop in Latin (commonly reprinted school book)[119]		4,000
1711. Settle's *City Ramble* (play)[120]		750
1711. *Works of George Farquar*, second edition[121]		1,000
1712. An edition of Clarendon's *History*[122]		1,500
1714. Third edition[123]		1,000
1714. Ford's *Perkin Warbeck, A Tragedy*[124]		1,000
1713. Newton's *Philosophiae Naturalis Principia Mathematica*, second edition, Cambridge Widely distributed to selected recipients and libraries in many countries of Europe[125]	15 in quires	711
1715. Pope's Homer's *Iliad*, volume i[126]		2,000
1716. Volume ii[127]		1,250
1716. Addison's *Freeholder*[128]		3,000
Most plays, early eighteenth century		750 or 1,000
1717. Gay's *Three Hours after Marriage*[129]		2,500
An edition before 1743, Aristotle's *Problems* (women's bodies)[130]		3000

---

[114] Plant 101.   [115] Capp 23, quoting primary sources.   [116] *Ibid.* 247, quoting primary sources.
[117] Prices from *A Catalogue of the Most Esteemed Modern Books* (1751).
[118] Quoted by D. F. McKenzie in *Making Meaning, 'Printers of the Mind' and Other Essays* edited by Peter D. McDonald and Michael Suarez (Amherst 2002) 24.
[119] Keith Maslon and John Lancaster, eds., *The Bowyer Ledgers* (1991).
[120] *Ibid.* 101.   [121] *Ibid.* 49.   [122] Harry Carter, *A History of Oxford University Press* (1975) i, 306.
[123] Bowyer Ledgers 220.   [124] *Ibid.* 209.   [125] McKitterick ii, 104 from original documents.
[126] Bowyer Ledgers 251.   [127] *Ibid.* 289.   [128] *Ibid.* 319.   [129] *Ibid.* 369.
[130] Trade sale catalogue, 4 August 1743.

Appendix 1 (*cont.*)

		Print run
Don Quixote by Skelton, 12mo		3,000
Human Prudence (conduct book)		1,500
1720 and **1722**. Wright's *Travels through France, Italy, &c*, two vols. 4to, with plates[131]	24	1,000
Herbert's *History of England*, three vols.[132]		1,000
1721. An edition of Clarendon's *History*[133]		
1729. Two editions of Gay's *Polly*, 4to[134]		10,500
1730. *A Letter from the West*[135]	6	
An edition before 1732, Butler's *Hudibras*, 12mo[136]		4,000
An edition before 1732, Stanhope's *Kempis*		5,000
Recent editions before 1732, Ovid, Horace, Virgil		2,000 or 3,000 each
1733. Sale's translation of the Koran[137]		1,500
1737. Le Sage's *Bachelor of Salamanca*, volume i		1,000
1739. Volume ii[138]		750
1738. Boyle's *Lecture sermons*, folio[139]		750
1742. Eliza Haywood's *Secret Histories, Novels, and Poems*, fourth edition[140]		1,000
1742. Chillingworth's Works folio	16	1,000
1743. Dodsley's *Collection of Old Plays*[141]		1,000
1755. Young's *Night Thoughts*, 8vo, printed by Samuel Richardson for Millar[142]		750
1755. Young's *Centaur Not Fabulous*, third edition, 12mo, printed by Samuel Richardson for Millar[143]		2,500

Teaching and reference books

	Print run
An edition before 1732, Littleton's *Latin English Dictionary*[144]	6,500
1734. Bailey's *Exercises*, 9th edition[145]	5,000
1736. Catechism, each impression[146]	5,000
1737. *Young Man's Companion*[147]	5,000
1763. Delphin classics, Virgil, Horace, Ovid[148]	normal editions 3,000
1763. Watts's *Hymns*[149]	normal editions 5,000

[131] *Ibid.* 9 February 1743/4.   [132] *Ibid.* 14 March 1719/20.
[133] Harry Carter, *A History of Oxford University Press* (1975) i, 306.   [134] Bowyer 58.   [135] *Ibid.* 62.
[136] And following two items. Daniel Midwinter and Aaron Ward valuation, 1732, BL add. mss. 44, 849.
[137] *Ibid.* 41.   [138] *Ibid.* 267.   [139] *Ibid.* 103.   [140] *Ibid.* 263.   [141] William Strahan archives.
[142] Receipted invoice by Samual Richardson, unpublished manuscript, Ac.
[143] *Ibid.*   [144] Midwinter and Ward valuation.   [145] Ackers ledger 46.
[146] Trade sale catalogue, 15 March 1736/7.   [147] Ackers ledger 92.
[148] Trade sale catalogue, 21 April 1763.   [149] Trade sale catalogue, 21 April 1763.

Appendix 1 *(cont.)*

Chambers's *Cyclopaedia*

1778. Sold in 418 weekly numbers, making four large volumes, 5,000 numbers sold each week[150]

Scottish print runs during the high monopoly period in England[151]

1754. Hume's *History of Great Britain*, 4to	2,000
1750s. Sermons	usually 500
of which 200 or 300 copies were sent to London to be sold in England	
1760. Henry's *Commentary on the Old and New Testaments*	1,000
1760. Swift's *Works*, two volumes (out of statutory copyright)	1,000
1760. Sully's *Memoirs* (out of statutory copyright)	1,000
1764. Reid's *Inquiry into the Human Mind* (first publication)[152]	750
1769/72. Brooke's *Fool of Quality* (pirated offshore, not out of statutory copyright)[153]	3,000
1771. *Encyclopaedia Britannica*, three volumes 4to, sold in numbers[154]	na
1776. Second edition, ten volumes	1,500
1789. Third edition	10,000
1771/72. Smollett's *Humphrey Clinker* (out of statutory copyright)	3,000
1774. Chesterfield's *Letters* (out of statutory copyright)	1,500
Of which 1,000 sent to England	
1775. *Works of Laurence Sterne* (pirated, not out of statutory copyright)	1,000
Bibles, Testaments and prayer books exported to America, 1764–71	20,000

Books free of statutory copyright, reprinted in Scotland, and sold in England at prices about two thirds or a half London prices, 1759[155]

A printed catalogue consisting of 177 titles in many types of printed literature, including classical Latin authors and textbooks, was available to booksellers throughout the English-speaking world by 1764.

---

[150] Rees and Britton 50.
[151] Where not otherwise noted the figures are quoted by Warren McDougall, 'Smugglers, Reprinters and Hot Pursuers' in Myers and Harris ed., *1550–1990*, from legal records. See also the print runs of editions of the works of Adam Smith in appendix 9.
[152] Robert Fleming and Patrick Neill ledgers, NLS.
[153] Quoted by McDougall 173, from legal records.   [154] Timperley 727, with later editions.
[155] *A Catalogue of Books printed for Alexander Donaldson, Bookseller in Edinburgh; and sold at his shop near Norfolk-street, in the Strand, in London, and at Edinburgh; Also by the Booksellers of Great Britain, Ireland, and America* (Edinburgh 1764) 19, CUL Munby d.157. See also the list in a letter sent by John Whiston on behalf of the London publishers to the booksellers of Oxford, Cambridge, and elsewhere, transcribed in *Petitions and Papers Relating to the Bill of the Booksellers* (1774).

Appendix 1 *(cont.)*

Irish offshore reprinting. Print runs of Irish reprints of titles published in Great Britain before 1800[156]

Many copies were illegally exported to Great Britain and to the British colonies in North America

1777. Hurd's *Sermons*	500
1777. Robertson's *History of America*	250
1777. Another edition	1,000
1777. Gordon's *Tacitus*	500
1770. *Annual Register*, reprinted annually	750
1777. Thicknesse's *Travels*	1,000
1778. Enfield's *Speaker*	2,000

Frequently reprinted in editions of similar length. For the huge circulation of this school textbook during the romantic period see appendix 6

1778. Beattie on Truth	500
1778. *Beauties of The Spectator*	1,500
1778. Robertson's *History of Scotland*	1,000
1779. Kaimes's *Sketches of Man*	1,500
1779. Hume's *Essays*	1,500
1779. Hume's *History of England*	2,000, reduced to 1,000 during manufacture
1779. *Abelard and Heloise*	2,500
1780. Moore's *Tour of France*	1,500
1781. Johnson's *Lives of the Poets*	1,500
1781. *Seven Champions of Christendom* By Richard Johnson, first published 1596, and part of the frozen popular canon. The cost figures show that this was a book-length version, not a chapbook	3,000
1781. *Fatal Effects of Inconstancy* Probably an unrecorded Dublin reprint of the 1774 London novel translated from the French[157]	500
1782. *George Bateman, A Novel* Probably an unrecorded Dublin reprint of the London title published in the same year[158]	500
1782. Ferguson's *Rome*	1,500
1783. *Adelaide and Theodore*[159]	500

[156] Extracted from two surviving ledgers of Graisberry, a Dublin printer, Trinity College, Dublin 10314 and 10315.
[157] Raven i, 220.   [158] By Elizabeth Blower, Raven i, 312.   [159] *Ibid.* 321.

	Print run
An immediate Dublin offshore reprint of a circulating library novel published in London	
1784. *Lives of the Admirals*	1,000
1783. Buchan's *Domestic Medicine* For the large sales of this book see chapter 14.	2,000
1785. Sheridan's *Life of Swift*	500
1797. Mrs Bennett's *The Beggar Girl* An immediate Dublin offshore reprint in three volumes of a popular Minerva Press novel published in London in seven volumes earlier in the year[160]	750

American colonial printing

	Print run
1640. *Whole Booke of Psalmes*[161]	1,700
1661. Indian Bible, New Testament[162]	1,500
1663. Indian Bible	1,000
1710. *A Confession of Faith* (Saybrook platform)[163]	2,000
1759. *New England Psalter*[164]	30,000
Date uncertain *Poor Richard's almanac*[165]	10,000
1760s and **1770s**, Ames's almanac[166]	50,000 to 60,000
1764. A pamphlet on a local Maryland question[167]	500
1765. Smith's *History of New Jersey.*[168]	600
1748. Menonite Martyr book (in German)[169]	1,300
End of eighteenth century, local sermons[170]	typically 400

American colonial books published in London

	Print run
1759. For Benjamin Franklin	
Enquiry concerning the Indians[171]	1,000
Inoculation, additional sheet	2,000
Review of Constitution of Pennsylvania	2,000
1766. *Considerations on Taxing America*	500

Examples of individual works which sold well, high monopoly period, England

Pope's Works[172]

---

[160] *Ibid.* 707.   [161] Noted by Lehmann-Haupt 40.   [162] Wroth 17.   [163] Wroth 21.
[164] *CBAW* 51.   [165] *CBAW* 51.   [166] *CBAW* 51.   [167] Wroth 182.   [168] Wroth 183.
[169] Noted by Lehmann-Haupt 40.   [170] *CBAW* 51.   [171] Strahan archives.
[172] Summarised from Donald W. Nicol, *Pope's Literary Legacy* (Oxford 1992).

Appendix 1 *(cont.)*

The property was worth more than those of Shakespeare and
Milton combined.
The editions of 1751–4, to give one example for which
accounts survive, produced at a net profit of over
£5000

1752. Large 8vo, nine volumes	1,500 sets
1751. Crown 8vo (smaller)	3000
1752. Large 8vo second edition, nine volumes	750
1752. Crown 8vo (smaller), second edition, nine volumes	2,500
1754. Pot 8vo (cheap paper), ten volumes	3,000

After 1774, when perpetual copyright ceased, Pope's works
became cheap and plentiful

James Thomson[173]
The Seasons
Between 1751 and 1770   11,250
Collected Poems
Between 1751 and 1770   14,250
See also appendix 6

James Hervey's *Meditations among the Tombs*

1750. Eighth edition, printed by Samuel Richardson[174]	2,500
1751. Ninth edition, printed by Samuel Richardson	2,500
1753. Tenth edition, printed by Samuel Richardson	3,000

After 1774 the book became cheap and plentiful.

Johnson's *Rasselas*[175]

1759. First edition	1,500
1759. Second edition	1,000
1759. Third edition	1,000
1765. Fourth edition	1,000

After 1774 the book became cheap and plentiful

Goldsmith's *Vicar of Wakefield* [176]

1766. First edition, two volumes 12mo	1.5	na

Goldsmith was paid 420 shillings in 1762[177]

1766. Second edition[178]	1,000
1766. Third edition[179]	1,000
1769. Fourth edition[180]	1,000

---

[173] Harlan 146, from Strahan archives.
[174] Noted by Keith Maslen, *Samuel Richardson, Printer of London* (Otago 2001) 91 along with the following two records.
[175] Harlan 81 from Strahan archives.   [176] Strahan archives and Harlan 89.
[177] Welsh 59 from an original document.   [178] Strahan archives.   [179] Strahan archives.
[180] Strahan archives. Another version Welsh 61.

Appendix 1 (*cont.*)

		Print run
Some time after 1774 benefited from the brief copyright window and became cheap and plentiful. For example		
1808. *Walker's Classics* edition, one volume[181]		5,000
1811. *Walker's Classics* edition, one volume[182]		5,000
Smollett's *Roderick Random*[183]		
1748. First edition		2,000
1748. Second edition		3,000
1749. Third edition		1,500
1754. Fourth edition		1,000
1759. Fifth edition		1,000
1763. Sixth edition		1,000
1768. Seventh edition		1,500
1769. Eighth edition		1,500
Ninth edition[184]		1,500
1780. Tenth edition, 12mo[185]		1,500
After 1774 benefited from the brief copyright window and became cheap and plentiful		
1792. 'new edition' Pretenders' edition[186]		1,500
1807. Another edition[187]	5	5,000
[Mackenzie's] *The Man of Feeling* (a novel of sensibility)		
1771. At expense of the author	2.5	750
Second edition	2.5	750
Third edition	na	1,000
1774. Fourth edition, published by Cadell	na	1,000
1774. Fifth edition	na	1,000
1791. Tenth edition[188]	na	1,000
Benefited from the brief copyright window and became cheap and plentiful		
Smollett's *History of England*[189]		
1754/58. First edition 4to, four volumes	63	1,000
1758/60. Second edition 8vo, 11 volumes	66	2,000
1758. Third edition in numbers, 1 to 14	0.5 each	13,000
15 to 36	0.5	11,000
Price of the whole book in numbers	18	
Only a few books were published in numbers during the high monopoly period		

[181] Longman archives.   [182] Longman archives.   [183] Strahan archives.
[184] Strahan archives.   [185] Zachs 293 from Murray archives.
[186] Zachs 388 from Murray archives.   [187] Longman impression books.   [188] Strahan archives.
[189] Simplified from figures quoted by Hernlund.

Appendix 1 *(cont.)*

		Print run
Circulating library and other novels[190]		
1761. Mrs Frances Sheridan, *Memoirs of Miss Sidney Biddulph*, three volumes[191]		1,000
1761. Second edition[192]		750
1763. [Frances Brooke] *Lady Julia Mandeville*, two volumes[193]		750
1763. Second edition[194]		750
1763. Third edition[195]		1,000
1765. Fourth edition[196]		750
1765. *History of Miss Indiana Danby by a Lady*, two volumes[197]		750
1768. *The Modern Wife*, two volumes[198]	6	750
1768. *The Visiting Day. A Novel*, two volumes[199]	6	750
1770. *Fatal Friendship. A Novel, by a Lady*, two volumes[200]		750
1771. *Memoirs of Mr Wilson; or the providential adultery*, two volumes. For Francis Hall, at his circulating library, near the new church, in the Strand[201]		500
1771. *The Fault was all his own. A Novel, by a Lady*, two volumes[202]	6	500
1774. (Henry Brooke's) *Juliet Grenville*, three volumes[203]	9	2,000
1777. Thistlethwaite's *The Child of Misfortune*, two volumes[204]	6	800

School books, typical edition sizes

1711. Ovid's *Metamorphoses*, in Latin[205]	3,000
1711. Aesop in Latin[206]	4,000
1716. Another edition[207]	4,000

Long-run school-teaching texts

Thomas Dyche, *A Guide to the English Tongue*
1709 until the end of the romantic period ?500,000

During the 1730s production was about 10,000 a year; in the 1740s about 20,000 a year still rising[208]

1764. Forty-fifth edition.
Only a handful of copies have survived[209]

Thomas Dilworth, *A New Guide to the English Tongue*
1740 until the end of the romantic period ?200,000

[190] Prices from *General Catalogue* (1786). [191] Bowyer Ledgers, 4297. [192] *Ibid.* 4318. [193] *Ibid.* 4423. [194] *Ibid.* 4434. [195] *Ibid.* 4445. [196] *Ibid.* 4438. [197] *Ibid.* 4442. [198] *Ibid.* 4723. [199] *Ibid.* 4712. [200] *Ibid.* 4817. [201] *Ibid.* 4840. [202] *Ibid.* 4869. [203] Garside, Raven, and Schöwerling i, 219. [204] Zachs 277 from Murray archives. [205] Bowyer Ledgers 73. [206] *Ibid.* 78. [207] *Ibid.* 336. [208] Ackers ledger. [209] D. F. McKenzie, 'The Economies of Print, 1550–1750' 390.

Appendix 1 (cont.)

		Print run
Royal Battledore, or First Book for Children, a cardboard version of the hornbook		
Between 1771 and 1780[210]		100,000 sold

The beginnings of a children's book industry

1744. Newbery obtained 'royal licences' to make certain abridgements of religious, history, and literary books for the use of children.

1745. *Circle of the Sciences*, ten volumes Newbery obtained a royal patent for fourteen years forbidding abridgement[211]		1,500 each
1745. *Nurse Truelove's Christmas Box* (half sheet)[212]		14,000
1745. *Nurse Truelove's New Year Box* (one sheet)		6,000
1746. *Lilliputian Magazine*, monthly		4,000 falling
1760. *World Displayed*, monthly		1,500 falling
1766. *The History of Little Goody Two Shoes . . . with the means by which she acquired her Learning and Wisdom, and in consequence therof her Estate*	0.5	na

Many later editions

1774. *Select Fables of Aesop and Others*[213]	0.5	2,000
1776. Boyce's *New Pantheon*, fifth edition[214]		2,000

Newbery and his many successors continued to provide similar books for children through the romantic period and beyond. See also appendix 7

Market value of private intellectual property rights, prices obtained at the closed book industry sales[215]

See also Shakespeare in appendix 12	*Price*
1764. Defoe's *Robinson Crusoe*, two volumes	£68
1764. Bunyan's *Pilgrim's Progress*	£196
1766. Delphin classics Horace	£150
1767. Milton's *Paradise Lost*	£900
1767. *The Spectator*	£1,228
1769. Thomson's *Seasons*	£479

---

[210] Welsh 172 from Collins the printer's archival records, whose whereabouts are now unknown.
[211] Welsh 186.   [212] Strahan archives, and following three items.
[213] Welsh 168.   [214] Welsh 177.   [215] Calculated from figures in Strahan archives 48,804.

Appendix 1 *(cont.)*

	Print run
Monopoly franchises sold by the state[216]	

1762. Exclusive right to print law books, twenty seven years, a　　　　　£2,500
secondary market price

1770. Exclusive right, along with presses at Oxford and Cambridge,　　£850 per annum
to print Bibles and prayer books in England

Offshore, other than Ireland

Sixteenth century

Examples of books available for illegal importation to England, and later Great Britain, showing the changing nature of the unsatisfied demand at home

1550s. English-language-books prohibited in England but produced
offshore in the Netherlands

	Shillings
Average buying price in Netherlands	1.1
Selling price in south of England[217]	2.3 to 2.6

Seventeenth century

Scotland

1607. Shakespeare's *Venus and Adonis* printed offshore in
Edinburgh[218]

Holland

Bibles, prayer books, Greek and Latin classics, with a few bestselling
English titles mid seventeenth century. Lewis Bayley's *Practice of
Pietie*, 'ten thousand at a time'[219]

Eighteenth century

Hobbes's *Leviathan*[220]

1710s and **1720s**. Books printed in 'pocket volumes' by T. Johnson,
The Hague, at a time when many of the English editions were
only available in expensive folio[221] Butler, Congreve, Cowley,
Dryden, Milton, Pope, Prior, Waller

---

[216] Calculated from figures in Strahan archives quoted by Harlan.
[217] Quoted by David Loades, 'Books and the English Reformation prior to 1558' in Gilmont 270 from Foxe's *Martyrs*.
[218] Timperley 450.
[219] Quoted by Alastair J. Mann, 'The Atlas of the 'Flemish Priest' 15, in *Publishing History*, 2 (2001).
[220] Noel Malcolm, *Aspects of Hobbes* (Oxford 2002) 336–82.
[221] A full list with prices in Edmund Smith, *Phaedra and Hippolitus* (1711) CUL. Advertisement bound in a copy of Johnson's reprint of Prior's *Poems* (1720), Ac.

Appendix 1 *(cont.)*

Addison's *Remarks on Italy*, Swift (Mandeville's) *Discourse on Free Thinking*
Over fifty plays, including Shakespeare

1780s. T. Barrois, Paris, 1783[222]
Dictionaries and text books, Telemachus in English, Fielding's *Tom Jones*, Sterne's
Sentimental Journey, Brydone's *Sicily*, Swift's *Gulliver's Travels*, Goldsmith's *Vicar of
Wakefield.*, Thomson's *Seasons*, Young's *Night Thoughts*, Prior, Mallet, Lisle, Parnell,
Goldsmith's poems, Addison, Pope, Milton, Gay, Moore's *Fables for the Female Sex*

1790s. J. J. Tourneisen of Basel, 1791[223]
Texts of the Enlightenment in Great Britain, sold at well below London and Edinburgh
prices

Impact of book prices on potential access

A long run indicator of the value of money

1395–1554. Annual rent of a small bookshop/living room in Paternoster Row, the centre of the London book industry, fixed in shillings[224]	26.66

Indicators of incomes, early modern period	*Income (shillings)*
1526. Annual salary of a rector, Lincoln diocese[225]	253.6
1526. Annual salary of a curate, Lincoln diocese[226]	103
1546. Annual salary of an incumbent/schoolmaster of a Gloucestershire parish[227]	220
Mid sixteenth century, average annual pay of a schoolmaster[228]	129.5
1569/70. Daily wages of a London carpenter[229]	1.4 to 1.5
Mason, daily	1
Labourer, daily	0.9
1571. Annual salary of a headmaster of a school in Southwark[230] plus fees from pupils	266.6
1635. Journeyman printer, weekly,[231]	8

Indicators of incomes, high monopoly period[232]	
Senior captain, Royal Navy, per day	20
Lieutenant per day	5

---

[222] Advertisement bound in a copy of Sterne's *Sentimental Journey* (second edition, Barrois, 1783), Ac.
[223] In a copy of Robertson's *Scotland* (1791 edition), Ac.   [224] *CHBB* iii, 130.   [225] *Ibid.* 232.
[226] *Ibid*. 232.   [227] Plant 42.   [228] *Ibid.*
[229] Examples taken from payments made by the Stationers' Company for work to their hall in London which required payments to a range of tradesmen, individually recorded. Arber i, 423, 449, and i, 455.
[230] Plant 42.   [231] Blagden 128.
[232] Official figures reproduced in almanacs, e.g. *Rider's British Merlin for 1764*.

Appendix 1 *(cont.)*

Captain's clerk, per week	33 to 45
Carpenter per month	40 to 80
Gunner per month	40 to 80

'In general that the wages of Men is, for the most part, from 1s to 2s 5d [2.5 shillings] per day; and the wages of Women from 4d [0.3 shillings] to 1s throughout the Kingdom' Josiah Tucker's *Instructions to Travellers*, 1757.[233]

Indicators of incomes, romantic period and later

Because many politicians, churchmen and others held several offices and sinecures simultaneously, it is difficult to establish total incomes. Spencer Percival, while prime minister, is said, for example, to have drawn £25,000 from various public appointments.
Royal Navy, 1816 onwards, per week[234]

Treasurer to the Navy	1,663
Secretary to the Admiralty	1,538
Captain,	
1st rate	300
4th rate	182
Gunner	40
Cook	8
Half pay [pension]	
Captain, first hundred names by seniority	101
others	87 to 73
Surgeon, six years service	42
Pensions	
Widow of an admiral	46
Widow of a gunner	9.6
Widow of a cook	nil

Romantic period. Estimates of the size of the British reading public

	Size of population (000s)
Edmund Burke, 1790s[235]	80
Burke's 'political nation,' a term commonly equated with those who read newspapers, 1790s[236]	400
Edinburgh Review, 1804	80
Edinburgh Review, 1814, 'probably not less than 200,000 persons reading for amusement and instruction among the middle classes of society'	

---

[233] Quoted by Cochrane 18.

[234] *Navy List*, 1817. The civil pay rates are taken from *The Patriot* (1810).   [235] Altick 49.

[236] Quoted by Hannah Barker, *Newspapers, Politics, and Public Opinion in Late Eighteenth Century England* (Oxford 1998) 4, from *First Letter on a Regicide Peace* (1796).

Appendix 1 (*cont.*)

Indicators of social classes, United Kingdom including Ireland, 1814[237]

	Number of people (000, 000s)
'Respectable middle classes'	1.5
'Shopkeepers, small farmers'	2.8
'Artisans, mechanics, servants, paupers, vagrants'	11.9
'Army and navy'	1.0
	17.2

Tax returns, 1852[238]

Pounds per year	Shillings per week equivalent	Number of people (000s)
£400 and over	164	27
£150 to £400	58 to 164	83
		110

---

[237] Discussed by Altick 81. [238] Summarised from Altick, *Writers* 141.

Appendix 2 Intellectual property and textual controls. Custom, law and practice[1]

ENGLAND (guild period)

Private intellectual property

Late fifteenth and early sixteenth century, some apparently competitive printing of similar texts, notably *The Ship of Fools, Dives and Lazarus*, and Latin–English dictionaries.[2]

1533. A printer complains that another printer had reprinted a text which he had been the first to print.[3]

From the late fifteenth century, members of the printed-book industry, by the act of printing, take into their ownership the exclusive right to print many works that had previously circulated in manuscript.[4]

1557. The Stationers' Company is incorporated by royal charter, formalising previous arrangements, practices, and relationships with the state. A register of intellectual properties is established into which new titles can, for a fee, be entered by members as proof of intellectual property ownership. Assignments of properties are also entered in the register from time to time. Regulations for establishing the ownership of disputed rights.

Later sixteenth century. The ownership of many intellectual properties passes from the printers to the booksellers.

1583. A Privy Council report recommends that the first printer of a text should have it 'as a privilege', i.e. as if the monopoly right had been specifically conferred by the state.[5] This can be regarded as a formal legal intellectual property regime.

Monopolies conferred, franchised, or guaranteed by the state

1504. First recorded royal privileges on the model of those conferred in continental jurisdictions. Henry VIII grants an exclusive right to the king's printer to print royal proclamations, statutes, and other government documents.[6]

1547. Almanacs and prognostications are included in the Letters Patent given to the king's printer, and then to the Stationers' Company.[7]

1553. The government grants an exclusive right to print law books, including law books to be published in the future.[8]

---

[1] The series of articles by John Feather on the book-trade and the law in *Publishing History*, 12 (1982); 22 (1987); and 24 (1988), consolidated in his *Publishing, Piracy, and Politics* (1994), is an important source, but it needs to be corrected in several respects, particularly with regard to the legal force of the Act of 1710, the fact that it applied to the whole of the then United Kingdom, and the law and the practice of publishing in Scotland before 1774. It is, of course, impossible to deduce the actual business practice of an industry from descriptions of the law.

[2] Loewenstein 67.

[3] Noted by John J. Lowndes, *An Historical Sketch of the Law of Copyright* (1840) 5.

[4] Many of the privatisations seem to have occurred before the registers began, but a few are noted later, including *Raynolde the Fox* in 1560, Arber i, 152, and *Pers Plowman* also in 1560, Arber i, 153.

[5] Arber ii, 794. Document quoted by Blagden 119.

[6] Feather, *Publishing* 11. Clegg 8. Some works printed by Pynson record the privilege in their colophon. Information kindly supplied by Meraud Grant Ferguson.

[7] Plant 101.   [8] Feather, *Publishing* 12.

Sixteenth century. Government issue, often in return for payment, letters patent conferring monopoly franchises to publish and sell certain texts and whole classes of books. Some of these letters patent contain provisions for maximum prices.[9]
Some printer/publishers resist this state assumption of an authority which had previously not existed, but are gradually obliged to submit.

After 1603. The Stationers' Company, having been endowed with many valuable intellectual properties, becomes the state's principal agent in enforcing the state's textual and cultural policies, including controls on the total size of the industry, gradually bringing most printers and booksellers within its jurisdiction.

Examples of the financial value of conferred intellectual property rights

Date uncertain. Sir Richard Coningsby accepts letters patent to collect the duty on playing cards in settlement of a state debt of £1,800.[10]

1614. The Stationers' Company buys the Psalms patent for £600.[11]

1624. The Stationers' Company offers to buy out Symcock's patent to print ballads for £200 or £300 per annum.[12]

1626. Caleb Morley offers £50 per annum for state endorsement of a Latin book.[13]

1631. The Stationers' Company buys the patent for Speed's *Genealogies* for £700.[14]

Intellectual property rights formally linked with official state/ecclesiastical textual controls

The privilege system ensures that no text unacceptable to the state or ecclesiastical authorities can benefit from the state's protection of intellectual property.

1546. The printer of any English book, ballad, or play is required to present the first copy to the mayor, retaining the rest of the edition for two days (to enable it to be stopped).[15]

1559. No book to be licensed for printing unless it had been passed by censors appointed by the state.[16]

1586. Decrees of Court of Star Chamber confirm the powers of the Stationers' Company and the privileges of patentees. Powers of censorship, previously mainly a matter of self-censorship within the industry, are given to the ecclesiastical authorities.

From 1595. Ecclesiastical censorship tightened.[17]

1599. The ecclesiastical authorities issue directions for tighter textual controls. Plays may only be printed if they have been 'allowed by suche as have aucthorytie'.[18]

---

[9] For example the privilege to print the works of Hieronimus Zanichus in 1605. Greg, *Companion* 153.
[10] Arnold Hunt, 'Book Trade Patents 1603–1640' in Hunt, Mandelbrote, and Shell 30.
[11] A selected list with other examples is given in Hunt, 'Book Trade' 29.
[12] *Ibid.* 35.   [13] *Ibid.* 31.   [14] *Ibid.* 31.   [15] *CHBB* iii, 15.
[16] Feather, *Publishing* 15.   [17] Clegg 58.
[18] Quoted by S. Schoenbaum, *Shakespeare, Records and Images* (1981) 204. See also Clegg.

Appendix 2 *(cont.)*

4 June 1599. 'The bishops' bonfire' of books ceremonially burned.

1607. Copies to be entered only by freemen resident in London, no freeman to help anyone else enter a copy, and no copy to be printed without having been entered.[19]

1623. 'A Proclamation against the disorderly Printing, uttering, and dispersing of Bookes, Pamphlets &c.'. Severe measures to be taken against anyone who prints or imports books in contravention of the censorship, intellectual property rights, or of the state-conferred monopolies and franchises. Adds a new prohibition against texts which, though lawful, are contrary to the general intention of the decree.[20]

1624. 'Proclamation against Seditious, Popish, and Puritanicall Bookes and Pamphlets'.[21]

1628. Controls on the second-hand trade.[22]

Between 1603 and 1640 over seventy new letters patent are issued which confer monopoly rights relating to printed texts.[23]

Tightening of intellectual property and textual control regime across the whole printed-book industry

From about 1600. Clamp-down on anthologies, abridgements, adaptations, and quotations. See chapter 4.

1620s. Stationers' Company fines any member who prints a book without formally entering it.[24]

1630. The Bishop of London, the official censor to whom the Stationers' Company was responsible in their role as delegated licensers, orders that the printer of every book must print his name in it.[25]

1632. William Prynne publishes *Histriomastix*, a puritan attack on stage plays, which contains disrespectful remarks about the royal family. In 1634 he is ordered to be imprisoned for life, to be fined £1,000, and to have both his ears cut off. Later he is fined another £1,000, the remaining parts of his ears are cut off, and he is branded on the cheeks.

1637. The Star Chamber decrees that the overall size of the industry be reduced to twenty master printers. Severe penalties for any one who prints 'any book or books of divinity, law, physic, philosophy, or poetry' without licence. Many other measures, including a specific requirement for reprints to obtain a new licence, and textual control of paratexts. All 'titles, epistles, prefaces, proems, preambles, introductions, tables, dedications, and other matters and things whatsoever thereunto annexed'.[26]

For the effects on the texts of Shakespeare's Sonnets see chapter 8.

---

[19] Jackson 31

[20] *STC* 8714, 8715. Full text in Greg, *Companion* 219. I have included corrections made in the second edition.

[21] Full text in Greg, *Companion* 228.   [22] Greg, *Companion* 240.   [23] Hunt, 'Book Trade' 27.

[24] Many examples in Jackson.   [25] Quoted by Todd vii.

[26] Quoted by W. W. Greg, 'Samuel Harsnett and Hayward's *Henry IV*' in *The Library*, (1956) 8.

Appendix 2 (*cont.*)

Civil War, Commonwealth, and Protectorate

1641. Abolition of the Court of Star Chamber and High Commission. By abolishing the instruments of state and ecclesiastical censorship, the state effectively abolishes the legal basis of intellectual property.

1643. A Remonstrance by Stationers' Company petitioning for a return to state regulation, including licensing/censorship, intellectual property protection, and trade privileges.[27]

1643. Parliament reinstates most of the previous regime of pre-censorship.[28] The occasion of Milton's *Areopagitica*.

Civil war. Most printing presses are employed in printing official documents, pamphlets and newsletters. Textual control to some extent breaks down.

1649. Licensing Act. Strict pre-censorship reaffirmed.[29]

State licensing period

1660. Licensing of almanacs, i.e. pre-censorship of the tolerated illegitimate supernatural by state-appointed censors, is re-introduced.[30]

1661. A bill to give the responsibility for licensing print back to the ecclesiastical authorities is defeated.[31]

1662. Licensing Act. General pre-censorship formalised. The office of state-appointed Licensor of the Press is re-introduced.

1663. Roger L'Estrange, the Licensor of the Press, prints *Considerations and Proposals in order to the Regulation of the Press*, proposals intended to enable the state to control all the print to be permitted to circulate. He argues that, since it is hard to control authors direct, the best method is to impose tight controls, and heavy penalties, including death, mutilation, and public shaming, on members of the print industry, among whom he includes not only printers, booksellers, type-founders, and manufacturers of presses, but 'stitchers, binders, stationers, hawkers, mercury-women [sellers of newspapers] pedlars, ballad-singers, posts, carryers, hackney-coachmen, boatmen, and mariners'. He advises a drastic reduction in the size of the industry as a whole and state licensing of all printed materials.[32]

1663. John Twyn, hanged, drawn, and quartered for publishing *A Treatise on the Execution of Justice*. The death penalty on printers of other works is commuted to a series of severe punishments.[33]

1684. The Stationers' Company's royal charter is renewed. The rights to perpetual intellectual property are made explicit.[34] But the state also continues to give licences for shorter periods, such as fourteen years.[35]

1689. 'Glorious Revolution'.

[27] Quoted by Gadd 144.   [28] Gadd 149.
[29] Quoted by Robert Maugham, *A Treatise on the Laws of Literary Property* (1828) 14.
[30] Timperley 529.   [31] Feather, *History* 51.   [32] Reprinted in full in Timperley 532.
[33] Timperley 540.   [34] Blagden 194.
[35] The full text of such a licence of 1693 is given in Dunton 153.

Appendix 2 (*cont.*)

1694. Foreseeing the lapse of the Licensing Act, the industry's leaders operating through the Stationers' Company strengthen internal regulations on the obligation to respect the intellectual property of members.[36]

1695. Licensing Act allowed to lapse.

SCOTLAND (becomes part of United Kingdom of Great Britain in 1707)

1507. James IV accords royal privilege to Chapman and Myllar to set up a printing press in Edinburgh, with a prohibition on imports from elsewhere (mainly from England) of the texts they print.[37]

Sixteenth century. Licensing of printing introduced, to be exercised by the burghs, or in the case of some texts, by the state.

1580s and **1590s.** Legislation to control many aspects of the printed-book industry.

1604. James VI and I, on his accession to the English throne, instructs the town council of Edinburgh to prohibit unlicensed printing, a duty which they perform with the same vigour as the Court of Star Chamber in England.[38]

Throughout the early modern period, severe penalties, including death, are applied against those who break the textual controls, especially on matters relating to the official supernatural. These controls are operated in combination with more general laws against blasphemy and against criticising state and ecclesiastical institutions, and were often exercised with great severity.[39]

1661, 1663. Two men are put to death for allegedly having written a text which blamed the defeat of Covenanting on 'an ungodly king'.[40]

1698. The last case of a man being put to death for denying a doctrine of the official supernatural as it was promulgated at the time.[41]

Until 1710. Scottish governments frequently grant monopolies of differing lengths of time, latterly, usually nineteen years, under letters patent or privilege. In Scotland, unlike in England, intellectual property was always regarded as a conferred privilege for a limited time.[42]

IRELAND (becomes part of United Kingdom of Great Britain and Ireland in 1801)

Until 1800. Apart from some letters patent relating to compulsory and semi-compulsory texts, no copyright protections existed. During the eighteenth century, many books in statutory copyright in Great Britain are immediately reprinted in Ireland, partly for local sale and partly for illegal export to Great Britain and to the British colonies in North America.

---

[36] Quotatations are given in Augustine Birrell, *The Law and History of Copyright* (1899) 80.
[37] *CHBB* iii, 14.   [38] Timperley 449.   [39] Summarised from Mann.
[40] Guthrie and Johnston, see Mann 182.   [41] Mann 177.
[42] See Mann, and William J. Couper, 'Copyright in Scotland before 1709' (Records of the Glasgow Bibliographical Society, 1933) and Warren McDougall 'Copyright Legislation in the Court of Session, 1738 to 1749 and the Rise of the Scottish Book Trade' in *Transactions of the Edinburgh Bibliographical Society* (1988). Many of the early Bible patents are reprinted by Lee.

Appendix 2 (*cont.*)

1801. Terms of the British Act of 1710 are extended to Ireland and other British territories in Europe.

UNITED KINGDOM OF GREAT BRITAIN. High monopoly period

Statutory copyright, 1710

Act of the British Parliament, Queen Anne's Act 'for the encouragement of learning'. The author of any book not yet published is given the sole right of printing it for the term of fourteen years from publication 'and no longer'. If the author is still alive at the end of the first fourteen year term, provision is made for a second term of fourteen years, making a maximum of twenty-eight years in all circumstances. Fourteen years is the same time limit as for patents for inventions and innovations. Texts for which the right to copy had already been assigned by an author to a bookseller (that is all existing printed texts) are protected for twenty-one years and there are other transitional measures.

The legislation includes provisions against excessive prices and profits. No evidence has been found that they were ever applied.

1731. Transitional period expires. All texts other than the most modern pass out of statutory copyright. For attempts to exercise such rights see chapters 6 and 8.

ENGLAND. High monopoly period

After 1731. Despite the unambiguous words of the 1710 statute, the London publishers claim that they still have perpetual intellectual property rights both on individual titles and on the classes of books over which formal monopoly had been conferred or franchised by the state. The English courts give injunctions against those who attempt to reprint books outside the statutory time limits. In England, but not in Scotland, perpetual intellectual property is allowed to continue in practice.

For a fee of about £10, compared with 0.5 shillings for registration in the Stationers' Register, some publishers obtain 'royal licences' for individual titles which reinforce the statutory and the claimed common law property rights. Many licences relate to music, which is easily copied into manuscript, and compilations such as encyclopaedias which might have been thought to invade the property rights in the source books. Some licences also forbid the making of extracts.[43]

1734. 'Hogarth's Act'. Statutory copyright protection is explicitly applied to engravings.

1739. Legal prohibition of imports for sale of any book published in Great Britain during the previous twenty years.

SCOTLAND. Publishing within the statutory regime of the 1710 Act during the high monopoly period in England

---

[43] See the list in Shef Rogers, 'The Use of Royal Licences for Printing in England, 1695–1760: A Bibliography' in *The Library*, 7th series, 1, 2 (2000). The full version of the one given to Newbery for *The Circle of the Sciences*, a compilation for children, is quoted by Welsh 111.

Appendix 2 *(cont.)*

1740s and **1750s**. The Scottish courts, following the 1710 Act, deny the lawfulness of perpetual copyright and refuse to injunct the reprinting of books which are in the public domain under the provisions of the Act.

1763. The Edinburgh publisher Donaldson opens a shop in London selling Scottish reprints of books out of statutory copyright at below London prices. Several lawsuits are mounted in England aimed at preventing him.

1768. On the death of Andrew Millar, the original publisher, a group of London booksellers, including Thomas Becket, pay a large sum for the purported perpetual copyright of Thomson's *The Seasons*, a work first published in 1726, and out of statutory copyright. The title is sold more cheaply in London by Donaldson.

GREAT BRITAIN. The end of perpetual copyright

1773. Lawsuits in Scotland and England to determine the lawfulness of perpetual intellectual property in England.

1773. The Scottish Court of Session confirms that there has never been such a right in Scotland.

1774. The House of Lords, as supreme court for civil cases in Great Britain, determines, in the case of Donaldson *v.* Becket, that the law of Great Britain is as set out in the statute of 1710. Perpetual copyright is confirmed to be unlawful, and all injunctions are dissolved.

After 1774. Some formal conferred monopolies, notably those for English-language Bibles, which derived from legislation other than the 1710 Act, continue to be lawful, but in practice are weakened by the publication of new translations on which separate intellectual property rights are asserted.

After 1774. A group of English booksellers attempts to prolong perpetual copyright in practice, but, with exceptions, are unsuccessful.

UNITED KINGDOM OF GREAT BRITAIN AND IRELAND

The brief copyright window and the old canon

c. 1780–1808. A body of texts, 'the old canon', which enter, or in the case of old ballads, re-enter, the public domain under provisions of the 1710 Act become cheap and plentiful, and are entrenched in the educational system. For the immense effects see chapter 7.

Tight controls are reimposed during the romantic period

1790. Printing presses require a state licence.[44]

1798. Commercial lending of newspapers forbidden by law.

1798. Williams, keeper of a reading room, is convicted of lending a newspaper to read, and taking one penny [0.08 shillings] for the use of it, and fined £5.[45]

---

[44] Timperley 770.   [45] Timperley 799.

Appendix 2 *(cont.)*

1799. Pitt proposes tight controls on the whole industry, aimed especially at discouraging 'cheap' literature.[46] The measures enacted included tight controls on manufacturers and suppliers of type and of presses; a legal requirement that the printer print his or her name and full address on the first and last pages of every book, and that every printer keep a register of his customers.[47]

1811. Following a petition to parliament, the scale of summary fines is reduced.[48]

1839. Registration of printing presses ended.

Closing of the brief copyright window

1808. Copyright is extended from fourteen to twenty-eight years, subject to certain deposit requirements.

1814. Copyright is extended to an unconditional twenty-eight years or life of author if longer. The extension is applied to books already published by living authors. Posthumous works are given a copyright period of twenty-eight years.

1836. Changes in deposit requirements. Agitation for extension of copyright period mainly by publishers and authors, including Wordsworth and Dickens. A bill to extend copyright to sixty years, 'Talfourd's bill', is defeated.

Long copyright re-established

1842. Copyright is extended to author's lifetime plus seven years or forty-two years from publication, whichever is the longer. Measures against foreign imports.

ENGLISH-SPEAKING NORTH AMERICA

Colonial period

Evidence that the English common law and trade customs relating to intellectual property were applied in the colonies.

1637. 'A Decree of Starre-Chamber, concerning Printing'. Adding to existing body of ordinances, it controls what may be legally printed 'in this Realme or other his Majesties Dominions', and explicitly affirms the rights and privileges of the Stationers.[49]
The many almanacs printed in the colonies are 'Published by Authority', implying that a waiver had been given to the monopoly of the Company of Stationers.[50]

1667/68. Green, printer of Cambridge, Massachusetts, reprints certain London pamphlets, but is stopped by the magistrates.[51]

1668. Johnson, a printer, is fined for reprinting a book recently printed in London without the approval of the licensers of the press.[52]

1673. Copyright protection for a term of years granted by General Court of Massachusetts.[53]

---

[46] Quoted by Todd viii from *Parliamentary Register*, ser. ii, i vol. viii (1799) 460.
[47] Summarised from Todd.   [48] Todd x.   [49] Timperley 490.
[50] *CBAW* 95.   [51] *CBAW* 90.   [52] Evans 1, 26.   [53] Wills xv. Noted also by Lehmann-Haupt 99.

Appendix 2 (*cont.*)

1686. John Dunton, a London publisher/bookseller on a visit, is made a freeman of Boston, perhaps as a precondition of being allowed to conduct business.[54]

1689. A local Maryland pamphlet, reprinted in London, includes the usual formula by which the agreement of the first printer/owner is acknowledged.[55]

1689. Bradfield of Pennsylvania prints certain texts without approval of the Governor, the official licensor, and is stopped.[56]

1770. William Billings petitions Massachusetts General Court to grant him the 'exclusive privilege' of printing and selling his book of church music, but the governor refuses to sign.[57]

1781. Andrew Law given the 'exclusive patent' by Connecticut general assembly to print *The Singing Master's Assistant*, for five years.[58]

UNITED STATES

1787. Article 1, section 8 of the United States Constitution, adopted by the Constitutional Convention, gives congress the power 'to promote the progress of science and the useful arts, by securing, for a limited time, to authors and inventors, the exclusive right to their respective writings and inventions.'[59]
By 1786 all states except Delaware had passed copyright acts, closely modelled on the law in Great Britain, i.e., that, in accordance with the Act of 1710, it is a property right belonging to an author which could be assigned for fourteen years with provision for another fourteen if the author was still alive. Registration was required. Copyright could be withdrawn if the author 'did not furnish the Public with sufficient editions'. Prohibitions against excessive prices.

1790. First federal copyright law. Confirms for authors resident in the United States a copyright period of fourteen years plus right of extension for a further fourteen. Closely modelled on the British brief copyright window regime, and with no protection for works first printed abroad.

1803. All copyrighted works required to carry a printed note giving information on where the copyright was granted and registered.

1831. Copyright period extended to twenty-eight years with provision for a further fourteen.

1891. The United States, having become a net exporter of intellectual property, joins the international copyright treaties, and thereafter presses other countries to join in a global intellectual property regime.

Long copyright internationalised and further lengthened

1844. The British government is empowered by parliament to make reciprocal copyright treaties with foreign states. Between 1846 and 1886 sixteen treaties are concluded with European governments.

---

[54] Dunton.   [55] See Wroth 40.
[56] Quoted in *CBAW* 204. For an extract see chapter 19.   [57] Wills xvi.
[58] Wills. xvii.   [59] Wills. xv.

Appendix 2 *(cont.)*

1911. Copyright is extended to life of author plus fifty years. The Act enables the United Kingdom to join the Berne International Copyright Convention with a uniform copyright regime throughout the British Empire. (Canada did not ratify until 1924.) At the time of this consolidating Act there were twenty-two separate acts of parliament relating to copyright in force in the United Kingdom. Registration is abolished.

1891. With the accession of the United States to the international copyright treaties, offshore publication of English language texts as a means of evading intellectual property ceases, although pornographic and other prohibited texts continue to be produced in Paris.

Twentieth century. Further changes which extend the range of texts on which intellectual property can be claimed, and lengthen the period of private ownership.

Appendix 3 Intellectual property. Rights of authors and performers, anthologies and abridgements

RIGHTS OF AUTHORS

From the arrival of printing, authors sell their manuscripts outright, with the implied intellectual property rights. Others accept payment in the form of free copies, or pay for the printing from their own funds.

Many works are printed from manuscripts, from memorised versions, and from orally delivered sermons without the consent, and against the wishes of the author.[1] This also creates perpetual intellectual property ownership rights in the hands of the printer/publishers. Intellectual property did not extend to authorial plagiarism except in so far as it may have infringed the intellectual property rights of printer/publishers.[2]

1641. Stationers' Company forbids the printing or reprinting of 'any thing' without the consent of the author. Appears to be the first formal right.[3]

1666. The property rights of 'the Author of every *Manuscript* or Copy' are referred to in a document issued by the booksellers.[4]

1695. A complaint that the London booksellers will not let anyone else sell newly printed books, even if they are produced at the expense of the author, and that they insist on a minimum print run of 200.[5]

1710. Intellectual property is, by statute, decreed to be originally an author's right which the author may transfer to a publisher for a period of time limited by statute.

RIGHTS OF PERFORMERS[6]

1833. Dramatic Copyright Act. Copyright extended for the first time to dramatic performances, even if there is no published text.

1835. An Act to prevent the publication in print of delivered lectures without the consent of the lecturer.

ANTHOLOGIES

The pre-1600 flurry of printed literary anthologies which draw on previously printed works

Poetry miscellanies

1557. *Songs and Sonnettes* . . . known as *Tottel's Miscellany*

---

[1] Many examples noted by Bennett, *1603–1640*.
[2] For attempts by authors to take control of their texts see Loewenstein.
[3] Quoted by Kernan 72 from Arber.   [4] Quoted by Blagden 153.
[5] These details emerge from a series of letters by Isaac Chauncey to Thomas Edwards, National Library of Wales, Rhual manuscripts, summarised in *A Schedule of the Rhual Manuscripts and Documents*, National Library of Wales (1949) no. 77.
[6] Discussed in chapter 18.

Appendix 3 (*cont.*)

The first printed anthology of English verse.[7] Includes passages from Chaucer previously printed.[8] Also two poems by John Hall printed in 1549.[9] Some of the pieces in the collection were registered as ballads in their own right.[10]

1576. *The Paradyse of Daynty Devices*
A collection of *sententiae*.[11]

1578. *A gorgious gallery of gallant inuentions . . . By T. P.*
Includes some pieces from *Tottel's Miscellany, The Paradyse of Daynty Devices*, and other printed predecessors, including the Willow Song sung in Shakespeare's *Othello*.[12]

1584. *A Handful of Pleasant Delights*
Ballads which had previously been printed as broadsides, including a version of *Greensleeves*.[13]

1588. *A Banquet of Dainty Conceits*
While purporting to be an anthology, the book is actually a collection of weak pieces by one author.

1591. *Britton's Bowre of Delights*
In 1592 Breton declared that the book had been published without his knowledge with 'many things of other men mingled with a few of mine'.[14] Includes material previously printed in *Tottel's Miscellany*.[15]

1593. R. S. editor, *The Phoenix Nest*
Includes three pieces previously printed in *Britton's Bowre of Delights*, but textually different.[16]

1596. *The Garland of Good Will*
Many pieces, some of them abridgements by Thomas Deloney, that had previously been printed. The book appears to have been almost continuously available until c. 1800.[17]

1597. *The Arbor of Amorous Deuises*
'By N. B., [Nicholas Breton]'.[18] Contains pieces from *Britton's Bowre of Delights* and by others, including Sidney, and some from *Tottel's Miscellany*.[19]

1598. (Francis Meres) *Palladis Tamia; Wits Treasury, being a second part of Wits Commonwealth*

---

[7] A summary is given by A. H. Bullen in his edition of *England's Helicon* (1899), with some corrections made by Rollins, *England's Helicon*. See also Pomeroy.

[8] Hyder Edward Rollins, ed., *Tottel's Miscellany (1557–1587)* (Cambridge, Mass. 1966) ii, 80.

[9] John Hall, *The Court of Vertue* (1565), edited by Russell A. Fraser (1961) xiii. Some pieces from this miscellany were entered as ballads.

[10] Rollins, ed., *Tottel's Miscellany* ii, 144.   [11] An assignment in Arber ii, 414.

[12] Notes in the edition by Hyder E. Rollins (Cambridge, Mass. 1926).

[13] Notes in the edition by Hyder E. Rollins (Cambridge, Mass. 1924). For what appears to be a dispute about this title some years earlier in 1576 see Greg and Boswell 86.

[14] Quoted *DNB* 1187. 'The Arbour of Amorous delightes, by N.B. gent' was entered on 6 January 1594. Arber ii, 643.

[15] Rollins, ed., *Tottel's Miscellany* ii, 157.   [16] Rollins, ed., *Phoenix Nest*, xxxii.

[17] See Bew's list summarised in appendix 4.

[18] Alexander Grosart, *The Works in Verse and Prose of Nicholas Breton* (1879) i, 44.

[19] *DNB*.

Appendix 3 *(cont.)*

Described in later editions as 'a treasurie of similes' and 'a treasurie of goulden sentences'. Includes an index of 'the Commonplaces into which these Similitudes are digested' and a list of 'The Authours both sacred and profane, out of which these similitudes are for the most part gathered.' The editor drew on a handful of English language books and translations.[20]

1599. *The Passionate Pilgrim by W. Shakespeare*
While appearing to be a collection of poems composed by Shakespeare, the book is a miscellany of pieces, some apparently only previously existing in manuscript, and others, including those of Shakespeare, previously printed.

1600. *Bel-vedere or the Garden of the Muses*[21]
Poetical quotations or *sententiae*, seldom more than a couple of lines. Some from Shakespeare's *Love's Labour's Lost*.
It is to the flurry of printed miscellanies that Iudicio, the critic in *The Second part of the Return from Parnassus* (c. 1601, printed 1606) alludes:
'. . . there starts vp every day an old goose that sits hatching vp these eggs which have ben filtcht from the nest[s] of Crowes and Kestrells. Heeres a booke, Ingenioso, why, to condemne it to Cloaca, the vsual Tiburne of all misliving papers, were too faire a death of so foule an offendor.'[22]

1600. *England's Helicon*[23]
A full anthology. Three-quarters of the text had already appeared in print.[24]

1613 reregistered.[25] 1614 reprinted with additions
'Nowe if any Stationer shall finde faulte, that his Coppies are robd by any thing in this Collection, let me aske him this question, Why more in this, than in any Divine or humane Authoure? from whence a man (writing of that argument) shall gather any saying, sentence, simile, or example, his name put to it who is the Author of the same.'[26]

1600. *Englands Parnassus*[27]
A large collection of pieces, some quite long, drawn from many recent authors, arranged in the form of an alphabetical dictionary of topics. Shakespeare is quoted ninety five times. It seems unlikely that the publishers owned the intellectual property in all of these texts.

Undated, but 1601. *Love's Martyr*
Includes pieces by Shakespeare, Jonson, Marston, Chapman. Uncertain how far it draws on previously printed texts.

1602. (Davison's) *Poetical Rhapsody never yet published*
Apparently mainly taken from previously unprinted pieces.
The last substantial Elizabethan miscellany.[28]

---

[20] Rollins, *England's Helicon* 49, quoting earlier studies.
[21] Arber iii, 168.   [22] *The Three Parnassus Plays (1598–1601)* edited by J. B. Leishman (1949) 230.
[23] Arber iii, 169, spelling modernised.   [24] Pomeroy 23.   [25] Arber iii, 538.
[26] From the editor's preface 'To the Reader, if Indifferent'.
[27] Arber iii, 173. Reregistered 1609. Arber iii, 420. My summary of the Shakespeare extracts is taken from the description of the book by Frederick C. Wellstood, *Catalogue of the Books, Manuscripts, Works of Art, Antiquities, and Relics exhibited in Shakespeare's Birthplace* (Stratford-upon-Avon 1937) 142.
[28] Noted as such, for example, by Bennett, *1603–1640* 193, but without offering an explanation.

Indications that a regime to control the use of quotations from printed books unauthorised by the intellectual property owners is being put in place

1578. A printer is fined for 'printinge in a ballad of his iii staves, out of another ballad, of Edward Whyte'.[29]

1602. Stationers' Court orders that psalms be not printed in future editions of Ascham's *English Schoolmaster*.[30]

1603. A member is fined for including a version of a list of Queen Elizabeth's funeral procession that he had apparently taken, although with some amendment, from Chettle's *Mourning Garment*. The passage reproduced, a self-evidently public matter, was only five pages long.[31]

1615. Thomas Langley is required to assign his copy of Markham's *Method*, a book 'supposed to be taken out of a Copie of Mr Jacksons', to Jackson for 45 shillings.[32]

1615. Thomas Snodam pays a fee to be allowed to print 'sacrid himmes by Joyce Taylor taken out of the psalmes which belong to the Company [of Stationers]'.[33]

1618. A publisher is forbidden to quote from *The Practise of Piety* in *The Father's Blessing*.[34]

1619. Jaggard, a printer, complains that an author has 'borrowed most of his materialles out of other mens Copies'.[35]

1620. George Wither, having prepared versions of biblical songs and prayers, and obtained permission to print them, finds his permission withdrawn.[36]

1628. Stationers' Company gives permission for a quotation from a printed book, adjudicating the ownership.[37]

1628. Francis Coules is fined by the Stationers' Company for 'printing a song taken out of the Crumes of Comfort'.[38] For the huge sales of Sparke's *Crums*, one of the bestselling books of the age, see appendix 1.

1636. 'a booke called The English Hellicon and Witts delight or the Muses Recreation . . . collected by T. M' entered in Stationers' register.

1637. Re-entered with compiler's name given in full as Thomas May

1642. Re-entered

---

[29] Arber ii, 848.   [30] Greg and Boswell 88.
[31] Arber ii, 836. The entry does not make clear that only a passage was copied, but the phrase 'contrary to order' implies that some general or particular prohibition was already in place. The prime property is *Englands mourning garment . . . To the which is added the true manner of her emperiall funerall* (1603) *STC* 5121. The encroachment is *Elizabetha quasi viuens Eliza's funerall . . . By H.P.* (1603) *STC* 19,803.5 and 19804.
[32] Jackson 86, 95. As the book appeared, there was little overlap.   [33] Jackson 456.
[34] Feather, *Publishing* 22 from Jackson 105.
[35] 'William Jaggard, The Printer', in Augustine Vincent, *A discouerie of errours in the first edition of the catalogue of nobility* (1622) *STC* 24,756.
[36] Arber iv, 43. The occasion for his book, discussed in Arber iv, 12.   [37] Jackson 201.
[38] Jackson 476. *STC* 23,016. The verses were probably printed as a broadside or godly ballad.

Appendix 3 *(cont.)*

1644. Re-entered. No copy of any book with these names, familiar from earlier anthologies, has been found. The multiple entries may signify that the compiler or printer was encountering difficulties in obtaining a printing licence which, by this date, was required for reprints as well as for new titles, or that, despite the entries, his right to publish such anthologies was successfully resisted by the owners of the primary texts.[39]

Printed 'common places', in the form of substantial quotations continue to be produced occasionally

1655. (John Cotgrave) *The English Treasury of Wit and Language, Collected Out of the most, and best of our English Drammatick Poems, Methodically Digested into Commonplaces For General Use*
An anthology of short pieces from dramatic writings, no authors named. Seems to have been compiled with the encouragement of Humphrey Moseley the publisher who at this time claimed ownership of many of the plays drawn upon.[40] *Wits Interpreter*, 1655, by the same compiler, although appearing from the title page and frontispiece to draw on older authors such as Shakespeare, it mainly consists of newly written verse.[41]

1657. Joshua Poole's *English Parnassus, Or A Helpe to English Poesy*
Rhymes and short phrases and conceits, useful to writers of poetry.

1702. Edward Bysshe, *The Art of English Poetry*
Mostly short extracts from the printed works of a wide range of older authors, mainly dramatists, including Shakespeare, arranged alphabetically by topic. The book was avowedly intended as a help to potential poets, but could also serve as a collection of *sententiae*.
8vo. Reprinted 1708, 1710, 1718, 1725, tranched down to 12mo, 1762. Ceased to be demanded after poetic anthologies become possible after 1774.

1714. Edward Bysshe, *The British Parnassus, or Common-place of English Poetry*

1738. Thomas Hayward, *The British Muse, or A Collection of Thoughts, Moral, Natural, and Sublime, of our English Poets*
A large collection, which includes a critique of the inadequacies of the five previous 'poetical commonplace books' published since *Belvedere*.

Others

1640 and much reprinted until eighteenth century. *Wits Recreations*. Short epigrammatic verses from English authors, although not Shakespeare. The practice of courtesy taught by *sententiae*.[42]

1724. *Thesaurus Dramaticus*, 2 volumes, of which about a quarter are from Shakespeare. Status unknown, too early to be a publication which attempted to take advantage of the statutory right accorded by the 1710 Act.[43]

[39] Rollins, ed. *Tottel's Miscellany* ii, 72.   [40] Kewes, *Authorship* 110.
[41] Discussed by Marotti 273.   [42] Discussed by Marotti 267.
[43] See H. L. Ford, *Shakespeare 1700–1740* (Oxford 1935) 58.

1737. *Beauties of the English Stage*, two volumes, with a few passages from Shakespeare. Status unknown.

1744. Dodsley's *The Preceptor.*[44] Compiled for school use 'though for the higher classes'.

1750. *The Works of Celebrated Authors, of whose writings there are but small Remains.* Two volumes. Tonson, the publisher may have claimed ownership of the intellectual property in all of the authors anthologised.

1761. James Burgh, *The Art of Speaking*[45]

1762. *The Poetical Miscellany*[46]

1767. (Oliver Goldsmith) *Beauties of English Poesy*, status unclear. Goldsmith says the book was suggested by his bookseller.

Brief copyright window and later

After 1774. A huge spate of anthologies are published which draw on the old-canon texts which came out of effective copyright in that year.

ABRIDGEMENTS

English-language biblical and apocryphal biblical texts. Evidence of a clamp-down on abridgements and adaptations, around 1600

1550. Thomas Paynell, *The piththy* [sic] *and moost notable sayinges of al scripture.*
A substantial abridgement of the English-language Bible.[47] Appears to be a publication by an individual without the direct involvement of the ecclesiastical authorities.

1579. Robinson's *Vyneyard of Vertue*[48]

Before 1598. *A hedgerovv of busshes, brambles, and briers . . . by I. D.*[49]
Quotations from the Bible arranged under different sins and vices.

1597. Middleton's *Wisdom of Solomon Paraphrased*
No others found.

* * *

1643. (during English Civil War) *The Souldiers Pocket Bible*
A sixteen-page pamphlet which lists passages of the Bible, mainly from the Old Testament, which describe military duty. Compiled and licensed by Edmund Calamy. A *Cavalier Soldier's Prayer Book* produced by the royalists was printed in 1648. *A Christian Soldier's Penny Bible* was produced in 1693.[50]

Evidence that printed ballad versions of biblical texts were frequent before 1600

1563/4. Sampson and Delilah[51]

---

[44] See Michael 165.   [45] Michael 173.   [46] *Ibid.* 174.   [47] *STC* 19,494.
[48] See W. W. Greg, 'Richard Robinson and the Stationers' Register' 408, in *Modern Language Review* (1955).
[49] *STC* 6170.   [50] Harrold R. Willoughby, *Soldiers' Bibles through Three Centuries* (Chicago 1944).
[51] Arber i, 237.

Appendix 3 *(cont.)*

Many other examples not noted here[52]

1592. 'The storye of Susanna beinge the xiith Chapter of Daniell . . .'[53]

1595. Mary Magdalen from twentieth chapter of St John[54]
There are few if any registrations of ballad versions of biblical stories after this time.

The end of dramatic adaptations of biblical and apocryphal biblical texts

Until the end of the sixteenth century, a high proportion of dramatic performances were adaptations of themes drawn from biblical and apocryphal biblical texts. The most common themes were Adam, Joseph, David, Esther, and Susannah.[55] At some time around 1600, however, the use of the Bible as a source material seems to have ended, without any known exceptions.

The last printed plays drawn from biblical texts

1568. *A newe and wittie Comedie or Enterlude, newly imprinted, treating upon the Historie of Iacob and Esau, taken out of the xxvii. Chap. of the first boke of Moses entituled Genesis.*[56]

1577. *A Tragedie of Abraham's Sacrifice . . taken out of the two and twentieth chapter of Genesis*[57]

1578. Thomas Garter, *The Commody of the moste vertuous and Godlye Susanna*

1594. Entry in Stationers' Register, Robert Greene's *History of Jobe* (lost)

1594. Entry in Stationers' Register, George Peele's *David and Bethsabe*

1599. First surviving printed copy, apparently a first edition.[58]

1639. *Christ's passion*, 'a tragedy with annotations by George Sands'.[59] An exception to the main pattern, unexplained.

Abridged 'ballad versions' of longer literary works common before 1600, but only a few later

1564/5. A book entitled 'the story of kynge Henry the IIIIth and the Miller of Tamowthe' is registered.[60]
Date unknown but before 1600. A ballad version of which a copy is extant.[61]

1599. *Edward IIII, and the Tanner of Tamworth* is registered as a play[62]

1600. Then simultaneously as a 'merye pleasant and delectable history' (i.e. as a prose version or chapbook), and as 'a ballad of the same matter that was printed by her husband John Danter'.[63]

---

[52] Arber i, 260, i, 77, i, 415, i, 416, i, 408, i, 435, ii, 320, ii, 359, ii, 376, ii, 430, ii, 487.
[53] Arber ii, 620.   [54] Arber iii, 45.   [55] Roston 55.
[56] Entered in Stationers' Register. See Greg i,1.
[57] W. W. Greg, *A Bibliography of the English Printed Drama to the Restoration* (1939) no. 77.
[58] *Ibid.* no. 160.
[59] *STC* 12,397. See W. W. Greg, *Licensers for the Press, &c. to 1640* (Oxford 1962) 40.
[60] Arber i, 264.   [61] Livingston, no. 229.   [62] Arber iii, 147.   [63] Arber iii, 173.

Appendix 3 (*cont.*)

1595. A ballad version of Greene's *Pandosto*, first published in 1588.[64] Shakespeare's *The Winter's Tale* makes use of common sources.[65] 1672. *Dorastus and Fawnia*, apparently a new abridgement of *Pandosto*, made for one of the Ballad partners, the main text still on sale unabridged in the meantime.
Date uncertain. *Argalus and Parthenia* from Sidney's *Arcadia* (1590).[66]

1592. Some years before Marlowe's play of the same name, a dispute between rivals about who had been the first to print what appears to be the chapbook or ballad version of *Doctor Faustus*.[67] Dr *Faustus*, the play, registered 1601.[68]

1594. 16 May, a ballad version of the *Jew of Malta* registered.[69]

1594. 17 May (Marlowe's) *Jew of Malta* registered.[70]

Date uncertain. *Christ's Tears over Jerusalem*, from Nashe's play, 1595.

Date uncertain. *Fed her Father*, abridged from a work registered 1596.[71]

Date uncertain. *Fortunatus*, abridged from Dekker's comedy, *Old Fortunatus*, 1600, based on a German Volksbuch of 1509, dramatised by Hans Sachs in 1553.[72]

Date uncertain. *The Gentle Craft*. Abridged from Deloney's book, 1598, which was based on traditional stories.[73] Dekker's play was registered 1599.

7 March 1597. *Jack of Newbury*, Deloney's book, composed from a traditional story, registered.[74] 8 July 1597 a ballad version registered.[75]

Date uncertain. *Long Meg of Westminster*, from a jest book not later than 1582. Used by Deloney in *The Gentle Craft. Part 2*, registered 1597.

Date uncertain. *St George*, and several other stories including *Valentine and Orson*, from Johnson's *The Seven Champions of Christendom* (1596).[76]

c. 1599. *The Story of David and Bersheba*, from Peele's play, *The Love of David and Bersheba*. Or possibly from the interlude 'Of the two sinnes of Kynge David' entered 1561/2.[77]

c. 1599. *The Spanish Tragedy.* From Kyd's play of the same name, first printed 1599.[78]

1600. *Valentine and Orson* registered as a play[79]

1601. *Don Sebastian* registered, and the ballad version registered to another owner two weeks later.[80]
No registrations of ballad versions of newly published plays or other literary works are recorded after this time.

1603. Some ballads, apparently derived from longer works, are entered 'so they belong to no other man', including *Arthur of the Round Table*, and *Wandering Prince of Troy*.[81]

---

[64] Francis Sabie, *The Fissher-mans Tale and Flora's Fortune*. Noted by Newcomb 82.
[65] See J. H. P. Pafford, ed., *The Winter's Tale* (1963), and Newcomb.
[66] Described in later printings as 'a Choice Flower gathered out of Sir Philip Sidney's Rare Garden'. See Ashton 483. Entered in Stationers' Register, 1629, with certain verses by Quarles, Arber iv 209, probably a re-registration. The story was still in Bew's list in the late eighteenth century under the title *The Unfortunate Lovers*.
[67] Feather, *Publishing, Piracy and Politics* 26. [68] Arber iii, 171. [69] Arber ii, 649.
[70] Arber ii, 650. [71] Arber iii, 64. [72] Arber iii, 156. [73] Deloney 522.
[74] Arber iii, 81. See also Deloney 506. [75] Arber iii, 81 and 87. [76] Arber iii, 64.
[77] *Roxburghe Ballads*, edited by C. H. L. P. Hindley (1873–4) ii, 270.
[78] *Ibid.* 453. [79] Arber iii, 159. [80] 30 March and 12 April. Arber iii, 182. [81] Arber iii, 326.

Appendix 3 *(cont.)*

1614. White, a ballad publisher, pays a fee 'for printing of a ballett of Hero and Leander.'[82] This marks a change of registration practice, omitting 'entering for his copy', the normal formula. The entry seems unrelated to Chapman's translation, entered in 1616.[83]

1615. A similar entry 'the ballett of Dulcina', entered 1611.[84]

1620. Similar entries for ballads of 'the wandering Jew' and 'I pray begin again.'[85] This form of entry, that I cannot explain, then ceases.

Direct evidence for the discouragement of abridgements

1621. An abridgement of Foxe's *Book of Martyrs* granted letters patent but is later refused a printing licence on the grounds that it would damage the sales of the main work.[86]

1624. A patent given for an abridgement of Camden's *Britannia*.[87]

1620s. The granting of Letters Patent for abridgements, that is the attempted creation by the state of a whole new class of intellectual properties of which the state could sell franchises, is successfully resisted by the Stationers' Company.[88]

1631. Dispute about an abridgement of Foxe's *Martyrs*.[89] Archbishop Laud refuses to grant licences on the grounds that 'abridgements, by their brevity and their cheapness, in short time work out the authors themselves'.[90]

1633. An abridgement of Gerrard's *Herbal* [medical] is forbidden.[91]

1635. An authorised abridgement of Breton's *Uncasing of Machivil's Instructions*.[92]

1681. Abridgements without consent are explicitly forbidden by the Stationers' Company's Ordinances. 'Copy or Copies, Book or Books, or any part of any such Copy or Copies, Book or Books.'[93]

1711. A fee paid for permission to print 400 'collections' out of Tully's *Offices* [Cicero's *De officiis*, a much favoured source of *sententiae*].[94]

1740. Courts confirm that an abridgement is a 'new work' entitled to copyright protection.[95]

---

[82] Arber iii, 549.   [83] Arber iii, 594.   [84] Arber iii, 567.   [85] Arber iv, 40.
[86] Arnold Hunt, 'Book Trade Patents 1603–1640' in Hunt, Mandelbrote and Shell 33, 48.
[87] *Ibid.* 33.   [88] *Ibid.*   [89] Jackson 236.   [90] Quoted by Hunt 'Book Trade' 30.
[91] Jackson, 255.   [92] *STC* 37,04.9.
[93] Arber i, 23. This is more explicit than a similar provision in the Ordinances of 1678. Arber i, 16.
[94] Bowyer Ledgers 70. No copy traced.
[95] In Gyles *v.* Watson quoted by Rose 51.

Appendix 4 Intellectual property. Popular literature, England

Ballads amongst the largest classes of printed books in the first century of print

Late fifteenth century, romances printed by Caxton, Wynken de Worde, and others

c. 1513. First extant printed ballads and romances.[1]

Ballads printed in England before the registers start in 1557.	na
Estimated number of ballad titles printed 1550 to 1600.[2]	3,000
Ballads entered in the registers 1557 to 1600.[3]	1,500

1560. An inventory shows 796 ballads in the cupboard of the Stationers' Company, apparently copies of books entered that year in a register which has since been lost.[4]

1585. Inventory of Roger Ward of Shrewsbury includes 'i Reame 6 quires ballates' and i boxe for ballates'.[5]

Examples of traditional oral and manuscript songs and stories being printed and the implicit intellectual property rights taken into private ownership

1520. A reference to 'Syr Eglemour' being sold for 3.5 pence, 'Robin Hod' for 2 pence, and many ballads for half a penny.[6]

1520. Reference to 'notbrone mayde' (nutbrown maid) and 'kesmes corals' (Christmas carols) being sold for one penny.[7]

1521. First surviving fragment of a printed Christmas carol.[8]

1561/2. *The Holly and the Ivy* (Christmas carol) registered.[9]

1561/2. *Tom Long the Carrier* registered.[10]

1561/2. *Patient Grizzel* registered.[11]

1561/2. Christmas carols, several registered to one printer.[12]

The move to monopoly

1575. The English state attempts to establish a 'privilege' for all ballads and books up to twenty-four pages, i.e. all texts which could be printed on a half, on one, or on two printed sheets folded, almost the whole of popular literature.[13]

1586. A printer/publisher registers 123 ballads.[14]

1612. In order, as they claimed, to correct recent abuses, the Stationers' Company gives the sole right of printing ballads to five printers.[15]

1618. Licensing of chapmen.

---

[1] Thomson 28.   [2] Watt 11, 42.   [3] Watt 42.   [4] Arber i, 143.
[5] See Alexander Rodger, 'Roger Ward's Shrewsbury Stock: An Inventory of 1595' in *The Library* (1958).
[6] Dorne 79. Another early account book (Godfrey) *Garrett Godfrey's Accounts c. 1527–1533* edited by Elisabeth Leedham-Green, D. E. Rhodes, and F. H. Stubbings (Cambridge Bibliographical Society 1992), contains, no. 945, a note of a sale of four ballad books 'off a quer and <a h>aff'.
[7] Dorne 87, 120, 128 and elsewhere.   [8] Dorne 152.   [9] Arber i, 176.   [10] Arber i, 177.
[11] Arber i, 309.   [12] Arber i, 402.   [13] Greg's *Companion* 17.
[14] Thomson 38, Rollins, 20, from Arber ii, 452.   [15] Thomson 41. Full text in Jackson 53.

Appendix 4 (*cont.*)

1619. Symcock is given letters patent for the exclusive right to print items on one side of the paper, including ballads. The patent is renewed in 1628. A period of fierce competition and litigation between the state and the Stationers' Company ensues.[16] The Stationers maintain their control.

1624. Establishment of the Ballad Partners, a syndicate within the Stationers' Company.[17] The Partners seem to have reassigned the property rights of other works which they held, including those in Shakespeare's plays, and to have bought up ballad titles as they became available, as part of a general move to divide the book market into sectors.[18]

1624. 128 old ballads re-registered at a bulk price 'provided that this entrance shall not preiudice any other man that have any Interest to any of them by any former Entrance or otherwise'.[19]

Outsider printer/publishers, resisting the move to monopoly, sell ballads at prices 25 per cent less than those of the Ballad Partners, on higher quality paper, but are driven out of business. Minimum price of Ballad Partners ballads 13.33s a ream.[20]

1649–1655. Commonwealth. The ballad trade is suppressed by law, although the trading and entering of titles continues.[21]

1656. The Ballad Partners combine to form what is in effect a single firm, producing to a uniform design and format, and pooling their production and storage facilities.[22]

1666. Fire of London. The warehouse of the Ballad Partners is destroyed, but re-established on a new site.

1675. 196 ballads and chapbooks registered, some very ancient.[23]

1685. About 300 ballads and chapbooks, some very ancient, in the ownership of William Thackeray.[24]

1695. Lapsing of state licensing. In the legal vacuum, the printer Onley prints many ballads in which an intellectual property was held by the Ballad Partners.[25] The lifting of restrictions on the number of printing presses leads to a rapid growth in the printing of locally composed ballads outside London, but the older favourites are only printed in London.

'We had besides a class of humbler authors and Poets, astronomical fortune tellers, authors of scriptural tracts and Hymns for places of Worship; dabsters in Jest Books, Joe Millers of the day, and ballads for country fairs and the husbandman's coarse illiterate merriment.' Luke Hansard, describing his work in a printing house in Norwich.[26]

---

[16] Hunt 50.
[17] A copy of the agreement of 1689 which probably includes many features agreed and operated earlier is transcribed in Thomson 279. The ballad warehouse had already existed for so long in 1689 that it was called 'antient'. See Thomson 67.
[18] For Shakespeare see chapter 8.   [19] Arber iv, 131.
[20] Arnold Hunt 'Book Trade Patents 1603–1640' in Hunt, Mandelbrote, and Shell 35.
[21] Thomson 46.   [22] Thomson 66.   [23] Thomson 70, from Arber ii, 496.
[24] List reproduced from the manuscript in the BL Bagford papers in *Bagford Ballads* edited by Joseph Woodfall Ebsworth (Hertford, 1878–80) i, liii. The fact that the names are 'Printed for' shows that Thackeray was owner at least in part.
[25] Thomson 82, quoting Dunton.
[26] *Autobiography of Luke Hansard* . . . edited by Robin Myers (1991).

Appendix 4 (*cont.*)

The intellectual property in any newly written ballads which proved commercially successful was usually bought by the Ballad Partners and added to the portfolio.

High monopoly period

1712. 174 ancient ballad and chapbook titles, a large part of the ancient popular canon, are reregistered for copyright under the 1710 Act, in some cases in versions of different length, so confirming that the then owners can take advantage of the transitional provisions and maintain their monopoly until 1731.

Date unknown, early eighteenth century. Black letter ('Gothic') type, is replaced with roman type. Woodcuts are re-engraved. The management of the whole business, manufacturing, storage, and sales, is remitted to a professional agent.

1723/5. *A Collection of Old Ballads. Corrected from the best and most Ancient Copies Extant.* 159 ballads published in book form during the transitional period allowed by the 1710 Act while perpetual intellectual property was still fully legal.[27] The editor of the second volume says he would have included more but for fear 'of being thought an Invader of other Men's properties'.

Battley, one of the publishers, is recorded as the previous owner of a list of chapmen's books sold at the closed trade sale of 21 April 1763. Copy in the Murray archives, which gives the buyer as Wilkie, later the Treasurer of the Stationers' Company, who bought all the chapmen's book shares on offer.

Other printed collections, edited by Percy, Ritson, Evans, and others also brought versions of the old ballads, hitherto mainly circulating individually, to the mainstream book buying public.

1754 and **1764**. Extant wholesale catalogues of the now almost fully monopolised ballad trade.[28]

'. . . I went to the old printing-office in Bow Church-yard kept by Dicey, whose family have kept it fourscore years. There are ushered into the world of literature *Jack and the Giants, The Seven Wise Men of Gotham,* and other story-books which in my dawning years amused me as much as *Rasselas* does now. I saw the whole scheme with a kind of pleasing romantic feeling to find myself really where all my old darlings were printed. I bought two dozen of the story-books and had them bound up with this title, *Curious Productions.* James Boswell, 1763.[29]

---

[27] The title page of the third edition of volume i (1727) notes that the book was 'Printed for J. Roberts in Warwick-Lane; D. Leach, in Black and White-Court in the Old Baily; and J. Battely, at the Dove in Pater-Noster-Row, the same three publishers as are mentioned in volume ii although with a slight difference in spelling and one change of address. This is a different list from those who published the first edition of the first volume whose imprint shows Roberts as the sole owner at that time, with the books being sold also by Brotherton, Bettesworth, Pemberton, Woodman, and Stag. The three volumes were reprinted in a facsimile edition c.1900. An advertisement list of D. Leach, one of the three publishers, inserted at the end of the copy of volume ii (1726), Ac, claims high sales.

[28] See bibliography: 'Book trade catalogues. Popular literature'.

[29] *Boswell's London Journal 1762–1763,* edited by Frederick A. Pottle (1950) 299. Boswell's collection, with others collected later, is in the Child Memorial, Harvard.

Appendix 4 *(cont.)*

Towns outside London where Dicey had named agents, probably his tied-in distribution network, mid-eighteenth century[30]

Northampton, Aylesbury, Bicester, Coventry, Harborough, Tring, St Albans, Cambridge, Newport Pagnell, Stony Stratford, Derby, Leeds, York (Gent), Newcastle (White), St Ives.

Ballads as visual decoration

The traditional woodcut images show the same long continuity.

'If o'er the Chymney, they some Ballad have
Of Chevy Chase, or of some branded slave
Hang'd at Tyburne, they their matins make it
And vespers too, and for the Bible take it.' Abraham Holland, 1624.[31]

     'ballads pasted on the wall
Of Chevy Chase and English Moll,
Fair Rosamond and Robin Hood
The little Children in the Wood.'

Said to be in every cottage. Goldsmith's *The Deserted Village* (1770).[32]
'"Death and the Lady", a figure half skeleton, half female – "Keep within compass", a beau with cocked hat, scarlet coat, &c., standing between the two legs of a pairs of compasses, and other showy, admonitory, pictures, were to be seen in the farm-houses and cottages in Wiltshire, in my youth-days.' Thomas Rees.[33] The print of 'Keep within compass' had been available at least since 1619.[34]
'on the walls hung "Twelve Golden Rules of Good King Charles" and "Death and the Lady".' Thomas Cooper remembering his uncle's cottage in Lincolnshire c. 1812.[35]

The Duchess of Suffolk's Calamity. An example of a long-lived ballad later believed to have emanated from 'the folk' but actually an abridgement of a longer text written and printed before 1600

Before 1602. Included in *Strange histories, of kings, princes, dukes, earles, lords, ladies, knights, and gentlemen*, metrical versions of stories from Holinshed's *Chronicles* compiled by Deloney, of which an edition, not the first, was printed in 1602.[36] Several later printings under different titles.[37]

---

[30] Noted in a copy of *Bird's Lamentation*, Harvard no. 684.
[31] Quoted by Tessa Watt in 'The Broadside Trade 1550–1640' in Myer and Harris, *Spreading*.
[32] English Moll is Moll Flanders, for which see chapter 4.
[33] Rees and Britton 83.
[34] See William St Clair and Irmgard Maassen, eds., *Conduct Literature for Women, 1500–1640* (2000) vi, 1, where the printed image is reproduced in facsimile.
[35] Cooper 20
[36] Man 585. Reregistered 1614, Arber iii, 557. For examples of how Deloney's versions are 'too often little more than metrical versions of the prose', see Man xxxviii.
[37] Man 585.

1624. In the Ballad Partners stock.[38]
1723/25. Reprinted in *A Collection of Old Ballads* and other collections.
1764. In the ballad trade's wholesale catalogue.
Romantic period. Disappears in the mass extinction.

Merging of the ballad/chapbook tradition with the old canon

'A Catalogue of Chapmen's Books' printed by J. Bew, c. 1800.[39] Many different books on religion, sermons, prayers, devotional exercises, religious conversion, advice on living and on dying, antidotes to melancholy. Bunyan, about a dozen titles and abridgements. Tolerated illegitimate supernatural, *Hocus Pocus, Tales of the Fairies, History of Witches and Wizards*. Many ancient chapbooks and ballads including *Garland of Good Will* (see appendix 3), *Argalus and Parthenia, Friar Bacon, Fifteen Comforts of Matrimony, Fair Rosamond, Jane Shore, Don Bellianis, Guy of Warwick, Seven Champions of Christendom, Valentine and Orson*. Pseudo-Aristotle's *Problems* and other related texts that offer pre-modern information and advice about women's bodies, sex, conception, birth control (mostly misleading).[40] Guides to husbandry, farriery, letter writing, arithmetic. (Defoe's) *Robinson Crusoe, Religious Courtship* (conduct). Lives of thief takers, thieves, housebreakers, highwaymen, London bawds. 'Select Novels for the Instruction and Entertainment of Youth' (abridged). *Amelia, David Simple, Female Quixote, Gil Blas, Joseph Andrews, Peregrine Pickle, Pamela, Roderick Random, Tom Jones* bound together in two volumes 4 shillings, or available at 0.5 shillings each. Bew also offered to supply 'country shopkeepers' with 'Bibles, Common Prayers, Testaments, Psalters, Spelling Books, modern books of all kinds, great variety of Plays, and all sorts of School books'.

Chapbooks of the Gothic 'Blue books'

List of J. Arliss, 1810 and later.[41]
'New pamphlets' price 0.5 shillings all with an illustration, each 36 pp., i.e. each a sheet and a half, also sold in numbers. Many appear to be abridgements of Minerva Press and other modern out-of-copyright novels.[42]
Much read by P. B. Shelley when he was a schoolboy.[43]

The mass extinction of the old ballads during the romantic period. Examples of long survival and sudden disappearance

Bevis of Southampton and *Guy of Warwick*

c. 1200. Both appear in France in manuscript versions.

---

[38] Arber iv, 131.   [39] Advertisement in Bew.   [40] See chapter 4.
[41] Advertised with other works, including children's books, in *Select Tales, Or Choice Repository*, vol ii, no 12, Ac. Examples in John Johnson and Ac.
[42] Noted by Cruse, *Englishman* 150.
[43] See Thomas Medwin, *The Life of Percy Bysshe Shelley* (1913 edition) 25.

c. 1300. Both appear in England in manuscript versions.[44]

Men speke of romances of prys,
Of Horn child and of Ypotys,
Of Bevis and sir Guy
      Geoffrey Chaucer, *Tale of Sir Thopas*, c. 1387

1400. *Guy of Warwick* recorded in the inventory of manuscript books of a monastic library, Titchfield.[45]

1490s. *Guy of Warwick* recorded among the books, probably manuscript, bequeathed to the Benedictine Monastery, Leicester.[46]

c. 1493. A fragment of a version of *Bevis* printed in England by Wynken de Worde survives.[47] Wholesale price 0.8 shillings bound.[48]

c. 1500. Both *Bevis* and *Guy* in print in England.[49]

1525. A royal privilege granted in France for the printing of *Guy de Warwich*.[50]

1539. 'Englishmen have now in hand in every Church and place, almost every man, the Holy Bible and New Testament in their mother tongue, instead of the old fabulous and fantastical books of the *Table Round, Launcelot du Lac, Huon de Bourdeaux, Bevy of Hampton, Guy of Warwick*, & and such other, whose impure fifth and vain fabulosity the light of God has abolished utterly.' *Summary of Declaration of the Faith, Uses, and Observances of England* (1539).[51]

1558. 'Bevys of Hampton' entered. One of the first when the registers open after the chartering of the Stationers' Company.[52]

1560. Another entry[53]

c. 1570
. . . blind harpers or such like taverne minstrels that give a fit of mirth for a groat, & their matters being for the most part stories of old time, as the tale of Sir Topas, the reports of Bevis of Southampton, Guy of Warwick, Adam Bell and Clymne of the Clough, & such other old romances or historical rimes. George Puttenham.[54]

1592. *Guy* registered as printed as a ballad, with the tune.[55]

1598. Among the romances condemned by name in Francis Meres.[56]

---

[44] Watt 14. For an edition of some of the early mss. see Eugen Kölbing, *The Romance of Sir Beves of Hamptoun* (Early English Text Society 1885).
[45] *CHBB* iii, 239.   [46] *CHBB* iii, 237.
[47] In the Bodleian. *STC* 1987, Bennett, *1475 to 1557* 244.
[48] H. R. Plomer, 'The Lawsuits of Richard Pynson' in *The Library* (1909) 127.
[49] Kölbing, *Romance* viii. Bennett, *1475 to 1557* 252.
[50] Quoted from an original document by Armstrong 294.
[51] Quoted by Mumby 57.   [52] Arber i, 95.   [53] Arber i, 156.
[54] Quoted by Watt 13. Another warning against 'Robin-hode, Clem of the Clough, wyth suche lyke' in a book of 1550, quoted by Bennett, *1475 to 1557* 58.
[55] Watt 14.   [56] Francis Meres, *Palladis Tamia* (1598) 269.

Appendix 4 (*cont.*)

1615.

Next after him your Country-Farmer views it,
It may be good (saith he) for those can use it.
Shewe mee King Arthur, Bevis, or Syr Guye
These are the Books he onely loves to buye. Henry Parrot.[57]

1630. An offshore edition in Scotland.[58]

1666. Bunyan describing the books he read before his conversion,
'Give me a Ballad, a News-book, George on Horseback, or Bevis of Southampton, give
me some book that teaches curious Arts, that tells of old Fables; but for the Holy
scriptures, I cared not. And as it was with me then, so it is with my brethren now.'[59]

1682 Both reregistered.[60] 1698, reregistered again.[61] 1712, reregistered again after the Act of
1710.

1742. *Guy* among recommended reading of Joseph Andrews, a serving man, in Fielding's
novel of that name.[62]

Eighteenth century. Both appear in several versions in the ballad trade wholesale
catalogues of 1754 and 1764.

About 1750. Thomas Gent produces versions in York in defiance of the London
'owners'.[63]

After 1774, both are reprinted in provincial towns.[64]

c. 1800. *Guy* available on Bew's list of chapmen's books. See above.

1805. 'The printed work [i.e. full version of *Guy*], however, is extremely rare, having been
superseded by a modern abridgement in prose, or rather perhaps in blank verse printed
like prose, which is to be found at almost every stall in the metropolis.' Ellis's *Specimens of
Early English Metrical Romances*.[65]
During the romantic period, neither story was accepted into the children's book repertory
and they ceased to be reprinted except in scholarly editions.

---

[57] Quoted by Watt 257.   [58] Noted by Aldis.   [59] Quoted by Spufford 7.   [60] Arber iii, 110.
[61] Arber iii, 477.   [62] Noted by Newcomb 235.   [63] Thomson 118.   [64] Thomson 124.
[65] *Specimens of Early English Metrical Romances* ii, 3.

Publishing a new title

Longman's costs and margins for a new copyrighted title, as declared to parliament, 1818, excluding overheads and any payments to the author.[1]

A 4to edition, 250 copies

Manufacturing costs	Price (shillings)	Percent of total cost
Setting the type	1,610	33
Paper	1,110	23
Pressing	530	11
Boarding	380	8
Total manufacturing costs	3,630	75
Selling costs, advertising	1,200	25
Total costs	4,830	100
Implied unit cost of manufacture	15	
Implied unit cost with advertising	19	
Retail price	31.5 to 42	
Sale price to retailers	23.6 to 31.5	

An 8vo edition of a new title, 750 copies

Manufacturing costs		
Setting the type	450	21
Paper and pressing	450	21
Total manufacturing costs	900	43
Selling costs, advertising	1,200	57
Total costs	2,100	100
Implied unit cost of manufacture	1	
Implied unit cost with advertising	3	
Retail price	10	
Sale price to retailers	7.5	

Competitive non-monopoly publishing

Symonds's edition of Thomson's *The Seasons*, out of legal and pretender copyright, and requiring no payment to authors, 1803.

Production costs for an edition of 4,000 copies.[2]	756	
Unit cost per copy		0.19
Retail price		1

Walker's Classics edition of Gray's *Poems*, pretender copyright, 1814.

Production costs for an edition of 4,000 copies.[3]

Printing	480	30
Covers and hot-pressing	133	8

[1] Compiled from answers given by Owen Rees of Longman, *Select Committee*.
[2] Whittingham archives, 41,902. [3] Longman archives, impression book.

Appendix 5 (*cont.*)

Paper	489	31
Plates	418.5	26
Other costs	63	4
Total costs	1,583.5	100
Implied unit cost	0.4	
Retail price	0.66	

The whole edition was pre-sold in lots ranging
from 100 to 600 copies

An example of the effects on print runs of the 1774 decisions

(Defoe's) *Robinson Crusoe*

High monopoly period	*Price (shillings)*	*Print run*
1719. First edition[4]		1,000
1719. Three more editions, each		1,000
An edition before 1754. Two volumes[5]	5	1,500
An edition before 1764. Two volumes[6]	5	1,500

Copyright pretenders' editions after 1774[7]		
1784		2,000
1790		2,000

'My library, that is to say, the library of my father's house, consisted of an old octavo
bible . . . a church prayer book, the Dyche [Dyche's *Guide to the English Tongue*, a
standard school book], and a book of pious ejaculations which belonged to my
grandfather . . . I had heard of such a book as Robinson Crusoe. I longed to see it. My
uncle . . . had it. I made repeated journeys to his house, more than three miles distant, to
beg the loan of it but it was always lent to some body or other. I was very near having it
once, for it had only been lent to somebody the evening before I got there.' Thomas
Dolby, a thatcher in Lincolnshire, writing of his childhood in the 1790s.[8]

1807. *Walker's Classics* edition[9]		5,000
1810. Barbauld's edition[10]		1,500
1817. *Walker's Classics* edition[11]		4,000

Some monopoly breakers' editions after 1774

From 1788. Harrison		? up to 10,000
From 1790s. Cooke		?5,000

Many other editions, including some rewritten, abridged, and illustrated, plus children's
versions. The book also became one of the cheap and plentiful titles included in

[4] K. I. D. Maslen, 'Edition quantities for *Robinson Crusoe*' in *The Library* (1961).
[5] Trade sale catalogue, 7 November 1754. Price from *A Catalogue of the Most Esteemed Modern Books* (1751).
[6] Trade sale catalogue, 20 September 1764.   [7] Longman copyright ledger, i, 172.
[8] Thomas Dolby, *Memoirs* (1827).   [9] Longman archives, impression book.
[10] Longman archives. Some confirmatory figures are also in the Richard Taylor archives.
[11] Longman archives, impression book.

Appendix 5 *(cont.)*

old-canon series, often sold very cheaply in parts.[12] For example, in the 1820s, Fairburn's edition, with excellent engravings, sold in weekly parts at one penny each.[13]

1808. Suttaby's edition, 24mo.[14]	4,000
1822. A Tegg edition.[15]	4,000
1826. Darton's children's edition.[16]	3,000
Gall and Inglis's Victorian stereotyped edition.[17]	39,000

Publishing 'on commission'

Percy Bysshe Shelley's *Laon and Cythna*, renamed *The Revolt of Islam* (1817), 750 copies 8vo. All costs paid by the author.[18]

	Price (shillings)	Percent of total
Printing 19 sheets	1,216	51
Printing another leaf[19]	15	0.6
Alterations in proofs	66	2.8
Paper	1,061.5	44.9
Labels	7.5	0.3
Total	2,366	100

The costs of the extensive alterations undertaken at the printer's request in order to avoid the risk of criminal prosecution are not known. *Laon and Cythna* was advertised twice, another cost to Shelley that does not appear in the table.[20]

Unit cost of manufacture	3
Estimated total unit cost to Shelley[21]	7
Unit retail price	10.5
Unit retail price at which the book was reissued in 1829, purporting to be a new book	10.5
Unit price at which stocks later sold to a remainder dealer[22]	0.5
Unit retail price of remainders on sale to the public	2.5

'The Paper and Printing are equally bad but it was done as cheap as possible.' R. Triphook, an employee of the publisher.[23] For evidence that Shelley was overcharged for the paper as well as the printing, see 'Paper per ream' below.

---

[12] For a full list see Robert W. Lovett, *Robinson Crusoe, A Bibliographical Checklist of English Language Editions* (New York 1991).

[13] Ac.   [14] Whittingham archives, 41,926.   [15] Whittingham archives, 41,926.

[16] Adlard ledger.   [17] Gall and Inglis impression book.

[18] Oxford, Bodleian Library, ms. Shelley adds. c. 12, folio 7. Transcribed in *SC* v, 160. For the sales see appendix 9.

[19] As the physical make up of the book shows. See Thomas J. Wise, *A Shelley Library* (1924) 49. This was a charge for printing leaf d, the text requiring slightly more than nineteen sheets.

[20] Robinson 191.

[21] Unit cost of manufacture plus my estimate of costs of amendments and advertising.

[22] H. Buxton Forman, *The Shelley Library* (1886) 77.

[23] Quoted by Robinson 191 from an original manuscript in Bodleian.

Appendix 5 (*cont.*)

Publication by subscription

1795. Ann Batten Cristal's *Poetical Sketches*
About 150 names, relatives and personal friends, mostly women, and prominent dissenters, including Amelia Alderson, later Opie, and Mary Wollstonecraft. Also Surrey Reading Society, and Reading [town] Society.

1802. Clio Rickman's *Poetical Scraps*
Many prominent dissenters and radicals

1812. Robert Forbes' *Poems Chiefly in the Scottish Dialect*
600 named subscribers, mainly living in and around Edinburgh

1813 W. S. Walker's, *Gustavus Vasa*
About 1,000 names, many royal, noble, rich, or connected with Eton. The preface tells how Walker began the poem when he was eleven, although he did not finish the first part till he was seventeen, and includes his detailed proposal for the remaining books.

1832. Leigh Hunt's *Collected Poems*
Noblemen, politicians, authors, editors, publishers and literary men drawn mainly from the liberal wing of society, including some who had little money of their own, come together to support an old man down on his luck. About 120 names in the first list including Campbell, Carlyle, Coleridge, Godwin, Lamb, Landor, Macaulay, Southey, and Wordsworth.[24]

Publishing with shared net profits

(Mary Shelley's) *Frankenstein*, novel, three volumes, 500 copies. Publisher's account to the author, January 1818, simplified.[25]

Costs	Price (shillings)	Per cent of total cost
Printing	752	32.4
Correction and labels	111.5	4.8
Paper	705	30.4
Boarding for 33 sets given away[26]	49.5	2.1
Advertising	550	23.7
Advertising in Scotland	150	6.5
Total	2,318	100
Unit cost of manufacture	4.6	
Retail price	16.5	
Income		
41 copies given away free	0	
459 copies sold to booksellers at 10.5 shillings each	4,819.5	
Total gross profit margin (Income minus cost)	2,501.5	

[24] Printed prospectus, dated April 1832, inserted in a copy of Leigh Hunt's *Lord Byron and Some of his Contemporaries*, Ac.
[25] Bodleian ms. Shelley adds. c. 12, f. 9, transcribed in *SC* v, 397. For the publication history and sales see chapter 18.
[26] The manuscript about the wording of which the editors of *SC* were doubtful, reads, to my eye, 'Boardg. 33 Sets given away'.

Appendix 5 *(cont.)*

Of which one-third to author	833.8	
two-thirds to publisher	1,667.7	

Publishing a bestseller with shared net profits

(Walter Scott's) *Rob Roy*, three volumes, 1817, 10,000 copies. Publisher's account, simplified.[27]

Costs		
Printing 42.5 sheets at 189s a sheet	8,032.5	26.2
Reprinting a large section of volume 3	115	0.4
Small letter printing	403	1.3
Transcribing the ms to preserve anonymity	378	1.2
Paper at 23s a ream	21,735	71.8
Advertising	0	0
Total	30,663.5	100
Unit cost of manufacture	3	
Unit retail price	24	
Income		
10,000 copies sold at 15.75 shillings	157,500	
minus costs	30,683.5	
Declared net profits of which half to Scott, half to the publishers	126,86.5	

English provincial printing, low cost/low price, wide margin

Illustrations of Sterne by John Ferrier, 1798
Printed in Warrington for Cadell and Davies.[28]

	756 copies
Printing and paper	618 shillings
Manufacturing cost per copy	0.8
Retail price.[29]	6

Johnson's *Rasselas*, 1804
Printed in Banbury

	1,086 copies
Printing and paper	887 shillings
Manufacturing cost per copy	0.8
Retail price as sold by Tegg and others in London.[30]	5

Provincial verse, on commission, *Modern Accomplishments*, 1813
Printed in Banbury[31]

	500 copies
Printing and paper	525 shillings
Manufacturing cost per copy	1.05
Retail price if any sold	?6

[27] Longman archives.
[28] Printing bill by George Nicholson, unpublished manuscript, found in a copy of a book described in a catalogue of second-hand books by Ximenes, bookseller, February 1998.
[29] *London Catalogue.*
[30] Calculated from contemporary financial accounts transcribed in *John Cheney and His Descendants, Printers in Banbury since 1767* (Banbury, privately printed 1936).
[31] *Ibid.*

Costs and prices of ballads and chapbooks

1764. Height of the high monopoly period[32]

Old ballads per ream, wholesale	8
Implying unit cost for a one sheet ballad	0.004
Retail price from a chapman	thought to be 0.08
Production cost in Banbury, per ream[33]	5.5 (0.08 a sheet)
Retail prices mentioned by John Clare[34]	
Chapbooks	0.5

1820s. 'Small books,' some with coloured illustrations.[35] one penny [0.08 shillings], a half penny [0.04 shillings], or a farthing [0.02 shillings]

1825. Manufacturing cost of 4,000 copies of *Children in the Wood*, a favourite old chapbook title, one sheet and wrappers.[36]   132.5 shillings

Implying a unit cost to the publisher of   0.03 shillings

Publishing of unlawful books and books which would not be handled by the regular trade

Carlile's Joint Stock Book Company, 1826/7[37]
The company's declared aims were 'to publish complete editions in the English language of the works of standard authors who have written, in any language, with a view to human improvement'.
Capital £357.[38] Investors from outside the book trade had subscribed for shares on which a minimum of 5 per cent was promised a preference share, fully transferable. Anonymity of investors guaranteed. Rent £15.
Eight titles published in the first year, all in editions of 1,000 copies except for Shelley's *Queen Mab* of which 2,000 were printed. The sales of all titles in the year were mostly less than 10 per cent of the numbers produced. The company, whose stocks were frequently seized for non-payment of fines levied under the blasphemy laws, went out of business in 1828.

[32] Wholesale prices in *A Catalogue of Maps, Prints . . . Printed and sold by Cluer Dicey and Richard Marshall* (1764). See chapter 17.

[33] See C. R. Cheney, 'Early Banbury Chap-Books and Broadsides', in *The Library* (1936).

[34] For the titles and occasional prices of the books Clare read see 'Sketches of the Life of John Clare, written by Himself . . . March 1821', in *John Clare's Autobiographical Writings*, ed. Eric Robinson (1983) 2, 3, 40, 56.

[35] Quoted in Simon Roscoe and R.A. Brimmell, *Lumsden of Glasgow* (1981).

[36] Adlard ledger for Darton, the children's book publisher.

[37] *Prospectus of the Joint Stock Book Company, established January 1, 1826, under the Direction of Richard Carlile*, n.d. [1827]. Tipped in a copy of Carlile's edition of Volney's *Ruins*, Ac. Other details in Joel H. Wiener, *Radicalism and Freethought in Nineteenth Century Britain, The Life of Richard Carlile* (1983) 123, drawing on information in Carlile's journal, *The Republican*.

[38] Calculated back from the figure for interest at 5 per cent.

Appendix 5 *(cont.)*

Printing costs of three volume novels, setting per sheet

Although some variation is to be expected, related, for example, to format and to the clarity of the manuscript copy, the differences between the figures are too great to be explained by such factors.

Publisher paying	Price (shillings)
Twelve novels published by Longmans, 1816 to 1818[39]	30 to 40
There are a few outside this range, including Porter's *Fast of St. Magdalen*, 1818	56.5
High quality Scottish provincial printing, 1826[40]	23 including corrections

Author paying or divided profits	
(Mary Shelley's) *Frankenstein*, 1818	32
(Austen's) *Mansfield Park*, 1814[41]	
volume i	47
volume ii	47
volume iii	48
(Austen's) *Emma*, 1816[42]	
volumes i and ii	81
volume iii	80

Author part owner of the printing firm[43]	
[Scott's] *Guy Mannering*, third edition, 1815	55
(Scott's) *The Antiquary*, 1816	119
(Scott's) *Rob Roy*, 1817	189
(Scott's) *The Monastery*, 1819	189

Paper per ream, standard quality as used for novels, shillings per ream

Publisher paying	
Actuals paid by Joseph Johnson, 1804, differing amounts.[44]	
Large order from Cowan, Scotland	19.5
Others	21, 22, 23
Large order from Scotland for Longman, 1812[45]	21
Twelve novels published by Longmans, 1816 to 1818[46]	24 to 27
Galt's novels published by Blackwood, 1820–1822	23
High quality Scottish, 1826[47]	20

Author paying or divided net profits	
(Scott's) *The Antiquary* (1816)	24.5
(Mary Shelley's) *Frankenstein* (1818)	30
(Austen's) *Mansfield Park* (Second edition 1816)[48]	35

---

[39] Longman archives.
[40] *St Andrews University Library Catalogue* (Tullis Press, Cupar, Fife 1826). See D. W. Doughty, *The Tullis Press, Cupar 1803–1849* (1967) 11.
[41] Calculated from figures in Murray archives, quoted by Gilson.
[42] *Ibid.*   [43] Longman archives.   [44] Joseph Johnson ledger.
[45] Longman to Cowan 1 October 1812. Longman i, 97, 361.   [46] Longman archives.
[47] *St Andrews University Library Catalogue*. See Doughty, *Tullis Press*, 11.
[48] Calculated from figures from Murray archives quoted by Gilson 59.

Appendix 5 *(cont.)*

(Austen's) *Emma* (1816)[49]	37
(Scott's) *Waverley* (Seventh edition 1817)	23
(Austen's) *Northanger Abbey*, and *Persuasion* (1818)	26
(Hope's) *Anastasius*, 1819	26.5

Nature of contract unknown

(Ferrier's) *Marriage* (Second edition 1819)	42

Start up costs for a printing business, 1820[50]

Box of cuts and metal ornaments	100
Stanhope press	900
272 pounds long primer at 1.5 shillings	408
185 pounds small pica at 1s 10d	339.1
12 pounds printing ink	25.5
Total	1,772.6

Illustrations

1826, for cheap print.[51]

Drawing per picture	42 to 63
Cutting per drawing	42 to 63

1829. Payments to J. M. W. Turner for the right to engrave twenty-nine pictures[52]	£152.25
Payments to the engraver, each[53]	£20 to 30

Advertising

New Monthly Magazine, shillings, 1824.[54]

	Each	Six insertions
Sixth of a page	10.5	57
150 words	15	78
Three-quarters of a page	31.5	168
Entire page	42	228

    The figures include stamp duty

Stamp duty, 1815[55]

Advertisements, each	3.5
Pamphlets per sheet	3.0
Newspapers	0.33

In 1819 'matters of devotion, piety, and charity' were exempted[56]

---

[49] Figures from Murray archives quoted by Gilson 68.

[50] Supplied to Inskipp of Battle, Whittingham archives, 41,924.

[51] Quoted from accounts for the *Everyday Book* by Frederick Wm. Hackwood, *William Hone, His Life and Times* (1912) 247.

[52] P. W. Clayden, *Rogers and His Contemporaries* (1889) ii, 6.

[53] *Ibid.*   [54] Advertisement among Blackwood archives.

[55] C. D. Collet, *History of the Taxes on knowledge* (1933) 9.   [56] Altick 328.

Appendix 5 *(cont.)*

Binding

Fine Binding, 1818, shillings per volume	
Full morocco by Lewis[57]	55
Standard prices, c. 1810, Cooke's cheap editions, shillings per volume[58]	
12mo in sheep	0.75
12mo in calf	1.25
Standard wholesale prices, 1818, shillings per volume[59]	
18mo or 12mo in sheep	0.5
if thick,	1.0
in calf lettered	2 or 2.5
Octavo, in sheep	1 or 1.5
in calf lettered	2.5 to 3.5
Quarto, in calf lettered	6.5 to 9.0

Waste paper

Selling price per pound weight, 1826 and 1827.[60]	0.33

Lectures

1814. Mr Webster at Taunton on mechanical and chemical philosophy	
Twelve transferable tickets	24
Single admission[61]	5
1818. Coleridge at Philosophical Society of London, Fleet Street	
Whole course, 14 lectures	42
Whole course for a gentleman and a lady	63
Single lecture[62]	5
1822. Hazlitt at Andersonian Institution, Glasgow. One lecture on Milton and Shakespeare[63]	5

'He was going to give lectures at Glasgow next week for which he was to have l 100 [2,000 shillings].' Diary of Mrs Hazlitt.[64]

1827. Michael Faraday at the Royal Institution, six lectures on elementary chemistry. Non subscribers, whole course	21
Children	10.5

---

[57] Quoted by Charles Ramsden in his *London Bookbinders, 1780–1840* (1952).
[58] Advertisement in Smollet's *History and Adventures of an Atom* (plate dated 1810, n.d.), Ac.
[59] Advertisement, signed W. Bent, dated 16 October 1818 in *The Modern Catalogue of Books* (1818), Ac.
[60] Adlard archives.
[61] Printed prospectus, quoted in the catalogue of Waller, an autograph dealer, 1856, Ac.
[62] *Literary Remains of William Hazlitt . . . by his son* (1836) ii, 41, quoting *Glasgow Herald*.
[63] *Literary Remains of William Hazlitt . . . by his son* (1836) ii, 39.
[64] Prospectus reproduced in Celina Fox, *London, World City 1800–1840* (1992) 348.

Appendix 5 *(cont.)*

Early stereotyping, low price/expected large and continuing large sales

Thomson's *The Seasons*, pretender copyright, for *Walker's Classics*, 1812
Production costs for an edition of 6,000 copies, to be made with existing stereotype plates:

	£rounded	Per cent of total cost
Printing	72	36
Covers	6	3
Hot-pressing	5	2.5
Paper	76	38
Paper for covers	6	3
Plates repairing	17	8.5
Working the plates	12	6
Paper	5	2.5
Expenses and incidentals	1	0.5
Totals	200	100

Books stereotyped by 1810, i.e. expected to be long-term best sellers[65]

Dictionaries, school readers, histories of England, Greece, Rome, arithmetic books, Latin text books, Cornelius Nepos, in Latin and English. Religious, conduct, and advice books. The New Testament in Latin, French and Welsh, *The Whole Duty of Man*, Bunyan's *Pilgrim's Progress*, (Dodsley's) *Economy of Human Life*, Gregory's *Father's Legacy*.[66] Literature *Elegant Extracts* (standard old-canon anthology, see appendix 6), *Tatler, Spectator, Guardian, Rambler, Adventurer, World, Connoisseur, Idler, Mirror, Lounger, Observer, Looker-On*. History *History of England* by Hume, continued by Smollett. Poetry Milton,[67] Cowper, Shakespeare, Thomson's *Seasons*, Bloomfield. Novels. Johnson's *Rasselas*, Goldsmith's *Vicar of Wakefield*, Sterne's *Sentimental Journey*, Defoe's *Robinson Crusoe*

Others known to have been stereotyped by 1816[68]

Beattie's *Essay on Truth*, Bunyan's other works, Gessner's *Death of Abel*, Doddridge's Works, Hervey's *Meditations*, Mason on Self Knowledge, Addison's *Essays on the Imagination*, Goldsmith's *History of England* (school book abridgement), Cotton's *Visions*, Gray, Moore's *Fables on the Female Sex*, Somerville's *Chase*, Watts's *Divine Songs*, Mackenzie's *Man of Feeling*

Stereotyping, end of romantic period

Mary Shelley's *Frankenstein* (with part of *The Ghost Seer*), in copyright, *Bentley's Standard Novels*, 1831, first two impressions of 4,020 copies[69]

---

[65] Advertisement by Walker, Reading. [66] For Gregory see also appendix 9.
[67] I have seen a copy dated 1808.
[68] Summarised from sale catalogue of Wilson's stock, reprinted by Turner. Since Wilson refused to use the technology to print anything 'against Religion' this may be an unrepresentative list.
[69] Calculated from the figures in Bentley's account, reproduced by Gettman, rearranged, converted into shillings, and slightly simplified. The Strahan figures for the same work exclude the twenty overcopies.

Appendix 5 (*cont.*)

Procurement costs	Price (shillings)	Per cent of total cost
Payment for copyright	600	6
Manufacturing costs		
Composing and correction	1,010	
Stereotype	720	
Pressing	1,220	
Paper	2,920	
Design and engraving	740	
'Working paper'	403	
Binding and labels	1,560	
Total manufacturing costs	8,573	80
Selling costs		
Advertising[70]	1,520	14
Total costs	10,693	100
Implied unit cost	2.7	
Implied unit cost without procurement, engraving or advertising costs[71]	1.9	
Retail price	6	
Price to retailers	4.5	
Gross margin after all costs.[72]	1.8	
Receipts from sales after first year	12,100	
Gross profit after first year	1,360 plus unsold stock[73]	
Implied return to author per copy sold	0.16	
Cost of a reimpression of 500 copies.[74]	198	
Unit cost	0.4	
Gross margin	4.1	
Estimated implied return to author per copy sold over the whole edition.[75]	0.1	

Scott's *Marmion*, 'People's Edition', 1837[76]

Unit cost per copy for initial edition of 3,130 copies, including stereotyping and advertising less than 0.5 shillings
Unit cost of follow up editions made from same plates less than 0.3 shillings
By 1842, c. 14,000 copies had been sold at prices less than 1 shilling
By 1867 another 16,000 had been sold.

---

[70] Averaged over each volume in the series.
[71] Calculated in order to throw light on the economics of other types of stereotype publishing at this time, such as *Don Juan*.
[72] That is price to retailers minus costs of investment and production.
[73] 520 copies, 223 in sheets; 107 copies had been given away gratis.
[74] Working twelve sheets at 14 shillings, plus cold pressing twelve reams. Strahan archives. It is not clear whether the figures include binding.
[75] Fee for copyright divided by 6,250.   [76] Chambers archives.

Appendix 5 *(cont.)*

Tracts sold at subsidised or predatory prices or given away free

Chapbook lookalikes. Cheap Repository Tracts, 1795–98.[77] For numbers printed see appendix 7, 569.

	Price (shillings)
Manufacturing unit cost for order of 4,000[78]	0.07
Retail price	0.8
Wholesale price, after subsidy, to the chapman	0.03
Chapman's margin	0.77
Wholesale price after subsidy, for giving away,	0.06
Revised wholesale price to the chapman	0.02
Chapman's margin	0.78

In the first year, over two million copies were said to have been sold or given away.[79]

Rivington's Publications for Society for Promoting Christian Knowledge[80]	
Retail price	usually free
Prices to distributors for giving away, sixteen-page book, unillustrated,	
For 12 copies	0.8
For 25 copies	0.6
For 50 copies	0.6
For 100 copies	0.5

Internal transport

1828. Books from Leith to London, by sea, sail or steam in 'bales' and 'parcels'[81]	4 and 5 shillings

Exporting to the American colonies, pounds

Colonial period

1679. A consignment of books, journals, and stationery, London to Boston[82]	
Books &c	108
Shipping and commission charges	2.3
Shipping costs as a proportion	just over 2 per cent
1772. A small order, peacetime, from London[83]	
Books	222.5
Shipping	2.5
Shipping costs as a proportion	just over 1 per cent

---

[77] Actuals from Spinney. [78] Whittingham archives 41,901. [79] Noted on copies, Ac.
[80] Advertised in *The Mercies of The Mosaic Law*, Ac. [81] Receipts in Bell and Bradfute archives.
[82] Simplified from a document transcribed by Ford 81. [83] Knox 238.

Appendix 5 *(cont.)*

After independence

1794. Wartime. A large order for Messrs Henry and
Patrick Rice, Philadelphia, despatched from Edinburgh[84]

About 300 books, many multi-volume, mostly sent in semi-manufactured state in sheets	1,654
Three trunks	46
Mats and ropes	6
Carriage to Leith (port)	2
Freight, primage, shore dues, shipping expenses	33
Insurance	76
Total	1,817
Carriage, insurance, and freight (cif) as percentage of order	10 per cent
Cif, taking account of the continuing and resale value of the trunks	about 7 per cent

Lackington's remainder business, volumes in stock available for sale according to his own claims[85]

1784	30,000
1792	90,000
1796	100,000
c. 1810 'Temple of Muses'	1,000,000
Annual sales	100,000

'Not an Hour's Credit will be given to any Person, nor any Books sent on board Ships, or into the Country before they are paid for.'

Victorian long-run reprinting

Routledge's *Poems of Lord Byron*, containing everything out of copyright, 1859.[86]
Production costs of plates for four expected editions of 1,000 copies each, stereotyped.

	Price (shillings)	Per cent of total cost
Printing (composing and stereotyping)	1,371	68
Drawing and engraving the plates	504	25
Mr Robson, editor	150	7
Total costs	2,025	100
In four editions of 1,000 copies	506	25
First edition		
Share of production costs	506	28
Machining	308	17
Paper	908	50
Paper for the plates	92	5
In four editions of 1,000 copies	1,814	100

[84] Bell and Bradfute day book.   [85] Figures from James Raven, 'Selling One's Life' in Brack.
[86] Routledge archives.

Appendix 5 *(cont.)*

Unit cost per copy	1.8
Retail price	5
Gross margin per copy if edition sold out	about 2
Unit cost after 4,000 copies sold	less than 1

1887 Reprint of 10,000 copies
Many tens of thousands of copies already sold
   in earlier reprints at 5, 3.5, 2.5 shillings,
   some unillustrated.

Unit cost per copy	0.3

Long-run reprinting from stereotypes

Warne's Edition of *Byron's Poetical Works* (1868)
All out of copyright[87]

Initial cost (making stereotypes and engraved illustrations) rounded	9,000	
Initial print run, without illustrations		24,000
with illustrations		6,000
Sold in first two years		50,000
Total later costs to 1893 in adding new material, new illustrations, repairing stereotypes, and new blocks for different styles of binding		565
Cumulative sales 1868 to 1893, including about 8,500 copies of luxury editions.		177,000

The stereotypes continued to be used to produce new impressions at least until the 1920s.

1937. The plates sent to be melted probably as part of the rearmament drive.

Falling prices as titles go out of copyright

Editions of *Poetical Works* of Byron	*Price (shillings)*
1810s Murray 1819. Works published to 1819 only	42
1820s Galignani 1826. Everything	20
1830s Murray. Everything	45
1840s Murray. Everything	12
Daly. Out of copyright works only.	7.5
Bohn. Out of copyright works only.	5
1850s Milner. Out of copyright works only.	5
1860s Nimmo. Almost everything	3.5
Gall and Inglis. Almost everything	3.5
1870s Moxon. Everything	3.5
Routledge. Everything	3.5
Warne. Everything	3.5
1880s Ward Lock. Everything	2
Warne. Everything	1.5
1890s Dicks. Everything	1

---

[87] Warne archives.

Appendix 5 (*cont.*)

The mechanisation of book manufacturing

'This afternoon we visited Messrs Clowes' printing office, which is the largest in London – indeed I should suppose the largest in the world. We were first conducted through the machine-rooms, in which were about 20 machines, throwing off at the rate of 750 sheets, printed on both sides, per hour. These machines were driven by steam.' Diary of the son of the Glasgow publisher, William Collins, 1837.[88]

Offshore publication of English-language texts, British import taxes, 1830s, shillings per hundredweight[89]

Books printed before 1801	20
Books printed since 1801	100

Baudry's List, 1827. Retail in Paris

	Francs	Sterling equivalent
Byron, seven volumes	70	56
twelve volumes	36	29
Campbell, two volumes	6.5	5.2
Scott, *Poetical Works*	14	11.2
Lady of the Lake	4.5	3.6
Lay of the Last Minstrel	5	4
Moore, *Loves of the Angels*	2	1.6
The Living Poets of England.[90]		
Large two-volume anthology	18	14.4

Galignani's *Collected Poetical Works*, in one volume.

1. Byron	1826, and later reissues and reprints
2. Moore	1827, and later reissues and reprints
3. Scott	1827, and later reissues and reprints
4. Wordsworth	1828, reissued with undated title page 1835
5. Southey	1829, reissued with undated title page 1835
6. Crabbe	1829, reissued with undated title page 1835
7. Rogers, Campbell, Montgomery, White, Lamb	1829, reissued with undated title page 1835
8. Milman, Bowles. Wilson, Cornwall	1829, reissued with undated title page 1835
9. Coleridge, Shelley, Keats	1829, but actually 1830, reissued with undated title page 1835
10. Hemans	1839

Prices 20fr. and 25fr. (16 shillings and 20 shillings), more for large paper versions.[91]
'Splendid Editions. Cheapness and Portability . . . One Sixth of the London prices . . .'
'In thus publishing the Works of the most celebrated Poets of modern times, including all their suppressed Poems and others not found in the London editions, Messrs Galignani

---

[88] Quoted by Keir 121.   [89] Noted by Frederick von Raumer, *England in 1835* (1836) iii, 58.   [90] For this anthology see also chapter 15.   [91] From advertisements in copies, Ac.

Appendix 5 (*cont.*)

have had in mind to facilitate their acquisition by reducing them to a compact form, offering them at a low price, and avoiding a heavy expense in binding, thus rendering them profitable to the Traveller and available to the Economist.' Advertisement.[92]

Prices of Galignani books in France, 1830s

	Wholesale French francs	Retail Sterling shillings	French Francs	Sterling shillings
Byron	7	5.6	11	8.8
Moore	15	12	20	16
Wordsworth	9	7.2	12	9.6

In 1840 A. D. English of Hull offered Byron's *Collected Works* in one volume, at 18 shillings compared with Murray's lowest price of 42 shillings.[93]

Galignani's novels in three volumes, unbound, representative prices

	Francs	Sterling equivalent
(Scott's) *Waverley* c. 1826.[94]	13	10.5
(Scott's) *Waverley* c. 1831.[95]	7.5	6.
British price of three-deckers novels.		20 to 31.5

Baudry and Galignani's *Ancient and Modern British Authors*, one volume

	Francs	Sterling equivalent	Bound
[Scott's] *Waverley*	10	8	8
British price of three deckers.		31.5	39

United States

Costs of setting up a two press printing shop, 1802[96]

The printing presses	$75 and $95
Total cost of all type, furniture, and other equipment needed	$650

Comparative retail prices

Hobhouse's *Journey to Albania*, 1810, two vols 4 to, with plates, not reprinted in England	105 shillings
An American reprint, with plates, 1817[97]	$4.50 equivalent to below 20 shillings

---

[92] *Ibid.* [93] Gillyat Sumner collection, Bodleian.
[94] Advertisement in *Poetical Works of Southey* (1826), Ac.
[95] Advertisement in *Poetical Works of Scott* (1831), Ac. [96] Silver 29, from a document.
[97] See Accardo 19.

Appendix 5 *(cont.)*

American offshore reprinting of a British bestseller

(Scott's) *Woodstock*, 1826[98]
Costs of producing 9,000 copies, in which equity shares were taken by eight other
    printer/publishers

	$3,734.45	sterling equivalent shillings	29,900
profit	$2,216	sterling equivalent shillings	17,700
unit cost of production	$0.4	sterling equivalent, shillings	3.2
Retail price in the United States	$1.75	sterling equivalent, shillings	8
Minimum retail price in Great Britain	31.5		
at this time.			

Despite the disparity in population, the American print run may have been longer than
that of the British edition from which it was copied.

British offshore reprinting of an American bestseller

Harriet Beecher Stowe's *Uncle Tom's Cabin* (1852)
Gall and Inglis printings.[99]

1852. September, Three printings at various prices	90,000
1852. December	5,000
1853. March	5,000
Routledge printings.[100]	
1853–1856	27,000
Total sales, all publishers, 1852/3 estimated.[101]	1,500,000

American offshore pirate editions, cloned from Galignani

Grigg of Philadelphia's list of poets and prose writers whose works were printed in one
volume, 1831.[102]
Byron, Burns, Cowper and Thomson, Coleridge, Shelley, and Keats, Goldsmith, Milton,
Young, Gray, Beattie and Collins, Moore, Scott, Sterne, Rogers, Campbell, Montgomery,
Lamb, and Kirke White
'Cheapness and Portability . . . Grigg's Splendid Library Editions'
Advertisement copied almost verbatim from Galignani's editions[103]

Reprinting history of an American clone, showing the long productive life of stereotype plates[104]

*The Poetical Works of Coleridge, Shelley and Keats. Complete in One Volume. Stereotyped by
J. Howe*

1831. Philadelphia:

---

[98] Calculated from the archival information transcribed by Kaser 30.
[99] Gall and Inglis archives.
[100] Routledge archives.   [101] Altick 384. Partly based on archival sources and publishers' claims.
[102] Advertisement in *Poetical Works of Milton, Young, Gray, Beattie, and Collins* (Philadelphia 1831), Ac.
[103] Advertisement in *Poetical Works of Milton, Young, Gray, Beattie, and Collins* (Philadelphia, 1831), Ac.
[104] Summarised from J. R. MacGillivray, *Keats, A Bibliography and Reference Guide with an Essay on
Keats's Reputation* (Toronto 1968).

Appendix 5 (*cont.*)

An almost exact line-for-line copy of the Galignani edition of 1830. The works of the three poets were paginated separately, as in Galignani, so that they could be sold separately, and the complex illustration was copied in exact detail.

'I now hear that the work is on sale in the eastern Cities and have sent for a copy: the volume advertised contains "Shelly, Colridge and Keats poems."' George Keats, the poet's brother, in a letter from Louisville, November 1830.[105]

Reimpressions or reissues 1831, 1832, 1834, 1835, 1836, 1838, 1839, 1844, 1847, 1849, 1853, and n.d.

Germany

Tauchnitz, Leipzig, 1842 onwards[106]

Each volume 1.5 shillings, some romantic period authors, but mostly recent novels, reprinted on condition that they were not commercially sold in Britain.

Victorian publishing for global markets

Much information about the initial publishing of the works of Dickens is recorded by Robert L. Patten, *Charles Dickens and His Publishers* (1978). Information on print runs after works came out of copyright is rare.

Dickens's *Barnaby Rudge*, Warne's Notable Novels, double columns, stereotyped	*Shillings*	*Print runs*
1884–94	0.5	28,000
1895	0.5	4,000
Plates melted 1916[107]		
Catherine D. Bell, *Ella and Marian*		
1866–76. Cased editions	3.5	7,000
1879–93. Price reduced	2.5	4,000
1879–93. Paperback	1	10,000
Plates melted 1915[108]		

Examples of routine Victorian fiction at the end of the three-decker era, showing the shope of the demand curve and relative sizes of colonial editions

Mrs J. H. Needell, *Stephen Ellicott's Daughter*, published by Warne.[109]
British editions

January 1891, three volumes	31.5	550
Probably sold almost exclusively to circulating libraries		
April 1891, one volume, stereotyped.	6	1,000

---

[105] *Keats Circle* i, 332.
[106] From William B. Todd and Ann Bowden, *Tauchnitz International, Editions in English 1841–1955* (Bibliographical Society of America 1988). Like Galignani before him Tauchnitz paid a small fee and was not technically a pirate.
[107] Warne archives.   [108] Jarndyce Catalogue, 141 (Spring 2001) item 44.   [109] Warne archives.

Appendix 5 *(cont.)*

January 1893, one volume stereotyped, reimpression	6	500
Produced in plain buckram		
May 1895, one volume, illustrated boards, 'yellowback'	2	2,396
1902. Paperback, double columns	0.5	na
Frances Hodgson Burnett, *His Grace of Ormonde*[110]		
1897 onwards. Total production cloth		14,500
Total production, paperback sold at sixpence		52,000
[0.5 shillings] 1899 onwards		
Overseas editions	na	1,500
April 1891, Colonial edition		
January 1892, Colonial edition, reimpression	na	2,000
Date unknown. American edition, apparently printed	na	na
locally from the same plates as the British and		
Colonial editions.		
1937. Plates melted		
Mrs J. H. Needell, *Passing the Love of Women*		
1892. Three volumes	31.5	550
January 1893. One volume	6	1,000
January 1893. Colonial edition	na	1,500
1937. Plates melted		
Mrs J. H. Needell, *Unstable as Water*		
1892	6	1,000
Colonial edition	na	1,500
1937. Plates melted		
Mrs J. H. Needell, *Philip Methuen*		
January 1893	6	1,500
April 1893. Colonial edition	na	1,500
1937. Plates melted		

Routledge's sales, 1898, the single year for which an archival record has been found, showing the scale of the overseas trade, pounds

Total sales	3,890
of which foreign, probably mainly colonial editions	808
of which New York, perhaps fees for hire of plates	80

---

[110] Warne archives still with firm.

Appendix 6 The old canon

Works released into the public domain by the outlawing of perpetual copyright in England in 1774, which were selected by publishers, and which subsequently became deeply entrenched in national reading in the romantic period and later. Prices in shillings.

The first formal canons in series of the 'British' and of the 'English' poets devised in Edinburgh

The British Poets

Edinburgh. 1773. Forty-three volumes, 12mo. The selection made by Hugh Blair.[1] The series is made up from the individual books of the *English Poets*, printed by Foulis (Glasgow, various dates before 1775). No introductions, prefaces, or illustrations.[2]
Price 1 shilling fine paper, probably 0.75 shillings common paper.
In 1777 Foulis's stock books record holdings of 9,815 volumes of the fine paper version, plus 17,501 of the cheaper version.
Authors included, some abridged. Milton, Butler, Cowley and Denham, Waller, Dryden including translation of Virgil, Garth, Prior, Pope including translation of Homer, Gay, Swift, Addison, Young, Parnell, Thomson, Akenside, Gray and Lyttleton, Shenstone, Collins and Hammond. In 1776 a forty-fourth volume, Beattie, one of the last poets to slip through the brief copyright window.[3] Not sold in England.[4]

The Edinburgh poetry canon made available in a cheap uniform series in England

The Poets of Great Britain Complete from Chaucer to Churchill (later to Cowper). John Bell, Edinburg [sic], at the Apollo Press, by the Martins

1776–1782. 109 volumes, 18mo, with introductions and engravings. Individual volumes 1.5 shillings.
Initially 3,000 of each were printed. Many were reprinted in editions of similar size, in some cases more than once.[5] 378,000 volumes printed. The first edition out of print by 1805.[6]

---

[1] For Blair's pervasive influence see chapter 14.

[2] The trade prices are given in *A Catalogue of Books, Being the Entire Stock in Quires of the late Robert and Andrew Foulis* (Glasgow 1777), copy in Glasgow. The retail price would normally be about a third higher.

[3] Advertisement in copy of Collins, Ac. A full run in NLS. For the Foulis editions see Philip Gaskell, *The Foulis Press* (1986), from which the information on prices and stocks is taken. The involvement of Blair is noted by Robert Anderson in his preface to *The Works of the British Poets, with Prefaces Biographical and Critical*, noted below.

[4] See the 1773 letter of William Strahan, the leader of the London booksellers, refusing to allow the *British Poets* to be sold retail in England, quoted by Bonnell 'Bookselling'.

[5] In addition to the sources used by Bonnell, the Whittingham archives show a reprinting of Lansdowne's works in 1793 of 1,000 copies.

[6] Constable i, 176.

Appendix 6 *(cont.)*

Milton, Pope, Dryden, Butler, Prior, Thomson, Gay, Waller, Young, Cowley, Spenser, Parnell, Congreve, Swift, Addison, Shenstone, Churchill, Pomfret, Donne, Garth, Denham, Hughes, Fenton, Dyer, Lansdowne, Buckingham, Savage, Roscommon, Mallet, Somerville, Collins, Hammond, Cunningham, Broome, King, Rowe, Tickell, Akenside, Lyttleton, G. West, J. Philips, A. Philips, E. Moore, Armstrong, Smith, Watts, Pitt, Gray, R. West, Chaucer.

The Poets of Great Britain, 18mo., 124 volumes bound as sixty two

London, 1807. A reprint of Bell's *Poets*, called Bagster's edition, illustrated.[7] 1,000 sets printed

The Works of the British Poets, with Prefaces Biographical and Critical,
by Robert Anderson

Edinburgh, 1793–1807, 8vo. Thirteen volumes, also sold in parts. Double columns, published by a consortium of Edinburgh and Glasgow publishers/printers. The first collected edition to reprint the works of the older authors in full.
Chaucer, Surrey, Wyatt (i.e. *Tottel's Miscellany*), Sackville, Spenser, Poems of Shakespeare (works other than the plays), Davies, Drayton, Carew, Suckling, Donne, Daniel, Browne, P. Fletcher, G. Fletcher, Jonson, Drummond, Crashaw, Davenant, Milton, Cowley, Waller, Butler, Denham, Dryden, Rochester, Roscommon, Otway, Pomfret, Dorset, Stepney, Philips, Walsh, Smith, Duke, King, Sprat, Halifax, Parnell, Garth, Rowe, Addison, Hughes, Sheffield, Prior, Congreve, Blackmore, Fenton, Granville, Yalden, Pope, Gay, Pattison, Hammond, Savage, Hill, Tickell, Somerville, Brome, Pitt, Blair, Swift, Thomson, Watts, Hamilton, A. Philips, G. West, Collins, Dyer, Shenstone, Mallet, Akenside, Hark, Young, Gray, R. West, Lyttleton, E. Moore, Boyce, W. Thompson, Cawthorne, Churchill, Falconer, Lloyd, Cunningham, Green, Cooper, Goldsmith, P. Whitehead, Brown, Grainger, Smollett, Armstrong, Wilkie, Dodsley, Shaw, Smart, Langhorne, Bruce, Chatterton, Graeme, Glover, Lovibond, Penrose, Mickle, Jago, T. Scott, Johnson, W. Whitehead, Jenyns, Logan, Warton, Cotton, Blacklock. Translations from Greek and Latin classics. Sold out by 1805.[8]
'To good old Anderson the poets and literature of the country are deeply beholden.' *Quarterly Review*.[9]

The Cabinet of Poetry, Containing the Best Entire Pieces to be found in the Works of The British Poets

1808. Six volumes, portraits, with a long introduction by the editor Samuel Pratt. Milton, Cowley, Waller, Butler, Denham, Dryden, Rochester, Pomfret, Phillips, King, Spratt, Halifax, Parnell, Garth, Rowe, Addison, Hughes, Buckingham, Fenton, Yalden, Gay, Prior, Pope, Tickell, Somerville, Pattison, Hammond, Savage, Hill, Broome, Swift,

---

[7] Longman impression books. Described as 'Johnson's British Poets'.
[8] Constable i, 176.   [9] Quoted by Lowndes, no date given.

Falconer, Watts, Thomson, Mallet, Phillips, Hamilton, Collins, Dyer, Shenstone, Akenside, Young, Gray, West, Lyttleton, E. Moore, Thompson, Cawthorn, Churchill, Lloyd, Cunningham, Green, Cooper, Goldsmith, Grainger, Smollet, Armstrong, Brown, Dodsley, Smart, Langhorne, Bruce, Chatterton, Shaw, Lovibond, Penrose, Mickle, Jago, T. Scott, Johnson, W. Whitehead, Jenyns, Graeme, Glover, Logan, Warton, Cotton, Blacklock, Mason, Burns, Beattie. Perhaps extracted from Anderson's edition.

The London book industry's response to the Edinburgh challenge

The Works of the English Poets . . . with Prefaces Biographical and Critical by Samuel Johnson.

1779–81. Originally seventy-five volumes 12mo, then sold as individual titles.[10] Renamed *The Works of the Most Eminent English Poets*, or simply *Johnson's Poets*. Some volumes, a second edition.[11]   3,000   3,000

1780. *The Lives of the most eminent English poets*, four volumes, 8vo.[12]   3,000

1793, Dublin, eight volumes. Offshore pirated edition. Out of print by 1805.[13]

1810. London. Johnson's *Poets* was officially reprinted without the prefaces in seventy-five volumes. 168s.[14]   1500 or 1250 each
Addison, Akenside, Armstrong, Butler, Blackstone, Cowley, Congreve, Collins, Churchill, Cawthorne, Cunningham, Dorset, Dryden, Dryden's Virgil, Dilke, Dyer, Denham, Fenton, Falconer, Garth, Gay, Goldsmith, Green, Gray, Halifax, Hughes, Hammond, Johnson, Jenyns, King, Lansdowne, Lloyd, Langhorne, Milton, Mallet, E. Moore, Otway, Pomfret, Parnell, Pope, Pope's Homer, Pitt, Pitt's Virgil, Philips, Rochester, Roscommon, Rowe, Rowe's Lucan, Smith, Sprat, Sheffield, Somerville, Savage, Swift, Shenstone, Stepney, Tickell, Thomson, Waller, Walsh, Watts, Yalden, Young, Whitehead.

Editions produced by publishers in England taking advantage of 1774

The Poetical Magazine; or Parnassian Library

Begins c. 1780. 18mo. Copied from Bell. Price 0.5 shillings. No list of titles found.[15]

The Literary Miscellany

1790s. 12mo. A series of reprints, in prose and verse, published by George Nicholson of Ludlow, later of Manchester. Paper covers 1 shilling or less except for Milton 1.5 shillings and Cotton 1.25 shillings.[16]

[10] *London Catalogue* (1799).
[11] Harlan 171 from Strahan's printing records of some of the volumes.
[12] Zachs 296 from Murray archives.   [13] Constable i, 176.
[14] Advertised at this price by Cawthorn in, e.g., Byron's *English Bards and Scotch Reviewers* (1809 onwards). The print runs, more for the lives than for the works, are apparently those noted for 1806 in John Nichols's ledger of purchase and disposal of copyrights 1769–1815, CUL, add. 8226.
[15] Bonnell 'Bookselling' 151.   [16] Publisher's advertisement, n.d., Reading University Library.

Appendix 6 (*cont.*)

Armstrong, Gray, Collins, Prior, Lyttleton and Goldsmith, Gay, Pope, Jenyns, Parnell, Blair, Milton, Shenstone, Cotton, *Elegies*. Nicholson also reprinted many conduct books, some abridged, for sale at equally cheap prices.

Lists of T. Willis, H. D. Symonds and others, 1799 onwards[17]

24mo. Each with a plate and life of the author. Printed by Whittingham 'adopted for the pocket, and embellished with elegant Frontispieces'. Some recorded initial print runs.[18]

	Price (shillings)	Print run
Young's *Night Thoughts* (and other works)	2.5	2,000
Milton's *Paradise Lost*	2.5	2,000
Thomson's *Seasons*[19]	1	4,000
Somerville's *The Chase*	0.5	2,000
Gray's *Poetical Works*	0.5	4,000
Goldsmith's *Poetical Works*	0.5	4,000
The Wreath (poems on death)	1	4,000

'The favourite poets of my juvenile days . . . Thomson, Young, Gray, Milton, Cowper'. George Miller, a country bookseller, 1833.[20]

Cooke's *British Poets*

1798 onwards, 18mo. Illustrated. Published in eighty parts at 1.5 shillings, on fine paper at 2 shillings.[21] Individual volumes were available at 0.5 shillings a week in parts.[22] Chaucer, Spenser, Donne, Waller, Milton, Butler, Denham, Cowley, Dryden, Roscommon, Cunningham, King, Prior, Lansdowne, Pomfret, Swift, Congreve, Addison, Rowe, Watts, J. Philips and Smith, Parnell, Garth, Hughes, Fenton, Tickell, Somerville, Pope, Gay, Broome, Young, Savage, Pitt, Thomson, A. Philips, Dyer, G. West, Lyttleton, Hammond, Collins, E. Moore, Shenstone, Mallet, Armstrong, Gray, R. West, Akenside, Buckingham, Churchill.

'I bought them over and over again, and used to get up select sets that disappeared like buttered crumpets; for I could resist neither giving them away nor possessing them.' Leigh Hunt on his early reading of Cooke's Poets.[23]

'They not only afforded me much amusement and instruction, on repeated perusal and examination, but, I believe, created that love of literature and art which progressively rose to a confirmed passion.' Dr Thomas Rees.[24]

---

[17] Advertisements in copies of Thomson's *Seasons*, Goldsmith's *Poetical Works*, and Goldsmith's *Essays* (1803), Ac. Symonds appears to have taken over the business. Some of the prices quoted are a little cheaper.

[18] Whittingham archives, BL add. mss. 41,902.   [19] For the costs of this book see appendix 5.

[20] (George Miller) *Latter Struggles in the Journey of Life* (1833).

[21] Advertisement on cover of *The History of Nourjahad* (1814), Ac.

[22] Advertisement sheet, no date, Reading University Library. Another list bound in Smollet's *History and Adventures of an Atom* (n.d., plate dated 1810), Ac.

[23] Quoted by Altick, *Writers* 177, from Augustine Birrel, *Essays about Men, Women, and Books* (1894) 143.

[24] Rees and Britton 27.

Appendix 6 (*cont.*)

'I knew there were poets and when Cooke's Poets commenced, I bought the poems of Thompson [sic] and Goldsmith, as they came out, in weekly numbers . . . They were the first poems I read and I derived from them lasting benefit. The simplicity and tenderness of "The Deserted Village" and "The Traveller", and the just descriptions and noble sentiments of the "Seasons" refined and elevated my mind. I saw nature with a new-born sight; in its quiet scenery I felt emotions of peaceful delight unknown to me before – my affections went forth to every living thing; my heart expanded with rapturous joy.' William Hone, the radical bookseller.[25]

'In the morning of the second day, we breakfasted luxuriously in an old fashioned parlour [in an inn at Linton in Devonshire] . . . It was in this room that we found a little worn out copy of Thomson's Seasons, lying on the window ledge, on which Coleridge exclaimed "*That* is true fame."' William Hazlitt, describing a journey with Coleridge in 1798.[26]

'You never see on a stall one of Cooke's books but it is soiled by honest usage . . . the thousand thumbs that have turned over its pages with delight.' Augustine Birrell, 1894.[27]

Suttaby's list

From about 1808 for many years.[28] 'Uniform Editions' 24mo. Frontispiece and engraved title with illustration. Paper covers. To judge from scattered archival sources, editions were of 2,000 to 3,000 copies and frequently reprinted.[29] Many titles available at 1 shilling or even less.

Nicholson of Stourport's editions, 1814 and later.[30]

Milton 2 shillings; Cowley, &c 1.5s; Addison 1.4s; Prior and Parnell 1.4s; Pope 2.75s; Gay 1s; Somerville & 2s; Thomson 1.5s; Blair 0.5s; Collins and Jenyns, 1s; Shenstone 1.5s; Gray, 0.75s. Lyttleton 1s; Goldsmith 1s; Armstrong 1s; Hammond 1s; Cotton 1.5s.

Thomas Tegg's list, about 1818

Tegg was in business for most of the early nineteenth century, specialising both in remainders reissued with new title pages and in editions specially printed. In 1841 he was said to be the richest bookseller in the country.[31] No full list of titles has been found, but most of the core of the old canon appear to have been available at all times, frequently reprinted in substantial editions. For example, Whittingham printed the following titles for Tegg in 1818 and 1819.

Thomson's *Seasons*	5,000
plus another edition in 1822	4,000
Goldsmith's *Poems*	5,000
Butler's *Hudibras*	4,000
Cowper's *Poems*	4,000

[25] Hackwood 47. For Hone list see appendix 11.
[26] In *My First Acquaintance with Poets*. The remark could have applied to any of the many editions.
[27] Quoted by Altick, *Writers*, from *Essays about Men, Women, and Books*.
[28] Advertisement on cover of *The Poetical Works of Dr Goldsmith* (1818), Ac.
[29] Whittingham archives, BL add. mss. 41,925 and 41,926.
[30] Advertised in *The Advocate and Friend of Woman*, plate dated 1814, but the book probably sold later, Ac.
[31] For Tegg's career, see Barnes and Barnes and James Grant, *Portraits of Public Characters* (1841) i, 29.

Appendix 6 *(cont.)*

Some other popular old-canon prose works, including (Cottin's) *Elisabeth*, Johnson's *Rasselas*, More's *Sacred Dramas*, and *Search after Happiness*, (St Pierre's) *Paul and Virginia*, Quarles's *Emblems*, Dodd's *Prison Thoughts*, Dodd's *Reflections on Death, Letters of Junius*, and Goldsmith's *Vicar of Wakefield* and *Citizen of the World*, were supplied to Tegg in similar quantities at this time. Many were printed in more than one edition.[32]

Books broken and sold in parts

List of J. Parsons, a numbers bookseller, 1798

	Price (shillings)
Milton's *Paradise Lost*, twelve numbers at	1.5
Young's *Night Thoughts*, seven numbers at	2.5
Thomson's *Seasons*, six numbers at	1.5
Plus Bunyan's *Pilgrim's Progress*, ?ten numbers at	1.5

Other prose works are noted below.[33] Cooke's editions sold in parts about a third of these prices.
'Oh! how my heart was delighted by the display of magnificence and varied wealth which this man's [a travelling numbersman] portfolio contained. There were various Bibles, various histories, various poems. There was John Bunyan's "Pilgrim"; "Robinson Crusoe"; "The Arabian Nights"; "Drelincourt on Death"; "Hervey's Meditations"; "Pamela or Virtue Rewarded"; "The History of Henry, Earl of Westmoreland", and many others.'
John Kitto, a self-taught scholar, recalling the reading in about 1816.[34]

The copyright pretenders bring down the price

List of Vernor, Hood, and Sharpe, turn of the century and later

Whittingham's ledgers note the printing of editions of 1,500 of Milton, and 2,000 of Thomson at the turn of the century. The firm's list for c. 1815, 18mo, includes the following poets at prices mostly around 3 shillings. The list can be regarded as creating an inner core of the old canon. In order advertised.[35]
Cowper, Bloomfield, Burns, Beattie, Young's *Night Thoughts*, Thomson's *Seasons*, Butler's *Hudibras*.

Sharpe's *Cabinet Edition of the British Poets*

Begun 1805. 18mo. Published by the pretenders to the copyrights in response to Cooke's edition. 134 numbers in seventy volumes. With portraits and illustrations. 2.5 shillings per part, or 2 shillings without plates.[36] The ledgers of Whittingham the printer show that 3,000 copies were printed of the first three authors in the series. For the second Thomson

---

[32] Whittingham archives, BL add. mss. 41,884.   [33] Advertisements in *The Idler* (1798), Ac.
[34] Quoted by Altick 265.   [35] Advertisement sheet, no date, Reading University Library.
[36] Lowndes.

Appendix 6 (*cont.*)

volume the initial print run was reduced to 2,500, and for Cunningham to 2,000. For Pope only 1,750 copies were ordered and that remained the normal initial print run for the volumes down to and including the first two volumes of Young, apart from Falconer and Day of which 2,000 were printed. After that the print run was reduced to 1,500.[37] Copies of a few of the lesser poets were still available as remainders in the 1830s.[38]

Collins and Gray, Milton, Goldsmith and Beattie, Thomson, Cunningham, Akenside, Hammond and Lyttleton, Pope, Falconer and Day, Somerville, Mallet, T. Warton, Young, Cotton, Butler, Langhorne, Gay, Glover, E. Moore, Dryden, Swift, Smollett, Bruce and Logan, Tickel, Philips, Addison, Dyer, Denham, Burns, Savage, Blair, Glynn and Boyce, W. Thompson, Jenyns, Parnell, Prior, Armstrong, Shaw, Lovibond and Penrose, Churchill, Watts, Green and Jago, J. Scott, Garth, Sir W. Jones, Mickle, Hoyland, J. H. Moore, Headley, and Russell, Oram, Bampfylde, and Lovell. Plus a Supplement of twelve parts, *Select Works of the Minor Poets.*

More limited canons

Crosby's list

1808 onwards, 12mo. 1 shilling and upwards.[39] A selection of the most popular titles, some taken over from Suttaby including, the following poets, in order advertised.

Pope's Homer, Dryden's Virgil, Young, Milton, Pope, Shenstone, Beattie, Akenside, Thomson, Gray, Somerville, Falconer, Goldsmith, Johnson, Collins, Hammond.

On the list of John Taylor 1812[40]

	Print run
Johnson's *Rasselas*	1,500
Johnson's *Sermons*	1,000
Young's *Night Thoughts*	1,000

Attempts by the pretender copyright holders to offset the shortcomings of Johnson

The Works of the English Poets from Chaucer to Cowper, including the Series edited . . . by Dr Samuel Johnson . . . the Additional Lives by Alexander Chalmers

1810. A large library edition, produced by a consortium of publishers. twenty-one volumes in double columns, with portraits.

400s	1,500

---

[37] Whittingham archives, BL add. mss. 41,902.
[38] Two-volume set in publisher's binding of the 1830s containing the works of Glynn, Smollett, Logan, Addison, Collins, Gray, Garth, Hoyland, J. H. Moore, Russell, Oram, Lovell, and Bampfylde, Ac.
[39] Advertisement in Gillyat Sumner collection, Bodleian.
[40] John Taylor commonplace book III.

Appendix 6 (*cont.*)

Johnson's list but also includes some authors such as Gower and Drayton not normally found. The publishers paid a fee of 2,000 shillings for the right to include Cowper whose works were not quite out of copyright.[41]

Copyright pretenders reduce their prices further

Walker's British Classics[42]

1814. Published by previous copyright holders, now operating as copyright pretenders. Recommended as school books, prize books, or presents.'[43] Prices 1 to 3 shillings
Normal initial print run   5,000
Some such as Thomson.[44]   6,000
Some titles were stereotyped and kept in print for many years
'I read the old novels and old poems again and again . . . At this time there were published charming little volumes of verse and prose, as Walker's Classics, one of which was generally in my pocket.' Charles Knight, later a pioneer of cheaper books.[45]
'Cowper I have, but it is not half his poems, being Walker's pocket one.' John Clare, the Northamptonshire poet, 1820.[46]

Whittingham's lists

Whittingham had begun as a printer whose business was mainly in business prospectuses, visiting cards, posters, advertisements, labels, almanacs, and a few books. Because of the high quality of his printing he was soon receiving orders for a wide range of types of book printing from all the main publishers of the early part of the nineteenth century. An entry in the 1795 ledger written in a coded mixture of letters and numbers notes his first, apparently secret, venture into publishing, probably in breach of some agreement or contract. 'Wh3tt3nghi7 4@ h3s 4w@ icc45@t' (Whittingham on his own account) consisting of 2,000 copies of Thomson's *Seasons* and of Young's *Night Thoughts*, two books for which he was receiving many orders.

Whittingham's *Cabinet Library*

1820s. A few shillings each. Part of a longer series begun earlier, Whittingham's *British Poets* (1822) 100 volumes, foolscap 8vo, 500 shillings or with the plates from Sharpe's edition, 700 shillings.[47] Several thousand copies were printed of each of the most popular authors. In 1830 Whittingham reprinted some of the more popular titles, including Thomson, Collins, and Cowper in editions of 2,000. At this time he also appears to have

---

[41] Longman archives, and Whittingham archives.
[42] For the production costs of a typical *Walker's Classics* book see appendix 5.
[43] Advertisement on cover of *The History of Nourjahad* (1814), Ac.   [44] Longman archives.
[45] Charles Knight, *Passages of a Working Life* (1863), i, 70.
[46] Mark Storey, ed., *The Letters of John Clare* (Oxford 1985) 35.
[47] Lowndes. Thomson is omitted from his published list but this is probably a mistake. According to Lowndes some of the memoirs were written by Dr Symmons, Mr Singer, and Mr Davenport.

Appendix 6 (*cont.*)

made stereotypes from which impressions of 1,000 were taken as need arose.[48] Mostly the same authors as in Bell, Johnson, and Cooke. In 1825 Tegg was advertising many titles at 2 shillings and upwards, said to be 25 per cent below normal.[49]

British Classics

c. 1820. Published by a consortium of London publishers.[50]
'British' enabled Falconer and Thomson, who were Scottish not English, to be included.

John Bumpus's *New Editions of Popular Standard Books*

1824. 18mo, with illustrations.[51]

Dove's *English Classics*

1825 onwards, a few shillings each, illustrated.[52] Published by a consortium, unnamed, using the king's printer with the royal arms. The use of the word 'Proprietors' maintained the claims of the copyright pretenders.
Mostly the same authors as in Bell, Johnson, and Cooke, but also including Byron's *English Bards and Scotch Reviewers, Hours of Idleness* (copyright not enforceable) and (Byron's) *Don Juan* (copyright not enforceable).

Allman's *New English Classics*

mid 1820s onwards, illustrated.[53] Includes (Byron's) *Don Juan*.

The main old-canon poets printed in the tiniest of formats, the cheapest achievable at the limits of manufacturing technology

Jones's *Cabinet University Edition of the British Poets*[54]

1825. 12mo. Four volumes, double columns. Scarcely readable with the naked eye. *Extra cloth boarding* (i.e. rebinding not necessary, an innovation in selling practice which reduces further the price to the reader). 10.5 shillings each.
'Comprising in 4 pocket volumes nearly as much as the sixty volumes of Dr Johnson's edition of the Poets, and at one sixth the price!!' Advertisement.[55]

---

[48] BL add. mss. 41,885.   [49] Tegg's *Select Library*.
[50] Advertisements in a copy of Johnson's *Lives of the Poets* (1820), Ac.
[51] Advertisement in Goldsmith's *Poetical Works* (1824), Ac.
[52] Advertisements and lists on covers of More's *Sacred Dramas* and of Goldsmith's *Citizen of the World* (1825), Ac. Goldsmith's *Citizen of the World*, notes twenty-one firms.
[53] Advertisement list on cover of Zimmerman's *Solitude* (1830), Ac.
[54] Advertisement in copy of Diamond Classics edition of Hayley's *Triumphs of Temper* (1830), Ac. For Jones's so-called 'Modern Poets of Great Britain' see below.
[55] Advertisement in a copy made up from numbers, Ac.

Appendix 6 *(cont.)*

1. Milton, Cowper, Goldsmith, Thomson, Falconer, Akenside, Collins, Gray. Somerville
2. Kirke White, Burns, Beattie, Gay, Shenstone, Butler, Byron's *Select Works* (those on which copyright not enforceable)
3. Hannah More, Pope, Watts, Hayley, Mason, Prior, Grahame, Logan
4. Dryden, Lyttleton, Hammond, C[harlotte] Smith, Richardson, Bloomfield, Gifford, Canning.

Jones's *Diamond Poets*

1820s. In numbers of 0.5 shillings. Prices of complete works of each author depending on length, Milton, 6.5, Young 3.5 shillings.

1823. Shakespeare's *Poems*[56]   4,000
Each author available at 1 shilling or in weekly numbers, 'at less than one fourth of the price of other editions'.[57] Most of the same authors are included as in the editions of Bell, Johnson, and Cooke.

The old canon, prose literature

Harrison's *Novelist's Magazine*

The first cheap series, begun November 1779 and continued though the 1780s. Arranged by the titles, as in the booksellers' and circulating library catalogues of the time, although the names of the authors were also given. Illustrated with engravings from pictures by contemporary artists. Published in successive numbers, over several years.
0.5 shillings each part. In 1794 Bell and Bradfute of Edinburgh was buying sets of twenty-three volumes bound in boards at 155 shillings, implying a retail price of about 180 shillings.[58] No print runs are known but at one time 12,000 copies were said to have been sold weekly.[59]
(Hawkesworth's) *Almoran and Hamet*; (Fielding's) *Joseph Andrews*; (Langhorne's) *Solyman and Almena*; (Goldsmith's) *Vicar of Wakefield*; (Smollett's) *Roderick Random*; (Voltaire's) *Zadig*; (Combe's) *Devil on Two Sticks*; (Morell's) *Tales of the Genii*; (Fielding's) *Tom Jones*; (le Sage's) *Gil Blas*; (Defoe's) *Robinson Crusoe*; (Sterne's) *Tristram Shandy*; (Guelette's) *Chinese Tales*; (Dodd's) *The Sisters*; (Smollett's) *Peregrine Pickle*; (Marmontel's) *Moral Tales*; (de Mouhy's) *Fortunate Country Maid*; (Kelly's) *Louisa Mildmay*; (Langhorne's) *Theodosius and Constantia*; (Smollett's) *Count Fathom*; (Cervantes's) *Don Quixote*; (Sterne's) *Sentimental Journey*; (Swift's) *Gulliver's Travels*; (Smollett's) *David Simple*; (Smollett's) *Launcelot Greaves*; (Lennox's) *Female Quixote*; (Fielding's) *Journey from this World to the Next*; (Kimber's) *Joe Thompson; Adventures of Peter Wilkins*; (Eliza Haywood's) *Betsy Thoughtless*; (Ambrose Philips's) *Persian Tales*; (Richardson's) *Clarissa*; (Marivaux's) *Virtuous Orphan*; (Lady Susannah Fitzroy's) *Henrietta*; (Fénelon's) *Telemachus*; (Eliza Haywood's) *Jemmy and Jenny Jessamy; Arabian Nights*; (Smollett's) *Humphrey Clinker*; (Goldsmith's) *Pompey the Little*; (Sarah Fielding's) *Ophelia*; (Guelette's) *Tartarian Tales*;

---

[56] Whittingham archives.
[57] Prospectus, n.d. 1820s, Gillyat Sumner collection. Also advertisements in surviving books in parts, Ac.
[58] Bell and Bradfute archives.
[59] Copy of the series in Bodleian. Described by Sadleir. Some further details in Rees and Britton.

Appendix 6 *(cont.)*

(Richardson's) *Pamela*; (Grasigny's) *Peruvian Tales; Gaudentio di Lucca*; (Smollett's)
Adventures of an Atom; (Quarles's) *English Hermit; Sincere Huron*; (Sherebeare's) *Lydia*;
(Mrs F. Sheridan's) *Sidney Bidulph*

> Our nicer palates lighter labours seek,
> Cloy'd with a folio-*Number* once a week;
> Bibles, with cuts and comments, thus go down:
> E'en light Voltaire is *number'd* through the town.

From George Crabbe's *The Library* (1781). Crabbe is referring to Voltaire's novel *Zadig*,
not to his philosophical works, none of which is known to have been sold in numbers.[60]

The Entertaining Museum, or Complete Circulating Library

Early 1780s. A series of reprints of essays, novels, translations from French, Spanish,
Italian, and German. No list found, but the series included at least twenty-six volumes,
illustrated, beginning with *Sir Launcelot Greaves*, and *Tom Jones*, and including *Gil Blas*,
The Vicar of Wakefield, and *Gulliver's Travels*.
Sold in numbers of 0.5 a week or 0.75 shillings bound.[61]
'The moderate price of this book deserves also to be noticed; as by such means books in
England come more within the reach of the people; and of course are more generally
distributed among them.' Carl Phillip Moritz, a visitor from Germany, *Travels in Several
Parts of England in 1782.*[62]

Hogg's *New Novelist Magazine*, early 1790s

8vo, illustrated. Available in ninety-four weekly numbers at 0.5 shillings each.[63] Similar to
Harrison's *Novelist Magazine*.

Cooke's *Select Novels*, begun late 1790s[64]

Arranged by title, unlike Cooke's *Select Poets* which is arranged by author. Unlike the
series by Harrison and Hogg, which in appearance resembled the newspapers of the time,
Cooke's Novels, consisting entirely of eighteenth-century novels and translations with
most of the same titles as were in Harrison's *Novelist's Magazine*, were books of pocket
size, easily carried, and concealed. Prices a shilling and upwards, or in numbers of 0.5
shillings. By about 1803, many of the prices had been reduced yet further.[65] Kept available
over many years.
'Tom Jones . . . came down in numbers once a fortnight in Cooke's pocket editions. I had
hitherto read only in schoolbooks and a tiresome ecclesiastical history . . . But the world I
found . . . was to me a dance through life, a perpetual gala-day.' William Hazlitt.[66]

[60] Lines 189ff.
[61] Copy of *Gulliver's Travels* with advertisement seen at a book fair in London 1996.
[62] 1924 edition, 44.   [63] Advertisement in copy of *Don Quixote* (c. 1791), Ac. Curwen 368.
[64] Trade advertisement, n.d., Reading University Library. Another in copy of *Rasselas* (n.d.) Ac.
[65] Advertisement in copy of *Belisarius*, n.d., but inscriptions show that it is before 1803.
[66] 'On Reading Old Books' in *The Plain Speaker*.

Appendix 6 (*cont.*)

Sharpe's *Novelist's Library*

Copyright Pretenders edition. 'Cabinet edition of the most celebrated novels in the English language.' Prospectus, 1809.[67] Illustrated.

The British Novelists, with an essay and prefaces, biographical and critical, by Mrs Barbauld

1810 Fifty volumes, 18mo. Arranged by title of novel, with the name of the author mentioned in the prefatory material. A copyright and copyright pretenders edition.[68]

	252 shillings the set.	mostly 500, 750 and 1,000
Defoe's *Robinson Crusoe*		1,500
1820. Second edition.[69]	210 shillings the set.	1,000

British Novelists

'comprising every Work of acknowledged Merit which is usually classed under the Denomination of Novels'. Prospectus.

1810 to **1816**. 8vo. five vols.[70] Every Saturday, one shilling each number, with an illustration.

1825. Tegg's price for the five volumes[71]	55 shillings	na

Ballantyne's *Novelist's Library*[72]

1821 to **1825**. Arranged by title, with the name of the author mentioned in the prefatory material which was written by Sir Walter Scott. Ten volumes. Originally 280 shillings, reduced to 105. Fielding, Smollett, *Don Quixote*, *Gil Blas*, Combe, Johnston, Sterne, Goldsmith, Johnson, Mackenzie, Walpole, Reeve, Richardson, Swift, Bage, Radcliffe.

Whittingham's *Novelist's Library*[73]

1823. Forty volumes, 16mo, illustrated. Arranged by title. The series is a mixture of the older novelists of the earlier lists and of the latest modern novels to fall out of copyright before the closing of the brief copyright window. The choice appears to have been mainly copied from those in Barbauld's edition, split into shorter volumes.

After the union with Great Britain, Irish reprints of out-of-statutory-copyright titles could now be freely exported to Great Britain

Some Dublin reprints.[74]

[67] Trade advertisement, Reading University Library.
[68] Longman archives. Some confirmatory figures in the Richard Taylor archives.
[69] Longman archives.   [70] Lowndes.   [71] Tegg's *Select Library*.
[72] Lowndes, and Michael Sadleir, *XIX Century Fiction, A Bibliographical Record* (1951).
[73] Sadleir, *XIX Century Fiction* ii, 17.   [74] Graisberry ledgers.

Appendix 6 (*cont.*)

1802. (Grasigny's) *Peruvian Tales*	500
1802. Milton's *Paradise Lost*	1,250
1802. (Goethe's) *Sorrows of Young Werter*	5,000
1804. Akenside's *Pleasures of the Imagination*	1,000
1805. *The Spectator*	1,500

Prices fall to what was probably the lowest levels in relation to incomes since the arrival of printing

Limberd's *British Novelist*

c. 1823 onwards, illustrated, double columns, printed separately at about 0.5 shillings a volume. Also available in numbers of sixteen pages priced at two pence [0.17 shillings]. No complete list found. Titles included the best-known novels by Goldsmith, Mackenzie, Reeve, Inchbald, and Walpole.

'On the appearance of this last named work [*Castle of Otranto*] Mr Simpkin of Simpkin and Marshall [leading London publishers] called on Mr Limberd and begged of him to give up the two penny numbers as he was ruining the trade by bringing out such cheap books.'[75]

Limberd was denied access to the usual outlets. In Manchester his distributor was a tinman.[76]

Roscoe's *Novelist's Library*

1831 to 1833. Seventeen volumes, illustrated, 5 shillings a volume. Arranged by title, with the name of the author mentioned in the prefatory material. Contains only old canon titles.[77]

British and English Classics

The name given to the series of essays, originally printed as serials and reprinted in book form, which became available to be reprinted after 1774. The favourite was *The Spectator*, but *The Adventurer, The Connoisseur, The Guardian, The Idler, The Lounger, The Mirror, The Observer, The Rambler, The Tatler,* and *The World* were also much reprinted and anthologised. These essays, which combined story telling with moral lessons, were regarded as especially suitable for reading by women. The same range of copyright pretender and new publishers reprinted the 'English classics' as reprinted the poetry and the novels. A few indications.

Harrison's *British Classics*

1790s. Eventually eight volumes.

---

[75] *The Bookseller*, 1859, 1326, 30 November 1859.   [76] Altick 267.
[77] List of titles in Sadleir, *XIX Century Fiction*.

Appendix 6 (*cont.*)

The British Essayists[78]

Published by the copyright pretenders, some print runs.

1803. Forty-five volumes   1,500
1817. Forty-five volumes   1,000
1823. Thirty-eight volumes   1,000

'British Classics' on the list of J. Parsons, a numbers publisher, 1798

Rambler, Spectator, Idler, World, Connoisseur, Adventurer, Tatler, Guardian,
Ninety-eight numbers at 0.5 shillings per number, making thirty-six volumes.[79]

Cooke's *British Classics,* c. 1803[80]

Goldsmith's *Essays* and *Citizen of the World*
Idler, Adventurer, Rambler, Tatler, Guardian, Connoisseur, World, Mirror.

1820s. Jones's edition of all the essayists, in numbers of 0.5 shillings[81]

The Spectator in one volume, illustrated[82]   15 shillings
The others at similar prices.[83]
1825. A Tegg edition, forty volumes   115.5, discounted from 180 shillings.[84]

Plays

A body of older plays, including the works of Shakespeare, some other Elizabethan and
Jacobean plays, the Restoration comedies, and many eighteenth-century plays, including
farces, became available in series at much lower prices. The books, usually with one
illustration, in a format akin to chapbooks, usually sold at 0.75 reducing to 0.5 each, both
in collected editions and individually. The collections included Bell's *British Theatre*;
Cumberland's *British Theatre*, Bumpus's *English Theatre*; Dolby's *British Theatre*, and later
French's and then Dicks's *Standard Plays*. For Shakespeare see appendix 12.
Cooke's *British Theatre*, one of the first, included over ninety plays, each illustrated by one
of the leading artists of the day, including Stodhart, Fuseli, and Opie.[85]
Prices continued to fall, as the prices of newly printed works rose. By the 1820s, the play
reprints were made from stereotype plates and prices fell further until many were available
at a penny (0.08 shillings).[86]

Music

(Harrison's) *New Musical Magazine*
1783–6[87]   1.5 shillings each part   1,500

[78] Production figures from Strahan archives, 48,813.   [79] Advertisements in *The Idler*, 1798, Ac.
[80] Advertisement in copy of *Belisarius*, n.d., but inscriptions show it is before 1803.
[81] Advertised in copy of *The Mirror and Lounger* (1827), Ac.   [82] *Ibid.*   [83] *Ibid.*
[84] Tegg's *Select Library.*   [85] Advertisement in Cooke's edition of *New Bath Guide*, n.d., Ac.
[86] Advertisements in surviving copies, Ac.
[87] Nancy A. Mace, 'Litigating the Musical Magazine' in *Book History* 2 (1999) 135.

Appendix 6 (*cont.*)

The first of many publications that drastically brought down the price of musical and operatic texts released into the public domain by 1774.

Conduct literature

The most commonly reprinted titles sold at prices as low as 1 shilling and 1.5 shillings by many of the same publishers such as Cooke and Nicholson, alphabetical.[88]
Bunyan's *Pilgrim's Progress*; Chapone's *On the Improvement of the Mind* and Gregory's *Father's Legacy:* Chesterfield's *Letters*; Doddridge's *Rise and Progress of Religion*; Dodd's *Reflections on Death* and *Thoughts in Prison:* (Dodsley's) *The Economy of Human Life*; (Fénelon's) *Telemachus*; Franklin's *Essays*; (Gessner's) *Death of Abel*; Hervey's *Meditations among the Tombs*; Mason's *On Self Knowledge*; Melmoth's *Great Importance of the Religious Life*; Mrs Rowe's *Devout Exercises of the Heart*, and *Friendship in Death* Sherlock *On Death*; Sturm's *Reflections on the Works of God*; Watts's *On the Improvement of the Mind* and other works; Zimmerman's *On Solitude*

Some Scottish and English provincial publishing lists

Books 'printed and sold by' William Phorson of Berwick, on the Scottish border, 1789.[89] Over sixty titles, verse and prose, some very ancient. Phorson seems to have taken a share in the equity of many titles being reprinted by consortia in several towns in Scotland. Berwick, just across the English border, was a frequent stopping place for the coastal shipping between Edinburgh and London, and it seems likely that many of Phorson's books were intended to be sent to London for sale in England. Prices lower than even the cheapest in England. Some recorded Scottish print runs
Beattie's *Poems*, 18mo, for Bell and Bradfute, Edinburgh, 1804.[90] 2,500
Johnson's *Works*, 18mo, 1814.[91] 500 or 1,000 each volume

An outpouring of verse and prose anthologies drawn from the works freed from private ownership after 1774

A spate of anthologies of English literature, many printed in provincial towns. Almost all draw on the old canon, reaffirm theories of natural theology, and emphasise the morally improving power of literature.

The Poetical Miscellany . . . for the Use of Schools

1778. Third edition. No trace of a first edition found.

Poems on Various Subjects: Selected to Enforce the Practice of Virtue, and to comprise in one volume The Beauties of English Poetry by E. Tomkins

1780. About half a dozen editions before 1800, and many later. The 1823 edition, sold at 3 shillings, appears to be stereotyped.[92] Still being reissued, with a few more modern pieces added, in 1837.

---

[88] Based on the advertisements found on unbound copies of old-canon books, Ac, and on the printed prospectuses in the collection at Reading University Library.
[89] Printed list of 'Books Printed by William Phorson'. Bell and Bradfute archives.
[90] *Ibid.*.   [91] *Ibid.*.   [92] Ac.

Appendix 6 *(cont.)*

The Lady's Poetical Magazine, or Beauties of English Poetry

1781. Illustrated. Published by Harrison, one of the first reprinters of novels.

Beauties in Prose and Verse Selected from the Most Celebrated Authors . . . The Whole calculated to Exhibit the most striking Picture of Virtue and Vice to the Minds of Youth

Beauties of Milton, Thomson, and Young

1783. Stockton.[93]

Elegant Extracts, or Useful and Entertaining Pieces of Poetry.

1785. A large anthology in two volumes, edited by Vicesimus Knox, prepared by the copyright pretenders, which sold in large editions throughout the romantic period. Intended for schools and libraries, and also much used for reading aloud in families. Stereotyped by 1810. There were similar volumes of *Elegant Extracts* in prose and *Elegant Epistles* whose publishing history was similar.
Various later editions at tranched down prices. Available in one volume in 1792 at 10.5 shillings.[94] In 12 monthly numbers in 1810 at 2.5 shillings.[95]
Between 1796 and 1824[96]   at least 23,000
1,500 of the 1810 edition were sold in parts.[97]
1825 Tegg's price   12.5 discounted from 15s[98]
'. . . a shelf or two of beauties, *Elegant Extracts* and Anas form nine tenths of the reading of the reading public'. Samuel Taylor Coleridge, 1817.[99] By -'Anas' Coleridge meant the literary columns of the reviews which were given headlines such as 'Byroniana'.

Poems for Young Ladies in Three Parts. Devotional, Moral, and Entertaining. (Selected by Dr Goldsmith) 1785

Select Lessons in Prose and Verse from Various Authors, Designed for the Improvement of Youth

1785. Tamworth. Several editions[100]

Select Beauties of Ancient English Poetry

1787. Two volumes. This collection includes extracts from poets excluded from Johnson's selection.

The Cabinet of Genius containing Frontispieces and Characters

1787 onwards until early 1790s. Sold in parts of six to fourteen pages. Each contains a poem with a splendid stipple engraving.

---

[93] Bodleian.   [94] Price from Scatcherd's advertisement in Walkingame's *Tutor's Assistant*, (1792) Ac.
[95] Prospectus for Sharpe's Edition, Reading University Library.
[96] Longman archives, John Taylor commonplace book.   [97] Whittingham archives, 41,925.
[98] Tegg's *Select library*.   [99] *Biographia Literaria*, chapter 3.   [100] Ac.

The Beauties of the Poets: Being a Collection of Moral and Sacred Poetry from the Most Eminent Authors, compiled by the Rev. Thomas Janes, of Bristol

Editions dated 1777, 1788, 1790, 1800[101]	4 shillings bound
1806 edition[102]	
Available in two types of paper, totalling	2,000
1806. Another printing	200
1810. An edition[103]	750
1810. Another, smaller format	1,500

[Henry Waylett, selector], *Beauties of Literature*

1791. Lewes. Two volumes. Verse and prose. Published by subscription, including copies taken by several members of the Shelley family. May have been part of the childhood reading of Percy Bysshe Shelley.

The Poetical Epitome, or Elegant, Extracts Abridged . . . for the Improvement of Scholars at Classical and other Schools, in the Art of Speaking, in Reading, Thinking, Composing, and in the Conduct of Life

1792.	na	na
A reissue of 1806[104]		5,000
An abridgement of *Elegant Extracts*		

The Beauties of Thought on Various Subjects in Prose and Verse Selected from the Best Authors. Calculated for the Improvement of the Minds of Readers of Every Class

1793. Bridlington (and other towns in Yorkshire). Arranged by topic, for example, 'Gratitude' 'Mortality'. Mainly prose.[105]

Modern Beauties in Prose and Verse, selected from the most eminent authors

1793. Darlington. Financed by subscription

Roach's Beauties of the Modern Poets of Great Britain, Carefully Selected & Arranged in Three Volumes

Roach's Beauties of the Poets of Great Britain, Carefully Selected & Arranged from the Works of the Most Admired Authors, Particularly Milton, Pope, Dryden, Thomson, Addison, Goldsmith, Johnson, Young, Blair, Gray, Prior, Shenstone, Mallet, Cowper, Collins, Parnell, Beattie, Moore, Chatterton, Buckingham, Duncombe, Armstrong, Percy, Cotton, &c &c In Six Volumes

1793 onwards. 12mo., with an illustration. Sold in twenty-four parts of about sixty pages each, 0.5 shillings.[106]

---

[101] Price from Scatcherd's advertisement in Walkingame's *Tutor's Assistant* (1792), Ac.
[102] Longman impression books.
[103] Longman impression books. Also Whittingham archives 41,925.   [104] Longman archives.
[105] Bodleian.   [106] Ac.

Appendix 6 (*cont.*)

T. Woolston editor, *The Young Gentleman and Lady's Poetical Preceptor; Being A Collection of the Most Admired Poetry: Selected from the Best Authors. Calculated to form the Taste to Classic Elegance; And while it Delights the Fancy, to Improve the Morals, and to Harmonize the Heart.*

No date, after 1794. Coventry. A substantial anthology, with no Shakespeare, some Milton, and the usual eighteenth-century authors.

(Rachel Barclay) *Select Pieces of Poetry intended to Promote Piety and Virtue in the Minds of Young People*

London 1795

The Domestic Instructor. Selected principally from celebrated authors, with original pieces . . . Adapted for Private Families and Schools, by J. B. Webster

London c. 1800.

The Beauties of Sentiment, or Select Extracts . . . Divine, Moral, Literary, and Entertaining

1801. Two volumes. Volume i is mainly religion, volume ii old-canon authors.[107]

The Beauties of Modern Poetry

Carlisle 1801. Includes a few pieces by contemporary writers

British Poetical Miscellany

Huddersfield, n.d., c. 1800, three editions. Unusually this anthology includes many pieces from contemporary authors, probably in defiance of intellectual property conventions.

An Essay on the Beauties of the Universe, Selected from the Most Eminent Authors . . . designed for the Amusement and Instruction of Youth

1803. Mainly from Thomson, Akenside, Mallet, Young, and Rowe

Poetical Beauties of Modern Writers

1803. Second edition. Includes some pieces by contemporary authors.
'It has long been the subject of observation, that of every SELECTION hitherto published, three-fourth parts have been occupied by extracts from POPE, MILTON, THOMSON, &c &c.' Preface by S. J. dated 1794.

---

[107] Bodleian.

Appendix 6 (*cont.*)

The Beauties of the Poets

c. 1808. Extracts from Bell's *British Poets*, including many complete works, sold in double-columned sheets as supplements to his weekly magazine, *La Belle Assemblée*. Also available in book form as *Poetical Extracts*.[108]

The Elegant Preceptor . . . Instructions in Morality and. . . . Accomplishments. From the Works of the Most Eminent Writers

1808. A third edition 1809. A prose anthology

John Evans, ed., *Flowers of Genuine Poetry, Ancient and Modern, Consisting of a Pleasing Variety of Popular, Instructive, and Entertaining Narratives and Tales in Verse*

1808, and available later. Tiny print.

Beauties of the Muses

1808. A series of books, all of twelve pages, that is one sheet, with abridgements and some new pieces, including Wordsworth's *Goody Blake and Harry Gill*.[109]

The Muses' Bower, embellished with the Beauties of English Poetry

1809. Four volumes

The Young Gentleman & Lady's Instructor; or New Reader and Speaker

1809. At least two editions. Includes an extract from Wollstonecraft's 'On Sensibility'.[110]

Eliz. Hill, *The Poetical Monitor*, and *A Sequel to the Poetical Monitor . . . adapted to Improve the Minds and Manners of Young Persons*

n.d. Many editions. Not clear how many of the pieces are newly composed. An eleventh edition of 1831 consisted of 1,200 copies.[111]

British Bards . . . from Spenser to Cowper

1810. An anthology in three volumes. Many editions throughout the period.

---

[108] Ac.
[109] Copy in BL. Whether the intellectual property owners of Wordsworth's piece gave permission is not known.
[110] Ac.   [111] Strahan archives 48, 848.

Appendix 6 *(cont.)*

The Poetical Bouquet, selected from the works of the most eminent British Poets

Elegant Miscellaneous Extracts. Watts, Hervey, Newton, Young, Blair, Sturm
A New edition

1813. Woodbridge. Mainly religious prose

J. Doncaster, *Friendly Hints Principally Addressed to the Youth of Both*
Sexes . . . partly original but chiefly selected from the most approved authors

1815. Chester. Several editions

Poems Selected from the Works of Approved Authors

1818. Dublin.[112]   0.5 or 0.66 shillings bound in sheep   na

Dr Aikin's *Select Works of the British Poets*

1820. A large anthology in one volume, closely printed in double columns[113]
                                        18 shillings   1,000
Reissued 1831. New editions with Supplement, 'as near to the present time as the claims of
copyright would allow'. 1845, 1849
The 1845 edition was stereotyped and the book was kept in print for many decades, being
advertised, for example, in Longman's list of 1865. The plates were still in the inventory in
1871.[114]
An edition in ten volumes 18mo, 1821. 40 shillings.[115]

The Bee, A Selection of Poetry from Approved Authors

1822. A school book probably for younger children

John Bullar, compiler, *Selections from the British Poets*

1822. Southampton. Since this anthology contained a few pieces which were still in
copyright it was subjected to legal action.[116]

The Poetical Bouquet

1822. Shrewsbury

Twenty Six Choice Poetical Extracts Selected from Celebrated Authors

c. 1823. Engraved with an illustration on cards so that they could be used as rewards.
2 shillings and 2.5 shillings. With other similar books.[117]

---

[112] Ac.   [113] Longman archives.   [114] Longman archives. Catalogue of stereotype plates 1819–74.
[115] Lowndes.   [116] See chapter 11.
[117] Ac. Others are listed in the inserted *Catalogue of Books and Fancy Articles, published and sold by*
R. Miller, in copy of the Ben Jonson volume, Ac.

Appendix 6 (*cont.*)

Joseph Belcher, compiler, *Poetical Sketches.*

1825. The compiler noted that he is keeping down the extracts from 'Milton, Young, Cowper, &c' because these poets are 'so very generally known and possessed that . . . to include more would be felt as a tax on the reader'.

The Select British Poetical Cabinet

1825. Two volumes   10.5 shillings   na
Appears to be made up of extracts from Sharpe's edition of the *British Poets*, intended to make available the many engravings in that series.

1826. *Beauties of the Poets of Great Britain*

Three volumes, illustrated

Anthologies of authors

Many volumes of selections from the works of the individual authors, many containing the word 'Beauties' in their titles. For example, the trade catalogues note *Beauties of Addison, Beattie, Blair, Burke, Fénelon, Genlis, Hervey, Johnson, Paley, Pope, Rousseau, Shakespeare, Sterne, Sturm, Thomson, Young* and others in verse and prose. Some recorded Tegg reprint editions are of 3,000 copies.[118]

Anthologies and compilations on other topics, many intended for use in education

'Beauties' and other anthologies arranged by subject, mainly drawn from out-of-copyright texts, including encyclopaedias, such as beauties of antiquities, drama, biography, history, letters on common and important occasions, oratory, divinity, and science, as well as adaptations, sale in parts and other forms of text made possible by 1774. For example Cooke's *Universal Geography*, a series of abridgements of voyages and travels, mainly from the eighteenth century, illustrated, available in 100 numbers at 0.5 shillings.[119]
William Mavor, a schoolmaster who worked for Longman, produced dozens of textbooks on natural history, voyages and travels, biography, botany, history, health, classics, and religion, as well as anthologies. Many were sold in hundreds of thousands, maybe millions, of copies, stereotyped, and kept in print for decades. Longman printed some of Mavor's textbooks on specially watermarked paper to make piracy easier to detect. Mavor, who seems to have been paid either nothing or a small fee as compiler, died in extreme poverty.[120] Lists of the astonishing numbers of such books that were then available are included in David Blair [pseud.], *The Universal Preceptor: or General Grammar of Arts, Sciences, and Useful Knowledge* (1831 edition).

[118] Whittingham archives. See also Barnes and Barnes 48.
[119] Advertisement in Cooke's edition of *New Bath Guide*, n.d., Ac.
[120] Royal Literary Fund archives.

Appendix 6 *(cont.)*

Anthologies intended for schools, entrenching the old canon into the educational system

Many verse anthologies were intended to be used in schools. The following, which were sold in hundreds of thousands of copies across the whole English-speaking world, were specifically intended to link the teaching and reading of selected passages of English literature with moral education, cultivation of taste, and national values.

(Enfield's *Speaker*) *The Speaker: or Miscellaneous Pieces Selected from the Best English Writers*

1774. The first standard selection for schools. Frequently reprinted in new impressions of 5,000 or 6,000 copies each. Stereotyped as early as 1808.[121] Longman's set of the plates was repaired in 1850 and 1851, and sold in 1874.[122]
'Only you're obliged to remember it [Latin] while you're at school, else got to learn so many lines from "Speaker"'. Tom in Eliot's *The Mill on the Floss*, 1860 but set earlier.[123]

(Murray's *Reader*) *The English Reader: or Pieces in Prose and Poetry, Selected from the Best Writers, Designed to assist young persons to read with propriety and effect; to improve their language and sentiments; and to inculcate the most important principles of piety and virtue*

1799. By 1833 had reached a twenty-second regular edition, usually of 10,000 copies each. Stereotyped.[124] Longman's set of plates bought in 1852 was eventually sent for melting in 1867[125]

Introduction to the English Reader (extracts for younger readers)

1801. Thirty-two regular editions by 1839, usually of 10,000 copies each. Stereotyped.[126]

Murray's *Sequel to the English Reader*

1800. Seven regular editions by 1829, usually of 6,000 copies each. Stereotyped.[127]

Murray's *English Exercises*

1808. Thirty-eight editions before 1839.

---

[121] Noted on title page, Ac.   [122] Longman archives. Catalogue of Stereotype Plates 1819–74.
[123] George Eliot, *The Mill on the Floss*, edited by A. S. Byatt (1979) 236.
[124] Tieken-Boon van Ostade 39 and 223. Many later editions.
[125] Longman archives. Catalogue of Stereotype Plates 1819–1874.
[126] Tieken-Boon van Ostade 39 and 223.   [127] *Ibid.*

Appendix 6 (*cont.*)

Classical English Poetry for the Use of Schools and Young Persons in General by William Mavor, LLD

1824. Another standard school textbook.
Reprinted, latterly from stereotypes, in numerous new impressions of thousands of copies each over several decades.

Many other similar 'readers' and 'speakers' all of which also drew almost exclusively on old-canon authors, such as *The Pleasing Instructor*, Ewing's *Principles of Elocution*, Mavor's *New Speaker*, and various catechisms by Pinnock. Some specifically designed for the teaching of girls and young women include *The Female Reader* (Said to be by 'Mr Cresswick' but actually by Mary Wollstonecraft) (1798), and *The Lady's Preceptor*, said to be by Mr Cresswick. All these books classify the selected poetry and prose by its intended moral and emotional effect rather than by author.

Examples of abridgements of texts which ceased to be privately owned after 1774

Some examples from Newbery[128]

1777. *Maxims of Chesterfield*

1782. *Holy Bible abridged*

1797. *Johnson's Poets abridged*

1800. Mavor's *Plutarch, selected and abridged*

Novels, priced at 1 shilling

1784. Fielding's *Joseph Andrews*[129]

1789. Fielding's *Tom Jones*[130]

1789. Richardson's *Clarissa*[131]
See also Bew's list in appendix 4.

The old canon continued as a uniform reprint series into Victorian times, with prices falling further as a result of stereotyping

Scott and Webster's *English Classic Library*

1834. 100 volumes planned, poetry and prose, illustrated with frontispieces and vignettes. Bound in cloth. 2 shillings and upwards.[132] Scott and Webster were successors to Dove, successors to the pretender copyright 'English Classics'. The publishers claimed to have made a reduction of 'fully one third' from former prices, and all pretence to copyright ownership is now abandoned. Many titles stereotyped.
'Thus the publishers will be enabled to place for many years the most valuable literature in the world within the reach of the Young and the Working Classes', prospectus.[133]

---

[128] Welsh 343, 346.   [129] *Ibid.* 219.   [130] *Ibid.*   [131] *Ibid.* 299.
[132] Prospectus and advertisement in Cowper's *Poems* (1834), Ac. Scott and Webster were 'Successors to Mr Dove' and took over his stock.
[133] Advertisement, Ac.

Appendix 6 (*cont.*)

The Aldine Edition of the British Poets, with Original Memoirs and Portraits

Pickering, **1835–53**. 12mo. stereotyped. Bound in cloth, 5 shillings each volume.[134] Initial print run, 1,000 copies, then reprinted from the stereotype plates in accordance with demand.[135]
Akenside, 1845, Beattie, 1853, Burns, 1839, Butler, 1835, Chaucer, 1852, Churchill, 1844, Collins, 1853, Cowper, 1851, Dryden, 1852, Falconer, 1836, Goldsmith, 1853, Gray, 1853, Kirke White, 1853, Milton, 1852, Parnell, 1852, Pope, 1852, Prior, 1835, Shakespeare, 1853, Spenser, 1852, Surrey, 1853, Swift, 1853, Thomson, 1847, Wyatt, 1853, Young, 1852.

Bohn's *Cabinet Edition of the British Poets*

1851. Four volumes, 14 shillings, tiny print, each author available separately. Jones's *Cabinet Edition* of 1825 reissued with a new title page.

Nichol's *Library Edition of the British Poets*, with Memoirs and Dissertations by the Revd George Gilfillan

1853–60, 8vo, forty-eight volumes. Bound in cloth, by subscription 168 shillings or 4.5 shillings per volume.[136]
Addison, Gay, Somerville, Akenside, Armstrong, Blair, Bruce, Logan, Beattie, Denham and Falconer; Bowles, Burns, Kirke White and Graham, Milton, Pope, Prior, Scott, Shakespeare and Surrey, Shenstone, Spenser, Thomson, Waller, Wyatt, Young.

The old canon comes to an end as a formal series as the poets of the romantic period come out of copyright

List of James Blackwood

1860s.[137] 'Universal Library of Standard Authors', 5 shillings. Includes Goldsmith, Burns, Scott, Milton, Young, Gray, Beattie, Blair, Collins, Thomson, Kirke White. 'Blackwood's Edition of the Poets,' illustrated 3.5 shillings.

Choice Selections from Spenser to Montgomery

Longfellow (copyright not enforceable), Pope, Burns, Milton, Scott, Cowper, Kirke White, Crabbe

Nimmo's *Large Print Unabridged Library Edition of the British Poets from Chaucer to Cowper*

1869. Forty-eight volumes, with portraits. 4 shillings each.[138] Probably derived from earlier editions.

---

[134] Lowndes. [135] Whittingham archives, BL add mss. 41,886. [136] Lowndes.
[137] Advertisement, n.d., in *The Poetical Works of the Rev. George Crabbe* (n.d.), Ac.
[138] Nimmo's advertisement, dated 1869, in *The Poetical Works of Lord Byron* (n.d.), Ac.

Appendix 6 (*cont.*)

Wyatt, Spenser, Shakespeare and Surrey, Herbert, Waller and Denham, Milton, Butler, Dryden, Prior, Thomson, Johnson, Parnell, Gray, and Smollett, Pope, Shenstone, Akenside, Goldsmith, Collins, and T. Warton, Armstrong, Dyer, and Green, Churchill, Beattie, Blair and Falconer, Burns, Cowper, Bowles, Scott, Chaucer, Crawshaw and Quarles, Addison, Gay, and Somerville, Young, Percy's *Reliques, Specimens of Less Known Poets*, Kirke White and Grahame.

The last old-canon poetry lists

Bell's *New Aldine Edition of the English Poets*

1866 onwards. A reissue by Bell and Daldry of the *Aldine Edition* of Pickering in fifty-two volumes.[139] 8vo, cloth.[140]
A few authors who had by now gone out of copyright and were attracting interest were added, including Blake, Chatterton, and Keats, but no attempt was made to match the series of romantic poets being published by Routledge, Warne, and others.

Bell's English Poets

Begun **1870**. Fortnightly volumes 1.25 shillings cloth[141]
Discontinued

Old-canon cultural categories

Most anthologies classified the contents by their expected moral and emotional effect on readers rather than by the names of their authors.

Elegant Extracts

Sacred and Moral, Didactic, Descriptive, Narrative and Pathetic, Dramatic, Sentimental, Lyrical, and Ludicrous

Murray's *Reader*

Narrative, Didactic, Descriptive, Pathetic, Promiscuous

Enfield's *Speaker*

Narrative, Didactic, Argumentative, Orations and Harangues, Dialogues, Descriptive, Pathetic

---

[139] *London Catalogue of Books, 1863–72* (1873).
[140] *English Catalogue of Books, 1872–1880* (1882). Supplemented by advertisement in copy of Collins (n.d.), Ac.
[141] Advertisement in copy of Jonson, Ac.

Appendix 6 (*cont.*)

Mavor's *Classical English Poetry*

Pastoral, Lyric, Didactic, Descriptive, Elegiac

The Casket of Gems, Choice Selections from the Poets, mid-Victorian

Sacred, Didactic and Moral, Descriptive, Works of Nature, Beauties and Enjoyments of the Country, Scenery, Pastoral, the Seasons and the Months, Natural Phenomena, Characters, Natural History, Animals, Epic, Narrative, and Pathetic, Elegiac, Lyrical, Ballads, Songs, and other Lyrics, the Social and Domestic Affections, Love of Home and Country, Sonnets, Genius.

Fugitive Poetry 1600 to 1878 In *Lansdowne Poets* series, 1878

Sacred, Moral, Natural and Descriptive, National, Social, and Domestic, Lyric and Legendary, Humorous, Elegiac, Epigrams, Epitaphs

Appendix 7 Romantic period. Book production arranged by literary genre

Prices and print runs of the main types of printed books in the English language made available for sale in Great Britain and elsewhere in the romantic period and later. Prices in shillings, retail before binding.

The official supernatural, primary texts

Bibles, psalms, and prayer books

The crown privilege to print and sell the Authorised (King James) Version of the Bible, the *Book of Common Prayer*, the psalms in English, and certain other standard printed texts of the Church of England remained in the hands of the king's printer in London and the university presses of Oxford and Cambridge. Similar monopoly franchises were in the hands of the king's printers in Scotland and in Ireland. The privileged presses enjoyed fiscal subsidies, such as exemption from paper tax. After the 1774 decision to outlaw perpetual private intellectual property throughout Great Britain, a new Act of Parliament confirmed that the crown privileges were unaffected. Although, with the proliferation of the new annotated versions of English-language Bibles, the monopoly was weakened, the production of the printed texts of the official supernatural remained far higher.[1] Some scattered indicative figures, rounded.

England

1808–15. Cambridge University Press.[2]

Bibles	392,000
Testaments	423,000
Prayer books	194,000

1808–15. Oxford University Press

Bibles	460,000
Testaments	386,000
Prayer books, catechisms, psalters, etc.	200,000

1829. King's printer in London, annually[3]

Bibles	51,500
Testaments	76,000

1821–30. Total production[4]

	Bibles	New Testaments	Prayer books	Psalms
King's printer	565,500	591,000	178,500	168,000
Oxford	1,253,000	1,221,500	2,269,000	2,040,000
Cambridge	380,500	484,000	481,000	358,500
Total	2,199,000	2,296,500	2,928,500	2,566,500

---

[1] 'On the Crown Privilege of Printing Bibles, &c,' in *Gentleman's Magazine* (1819).
[2] Timperley 861.   [3] Timperley 908.
[4] Quoted from official sources used by Eliot and by G. E. Bentley, Jnr, "The Holy Pirates: Legal Enforcement in England of the Patent in the Authorised Version of the Bible ca.1800' in *Studies in Bibliography*, 1997.

Appendix 7 *(cont.)*

1810. *Book of Common Prayer*, total printed in various formats for Scatcherd and Co. in this one year[5]	75,000

Scotland[6]

1816. Glasgow University Press, annually[7]	
Bibles	200,000
Before the abolition of the Bible patent in 1839	annual average under 80,000
1854–58	annual average 225,000
1860	300,000

Free distribution

1790s, annual distribution by Society for Promoting Christian Knowledge[8]	5,000
Between 1804 and 1819. Distribution at heavily subsidised prices by British and Foreign Bible Society	over 2.5 million
1805–23. Distribution within Great Britain of Bibles by the British and Foreign Bible Society, stereotyped[9]	over 3.1 million

Non-official English-language Bibles

1802. Priestley's Bible in folio[10]	5,000

Non-official English-language Bibles sold to low income readers in numbered parts

c. 1811. *Kelly's Family Bible*, edited by Revd John Malham, illustrated, sold in 173 numbers, total sold[11]	80,000
1811. Copies printed of each part of Malham's Bible[12]	5,000
1813. Copies printed of each part of Knight's Bible[13]	5,000
1810s to about **1830.** Twelve separate editions of Bibles sold by Kelly	250,000
Life of Christ	100,000
After 1834. *Guide to Family Devotion*	30,000
Before 1850. Brown's *Self-Interpreting Bible*[14]	10,000

---

[5] Whittingham archives 41,925.   [6] Quoted by Keir 169 from evidence given to a Select Committee.
[7] Timperley 864.
[8] Quoted by Scott Mandelbrote, 'The Bible and its Readers' in Isabel Rivers, ed., *Books and Readers, New Essays* (2001) 48.
[9] Quoted by Lee 201.   [10] Fell's *Kelly* 83.   [11] Curwen 367.
[12] Clowes ledger.   [13] Clowes ledger.   [14] Fell's *Kelly* 135.

Appendix 7 (*cont.*)

The official supernatural, secondary writings

Besides sermons such as those of Hugh Blair, which were published commercially, earning high rewards for authors and publishers, many books on religion were financed from church or other funds available to the author, with copies being distributed free to selected recipients. Some recorded print runs:

1770. Bethune's *Essays*, two volumes, at his own expense	1,000
1790 and later. Logan's *Sermons*, five editions[15]	5,000
1790. *Sermons on Liberty and Equality* (Edinburgh), not identified[16]	60
1791. Carr's *Sermons*, two volumes[17]	1,500
1797. Mair's *Sermons*	1,250
1806. Logan's Sermons, fifth edition[18]	1,000
1809. Lindsey's *Sermons*, 8vo, two volumes[19]	750
1809. Coggan's *Sermon on the Death of Mr Ralph*[20]	175
1816. Disney's *Sermons*, four volumes[21]	500
1827. Keble's *Christian Year* [verse] before 1873[22]	379,000
Early nineteenth century. Two editions. Scott's *Commentary on the Bible*[23]	7,000

Official calendar and the tolerated illegitimate supernatural

After 1775, when the monopoly on selling almanacs in England was abolished, many more almanac titles were published, including many which did not contain astrological texts or forecasts.[24] However, the Stationers' Company continued to dominate the market, partly by buying out rivals. Almanacs which included elements of the tolerated illegitimate supernatural remained the majority.

Some estimates of total production

1768	107,000
1789	220,000
1800	353,000
1800. Stationers' Company almanacs	571,000

of which *Vox Stellarum*, '*Old Moore*', with its astrological information and prognostications was 62 per cent. Less than 10 per cent of the total of Stationers' Company almanacs were unsold.[25]

1837. Stationers' Company almanacs, the all-time high[26]	637,000

Vox Stellarum, '*Old Moore*'[27]

1768	107,000
1789	230,000

[15] Bell and Bradfute archives, order from Neill, printers.   [16] Bell and Bradfute archives.
[17] *Ibid.*   [18] *Ibid.*   [19] Richard Taylor check books.   [20] *Ibid.*   [21] *Ibid.*
[22] Total sold during copyright period, quoted by Altick 386.   [23] Fell's *Kelly* 142.
[24] Houston 185.   [25] Myers 85.   [26] *Ibid.*   [27] Capp 263, quoting primary sources.

Appendix 7 (*cont.*)

1802	365,000
1810s. '*Old Moore*' annual order to one printer[28]	100,000
1839	560,000

In 1802 alone the profits from *Old Moore* were £3,000, greater, as one
contemporary remarked, than those of many German principalities.[29]

Ancient classics

Huge numbers of the Greek and Latin classics, especially Horace and Virgil, many
intended for schools

History

Besides histories of the Greek and Roman world, some of the modern histories written in
the eighteenth century in multi-volume editions were frequently reprinted and abridged
for sale at cheaper prices. Such books were frequently bought by subscription libraries and
book clubs.

Some scattered recorded print runs of reprints and of newly published works.[30]

Reprints

1804. Ferguson's *History of Rome*, five volumes[31]	1,000
1809. Robertson's *History of Scotland*, eighteenth edition[32]	1,500
1817. Another edition	1,000
1817. Another edition	1,000
1817. Robertson's *Charles V*, four volumes	1,000
1809. Robertson's *History of India*, fifth edition[33]	1,500
1817	750
1790. Hume's *History of England*, in forty-eight numbers[34]	3,000
1818. eight volumes	1,500
Smollett's continuation of Hume's *History*	1,500
1823. Both reprinted	1,500
1813. Kelly's edition of *History of England* in numbers.[35]	5,000
1820. Another edition in numbers.[36]	10,000

New works, retail price, and print runs

	Shillings	Print run
1808. Fox's *History of the Early Part of the Reign of James the Second*, 4to	36 and 52.5	5,750
1818. Hallam's *Middle Ages*, two volumes, 4to[37]	63	750

---

[28] Richard Taylor archives.   [29] Noted by Capp 263.   [30] Strahan archives.
[31] Annotated *Catalogue of Books in Quires*, Bell and Bradfute, 1804, NLS, Acc. 10,062.
[32] Strahan archives.   [33] *Ibid.*   [34] *Ibid.*   [35] Clowes ledger.
[36] Clay archives.   [37] Murray archives.

Appendix 7 (*cont.*)

Reprinted in 8vo at	36	na
1822. Southey's *War in Spain*, volume i		1,250
Second edition		300
Third edition		500
1827. Volume ii		1,750
1825. Leake's *Outline of the Greek Revolution*	7.5	250
Of which seventy-seven sold		
1826. Reprinted		750
Of which 403 copies were remaindered[38]		

Biography

1802. Hayley's *Life of Cowper*[39]	1,000 plus 250 royal
1813. Southey's *Life of Nelson*[40]	3,500
Many subsequent editions	na
1831. Family Library edition[41]	11,000
1823. Miss Aikin's *Memoirs of King James the First*[42]	1,000
1824. Hayley's *Life of Cowper*[43]	750

See also the *Memoirs of Harriette Wilson by Harriette Wilson*
and the biographies by Thomas Moore noted in appendix 9.

Topical events

1809. Salvo's *Escape of Mrs Spencer Smith*[44]	250
1811. Johnstone's *Trial for Deposing Governor Bligh*[45]	500
1814. Labaume's *Invasion of Russia*[46]	1,000
1814. Second edition	1,000
1814. Third edition	1,500
1814. Fourth edition	1,500
1815. Second edition in 12mo	1,000
1815. Second edition in 12mo	1,500

Voyages, exploration, descriptions of foreign countries, and accounts of travels at home and abroad

Travel books often appeared first in 4to, and only if commercial interest was high, were they reprinted in 8vo. Later the two-volume 8vo format seems to have been preferred. For most travel books, a small expensive edition was all that ever appeared, and a high

[38] *Ibid.*   [39] Johnson ledger, printing order.   [40] Murray archives.   [41] Whittingham archives.   [42] Richard Taylor check books.   [43] Longman archives.   [44] Richard Taylor archives.   [45] *Ibid.*   [46] Clowes ledger.

Appendix 7 *(cont.)*

proportion of copies of all editions were remaindered. Many were illustrated by engravings and maps.

The publishers frequently drew on books first published in other European languages, for which permission to translate was not required, sometimes, as in the case of Humboldt, paying an extremely high price to obtain a copy of the original language edition, imported with difficulty in war time. In the 1810s Phillips published a series of translated abridgements of contemporary books of travel first published in full in other languages and not yet translated into English.

Some recorded examples[47]

Holmes's *Tour in Ireland in 1797*		
1801. 8vo	9	750
Cruttwell's *Tour through Great Britain*		
1801. 8vo, six volumes	48	1,500
White's *Aegyptiaca*		
1801. On commission.[48]	omitted from trade catalogues	750
Sonnini's *Travels in Greece*		
1801. 4to	52.5	250
In 8vo	27	1,000
Pallas's *Travels in Russia*		
1801 and 1803. Two volumes, 4to	147	750 plus 50
A later 8vo edition, four volumes	20	na
Marchand's *Voyage round the World*		
1801. Two volumes, 4to.	73	250
In 8vo	31.5	750
Links's *Travels in Portugal*		
1801. 8vo	9	750
Adams's *Guide to Madeira*		
1801.	na	500
Denon's *Travels in Egypt*		
1802. 4to	84	250
In 8vo, three volumes	42	1,000
1803. Reprinted		500
1810. *Sir William Jones's Poems*, Two volumes.	12	1,000
Campbell's *Tour through North Britain*		
1803. Two volumes, 4to[49]	42	750
Muirhead's *Travels in France &c in 1787 and 1789*		
1804. 8vo	7	750
Heriot's *History of Canada*		

[47] From Longman archives except where shown.   [48] Besterman 129.
[49] Longman impression books. Richard Taylor archives suggest only 500 for volume i.

Appendix 7 (*cont.*)

1804. 8vo	12	1,000
Card's *Revolutions in Russia*		
1804. Second edition, 8vo	12	500
Description of Latium		
1805. 4to	na	750
Burnett's *View of Poland*		
1807.	7	1,000
Volume vii of *Asiatic Researches*. Selected as typical of annual production.		
1807. 4to		170
In 8vo		1,250
In 4to, twelve volumes, price in 1818[50]	399	na
In 8vo, twelve volumes, price in 1818[51]	162	na
Sir William Jones's *Works*, six volumes, 4to[52]	210	na
Thirteen volumes, 8vo	136.5	na
Gell's *Ithaca*		
1807. 4to, with plates	52.5	500
Author received £200		
Parsons's *Travels in Asia and Africa*		
1808. 4to	25	500
Bourgoing's *Modern State of Spain*[53]		
1808. Four volumes, 8vo plus folio atlas	63	1,500
Account of Jamaica and its Inhabitants		
1808. 8vo	7.5	750
Laborde's *Spain*		
1809. Five volumes, 8vo	73.5	1,250
Letters from Canada		
1809. 8vo	na	1,000
History of Chile		
1809. Two volumes	na	1,000
Humboldt's *Researches in America*		
1810. Two volumes plus atlas.	31.5	1,000
Longman's accounts note that they obtained a copy of the French version for £63 and onsold it to Sir James Mackintosh for £42.		
Wilkie's *History of Mysoore*		
1810. Volume i, 4to	na	500
Southey's *History of Brazil*		
1810. 4to, volume i	na	750
1817. 4to, volume ii	na	750
1819. 4to, volume iii	155 the three	750

[50] *London Catalogue* (1831).   [51] *Ibid.*   [52] *Ibid.*
[53] Richard Taylor archives.

Appendix 7 (*cont.*)

Marsden's *History of Sumatra*		
1810. 4to with plates, folio	73.5	750
Hamilton's *Egypt*		
1810. 4to	84	750
Campbell's *Tour through North Britain*		
1810. 4to, two volumes.	105	500
Lambert's *Travels through Canada and the United States*		
1813. octavo, three volumes.	30	750
Pouqueville's *Travels in the Morea*		
1813. 4to	42	750
Keating's *Travels to Morocco*		
1815. 4to	63	500
Klapwroth's *Travels to the Caucasus*		
1815. 4to	42	500
Elphinston's *Caubel*		
1815. 4to	73.5	750
1824. 8vo[54]	42	500
Walpole's *Memoirs relating to European and Asiatic Turkey*		
1817. 4to	63	500
Second edition, 4to[55]	63	500
Neale's *Travels through Germany, Poland &c*		
1817. 4to, coloured illustrations[56]	42	500
Lewis and Clarke's *Travels in North America*		
1817. 4to	52.5	250
Later 8vo edition	42	na
McLeod's *Voyage in the Alceste*		
1817. 8vo[57]	9.5	1,250
1817. Second edition	9.5	3,500
1819. Third edition	9.5	3,000
Daniell's *African Sketches*		
1820. Folio, magnificent coloured illustrations	110	250
Leake's *Athens*		
1821	30	750
1835. 325 copies were remaindered to Tegg in quires[58]		
1823. Gell's *Morea*, with plates[59]	15	1,000
Leake's *Asia Minor*		
1824. 8vo[60]	18	750
325 copies remaindered[61]		

---

[54] Murray archives.   [55] Strahan archives.   [56] *Ibid.*   [57] Murray archives.   [58] *Ibid.*
[59] Whittingham archives, 48,862.   [60] Richard Taylor check books.
[61] Noted by Barnes and Barnes 53.

Appendix 7 (*cont.*)

Denham and Clapperton's *Travels in Africa*
1827. Two volumes   36   1,500
1,167 copies remaindered.[62] Previously published in 4to

Lieutenant Rose's *Four Years in South Africa*
1829[63]   10.5   750
170 copies remaindered

Lieutenant Hardy's *Travels in Mexico*
1830   16   1,250
Nearly 600 copies remaindered

Caillié's *Travels to Timbuctoo*
1830. Two volumes   30   1,500
650 copies remaindered

Captain Moorsom's *Letters from Nova Scotia*
1830   12   750
300 copies remaindered

Lander's *Records of Clapperton's Expedition* (Africa)
1830. Two volumes   21   1,250
200 copies remaindered

Webster's *Travels through the Crimea, Turkey, &c*
1830. Two volumes   32   750
350 copies remaindered

Trant's *Greece*
1830   16   500

Temple's *Travels in Peru*
1831. Two volumes   32   1,000
200 copies remaindered

Kotzebue's *Second Voyage round the World*
1830. Two volumes   21   750
200 copies remaindered

Mackenzie's *Notes on Haiti*
1831. Two volumes   21   750
200 copies remaindered

Dobell's *Travels in Kamtshanka and Siberia*
1831. Two volumes   21   750
200 remaindered

Burckhart's *Notes on the Bedouins and Wahabys*
1831. One volume 4to   52.5   250
Two volumes, 8vo   24   500
324 copies remaindered

---

[62] *Ibid.*
[63] Except where shown, the information on the remaining titles in this section is taken from Bentley archives. BL add. mss. 46,674.

Appendix 7 *(cont.)*

Beechey's *Voyage to the Pacific*

1831. 4to	84	500
Two volumes, 8vo	38	750
Third edition	38	750

Stewart's *Visit to the South Seas* (reprinted from an American edition)

1831. Two volumes	21	500

Art

Burke's *Philosophical Enquiry* can be taken along with Blair's *Essays* (see appendix 9) as the two main theoretical statements of the nature of art and literature which were widely read and accepted during the romantic period.

1806. Flaxman's *Odyssey* and *Iliad*[64]
250 sets with some overcopies

1808. 50 more sets of each

1807. Landseer's *Lectures on Engraving*[65]		750
1809. John Opie's *Lectures on Painting*[66]	21	1,000
1816. *Report of the Select Committee on the Elgin Marbles*[67]	9	750
1817. Burrows's *Elgin Marbles*[68]	20	500
1820. Fuseli's *Lectures on Painting*[69]	12	250

Plate books

1783. *Ionian Antiquities*. First part[70]	252	200
1797. *Ionian Antiquities*. Second part Published by subscription for the Society of Dilettanti[71]		500
1809. *Specimens of Antient Sculpture* Published by subscription for the Society of Dilettanti[72]		350
1786–1796. Gough's *Sepulchral Monuments*[73] Many copies were destroyed by fire in the warehouse		250
1812. *Cambria Depicta*[74]		300
1812. Ackerman's *Repository of Arts*[75]	na	1,500
1817. Flaxman's designs for Hesiod, engraved by Blake[76]	52.5	200

---

[64] Longman impression books.   [65] *Ibid.*   [66] Richard Taylor archives.   [67] Murray archives.
[68] Richard Taylor check books.   [69] Strahan archives.
[70] Lionel Cust and Sidney Colvin, *History of the Society of Dilettanti* (1898) 100.
[71] Peter Isaac, ed., William Bulmer, *The Fine Printer in Context, 1757–1830* (1993) 53.
[72] (Sharon Turner) *Reasons for a Modification of the Act of Anne respecting the Delivery of Books and Copyright* (1814) 42.
[73] *Ibid.*   [74] Clowes ledger.   [75] *Ibid.*
[76] G. E. Bentley Jr, and Martin K. Nurmi, *A Blake Bibliography* (1964) 113 transcribed from Longman archives.

Satire with coloured plates

1819. [A. Burton] *Johnny Newcombe in the Navy*[77]   21   1,500

Natural history

1806. Graham's *Birds of* Scotland[78]   1,500

1806. *Forsyth on Fruit Trees*, fourth edition[79]   2,000

1810. Fifth edition   1,500

1807. Smith's *Botany*   1,000
Mr Sowerby was paid 195 shillings for colouring twenty-four sets of the plates.

1808. Second edition   1,500

Anti-Slavery Campaign

A Baptist pamphlet

1791. *An Address to the People of Great Britain, on the propriety of abstaining from West India Sugar and Rum.* (By William Fox, Baptist minister and founder of the Sunday-School Society.) Price one penny, four for three pence, nine for sixpence, nineteen for a shilling, or fifty for two shillings and sixpence. The 24th edition notes 'price a Halfpenny, 13 for 6d, or 50 for 1s 9d . . . Persons in the Country, ordering 1000 may have an Edition worked off, with their Names and Residence in the Title.'[80]
Copies circulated in 1790s   ?100,000

Thomas Clarkson, the abolitionist compaigner, 'wrote to Josiah Wedgwood urging him to have a bookseller order a thousand copies of Fox's pamphlet, An Address to the People of Great Britain on the propriety of abstaining from West India Sugar and Rum . . . To this letter Clarkson adds that the "Sugar Revenue has fallen off £200,000 this quarter." Wedgwood immediately replied, ordering two thousand copies.'[81]

Anti-Slavery Society

Number of pamphlets circulated, rounded[82]

---

[77] Shaylor 206, quoting an original letter.   [78] Longman impression books.   [79] *Ibid.*
[80] Quoted by Raven in James Raven, ed., *Free Print and Non-Commercial Publishing since 1700* (Aldershot 2000) 72 from primary sources.
[81] Initial prices from copy of sixth edition, 1791, BL. According to (William B. Gurney), *Some Particulars of the Lives of William Brodie Gurney and his Immediate Ancestors. Written Chiefly by Himself* (1902 'printed for family circulation only'), BL '250,000 were printed, and they had for a time a great effect' and although that figure cannot be easily reconciled with the other indications, the circulation was undoubtedly huge and unprecedented. Many library catalogues, following an old error, have wrongly attributed the authorship to William Fox, an attorney. I am grateful to Tim Whelan for providing the essential information and for making available to me the results of his work in examining the many editions, assessing the evidence, and correcting the authorial attribution.
[82] E. L. Griggs, *Thomas Clarkson: The Friend of Slaves* (1970) 69.

Appendix 7 *(cont.)*

1823	202,000
1824	146,000
1825	236,000
1830	over 500,000

Publications of the Society for Effecting the Abolition of the Slave Trade, many copies distributed free, 1788.[83]

Clarkson's *Essay on the Slavery and Commerce of the Human species*	2,325
Falconbridge's *Account*	6,025
Various pamphlets and reports	4,000 to 10,000
Engraving of a Slave Ship, copper	1,700
woodcut	7,000

Pamphlets

With a few exceptions, such as those by Burke and by Paine noted in appendix 9, the usual print run of pamphlets from the 1790s onwards appears to have been 500 or 750, with no obvious rise even in the 1820s, when the reading nation as a whole was much larger. Many pamphlets were printed at the expense of the authors and were circulated free to friends and colleagues as can be seen from the many presentation inscriptions to be found in surviving copies. Some recorded examples.

1793 *Burke's Address to the Swinish Multitude* (not identified)[84]		500
1796. Epistle from Sheridan to Dundas[85]		500
1796. 'For printing a Reply to Burke' (title not named, for Jordan)[86]		500
1809. Ricardo on Bullion and Banknotes[87]	na	250
1812. Owen's *New View of Society*[88]	6	500
1812. Hollis's *Free Thoughts*[89]	na	250
1821. Bentham's *On Jury Packing*	10.5	500
second edition		750
1818. Hague on Capital Punishment[90]	na	500
1823. (Blaquiere's) *Appeal from the Greek Committee*	na	500
1823. Bowring's *Appeal*	na	500
Second edition		250

---

[83] Quoted by James Walvin, 'The Public Compaign in England against Slavery, 1787–1834', in David Eltis and James Walvin, eds., *The Abolition of the Atlantic Slave Trade* (Madison 1981) 76, from *Accounts of the Receipts and Disbursements of the Anti-Slavery Society* (1831) in Goldsmith's Library, University of London.

[84] Whittingham archives 41,901.   [85] *Ibid.*   [86] *Ibid.*   [87] Murray archives.
[88] Richard Taylor archive check books.   [89] *Ibid.*   [90] *Ibid.*

Appendix 7 *(cont.)*

1823. Sir George Rose *On the Slave Trade*   na   500
Of which Rose took seventy copies for distributing free[91]

Newly composed poetry published during the brief copyright window before 1808

List of Cadell and Davies, c. 1800, 12mo with illustrations[92]

For newly published books of verse in the 1790s and 1800s the usual price appears to have been 5 or 6 shillings and the print run per edition 500 or 750.

Books of verse, many printed on commission at author's expense and not listed in trade catalogues

1802. William Preston's Poems, Dublin[93]   250

1806. Miss Patrickson's *Poems*, Two volumes[94]   500
On subscription. The author claims to have written the poems
  at the age of fourteen.[95]

1809. Bland's *Poems*[96]   9   500

1809. Barlow's *Columbiad*[97]   15   500

1809. *Britannia, A Poem*, 4to[98]   15   250

1811. Lofft's anthology of Sonnets, five volumes[99]   750

1811. Wilson's *Romance, a Poem* (at author's expense)[100]   250

1812. *The Thirty Nine, a Poem* (one sheet for Eaton)   500

1814. Merivale's *Ode on the Deliverance of Europe*   250
100 copies sold by 1817[101]

1821. Norwich. *Poems; Being the Genuine Compositions of*   6   2,000 subscribers
  Elizabeth Bentley of Norwich. Sold by the author
The author is said to have learned about Nature and God from
  Milton, Pope, Thomson, Collins, Gray, Goldsmith.

1832. Medwin's *Prometheus Bound*[102]   na   500

Novels published at author's expense

1798. (Miss Holford, aged 17)
Calaf, two volumes   7   500

---

[91] Murray archives.
[92] Advertisement in Somerville's *Chase* (1800), Ac. Price of Somerville from *London Catalogue*.
[93] Graisberry ledgers.   [94] Richard Taylor archives.
[95] J. R. de J. Jackson, *Romantic Poetry by Women, A Bibliography, 1770–1835* (Oxford 1993) 252.
[96] Richard Taylor archives.   [97] *Ibid.*   [98] *Ibid.*   [99] *Ibid.*
[100] Clowes ledger. Wilson was author of the *Poetical Magazine*.
[101] Peter Isaac, ed., *Willam Bulmer, The Fine Printer in Context, 1757–1830* (1983) 91.
[102] Whittingham archives.

Appendix 7 (*cont.*)

Printed at author's expense at a loss of some 400 shillings.[103]

1800	na	na
1825. (Holford's) *Calaf*[104]	na	500
(Mary Barker's) *Welsh Story*		
1798. Three volumes[105]	10.5	750
The author, who took 135 copies, lost about £48		

New three volume novels

For information about the prices and print runs of novels of Austen, Burney, Godwin, Hope, Porter, Scott, Mary Shelley, and Trelawny see appendix 9. Examples of print runs of others

1790s. Hookham and Carpenter novels, mostly[106]		500 or 750
1809. *Caroline Ormsby* (for Colburn)[107]		500
1811. Second edition		500
1810. *Sophia, Or Dangerous Indiscretions*[108]	16	500
1814. De Stael's *Germany*[109]	36	750
1818. *Lionel*[110]	21	500
Most other Longman novels		500 or 750
1819. Ferrier's *Marriage*, second edition		1,500
1826. Tranched down to two volumes	21	1,000
1822. *Lemira of Lorraine* (for Whittaker)[111]		500
1824. (Laetitia Matilda Hawkins) *Annaline* (for Carpenter)[112]		1,000
1825. *Tales of Fault and Feeling*[113]	21	500
1830. (Mrs Sheridan's) *Carswell, or Crime and Sorrow* 500 copies wasted, 500 copies remaindered.[114]	10.5	1,500
(Lady Charlotte Bury's) *Separation* (silver fork novel) **1830.** Three volumes.[115] 300 remaindered	27	'supposed to be' 1,250
(Miss Sedgwick's) *Hope Leslie, or Early Times in Massachusetts* (reprinted from an American edition) **1830.** Three volumes.[116] 421 copies remaindered	21	442

[103] Garside, Raven, and Schöwerling, 1798, 30.   [104] Adlard ledger.
[105] Hookham archives and Garside, Raven, and Schöwerling, 1798: 15.
[106] Hookham archives. Other examples in Garside, Raven, and Schöwerling.
[107] Richard Taylor archives.   [108] Longman archives.
[109] Clowes archive for volume iii.   [110] Longman archives.
[111] Whittingham archives 41,926. See Garside, Raven, and Schöwerling ii, 528.
[112] Whittingham archives 41,926. See Garside, Raven, and Schöwerling ii, 579.
[113] Adlard ledger.   [114] Bentley archives. BL add. mss. 46,674.   [115] *Ibid.*   [116] *Ibid.*

Appendix 7 (*cont.*)

Society romances sold cheaply in parts

1827. (Hannah Maria Jones's) *Rosaline Woodbridge*[117]	60,000 parts printed
1824. (Hannah Maria Jones's) *Gretna green or the Elopement of Miss D – with a gallant son of Mars. With plates.*[118]	each part 500

Minerva Press novels, c. 1815

About 100 titles were advertised, some in multi-volume editions, at about 5 shillings a volume.[119] No print runs recorded.

Bentley's Standard Novels and Romances, 1831 to 1855

For print runs of novels in the series by Austen, Burney, Godwin, Hope, Peacock, Porter, and Mary Shelley and Trelawny see appendix 9. Cumulative sales of some others to 1853, summarised and rounded.
Frederick Marryat, author of sea stories, was, in terms of copies of his works sold, by far the most popular in the series.

King's Own	10,000
Peter Simple	15,000
Mr Midshipman Easy	12,000
Jacob Faithful	11,000
Newton Forster	8,000
Japhet	10,000
Phantom Ship	4,000

Other titles which sold well

Red Rover	8,000
Water Witch	8,000
Works by J. Fenimore Cooper, mainly adventure stories set in North America	
Last of the Mohicans	6,000
Several other titles by Cooper	6,000
De Stael's *Corinne*	6,000
Beckford's *Vathek* with Walpole's *Castle of Otranto*	6,000
Susan Ferrier, several titles	4,000
Mary Brunton, several titles	3,000

Between 1849 and 1855, 180,000 books sold. By 1855 annual sales had fallen to 22,000, having been 56,000 in 1850.

Printed plays

The texts of large numbers of new plays were published in book form immediately after the first performance, in order to catch the market, sometimes being printed on a Sunday.

---

[117] Clay archives.   [118] *Ibid.*
[119] 'New Publications printed for A. K. Newman and Co.' bound in a copy of *Letters of Abelard and Heloise* (1815), Ac.

Appendix 7 (*cont.*)

The usual print run appears to have been 250 or 500, with reprints of the same length, presumably from type kept standing.[120] Occasionally a play did unusually well, such as Maturin's *Bertram*, noted in appendix 9. For other examples, see Coleridge and Godwin in appendix 9.

Music

1811. *Irish Melodies* (by Thomas Moore)[121]   1,000

1812. Another edition   750

1812. *Indian Melodies*[122]   500

Fine Printing with Bodoni types[123]

1793. Gray's *Elegy*   100

1793. Cornelia Knight's *Lines addressed to Victory*   100

1794. Thomson's *Typographia*   175

Gift books and printed albums

Forget Me Not

1823[124]   10,000 sold

The Keepsake

for **1828**[125]   15,000 sold

Literary Souvenir[126]

for **1830**   10,000

for **1831**   9,000

for **1832**   9,250

for **1833**   6,000

for **1834**   5,500

New Year's Gift[127]

for **1830**   5,000

for **1831**   5,000

for **1832**   2,500

The Bijou[128]

1829   5,000

Comic Annual

---

[120] Examples in the Longman and Richard Taylor archives.   [121] Clowes ledger.   [122] *Ibid.*
[123] *Typographia* 313.   [124] Boyle, preface, quoting the publisher's claims.
[125] Publisher's claim quoted by Peter Manning in 'Wordsworth in *The Keepsake*', in Jordan and Patten 49.
[126] Longman impression books. Totals include large paper copies.
[127] *Ibid.*   [128] Whittingham archives 41,825.

Appendix 7 (*cont.*)

1833[129]   2,000
Many gift books appear to have been exported to the United States, and many
from America imported.

Chapbook stories taken into a new children's book industry

Phillips's chapbooks for children, 1804[130]
Blue Beard, Children in the Wood, Fortunatus, Robin Hood, and many of the other old
favourites of the chapbook canon adapted and made less coarse, produced in editions of
3,000.

Works specially written for children

For the children's books by Godwin and Charles Lamb, see appendix 9. Some others.
(Aikin and Barbauld) *Evenings at Home*[131]

1792–96. Six volumes

About ten editions before 1820	na	na
1823. Revised to obtain new copyright	10.5	3,000
1826	na	4,000
1836	5	3,000
1846. Stereotyped		1,500

1860. Plates offered to an American publisher
The book continued to be reprinted throughout the nineteenth century at the rate of
about 10,000 a decade. By the 1890s the price had fallen to 1 shilling.

1807. A translated edition of Fénelon's *Telemachus*[132]	na	5,000
1811. Robinson's *Scripture Characters*, four volumes[133]		3,000
1811. *Blue Beard* for Cawthorn[134]	na	1,500
1820s. Berquin's *Select Stories*[135]		3,000
French edition		3,000
1825. Mrs Hofland's *Daughter of Genius*[136]		2,000
1828		2,000
1825. Many titles published by Darton[137]		4,000
1826. Mrs Hofland's *Son of a Genius*[138]		2,000
1826. Mrs Hofland's *Officer's Widow*		1,500
1829		1,500

---

[129] Clay ledger 1289/3/3/3.   [130] Richard Taylor archives.
[131] Aileen Fyfe, 'Copyrights and Competition: Producing and Protecting children's books in the nineteenth century' in *Publishing History* (1999).
[132] Whittingham archives 41,926.   [133] Clowes ledger.   [134] *Ibid.*
[135] Zachs 336 from Murray archives.   [136] Harris ledger.   [137] Adlard ledger.
[138] Harris ledger.

Appendix 7 *(cont.)*

1834	1,500
1824/5. Mrs Dorset's *Peacock at Home*[139]	1,500
1828	1,500
1831	1,500
1834	1,500
Mrs Trimmer's *History of England*, two volumes[140]	
1827	1,000
1829	1,000

School textbook

1820s. Goldsmith's *History of England*, stereotyped[141]	36,000 annually

Books most commonly produced to be sold cheaply in numbers, later romantic period[142]

	Number	Price per number, shillings
Family Bible	100	0.5
Family Herbal	27	0.5
Pilgrim's Progress	14	0.5
Hervey's *Meditations*	10	0.5
Foxe's *Martyrs*	75	0.5
Plus many other religious and consolatory works		
Tracts (*Brave British Tar, On Drunkenness, Female Martyrs* and other titles intended to recommend the official supernatural and political ideology)		per hundred 2.3
Elegant Extracts	48	0.5
Milton's *Paradise Lost*	13	0.5
Cowper's *Poems*	26	0.5
Arabian Nights	50	0.5
Life of Wellington	72	0.5
Life of Nelson	25	0.5
Defoe's *Robinson Crusoe*	26	0.5
Goldsmith's *History of England*	27	1.0

Old-canon poetry and novels at various prices, usually 0.5 shillings a week.

---

[139] *Ibid.*   [140] *Ibid.*   [141] Phillips papers among Longman archives, Reading University Library.
[142] Summarised from catalogues of Brightly and Childs, Bungay, c 1810; Nuttal, Fisher, and Dixon, Liverpool and Hull, 1820s; Davies and Booth, Leeds, London, Birmingham, Newcastle, Hull, 1820s; Cumming, Leeds, Bradford, Hull; Kelly's, London, 1824; Charles Knight, London, 1830s. Gillyat Sumner collection, Bodleian.

Some print runs

Kelly's *Oxford Encyclopaedia*[143]	4,000
Hume's *History of England*	5,000
History of French Revolution	20,000

Playbills for Covent Garden theatre

1825–7. Print run per performance[144]	250

Religious and moral tracts sold at subsidised or predatory prices or given away free, shillings

Tracts. A few representative statistics[145]

1811. Christian Tract Society print order per title, for early titles, e.g. *Essay on Repentance, Letter from a Son to his Mother, Henry Goodwin*[146]	5,000
Reprints	1,000 to 5,000
1804. Religious Tract Society printed 314,000 copies. By 1815 had 124 local groups engaged in distribution.	
Between 1827 and 1867. Annual production of Society for the Promotion of Christian Knowledge	Rising from 1.5 million to 8 million
Between 1840 and 1850 Religious Tract Society distribution[147]	23 million
1844. The *Missionary*, monthly[148]	40,000
falling rapidly until 1861	3,000

Books written by British authors reprinted offshore in the United States, prices and print runs

Philadelphia Printing

1790s. Guthrie's *Geography* (British textbook)[149]	$16	2,500
Goldsmith's *Animated Nature* (British textbook)[150]	$9	3,000
Wollstonecraft's *Rights of Woman*, 1792[151]		1,500
Bunyan's *Divine Emblems*, 1796.[152]		4,250
Bunyan's *Divine Emblems*, 1808.[153]		3,500
1812 prices in Philadelphia[154]		
Goldsmith and Collins	$0.75	

---

[143] Fell's *Kelly* 153.   [144] Adlard ledger.
[145] Quoted by Altick 101. See also Leslie Howsam, *Cheap Bibles* (1991).   [146] Richard Taylor archives.
[147] Quoted by Watt 23.   [148] Gall and Inglis impression book.   [149] Bradsher 15.
[150] *Ibid.*   [151] Silver 173.   [152] *Ibid.*   [153] *Ibid.*   [154] Noted by Bradsher 82.

Appendix 7 *(cont.)*

(Scott's) *Marmion*		
Lady of the Lake, and *Lay of the Last Minstrel*	$1	
(Scott's) *Tales of the Crusaders*, 1825[155]		3,500
(Scott's) *Woodstock*, 1826[156]	$1.75	9,000
8,000 sold on first day[157]		
(Scott's) *Chronicles of the Canongate*, 1827		8,250
(Scott's) *Anne of Gerstein*, 1829		6,250
(Scott's) *Life of Napoleon Buonaparte*, 1827[158]		12,500
(Austen's) *Pride and Prejudice*, 1832		750
(Austen's) *Persuasion*, 1832		1,250
(Austen's) *Mansfield Park*, 1832		1,250
(Austen's) *Northanger Abbey*, 1833		1,250
(Austen's) *Sense and Sensibility*, 1832		1,000
(Austen's) *Emma*, 1833		2,000
Godwin's *Deloraine*, 1833		1,000
Babbage's *On the Economy of Machinery and Manufactures*, 1832		1,000
A clone from Galignani's Paris edition, stereotyped, *The Poetical Works of Rogers, Campbell, J. Montgomery, Lamb, and Kirke White*, 1829		1,000
(Ferrier's) *Destiny*, 1831		1,250
Hemans's *Songs of the Affections*, 1831		750
Lamb's *Essays of Elia*, 1828		500
(L. E. Landon's) *Golden Violet*, 1827		500
Leigh Hunt's *Lord Byron and Some of His Contemporaries*, 1828		1,000
Atlantic Souvenir (gift book), 1830s[159]		10, 000
The Gift [gift book], 1830s[160]		7,500

New York Printing[161]

(Defoe's) *Robinson Crusoe*, chapbook version, 1795	1,900
Campbell's *Pleasures of Hope*, 1800	500
Murray's *Reader* (British school textbook), 1817	3,000
(Defoe's) *Robinson Crusoe*, 1817	3,000
Chapone and Gregory (conduct books for women issued as one), 1827	2,000
Reprinted after earlier editions	na
Hemans's *Poetical Works* two volumes, 1828	2,000
The Token (gift book), 1820s[162]	4,000

Chapbook reprinting

1800. Philadelphia, *Cinderella*[163]	1,000
Cost of the edition to the printer/publisher, $8.5	

---

[155] Except where shown otherwise, all from Kaser.   [156] For the cost figures see appendix 5.
[157] Quoted in Charles A. Madison, *Book Publishing in America* (c. 1966), 8.   [158] *Ibid.* 11.
[159] Thompson 50.   [160] *Ibid.* 7.   [161] Duyckinck archives, except where shown otherwise.
[162] Thompson 7.   [163] Quoted by Victor Neuburg, 'Chapbooks in America' in Davidson 85.

Appendix 7 (*cont.*)

Books of American Origin	
Charlotte Temple, 1813. Regarded as one of the first 'American' novels, although originally published in London[164]	1,000
American Preceptor (American schoolbook) 1817. A Boston edition of 1811 is described as Forty Second[165]	10,000
Life of Franklin (chapbook) 1817.	3,000

[164] Duyckinck archives.   [165] Ac.

Appendix 8 Periodicals

Journals	*000s of copies*
1711. *The Spectator*, daily.[1]	3
1734. *Critical Review*[2]	1
1734. *London Magazine*[3]	4
Rising by 1739 to	8
plus reprints of earlier issues	1.5
1749. *Monthly Review*[4]	1
Rising to 1.5 by 1753, 2.5 by 1756, 3–4 by 1777	
1753–1756 *The World*, weekly[5]	2.5
1765. *Public Advertiser*, daily[6]	2
1771[7]	3.25
mid-century, *Gentleman's Magazine*[8]	10
1769. *Philosophical Transactions of Royal Society for the year 1768*[9]	0.75
Town and Country Magazine, monthly late eighteenth century[10]	14
Discontinued 1792	
1779. *The Mirror* (Edinburgh) weekly[11]	never more than 0.4
1787. Bell's *The World*, first issue[12]	4
New Annual Register, annual late eighteenth century[13]	7 to 8
1787. *European Magazine*[14]	2.5

Newspapers

1709. Said to be fifty-five regular newspapers appearing in a week[15]	na
1753. Copies sold annually in England.	7.5 million
1760. Copies sold annually in England[16]	9.5 million

Literary journals, 1797, monthly[17]

Monthly Review	5
By 1825, down to[18]	1.5

---

[1] Timperley 596.   [2] Ackers ledger 44.   [3] Ackers ledger 52.   [4] Strahan archives.
[5] Timperley 685.   [6] Woodfall's accounts.   [7] Woodfall's accounts.
[8] Estimate discussed in Ackers ledger 12.   [9] Bowyer ledgers 4784.
[10] Rees and Britton 38. Timperley 795.   [11] Timperley 744.   [12] Morison 8.
[13] Rees and Britton 38. Timperley 795.   [14] Upcott mss i, 97.
[15] Bowyer *Anecdotes* 493, with titles. The figure of fifty-five is arrived at by counting bi-weeklies as two, tri-weeklies as three, etc.
[16] Quoted in *Songs of the Press* (1833) from an official return to the House of Commons.
[17] Timperley 795.   [18] Strahan archives, 488, 846.

Appendix 8 *(cont.)*

Monthly Magazine	5
Gentleman's Magazine	4.5
British Critic	3.5
European Magazine	3.25
Critical Review	3.5
Universal Magazine	1.75
English Review	na
Analytical Review	1.5

The three main romantic period literary reviews

Edinburgh Review

Owned 50/50 Constable and Longman, its London distributor;
after the crash of 1826 owned wholly by Longman

	000s of copies sold
1814	13
1818	12
1824–26	11

Quarterly Review

Owned by Murray

1817, 1818	12–14
1830s	9–10

'We duly received your Review of Lalla Rookh, which was immediately sent to the
publishers of the Quarterly Review; and we hope it will be adopted . . . We shall credit
you with the value at the rate of 10Gs [210 shillings] p[e]r Sheet printed . . .' From a letter
from Longman to the Revd W. Shepherd whom they had commissioned 'entirely *entre
nous*' to write a favourable review, for which he would be liberally remunerated.[19] The
review was not printed.

'The Edinburgh and Quarterly reviews are now to be found in the houses of most of our
principal farmers [in Ireland] . . . and the merits and demerits of Scott, Campbell, and
Lord Byron, are now as common table talk here as in any part of the United Empire.'
Maria Edgeworth, 1820.[20]

Blackwood's Magazine

Owned by Blackwood

1817	4
one particularly successful number	10

---

[19] Longman and Co. to Shepherd, 17 November 1817, and 29 December 1817, Longman
archives i, 100, 173 and 195. To judge from the *Dictionary of National Biography*, Shepherd had no
specialist qualifications for reviewing *Lalla Rookh* other than a willingness to write favourably in
exchange for double payment.

[20] Quoted by Elfenbein 54.

Appendix 8 *(cont.)*

'A friend of mine in whose literary fame I take a sensible interest is about to publish a small volume under the assumed name of B. Cornwall . . . as I greatly admire my friend's poetical genius I trust my recommendation will awaken a kindred feeling in you, in which case you will favour him with an early and kindly Review. By so doing you will confer an obligation on me which I shall be happy to requite, in any other or in the same manner . . .'.[21] William Jerdan, editor of the London *Literary Review* to Blackwood, 1819. A favourable review appeared shortly afterwards.

Other reviews and magazines, romantic period[22]

Pigs Meat, each issue, 1793 (anti-Burke)[23]	1.5
Town and Country Herald, 1793[24]	1.1
Sunday Reformer[25]	1.5
Cobbett's Political Register[26]	
1802–36 under various titles, weekly	
1804	4
1815 said to read in a hundred clubs	
1816 Cobbett reduces the price to twopence	40 to 50
1817	8
Zachary Macaulay's *Christian Observer*, 1806[27]	0.5 rising quickly to 2.5
Edinburgh Annual Register, annual, 1808–1812[28]	1.5
The Enquirer, 1811[29]	0.75
Monthly Magazine, monthly, 1813	4.5
Ladies Annual Journal, 1813[30]	2
Monthly Review, monthly, 1813	4
European Magazine, quarterly, 1813	3
Gentleman's Magazine, monthly, 1813	2.75
Critical Review, monthly 1813	2
Anti-Jacobin Review, monthly 1813	2
British Critic, 1813	2
West of England Magazine, monthly 1813[31]	1.75 falling to 0.5
Eclectic Review	1.5
New Annual Register, annually, 1814, 1815, 1816[32]	1.5
London Magazine, monthly (estimate for 1821)[33]	2

---

[21] Blackwood papers.
[22] Mainly from a letter from Longman to Mr Cassan 23 August, 1813, Longman archives i, 99, 59. Many of the same figures quoted by Timperley 795.
[23] Whittingham archives 41902.   [24] *Ibid.*   [25] *Ibid.*
[26] M. L. Pearl, *William Cobbett. A Bibliograpical Account of His Life and Times* (Oxford 1953) 6071.
[27] *Ibid.*   [28] Constable archives.   [29] Whittingham 41925.   [30] *Ibid.*
[31] Richard Taylor archives.   [32] *Ibid.*
[33] 'we have sold . . . 1,900 of last no. of the Mag'. Taylor to his father 15 October 1821, Taylor archives, Matlock. In 1822 he estimates 1,600 which 'will not pay expenses'. Blunden 140.

Appendix 8 (*cont.*)

Westminster Review, monthly, 1824[34]	3
Phillips's *Critical Gazette*[35]	0.75
Rambler's Magazine, 1820s, scandalous, sales of one issue[36]	1.5
Ladies Magazine, 1831, monthly[37]	1

Literary newspapers

(John and Leigh Hunt's) *The Examiner*, weekly (estimate for 1810)[38]	between 7 and 8
Price in 1809 0.7 shillings of which 0.4 was stamp duty[39]	
Literary Gazette, 1826	5
Of which about 4,000 sold[40]	
Limberd's *Mirror of Literature*, 1823	80
Chambers's *Edinburgh Journal*, weekly, 1832[41]	50
Penny Magazine, 1832, weekly and monthly parts[42]	200
Leigh Hunt's London Journal, weekly, 1844[43]	5 falling rapidly to 0.5

Specialist[44]

1797. *Repertory*	1
1797. *Annals of Agriculture*	1
1797. *Nicholson's Journal*	0.75
1797. *Medical Review*	0.75
1803. *Transactions of the Dublin Society*[45]	0.3
1805	0.5
1803. *Transactions of Royal Irish Academy*[46]	0.5
1820s. *The Lancet* [medical][47]	1.25
1820s. *The Magistrate*[48]	1 or 1.25
1820s. *Cambrian Quarterly Magazine*[49]	0.75
1825. *Philomathic Journal*[50]	0.5 falling to 0.25

For children

1820s. *Juvenile Friend*[51]	1 or 0.75

'Two-penny Trash'

Chapbook size miscellanies, such as *The Tickler, The Nic-Nac, The Bee*, of which there were many in the 1820s.

---

[34] Strahan archives 48,820.   [35] Adlard ledger.   [36] McCalman 225.
[37] Strahan archives 48,897B.   [38] R. P. Howe, *The Life of William Hazlitt* (1947) 151.
[39] Edmund Blunden, *Leigh Hunt's "Examiner" Examined* (1928) 5.
[40] Bentley archives, BL add. mss. 46,674.   [41] Timperley 920.   [42] Quoted by Curwen 257.
[43] Bentley archives.   [44] From Timperley 795 except where shown.   [45] Graisberry ledgers.
[46] Graisberry ledgers.   [47] Adlard ledger.   [48] *Ibid.*   [49] *Ibid.*   [50] *Ibid.*   [51] *Ibid.*

Appendix 8 (*cont.*)

'Some journeyman printers who were out of work tried what a weekly two-penny of mischievous extracts would do; it answered so well that there were presently between twenty and thirty of these weekly publications, the sale of which is from 1,000 to 15,000 each.' Robert Southey, 1822.[52]

Newspapers

	000s
London dailies, 1780s, contemporary claims and estimates	
Total daily production in London	25
Morning Post	5
Public Advertiser (later *The Times*)	3 to 4.5
Daily Advertiser	5
Bell's Weekly Messenger, issue covering Nelson's funeral, 1805[53]	14

Newspapers published, titles[54]

	1782	1790	1821	1833
England	50	60	135	248
Scotland	8	27	31	46
Ireland	3	27	59	75
United Kingdom	61	114	216	369

Newspapers, numbers of copies circulated, millions[55]

1753	7.4
1760	9.4
1774	12.3
1780	14.2
1790	14
1791	14.8
1792	14.8
1793	17

London newspapers, 1833, those above 100,000 only, alphabetical, 000s[56]

The Age	308
Albion and Star (daily)	114
Bell's Weekly Messenger	293
Bell's New Weekly Messenger	118
Courier (evening daily, liberal, falling)	308

[52] Southey, *Life* v, 117. [53] See Morison 50.
[54] Quoted in *Songs of the Press* (1833) from an official return to the House of Commons.
[55] Timperley 806.
[56] Gomme, *Bibliographical Notes* 160, from official returns based on stamp duty.

Appendix 8 *(cont.)*

Globe and Traveller (daily)	573
John Bull (conservative)	124
Morning Advertiser (daily)	610
Morning Chronicle (daily)	772
Morning Herald (daily)	1,286
Morning Post (daily)	318
Record	121
St James's Chronicle (daily)	727
The Sun (daily)	289
Sunday Times	181
The Time (daily)	1,779
True Sun (radical republican)	287 falling
Weekly Dispatch	740

Radical Newspapers, 1833[57]

Poor Man's Guardian	16 weekly
Hetherington's *Destructive*	8

[57] Webb 61.

Information on some of the new and recent texts published, reprinted, and read during the romantic period. With a few authors, the record is quite full. With many others, the information is fragmentary. Prices in shillings, retail before binding.

Jane Austen[1]

Sense and Sensibility	Price	Print run
1811. 'by a Lady'. Three volumes[2] 'Printed for the author', i.e. 'on commission', with Austen or her family meeting all expenses *Sense and Sensibility*. Second edition	Fifteen for the three	na
1813. Three volumes[3] Again 'Printed for the author' on commission	18	na
1815. Still available Appears to have moved slowly and not to have sold out In the early 1830s when the novels were all out of print, Bentley bought those copyrights of which Austen had retained ownership from her family, and the others from the executors of Egerton, her first publisher.		
1832. One volume, *Bentley's Standard Novels*[4]	6	3,000
1837. Reimpression		1,000
1846. Reimpression	5	1,000
1853. Reimpression		750

Pride and Prejudice

1797. Austen's father wrote to the publisher Cadell asking if he would be interested in publishing the novel, but the offer was declined by return of post.

1813. After the success of *Sense and Sensibility*, the copyright of this new title was sold outright.
'By the Author of *Sense and Sensibility*'
Three volumes   18   na

---

[1] Mainly summarised from Gilson. Figures for the Murray editions from Murray archives.

[2] The estimate of '750 to 1,000', quoted in Austen, *Letters* 217, and elsewhere, was made by Sir Geoffrey Keynes who did not have access to the Murray archives or the actual figures for the later books. For a first novel published on commission, the records noted in appendix 5 and elsewhere suggest that a print run of 500 or 750 was more normal.

[3] Keynes suggested 750, but 500 looks more plausible in the light of information now available. The other later estimates commonly quoted, e.g. 1,250 for *Mansfield Park*, also appear to be too high.

[4] The figures taken from the Strahan printing archives are confirmed, with the addition of overcopies, by a note of about 1856 in the Bentley archive, BL add mss. 46,674.

Appendix 9 (*cont.*)

Pride and Prejudice. Second edition

1813. Three volumes	18	na
1815. Still available		
1817. *Pride and Prejudice.* Third edition		
Three volumes	12	na
Remaindered and some copies probably wasted		
1833. One volume, *Bentley's Standard Novels*[5]	6	2,500
1836. Reimpression from stereotype plates		500
1839. Reimpression		1,000
1846. Reimpression	5	1,000
1853. Reimpression	na	1,000

Mansfield Park

1814. 'By the Author of Pride and Prejudice'		
Three volumes	18	na
Mansfield Park. Second edition		
1816		
Three volumes, Murray	18	750
1820. 489 copies remaindered	2.5	
1833. One volume, *Bentley's Standard Novels*[6]	6	2,500
1837. Reimpression from stereotype plates		1,000
1847. Reimpression	5	1,000
1853. Reimpression		750

Emma

1815. Published by Murray, on commission		
'By the Author of Pride and Prejudice'		
Three volumes	21	Probably 2,000
1,250 copies sold in first year		
1818. 565 copies still available		
1820. 535 copies remaindered at 2 shillings		
1833. One volume, *Bentley's Standard Novels*[7]	6	2,500
1836. Reimpression from stereotype plates		750
1841. Reimpression	6	750

---

[5] Strahan/Spottiswoode archives. [6] Strahan/Spottiswoode archives.
[7] Strahan/Spottiswoode archives.

Appendix 9 *(cont.)*

1849. Reimpression	5	750
1851. Reimpression	3.5	750
1854. Reimpression	na	750

Northanger Abbey

1803. The manuscript sold to Crosby for £10 but he did not publish

1809. (before the success of *Sense and Sensibility*) Austen demands that he publish or she will go to another publisher. Crosby denied that he had breached the contract, but returned the manuscript in return for the original price.[8]

Northanger Abbey and *Persuasion*

1818. After Austen's death, published by Murray, on commission from the family. 'By the Author of Pride and Prejudice, Mansfield Park &c'. Austen publicly named as author for the first time.

Four volumes	24	1,750

1818. 1,409 copies sold

1821. 282 copies remaindered

1833. One volume, *Bentley's Standard Novels*[9]	6	2,500
1838. Reimpression from stereotype plates		1,000
1847. Reimpression	5	750
1851. Reimpression	3.5	750
1854. Reimpression	na	1,000

For print runs of early American reprints see appendix 7

1850 and **1851**, after expiry of copyright

Routledge paperback[10]	1.5 or 1	many thousands
1880s. Dicks's paperback[11]	0.5	? tens of thousands

From the 1850s Routledge sold about 2,000 copies a year from various editions, a figure that had broadly doubled by the 1880s, by which time there were other competitors in the market. *Pride and Prejudice* sold more than the other titles. But although Routledge's minimum price was reduced from 2.5 shillings to 2 shillings to one shilling and eventually to 0.5 shillings, sales even at that very low price were not much greater than those of the higher-priced editions.[12] In Victorian times, unlike Scott, Austen appears to have remained an author mainly for the middle classes.

Reverend Hugh Blair

See chapter 14 for the usefulness of Blair's works as a standard for reconstructing the official ideology of the romantic period. Blair published five successive volumes of

---

[8] Austen, *Letters* 174. [9] Strahan/Spottiswoode archives.
[10] *English Catalogue.* [11] Ac. For Dicks see chapter 21. [12] Routledge archives.

Appendix 9 (*cont.*)

Sermons, the first in 1778, the fifth in 1800, all of which were reprinted in numerous editions at high prices and tranched down.

Sermons

Cumulative production 1774–1815, volumes[13]   222,000
Before 1800 Blair's *Sermons* were also extensively reprinted in Ireland for illegal export to Great Britain.[14]

1801/2. A recorded Dublin edition[15]   1,000
Since Blair died in 1800, many of the copyrights fell within the brief copyright window, opening the way to a sharp fall in price.

1825. Tegg's edition, three volumes.[16]   10.5 discounted from 13.5   4,000

1825. Benbow's price[17]   6   na
Much anthologised in old-canon anthologies and school books.
Some examples of abridgements

1808. *Beauties of Blair*, Fifth edition[18]   1,500
'Dr Blair, whose famous sermons were once infallibly to be found on the shelves of every bookshop and library in the kingdom.'[19]

Lectures on Literature and Belles Lettres

A discussion of the nature and purposes of literature. It can be taken, alongside Burke's *Philosophical Enquiry*, as one of the two main statements of the nature of art and literature read during the romantic period. See chapter 14.
Cumulative production 1783–1814[20]   18,500

1825. An Edinburgh reprint[21]   na   2,000

William Blake

Most books were made and coloured individually in response to specific orders.[22] The prices charged also varied. Other copies were sold after his death.[23]
'Blake may have produced few if any more than the half-dozen contemporary copies which survive, and even these few he found difficult to sell.' G. E. Bentley, Blake bibliographer.[24]
With one exception, the works of Blake were not reprinted until the late nineteenth century when he was discovered by the pre-Raphaelites and others. Blake did not become readily available to be read until the mid twentieth century.

[13] Strahan archives.   [14] Some figures quoted by McDougall 173, from legal records.
[15] Graisberry ledgers.   [16] Whittingham archives 41,926.
[17] Advertisement list in *Poetical Works of Thomas Little*, Ac.   [18] Longman impression books.
[19] William Jaggard, *Shakespeare Bibliography* (Stratford-on-Avon 1911) 500.
[20] Estimated from Strahan archives.   [21] Oliver and Boyd archives.
[22] See the discussion in Joseph Viscomi, *Blake and the Idea of the Book* (Princeton 1993) 153.
[23] Summarised from G. E. Bentley, Jr. ed. *William Blake's Writings* (1978).   [24] *Ibid.*

Appendix 9 *(cont.)*

Robert Bloomfield[25]

The Farmer's Boy

1800. 4to	na	500
Published also in 8vo	na	na
Before 1802, five editions totalling about		20,000
1802. Sixth edition, 12mo	4	6,500
1809. Stereotyped.		
1802–22		31,000
1802, 1803. Dublin editions[26]		each 1,000

Rural Tales, Wild Flowers, Banks of Wye, Works, and other books

1803–26	4 to 5	at least 46,500
1830. Tiny paper-backed stereotyped editions[27]	0.5	na
Printed from stereotypes in Milner's *Cottage Library*, recorded sales to 1866[28]		60,000

Edmund Burke

Selected[29]

A Philosophical Enquiry into the Sublime and Beautiful

1757	3	500
1757. Second edition	3	na
1761, 1764, 1767, 1770		
1773. Seventh edition[30]	3	500
1776, 1782		
Out of statutory copyright 1785		
1787, 1793		
1799. Copyright pretenders	5	na
1801. 12mo[31]	na	1,500
1807[32]	na	1,500

Many cheap reprints, of which the print runs are unknown, 1766 Dublin, 1772. 1779. Basle. Berwick, 1796. Dublin. 1803. Montrose. 1812, 1810. Tegg. 1818. 1818. Glasgow. 1820, 1821, 1823, 1824, 1824, 1825, 1827.

---

[25] Mainly drawn from Bloomfield, with additional information on print runs from Longman archives. Prices from *London Catalogue.*
[26] Graisberry ledgers.   [27] Printed by R. Spettigue, perhaps pirated, Ac.
[28] Wroot 169.   [29] William B. Todd, *Edmund Burke, A Bibliography* (1964) 34.
[30] Todd 36 from Bowyer ledgers.   [31] Longman archives.   [32] *Ibid.*

Appendix 9 (*cont.*)

Can be taken, along with Blair's *Lectures on Rhetoric and Belles Lettres*, as one of the two main statements on the nature of art and literature read during the romantic period. See chapter 14.

Thoughts on the Cause of the Present Discontents[33]

1770	2.5	750
1770. Second edition	2.5	1,000
1770. Third edition	2.5	1,000
1770. Fourth edition	2.5	500
1775. Fifth edition	na	na
1784. Sixth edition	na	na

Reflections on the Revolution in France

1790	5	4,000
1790. Second edition	5	2,000
1790. Second edition, second impression	5	2,000
1790. Second edition, third impression	5	2,000
1790. Second edition, fourth impression	5	1,000
1790. Third edition, revised	5	2,000
1790. Fourth edition, mainly a reimpression, but with revisions	5	1,000
1790. Fifth edition, more revisions	5	1,000
1790. Sixth edition, more revisions	5	500
1790. Seventh edition, more revisions	5	1,000
1791. Eighth edition	5	500
1791. Ninth edition	5	1,000
1791. Tenth edition	5	500
1791. Eleventh edition	5	1,000
1792. Twelfth edition	5	1,000
Sold by Dodsley, while the title was in copyright[34]		18,000
Many subsequent editions. Total said to have been sold by the 1840s[35]		30,000

[33] Print runs from Todd and Bowyer ledgers.
[34] Timperley 793. This is a more believable figure than the 30,000 in 1791 alone quoted on page 772. Some figures for edition sizes of Burke's earlier works in Bowyer ledgers.
[35] Knight, *Old Printer* 222. It is not clear to which time period this estimate refers.

Appendix 9 *(cont.)*

Fanny Burney[36]

Evelina

1778. Three volumes, anonymous[37]	7.5	500 or 800
1778. Second edition, three volumes[38]	na	500
1779. Third edition	na	na
1810. An edition[39]	na	500

Evelina went out of statutory copyright during the brief copyright window and was frequently reprinted in cheaper editions.

Cecilia, Memoirs of an Heiress

1782. Five volumes	15	na

Burney sold the copyright for £250[40]

1783. Second. Five volumes	na	na

In 1787 the London publishers successfully sued the Edinburgh printer Anderson for pirating *Cecilia*, claiming as damages the loss caused by 3,000 'counterfeit' copies.[41]

An edition of 1820, three volumes[42]		750

Camilla

1796. Five volumes 'By the author of Evelina and Cecilia'[43]	21 for the five volumes	4,000

'By the author of Evelina and Cecilia'. Published by subscription. Over 11,000 members of the royal family, the titled aristocracy and upper income groups, a few booksellers who ordered more than one set, such as Cawthorn's British (circulating) Library who took twelve, a dozen named subscription libraries and book clubs, and numerous identifiable individual readers such as Miss J[ane]. Austen, Steventon.

1801. First three volumes reprinted.[44]	na	1,000

The Wanderer

1814. Five volumes, 'By the author of Evelina, Cecilia, and Camilla'.	42	3,000

Longman agreed to pay £1,500 for a first edition of 3,000, plus another £1,500 for five subsequent editions totalling £3,000 for 8,000 copies in all. The first edition was sold out three days before publication, but demand then slowed to a trickle.

1814. Second edition	42	1,000

461 copies sold by midsummer 1814

---

[36] Mainly from references in Burney.   [37] Burney iii, 43.   [38] *Ibid.* 174.
[39] Longman impression books.   [40] Garside, Raven, and Schöwerling i, 313.   [41] Strahan archives.
[42] Longman archives.   [43] Strahan archives.   [44] Strahan archives 48,817.

In 1817 Longman 'wasted' the remainder of the second and the whole of the third and fourth editions, 3,000 copies in all.
The book was not reprinted until 1988

Robert Burns

Poems, Chiefly in the Scottish Dialect

1786. Kilmarnock, published by subscription[45]	3	612
1787. Edinburgh, published by subscription[46]	5	2,894
1787. London. Third[47]	6	1,500

Several offshore editions in Dublin and Belfast

1793. London. Two volumes	na	na
1794, 1797, 1798, other editions	na	na

Many of Burns's works went out of copyright during the brief copyright window and became cheap and plentiful. He was the first author to be printed from stereotypes in Milner's Cottage Library. Recorded sales in that series.[48]

1837	10,000
1838 and **1839**	30,000
1840	7,000
1869. Accumulated sales	100,000
1895. Accumulated sales	183,333

Lord Byron

Selected.[49] For the special case of *Don Juan* see chapter 16.

Poems on Various Occasions

1807[50]	Private circulation	100

Hours of Idleness

1807. Printed and sold by Ridge of Newark, near where Byron lived	10.5	?500

[45] Account of printing costs rendered to Burns by Wilson, the local printer, reproduced from the original document in *The Bibliography of Robert Burns* (Kilmarnock 1881) 298.

[46] J. W. Egerer, *A Bibliography of Robert Burns* (1964) 6.   [47] Strahan archives.   [48] Wroot 169.

[49] Thomas J. Wise, *A Bibliography of the Writings in Verse and Prose of . . . Byron* (1932). The production figures were provided by the late John G. Murray from the Murray archives. Other information I have, by courtesy of the Murray family, taken direct from the Murray archives. For the publishing history of Byron's works, see St Clair, *Byron* although some of the conclusions of that article, particularly on multipliers, are modified by the present book.

[50] Leslie A. Marchand, *Byron. A Biography* (1957) i, 125.

Appendix 9 *(cont.)*

Probably printed at Byron's expense 'on commission' After Byron became famous, Ridge issued several unauthorised editions with false dates. Because the ownership of the copyright was uncertain, the book was reprinted cheaply by many publishers from the 1820s, becoming for a time, probably the most widely circulated and anthologised of his works other than *Don Juan*.

Imitations and Translations

An anthology prepared in association with Hobhouse[51]   10.5   750

English Bards and Scotch Reviewers

1810 onwards   6   ?about 20,000
Most were unauthorised editions with false dates as revealed by the watermarks in the paper[52]

Childe Harold's Pilgrimage, A Romaunt

1812. 4to	30	500
1812. 8vo	12	3,000
1812. 8vo	12	3,000
1814. 8vo	12	1,500
1814. 8vo	12	2,000
1814. 8vo	12	3,000

Other short poems were added in later editions. Murray frequently changing the title pages, pretending that there were ten editions when actually there were only six.[53] Many copies of the later editions which were unsold at the time were sold in sets of Byron's *Works* made up of remainders.

1819. As part of a two-volume edition of the whole poem   na   750
In 1823 600 still unsold
'*Childe Harold* . . . is on every table.' The Duchess of Devonshire, 1812.[54]

The Giaour

1813. 8vo, fourteen apparent editions to 1814 with frequent   5.5   12,500
changes to the text[55]

The Bride of Abydos

1813. 8vo, eleven apparent editions to 1815[56]   5.5   12,500

---

[51] Longman archives.   [52] See chapter 9.   [53] Murray archives.
[54] *The Two Duchesses*, edited by Vere Foster (1898) 376.   [55] See chapter 9.
[56] There are two 'fifth editions' entirely reset.

Appendix 9 (*cont.*)

The Corsair

1814. 8vo, nine editions to 1815	5.5	25,000

Ode to Napoleon Buonaparte[57]

1814. 8vo. Anonymous, first three editions	1.5	2,750
An extra stanza was added in order to lengthen the text and so escape the stamp duty on pamphlets.[58]		
Fourth, fifth, sixth and seventh editions total	1.5	1,250
There was no eighth edition		
Ninth and tenth editions total	1.5	1,000
Lord Byron named as the author on the title page		
1815. Eleventh edition	1.5	500
1816. Twelfth edition	1.5	1,000
1818. Thirteenth edition	1.5	na

Lara, A Tale (with *Jacqueline* by Samuel Rogers)

1814. 8vo 7.5, plus three editions to 1815	5.5	9,000

Hebrew Melodies

1815. 8vo	5.5	6,000
Sold out		

Adaptation of *Hebrew Melodies*

'She walks in Beauty like the Night', 'Jephtha's daughter' and other poems set to music and sold as songs by Isaac Nathan.

1829, each[59]	1.5 or 2	2,000

The Siege of Corinth

1816. 8vo. Four editions to 1818[60]	5.5	9,500

Childe Harold's Pilgrimage, Canto the Third

1816. 8vo	5.5	12,000

The Prisoner of Chillon

1816. 8vo	5.5	9,000

[57] Murray archives. The texts after the third all seem to be the same.
[58] Thomas J. Wise, *A Bibliography of . . . Byron* (1933) i, 99.
[59] Adlard ledger.   [60] Murray archives.

Appendix 9 *(cont.)*

Manfred

1817. 8vo	5.5	6,000
Second edition	5.5	1,000
Edition sold out		

Beppo

1818. 8vo Anonymous	5.5	500
Second edition	5.5	500
Third edition	5.5	500
Fourth edition. Four additional stanzas added but without any indication that the text was different	5.5	750
Fifth edition. Byron named as author	5.5	1,500
Sixth edition. Byron named as author	5.5	1,500
Seventh edition. Byron named as author	5.5	1,500
Eighth edition. Byron named as author	5.5	1,500
1822. 2,600 copes remaindered		

Childe Harold's Pilgrimage, Canto the Fourth

1818. 8vo	12	10,000

Mazeppa

1819. 8vo	5.5	8,000
By 1822, 7400 copies sold, 600 remaindered		

Marino Faliero

1821. 8vo	12	4,040
Remaindered		

Sardanapalus, The Two Foscari, Cain

1821. 8vo	15.5	6,099
Remaindered		

Letter to **** ***** [John Murray] *on the Rev. W. L. Bowles's strictures on the Life and Writings of Pope*

1821. 8vo	na	2,500
Byron added six pages of addenda which were included in the later impressions.		

Byron's *Observations upon 'Observations', A Second Letter to John Murray on the Rev. W. L. Bowles's strictures on the Life and Writings of Pope*, was not published until 1832.[61]

The Age of Bronze

1823. 8vo Published by Hunt, probably on commission[62]   2.5   3,000

The Island

1823. 8vo. Published by Hunt, probably on commission   5   3,000

Werner

1823. 8vo   5.5   5,000
4,900 sold in first year, plus eighteen for the press[63]

The Deformed Transformed

1823. 8vo. Published by Hunt, probably on commission   5   ?3,000

The Liberal, a periodical whose contributors also included Shelley, Leigh Hunt, Hazlitt, Mary Shelley and others

1822. First number   5   7,000
'Byron's Magazine or rather Hunt's "the Liberal" has arrived in town, but they will not sell it – it is so full of Atheism and Radicalism, and other noxious *isms*.' Thomas Carlyle from Edinburgh, 1822.[64]

1823. Second number   5   6,000
Only 2,700 sold by 1824

1823. Third number   5   3,000
          Fourth number   5   na

1824. Set of four numbers   21   na

1824. June, 8,285 single numbers remain unsold.
'The expected sale of the work in sets . . . altogether failed. Scarcely a single set has been sold since [September 1823] and not 25 copies in all of odd nos . . . A large number must be sold for waste paper . . .' John Hunt, the publisher.[65]

---

[61] Wise, *A Bibliography of . . . Byron* ii, 35.   [62] *Ibid.* and Byron, *Letters and Journals* x, 158.
[63] Byron, *Letters and Journals*, x, 70, from Murray archives. 'For the press' are review copies.
[64] Charles Richard Sanders (and others) *The Collected Letters of Thomas and Jane Welsh Carlyle* (Durham NC 1970) ii, 190.
[65] Quoted by William H. Marshall, *Byron, Shelley, Hunt, and 'The Liberal'* (Philadelphia 1960) 204.

Appendix 9 *(cont.)*

Collected Works

In addition to made-up collections of remainders, Murray published editions of the collected works. Since he did not own the copyrights of *Don Juan* and some other works until he bought them in 1829 no editions until that date are complete.

1818. Five volumes	2,000
1819. Three volumes	3,500
1827. Six volumes	2,500
Reprinted	2,500
1828. Four volumes	5,000
New edition	7,000

'In almost every under-graduate's room that I happen to enter, he [Byron] seems to have taken possession.' Revd Edward Berens, *Advice to a Young Man upon first going to Oxford*, in *Ten Letters from an Uncle to his Nephew* (1832).[66]

1831. *Life and Works*, multi-volume, stereotyped, each volume priced separately, see below. Initial print run, 10,000 to 15,000, with each volume reissued in impressions of 500 or 250 as demand arose.[67]

1837. Galignani-style, one volume edition, stereotyped Initial print   10,000 copies[68]
   run

25 impressions, totalling 75,000 copies sold between 1837 and 1899[69]

All Byron's works, including *Don Juan*, were continuously available from Murray in a variety of formats at gradually lowered prices during the copyright period and beyond. For the large sales of Byron's *Collected Works* produced after the copyrights expired, see chapter 21.

Thomas Campbell

Scattered indications[70]

The Pleasures of Hope

Campbell offered the book to the main publishers in Edinburgh and Glasgow, including Constable. Eventually the Glasgow University printer Mundell agreed to publish it on the basis that Campbell had the right to buy up to fifty copies at the trade price and would receive £10 if the book were to be reprinted.[71]

1799. First edition	na
1800. Second edition	2,000

---

[66] Revd Edward Berens, 'Advice to a Young Man upon first going to Oxford', in *Ten Letters from an Uncle to his Nephew* (1832) 151.
[67] Strahan archives.   [68] *Ibid.*
[69] *The Poetical Works of Lord Byron, Collected and Arranged with Notes by Sir Walter Scott, Lord Jeffrey, Professor Wilson, Thomas Moore, William Gifford, Rev. George Crabbe, Bishop Heber, J. G. Lockhart, Lord Broughton, Thomas Campbell, Twenty-Fifth Impression (75th Thousand) of this edition* (1867), Ac.
[70] J. Logie Robertson, ed., *The Complete Poetical Works of Thomas Campbell* (Oxford 1907), chronology.
[71] Timperley 664.

Appendix 9 (*cont.*)

Before 1806, nine editions, all of which appear to be separate printings.
'The lover presented it to his mistress, the husband to this wife, the mother to her daughter, the brother to his sister, and it was recited in public lectures, and given as a prize volume in schools.' Beattie's *Life of Campbell*.[72]
At some point, Longman bought the copyright from the then owner. By 1826 they had sold about 17,000 copies. Campbell later tried to reclaim the copyright under the terms of the 1814 Copyright Act.[73]
Many later editions.

Gertrude of Wyoming

Romantic verse tale relating to Wyoming, Pennsylvania

1809. 4to[74]	25	3,000
1810. Tranched down to 12mo[75]	9	2,000
1810. Third edition	9	2,000
Nine editions to 1825, totalling		?13,000

Poems (mainly Pleasures of Hope)

1809. Murray[76]	na	5,000
1836. Oliver and Boyd	5	5,000

Many later editions
Campbell's works were continuously in print, and readily available throughout the nineteenth century. See chapter 21.

Reverend Thomas Chalmers

1817. *Sermons*, known as *Astronomical Discourses*[77]		
Published in Glasgow and Edinburgh. Author		
received £1,800	12	6,000 in first 10 weeks
		20,000 in first year
1819. *Tron Church Sermons*	12	7,000
The book sold badly		
1819. *Importance of Civil Society*	1.5	6,000
Date uncertain, another edition	0.75	na
1819. *A Sermon on the Death of Princess Charlotte*	na	8,000
About 6,000 sold		
1837. *Works*[78]	na	8,000 in first year

---

[72] Quoted by Collins, *Profession of Letters* 83, from Beattie's *Life of Campbell* i, 265.
[73] Owen Rees of Longman to Stirling, 27 March 1826, Longman archives i, 102, 10B.
[74] Longman impression books.   [75] Longman impression books.   [76] Murray archives.
[77] Keir 31. For the reading of Chalmers see chapter 14.   [78] Keir 131.

Appendix 9 *(cont.)*

Hester Chapone

Letters on the Improvement of the Mind. Addressed to a Lady

1773. First published

1780s[79]   several editions of 1,500 each
About 1800 the book became available cheaply as one of the old-canon classics
Between 1800 and 1819[80]   more than 22,000

1824. Chapone's *Letters* and Gregory's *Legacy*, and Pennington's *Letter*

                                                        3   na

1829. Another edition[81]   na   3,000
Chapone's book was frequently praised, reprinted, anthologised, quoted from, and copied
by others. Surviving copies show that the books were frequently given as gifts to young
women by parents, godparents, friends, and by schools as prizes.

John Clare

Scattered references[82]

Poems Descriptive of Rural Life and Scenery

1820   5.5   1,000
'I shall want more of Clare's Poems before you can send them having at shop-shut only 1
copy left. Send another 25 p[er]. Coach if you can conveniently do so, *Immediately.* About
50 more, by Waggon will satisfy the town and neighbourhood which seem disposed to
buy freely.' Edward Drury, the retail bookseller in Northamptonshire, who had
championed Clare locally, to the London publishers.[83]

1820. Second edition, with minor changes   5.5   2,000

1821. Third edition reprinted with further minor   5.5   ?1,000
    changes
'Tell Clare if he still has a recollection of what I have done, and am still doing for him, he
must give me unquestionable *proofs* of being that Man I would have him to be – he must
expunge – expunge!' Letter from Lord Radstock who had begun a subscription to raise
money for Clare.

1821. Fourth edition reprinted with further changes, 5.5   ?1,000
    including the omission of the lines and sentiments
    objected to by Lord Radstock.

The Village Minstrel [volume ii]

1821   6.5   1,000
    By December 1821, 800 sold

---

[79] Strahan archives.   [80] Longman impression books.   [81] Whittingham 41926.
[82] Edition sizes from Chilcot. Prices from *London Catalogue.* Further bibliographic information from
    Barbara Estermann, *John Clare, An Annotated Primary and Secondary Bibliography* (1985).
[83] Quoted in Chilcot 91.

Appendix 9 (*cont.*)

1823. Second edition consisting of unsold sheets
1829. 1,250 sold of the two editions
'nearly £300 of copies unsold'

The Shepherd's Calendar

1827	6	1,000

By July 1829, only 425 sold
1831. Selling 'not above 12 in the year'

The Rural Muse

1835	7	na

Apart from a collected edition in 1873, Clare's poems were not reprinted until the mid-twentieth century

William Cobbett

Author of over 200 titles. His periodical, *Political Register* (see appendix 8) eventually ran to eighty-five volumes. Apart from a ledger of his early American publications, no publishing records found. Most of the information below comes ultimately from Cobbett's own claims and from reports by government ministers and agents all of whom had an interest in exaggerating the readerships. Cobbett, most of whose works were published by himself at low prices, adopted stereotyping as early as 1821.[84] Although the numbers of copies circulated were extraordinarily high, some of the claims should probably be discounted.[85]

Early pamphlets[86]

1796–1800 in America	mostly below 500

Paper against Gold

1815. Various editions, some as 'two-penny trash'
Cobbett claimed 30,000 as two-penny trash.

Address to the Journeymen and Labourers of England, Wales, Scotland and Ireland

1817. Estimate by Sir Robert Wilson	40,000 a week
Total distributed	'above half a million'

[84] The third edition of *Cottage Economy* (1821) is described on the title page as 'Stereotype edition'.
[85] See especially M. L. Pearl, *William Cobbett, A Bibliographical Account of his Life and Times* (Oxford 1953) from which the information is taken except when cited otherwise.
[86] Pierce W. Gaines, *William Cobbett and the United States* 1792–1831 (Worcester, Mass. 1971).

Appendix 9 *(cont.)*

These seem to be exaggerations put about, whether sincerely or not, by those who claimed that Britain was on the brink of a violent revolution.

A Grammar of the English Language

1818. First issue of 5000 sold out in a fornight, 13,000 in first months,   50,000 claimed
1822

Cobbett's Sermons

1821. By 1822 150,000 claimed. By 1828 211,000 claimed

Cottage Economy

1821. By 1828   50,000 claimed

Samuel Taylor Coleridge

Scattered references[87]

1796. *Poems* Sold out in six months	na	probably 500
1797. *Poems* (with poems by Lamb and Lloyd, their contribution not mentioned) second edition with additions.		probably 500
1803. *Poems* (with poems by Lamb and Lloyd, their contribution not mentioned) third edition.[88]	10.5	500

1816. *Christabel, Kubla Khan,* and *The Pains of Sleep*		
First edition	4.5	1,000
Plus 500 on special paper		
Second edition	4.5	500
Third edition	4.5	500
Sold out in December 1817.[89]		
1817. *Sibylline Leaves*[90]	10.5	750

Plays

1800. *Wallenstein parts 1 and 2*[91]   na   1,500
'Very few copies were sold, but after remaining on hand for sixteen years, the remainder was sold off rapidly at double price.'[92]

---

[87] Coleridge makes many references to the publication of his works in his correspondence. See Coleridge, *Letters*.

[88] Longman impression book.

[89] Edition sizes from Murray archives. See also Eric W. Nye, 'Coleridge and the Publishers, Twelve New Manuscripts' in *Modern Philology*, 1989.

[90] Price from a review in Galignani's *Weekly Repertory*, 1818.

[91] Longman archives. Coleridge was paid as translator not as author.   [92] Curwen 91.

Appendix 9 (*cont.*)

1813. *Remorse*, three editions   3   na
'The Wallenstein went to the waste basket. The Remorse, though acted twenty times,
rests quietly on the shelves in the second edition, with copies enough for seven years
consumption, or seven times seven.' Coleridge to Murray 31 August 1814.
Zapolya[93]   5.5   2,000
Said to have sold 1,000 copies in Christmas season 1817.

Prose

Biographia Literaria

1817. Two volumes   21   750

Table Talk[94]

1835. Two volumes   6   2,000
1836. Second edition   6   2,000
The main prose works were reprinted in Bohn's Standard Library in the 1850s, and
apparently kept available from stereotype reimpressions for much of the later Victorian
period. No print run figures found but the initial print runs of Bohn's Standard Library
editions was either 2,000 or 5,000.[95]

Collected poetical works

1828. Three volumes, Pickering.[96]   na   312
Sold out October 1828

1829. Three volumes, Pickering   36   500
Forty-six copies were still on hand (i.e. not yet sold) in June 1832.[97] For the 1834 edition,
1,000 copies were printed, then a further 500 from the stereotypes.[98] For the 1844 edition,
1,500 were printed.[99]
For Victorian editions see appendix 13.

George Crabbe

Selected [100]

1775. *The Candidate*   250
1781. *The Library.* Published by subscription   250

---

[93] Murray offered for an edition of 1,000, but the book was published by another publisher, Fenner. Smiles i, 304. Fenner went bankrupt in 1819.
[94] Strahan archives.   [95] *Ibid.*
[96] John Louis Haney, *A Bibliography of Samual Taylor Coleridge* (Philadelpia 1903) 12.
[97] Unpublished. Toronto University Library.   [98] Whittingham archives BL add. mss. 41,885.
[99] Whittingham archives, BL add. mss. 41,886 and 41,956.
[100] T. Bareham and S. Gatrell, *A Bibliography of George Crabbe* (1978), and Franklin P. Batdorf, 'The Murray Reprints of George Crabbe, A Publisher's Record', in *Studies in Bibliography* (1951–2).

Appendix 9 *(cont.)*

1807. *Poems*, eight editions before 1813   na

1810. *The Borough*, five editions   10.5   na

1812. *Tales*, five editions   12   na

1819. *Tales of the Hall*, two volumes   24   4,500
July 1822, 330 copies sold to remainder dealers at 2 shillings
'Extracts from these poems of Crabbe would be excellent for the poor . . . What a
different use Crabbe and Lord Byron made of the talents God gave them.' Maria
Edgeworth, 1819.[101]

1820. Three volumes   10   3,000

1830. 1,104 copies sold to a remainder dealer at 3 shillings. Tegg bought 722 sets at
2 shillings.[102]

1823. *Works*, five volumes   52.5   1,500

1829. Last 722 copies remaindered at 10 shillings[103]

1834. *Works*, eight volumes,   5 per volume   8,000
Sold out by 1841

1847. *Works*, one volume, Galignani style, stereotyped   2,000
Reprinted in impressions of 1,000 three times in the nineteenth century, but copies of the
final impression were still available in 1950.

Thomas De Quincey

His most famous work only[104]
Confessions of an English Opium Eater
Parts I and II originally printed in the *London Magazine*,   circulation about
     1822.[105]   2,000 copies

1822. First edition in book form[106]   5   1,000
De Quincey had intended to provide part III when the book was in proof. This was
never written but an appendix was included and subsequently printed in the *London
Magazine.*

1822. Second edition[107]   5   1,000

1823. Third edition[108]   5   ?1,000

1826. Fourth edition[109]   5   ?1,000

1845. W. Smith, a cheap edition, perhaps pirated   2   na

1856. 'Author's Edition'

---

[101] Maria Edgeworth, *Letters from England, 1813–1844* (1971) 169.
[102] Noted by Barnes and Barnes 53.   [103] Slightly different figure given by Barnes and Barnes 53.
[104] Mainly from J. A. Green, *Thomas de Quincey, a Bibliography* (1908).
[105] For estimates of production of the main literary magazines, see appendix 8.   [106] Chilcot, 163.
[107] To judge from the second edition of Clare's *Poems*, see above.
[108] Estimate based on what is known of Taylor and Hessey's normal practice for edition sizes.
[109] *Ibid.*

Appendix 9 (*cont.*)

Much altered and extended. Many subsequent reprints of both versions
Routledge, 1881–8   19,000
Many stories that *Confessions of an English Opium Eater* glamorised and encouraged drug taking, and caused at least six suicides.[110] A fictional example of the alleged effects of reading the book is in Conan Doyle's Sherlock Holmes story, *The Man with the Twisted Lip.*

Maria Edgeworth

A few indications only.[111] Edgeworth's texts differ from edition to edition as she consciously altered them in response to comments in published reviews.

Patronage

1814. Author named, four volumes[112]   na   ?8,000
8.000 copies said to have been sold on first day

1814. Second edition, some changes   na   3,000
1,500 copies said to have been ordered but sales slumped after reviews in the *Quarterly Review, Edinburgh Review*, and *British Critic*

1814. Third edition   na   na
Disrespectful remarks about doctors put in the mouth of a character in the novel were altered to approving remarks, in response to comments in the *British Critic.*

1825. In collected edition
Substantially rewritten by the author and her half-sisters   na   na

Halen

1834. Three volumes[113]   31.5   3,000
1834. Second edition
Bentley's Standard Novels, impressions, until 1853.[114]   6, falling to 3.5   6,500

Edward Gibbon

Some recorded print runs[115]

---

[110] See Grevel Lindop, *The Opium Eater, A Life of Thomas De Quincey* (1981).
[111] Bertha Coolidge Slade, *Maria Edgeworth, A Bibliographical Tribute* (1937). Descriptive with no prices or print runs.
[112] Summarised from *The Novels and Selected Works of Maria Edgeworth*, general editors: Marilyn Butler, Mitzi Myers; consulting editor, W.J. McCormack (1999).
[113] Whittingham archives.   [114] Bentley archives.
[115] Figures for the early editions in Strahan archives. Some are quoted and transcribed by J. E. Norton, *A Bibliography of the Works of Edward Gibbon* (1940), and by Nicolas Barker, 'A Note on the Bibliograhy of Gibbon, 1776–1802' in *The Library* (1963).

Appendix 9 *(cont.)*

The Decline and Fall of the Roman Empire

4to, volume i

1776	21	1000
1776. Second edition	21	1,500
1777. Third edition	21	1,000

'My book was on every table, and almost on every toilette.'[116]

1781. Fourth edition	21	500
1782. Fifth edition	21	750

4to, volumes ii and iii

1781	42	3,000
'Second edition'	42	old sheets
1789. Volumes i, ii, and iii		350

4to, volumes iv, v, and vi

1788	63	3,000

4to whole work, six volumes

1789	126	na, old sheets

Gibbon was said to have received £6,000 for the labour of his lifetime. The booksellers made £60,000.[117]

'One of those booksellers in Paternoster Row who publish things in numbers, went to Gibbon's lodgings . . . "Sir," said he, "I am now publishing a History of England, done by several good hands, I understand you have a knack at them there things, and should be glad to give you every reasonable encouragement." As soon as Gibbon recovered the use of his legs and tongue, he ran to the bell and desired his servant to show the encourager of learning downstairs.' Horace Walpole.[118]

4to whole work

1783. First six volumes	48	2,000
1788. First six volumes		1,500
1791. First six volumes		1,500
1797. First six volumes		1,500
1801. First six volumes		2,000
1790. Second six volumes	48	2,000
1791. Second six volumes		1,500
1796. Second six volumes		2,000

Until 1800, Irish piracies obtainable at about half London prices

1801. Second six volumes		2,250
1801–2. Twelve volumes, 12mo	48	2,000

Although copyright on the whole work probably expired in 1802, during the brief copyright window, the price continued to be high during the romantic period.

---

[116] Edward Gibbon, *Autobiography* (Everyman edition 1911) 145.
[117] Quoted by Goodhugh 41.　　[118] *Ibid.*

Appendix 9 *(cont.)*

1807. Twelve volumes, 8vo, plus extra sets of volumes i to vi[119]		1,500 plus 1,900 sets of volumes 1 to 6.
1807. Twelve volumes 'royal 18mo' (a small format)[120]		2,000
1807. Abridgement, two volumes	16	1,000

The abridgements usually omitted chapters 15 and 16, Gibbon's comments on the early history of Christianity, and other passages thought to undermine respect for Christianity and its institutions.
'Sceptical and deistical opinions have of late been plausibly advanced.' French and English history should be read for their moral lessons, but not Gibbon 'who was little of an Englishman'. *Advice from a Lady to her Grand-Daughters* (1808), one of many comments in conduct literature on the dangers of reading Gibbon.

1813. Twelve volumes[121]	84	2,000
1814. With the *Miscellaneous Works*, seventeen volumes		
1820s. Jones's edition, four volumes, also available in 0.5 shillings in parts.[122]	21	na
1820s. Bumpus's edition, twelve volumes[123]	63	na
1825. Tegg's price, twelve volumes[124]	56 said to be discounted from 96	
1826. Bowdler's edition 'adapted for families . . . by the omission of objectionable passages', five volumes	63	1,000
1831. One volume stereotyped		2,000

1838. One volume edition in Scott and Webster's stereotyped *English Classics* series (n.d. c. 1838). An abridgement by Revd Charles Hereford that claims 'That part of the work which embraces religious discussion has been wholly omitted.'

1838. Edition edited by Revd H. H. Milman, four volumes		1,250
1844. One volume stereotyped		500
1847. One volume stereotyped		500
1853. One volume stereotyped		500

Reverend Thomas Gisborne

An Enquiry into the Duties of the Female Sex

1796 to **1822** in thirteen editions[125]	more than 12,500

---

[119] Longmans impression books.   [120] *Ibid.*
[121] Print run confirmed by an entry in Taylor's manuscript commonplace book III, New York Public Library. Taylor and Hessey paid 68 shillings for a share of 1/128 despite the expiry of the legal copyright.
[122] Advertisements in copies of Jones's Diamond Classics, Ac.
[123] Advertisement in copy of *Letters of Junius*, Ac.   [124] Tegg's *Select library*.
[125] Strahan archives. Some of the editions for which no print runs are recorded may be reissued sheets.

Appendix 9 (*cont.*)

An Enquiry into the Duties of Men in the Higher and Middle Classes of Society in Great Britain

1794 to **1824**   more than 4,750

Sermons

1802 and six later editions   9,500

Walks in a Forest (poem on natural religion)

1797, and at least eight editions before 1819   6   about 6,000

Poems Sacred and Moral

1798, and later editions   6   about 4,000

William Godwin

An Enquiry concerning Political Justice[126]

Godwin accepted £735 for the copyright with provision for a further £315 if sales exceeded 3,000 in 4to or 4,000 in 4to and 8vo combined, but it is unlikely that such large numbers in 4to were actually printed.

1793. Two volumes, 4to   36   na
Pirated in Ireland

1796. Second edition, 8vo, heavily revised   16   na

1798. Third edition, 8vo, further revised   14   na
The book was taken by many reading societies
'I have known the circulation of an odd vol. of Godwin's Political Justice to convert a number of Orangemen to rationality who now form the nucleus of an extensive reform in other districts.' From a letter of 1838 from E. Burns, an agent for James Watson's books in Belfast.[127]

1842. Fourth edition, Watson, the radical bookseller,   5   na
two volumes, perhaps stereotyped
Also available in eleven parts at 0.5 or 63 numbers at 0.18 shillings

Caleb Williams

1794. Three volumes   18   na
1796. Second edition, three volumes   18   na

---

[126] Bentley, 'Copyright Documents'.   [127] Letters of E. Burns to Watson, BL add. mss. 46,345.

Appendix 9 (*cont.*)

1797. Third edition, three volumes	12	na
1816. Fourth edition, three volumes[128] Probably printed at the expense of Godwin or Shelley[129]	21	na
1830. Two volumes[130] 183 copies sold off	na	250
1831. One volume, *Bentley's Standard Novels* Seven subsequent reimpressions making a total of 7,250 copies before the series was ended in the 1850s[131]	6, later reduced	2,000
1834. Smith, one volume Produced immediately after the death of Godwin when the copyrights on the early versions expired	na, but very cheap	na
1838. One volume, Allman and Daly[132]	1.5	na
1839. Chambers edition, stereotyped[133] Sold out by 1842	na, but very cheap	4,283
1850. Reprinted Sold out by 1863	na, but very cheap	5,270
1841. *Novel newspaper*, a few pence, probably also available in parts, appears to be stereotyped, probably sold in tens or even hundreds of thousands of copies.[134]		
1853. Allman[135] Many later reprints including	1.5	na
Routledge's *Railway Library*, yellowback[136]	2	na
Warne's *Sixpenny Novels*, double columns, hard-to-read paperback[137]	0.5	na
The plates were melted as part of the armaments drive in 1915[138]		
The book was not reprinted until the 1960s, being omitted, for example, from *Everyman's Library.*		

St Leon (historical novel) four volumes[139]

1799. Four volumes	16	1,000
1800. Second edition, four volumes	16	na
1816. Third edition, four volumes	24	na

[128] *English Catalogue* gives the price as 18 shillings.
[129] Implied by the fact that Godwin had to meet the bills of the printers Hamilton and Davison. Letter of Fanny Imlay quoted in *SC* iv, 673.
[130] Bentley archives. BL add. mss. 46,674. [131] Strahan archives.
[132] Ac, price from *London Catalogue*. [133] Chambers archives.
[134] Ac. See Louis James, *Fiction for the Working Man* (1963). [135] *English Catalogue*.
[136] Advertisement in Porter's *Scottish Chiefs*, n.d., Ac.
[137] Advertisement in copy of Stevenson's *Ebb Tide* (1906), Ac. [138] Warne archives.
[139] Print run from a manuscript fragment of autobiography, Abinger papers. Bodleian.

Appendix 9 *(cont.)*

1831. One volume, *Bentley's Standard Novels*	6, later reduced	3,500
1835. Reimpression		750
1841. Reimpression		500
1850. Reimpression		1,000

Fleetwood (historical novel)

1805. Three volumes[140]	15	1,750
A copy noted as on sale in India[141]		
1831. One volume, *Bentley's Standard Novels*	6	3,000
1853. Reimpression	5	500

Lives of Edward and John Phillips

1815[142]	na	250
1817. Eighty-five copies still unsold, remaindered or wasted		

Mandeville (historical novel)

1817. Three volumes	21	na
Not reprinted until 1992[143]		

History of the Commonwealth

1824. Four volumes[144]	56	First volume 2,000, Later volumes 1,750
In 1827 available at 28 shillings.[145] Never reprinted		

Cloudesley (historical novel)

1830. Three volumes[146]	31.5	1,750
Over 500 copies remaindered		

Deloraine (historical novel)

1833. Three volumes	28.5	na

---

[140] Richard Taylor archives. A huge figure for a novel at this time.
[141] By Sir James Mackintosh, quoted by Blakey 123.   [142] Longman impression books.
[143] *Collected Novels and Memoirs of William Godwin* (1992).   [144] Richard Taylor archives.
[145] Goodhugh.   [146] Bentley archives. BL add. mss. 46,674.

Appendix 9 *(cont.)*

Books for children

(William Scolfield, pseudonym) *Bible Stories*[147]

1802   4 bound   2,500
In a review, Mrs Trimmer, author of a rival adaptation, warned parents 'to examine with
care every abridgement of the Bible, every selection from Scripture . . . since the sacred
Volume itself is frequently employed by the enemies of Religion, as an engine of
mischief'.[148]
Reissued with different title pages, renamed *Scripture Histories*, and still available many
years later.

(Edward Baldwin pseudonym) *History of England*
1806. First edition[149]   1,000

(Edward Baldwin pseudonym) *History of Rome*
1809. First edition[150]   1,000
Some of Godwin's children's books were still being reprinted, still under the pseudonyms,
as school texts in mid Victorian times and later.

The following titles, of which some publishing information has been found, were mainly
written by Godwin's friends.

Swiss Family Robinson (originally published as *Family Robinson Crusoe*)
1814. Two volumes[151]   1,500 each

(Mrs Mason, Lady Mountcashell) *Stories of Old Daniel*
1807, and many subsequent editions[152]   1,000 each

Eliza Fenwick, *Rays of the Rainbow*
1811[153]   2,000

Caroline Barnard, *The Parent's Offering*
1812   1,000

Mylius's School Dictionary of the English Language . . . To which is prefixed [Godwin's] *New
Guide to the English Tongue.*
1809. Copies sold by c. 1825[154]   60.000

See also Lamb, Hazlitt, and Mary Shelley

Play

Faulkener, 1807   500

[147] Print runs from Richard Taylor archives. For the particular interest of this book see St Clair, *Godwins and Shelleys*, and St Clair, 'Godwin as Bookseller'.
[148] Quoted by Marjorie Moon, *Benjamin Tabart's Juvenile Library* (1990) 44.
[149] Richard Taylor archives.   [150] *Ibid.*   [151] *Ibid.*   [152] *Ibid.*   [153] *Ibid.*
[154] Noted in printed advertisement for books published by M. J. Godwin, inserted in copy of *The First Book of Poetry* (1825), Ac.

Appendix 9 *(cont.)*

Late pamphlets

Letters of Verax (1815), and *Letter to a Young American* (1818)[155]   500 each

John Gregory

A Father's Legacy to His Daughters. Conduct book for women

1774 to **1813.**[156] Official editions   19,500
                                                              others na but many
                                                                      thousands

Frequently anthologised and quoted from by writers of other conduct books and school textbooks. There are also editions in which the book is printed with the similar works by Chapone, Lambert, and Pennington under titles such as *The Female Repertory, or Young Girl's Guide to Virtue; The Lady's Library; The Young Lady's Pocket Book and Parental Monitor.*

1836. Tilt's miniature edition[157]	1.5	na
'prettily bound in silk'	2	na
'very handsome in morocco'	3	na
1839. Another edition[158]	na	2,000

Available through much of the nineteenth century. Still advertised c. 1860 by Nimmo as a 'Two shilling Prize Book'.[159]

William Hazlitt

Selected.[160] Many of Hazlitt's writings appeared first in literary journals.

Free Thoughts on Public Affairs[161]

1806. Published at Hazlitt's expense   250

A New and Improved Grammar of the English Tongue[162]

1810. School book published by Godwin's Juvenile Library   1,000

Memoirs of the late Thomas Holcroft

1816. Three volumes[163]	21	1,000
Reprinted in 1852	na	na

---

[155] Richard Taylor archives.
[156] Strahan archives, Longman inpression books, Whittingham 41,926. See also Harlan 196.
[157] Advertisement in copy of Bacon's *Essays* (1836), Ac.   [158] Whittingham 41,926.
[159] In *Books and Authors*, n.d., Ac.
[160] See *Bibliography of William Hazlitt, Second edition revised by Geoffrey Keynes, Kt* (1981), and *Keats Shelley Review*, 1987. Few of Hazlitt's personal papers survive.
[161] Richard Taylor archives.   [162] *Ibid.*   [163] Longman archives.

Appendix 9 (*cont.*)

The Round Table

1817. Two volumes   14 each   1000

In 1815 Hazlitt agreed to an edition of 1000 copies, for a fee of £500, to be paid 'in half a year after publication'.[164]

Characters of Shakespear's Plays[165]

1817   10.5   1,000

1817. Second edition   10.5   na

Quarterly Review attacks Hazlitt's 'sedition' and 'senseless and wicked sophistry'[166]

'Taylor and Hessey told me that they had sold nearly two editions in about three months, but after the *Quarterly* review of them came out, they never sold another copy.' Hazlitt reporting a conversation with the publishers.[167]

A View of the English Stage

1818   12   na

Lectures on the English Poets. Delivered at the Surrey Institution

1818   10.5   na

1819. Second edition   10.5   na

Vicious attacks in *Quarterly* and *Blackwood's*

'I should like to send over an Edition of 1000 Lectures on the Poets, if I thought they would sell for more than waste paper, exclusive of Freight, for we have overprinted that Work. – But perhaps we had better make a short End of them in our own Hands. Taylor, the publisher, to a bookseller in Philadelphia. January 1820'.[168]

Lectures on the English Comic Writers. Delivered at the Surrey Institution[169]

1819   10.5   na

Publishers pay 'a handsome sum' for the copyright[170]

---

[164] Text of the contract transcribed in Stanley Jones, *Hazlitt . . . From Winterslow to Frith Street* (1989) 208.

[165] Robinson 189, Chilcot 69.   [166] Quoted by Chilcot 69.

[167] Quoted by W. Carew Hazlitt, *Memoirs of William Hazlitt* (1967) i, 228.

[168] *Keats Circle* i, 101.

[169] According to Patmore the audiences were mainly dissenters, quakers, and others generally unsympathetic. For examples of the expensive prices of admission to lectures see appendix 5.

[170] Hazlitt, *Memoirs* i, 239.

Appendix 9 *(cont.)*

Attacked by *New Monthly Magazine*
Probably remaindered

Political Essays

1819. Published by William Hone[171]	14	na
1840s. Remainders still available	6.5	na

Lectures . . . on the Dramatic Literature of the Age of Elizabeth

1820	12	?1,000

Stock transferred to Warren who reissues it as 'second edition'

1825. Tegg's price[172]	7.5	

Table Talk

1821 and **1822.** Two volumes.	14 and 16	na
1824. Second edition, two volumes.	28	na
1826. Remainder copies	15	

?1829. Another edition prepared by Hazlitt available from Galignani at 9 francs (7.2 shillings)

Liber Amoris

1823. Anonymous	7.5	na

Select English Poets, or Elegant Extracts from Chaucer to the Present Time

1824	30	na

An anthology, prepared by Hazlitt, with others.[173] Intended to supersede the standard old-canon anthology *Elegant Extracts*.[174] Suppressed by legal action by the intellectual property holders. Most copies appear to have been destroyed.[175]
In 1825 a large part of the book was reissued, as *Select Poets of Great Britain*, in essentials another old-canon anthology.[176]

	15	na

---

[171] See appendix 11.   [172] Tegg's *Select Library*.
[173] Hazlitt, *Memoirs* i, xxviii.   [174] See chapter 12.
[175] This is made explicit in the paratext and in the running titles. One copy in British Library, another in Bodleian. Copies made their way to the United States.
[176] Tegg who sold books cheap, including many in Ireland and the Australasian colonies, Griffin, a radical pirate, Baudry a French offshore pirate.

Appendix 9 (*cont.*)

The Spirit of the Age

1825. Anonymous   10.5   ?1,000

1825. Second edition, text substantially changed, anonymous   10.5   ?1000
Another version available from Galignani at 9 francs (7.2 shillings)

The Plain Speaker

1826. Two volumes (anonymous)   16 each   na

Notes of a Journey through France and Italy

1826. Hunt and Clarke   14   na
Originally anonymous, then author's name stamped on to the title page.

1829. Hunt and Clarke go bankrupt and their stocks are sold
off cheaply.[177]
Many of Hazlitt's essays and lectures were republished in the 1840s at the instigation of his son, and kept in print in one-shilling editions as part of Bohn's Standard Library. His essays on the poets were particularly popular.

Felicia Hemans

Selected. Information from Murray and Blackwood archives[178]

1816 *Restoration of Works of Art to Italy*   na   1,000
1828. 380 copies remaindered

1817 *Modern Greece*   5.5   500
1821. Second edition   5.5   750
1837. 535 copies remaindered

1819 *Tales and Scenes*   6.5   750
1823. Second edition   6.5   750
1837. 238 copies remaindered

1820. *The Sceptic*   3   750
1821   3   750
1837. 230 copies remaindered

1823 *The Siege of Valencia*   9.5   1,000
Sold out

---

[177] Blunden 188.

[178] Information on the early works from Feldman from Murray archives. The print runs of some of the later books I have taken from Blackwood archives, impression book, 30, 839.

Appendix 9 (*cont.*)

1823. *The Vespers of Palermo*	3	1,000
1825. *The Forest Sanctuary*	4.5	750
1828. First Blackwood edition	8.5	1,500
1829. Second edition	8.5	na
1835. Third edition	8.5	na
1828. *Records of Woman*	8.5	1,000
1829. Second edition	8.5	1,000
1830. Third edition	8.5	na
1833. Fourth edition	8.5	na
1830. *Songs of the Affections*	7	1,500
1835. Second edition	7	na
1834. *Songs and Hymns*	7.5	na

Hemans's works were readily available throughout the nineteenth century and beyond. As the poet of the 'domestic affections' she appears to have been one of the most often read poets at that time. See chapter 21.

John Cam Hobhouse

A Journey through Albania to Constantinople

1813. 4to, two volumes	105	na
1813. Second edition, probably reissued sheets	105	
1855. Heavily revised edition on commission[179]	na	500
1818. *Historical Illustrations to Childe Harold*	14	750
Second edition, made from same type[180]	14	1,250
See also Byron, *Imitations and Translations*		

James Hogg

Hogg received little education, except from reading. As a boy, his wages for herding a few cows for a neighbouring farmer for half a year were a ewe lamb and a pair of shoes, 'for shoes I had none'. Hogg's *Memoirs of the Author's Life* includes a good deal of information about the publication of his many books.[181]

The Mountain Bard (poems in the tradition of Border ballads)

1807[182]	10.5	1,000

---

[179] Murray archives.   [180] *Ibid.*
[181] James Hogg, *Memoirs of the Author's Life* edited with *Familiar Anecdotes of Sir Walter Scott* by Douglas S. Mack (1972).
[182] Constable i, 353.

Appendix 9 *(cont.)*

Published by subscription with the help of Walter Scott. Constable, the publisher, told him that 'nobody's poetry would sell' but agreed that if he could find 200 subscribers he would publish the book and give him as much for it as he could. Hogg found 500 subscribers.
Hogg made nearly £300, enough to enable him to buy two farms.

1821. Third edition.[183]	na	1,000

The Shepherd's Guide (on the diseases of sheep)

1807	na	na

The Queen's Wake (romantic poem)

1813	12	1,000

1813. 'Second edition', sheets reissued
When the publisher went bankrupt, Hogg received the remaining 490 copies at cost, which, to Hogg's surprise amounted to less than 3 shillings a copy, but which may have been lower.

1814. Third edition	12	na
1819. Fifth edition	12	na
1819. Sixth edition[184]	12	1,000

Pilgrims of the Sun (romantic poem)

1816[185]	7.5	1,000

Winter Evening Tales

1819. Two volumes, 12mo	14	1,562
Second edition.[186]		1,036

Jacobite Relics of Scotland

1819. Two volumes[187]	36	1,500

Queen Hynde (romantic poem)

1824	14	1,500

[183] Oliver and Boyd archives.
[184] Blackwood archives, impression book, 30, 839. Also Murray archives.   [185] Murray archives.
[186] Oliver and Boyd archives.   [187] Blackwood archives, impression book, 30, 839.

Appendix 9 (*cont.*)

The Three Perils of Man (prose)

1822. Three volumes   24   1,000

The Three Perils of Woman (prose)

1823. Three volumes   21   1,000

Private Memoirs and Confessions of a Justified Sinner[188]

1824. One volume, anonymous[189]   10.5   1,000
Published on half profits

1828. A large remainder said to have been reissued as *The Suicide's Grave*, but no copy has been found.
'Being a story replete with horror, after I had written it I durst not venture to put my name to it.' Hogg's *Memoirs*.

1837. Included in selected *Tales and Sketches*, as *The Private Memoirs and Confessions of a Fanatic*. Heavily bowdlerised to exclude the descriptions of religious fanaticism which are the heart of the book. Not available in the original version until 1924.

Thomas Hope

Anastasius (picaresque novel about Greece and Constantinople)

1819. Three volumes   31.5   750
1819. Second edition   31.5   1250
1819. Third edition   31.5   1,250
1817. Fourth edition   na   750
The publication of this novel, falsely attributed to Byron, marks the culmination of the policy of forcing up the price of three-decker novels. On the first two editions Murray and Hope together made a profit of £1,135.[190]

1836. *Bentley's Standard Novels* edition   6   3,000
1855. Reimpression   3.5   500

John Keats

Scattered references[191]

---

[188] Mainly summarised from the edition edited by John Carey (Oxford 1969). But see also the acrimonious correspondence about money transcribed by David Gove, 'With regard to the Justified Sinner' in *Notes and Queries* (September 2000) 324.
[189] Longman archives.   [190] Murray archives.   [191] The essential basis remains MacGillivray.

Appendix 9 (*cont.*)

Poems

1817. Published by Olliers probably on commission[192]
'Foolscap 8vo'[193]   6   ?500 or 750
Advertised in the *Morning Chronicle* and *The Times*, probably at Shelley's expense.[194]

1817. Stocks transferred to Taylor and Hessey
'We regret that your brother ever requested us to publish his book, or that our opinion of its talent should have led us to acquiesce in undertaking it. We are, however, much obliged to you for relieving us from the unpleasant necessity of declining any further connection with it, which we must have done, as we think the curiosity is satisfied, and the sale has dropped.' Olliers, informing Keats's brother that they are ending the arrangement.[195]

1824. Still being offered at original price

Endymion, A Poetic Romance

1818. April   9   ?500 or 750
Losses on one book to be offset against profits on others
'A few copies . . . have already been sold upon the strength of my recommendation to the booksellers.' Benjamin Bailey, a friend of Keats, to Taylor.[196]
'I have much pleasure in saying that Endymion begins to move at last – 6 copies have just been ordered by Simpkin & Marshall & one or two have been sold singly in the Shop – there is nothing like making a Stir for it.' Hessey, the publishing partner, to Taylor, October 1818.[197]
'My poem has not at all succeeded.' John Keats to his brother George, February 1819.[198]

1821. Still offered at original price[199]
Date unknown. Remaining copies sold as waste paper to Stibbs for 0.08s a pound. He binds and sells a few at 1.5s.[200]

Lamia, Isabella, The Eve of St. Agnes, and Other Poems

1820. 12mo[201]   7.5   ?1,000

---

[192] A suggestion by Robinson. Given the fact that almost all first volumes of poetry were published at the author's expense, the circumstantial evidence which Robinson notes makes his suggestion very likely.
[193] I.e. modest size.   [194] Robinson 188.
[195] Olliers to George Keats, 29 April 1817 quoted by Amy Lowell, *John Keats* (1925) i, 312.
[196] Bailey to Taylor 20 May 1818. *Keats Circle* i, 25.
[197] 23 October, i.e. six months after publication. *Keats Circle* i, 52.
[198] Keats, *Letters* ii, 65.   [199] Blunden 95.
[200] Chilcot 38, quoting Hewlett as the source, but as far as I can see, she does not offer a primary source nor a date.
[201] The usual Taylor and Hessey initial print run. That this is the figure tends to be confirmed by the references to 500 copies as the implied break even point according to the publisher's accounting conventions.

Appendix 9 *(cont.)*

'Hessey has subscribed [received promises of purchase from other booksellers] 160 of Keats – & sold *one Endymion* today.' Keats's friend Woodhouse, July 1820.[202]
'We have had some trouble to get through 500 copies of his work, though it is highly spoken of in the periodical works.' Taylor to John Clare, August 1820[203]
'Of Keats's poems there have never yet been 500 sold.' Taylor to Clare, 1822[204]

1828. Still offered at original price[205]

1820. Despite financial difficulties Taylor buys the copyrights of *Endymion* and *Lamia* from Keats for £100 each, offsetting Keats's debts of £70 and adding £10, so enabling the dying Keats to go to Italy.[206]
'Tell Taylor I shall soon be in a second Edition – in sheets – and cold press.' A message from the dying Keats.[207]

1821. Death of Keats

1829. Taylor and Hessey go bankrupt

The Poetical Works of Coleridge, Shelley, and Keats. Complete in One Volume

1829 (but actually 1830). Paris Galignani.

1835. Reissued without date[208]

1831. The Galignani edition was cloned and stereotyped in Philadelphia and frequently reissued in various impressions until the 1840s.[209]

1835. A proposal to reprint Keats's works turned down by Taylor, the then intellectual property owner. 'I fear that even 250 would not sell.'[210]

1838. Taylor still refusing permission
'Moxon told me that Taylor will neither give a second edition, nor allow another to give one.' Keats's friend Severn.[211]

1840. Taylor gives permission to Smith, a reprinter of cheap editions of out of copyright poets, to bring out two editions in different formats.

The Poetical Works of John Keats

1840. 'Smith's Standard Library'   2   probably more than 3,000[212]
Paper covers, double columns
Now available at the cheapest end of the market

1844. Another issue[213]

---

[202] Lowell ii, 428.   [203] Chilcot 48.   [204] Chilcot 51.
[205] Blunden 93.   [206] Chilcot 53.   [207] *Keats Circle* i, 182.
[208] For examples of the reading of this edition in Britain see chapter 15, 302. For the American clones see chapter 19.
[209] MacGillivray B2, 3, 4, 5, 6,7, 8, 9,10, 14, 18.   [210] *Ibid*. xlix.   [211] *Ibid*.
[212] To judge from the known print runs of similar editions produced at this time by Chambers.
[213] Library of Keats–Shelley Memorial, Rome.

Appendix 9 (*cont.*)

The Poetical Works of John Keats

1841. London: published for the Proprietors by William Smith, 113, Fleet Street
'Royal 8vo'.[214]   5   na

1852. Available at 2 shillings, probably remaindered[215]
'a scanty sale. Remainder copies . . . came early and stayed long on the market.' Sidney
Colvin, 1920.[216]

1845. Holman Hunt, the Pre-Raphaelite painter, comes across copies of first editions.
'These were in mill-board covers, and I had found mine in book bins labelled this lot 4d
[0.33s]'[217]

1840s. The Pre-Raphaelites decide to publish a reprint, but are stopped by the copyright
holder. The copyrights, all due to expire by 1848, were prolonged until 1862 by the 1842
Act.
'I have seen an Announcement of an Edition of Keats's Poems as being in preparation . . .
I should be sorry to be obliged to interfere, but if necessary I must take such Steps as the
Law authorises for the Protection of my Copyright.' Taylor to Moxon, 1845.[218]

1845. Taylor sells an equal right to the copyright to Moxon for £50[219]

1848. Publication of Monckton Milnes's *The Life and Literary Remains of John Keats.* The
corpus of Keats's published poetry is increased by a third. Some of his best poems,
including *La Belle Dame Sans Merci, When I have fears that I may cease to be*, and *Bright
Star* make their first appearance in book form.

1848. Holman Hunt's picture of 'The Eve of St Agnes' is exhibited, turning Keats into a
Victorian poet.

1854. First illustrated edition
After 1850 numerous new editions, many illustrated in Victorian style.[220] Continuously in
print ever since.

Reverend John Keble

1827. *The Christian Year*, copies sold before the expiry of   379,000
copyright in 1873[221]

Charles Lamb

Selected[222]

---

[214] Supplement to *London Catalogue of Books* gives price 5 shillings.
[215] Edmund Blunden, *Keats's Publisher* (1936) 220, quoting a contemporary catalogue.
[216] Sidney Colvin, *John Keats* (1920) 528. Although not a wholly reliable source, Colvin appears to be
drawing on direct experience of seeing the books.
[217] George H. Ford, *Keats and the Victorians* (New Haven 1944) 94.   [218] *Keats Circle* i, 115.
[219] *Keats Circle* ii, 128.   [220] See chapter 21.
[221] Noted by Altick 386 from John Collins Francis, *John Francis* (1888) ii, 193.
[222] See J. C. Thomson, *Bibliography of the Writings of Charles and Mary Lamb* (1908).

Appendix 9 *(cont.)*

A Tale of Rosamund Gray

1798[223]   2.5   na

John Woodvil (verse drama)

1802   3   na
Published by Lamb at his own expense. The book cost less than £50 to print, and Lamb
lost £25.[224]

Works (prose and poetry)

1818. Two volumes   12   na
Probably published on commission[225]
Lamb gave away at least thirty copies[226]

Essays of Elia

Had first appeared in the *London Magazine*, owned by Taylor and Hessey.

1823. Anonymous[227]   9.5   1,000
200 copies still available in 1828
No longer available by 1834

1836. Second edition   na   na
For the print runs of the earliest American reprint see appendix 7.
When the book came out of copyright many editions, including   21,000
   Routledge, 1881–8.[228]

Last Essays of Elia

Had first appeared in the *London Magazine*. For its circulation see appendix 8.

1833. Published in book form.   na   1,000
At some point the copyright of Lamb's works in verse and prose passed to Moxon.
'No *writing*, and no *word*, ever passed between Taylor, or Hessey, and me, respecting copy
right. This I can swear. They made a volume at their own will, and volunteered me a third
of profits which came to £30 which came to *Bilk*, and never came back to me.' Lamb to
Moxon 1833 when legal action was threatened.[229]
'Just as the "Last Elias" were ready for distribution, there has come from Taylor of the
"London", a threat to Moxon of applying for an INJUNCTION, unless he compensates

---

[223] Garside, Raven, and Schöwerling i, 749.   [224] E. V. Lucas, *The Life of Charles Lamb* (1905) i, 224.
[225] Robinson 186. At this time most or all of the Olliers' publications appear to have been financed in
     this way.
[226] References in *The Letters of Charles and Mary Lamb*, edited by E. V. Lucas (1905).
[227] Chilcot 163.   [228] Routledge archives.   [229] *Letters* iii, 357.

him for his copyright. The son of a bitch in a manger! neither to print, himself, nor <u>let</u> print.'[230] Lamb paid Taylor £30 to waive his claim.

Lamb's main works were kept in print by Moxon, who married his adopted daughter, during most of the nineteenth century.

Books for children, written with Mary Lamb, for Godwin's Juvenile Library

Tales from Shakespear, Mrs Leicester's School, Adventures of Ulysses, initial editions of 1,000 copies and frequently reprinted in editions of the same size until Godwin was obliged to sell the copyrights.[231]

Eight of the *Tales from Shakespear* were sold separately for 0.5 shillings, with illustrations.[232] These can be regarded as the first chapbook versions of Shakespeare since the ballad version of *Titus Andronicus*, 1594. See chapter 8 and appendix 12.

Letitia Landon (LEL)

Landon, who wrote frequently for the annuals, especially *Fisher's Drawing room Scrap Book* was amongst the verse authors most frequently anthologised in women's manuscript commonplace books. As far as her full length books are concerned, sales after 1825 were modest. Her total literary earnings over an extremely productive life, before her mysterious early death were only £2,585.[233] Her works encapsulate romantic feminity carried to its extreme in the annuals.

The Improvisatrice

1824   10.5   na

'Aware that to elevate I must first soften, and that if I wished to purify, I must first touch, I have ever endeavoured to bring forward grief, disappointment, the fallen leaf, the faded flower, the broken heart and the early grave.' Preface.

Several editions made immediately from moveable type. At some point stereotype plates were made but the reimpressions were short and infrequent.

1839 edition[234]   na   500

plates melted 1858[235]

The Troubadour

1825   10.5   na

Three editions in 1825. Landon received £600.[236]

---

[230] *Letters* iii, 358.   [231] Richard Taylor archives.
[232] *The Works in Prose and Verse of Charles and Mary Lamb* (Oxford, n.d. 1908) i, xxii.
[233] Jerdan iii, 185. But he has included one-off payments with fees she received annually for editing.
[234] Strahan archives.   [235] Longman archives. Catalogue of Stereotype Plates 1819–1874.
[236] Jerdan iii, 185.

Appendix 9 (*cont.*)

The Golden Violet

Half profits, with an advance of £200, 'altho' it is contrary to the usual practice of the house'.[237]

1826	10.5	2,000
1839		500
1844		500

The Venetian Bracelet

1829[238]	10.5	1,500
1844[239]		500

Romance and Reality

1831 (novel). Three volumes All sold[240]	31.5	1,000

Francesca Carrera

1834 (novel)	31.5	not more than 1,250

Works of LEL

Nonce editions from unsold sheets	na	na
1850. Two volumes[241]		1,000
1853		500
1855. Plates corrected		500

1874. Plates melted
The 1830s vogue for tragic feminine disappointment proved as transient as the butterflies, the blossoms, and faithless lovers, about which LEL wrote, and her works featured in only one of the editions of the romantic poets produced in late-Victorian times when the copy rights expired.[242]

Reverend T. R. Malthus

A few indications relating to his major work only.[243] Malthus's book was continuously revised and updated. The differences among the editions are substantial. The *Essay* was, for example, originally about 50,000 words, the fifth edition, 250,000.[244]

---

[237] Longman to Jerdan, 1 June 1826, Longman archives I, 102.   [238] Longman archives.
[239] Longman archives.   [240] Bentley archives. BL add. mss 46,674.
[241] Longman archives.   [242] See appendix 12.
[243] Mainly extracted from Patricia James, *Population Malthus* (1979). Prices, where given, from trade catalogues.
[244] John Maynard Keynes, *Essays in Biography* (1933) 117.

Appendix 9 (*cont.*)

An Essay on the Principle of Population

1798. Anonymous pamphlet   6   ?500
Malthus writes that he cannot conceive of a loving God condemning any of his creatures to 'eternal hate and torture'.

1803. Second edition, 4to, author named, text much revised   31.5   na
and enlarged. The heterodox passages are omitted.

1808. Third edition, two volumes 8vo, further revised   na   na

1807. Fourth edition, two volumes, 8vo   na   na

1815. Fifth edition. Three volumes, octavo, much revised[245]   42   1,500 plus 750

1826. Sixth edition. Two volumes[246]   na   1,500

1820. *Principles of Political Economy*   18   na

1836. Second edition, posthumous   na   na

Charles Robert Maturin

Bertram, A Tragedy

Performed at Drury Lane, with Kean in the title role, with great success.

1816   1,500

1816. Second edition   1,500

1816. Third edition   1,500

1816. Fourth edition   750

1816. Fifth edition   500

1816. Sixth to ninth editions[247]   250 each

Reverend Henry Milman

Historical verse dramas mainly on religious themes
The Fall of Jerusalem   8.5
Five editions totalling[248]   7,250
Martyr of Antioch   8.5   3,500

James Montgomery

Some of Montgomery's poems concern Christian missionary voyages. Montgomery also wrote and edited collections of psalms and hymns which sold in large numbers. He is sometimes confused with Robert Montgomery, author of bestselling religious poems in the 1830s.

[245] Murray archives. Price from Goodhugh 361.   [246] Murray archives.
[247] *Ibid.* I have not attempted to discover, by examining copies, how far these editions were made from newly set or from standing type.
[248] *Ibid.* Murray archives.

Appendix 9 *(cont.)*

Some recorded print runs[249]

The Wanderer in Switzerland and other Poems

First edition		na	na
Copyright bought by Longman			
1805. Second edition		6	1,000
1806. Third edition			2,000
Montgomery received an ex gratia payment of 600 shillings			
1808. Fourth edition			1,500
1811. Fifth edition			1,500
Eighth edition			1,500

West Indies

1810		6	1,500
1810			2,000
1814			1,000
1819			1,000
1822			1,000
1827 Seventh edition			750
Another edition			1,500
1827. Tenth edition			1,000
1832. Eleventh edition			500

The World before the Flood

1813. 8vo		9	1,000
1813. Second edition			1,500
1814. Third edition			1,500
Fourth edition			1,500
1818. Fifth			1,500
1822			1,000
1826. Seventh edition			1,000
1829. Eighth edition			1,000

Greenland

1819. 8vo		8	1,500
Third edition			750

---

[249] All from Longman impression books.

Appendix 9 *(cont.)*

Songs of Zion

1822	5	1,500
Second edition		750
1827. Third edition		750
'Works'		
1827. Seventh edition		1,000

Pelican Island (about Australia)

1827	8	1,000
1827. Second edition, 12mo		1,000
1827. Third edition		1,000
Montgomery's works were occasionally reprinted later		

Thomas Moore

Little's Poems

1812[250]	na	2,000
1817. Another edition[251]	na	2,000

Intercepted Letters, or Two-Penny Post Bag, 'by Thomas Brown'

1814. For Murray edition[252]	na	3,000
1818. Another edition[253]	na	1,000

Lalla Rookh

1817. 4to	42	1,000
Two further impressions of 750 appear to have been taken		1,500
1817. Second edition, quarto, included in the above figures		
1817. Third edition, 8vo	14	3,000
1817. Fourth edition, 8vo	14	1,000
1817. Fifth edition, 8vo	14	1,000
1817. Sixth edition, 8vo	14	1,500
1818. Seventh, Eighth, Ninth (perhaps a single impression), 8vo editions	14	3,000
1820. Tenth edition, 8vo	14	1,500
1821. Eleventh edition, 8vo	14	1,500

[250] Whittingham archives 41,925.   [251] *Ibid.* 41,926.   [252] Clowes ledger.
[253] Whittingham 41,926.

Appendix 9 *(cont.)*

1824. Twelfth edition, 8vo	14	1,500
1820s. Dugdale's pirated edition	na but not more than 1 to 2s	na
1825. Thirteenth edition, 8vo	14	2,000
1827. Fourteenth edition, 8vo	14	2,000

Tranched down again but without any great increase in the expected size
of the market.

1829. Fifteenth edition, 12mo[254]	5	2,000
1832. Sixteenth edition, 12mo	5	2,000
Seventeenth edition, 8vo		750
1835. 12mo	na	500

Many later editions, including local and foreign pirates.
Stereotype plates of an 8vo edition of the text were made in 1851 and sent
for melting in 1871.[255]
The 1855 *London Catalogue of Books* offered

16mo	5	na
32mo	2.5	na

1859, by which time the title was out of copyright, Gall and Inglis edition[256]

	1.5	3,100
1859. Routledge edition	1.5	na
1874. Another Routledge edition[257]	na	4,000

1817. Westall's *Illustrations to Lalla Rookh*
Engravings designed to be inserted in all three formats of the book. About 1,500 sets
appear to have been sold in the first few years after 1817. These reinforce the orientalism of
the texts.

The Loves of the Angels

Moore playfully included scenes of erotic love between human beings and angels.

1823. First edition, 8vo	9	3,000
second, third, fourth, fifth editions 1,000 each	9	4,000
1824. Dugdale's pirated edition[258]	1.5	na

Life of Sheridan[259]

1825. 4to	na	1,000
1825. Second edition, 8vo	31.5	1,500

---

[254] Format description used in the British Library catalogue. The Longman archive says foolscap 8vo,
a similarly small format.
[255] Longman archives. Catalogue of Stereotype Plates 1819–1874.
[256] Gall and Inglis archives.   [257] Routledge archives.
[258] Advertised on cover of Dugdale's edition of *The Poetical Works of Thomas Little* (1824), Ac.
[259] Longman archives.

Appendix 9 (*cont.*)

Three more editions in 8vo		4,000

Letters and Journals of Lord Byron, with Notices of his Life

1830/31. The 'authorised biography' first published in two volumes 4to.	84	1,750

An extremely high price. 1,050 sets were remaindered to Tegg[260]
Later reprinted and stereotyped in one volume and keep
  in print for most of the nineteenth century

1854. *Poetical Works*, in one volume, Galignani style, stereotyped, first impression[261]		2,000

Hannah More

One of the most prolific and commercially most successful authors of the romantic period. Selected titles only.[262] More was also responsible for the Cheap Repository Tracts, many of which she wrote.[263]

Strictures on the Modern System of Female Education

1799. Two volumes	12	1,000
By 1801, eight editions[264]		11,000
1799. *Remarks on the Present Mode of Educating Females; Being a Copious Abridgement of Miss Hannah More's Strictures*	na	na

A rare instance of an abridgement, presumably authorised by the intellectual property owners

Hints Towards Forming the Character of a Young Princess

1805	na	na

Several editions. More emphasises the importance of studying ancient and British history, but Hume to be read only with extreme caution, 'a serpent under a bed of roses.' She recommends memorising 'one select passage, one weighty sentence, one striking precept' (i.e. *sententiae*) from a range of books whose titles she lists. Novels are fabrications not knowledge, and some travel books are 'interlarded with infidelity'.

Coelebs in Search of a Wife (a conduct book in the form of a novel, with much advice on reading and its dangers)

1808. Two volumes	12	1,000
Between 1808 and 1826		14,500

---

[260] Noted by Barnes and Barnes 53.   [261] Strahan archives.
[262] Production figures from Strahan archives. Prices from *London Catalogue*. See also Roberts.
[263] See chapter 17.
[264] Preface to *Remarks on the Present Mode of Educating Females; Being a Copious Abridgement of Miss Hannah More's Strictures* (1799).

Appendix 9 *(cont.)*

Allegedly in sixteen editions, but the fourth, sixth, eighth, and tenth were not genuine editions.[265] Tranched down to 12mo in 1809

Practical Piety; or The Influence of the Religion of the Heart on the Conduct of Life

1810. Two volumes   10.5   1,000
Between 1810 and 1825 19,000 copies were printed in fourteen editions. Reading the works of Gibbon condemned

Moral Sketches of Prevailing Opinions and Manners, Foreign and Domestic; with Reflections on Prayer

1819   9   1,500
In the first two years 8,500 copies were produced in nine alleged editions

Amelia Opie, previously Alderson

Some indications[266]

Poems

1804–10. Six editions	6	5,000

Father and Daughter, A Tale

1804–24. Nine editions	4.5	over 7,000

Adeline Mowbray

1804. Three volumes, a novel with comments on Wollstonecraft and Godwin	13	2,000
1810. 'Third' edition	na	500

Simple Tales

1806. Four volumes	21	2,000
1809. Four volumes. 'Third'	21	1,000
1815. Four volumes. Fourth edition	21	500

Warrior's Return

1808	na	2,000

Valentine's Eve

1815. Three volumes	21	2,000

[265] Most of the editions were of 1,000 copies. When the publisher ordered an edition of 1,500 or 2,000 copies, he sometimes counted it as two. This practice is made explicit in the records of the printing of More's *Moral Sketches*.
[266] Longman impression books, confirmed and added to, in some cases, by Richard Taylor archives.

Appendix 9 (*cont.*)

Tales of Real Life		
1815. Third edition[267]	18	500
New Tales		
1818. Four volumes	28	2,000
1818. Second edition	28	1,000
Tales of the Heart		
1820. Four volumes	28	2,500
Madeline		
1822. Two volumes	14	1,500
Temper		
Second called third. Three volumes	21	1,000

Thomas Paine

Only a few reliable records found. Although the number of copies produced was unusually large, and the circulation unusually wide, some of the claims and estimates made and repeated, such as the 'many hundreds of thousands' of copies of *The Rights of Man* said to have been 'rapidly sold' after 1792, the '200,000 copies sold in the first year', mentioned in a contemporary pamphlet, and the 'hundreds of thousands of copies' [which made Paine's writings known] 'in every village on the globe where the English language is spoken' defy credibility when compared with what is recoverable from archival sources.[268]

The Rights of Man		
1791	2.5	na
The Rights of Man, Part Two		
1792	2.5	na

---

[267] Richard Taylor archives.

[268] The exaggerations seem to have begun with a remark in *Impartial Memoirs of the Life of Thomas Paine* (1793) quoted by Conway 141, and in a remark by Thomas Clio Rickman, *The Life of Thomas Paine* (Cousins's edition 1840s) 5, repeated by Conway 116. Although it is possible that editions have disappeared without trace, I have come across few, if any singleton survivors, as is the case, for example, with Byron's *Don Juan*, for which see chapter 16.

Appendix 9 (*cont.*)

The Rights of Man

1790s. Several editions   0.5   ?more than 20,000
'The original edition of the First and Second Parts of the RIGHTS OF MAN, having been expensively printed, (in the modern style of printing pamphlets, so that they might be bound up with Mr Burke's Reflections on the French Revolution,) the high price precluded the generality of the people from purchasing; and many applications were made to me from various parts of the country to print the work in a cheaper manner. The people of Sheffield requested leave to print two thousand copies for themselves, with which request I immediately complied. The same request came to me from Rotherham, from Leicester, from Chester, from several towns in Scotland; and Mr James Mackintosh, author of *Vindiciae Gallicae*, brought me a request from Warwickshire, for leave to print ten thousand copies in that county. I had already sent a cheap edition to Scotland; and finding the applications increase, I concluded that the best method of complying therewith, would be to print a very numerous edition in London, under my own direction, by which means the work would be more perfect, and the price be reduced lower than it would be by *printing* small editions in the country, of only a few thousands each.[269]
'French affairs [Burke] & the rights of Man engross all attention.' Murray, writing to Calcutta, October 1792.[270]
Johnson, Symonds, Phillips, Robinson, Holt of Newark, and other booksellers were imprisoned, some for as long as for two years, for selling *The Rights of Man, Part One.*

1817. Carlile discovers 900 copies unsold when Symonds went to prison
Other editions, 1819, 1820, 1821, 1826, 1837

1823. Copies in stock when Carlile's shop raided[271]   1,015

1792. *Paine's Political and Moral Maxims, Selected from the Fifth edition of Rights of Man Parts I and II by a Freeborn Englishman*
A low price digest

Letter to . . . Mr Secretary Dundas

1792[272]   0.3   1,000
Printed for distribution to its regional branches by the   (said to be 12,000)
   Society for Constitutional Information[273]
William Holland, a bookseller, was imprisoned for one year and required to pay fines and give securities for selling *Address to Addressers*.[274] Symonds, another bookseller, was sentenced to a further year and further fines; Ridgeway was sentenced to two years.

The Age of Reason, Part the First[275]

1795[276]   0.5   1,000

---

[269] See *The Writings of Thomas Paine*, edited by Moncure Daniel Conway (1895) iii, 64.
[270] Quoted by Zachs 229.   [271] *The Republican*, 21 February 1823.
[272] Whittingham archives 41,901 and 41,902. 'Paine's letters'.   [273] Webb 38.
[274] Timperley 777.   [275] Prices printed on surviving copies.
[276] Whittingham archives 41,902. The exact nature of the different editions at different prices is not clear, but the archives suggest that only 3,000 copies were produced in all.

Appendix 9 (*cont.*)

The Age of Reason, Part the Second

1795   2.5   1,000
'Mr Paine has written a second part. Mr Stone of Paris has sent me some of the copy. He
is printing a very large impression to send to America, but wants to sell me the copy for
English sale, not considering that the author being an outlaw can give no title and that
anyone may reprint it here.' Joseph Johnson, publisher to Joseph Priestley, September
1795.[277]
Second edition   1   1,000

The Age of Reason

Cheap edition by Eaton   0.5   na
'Infidelity is making rapid strides among us, especially among the young people of the
rational dissenters. Attacks on revelation are read with avidity, defences with indifference
if at all.' Joseph Johnson, the publisher, to his agent in the United States, sending fifty
copies of Lindsay's reply to *The Age of Reason*, 1796. Lindsay had given away nearly a third
of the edition of 1,000 copies.[278]

The Age of Reason, Part the Third

1812   2   na
It is not certain that this work is by Paine. The publisher Eaton, a veteran of the
persecutions of the 1790s, was prosecuted, convicted, imprisoned for blasphemous libel,
and stood in the public pillory, the last time in British history, so far, that this punishment
has been applied.

The Age of Reason[279]

1818. Carlile   6   1,000

1819. Carlile   various prices as low as 2.5   3,000

1819. Carlile   cheap parts   10,000
Besides Carlile, other publishers began to reprint Paine's works in a variety of formats and
editions, as collected works, individually, and in parts, with portraits, life, and other
related material, establishing Paine as the core author of the newly emerging radical
canon. See chapter 16.

Decline and Fall of the English System of Finance

1819–21. Carlile sells[280]   5,000

---

[277] Joseph Johnson letterbook, NYPL.   [278] *Ibid.*
[279] Information kindly supplied by Iain McCalman.
[280] R. Carlile, *Life of Tom Paine* (1821) 21. Information kindly supplied by Iain McCalman.

Appendix 9 *(cont.)*

Age of Reason

1820s. Benbow sells before 1823   'some thousands'
Paine's works were available at cheap prices during most of the early nineteenth century.

Reverend William Paley

Principles of Moral and Political Philosophy

1785. Not so much an original work as a conduct text book. Paley, although an untried author, received £1,000
By 1809 the book was in its seventeenth edition, with many editions, abridgements, and teaching texts available cheaply later.

1824. A Tegg edition[281]   na   1,500

A View of the Evidences of Christianity

1794. Two volumes   12   na
By 1819 the book was in its nineteenth edition.   ?20,000

1820. Available from Tegg[282]   9

1824. Available from the London consortium[283]   4.5

1824. A Tegg edition[284]   na   1,500
The book was later stereotyped by the Religious Tract Society
'Superficial readers had been dazzled by the splendid sophistries of Volney, and deluded by the imposing boldness of Paine. The whole hierarchy of the church, thus attacked in its very foundations by the champions of infidelity, and so amply provided with the means of remunerating its defenders, could not, therefore, overlook the well-timed publication of a work, popular in its execution, in which the truth and authenticity of the scriptures were so ably enforced: hence, the services of Mr Paley were at length crowned with a liberal, but well-earned, and by no means excessive reward [a bishopric].'[285] G. W. Meadley, *Memoirs of William Paley* (1809).

Natural Theology, or Evidences of the Existence and Attributes of the Deity

1802. First edition[286]   na   1,000

1802. Second, third, and fourth editions   na   each 1,000

1803. Fifth and sixth editions   na   together 2,000
Eighteen editions by 1818, tranched down from 12 to 7 shillings

1810. An edition.[287]   10.5   2,000
Total production of the order of   ?35,000

---

[281] Whittingham archives 41,926.
[282] Advertised on copy of Blair's *Sermons*, three volumes (1820), Ac.
[283] Advertised on copy of Herbert's *Poems* (1824), Ac.   [284] Whittingham 41,926.
[285] G. W. Meadley, *Memoirs of William Paley* (1809) 117.
[286] First five editions from Richard Taylor archives.   [287] Longman impression books.

Appendix 9 *(cont.)*

1820. Tegg's price	10.5s boards[288]	
1824. Tegg's edition[289]	6 said to be discounted from 9[290]	1,500
1825. Another Tegg edition[291]		1,500

Sermons

1808. Third edition[292]	10.5	2,000
1809. Fourth edition		2,000
By 1815, an eleventh edition		
1823. Tegg's edition[293]	4.5	1,500

Horae Paulinae

1810	8	1,500
1823. Tegg's edition[294]	4.5	1,500

Beauties of Paley

1810. Anthology	4.5	1,500

Paley's works were available, through cheap editions, anthologies, and abridgements, to a wide readership. As with Blair's *Sermons*, Paley's books were used by other churchmen, by teachers, and by others in authority in preparing their sermons and on other occasions. 'Paley, so little appreciated now, was for a generation or more an intellectual influence on Cambridge only second to Newton.' John Maynard Keynes, 1933.[295]

Thomas Love Peacock

Selected. Surviving evidence scanty[296]

Verse

All of Peacock's volumes of poetry named him as the author on the title page

Palmyra

1805	7	na

Published at author's expense on commission[297]

---

[288] Advertised on copy of Blair's *Sermons*.   [289] Whittingham archives 41,926.
[290] Tegg's *Select Library.* 1825 8vo. Ac.   [291] Whittingham 41,926.   [292] Longman impression books.
[293] Whittingham archives 41,926.   [294] *Ibid.*
[295] John Maynard Keynes, *Essays in Biography* (1933) 108.
[296] Mainly drawn from *The Halliford Edition of the Works of Thomas Love Peacock*, edited by H. F. B. Brett-Smith and C. E. Jones (1834), and Bill Read, 'The Critical Reputation of Thomas Love Peacock, with an annotated enumerative bibliography of works by and about Peacock from February 1800 to June 1958', Dissertation, Boston University Graduate School.
[297] Evident from the reference in a letter quoted in the Halliford edition of *The Works* viii, 188. It seems likely that all Peacock's poems were published at author's risk and lost money.

Appendix 9 *(cont.)*

The Genius of the Thames

1810   7   na
Peacock, in financial distress, is granted 420 shillings by
    Royal Literary Fund.[298]

1812. Second edition heavily revised[299]   7   na

1817. Remaining sheets reissued with new title page   5   na

The Philosophy of Melancholy

1812   18   na
Not reprinted until the twentieth century
In May 1812 Peacock was deep in debt, said to be on the verge of suicide, and rescued by
further grants from the Royal Literary Fund.[300]
'His literary productions have wholly failed.' Thomas Hookham, Peacock's publisher,
who also owned a circulating library, applying to the Royal Literary Fund for a third
grant, May 1813.
Thereafter Peacock was supported by Shelley until he took up a paid appointment at the
East India Office in 1819.

Rhododaphne, or The Thessalian Spring

1818. Anonymous   7   na
Shelley wrote a favourable review but, as far as is known,
    it was not printed.

Novels

None of Peacock's novels originally named him as the author

Headlong Hall

1816. One volume   6   na

1816. Second edition   6   na

1822. Third edition   6   na

Melincourt

1817. Three volumes, 'By the author of Headlong Hall'   18   na
By 1831 out of print[301]

1856. Reprinted as a yellow back   ?2   na

---

[298] See Nicholas A. Joukovsky, 'Peacock before Headlong Hall' in *Keats–Shelley Memorial Bulletin*,
    1985.
[299] A note of 1812 among the Constable archives, 864, records 72 copies of *Genius of the Thames* at 4/7,
    making £16/10, perhaps a reference to Ballantyne's sales.
[300] See Nicholas A. Joukovsky, 'Peacock before Headlong Hall' in *Keats–Shelley Memorial Bulletin*,
    1985.
[301] Advertisement in *Crotchet Castle* (1831).

Appendix 9 (*cont.*)

Nightmare Abbey

1818. One volume, 'By the author of Headlong Hall'   6.5   na
By 1831 out of print.[302]

Maid Marion

1822. One volume, 'By the author of Headlong Hall'   7   na
By 1831 out of print.[303]

The Misfortunes of Elphin

1829. One volume, 'By the author of Headlong Hall'[304]   7   750

Crotchet Castle

1831. One volume, 'By the author of Headlong Hall'[305]   7.5   750

Gryll Grange

1861. One volume, 'By the author of Headlong Hall'   7.5   na
Had appeared the previous year in *Fraser's Magazine*
Bentley's Standard Novels edition (*Headlong Hall, Nightmare Abbey, Maid Marian*, and *Crotchet Castle*)

1837. One volume   6   3,000
Maintaining the convention that poetry was written by named authors and novels by anonymous piece workers, Peacock asked not to be named. 'I thought I might very fitly preserve my own impersonality', he wrote,' having never intruded on the personality of others.' However, Bentley used Peacock's name in the advertisements printed on the endpapers.[306] Peacock reluctantly provided a preface signed 'The author of Headlong Hall', in which he declared that 'an old friend assures me that to publish a book without a preface is like entering a drawing-room without making a bow.'
No later impressions before the series ended in the 1850s.[307]
Apart from the four novels reprinted by Bentley, Peacock's works were not readily available until his *Collected Works* were published in three volumes in 1875.
'. . .the discovery in a warehouse about the year 1870 of a considerable stock of the first editions of Peacock . . . which were sold off at a few shillings each'. The editor of Peacock's *Collected Works*, 1934.

Robert Pollok

Born in 1798 near Glasgow to a family of farmers, Pollok was trained as a cabinet maker. After taking his degree at Glasgow University, he spent five years attending the divinity

---

[302] *Ibid.*   [303] *Ibid.*   [304] Edition size from Adlard ledger.   [305] *Ibid.*
[306] See preface to *Bentley's Standard Novels* edition.   [307] Strahan archives.

Appendix 9 (*cont.*)

college of the United Secessionist Church of Scotland. He wrote prose tales for children whose copyrights he sold for £15 and £21. At the age of twenty-seven, suffering from rheumatic fever, he read Byron's *Darkness*, and determined to write an epic poem to combat what he saw as its despairing sentiments. *The Course of Time*, in blank verse, was written over two years. Although the main theme is primarily religious, some of the poem is personal in the style of Wordsworth's *The Excursion* which occasionally it resembles. The book was an instant success.

'[Pollok] like the royal eagle, soars in the very path of descending light, towards the eternal sun, He is erect and triumphant, yet withal also pure and tender that he is the very poet of my heart.'[308]

Plans were made to enable Pollok to go to Italy for the sake of his health as Keats had done, but he died, at the age of twenty-nine, six months after the publication of his poem.[309]

The Course of Time

1827.[310]	10.5	750
Published by Blackwood on the basis of half profits, author retaining copyright.		
First eighteen months	na	12,000
First ten editions to 1830[311]	na	17,750
'His Immortal Poem is his Monument'. Inscription on Pollok's grave.		
By 1869 copies sold[312]		78,000
A later undated edition claim for copies sold		84,000

Jane Porter

A few indications[313]

Thaddeus of Warsaw

1805. Four volumes	18	500
1805. Second edition, four volumes	18	500
1805. Third edition, four volumes	18	500
1806. Fourth edition, four volumes	18	1,000
1809. Fifth edition, four volumes	18	750
Bentley's Standard Novels edition, 1830s to 1850s[314]		7,000

Hungarian Brothers

1808. Second edition, three volumes	16.5	750
Bentley's Standard Novels edition, 1830s to 1850s[315]		3,000

---

[308] Emma Tatham, quoted by Cruse, *Victorians* 68.
[309] Abridged from the memoir attached to later editions. More details in Keir.
[310] Blackwood archives, impression book, 30, 839.   [311] *Ibid.*
[312] Altick 387 quoting Margaret Oliphant, *Annals of a Publishing House* (1897) ii, 93.
[313] All from Longman impression books.   [314] Bentley archives.   [315] *Ibid.*

Appendix 9 *(cont.)*

Scottish Chiefs, A Romance

1810. Five volumes	35	2,000
Bentley's Standard Novels edition, 1830s to 1850s[316]		6,000

Ann Radcliffe

Most of Radcliffe's tales of terror, which always turn out to have a non-supernatural explanation, were first published anonymously in the 1790s. A few indicators.[317]

Romance of the Forest

1791. Three volumes, by 'the authoress of "A Sicilian Romance" &c'.[318]	9	750
Several later editions, including		
1806 edition, three volumes[319]	15	1,000

Mysteries of Udolpho

1794. Four volumes	20	1306
1794, 1795. Four volumes	na	1310
1806 edition. Four volumes.[320]	28	1,000

The Italian

1797. Three volumes, 'by the author of the mysteries of Udolpho, &c &c'[321]	15	2,000
1797. Second 'corrected'.	15	na

Sicilian Romance

1809 edition[322]	8	500

'The popularity of Mrs Radcliffe's works obtained such prices as had never before been paid for works of fiction. For the "Mysteries of Udolpho" she received £500, and for "The Italians" £800, nor were her Publishers the losers, for the sale was such as not only to cover all the expenses, but to reward them well for their liberality.' From *Memoirs of Mrs Ann Radcliffe* prefixed to Limberd's cheap edition of 1827.[323]

---

[316] *Ibid.*

[317] Print runs from Longman impression books. Other information from Garside, Raven, and Schöwerling.

[318] Print run from Hookham ledger i, which note 750 ordered from printer Gosnell. See also Garside, Raven, and Schöwerling i, 543.

[319] Longman archives.   [320] *Ibid.*   [321] Garside, Raven, and Schöwerling i, 727.

[322] Longman archives.

[323] The figures, and the huge difference from anything offered before and for long after, are confirmed by Raven in Garside, Raven, and Schöwerling i, 52.

Appendix 9 *(cont.)*

Samuel Rogers

The Pleasures of Memory

1792		250
Three more editions soon after	na	na
'Instantly became popular especially among the ladies'[324]		
1801 to **1816**, fifth to nineteenth editions, tranched down[325]		22,350
1838. Moxon's edition[326]	na	1,500

Italy

1822, part I; 1828 part II.
'From the publisher's point of view . . . a failure. So [Rogers] made a bonfire, so he described it, of the unsold copies, and set himself to the task of making it better.'

1830   28 or on India paper 63   10,000
Republished with a revised text. Magnificent engraved illustrations by Turner, Flaxman, Stodhart, and other leading artists, financed by Rogers at a total cost of £1,500 for this work and *Poems*.

1832. 6,800 sold. Rogers eventually covered his costs
Poems (a new edition of *Pleasures of Memory* &c)

1831   28 or on India paper 63   10,000
Republished with illustrations, financed by Rogers

1833. Most copies sold, costs covered
'For the next twenty years there were few drawing rooms in which one of these books was not on the table, and probably there were no cultivated people who had not turned to them again and again with ever increasing delight.'[327]

1838. Moxon's edition[328]   na   2,000

1847. Over 50,000 copies said to have been sold[329]
In 1850. Rogers, then aged eighty-seven, was offered the Poet Laureateship on the death of Wordsworth, but he declined. Rogers's works were readily available throughout most of the nineteenth century.

Sir Walter Scott

By far, the most popular author of the romantic period and later, both in verse and in prose, not only in Great Britain but in English-speaking communities elsewhere. Extensive though the following summary is, in order to save space, it omits Scott's many biographical works and editions, some of his less well-known verse and prose writings, musical adaptations, plays, and the many shorter pieces he published both individually and as contributions to other works. The figures also exclude offshore piracies from

---

[324] P. W. Clayden, *The Early Life of Samuel Rogers* (1887) 213.   [325] *Ibid.* 217.
[326] Whittingham archives 41,926.   [327] P. W. Clayden, *Rogers and His Contemporaries* (1889) ii, 7.
[328] Whittingham archives 41,926.   [329] Curwen 353. Probably an exaggeration.

Appendix 9 (*cont.*)

France, the United States, and elsewhere, some of which were imported in large numbers. For full bibliographical information about the publication history until 1836, readers should consult the impressive volume by Todd and Bowden.[330]

Writings in verse[331]

Minstrelsy of the Scottish Border

1802. Two volumes[332]	18	360, 360, and 720 each
1803. Second edition, three volumes	31.5	1,000
1806. Third edition	31.5	1,250
1810. Fourth edition[333]	36	1,250
1812. Fifth edition	36	1,500

The Lay of the Last Minstrel

1805 4to edition	25	750
1806. Second edition, 8vo	10.5	1,500
1806. Third edition	10.5	2,000
1806. Fourth edition	10.5	2,250
1806. Fifth edition	10.5	2,000
1807. Sixth edition	10.5	3,000
1808. 'Eighth' edition 4to, with *Ballads*	31.5	na
1808. Ninth edition, 8vo	10.5	3,550
1810. Tenth edition	10.5	3,250
1810. Eleventh edition	10.5	na
1811. Twelfth edition	10.5	3,000

---

[330] William B. Todd and Ann Bowden, *Sir Walter Scott, A Bibliographical History, 1796–1832* (Oak Knoll, Del. 1998).

[331] In addition to Todd and Bowden, see Ruff. There is much information about the first publication of the novels in James Corson, *Bibliography of Sir Walter Scott 1797–1940* (1943) and Greville Worthington, *A Bibliography of the Waverley Novels* (1931) although almost nothing on print runs, prices, and sales. Figures for production for many editions are found in the Longman archives, a source from which Lockhart took his estimates. The impression books of Constable do not appear to have survived – they are not among the Constable archives in the NLS and, according to a note in ms. 803, were no longer in the hands of the firm in 1932. There are however many scattered indications in the Constable archives that do survive, and in the Murray archives, some of which were quoted by Edgar Johnson, *Sir Walter Scott, The Great Unknown* (1970). Information on the lifetime editions is summarised from Todd and Bowden except where shown.

[332] Whittingham archives 41,902.

[333] Todd and Bowden 29, with the price, which I conjecture is a misprint, amended.

Appendix 9 *(cont.)*

1812. Thirteenth edition	10.5	3,000
1816. 'Fifteenth' edition	10.5	3,000
1823. Sixteenth edition	10.5	1,000
1825. 'new edition' foolscap 8vo (small size)	9	2,000

'In the history of British Poetry, nothing had ever equalled the demand for the *Lay of the Last Minstrel.*' Lockhart, Scott's son in law, in his *Life of Sir Walter Scott Bart.*, 1836.[334]

Marmion

1808. 4to edition	31.5	2,000
1808. Second edition, 8vo	12	3,000
1808. Third edition	12	3,000
1808. Fourth edition	12	3,000
1810. Fifth edition	12	2,000
1810. Sixth edition, two volumes	21	3,000
1811. Seventh edition, one volume, 8vo	12	4,000
1811. Eighth edition, one volume, 8vo	12	5,000
1815. Ninth edition	12	3,000
1821. Tenth edition	14	500
1825. 'new edition' foolscap 8vo (small size)	9	2,000
1825. Twelfth edition, octavo	14	500
1830. 300 copies reissued	na	
1830. 'new edition' foolscap 8vo (small size)	9	500

'The legitimate sale in this country . . . down to the period I am writing (May 1836) may be stated at 50,000 copies. I presume it is right for me to facilitate the task of future historians of our literature by preserving these details as often as I can. Such particulars respecting many of the great works, even of the last century are already sought for with vain regret; and I anticipate no day when the student of English civilisation will pass without curiosity the contemporary reception of the *Tale of Flodden Field.*' Lockhart.[335]

The Lady of The Lake

1810. Quarto edition	42	2,000
1810. Second edition, octavo	12	3,000
1810–30		a further 29,250

---

[334] Lockhart 123.   [335] *Ibid.* 156.

Appendix 9 (*cont.*)

Rokeby

1813. January, Quarto	42	3.000
1813. April, Second edition, octavo	14	6,000

The other 'editions' appear to have been reissues of unsold sheets.
'This, in the case of almost any other author, would have been splendid success.'
Lockhart.[336]

The Lord of the Isles

1815. 4to edition	42	1,750
1815. Second edition, 8vo	14	6,000
1815. Third edition	14	sheets from second
1815. Fourth edition	14	6,000
1815. Fifth edition	14	sheets from fourth

The Field of Waterloo

1815. Three editions	5	10,000

Collected verse writings

1806. Five volumes	105	na

Mainly made up of unsold copies of later editions
of individual poems.

1806. Six volumes	126	na

Mainly made up of unsold copies of later editions
of individual poems.

1812. Eight volumes	na	na

Mainly made up of unsold copies of later editions
of individual poems.

1813. Nine volumes	na	na

Mainly made up of unsold copies of later editions
of individual poems.

1813. Ten volumes	249	na

Mainly made up of unsold copies of later editions
of individual poems.

Poetical Works

1820. Twelve volumes	72	2,000
1821. Ten volumes	120	na
1822. Eight volumes	72	2,000

---

[336] *Ibid.* 309.

Appendix 9 *(cont.)*

1823. Ten volumes, 18mo	63	na
1825. Ten volumes, 8vo	na	na
1830. Eleven volumes, 18mo	63	na
1830. Eleven volumes, 8vo	120	na

Waverley novels

Waverley

1814. Three volumes, anonymous	21	1,000
1814. Second edition	21	2,000
1814. Third edition[337]	21	1,000
1815. Fourth edition	21	1,000
1815. Fifth edition	21	1,000
1816. Sixth edition	21	1,500
1817. Seventh edition	na	2,000
1821. Eighth edition	na	2,000
Before 1836[338]		40,000

Guy Mannering

1815. Three volumes, 'by the author of "Waverley".' Sold out on the day after publication	21	2,000
1815. Second edition	21	5,000
1815. Third edition	21	same sheets as second
1817. Fourth edition[339]	21	2,000
1820. 'Sixth' edition	na	na
In 1825 still selling about 200 a year[340]		
Sales before the collected edition of 1829		10,000
Before 1836 with collected editions, total domestic sales[341]		50,000

The Antiquary

1815. Three volumes, 'by the author of "Waverley" and "Guy Mannering"'.	24	6,000
1816. Second edition	24	same sheets as first
1818. 'Fifth' edition	24	na
1821. 'Sixth' edition	na	na
In 1825 still selling about 200 a year[342]		

[337] See Todd and Bowden 313 for the complex settings caused by the rush to produce copies for sale.
[338] Lockhart 300.   [339] Longman archives.
[340] Hurst Robinson to Constable, 5 July 1825, Constable archives, 23,608.   [341] Lockhart 310.
[342] Hurst Robinson to Constable, 5 July 1825, Constable archives, 23,608.

Appendix 9 (*cont.*)

Tales of My Landlord, 1st Series. Black Dwarf and Old Mortality

1817. Four volumes, 'Collected and arranged by Jedediah Cleishbotham'	28	2,000
1817. Second edition[343]	28	2,000
1817. Third edition[344]	28	2,000
1817. Fourth edition[345]	28	3,000

Scott would only agree to an edition of 6,000 when the publishers undertook to take some of Ballantyne's old stock, and to place further work with them.[346] The second printing was ordered before the first was put on sale. All the copies of the first three printings were sold in two months.[347]

1819. Fifth edition	28	na
1819. Sixth edition	28	old sheets

Rob Roy

1818. Three volumes[348]	24	10,000
1818. Second edition	24	same printing
1818. Third edition	24	same printing
1818. Fourth edition	24	3,000
Before 1836 with collected editions, total domestic sales[349]		40,000

Tales of My Landlord, Second Series, Heart of Midlothian

1818. Four volumes	32	10,000

Tales of My Landlord, Third Series, The Bride of Lammermoor and A Legend of Montrose

1819. Four volumes	32	probably 10,000

Ivanhoe

1819. Three volumes, 'by the author of "Waverley" &c'	30	probably 10,000
1820. Second edition	30	same printing
1821. Third edition	na	na
12,000 copies said to have been sold in three volumes despite the high price[350]		

---

[343] Murray archives. [344] *Ibid.* [345] *Ibid.* [346] Johnson, 549. [347] Constable, iii, 92.
[348] Longman archives. [349] Lockhart 358. [350] Lockhart 419.

Appendix 9 (*cont.*)

The Monastery

1820. Three volumes, 'by the author of "Waverley"'[351]	24	10,000
1820. Second edition	24	same printing

The Abbot

1820. Three volumes, 'by the author of "Waverley"'[352]	24	10,000

Kenilworth

1821. Three volumes, 'by the author of "Waverley", "Ivanhoe", &c'	31.5	10,000

Of first edition 7,145 copies shipped to London, 100 to Dublin, plus an unknown amount to booksellers in Scotland and England north of York.[353]

1821. Second edition	31.5	2,000

An Oxford bookseller lends copies of Waverley novels for reading at 1 shilling and 1.5 shillings.[354]

The Pirate

1822. Three volumes, 'by the author of "Waverley", "Kenilworth", &c'	31.5	10,000
1822. Extra copies printed in London		2,000
1822. Second edition	31.5	same printing
1822. Third edition	31.5	same printing

The Fortunes of Nigel

1822. Three volumes, 'by the author of "Waverley", "Kenilworth", &c'	31.5	Probably 10,000
1822. Second edition	31.5	same printing
1822. Third edition	31.5	same printing

'I was in town yesterday, and so keenly were the people devouring my friend Jingling Geordie, that I actually saw them reading it in the streets as they passed along . . . The smack Ocean, by which the new work was shipped, arrived at the wharf on Sunday; the bales were got out by *one* on Monday morning, and before ten o' clock 7,000 copies had been dispersed.' Archibald Constable, Scott's publisher, from London, May 1822.[355]

---

[351] Longman archives.   [352] *Ibid.*
[353] Constable archives, 23, 618, letter of 20 January 1821.
[354] Ledger of an Oxford bookseller 1819–23, Bodleian ms. Eng. His. b. 189.   [355] Lockhart 475.

Appendix 9 (*cont.*)

Peveril of the Peak

1822. Four volumes, 'by the author of "Waverley", "Kenilworth", &c'	42	na
1823. Second edition	42	same printing

Quentin Durward

1823. Three volumes, 'by the author of "Waverley", "Peveril of the Peak", &c'	31.5	na

First edition at least 8,180[356]

St Ronan's Well

1823. Three volumes, 'by the author of "Waverley", "Quentin Durward", &c'	31.5	9,800

Of which 7,000 shipped to London

1824. Second edition	31.5	same printing

Redgauntlet

1824. Three volumes, 'by the author of "Waverley"'	31.5	10,000

At least 7,150 copies sent to London[357]

Tales of the Crusaders. The Betrothed, The Talisman

1825. Four volumes, 'by the author of "Waverley", "Quentin Durward", &c'	42	na

In January 1826, as a result of a national banking crisis, the London firm of Hurst Robinson, distributor of the Waverley novels in southern England, was forced into bankruptcy by a cash-flow crisis, to be followed by Ballantyne and then Constable in Edinburgh. Stocks were sold off at low prices in an attempt to stave off ruin. Tegg, the remainder dealer claimed to have bought 'the best of Scott's novels at fourpence a volume'.[358] Scott surrendered all his assets, including unfinished manuscripts, into trust. He determined to pay off his debts by writing even more. Part of the response of the successor publishers was to tranche down the prices of titles already published, despite the existence of large unsold stocks.

Woodstock

1826. Three volumes, 'by the author of "Waverley", "Tales of the Crusaders", &c'	31.5	na

---

[356] Constable archives, note, no date, 23,620.   [357] *Ibid.*   [358] Quoted by Barnes and Barnes, 52.

Appendix 9 *(cont.)*

Chronicles of the Canongate, first Series. *The Highland Widow, The Two Drovers, The Surgeon's Daughter*

1827. Two volumes, 'by the author of "Waverley", &c'[359]   21   na

Tales of a Grandfather

1828. Three volumes, anonymous[360]   10.5   na
Published in the small format of 'royal 18mo in sixes'

1828. Second edition   10.5   na

1828. Third edition   10.5   same printing

1828. Fourth edition   10.5   same printing

1828. Fifth edition, text much revised   10.5   na

1829. Sixth edition   10.5   same printing
'Their reception was more rapturous than that of any of one of his works since Ivanhoe. The popularity of the book has grown with every year that has since elapsed; it is equally prized in the library, the boudoir, the schoolroom, and the nursery; it is adopted as the happiest of manuals not only in Scotland, but wherever the English language is spoken.' Lockhart.[361]

Chronicles of the Canongate, second series, *The Fair Maid of Perth*

1828. Three volumes, 'by the author of "Waverley", &c'   31.5   na

1828. Second edition   31.5   na

Tales of a Grandfather, second series

1828. Three volumes, anonymous   10.5   na

1829. Second edition   10.5   na
Anne of Gerstein

1829. Three volumes, 'by the author of "Waverley", &c'   31.5   na

Tales of a Grandfather, third series

1830. Three volumes, anonymous   10.5   na

Tales of a Grandfather, fourth series

1831. Three volumes   10.5   na

---

[359] Johnson, *The Great Unknown* 997.   [360] Todd and Bowden 662.   [361] Lockhart 674.

Appendix 9 (*cont.*)

Tales of My Landlord, fourth and last Series, *Count Robert of Paris*, and *Castle Dangerous*

1831. Four volumes, 'Collected and arranged by Jedediah Cleishbotham'	42	na

Life of Napoleon Bonaparte

1827. Nine volumes, 'by the author of "Waverley"'	94.5	6000
1827. Second edition	94.5	2000

Collected editions of the Waverley novels

Novels and Tales of the Author of Waverley

1819. Twelve volumes, 8vo	144	1,500
1822. Twelve volumes	144	same printing
1821. Twelve volumes, 12mo	120	1,500
1823. Twelve volumes, 18mo 'miniature edition'	84	na
Since 5,000 copies were sent to London the total printing was probably above 7,000		
1825. Twelve volumes, 12mo	na	old sheets

Historical Romances of the Author of Waverley (second series *Ivanhoe* to *Kenilworth*)

1822. Six volumes, 8vo	72	5,000
2,700 copies sent to London		
1822. Six volumes, foolscap 8vo (small size)	60	1,500
1824. Six volumes, 18mo (smaller size)	42	na
5,000 copies were sent to London		

Novels and Romances of the Author of Waverley (third series *The Pirate* to *Quentin Durward*)

1824. Seven volumes, 8vo	84	na
1824. Nine volumes, 12mo	67.5	na
1825. Seven volumes, 18mo	49	na
5,000 copies were sent to London		

'Who will buy Waverley at 21/- when you are selling it at 6/-?' Hurst Robinson protesting at the plan to produce a cheaper edition, shortly before the crash of 1825.[362]

---

[362] Hurst Robinson to Constable, 5 July 1825, Constable archives, 23,608.

Appendix 9 *(cont.)*

In 1826, in their desperation to raise money quickly, Scott's trustees ordered that the next series should be published virtually simultaneously in the three formats at three different prices, as was being done, although for other reasons, in the case of Byron's *Don Juan*.[363] The effect, as was foreseen, was to concentrate demand on the cheapest version.

Tales and Romances of the Author of Waverley (fourth series *St Ronan's Well* to *Woodstock*)

1827. Seven volumes, 8vo	84	1,500
1827. Nine volumes, 12mo	67.5	1,500
1828. Seven volumes, 18mo	49	1,500
1828. Seven volumes, second impression, 18mo	49	1,000

Tales and Romances of the Author of Waverley (fifth series *Chronicles of the Canongate* to *Castle Dangerous*)

1833. Seven volumes, 8vo	108	na
1833. Eight volumes, 16mo	82.5	na
1833. Six volumes, 18mo	63	na

Meanwhile Cadell, the new owner decided on a completely new edition of the whole series of Waverley novels, to be illustrated with plates of pictures drawn by leading artists. The texts were stereotyped, steam presses were used from about volume xii onwards, and the volumes were sold already bound in cloth. There were to be forty-eight volumes, each sold at 5 shillings, a new one appearing each month.

Cadell's *Collected Edition of the Waverley Novels*

1829–33. Forty-eight volumes	5 each	see below

Cadell's *The Poetical Works of Sir Walter Scott*, with Scott's extensive revisions

1833–34. Twelve volumes	5 each	see below

'The circulation of these works having hitherto been confined, to a great degree, to the wealthier ranks of society, the Proprietors have resolved to place them within the reach of readers of all classes, by republishing them in a less costly but at the same time more elegant shape and with the additional advantage of a periodical issue.' Cadell's Prospectus.[364]

Planned first impression 7,000 a volume, 'then made 10,000, – then 12,000, – then 15,000, – then 20,000'.[365] Initially sold 35,000 copies a month[366]

Still available in 1847 at 5 shillings a volume[367]

---

[363] See chapter 16.
[364] Publisher's prospectus quoted by Jane Milgate, *Scott's Last Edition* (Edinburgh 1987) 1.
[365] Quoted *ibid.* 33.   [366] Lockhart 701.
[367] *Catalogue of the Various Editions Now Completed of the Novels, Poetry, Prose Writings, & Life of Sir Walter Scott, Bart* (1847), Ac.

Appendix 9 *(cont.)*

Cadell's Sales, 1827 to 1849[368]

Waverley Novels	78,270 sets
Poetical Works	41,340 sets

Plus numbers issued in weekly parts

Novels	7,115,197
Poetry	674,955

In 1850/1 the firm was selling about 35,000 Waverley novels in various editions, plus about 12,000 *Poetical Works* in various editions.

1851. *Collected Poetical Works* in one volume
(Galignani style)[369]   5   8,000

In 1854, the firm decided to produce a *Railway Edition*, made with stereotypes and 'done up in fancy boards', to be sold, at roughly monthly intervals, at 2 shillings and at 1.5 shillings a volume, depending on binding.

Railway edition
Cumulative Sales of volumes sold   volumes

1853–4	31,000
1854–5	94,000
1855–6	106,000
1856–7	123,000
1857–8	129,000
1858–9	150,000
1859–60	185,000
1860–1	215,000

Railway and shilling editions
Price 1 shilling. Cumulative sales of volumes sold

1862–3	730,000
1863–4	1,051,000

Sixpenny edition
Price 0.5 shillings. Books were made from the same stereotype plates altered to suit the smaller paper size. Cumulative sales of volumes sold

Between 1866 and 1868	2,099,000

'The writer was travelling down to Wales, and at the London station he said "Boy, where are the Scott novels?" "Don't keep them he replied." "Don't keep them! Why not?" "Because, if we did, we would not sell anything else" . . . At every station the writer made the same inquiry and met with the same result." *Illustrated London News*, 25 September 1867.[370]

---

[368] Summarised from Corwen 138 who drew on figures prepared by Cadell's executor. In the absence of details it is difficult to judge the amount of reading which this enormous figure represents, but if there were twenty-four numbers per title, that would be the equivalent of nearly 300,000 books, maybe about 50,000 copies of each of the favourites.

[369] A. and C. Black minute book, NLS.   [370] Quoted by Curwen 153.

Appendix 9 (*cont.*)

1873, As soon as the copyrights expired, Dicks issued a 'Threepenny edition' in thirty-two volumes, that is at half the previous price, exremely low though that had been. Customers anywhere in the country could order by post, paying by sending half-penny postage stamps, available in any post office.

Many other publishers reprinted Waverley novels in a variety of formats, some abridged in paperback.[371]

William Shakespeare

See appendix 12

Mary Wollstonecraft Shelley

Monsieur Nongtonpaw

1808. A humorous picture book for children, written, or contributed to, by Mary Godwin when she was a child.[372]		1,000
1809. Second edition		1,000

Frankenstein, or, The Modern Prometheus

For a full discussion see chapter 18

1818. Lackington, three volumes	16.5	500
1823. Whittaker, two volumes[373]	14 unbound c. 19 bound	
1835. Still advertised in the *London Catalogue of Books*		
1831. *Bentley's Standard Novels*, one volume	6	3,500
1832. Bentley, new impression 3,170 copies sold to retail booksellers in the first year[374]		500
1833. An American edition[375]	na	1,000
1836. Bentley, new impression[376]		500
1838. *Romancist Library* offer refused Dates uncertain, Bentley price reduced to	0.17 5 and later 3.5	
1839. Bentley, new impression[377]		750
1847. Price reduced to	2.5	
1849. Bentley, new impression[378]		1,000
1855. Hodgson's 'Parlour Library' edition, perhaps pirated, includes 1817 preface and 1831 introduction		

---

[371] E.g. Cameron and Ferguson's 3d [0.25 shillings] edition of *Waverley*, Ac.
[372] Richard Taylor check books.
[373] This edition is not made from the same types as the first, as suggested by Lyles, but is a complete reprint in moveable type which includes some changes to the text.
[374] Strahan/Spottiswoode archives.   [375] Kaser 128.
[376] Strahan/Spottiswoode archives.   [377] *Ibid.*   [378] *Ibid.*

Appendix 9 (*cont.*)

Bound	1.5	na
Paper	1	na

1850s, 1860s, 1870s. Mostly out of print but protected by copyright.

1879. Becomes free of all copyright restrictions

1882 to 1899. Routledge[379]   40,000
One version   1
  Bound   0.5
  Paper   0.25
Most Routledge editions contain both the 1817 preface and 1831 introduction, but the Routledge World Library edition omits both, substituting a preface by the editor of the series which describes the moral purpose as 'vague and indeterminate'.

?1880s. Milner's 'Cottage Library'[380]   1   na

1883. Dicks's *English Library of Standard Works*[381]
In four weekly parts, paper covers   0.2   na
As part of a volume in paper covers, containing   1.5   na
  6 other novels and forty-eight short stories
Dicks's editions, which contained the 1817 preface and 1831 introduction, probably sold in tens or hundreds of thousands of copies.[382]

1893. Masterpiece Library
  'Penny Popular Novels' abridged   0.08   na
Omits both the 1817 preface and 1831 introduction, substituting a preface by the editor, W. T. Stead, which offers the, by now, conventional warning of the dangers of creating monsters which destroy their creators.
'Everybody has heard of *Frankenstein*. But comparatively few have read the weird and powerful novel which made the name of Frankenstein one of the symbol words of the language.'

1897. Gibbings, art-nouveau design and illustrations, published in partnership with a publisher in Philadelphia. Contains the 1817 preface and the 1831 introduction.
                                                              3.5   na

c. 1897. Downey's *Sixpenny Library*[383]   0.5   na

1909–10. Routledge sells about 1,000 copies

1910 to 1914. Routledge sells about 200 to 300 copies a year

1912. *Everyman's Library*.[384]   1   na, but probably 8,500

---

[379] Routledge archives, University College, London.
[380] No copy found, but advertised in Milner's lists over many years.
[381] The existence of this huge edition has not previously been noted as far as I can tell, probably because, being printed on frail paper, only a few copies have survived. *Frankenstein* was serialised in parts 18 to 23, and forms part of volume iii. A copy in Bodleian.
[382] Estimate based on the known sales of some of his other reprints.
[383] No copy found, but advertised in *The Vicar of Wakefield* (n.d. but c. 1897).
[384] Figures kindly supplied from the Dent archives at Chapel Hill by Professor Mark Reed. The dates given refer to dates of publication given on the title pages. The production figures are usually noted in the accounts of the previous years. In general about a third of the Everyman production was exported to the United States as part of the Dent/Dutton partnership.

Appendix 9 *(cont.)*

Contains the 1817 preface and 1831 introduction
Over 8,000 sold by 1918

1919–21	Out of print	
1922	New impression	na, but probably 4,000
1927	New impression	4,000
1930	New impression	4,000

Over 3,000 sold in 1931–2, time of the first release of the Whale/Karloff film.

1933	New impression	4,000
1939	New impression	4,000

From 1912 to 1940 sales to the retailers in the British market were typically well below 500 copies a year. The exceptions were 1912, the year of publication (2,250), 1930 and 1931 (1,000 and 750), 1932 (2,000), and 1933 (600).[385] The years of largest sales in the American market were 1913 (1,000) and 1922 (1,500). The surge in 1932 (600) is less marked than in the British market.

Frankenstein. Some stage versions[386]

Early favourites

1823	*Presumption, or the Fate of Frankenstein* later renamed *Frankenstein, or, The Danger of Presumption* Played thirty-seven times in its first season and frequently until 1850s[387]
1826	*The Man and the Monster* later retitled *Frankenstein, or, The Monster* 'a peculiar romantic, melo-dramatic pantomimic spectacle' Played frequently until 1840s
1826	Text of *The Man and the Monster* printed

Others

1823	*Another Piece of Presumption* (burlesque)
1823	*Humgumption; or, Dr Frankenstein and the Hobgoblin of Hoxton* (burlesque)
1824	*Frank-in Steam; or, The Modern Promise to Pay* (burlesque)
1826	*The Monster and the Magician., or, The Fate of Frankenstein* 'Melodramatic Romance'

Victorian

1849	*Frankenstein, or The Model Man* (dramatisation) Fifty-four performances in London West End
1850s	*The Man and the Monster* revived in Birmingham, Edinburgh, and perhaps elsewhere

---

[385] Rounded.

[386] Mainly summarised from Forry. Although the figures are likely to be reasonably complete with regard to performances in London, the record for other cities is fragmentary.

[387] Forry gives the figure of 37. The Birmingham playbill declares in 1824 that the piece had drawn '109 full houses last year at the English Opera House'. Forry 9.

Appendix 9 (*cont.*)

1865   Text of *Presumption, or the Fate of Frankenstein* printed

1867   Text of *The Man and the Monster* reprinted

1887   *Frankenstein, or, The Vampire's Victim*
        106 performances in London West End

Frankenstein as a popular expression[388]

1824   Canning in the House of Commons, To emancipate West Indian slaves 'would
        be to raise up a creature resembling the splendid fiction of a recent romance'

1824   'I never, like Frankenstein, made monsters at command.' From *Don Juan*,
        cantos XVII and XVIII, a piece of spurious Byroniana printed by Duncombe.[389]

1830   *Fraser's Magazine*. A state without religion is 'a Frankenstein monster'

1832   Reform Bill. At least three cartoons 'The Political Frankenstein'

1837   De Quincey. Godwin's philosophy is 'a monster created by Frankenstein'

1837   Carlyle *French Revolution*.[390] 'France is a monstrous Galvanic Mass'

1838   Gladstone notes in his diary that Sicilian mules 'really seem like Frankensteins
        of the animal creation'.[391]

1843   Punch cartoon. 'The Irish Frankenstein'

1848   Gaskell *Mary Barton* 'the actions of the uneducated seem to me typified in those
        of Frankenstein, that monster of many human qualities ungifted with a soul'.

1854   Punch cartoon 'The Russian Frankenstein'

1866   Punch cartoon 'The Brummagen [working class] Frankenstein'

1866   In Wheeler's *Dictionary of Noted Names*

1869   Cartoon 'The Irish Frankenstein'

1870   In Brewer's *Dictionary of Phrase and Fable*

1871   Tyndall's 'Fragments of Science for Unscientific People. Frankenstein's
        Chemistry.' Punch.[392]

1872   'I have had indirect influence on nearly every cheap villa builder between this
        [house] and Bromley; and there is scarcely a public house near the Crystal
        Palace but sells its gin and bitters under pseudo-Venetian capitals . . . One of
        my principal notions for leaving my present house is that it is surrounded by
        Frankenstein monsters of *in*directly my own making.' John Ruskin in a letter to
        the *Pall Mall Gazette*, on the influence of *The Stones of Venice* on English
        architecture.[393]

1882   Phoenix Park murders. Punch cartoon of Parnell 'The Irish Frankenstein'.

[388] The examples taken from Baldick with additions I have myself noticed.   [389] Ac.

[390] Baldick 92 shows, with numerous precise quotations, how deeply the Frankenstein story permeates
Carlyle's descriptions of the French Revolution. The book is not named directly, although in
Carlyle's *German Romance*, he speaks of the 'gory profundities of Frankenstein'.

[391] Quoted by Forry 36. Gladstone read the book in 1835. Print-out of Gladstone's reading kindly
supplied by the late Colin Mathews.

[392] Quoted by Forry 36.   [393] *The Complete Works of Ruskin* (1903–1912) x, 459.

Appendix 9 (*cont.*)

Valperga

1823. Three volumes   21   1,250
Publication was paid for by Godwin, which may account for the print run being higher
than the publisher Whittaker would have risked if he had had a direct financial interest in
the book's sales.[394] *Valperga*, was, in Mary Shelley's words 'never properly published', and
was rejected for *Bentley's Standard Novels* even when that series was short of suitable
titles.[395] Not reprinted until 1996

The Last Man

1826. Three volumes   27   na
A 'second edition' appears to be reissued sheets

Perkin Warbeck

1830. Three volumes[396]   31.5   750
228 copies remaindered
Mary Shelley received 3,000 shillings for the copyright.[397]

[**1834.** An American edition.[398]   na   1,000]

1857. Routledge buys copyright for 714 shillings and   3   6,000
    issues a reprint. Not reprinted until 1996

Lodore

1835. Three volumes[399]   31.5   750
Not reprinted until 1996

Falkner

1835. Three volumes. Not reprinted until 1996   31.5   na

Works for *The Cabinet Cyclopedia*, an educational series

Lives of the Most Eminent Literary and Scientific Men of Italy, Spain, and Portugal

1835 and **1837.** Three volumes, of which the initial print runs were 4,000, 3,500, and
2,500. No new impressions were made.[400]
Never reprinted

---

[394] Richard Taylor archives.
[395] Mary Shelley, *Letters* ii, 332.
[396] Bentley archives. BL add. mss. 46,674. The remainders were bought by Tegg. See Barnes and
    Barnes 52.
[397] Bentley archives.   [398] Kaser 128.   [399] Bentley archives.   [400] Strahan archives.

Appendix 9 (*cont.*)

Lives of the Most Eminent Literary and Scientific Men of France

1838 and **1839.** Two volumes, of which the print runs were 2,500 and 2,000.
No new impressions were made.[401] Never reprinted.

Percy Bysshe Shelley[402]

Scattered indications. For the pirated editions and the official edition of 1839, see
chapter 16 and appendix 11.

Queen Mab

1813. Privately printed for distribution, not for sale   250
'Shelley sent a copy to all the great Poets of the day.'[403]
1821. Extensive pirating begins
1822. Death of Shelley
Carlile buys remaining stock from a member of the trade, 180 copies remain

Alastor

1816   5   250
Printed at Shelley's expense. Murray declines to sell on commission, sold on commission
by Baldwin, Cradock, and Joy; and Carpenter.
1820. Copies still available

History of a Six Weeks' Tour (with Mary Godwin, later Shelley)

1817   4.5   na
Printed at Shelley's expense on commission
1829. Remaining stocks reissued as a new book by John Brooks,
a radical pirate.[404]

Revolt of Islam, originally entitled *Laon and Cythna*

1818   10.5   750
Printed and advertised at Shelley's expense. Financial accounts reproduced in appendix 5.
'Can't you *make* the Booksellers subscribe more of the Poem?' Shelley to his publisher,
January 1818.[405]

1829   10.5
Remaining stocks reissued as a new book by John Brooks, a radical pirate[406]
1840s or later. Bundles of twenty-five copies remaindered to the trade at sixpence (0.5s) a
copy. Sold retail for about 2.5 shillings.[407]

---

[401] *Ibid.*   [402] James E. Barcus, *Shelley, The Critical Heritage* (1975) 9.
[403] Mary Shelley to Moxon, 12 December 1838. Mary Shelley, *Letters* ii, 303.
[404] See appendix 11.   [405] Mary Shelley *Letters*, i, 593.   [406] See appendix 11.
[407] H. Buxton Forman, *Shelley Library, an Essay in Bibliography* (Shelley Society 1886). Forman was
    able to buy sheets from Brooks's family in the 1880s.

Appendix 9 (cont.)

'Mr Robert Browning, who has an unusually accurate memory for details, told me in 1876 that, when he was a youth, he met, in his wanderings about London, with a small bookseller who had for sale a large pile of copies.' H. Buxton Forman, a collector of rare books, 1886.[408]

Rosalind and Helen

1819	10.5	na
Regularly published by Ollier		

The Cenci

1819. Printed at Shelley's expense at Leghorn		250
Second edition by Ollier	4.5	Probably 500

Epipsychidion

1821	2	Probably 250
1823. 160 copies still available[409]		

Prometheus Unbound

1820	9	Probably 500

'Absolutely and intrinsically unintelligible . . . To his long list of demerits, he has added the most flagrant offences against morality and religion.' Fortunately 'he tempers irreligion and sedition with nonsense'. *Quarterly Review.*[410]
1824, still available

Adonais

1821. Printed at Pisa	3.5	250
Sold out		
Second edition	na	na

1824. Still available

1829. Reprinted in Cambridge, perhaps a result of interest in Shelley among an undergraduate club

Hellas

1821	3.5	na

'The sale, in every instance, of Mr Shelley's works has been very confined.' Ollier, Shelley's publisher, 1823

[408] *Shelley Library* 77.   [409] Robinson 209, quoting Ollier's list sent to Hunt.
[410] Barcus, *Critical Heritage* 254.

Appendix 9 *(cont.)*

Poetical Pieces

1823. 10.5 shillings. A made-up volume of remainders, *Prometheus Unbound, Hellas, The Cenci, Rosalind and Helen*

1831. Still being advertised.

Posthumous Poems

1824 15 500
Published by the help of a guarantee given by three friends of Mary Shelley
'Nothing would be better than to print 500 or 750 copies (if it pleases the Gods of wastepaper) for Mr Hunt to sell at two pence a pound three or four years hence.'
T. L. Beddoes, one of the proposed guarantors, arguing about the edition size.[411]
Publishers' accounts note the sale of 309 copies in two months, but after the intervention of Shelley's father, 160 copies in sheets and thirty-one in boards were withdrawn and consigned to Sir T. Shelley for destruction.[412]

Adam Smith

Some print runs and prices[413]

The Theory of Moral Sentiments

1759		1,000
1760. Second edition		750
1767. Third edition		750
1774. Fourth edition 4to		500
1781. Fifth edition		750
1790. Sixth edition[414]	6	1,000
1792. Seventh edition		1,000
1797. Eighth edition		1,000
1800. Ninth edition[415]	14	1,000

Eighty-four copies, a twelfth share, were taken by Bell and Bradfute in Edinburgh[416]

1804. Tenth edition[417]		1,000

[411] Quoted by Taylor 3.   [412] Manuscript account, NYPL, exhibited 1992.
[413] Strahan archives. Some of the figures confirmed by Bell and Bradfute archives. Other information derived from the Strahan archives about the early editions is noted in William Todd's note 'The Text and Apparatus' in Smith's *Wealth of Nations* 61.
[414] Price from *General Catalogue* 1786, perhaps per volume.
[415] Price from *London Catalogue* 1799.   [416] Bell and Bradfute archives.
[417] I take it that it is this edition whose printing is noted in the Longman impression book for 14 May 1801.

Appendix 9 (*cont.*)

1808. An edition mentioned by Bell and Bradfute, perhaps the tenth		1,250
1811. Eleventh edition	18	750

An Inquiry into the Nature and Causes of the Wealth of Nations

1776. Two volumes, 4to Smith received £500[418]	36	500
1778. 4to, second edition Unusually the price was raised	36	500
1784. 'Additions and Corrections to accommodate the purchasers of the former editions'	2	500
1784. Three volumes, third edition, revised, 8vo	18	1,000
1786. Fourth edition, 8vo[419]	18	1,250
1789. Fifth edition, 8vo	18	1,500
1791. Sixth edition, 8vo, after author's death	18	2,000
1793. Seventh edition	na	2,500
1796. Eighth edition[420]	21	2,500
1800. Ninth edition	na	na
1802. Tenth edition	na	2,000

1804 (legal copyright expiring after twenty-eight years)

1805. Eleventh edition, edited by William Playfair, an unsympathetic editor, who, besides providing a brief memoir, infiltrated extra chapters and added many notes that contradicted Smith's text. The purpose of the changes was partly to undermine what Smith wrote but mainly to enable the then intellectual property owners to claim a new copyright.[421]   27   2,000

'In the whole course of our literary inquisition, we have not met with an instance so discreditable to the English press . . . It may be given as a specimen of the most presumptuous book-making.' *Edinburgh Review*, 7 (1806) 470.

1808. Twelfth edition[422]	na	1,200
1812. Thirteenth edition[423]	27	1,250
1817. Fourteenth edition. Edinburgh	na	na
1819. Fifteenth edition, edited by J.R. McCulloch	na	na
1825. Tegg's price, three volumes, 8vo[424] Three volumes, 12mo	18 discounted from 27 10 discounted from 15	
1838. McCulloch's edition, stereotyped Reprinted	52.5 na	1,000 1,000

---

[418] Quoted by Cochrane 162.   [419] *General Catalogue* (1786) quotes a price of 21 shillings.
[420] Price from *London Catalogue* (1799).   [421] Price from *New London Catalogue* (1807).
[422] Longman impression books.   [423] Price from *The Modern London Catalogue* (1818).
[424] Tegg's *Select Library*.

Appendix 9 (*cont.*)

1795. *Posthumous Essays*[425]		1,000
1811. *Works of Adam Smith*	60s	750, plus 750 of *Moral Sentiments* and 1,250 of *Wealth of Nations*

Robert Southey

Selected. See appendix 7 for some of his travel and biographical works

Joan of Arc

1796. Two volumes. Bought from Cottle of Bristol.[426]	16	1,000
1805. Third edition, two volumes.[427]	16	500
1815. 'Fifth', edition, two volumes.	16	500
1801. *Poems*, volume i, fourth edition[428]	na	1,000
1802. *Poems*, two volumes	na	2,000
1806. *Poems*, volume ii[429]	na	1,000

Thalaba the Destroyer

1801–21. Four editions. two volumes[430]	16	totalling 3,500

Amadis de Gaul

1803. Four volumes[431]	21	1,000

Southey as translator was paid £100. 500 copies were sold in the first year.[432]

Madoc

1805. 4to[433]	42	500

'I can tell you nothing of the sale of *Madoc*, except that Longman has told me nothing, which is proof enough of slow sale; but if the edition goes off in two years, or indeed in three, it will be well for so costly a book.' Southey in a letter February 1806.[434]

1814. Second edition, two volumes	16	1,000
1815. Two volumes	16	1,000

Another edition of *Madoc*

1824. Two volumes[435]	16	500

---

[425] Strahan archives.   [426] Longman archives, bought from Cottle.
[427] Longman impression books.   [428] *Ibid.*   [429] *Ibid.*   [430] *Ibid.*   [431] *Ibid.*
[432] Southey, *Life* ii, 301.   [433] Longman impression books.   [434] Southey, *Life* iii, 27.
[435] Strahan archives 48,846.

Appendix 9 (*cont.*)

Remains of Kirke White

1807. Edited by Southey for the benefit of the family.[436]   750

1808. Second edition   1,500

1809   1,500

1810   1,500
Many more editions with long print runs

Letters from Spain and Portugal

1808. Two volumes   10.5   1,000

The Curse of Kehama

1810. 4to[437]   31.5   500
'Of *The Lady of the Lake*, 25,000 copies have been printed; of *Kehama* 500; and if they sell in seven years, I shall be surprised.' Southey in a letter.[438]

1811. Second edition, 12mo.[439]   14   750
The printers were asked to observe special secrecy in printing this edition, it being unusual to move straight from 4to to 12mo, and 'we wish to get the whole of the quarto off first'.[440]
'Thousands of people read my books . . . but they do not buy them – they borrow them, even those persons who are what they call my friends.' Southey to Coleridge.[441]

Carmen Triumphale for 1814

1815   5   500
The first of Southey's poems as Poet Laureate

Roderick the Last of the Goths

1814. 4to   42   500
Second, two volumes, 12mo   16   1,500

1815. Two volumes, 12mo   16   2,000

1818. Two volumes, 12mo   16   2,000
Another edition of *Roderick*

1826. Two volumes, sixth edition.[442]   16   1,000

Congratulatory Ode to His Royal Highness the Price Regent, His Imperial Majesty the Emperor of Russia, And His Majesty the King of Prussia

1814. 4to   na   250

---

[436] Longman impression books.   [437] *Ibid.*   [438] Quoted in Smiles i, 189.
[439] Longman impression book.   [440] Longman to Ballantynes, 5 July 1811. Longman archives.
[441] Southey, *Life* iii, 134.   [442] Strahan archives 48,846.

Appendix 9 *(cont.)*

Wat Tyler

1817. Pirated, see chapter 16

The Vision of Judgment

1820. 4to[443]   15   500
Sycophantic poem on the death and apotheosis of George III made famous by Byron's
attack. Never reprinted.

A Tale of Paraguay

1826[444]   10.5   1,500
Southey's prose works, notably his *Life of Nelson*, sold many more copies than his verse.
Southey was also a prolific and highly paid literary journalist. His main works were readily
available throughout the nineteenth century and beyond.[445] The one-volume edition
made in 1847 was not melted until 1895.[446]

Taylor family

Mrs Ann Taylor, afterwards Gilbert, of Ongar, often in association with her daughter Jane.

Hymns for Infant Minds

1810. A thirtieth edition by 1838, and many more during the Victorian period.

Maternal Solicitude for a Daughter's best interests

Some recorded print runs[447]
First edition, 1813   5   750
Second edition, 1814   1,000
Third edition, 1814   1,000
Fourth edition, 1815   1,250
Later editions until a twelfth 1830

*Practical Hints to Young Females on the Duties of Wife, a Mother, and a Mistress
of a Family*

1815. 5 shillings. A twelfth edition, 1826.

The Family Mansion, A Tale

More than one edition, 1822

---

[443] Strahan 48,844, and Longman archives.   [444] Strahan archives 48,846.
[445] Some figures for *Life of Nelson* in appendix 7, 555.   [446] Longman's register of stereotypes 287.
[447] John Taylor's commonplace book III. NYPL.

Appendix 9 *(cont.)*

Reciprocal Duties Of Parents and Children

Some recorded print runs[448]
First edition, 1814   750
Second edition, 1815   1,000
Third edition, 1815   5   1,000
Fourth edition, 1815   1,000

Correspondence between A Mother and her Daughter at School

1817. 5 shillings. A seventh edition, 1829

Display, A Tale for Young People (conduct fiction)

1815. A thirteenth edition by 1832

Edward John Trelawny

Adventures of a Younger Son

1831. Three volumes[449]   31.5   1,000
The text of Trelawny's manuscript version was substantially amended by Mary Shelley and by the printers. A full unexpurgated version was published for the first time by myself in 1978.[450] Copies of the first edition are found in remainder bindings.[451]

1835. *Bentley's Standard Novels*, one volume.[452]   6   2,500

1846. Bentley, new impression   1,000

1854. Bentley, new impression   2.5   500
Later 1850s Hodgson's 'Parlour Library'   1.5 and 1   na
Made from Bentley's plates, presumably by arrangement

Records of Shelley, Byron, and the Author

1878. Two volumes. A heavily revised version of his *Recollections of the Last Days of Shelley and Byron*, 1858.[453]   6   750

C. F. Volney

The Ruins, or A survey of the Revolutions of Empires

Translated from the French. Many   Sales before 1820[454]   about 30,000
editions, some very cheap, and in parts

---

[448] *Ibid.*   [449] Bentley archives.
[450] William St Clair, ed., *Edward John Trelawny, Adventures of a Younger Son* (Oxford 1974).
[451] Ac.   [452] Bentley archives.   [453] Whittingham archives.   [454] Carlile's estimate.

Appendix 9 (*cont.*)

Sales in 1820		10,000
1826. Another Carlile edition[455]		1,000

Jane West

Letters to a Young Man

1801–9. Three volumes. Five editions.[456]	21	totalling 4,500

Letters to a Young Lady

1806. Three volumes. Three editions.[457]   21   totalling 4,500
'The author warns against the "petticoat philosophist" [such as Wollstonecraft] who seeks for eminence and distinction in infidelity and scepticism, or in the equally monstrous extravagancies of German morality.'

The Mother (a poem)

1809	7	1,000

The Refusal (a conduct novel)

1810. Three volumes	21	2,000

Harriette Wilson

Memoirs

The autobiography of a society courtesan, written in order to extract money from clients.[458]

1825. Stockdale's original edition[459]

	each of 12 parts 2.5	7,000
	whole set 16	
The twenty-eight plates 'sketched and coloured from the life'[460]	27.5 or 2 each	na

---

[455] *The Republican*, 29 December 1826.
[456] Longman impression books.   [457] Longman impression books.
[458] See Frances Wilson, *The Courtesan's Revenge, Harriette Wilson, the Woman who Blackmailed the King* (2003).
[459] Price of parts from Stockdale the publisher's advertisement in (Harriette Wilson), *Paris Lions and London Tigers* (1825) BL. Price of a full set from advertisement on cover of Benbow's edition of *The Poetical Works of the late Thomas Little* (1825), Ac. Print run from *Memoirs of Harriette Wilson* (1831) Stockdale's eight volume edition iv, 20 (BL) which quotes the testimony of the printer's son in one of the trials. The figure is evidently for one of the parts which sold most copies when first published. Information about some other editions, all of which survive in only a few copies, kindly supplied by Steve Weissman.
[460] Stockdale's advertisement in *Paris Lions and London Tigers*, which forms part of the *Memoirs of Harriette Wilson*.

Appendix 9 *(cont.)*

At Stockdale's prices, the parts and illustrations are unlikely to have been sold, to any great extent, except to the richest sections of society.

1825. Onwhyn's pirated edition[461]   4   5,000
Stockdale claimed up to thirty-five legitimate editions but most appear to be made up from sheets of the first printing.

1825 onwards. When Stockdale was denied intellectual property rights, the way was opened for piracies abridgements, and adaptations, of all kinds, by Benbow, Duncombe, Dunbar, Douglas, Dugdale and others at lower prices and widening readership and many more illustrations. Some have false imprints. Within a few months the minimum price fell to 0.08 shillings a part.
'Delicate age! that purchased more than fifty thousand copies of the notorious Harriet Wilson's Memoirs!' *The Age Reviewed.*[462]

Mary Wollstonecraft

Thoughts on the Education of Daughters

1787   2.5   na
Still available in 1794[463]

Mary, a Fiction

1788   3   ?500
Still available in 1794[464]

Original Stories from Real Life (didactic stories intended to help the education of children)

1788   2   na
   With plates by William Blake   2.5
   Reprinted with revisions, 1791, 1796
1820 still available, illustrated, half bound[465]   2
Not reprinted until the twentieth century

Vindication of the Rights of Men (a pamphlet reply to Burke's *Reflections on the French Revolution*)

1790. Anonymous   1.5   na
   Sent to the printer as it was being written.[466] Probably subsidised by the publisher

---

[461] Stockdale the publisher quoting *English Law Reports*, volume 108, 65.
[462] (Robert Montgomery attrib.) *The Age Reviewed* (second edition 1828) ix.
[463] Bodleian advertisement.   [464] *Ibid.*
[465] Advertised by J. Bumpus in 1820 edition of *Letters of Junius*, Ac.
[466] Godwin in William Godwin, *Memoirs of the Author of a Vindication of the Rights of Woman*, edited by Richard Holmes (1987) 230, noted that, when she fell into a depression and had second thoughts in the course of writing the book, her publisher Johnson offered to throw aside the sheets already printed.

1790. Second edition, revised, author named   1.5   na
     Not reprinted until the twentieth century

Young Grandison

1790. Two volumes   6   na
     Translation of a French work
1795. Copies sold at reduced prices at trade sale[467]

The Female Reader (extracts, mainly old canon regarded as suitable reading for young women, published under the name of 'Mr Cresswell, Teacher of Elocution')

1790–1   3.5 bound   na
Still available in 1794[468]

Elements of Morality

1790–1
Heavily adapted translation of a work by Salzmann.   10.5   na
Three volumes with plates, some engraved by Blake.
Wollstonecraft's name does not appear.
Still available in 1794[469]

1795. Copies sold at reduced prices at trade sale[470]

1821. 'new and improved edition'[471]   2,000

A Vindication of the Rights of Woman

For the impact see chapter 14

1792   7   na

179. Second edition, small revisions[472]   7   na
In January 1792, Hookham, the fashionable bookshop and circulating library in London, ordered twelve copies, to be followed in the same year by five further orders of six each, making a total of 42 copies. It seems likely that most of these copies were intended for renting rather than sale.[473]
Reprinted in Boston, Philadelphia, and Dublin. Translated into French and German.

1795. Copies sold at reduced prices at trade sale[474]

1796. Third edition, further small revisions   7   na

---

[467] 24 February 1795, John Johnson xerox.   [468] Bodleian advertisement.   [469] *Ibid.*
[470] 24 February 1795, John Johnson xerox.   [471] Oliver and Boyd archives.
[472] Bodleian advertisement gives 6 shillings.   [473] Hookham archives, PRO.
[474] 24 February 1795, John Johnson xerox.

Appendix 9 *(cont.)*

'It seems not very improbable that it will be read as long as the English language endures.' William Godwin, Wollstonecraft's husband, in his *Memoirs of the Author of a Vindication of the Rights of Woman*, 1798, shortly after her death.

'The writings of Milton and Pope were familiar to her . . and she was a tenacious asserter of that doctrine which has recently been revived, and so warmly propagated by the late Mrs Woolstonecraft; THE EQUALITY OF THE SEXES.' John Prince describing his aunt, wife of a journeyman breeches-maker.[475]

1841. 'Third edition revised and re-edited'[476]   ?1   na
Paper covers. Probably stereotyped. Published by Strange, Cleave and other radical booksellers.

The existence of this edition, not previously noted, shows that the *Vindication* was not entirely forgotten by the Chartists. Indeed it may have been the most widely read edition before the twentieth century. However the book does not appear in the advertisement lists of Watson, Cousins, or other radical publishers, and it did not form part of the radical canon. See chapters 14 and 16.

A Vindication of the Rights of Woman with Strictures . . . by Mary Wollstonecraft New Edition with an Introduction by Mrs Henry Fawcett

1892   na   na

A Vindication of the Rights of Woman by Mary Wollstonecraft With an Introduction by Mrs Elizabeth Robins Pennell

n.d. [1892] Published to celebrate the centenary   1.5   na

The Rights of Woman was included in *Everyman's Library*, but otherwise was not easily available until the latter part of the twentieth century

Letters Written During a Short Residence in Sweden, Norway, and Denmark

1796   5   na
1802. Second edition   na   na
Not reprinted until the mid twentieth century.

William Wordsworth

Figures mainly derived from Longman archives[477]

---

[475] John Henry Prince, *Life, Pedestrian Excursions, and Singular Opinions* (1806) 35.
[476] Ac, no other copy known.
[477] Mainly summarised from W. J. B. Owen, 'Costs, Sales, and Profits of Longman's Editions of Wordsworth' in *The Library* (1957). Owen drew on the Longman archives. A record of the printing

Appendix 9 *(cont.)*

Lyrical Ballads

1798 6 500
Anonymous by Coleridge and Wordsworth. Provincial publication in Bristol. Most of the
edition sold to Arch of London[478]

1800. Second edition, two volumes 750 and 1,000

1802. Third edition 500

Poems, in Two Volumes

1807 28 1,000

1814. 230 copies remaindered

Convention of Cintra

1809 4 500
Prose pamphlet, financed by Wordsworth, sold by Longmans on commission
1810, 238 copies sold. 1811, 178 copies wasted

The Excursion

1814. 4to 42 500
'the poem is of a didactic nature . . . such as lovers of Cowper and Goldsmith will
recognise as something familiar and congenial'. *Quarterly Review*, 1814.[479]

Sales to June 1815	291
Sales to June 1816	40
Sales to June 1817	19
Sales to June 1818	19
Sales to June 1819	11
Sales to June 1820	25
Sales to June 1821	1
Sales to June 1822	1
Sales to June 1823	4
Sales 1823 to 1833	2

1834. Thirty-six copies remaindered

of *Lyrical Ballads* (1802), is in the Richard Taylor archives. The information in the archives is not
always reconcilable in detail with references in Wordsworth's letters. In cases where Owen does not
record the retail prices, I have supplied them from *The Modern London Catalogue* (1818), and from
later editions.

[478] *The London Catalogue* (1799) quotes 6 shillings as the price. Thomas J. Wise, *A Bibliography of
William Wordsworth* gives the price as 5 shillings. See also Cruse, *Englishman* 37, drawing on
Cottle's *Early Recollections*, and other sources.

[479] Donald Reiman, ed., *The Romantics Reviewed* (New York 1972), Part A, ii, 827.

Appendix 9 (*cont.*)

1820. 8vo edition	14	500
1824. Edition sold out		

Poems

1815. Two volumes	28	500
1820. Edition sold out		

The White Doe of Rylstone

1815. 4to   21   750
Longman contracted to print 750 copies, 'with the condition that no new edition be
published till our books are sold'. Longman to Wordsworth, 28 January 1815.[480]
'This, we think, has the merit of being the very worst poem we ever saw imprinted in a
quarto volume.' *Edinburgh Review*.[481]
'Do you know the reason why I published the "White Doe" in quarto?' 'No, what was it?'
"To show the world my own opinion of it.' A record of Wordsworth's conversation,
1820.[482]

1831. Copies still available

Thanksgiving Ode

1816   4   500
To 1824, 163 copies sold. 1834, 220 copies remaindered

Letter to a Friend of Robert Burns

1816. Prose   2.5   500
To 1824, 118 copies sold. 1834, 174 copies remaindered

Peter Bell

1819. Two editions   5.5   1,000
To June 1819, 701 copies sold. 1833, 139 copies remaindered

The Waggoner

1819   4.5   500
To June 1819, 241 sold. To 1833, 408 sold. 1833, 49 copies
   remaindered

The River Duddon

1820   12   500
To June 1821, 340 sold. 1834, 30 copies remaindered

---

[480] Longman archives.   [481] Quoted by Cruse, *Englishman* 52.   [482] Russell's *Moore* 272.

Appendix 9 (*cont.*)

Miscellaneous Poems

1821. Four volumes   32   500
To June 1821, 255 sold. 1826, edition sold out

Memorials of a Tour on the Continent

1822. Prose   6.5   500
To 1830, 345 copies sold. 1834, 124 copies remaindered

Ecclesiastical Sketches

1822   6.5   500
To 1833, 266 sold. 1833, 203 copies remaindered

A Description of the Scenery of the Lakes

1822 and **1823.** Two editions   5.5   1,500
1835. Sold out

Poetical Works

1827. Five volumes   45   750 plus 250 of
                                                                                    The Excursion

1832. Sold out

Poetical Works

1832. Four volumes   24   2,000 plus 500 of
                                                                                    The Excursion
1833. 1,600 copies still unsold
'Wholly inexplicable.' Wordsworth's comment.[483]
'There does not appear to be much genuine relish for poetical Literature in Cumberland;
if I may judge from the fact that not a copy of my Poems having sold there by one of the
leading Booksellers, though Cumberland is my native County. – Byron and Scott are I am
persuaded the only *popular* Writers in that line, perhaps the word ought to be that they
are *fashionable* Writers.' Wordsworth to Moxon, 1833.[484]
'You know I have not a Wordsworth, or even selections from him. These outlandish folks
don't know him. Daniel Macmillan, the future publisher, on the impossibility of buying
copies of Wordsworth in Glasgow, 1833.'[485]

1836. Sold out

Yarrow Revisited

1835   9   1,500
Second edition, from stereotypes[486]   500

---

[483] Merriam 136.   [484] Wordsworth *Letters*, second edn, v, 11, 633, c. 10 August 1833.
[485] Hughes 23.   [486] Strahan archives.

Appendix 9 *(cont.)*

1837. 322 copies unsold, stereotype plates sold to Moxon
1842. Moxon remainders the last copies at 0.9s each[487]

Poetical Works

1836. Six volumes	30	3,000
End 1837, 1,900 still in stock[488]		

1843. Wordsworth appointed Poet Laureate
1850. Wordsworth dies

The Prelude

1850[489]	6	2,000
For Victorian editions see chapter 21.		

---

[487] Merriam 99, 140.   [488] Merriam 136.   [489] Print run from Merriam 148.

Appendix 10 Libraries and reading societies

Estimated growth of circulating libraries in London[1]

Late seventeenth century	some
Early eighteenth century	few or none
1740–50	9
1770[2]	4
1770–80	19
1790–1800	26

The largest, the Minerva, was founded in 1775

Start-up period

'. . . though novels are a pretty light summer reading, and do very well in Tunbridge, Bristol, and the other watering places: no bad commodity for the West-India trade, neither; let 'em be novels, Master Cape'. From Samuel Foote's comedy *The Author*, first performed 1757.[3]

'The reading female hires her novels from some Country Circulating Library, which consists of about a hundred volumes.' *Annual Register for 1761*.[4]

'A man might as well turn his daughter loose in Covent garden [the theatre and prostitute area] as trust the cultivation of her mind to a circulating library.' The words of her father in George Colman's play *Polly Honeycombe*, 1760.

'A circulating library in a town is an evergreen tree of diabolical knowledge! It blossoms through the year. And, depend on it, Mrs Malaprop, that those who are so fond of handling the leaves will long for the fruit at last.' Sir Anthony Absolute in Sheridan's *The Rivals*, first acted 1775.

Output of new novels and romances, many intended for circulating libraries, published in London, by title[5]

1770s, annual average	31
1780s	38
1790s	66

Output of new novels and romances, many intended for circulating libraries, published in London and Edinburgh, by title[6]

1800s, annual average	77

---

[1] Stewart-Murphy 15. The range of estimates varies a good deal, and will probably have to be revised upwards as a result of current work being done by Robin Alston. See the on-line 'Library History Data Base'.
[2] Timperley 721.   [3] Quoted in part by Plant 57.
[4] Quoted by Collins, *Profession of Letters* 29.
[5] Summarised from Raven in Garside, Raven, and Schöwerling i, 72   [6] *Ibid.* ii, 73

Appendix 10 *(cont.)*

1810s	66
1820s	82

London, late eighteenth and early nineteenth century. Minerva Library, Leadenhall Street, London, founded 1775, early nineteenth century rates

	Shillings
Eighteen books in town or twenty-four in country	84
Twelve books in town, eighteen in country	63
Six books in town, twelve in country	42
Four books in town, eight in country	31.5
Two novels at a time	16
Non-subscribers, per volume per week	0.5 folio
	0.3 8vo
	0.25 12mo
	0.16 single plays, per day

Typical circulating libraries, early nineteenth century

Annual membership prices for borrowing one volume at a time

Hookham's, Bond Street (fashionable West End, with many titled clients, men and women)[7]	42
Barratt's, Bath, c. 1818 (fashionable resort), about 5,000 volumes	30
Greer's Belfast, about 1,500 volumes	30
Rowley's, Edmonton, c. 1820	21
Mrs Crew's, Liverpool, 1840, about 1,000 volumes	21
Warren's, Faversham	16
Pollocks, North Shields	14
Wilson's, Nottingham	8
Knaresborough, 1834, 300 volumes, mostly religious	4

'A respectable subscription library, a circulating library of ancient standing, and some private book-shelves were open to my random perusal, and I waded into the stream like a blind man into a ford.' Walter Scott, recalling his reading of old romances during his schooldays in Kelso in the early 1780s.[8]

'I can read their three-volume enormities to this day without skipping a syllable; though I guess nearly all that is going to happen from the mysterious gentleman who opens the work, in the dress of a particular century, down to the drying of tears in the last chapter.' Leigh Hunt.[9]

'An extensive circulating library supplied me with romances and novels which I read rapidly and incessantly . . . My mind had thus become enfeebled.' William Hone the radical bookseller.[10]

---

[7] For a reconstruction of the history of Hookham's, with many interesting details, see F. B. Curtis, 'Shelley and the Hookham Circulating Library in Old Bond Street' in *Keats-Shelley Memorial Bulletin*, 1982. Some ledgers of the 1790s in the Public Record Office, Kew.
[8] Lockhart 11.   [9] Quoted by Cruse, *Englishman* 97.   [10] Hackwood 54.

Appendix 10 *(cont.)*

Circulating libraries 'supply novels and high-seasoned productions for sickly or perverted appetites, but . . . as far as they exhibit the passions and foibles of mankind, amend the heart, and extend the influence of sentiment and sensibility, they must be regarded as useful establishments'. A traveller for the book trade, 1821.[11]

SUBSCRIPTION LIBRARIES AND BOOK CLUBS OWNED BY MEMBERS

The Liverpool Library, later the Liverpool Lycaeum

1757. Begins as a club of friends of a local schoolmaster. Periodicals bought collectively, circulated among members and kept in a cupboard.

1758. The principal merchants, professional men, and tradesmen found the Liverpool Library. Books to be bought, circulated, and kept. Entry subscription 31 shillings then 5 shillings annual fee. Amalgamated with a coffee-house club which brings a collection of books.

1759. First catalogue published, 450 books, 109 members.

1786. A 'spacious room' rented for twenty-one years.

1794. Entry subscription by now 105 shillings, annual fee 10.5 shillings. Collection consists of 5,095 volumes, annual expenditure on books 3,000 shillings.

1800. A fine new building, the Lyceum, built, combining library, reading room, and coffee and newsroom. Membership limited to 893 where it stays at least until 1889.

1801. 8,157 volumes

1830. 21,400 volumes

1850. 36,761 volumes

The Liverpool Athenaeum[12]

Opened 1799. 350 original subscribers, gradually extended

Admission fee, shillings	210
Annual fee	42
Expenditure after expenses, on books	66 per cent
on newspapers	33 per cent
Share price, 1800	600 shillings rising
All books kept, unless duplicates	

Hull Subscription Library

Founded 1775. In 1805 2,300 titles, 462 members including thirty-five women. Later, probably 1820s, In 1820s entry fee 210 shillings plus 21 shillings annually. Membership fully transferable.

---

[11] *Monthly Magazine* (June 1821).
[12] Extracted from *Catalogue of the Liverpool Library* (1814), with *Appendix* (1820).

Appendix 10 *(cont.)*

'. . . the proposer of the history of Tom Thumb, Jack Hickathrift, [chapbooks] a sixpenny [0.5 shillings] edition of Watts's Songs for Children or a two penny tract. [0.15 shillings] . . . has just a right to be offended . . . These have actually been put down in the Poll book!' From a letter of complaint about purchasing policy, 1812.[13]

Halifax Circulating Library (subscription library)[14]

Founded 1768, inspired by the libraries at Liverpool and Manchester. Original membership about 140, clergymen, gentry, lawyers, wool merchants, apparently mainly men but one titled lady.

1770. Bought shelves; 1781, engaged a paid librarian; 1785 hired a room; 1817, a house; 1824, then specially designed premises.
Initially a high entrance fee as well as annual subscription. Entry fee abandoned in 1800s. In 1815 subscription fee 25 shillings. Heavy fines for subscribing for a book before it had arrived at the library and been placed on the table for general inspection. Large fine (2.5 shillings) for borrowing a book without having it entered in the register. Initial purchases mainly history, law, trade, classics in translation, but also works of Swift, Dryden, Sterne. In 1790 decides to exclude all books on religion, a rule rigorously enforced. In 1797 orders the burning of books 'found to be of an indecent or immoral or blasphemous character'. Accepts *Gil Blas* and *Roderick Random*, but rejects as 'unsuitable for circulation' Boccaccio and Burton's *Anatomy of Melancholy.*

York Book Society, later York Subscription Library[15]

Founded 1794. Entrance fee 10.5 shillings plus annual subscription of 21 shillings. Met monthly. In 1796 had eighteen members all men, forty-nine books and some pamphlets. By 1803 had 131 members including eight women, two titled men, and nine clergymen. The collection of about 200 volumes was now rearranged by title instead of by date of acquisition. Almost exclusively new expensive books of history, travel, philosophy, and many contemporary political pamphlets. The library bought Godwin's *Political Justice*, Volney's *Ruins*, some works by Paine but not *Rights of Man*, some works by Wollstonecraft but not *Rights of Woman*. Only a few literary works had been bought by 1803, including Radcliffe's *The Italian*, Burney's *Camilla*, and Campbell's *Pleasures of Hope.*

Cirencester, Bibury, and Fairford Book Clubs, Gloucestershire, turn of the century[16]

The three clubs appear to have been similar in social composition and in their purchasing policy. In 1806 the Cirencester had a membership of twelve, all men, each paying

---

[13] Isaac Wilson, *Letter to Daniel Sykes . . . on Hull Subscription Library* (1812), Bodleian. *Laws of the Subscription Library at Kingston upon Hull* (n.d., 1820s), Bodleian.

[14] E. P. Rouse, 'Old Halifax Circulating Library, 1768–1866' in *Halifax Antiquarian Society Publications* (1911). The original minute books &c are lost but Rouse's notes and transcriptions are preserved in Calderdale District Record Office, Halifax.

[15] *Laws of a Book Society Established at York* (n.d., 1796), and annual updates for a few years later. John Johnson collection.

[16] Stevens ledgers.

21 shillings a year, plus an entry fee to build the revolving fund. The clubs each bought about thirty books and pamphlets a year, many concerned with current political, educational and religious questions, including especially Burke's *Reflections* and Paine's *Rights of Man*. They took many sermons, plus two conservative reviews, the *Anti-Jacobin* and the *British Critic*, with only a very occasional book of imaginative literature, including Rogers's *Pleasures of Memory*, Scott's *Ballads*, and Radcliffe's *Mysteries of Udolpho*. They sold all the books after they had done their rounds, netting a return of nearly half the original cost.

Book clubs in Hampshire, 1813

'The Miss Sibleys want to establish a Book Society in their side of the Country, like ours . . . What can be stronger proof of that superiority in ours over the Steventon and Manydown Society which I have always foreseen and felt. – No emulation of the kind was ever inspired by *their* proceedings; no such wish of the Miss Sibleys was ever heard, in the course of the many years of that Society's existence; – And what are their Biglands and their Barrows, their Macartneys & Mackenzies[17] to Capt. Pasley's Essay on the Military Police [policy] of the British Empire & the rejected Addresses.'[18]
'Ladies who read those enormous great stupid thick Quarto Volumes which one always sees in the Breakfast parlour there', Austen wrote shortly afterwards about the Sibley household, 'must be acquainted with everything in the World. – I detest a Quarto. Capt Pasley's book is too good for their Society. They will not understand a Man who condenses his Thoughts into an Octavo.'[19]

Bolton Union Book Club, previously known as Bolton Caledonian Book Club[20]

Established before 1806. Originally about twenty members, all men, many with Scottish names. In 1817 about thirty members all men, entrance fee 32.5 shillings, plus subscription of 2.5 shillings a quarter. Books allowed out for five weeks. Careful registers, note of damage, and fines. A valuation in 1816 showed a library of about 230 volumes. The entry fee appears to have been adjusted from time to time to reflect the growing value of the collection.
The room in the Ship where the books were kept served also as newsroom for a newspaper club of about forty or fifty members, all men, paying 16 shillings. In 1816 the newspaper club took *The Courier, Statesman, Cobbett's, Observer, Mercury, Anti-Gallican*, and local

---

[17] Books about Spain, China and Iceland, full titles in Austen, *Letters*, and 'General Index of Literary Allusions' in R. W. Chapman's edition of the novels of Jane Austen (1923 and later) v.
[18] Bestselling book of parodies of living poets by James and Horace Smith first published in 1812, Austen, *Letters* 198.
[19] *Ibid.* 206.
[20] The four surviving ledgers of the Gloucester bookseller Timothy Stevens offer a glimpse of three English provincial book clubs at the turn of the century when Stevens supplied the Bibury, the Cirencester, and the Fairford book clubs, and had started to deal with Mr Webb's New Book Society. Gloucester Public Library. For an account of the earlier period, see Paul Kaufman, 'A Bookseller's Record of Eighteenth Century Book Clubs', *The Library* (1960). There are a few entries as late as 1818 but the main record stops about 1807–8.

Appendix 10 *(cont.)*

papers of Carlisle, Liverpool, and Chester. Regular debates on general topics, e.g. 'whether love or anger be the stronger passion'.[21]

Bristol Library Society

By 1770s and 1780s the library contained many books on classics, history, travel. British and French Enlightenment writers, including Gibbon, Robertson and Hume's books of history, Montesquieu, Helvétius, Voltaire, Rousseau, were extensively borrowed, along with Chesterfield. Books on science were also among the categories most extensively borrowed. The library was used by Coleridge who presented a copy of his *Poems*, 1796.[22] By 1798 the membership was 198 including three women. At that time it contained 5,000 volumes. Extensive purchasing and borrowing records exist.
'It is recommended to the Committee to revise their sentence on [Coleridge's] Christabel. It is but 4/6 [4.5 shillings] and they have recently expended £4 4s [84 shillings] on a treatise on *Playing Cards*. 3,000 copies of Christabel were sold in the first fortnight. It is a curious attempt to make accent instead of syllables the measure of verse; besides it has excited considerable interest in this city from the Author's local connexions.' Note by a member, 1816.[23]
The records show the increasing and repeated attempts by some members to persuade the committee to buy modern novels, all rejected until 1814 with a decision to buy *Waverley*, the society then decided to buy every new novel by the author of *Waverley* as it came out, members eagerly writing the titles in the proposal book before the books were even published.

Luddenden Circulating Library, Yorkshire

Founded c. 1776. In 1818 it consisted of twenty-four members, all men, apart from widows who inherited their husbands' membership. Shares were hereditary, but not saleable, and the same family names appear in the membership lists during the society's long history. Met monthly. Bought and circulated four books a month, which were kept. In 1834 had about 1,000 volumes. In 1790s the society had bought Paine's *The Rights of Man* and *The Age of Reason*, as well as religious works. In 1830, at the time of the Reform Bill debates and the Revolution in France, the society decided 'to remove all the seditious, deistical, immoral, and other pernicious works'. About ten books, titles not known, were recommended for ejection.[23]

Ayr Library Society

Established 1762. Entry fee 1 shilling, annual fee 7 shillings, very cheap compared with prices in England, and the reverse of the usual proportion. The fee probably increased with the inflation which began in the 1790s. The committee met to select the books four times a year. During first forty years the society had a total of 103 members, ministers,

---

[21] Book receipts, a register book, and sundry other papers relating to the Bolton Caledonian Book Club and Bolton Union Book Club, Bolton Central Library.

[22] For the actual sales figures see appendix 6.

[23] 'Coleridge's Poems on Various Subjects, 8vo. The Gift of the Author Mr S. T. Coleridge, May 17 1796.' Donation book no. 99.

Appendix 10 (*cont.*)

physicians, writers, merchants, two tanners, a baker, a cabinet maker, and a watchmaker. In 1790 the society decided to exclude works of religious controversy and novels.

Kirkcudbright Public Library[24]

Established 1777 to buy 'the most valuable Books on ancient and modern history, voyages, travels, Belles Lettres. Agriculture &c.' A subscription library. About twenty members, all men. Shares in 1807 cost 123 shillings on admission. Many books on travel, history, religion, plus Bloomfield, Burns, Anderson's *British Poets*, thirteen volumes [old-canon collection]. All Scott's poems as they came out, Crabbe, all Byron, Hogg, Wilson, Miss Bowles, Barry Cornwall, Moore's *Lalla Rookh*, Waverley novels as they came out, Kirke White.

Wigton Subscription Library[25]

Established 1795. About forty members, local landowners, public officials, ministers of religion, professional men, a few merchants, a few women. Entry fee 21 shillings plus annual subscription (1810s and 20 shillings) 7.5 shillings. Shares heritable and disposable. Bought about ten books a year, concentrating on histories of various European countries, travel and exploration, science, agriculture, plus Bell's *British Theatre*, and a few old-canon novels. In 1806 decided to buy Scott's *The Minstrelsy of the Scottish Border*, then all Scott's own poems as they came out 'second hand if possible'. Also Cowper, Campbell, Crabbe, Rogers, Hogg, Byron in six volumes ('a cheap edition'), Moore ('a cheap edition') Moore folio music, sent back on grounds of expense. After *Waverley*, they bought all the works of the author of *Waverley* as they came out, in some years a third or more of all the books bought. By the 1830s they were buying many novels, especially Bentley's Standard Novels. No sign of interest in Wordsworth, Shelley, or anything controversial. In 1831 the committee was invited to 'enquire the price of *Lalla Rookh*'.

The Eclectic Book Society, London[26]

Founded 1807. During 1813 to 1820, the club consisted of twelve members, all men, all evidently well-off, all carefully selected by the other members. Entry fee on election 105 shillings of which two thirds was returned when a member left, a figure changed in 1817 into a fee of 42 shillings not returnable. Members paid 1 shilling a month, and with fines and the income from sales, this enabled the society to buy four or five books a month selected by the members in rotation, all of which were circulated to every member.[27] The club took a wide variety of books on travel, antiquities, history, economics, church matters, and conduct literature. The club also took half a dozen literary journals including the *Edinburgh* and the *Quarterly Reviews*, sometimes cancelling their subscription when

---

[24] Summarised from the surviving archives, Hornell Museum, Kirkcudbright.
[25] *Ibid.*   [26] Guildhall Library, London, mss. 988A.
[27] Minute book for the years 1813 to 1820. Guildhall Library, London, mss. 988A.

Appendix 10 *(cont.)*

an article caused offence, and renewing it at the next meeting. All books were sold after the annual dinner.

An unidentified book club, London, 1822

Twelve members meeting in each others' houses four times a year. Annual income 360 shillings plus 160 shillings from sale of books. Booksellers' discount of 10 per cent defrays the expenses. Fines for delay 3d [0.25 shillings] a day; omitting to write in the date 1 shilling; failing to attend 2.5 shillings.

'The Liberals', a London working men's book club, c. 1821

Working men who paid a small subscription towards the foundation of a select library of books for circulation. Met two evenings a week for discussion on literary, political, and philosophical topics.
'. . . laid the foundations of what little knowledge I possess'. William Lovett, a Chartist leader.[28]

Miles Platting Reading Society, a radical book club, 1820s

Established 1820 to 'extend the circulation of such writings . . . [which] dispel the thick mist of ignorance, and burst the shackles of delusion [e.g. the unlawful books published by Carlile]'. Membership about twenty. Subscription sixpence [0.5 shillings] or more if a member wished. Every member chose a book to buy as soon as his accumulated subscriptions permitted. The books were circulated to all members, kept for a month and then returned to the proposer as his private property. Met every second Sunday. In its first three years the society bought and circulated 150 books.[29]

MECHANICS INSTITUTES LIBRARIES, 1826

Summarised from replies to a questionnaire about the state of progress from Henry Brougham sent to twenty-five institutes in large and small towns in England and Scotland.[30]

Birmingham

Annual subscription rates 42 shillings, 21 shillings, 12 shillings, and 6 shillings. The higher rates were for patrons and supporters, about thirty to forty at 12 shillings, only one member at 42 shillings. The reason for lack of support was said to be fear that the mechanics would combine to form trade unions.
Main rate for mechanics 12 shillings, the lower rate for apprentices

---

[28] *The Life and Struggles of William Lovett in his Pursuit of Bread, Knowledge, and Freedom* (1876) 34.
[29] *The Republican*, (1823) 635.
[30] Archives of Society for the Diffusion of Useful Knowledge, SDUK/22.

Appendix 10 *(cont.)*

Membership steady at about 250
Using the Scotch church for lectures

Manchester

Eleven local patrons each gave £600
About 700 members

Ashton under Lyme

Had been about 500 members but reduced to about 100 as a result of economic recession.

Ayr

About 100 ordinary members, with about fifty honorary members paying 42 shillings.

Devonshire and Stonehouse

Lost about half its money with the crash of a local bank. Life membership for £10 or a gift of £20 worth of books.

Lectures

Most institutes reported lectures on mechanics, chemistry, and mathematics, all well attended.

Libraries

Manchester about 1,400 titles of which about half had been donated, Leeds about 300, Dunbar about 200
Almost all had extensive holdings of books on chemistry, engineering, mathematics, and science and technology. Many also took books on travels, philosophy, and history, many modern and expensive. Smith's *Wealth of Nations* and Gibbon's *Decline and Fall* were common, along with Paley. Some extremely expensive books were occasionally held, for example, five volumes of Palladio's *Architecture* at Leeds. Many libraries had a few old-canon prose and verse works including conduct books, notably Thomson's *Seasons* and Pope's *Homer*, but others had no imaginative literature of any kind. Despite standing rules against 'sectarianism' Hackney Institute accepted five volumes of tracts from the Christian Tract Society and the Society for Promoting Christian Knowledge on the grounds that they were moral rather than religious. Dunbar Institute made sure that all 'frivolous, irreligious, and polemical books' were carefully excluded.
No institute which reported its holdings seems to have taken any romantic-period literature poetry or novels apart from Stockton which had a copy of Wordsworth's *Lyrical Ballads*, two volumes. No sign of Byron or Scott, or Waverley novels in any library. All institutes reported heavy and frequent borrowing by the mechanics. All said the mechanics wanted more 'general literature'.

Appendix 10 *(cont.)*

Science 'elevates the faculties above low pursuits, purifies and refines the passions, and helps our reason to assuage their violence'. Lord Brougham, one of the founders of the Mechanics institutes movement and of the Society for the Diffusion of Useful Knowledge.[31]

Mechanics institutes libraries in Yorkshire, 1842

In larger towns about 2 per cent of population members, in smaller towns much higher. Thirty-eight libraries, with 38,000 volumes, 73,000 borrowings by 7,900 members.[32]

COUNTER-ENLIGHTENMENT LIBRARIES IN RURAL AREAS

Lewes Mechanics Institution, Library, 1827

About 250 volumes, some confined. Only one volume lent at a time, fourteen days. Heavy fines. Mainly history, ancient classics in translation, voyages and travel, science, technology, economics, philosophy, conduct, reference, one novel (Galt's *Ayrshire Legatees*), old-canon anthologies, Enfield's *Speaker*, Murray's *Reader*. No politics or religion.

Westgate Library, Lewes, 1825

About 350 volumes. Open to the public. The books were kept in the vestry of the Unitarian Chapel. Miss E. Shelley, perhaps a relative of the poet, was one of about fifty subscribers. The main holdings were books of religion, travel, history, and conduct. 'All meetings to be concluded with a prayer.'[33]
'[In Scotland] they have book societies and send new books to and fro to one another with an alacrity and punctuality that are most delightful . . . When I have been pedestrianising in that country, I have frequently accosted men at their work . . . and found them well acquainted with the latest good publications, and entertaining the soundest notions of them, without the aid of critics. Such men in England would probably not have been able to read at all.' William Howitt, 1838.[34]

Magazine societies, 1821 estimate

Typically ten to twelve members. Subscription 20 shillings or 21 shillings
Main holdings *Monthly Review, Monthly Magazine, Edinburgh Review, Quarterly Review*

---

[31] Quoted by James Secord in 'Progress in Print' 378 in Marina Frasca-Spada and Nick Jardine, eds., *Books and the Sciences in History* (2000), from (Brougham's) *Objects, Advantages, and Pleasures of Science* (1827), of which 33,100 copies had been sold by 1829.
[32] Figures quoted by Earl of Carlisle, 'On the High Position attained by Mechanics' Institutes in Yorkshire', *Lectures and Addresses* (1852) 92.
[33] Copies of catalogues and rules of Lewes, Westgate and Southover Societies. London Library.
[34] *Ibid.* Quoted by Kaufman from Samuel Smiles, *Lives of the Engineers* (1861) ii, 492.

Appendix 10 *(cont.)*

NEWSPAPER SOCIETIES, 1821 ESTIMATE

Six, seven or eight persons pay 0.5 shillings a week, to buy one London paper and two or three provincial papers. In poorer districts twelve or fourteen persons pay 1 penny a week, buy one or two provincial papers.

Total number of magazine and newspaper societies in 1821 – 750

FREE PUBLIC LIBRARIES

1849–52. Reports by the Parliamentary Select Committee on Public Libraries which describe the poor level of education and widespread lack of access to books.

1850. Public Libraries Act (to be followed by others)[35]

---

[35] John Minto, *A History of the Public Library Movement in Great Britain and Ireland* (1932).

Types of print available outside the mainstream book industry. No archival records are known to have survived, but occasional figures are recorded. My main sources are surviving copies of the books, some of which carry advertisements.

William Hone, 1810s and 1820s[1]

Hone composed and published political satires, many illustrated with woodcuts by Cruikshank. They included *The Political Litany*, a parody of the biblical ten commandments, for which he was unsuccessfully prosecuted. Most of Hone's publications were lawful. Some pamphlets claim to have been reprinted in as many as forty-eight editions. No information on print runs found. The prices were low compared with those of other new books, his pamphlets being usually one shilling or less.

Richard Carlile and family, 1820s and 1830s[2]

Although Carlile was in prison for many years for publishing offences, he managed to keep his publications on the market. The main business was in the works of Paine (including the dubious part III of *The Age of Reason*; Volney's *The Ruins of Empire*; Palmer's *The Principles of Nature*; philosophical works by Godwin and other radical and sceptical writers; pamphlets by Robert Owen and Robert Dale Owen, and advice on birth control. Some recorded print runs are noted in appendix 9 'Thomas Paine' and 'C. F. Volney'. In 1823 the authorities are said to have seized 50,000 books and pamphlets, including over 1,000 copies of *The Rights of Man*.[3]
Every Woman's Book, a book of advice on birth control said to have sold 5,000 copies by 1826.[4]

William Clark, 1820s

Only a few books are known. Clark had worked for Carlile, and appears to have later set up on his own, possibly as a front man for Carlile.

William Benbow, 1820s

His list included pirated reprints of most of Byron's works sold in paper covers for a shilling or less.[5]
'When I published English Bards and Scotch Reviewers, few except gentlemen had read the work, but in cheap form it was soon in the hand of every mechanic in the kingdom who has a taste for reading.' Benbow in 1825.[6]

---

[1] Summarised from catalogues in *The Second Trial of William Hone* (1818), and *The Political Showman* (1821), Ac.
[2] Advertisements and surviving copies. Other information from Joel H. Wiener, *Radicalism and Freethought in Nineteenth Century Britain, The Life of Richard Carlile* (1983).
[3] *The Republican* (1823) 240.   [4] *The Republican* (1826) xiv, 443.
[5] Advertisement lists in *Cobbett's English Grammar* (1820), and *Poetical Works of Thomas Little* (1825), Ac. See also McCalman.
[6] W. Benbow, *A Scourge for the Laureate* (n.d. c. 1825).

Appendix 11 (*cont.*)

Philosophical Dictionary
Extracts from French enlightenment philosophers
Oraculum or Book of Fate
Decameron of Boccaccio
Vicar's *English Worthies*
The Rights of the People
William Lawrence's *Lectures*
A book on anatomy by a famous surgeon, declared unlawful and possibly blasphemous
because it saw no need to postulate the existence of a soul. The first edition, *Comparative
Anatomy* (1807), had been produced in an edition of 750 copies, so that the banning seems
to have caused pirate reprinting at lower prices with greater impact.[7]
Lewis's *The Monk* in three volumes (not pornographic but not fully respectable)
Poems of Thomas Little (i.e. Thomas Moore)
Maxims of la Rochfoucault
Benbow's *Religious Tracts*
'designed as an antidote to the baneful system of Methodistical Cant, Hypocrisy, and
Blasphemy which is deluding the Unwary and Credulous people of this country'.
Advertisement.
The Crimes of the Clergy, two volumes. (Examples of financial, sexual, and other abuses)
Basia of Secundus. (Mildly erotic)
Translation of Louvet's *Amours . . . de Faublas*
A transvestite French novel with erotic plates for which Benbow was successfully
prosecuted for obscene libel. Lockhart suggested in 1821 that in *Don Juan* Byron had
copied *Faublas*, described as 'a book which is to found on the tables of Roués, and in the
desks of divines and under the pillows of spinsters – a book, in a word, which is read
universally'.[8]
Harriette Wilson's *Memoirs* in full and in parts
Cobbett's *A Grammar of the English Language . . . Intended for the Use of Schools, and of
Young Persons in general; but more especially for the Use of Soldiers, Sailors, Apprentices, and
Plough-Boys*. Tens of thousands of copies sold
Plus pamphlets, satires, plays, squibs, prints, and periodicals, many at less than
a shilling

Books published by Benbow in association with 'Erasmus Perkins'

Shelley's *The Cenci*

Shelley's *Miscellaneous and Posthumous Poems*

*Melodies, Irish and National, by the Celebrated British Poet, Thomas Moore, Esq. Verbatim
from the London edition of 1822*
1822. Pisa (actually London). Presso Erasmo Perchino. Prezzo Paoli
138 pp. 'Avviso' initialled E. P. (Erasmus Perkins)
A false imprint by Benbow and Perkins for which Benbow was successfully prosecuted in
1822 for omitting the name of the printer[9]

---

[7] Strahan archives.   [8] Strout 21.
[9] See Charles Henry Taylor, *The Early Collected Editions of Shelley's Poems*, Yale Studies in English 140
(1958) 11, quoting *The Examiner*, 25 May 1823.

Appendix 11 (*cont.*)

William Dugdale, 1820s and later

Reprints of Byron at around a shilling, works of Moore, French pornography with 'superb and fascinating plates' at prices of more than 20 shillings. Harriette Wilson's *Memoirs* in full and in parts.

'Judging from the contents of Dugdale's window, the literature of the working class . . . a *mélange* of sedition, blasphemy, and obscenity.' *The Times*, 1848[10]

'Dugdale, after a score of imprisonments, still perseveres in the sale of indecent prints.' *The Bookseller*, 1868[11]

J. J. Stockdale, mainly 1820s and later[12]

The younger Stockdale is best known for having published *The Memoirs of Harriette Wilson*. Besides political pamphlets, and some early works by Shelley, he also published semi-pornographic satire, possibly as part of a political agenda.

Other pirates, 1820s

Byron's *The Prisoner of Chillon*, London, 1817, no publisher or printer named.[13] W. P. Chubb, printer, Byron's *The Prisoner of Chillon*, 1824
Thomas Wilson, Byron's *The Bride of Abydos*, 1825
Thomas Colmer, Byron's *Childe Harold's Pilgrimage*, 1827
H. Gray, 1822; Crofts, 1830, Byron's *Cain*
Childe Harold's Pilgrimage. Complete, by Lord Byron. 1827. Paris (but probably London)[14]
A copy was owned by Branwell Bronte at Howarth[15]
Childe Harold's Pilgrimage. A Romaunt. By the Right Hon. Lord Byron
n.d. c. 1829. London. John Duncombe, a theatrical publisher who also published a fake continuation of *Don Juan*[16]

John Brooks, late 1820s and early 1830s[17]

Shelley's *The Revolt of Islam* (remaindered)[18]
Shelley's *The Cenci* (remaindered)
(Shelley and Mary Shelley) *Six Weeks Tour* (remaindered)
The Reformer's Library (five volumes of works of sceptical philosophers)
Bolingbroke's *Patriot King*. Works of Paine, Robert Owen, and Robert Dale Owen
Reformer's Catechism
The People's Charter
Books challenging the consistency and historical truth of the Bible

---

[10] Quoted by Thomas Frost, *Reminiscences of a Country Journalist* (1886) 53.
[11] 'Mischievous Literature' in *The Bookseller* (1868), 445.
[12] Stockdale.   [13] Copy in Bodleian.
[14] The type looks English and the printers' key signatures are in letters and numbers, not numbers as in most French books. In a copy I have seen in original boards, the boards are made from English publishers' waste.
[15] Copy of title page kindly supplied by Christine Alexander from the original at Haworth.
[16] Ac.   [17] Summarised from printed advertisement leaf tipped in copy of *The Yahoo* (1830), Ac.
[18] Remaindered sheets of the original edition.

Moral Physiology (birth control)
The Yahoo (verse satire falsely claiming to have been printed in New York)
Sir James Lawrence, *The Etonian Out of Bounds* for Erasmus Perkins, 1834
In 1827 a man charged with stealing books from Brooks's shop was acquitted, when the court ruled that Brooks, as an avowed deist who did not fear punishment after death, could not be trusted to tell the truth.

Charles Daly, 1820s to 1840s

Began as a dealer in waste paper before branching into remainders and then his own publications.[19] Tiny print stereotyped on large 'elephant' or 'imperial' sheets folded into the tiny square size of 32mo. Since many books are undated the dates of manufacture and sale are uncertain. Prices not known but probably cheap and falling.

William Strange, 1830s and 1840s

Political pamphlets, including a reprint of Wollstonecraft's *Rights of Woman*. He also published out of copyright literary works in paper covers, extremely cheaply, notably Milton, Scott's *Marmion*, some romantic tales by Byron, and plays at a penny each.

James Watson, 1830s to 1850s

Mostly Watson's own publications, retail in London and wholesale to the network of radical bookshops which, by the 1830s, existed in all the main industrial cities. Watson was a successor to Carlile for whom he had worked, and took over stock from Brooks and others. Prices usually less than 1 shilling, and many far lower. Longer works, e.g. Godwin's *Political Justice* (see appendix 9 'William Godwin'), were available in numbers. Most of his books were stereotyped and published in paper wrappers.[20]
Watson sold many works by and about Tom Paine; Volney's *Ruins*; liberal and sceptical writers, English and French; pamphlets questioning the literal truth of the Bible, including the findings of geology; Lawrence's *Anatomy*, economic, and political pamphlets by Owen, Holyoake, and others; advice on birth control; grammars, mathematics, science, advice of farming, and other self education, Chartist songs, including some from Shelley, and a few literary works by working men including Thomas Cooper's prison epic, *The Purgatory of Suicides*.

B. D. Cousins, 1830s until 1850s[21]

Much the same as Watson

John Cleave, 1840s and later

No list found. Seems also to have been similar to Watson's

---

[19] Adlard ledger shows him buying waste copies of *The Medical Journal* in 1826.
[20] Advertisements in his books. Last date seen on a title page 1850, Ac.
[21] Advertisement in copy of *The Life of Thomas Paine* (n.d.) Ac.

Appendix 11 *(cont.)*

Abel Heywood, Manchester, 1830s and later

No list found. Heywood seems to have sold books from Watson in London as well as publishing some of his own. He became Lord Mayor of Manchester.

Freethought Publishing Company, mid and late Victorian[22]

Pamphlets by Charles Bradlaugh, Annie Besant, Edward Aveling, and others which contest the truth of the Bible, condemn the power of the church, criticise the existing distribution of wealth and income, and call for reform of marriage. Plus Tom Paine, Voltaire's *Philosophical Dictionary, The Works of Shelley*, 'The poet of Atheism and Democracy', in four volumes, 2 shillings each, Shelley's *Song to the Men of England*, set to music 0.16 shillings. 'THREE HUNDRED AND TWENTY SECOND THOUSAND'. Advertisement.

Shelley's *Queen Mab*. Publication

	Prices (shillings)	Print run

To save space I have not transcribed all the title pages.

Queen Mab, A Philosophical Poem, With Notes, By Percy Bysshe Shelley
1813. Privately printed   na   250
180 undistributed copies were sold to collectors many years later[23]

Queen Mab, A Philosophical Poem, By Percy Bysshe Shelley
1821. New York (but actually London), 12mo. The $\varepsilon\pi$ on the engraved title page and the ¶ of the added preface are codes for Erasmus Perkins. The eagle and snake wand also appears on the engraved title of Benbow's *Don Juan*.[24] Title pages are found in Gothic and Roman implying that there were several issues.

Queen Mab. By Percy Bysshe Shelley
1821. 8vo. Imprint 'Printed and Published by W. Clark, 201, Strand. T. M.' (i.e. Thomas Moses, a printer, who probably financed the publication). Two versions, original and expurgated.
1822. Printed and published by R. Carlile. Made from Clark's unexpurgated version but with a new title page. Some copies also have a slip pasted over the previous imprint 'Printed and Published by R. Carlile, 55, Fleet Street'.

Queen Mab by Shelly [sic] 5 shillings.
In Dugdale's advertisement list 1823. No copy found

Queen Mab, By Percy Bysshe Shelley
1826. Printed for the Joint Stock Company, and Pubished [sic] by Richard Carlile, 32mo.[25]
                                 2.5 in boards   2,000
'Queen Mab and [Paine's] Good Sense are the best selling books which the company has printed.' Carlile, 1826.[26]

---

[22] Advertisement in *The Three Trials of William Hone*, reprinted c. 1880, ac.
[23] W. H. Wickwar, *The Struggle for the Freedom of the Press* (1828) 263.
[24] See St Clair, *Godwins and Shelleys*, 512–18, and illustration.
[25] Accounts of the Joint Stock Company in appendix 5.
[26] *The Republican* (1826) 96.

Appendix II *(cont.)*

1829. 8vo. 'Printed by R. Brooks, Oxford Street'   9
an unregistered name.
Queen Mab. Or the Destiny of Man. A Philosophical Poem. By Percy Bysshe Shelley
Revised Edition Free from All Objectionable Passages
1830. Stephen Hunt. 12mo. Notes and 800 lines of verse omitted

The Beauties of Percy Bysshe Shelley . . . . and a revised edition of Queen Mab, free from all the
objectionable passages. With a biographical Preface.
1830. Stephen Hunt. Several reimpressions and   3.5
reprinted editions.

Queen Mab. By Percy Bysshe Shelley.
1832. Printed and published by Mrs Carlile and Sons

Queen Mab with Notes. By Percy Bysshe Shelley
1832. London: John Brooks, 18mo   1.5
Yellow paper wrappers have been bound round sheets from Carlile's edition. The first
really cheap version

Queen Mab, or, The Palace of Prophecy
No date. Probably between 1832 and 1835. London. W. Medhurst. 12mo. Only known
from one copy.[27]

The Works of Percy Bysshe Shelley, With His Life. In Two Volumes
1834. Printed and published by John Ascham. 12mo. There were to be ten parts, each
costing 1 shilling. Only a few copies of the individual parts survive.[28] The engraved title
page found in some copies, with its similarity to the Benbow/Perkins edition of *Queen
Mab*, 'New York', 1821, and its Greek *p* in Πolborn suggests that this edition may have
been promoted or financed by Erasmus Perkins.

*Queen Mab; A Philosophical Poem; with notes. By Percy Bysshe Shelley. To which is added, A
Brief Memoir of the Author*
N.d. probably first around 1835, the version with the Memoir. 1840 or 1841. James Watson.
Watson sold copies of this version for many years, with different title pages, at 1 shilling
paper or 1.5 shillings stitched. The stereotypes were in continuous use until 1861.[29]

Queen Mab. By Percy Bysshe Shelley
No date but c. 1835. Fr. Campe, Nuremberg and Paris. A foreign pirate which appears to
have circulated in Britain.[30]

In 1834 Edward Moxon, the main publisher of poetry of the post-romantic period, aware
of Shelley's growing reputation and seeing the success of the pirates, offered Mrs Shelley
£600 if she would bring out an official edition, and renewed his offer in 1835.[31]

*The Beauties of Percy Bysshe Shelley, Consisting of Rosalind and Helen, Posthumous Poems,
Revolt of Islam, Queen Mab, and Prometheus: unbound* [sic] with portrait of the author.

---

[27] Pforzheimer collection. NYPL.
[28] One set in NYPL, Arents collection. *Rosalind and Helen* and *Posthumous Poems*, Ac.
[29] Forman, *Shelley Library* 56. He dates the first edition from the date of the arrival of the book in British Museum.
[30] The Bodleian copy has an English inscription of 1835. Campe also printed editions of Byron, Ac.
[31] Mary Shelley, *Letters* ii, 198.

Appendix 11 *(cont.)*

The Works of Percy Bysshe Shelley
1836. Daly. No printer's name. Tiny print in one fat little volume. Daly continued to sell copies of this edition in various versions, with new title pages bearing later dates, at least until the authorised *Poetical Works of Percy Bysshe Shelley* was published in 1839, and probably later.

The Poetical Works of Percy Bysshe Shelley edited by Mrs Shelley
1839. Moxon. Four volumes   20   2,000[32]
Moxon disposed of many copies shortly after publication at a trade sale at the unusually low price of 10.5 shillings, equivalent to an almost immediate remaindering.[33]

The Poetical Works of Percy Bysshe Shelley edited by Mrs Shelley
1839. Moxon. 1 volume, 8vo. 'Uniform with the Works of Lord
Byron' i.e. Galignani style.[34]   12
Some passages of *Queen Mab* were blocked out with asterisks, and the notes cut back, partly because this was what Mary Shelley said Shelley would have wanted, but also in order to protect Moxon's copyright. In 1840, a group of authors and booksellers brought an action for blasphemy against Moxon, teasing the authorities to acknowledge openly that the law had always been enforced only against cheaper books. The case was decided against Moxon but no action was taken. The omissions were restored in the next edition, but removed again later. In 1844, Moxon registered the four volume, self-censored, version for copyright.[35]

Shelley's Poetical Works
1844. 32mo, cloth, 2.5 shillings. Advertised by G. Nodes in his list of 'Cheap Standard Works'.[36] No copy found, perhaps a version of the Daly edition

The Poetical Works of Percy Bysshe Shelley Complete
1845. No name of publisher or printer. Tiny print in fat little volumes. Preface as in Daly's edition but a complete reprint probably by Daly. Some copies contain a plate showing Shelley looking Byronic. Another version, 1851.

The Poetical Works of Percy Bysshe Shelley Complete in Two Volumes
N.d. (post 1845) London; W. Dugdale. 32mo. Tiny print in two fat little volumes. Volume i appears to be the same as Daly's edition: volume ii includes a new printing of all the poems first published in the authorised edition of 1839, and includes an engraving of Severn's picture of Shelley composing *Prometheus Unbound* in the Baths of Caracalla in Rome, first exhibited in 1845.

The Poetical Works of Percy Bysshe Shelley Complete in Two Volumes
N.d. (post 1845) London; W. Dugdale (The street number scratched out from the stereotype in both volumes). Tiny print in fat little volumes reset. Price 4.5 shillings the two volumes or 4 shillings cash.[37]

(Byron's) *Don Juan*

Many of the books noted below are only known from copies in the author's collection, and there may have been more editions and impressions of which no copies

---

[32] *Ibid.*, 300.   [33] Hughes 89.   [34] Advertisement in *Publishers Circular*, December 1839.
[35] Stationers' Company Registers, unpublished.
[36] Advertisement in Nodes's edition of *Don Juan* (1844), Ac.   [37] Ac.

Appendix II (*cont.*)

have been found or which have not survived. To save space I have not transcribed all the title pages.

Don Juan
1819. Printed by Thomas Davison
4to. First edition   31.5   1,500
Official
The book names neither author nor publisher, but only the printer as required by law. Several passages are asterisked.

Don Juan. An Exact Copy from the Quarto Edition
1819. Published by J. Onwhyn. 4 Shillings. 8vo. Imprint of E. Thomas, Printer, Denmark-Court, Strand.
Poor quality paper, without even paper covers. The first piracy. Little is known of Onwhyn except that he had earlier been convicted of seditious libel, and later pirated Harriette Wilson's *Memoirs*, employing Thomas as the printer.

Don Juan
1819. Paris. Galignani reprints the London edition instantly. Price 3 francs, sterling equivalent 2.4 shillings or 6 francs 'vellum paper'.

Don Juan. A New Edition[38]
1819. Printed by Thomas Davison
8vo   9.5   3,750
Official. Murray tranches down to 8vo sooner than usual.[39] The edition was sold out by about 1822. Another 750 copies were printed but 288 copies were still unsold in 1843.[40]

Don Juan Illustrations
1819. Murray commissions a series of illustrations for binding into the book, but abandons the enterprise and destroys the pictures, presumably in reaction to the condemnation of *Don Juan* by many of his former customers.[41]
From the beginning *Don Juan* mutates into a new forms. There are many fakes, false continuations, parodic imitations, theatrical versions, operatic versions which link Byron's *Don Juan* with other versions of the story, and pornography.[42] But the prime printed text continues to be dominant.

Don Juan. An Exact Copy from the Quarto Edition
1820. Printed for Sherwin and Co. 8vo. 4 shillings. 8vo. Pirate. Almost a forgery. Resembles the official Murray 8vo edition in everything but price.

Don Juan. A New Edition.
1820. Printed by Thomas Davison, 8vo   9.5   nil
Official. A reissue of sheets of the 1819 edition, with some corrections

Don Juan
1820. Printed by Thomas Davison, 'Crown 8vo'   7   3,500

---

[38] Wise, with further details from Murray archives.
[39] Peter Isaac, 'Byron's Publisher and his Spy . . . Murray's Printers 1812–1831' 14, in *The Library* (1977). I have amended the figure for the print run from Murray archives.
[40] Murray archives.   [41] *Ibid.*
[42] Many are noted in Samuel C. Chew, *Byron, His Fame and After-Fame* (1914).

Appendix II (*cont.*)

Official, but tranched down to a size only a little larger than 12mo. The speed with which he tranches down is another sign that Murray had lost many traditional customers.[43]

Don Juan, Cantos III, IV, and V
1821. Printed by Thomas Davison, 8vo   9.5   1,500
Designed to allow it to be easily bound with the volume containing the earlier cantos. Official. First publication of the next part of the poem.

Don Juan, Cantos III, IV, and V
1821. Printed by Thomas Davison, Crown 8vo   7   4,500
Murray's 'small paper' edition issued simultaneously with the 8vo. Another publishing innovation. Murray abandons hope of being able to tranche down and starts with a cheap format.
The injunctions against the pirating of cantos I and II do not prevent the same two London pirates publishing new piracies when the next part of the poem is published.

Don Juan, Cantos III, IV, and V
1821. Published by J. Onwhyn, 8vo. Imprint of E. Thomas   4   na

Don Juan, Cantos III, IV, and V
1821. Printed for Sherwin and Co.   4   na

Don Juan, Cantos III, IV, and V
1821. Paris. Galignani again instantly reprints the London edition

Don Juan A Correct Copy from the Original Edition
No Date, but 1821 or 1822. Printed and Published by   6.5   na
John Fairburn, 8vo. Imprint of G. Smeeton
Contains six comic coloured plates in the style of Regency theatre prints. Smeeton and Fairburn were publishers of theatrical, satirical and pornographic prints. The engraved title page includes a vignette portrait of Byron. Although he is not named, the image is already recognisable by readers. This vignette is the first direct indication in any edition that *Don Juan* was written by Byron.[44]

Don Juan. In Five Cantos. A New Edition, With Notes And Three Engravings after Corbould
N.d. but probably 1821. Printed by and for Peter Griffin. 12mo. Small print, five stanzas per page. One of the illustrations shows the Don looking like Byron, half naked on a beach.

Don Juan. A New Edition
1822. Printed by Thomas Davison, 8vo   9.5   na
A genuinely new official edition of Cantos I and II

Don Juan. Cantos III, IV, and V Fifth Edition, Revised and Corrected
1822. Printed by Thomas Davison. 8vo   9.5   na
A new edition incorporating many changes of text demanded by Byron. By calling this book a 'fifth edition', Murray exaggerates his previous sales. 'The Author repeats (as before) that the former impressions (from whatever cause) are full of errors. – And he further adds that he doth humbly trust – with all due deference to those superior

---

[43] Murray archives.
[44] When Byron's difficulties with Murray first became apparent in 1819, Fairburn had offered to become Byron's publisher. Byron, *Letters and Journals* x, 53.

persons – the publisher and printer – that they will in future less misspell – misplace – mistake and mis-everything, the humbled M.S.S. of their humble Servant.' Note by Byron 1821.[45]

Don Juan. Cantos 1 to v A New Edition
1822. Printed and Published by T. Dolby. 12mo.   3   na
Contains three satirical plates, available in coloured and uncoloured versions. Another mutation into a more popular form

Don Juan, Cantos 1 to v
1822. Benbow. 12mo   2.5   'thousands'
Later reissued with a new title page 'Benbow, Printer and Publisher, at the Byron's Head, Castle-Street, Leicester-Square' with an engraved frontispiece of a statue bust of Byron. Benbow also provided an elaborately engraved title page designed round the winged wand of Mercury (cadaceus), a device he also used for his piracy of Shelley's *Queen Mab*. By calling his shop 'The Byron's Head', like a tavern, but also reviving the tradition of bookshop names of earlier centuries, Benbow enables the word 'Byron' to appear for the first time in any copy of the poem, official or pirate. Some surviving copies are disguised to look like volumes of plays, presumably for readers who wanted to conceal what they were reading. It is Benbow's shop, and the others which stocked his books, that Southey calls 'preparatory schools for the brothel and the gallows'.

Don Juan. With a Preface by a Clergyman
1822. Printed by and for Hodgson & Co. 12mo. Portrait. The preface, which might at first sight be thought to be a pirate's joke, is evidently sincerely meant, perhaps genuinely written by a clergyman.
"This work, entitled DON JUAN, seems, I know not why, a sort of common property among the booksellers: for we have had editions of all sorts and sizes; from the original superb quarto, to the shabby "two penny trash", or weekly instalments of about twenty four duodecimo, badly printed pages. It has been, and still is, one of the most popular poems of the present day.' Preface.
Another version dated 1823

Many cheap magazines made from one folded sheet, such as *The Hive, The Indicator, The Portfolio, The Nic Nac*, and *The Tickler*, carried extensive quotations from *Don Juan*.

Poems of the Right Honourable Lord Byron; With his Memoirs
1823. Published by Jones and Company. 8vo. *Hours of Idleness, English Bards and Scotch Reviewers, Poems on Domestic Circumstances*, and *Don Juan Cantos 1 to v* (i.e. all the poems of which the copyright was unenforceable).
Pirate. Small print, double columns. Portrait. For the first time Byron is named as author on the title page. This version, with its misleading title, was available in parts at 1 shilling and in weekly numbers at 0.5 shillings.[46]
In 1822 Byron decides to break with Murray, but he has difficulty in finding another publisher. In 1823 he agrees that John Hunt should publish the next cantos as they are

[45] Mrs James T. Fields, *A Shelf of Old Books* (1894) 75. The present whereabouts of the original manuscript are unknown.
[46] Advertisements in copies of Jones's books. I have never come across a copy of a part or a number of *Don Juan*, but have seen copies of parts of the other books in the advertised series.

Appendix II *(cont.)*

written, Byron taking half net profits. All hope of tranching down is abandoned. Each successive book is published simultaneously in three formats.

Don Juan. Cantos VI, VII, and VIII
1823. John Hunt. 8vo   9.5   1,500
Official. This version follows the format of Murray's 8vo editions closely, with no mention of Byron's name on the title page

Don Juan. Cantos VI, VII, and VIII
1823. John Hunt, 'small paper'   7   3,000
Official. This version too matches Murray's edition in price and edition size

Don Juan. Cantos VI, VII, and VIII
1823. Printed for John Hunt. 18mo 'common edition'   1   16,000
An entirely new way of publishing, high volume at very low price
When the next cantos arrive from Byron, they are published in the same way

Don Juan. Cantos IX, X, and XI
1823. John Hunt. Again published simultaneously in three formats
8vo   9.5   1,500
'small paper'   7   2,500
'common'   1   17,000

Don Juan. Cantos XII, XIII, and XIV
1823. Printed for John Hunt. Again published simultaneously in three formats, same prices. Edition sizes not recorded, presumably much the same.

Don Juan Cantos XV and XVI
1824. Printed for John and H. L. Hunt. Again published simultaneously in three formats, same prices. Edition sizes not recorded, presumably much the same.

As new cantos are published, they are immediately reprinted in pirate versions which match the 'common' edition in their design so closely that they can almost be regarded as forgeries. These versions are sold at the same price of 1 shilling. Among the imprints found are those of Benbow, Dugdale, Hodgson, Sudbury, Dickinson, and Mitford, some of whom may have been front men.
Galignani also again instantly reprints each part of the poem as it comes out. Price 3 francs, sterling equivalent 2.4 shillings.
'I have ascertained from a young Man who was in Galignani's office in Paris – that *DJ* is by far the most popular – so much so – that G always prints several hundred extra copies of that only – in addition – when he makes a new edition of the whole works.' Byron in a letter, 1823.[47]
April 1824. Death of Byron. The pirates, foreseeing an expected demand for copies of the whole poem, which could not be met by the regular publishers, are quick to exploit the opportunity.

Don Juan I to XVI
1825. Sudbury. 18mo   7.5   na
This is a made up edition of individual parts, without a single title page or continuous pagination. Perhaps the first single volume edition of the whole poem.

----

[47] Byron, *Letters and Journals* x, 134.

Don Juan, a Poem by Lord Byron
Galignani makes available the whole poem in three volumes. Price 15 francs, sterling equivalent 7.2 shillings.[48]
The next few years see a huge outpouring of pirate reprints of the whole poem, offered in many shapes and sizes. The poem is now reprinted outside London, and is found on the lists of reprint publishers who normally published only old canon works.

Don Juan, A Poem. By Lord Byron In Two Volumes
1825. Edinburgh. Printed for James Kay. 12mo. Two volumes. Engraved portrait after Harlowe. Kay was an artist and printer of satirical prints.

Don Juan. Cantos VI–VII – and VIII
1825. Printed for Hunt and Clarke. 8vo. Official. Hunt, having run out of copies of his print run of 3,000 copies of the 8vo *VI*, *VII*, and *VIII* reprints this volume only, so that 8vo sets of the whole poem can be made up.

Don Juan. Complete by Lord Byron
N.d., but probably 1826 or 1827. Printed and published by J. F. Dove. 24mo. Text closely printed, seven stanzas to the page and numbered, scarcely readable with the naked eye. *Don Juan* is now included in Dove's *English Classics* which are otherwise all old canon.[49]

Don Juan, Complete; English Bards, and Scotch Reviewers; Hours of Idleness, The Waltz; and all the other minor poems: By Lord Byron
1826. Printed for the proprietors of the *English Classics*, by J. F. Dove. 12mo. 6 shillings. Five stanzas to the page, very closely printed. Another version is dated 1827.
This edition includes a number of asterisked passages which were printed in full in the original. Dove, it seems, is being even more careful not to offend his customers than Murray, probably because he includes the poem among his old-canon *English Classics*

Don Juan. By Lord Byron
1826. Printed for the booksellers. 8vo. Imprint of Thomas White, Printer, Johnsons [sic] Court.
Produced to be bound with the 8vo editions of Byron's works published by Murray and Hunt. As in earlier centuries it is the printers who are the entrepreneurs, supplying the retail booksellers and selling direct to customers.

1826. Printed for the booksellers. 16mo. Imprint of Thomas White. Another version produced to be bound with the 'small paper' editions of Byron's works published by Murray and Hunt.

1826. 'Printed for the Proprietor'. 16mo. Imprint of Thomas White. Tiny print, five stanzas per page, scarcely readable. Printers key signatures numbers not letters, unusual for an English book. Engraved portrait after Phillips.

Don Juan, in Sixteen Cantos. By Lord Byron, Complete in One Volume
1826. Printed for William Clark 16mo. Engraved portrait after Phillips reversed. Tiny print scarcely readable. Imprint of W. Wilson, printer. A copy in original publishers' cloth gives price at this time 5 shillings. A biographical note initialled W(illiam) C(lark) praises Byron for his love of freedom and his attack on the evils and hypocrisies of society, but it is

---

[48] Not seen. So described in Galignani's advertisement lists, c.1830. The edition was probably made up from the original parts which were still available at 3 francs each.
[49] See appendix 6.

Appendix II (*cont.*)

to: '*Don Juan* that he will owe his immortality.' Perhaps the same William Clark as pirated Shelley's *Queen Mab* in 1821. No W. Wilson was registered as a printer at the stated address.

1827. Printed for J. Thompson, 16mo. Some copies with engraved portrait of Byron after Phillips. Imprint of Plummer and Brewis, Printers.
Made from the same type as Clark's edition, probably stereotyped. Impressions are found with the dates 1829, 1830, and 1832 on the title pages.

Don Juan in Sixteen Cantos. By Lord Byron. Complete in One Volume, with a short biographical Memoir of the Author
1827. Printed for T. and J. Allman. Pirate. Allman, an old-canon reprinter, continued to reprint this edition for many years. Later editions with variations, which appear to be essentially reimpressions from the same plates, have been found dated 1829, 1833, 1834, 1835, 1841, 1848, 1849, 1851, 1852, 1853, and 1854, and there are likely to have been others.

1827. Printed and published by J. F. Dove. The sheets of the earlier edition appear to have been entirely reprinted to get rid of the self-imposed expurgations.

Don Juan by Lord Byron
1828. Printed for the Booksellers. 16mo. Two volumes. Imprint of Hamblin Printer.

Don Juan. In Two Volumes
1828. Thomas Davison. Two volumes with two plates one of which shows Don Juan looking like Byron. Two versions of the book were published on different paper sizes from the same print.[50]

'foolscap 8vo' version	9	1,000
18mo version	4	4,000

Murray and Davison, having seen the success of the pirates, decide to do some pirating themselves, reprinting the cantos published by Hunt as well as those whose intellectual property Byron had assigned to Murray. They also copy the pirates in still keeping Byron's name off the title page, while confirming his authorship by an illustration. Murray and Davison split the costs and profits.[51] The accounts for this book were not entered in Murray's normal ledgers.

Don Juan; Hours of Idleness; English Bards and Scotch Reviewers; The Waltz; and Other Poems. By Lord Byron. In Two Volumes
1828. J. F. Dove. Engraved frontispiece by Corbould in each volume. Provided at the back of these books in their unbound state are two extra title pages and six labels to enable customers to add *Don Juan* to the six-volume official Murray set of Byron's *Works*. Another version, 1829

The Beauties of Don Juan; Including only those Passages which are Calculated to Extend the Real Fame of Lord Byron
1828. Printed for James Cawthorn. Two volumes (although only one seems to have been printed and it is complete). 16mo. 12 shillings. The editor dedicates the book to his sister. He regrets that the poem has 'remained a sealed volume to the fairest portion of the community'.[52]

---

[50] Isaac, 'Byron's Publisher' 14.
[51] McGann suggests, in *Complete Poetical Works*, v, xix, that this is an authorised Murray edition, issued 'for copyright purposes', but Murray did not own the copyright of cantos VI to XIV in 1828.
[52] Edward Berens, *Advice to a Young Man upon first going to Oxford* (1832) 159.

1828 written as M, DCCC, XXVIII. London: no name of printer nor of publisher given anywhere. Tiny print, six stanzas to the page. Pirate. The only known copy has been finely bound in full green morocco, gilt edges, with a foldover flap like a map, apparently a book specially manufactured to be kept in the pocket when travelling. For references to travelling with *Don Juan* in the works of Dickens and Thackeray, see chapter 20.

1829. London, printed for the booksellers. 12mo. Two volumes. Portrait after Phillips published by Bumpus 1824, now much worn. Printed by James Starke. There are at least two versions, one more closely printed than the other, differences in the quality of the paper, and other evidence that more than one impression was made. Pirate.

1829. London: Printed by C. and Z. Morris. 24mo. Portrait from Phillips reversed. Price 5 shillings. Tiny print, scarcely readable. Six stanzas to the page numbered at the top. Charles Morris registered at this address 1828, Zachariah Morris registered at another address in 1835. Reissued under different title pages in 1831, 1833, 1835, and perhaps other years. The first stereotyped version whose plates were used by various publishers until at least 1875 and perhaps later.

In 1829 Hunt went bankrupt. In 1830 their stock, including their Byron copyrights, was sold to Murray for £3,885, apart from the copyright of their interest in *Don Juan* which was bought in at £325. That price implied that, despite all the piracies, and the passing of eleven years since the poem first began to appear, a good return was still thought to be achievable. Murray acquired the copyright soon after, and in 1832 published a new edition of Byron's *Complete Works*. This new edition includes for the first time the parts of *Don Juan* that had been asterisked in all earlier editions, and the dedication to Southey, the full extent of whose obscenity was probably by now lost on many readers unfamiliar with Regency slang. The 1832 edition is the first edition of *Don Juan* with the text as Byron wrote it.

Murray's edition establishes a claim to a new copyright. Many of the pirates now incorporated the texts of the previously asterisked stanzas, including those about syphilis, but only two are brave enough to reprint the dedication. The word 'Complete' slides from meaning that all sixteen cantos are included towards the notion of 'unexpurgated'. The pirates also dropped the Latin epigraph. Despite the huge sales, the book continued to be reprinted in numerous new editions.

1833. Printed for Scott and Webster. 18mo.
Scott and Webster, reprinters of old canon, took over Dove's stock and stereotype plates. Other versions from the same plates 'Printed for the Booksellers' 1835. Another undated.

1834. Mayhew, Isaac, and Co. Two volumes. 'Royal 64 mo'. Probably the smallest book size attainable by the technology of the time, tiny format, tiny print, almost unreadable by the naked eye. Probably made from stereotypes. Only one copy known.

1834. Printed and published by R. Carlile, Jr. Carlile's version is unusual in illegally pirating the new full text published by Murray in the previous year on which copyright was enforceable.

1835. Printed for J. Thompson. Frontispiece illustration of the Westall picture used in the Murray Davison edition of 1828, showing the boy looking like Byron.
Sheets of Carlile's unexpurgated edition of the previous year

1835. Printed for the Booksellers. Portrait. Imprint of B. D. Cousins

Appendix 11 *(cont.)*

Very tight printing, six cantos per page, numbered at the foot. This edition is manufactured from the Morris stereotype plates although there are differences.

1835. Scott, Webster, and Geary
Made from same plates as 1833 edition

Don Juan. Complete in Sixteen Cantos By Lord Byron. With Choice Extracts from his other poems
1836. Published by Matthew Hendrie. 24mo. Imprint of Richardson, Hutchison, and Co. printers. Tightly but clearly printed, five stanzas to the page, numbered. This version too appears to have been stereotyped and the plates used by various publishers for many years.

Don Juan; in Sixteen Cantos. by Lord Byron. With Illustrations
1837. London: Charles Mason. 32mo. Extremely small type scarcely readable in a fat little volume. Numerous engraved illustrations, more saucy than erotic, showing the Don looking like Byron.

1837. John Murray, Albemarle Street. 12mo. 5 shillings. Full text, including *Beppo*. Illustration and much editorial material. Official. This is Murray's unsuccessful attempt to take back some of the market by printing a better edition at a highish price. Initial print run 5,000.[53]

1837. William Mark Clark. 12mo. The only known pirate version other than Carlile's to risk pirating the new full text.

N.d., first published before 1838. Cornish and Co. Royal 64mo. 1.5 shillings. Tiny format, tiny print, almost unreadable. Portrait after Phillips much worn. No printer's imprint. This edition is from the same plates as the Mayhew Isaac edition of 1834, although they are now more worn. The key signatures are different.[54]

1838. J. Smith, 32mo at 5 shillings, 24mo at 3.5 shillings. No copy seen.[55]

1839. Charles Daly. A version of Mason's edition of 1837. Price 2.5 shillings or 3.5 shillings 'in rich silk'. Other versions have been found dated 1839, 1849, and undated. Still being advertised in the 1850s. Published both with and without illustrations. Frontispieces differ. The Daly editions are in the same tiny format as his editions of Shelley's *Works*.

1842. Glasgow. Published by George Love. Cloth. Portrait after Sanders. Price appears to have been 2 shillings. From the same stereotype plates as Hendrie's edition.

Don Juan, By Lord Byron, In Sixteen Cantos
1844. G. Nodes. Reissue of the version of Scott and Webster, itself taken over from Dove.

1846. Published by the booksellers. 16mo. Frontispiece and vignette. Small print, numbered lines, black encircling border. A few select poems at the end, not clear why they were selected, some spurious.

---

[53] Strahan archives.
[54] Advertised in a copy of John Calvin, *Institutes of the Chistian Religion* (1838). Published by S. Cornish and Co, Ac. Price 1.5 shillings. 'In one volume royal 64mo, beautifully printed in Diamond type, cloth extra, gilt label, price 1s 6d. Byron's Don Juan with the last corrections of the Author. This is the smallest as well as the most elegant edition that has yet appeared.'
[55] Advertised on back board of *The Miscellaneous Poems of Lord Byron* (1828), Ac. Perhaps made from the Mason or Thompson/Clark plates in which Joseph Smith may have taken a share, although the *Miscellaneous Poems* is apparently his own printing.

1849. H. G. Bohn. Stereotyped, very worn. 2.5 shillings. Pirate. Contains a picture of the Don and Haidee being discovered in bed.

1850 and later without date. Manchester: Printed and published by Thomas Johnson. Uses the same stereotype plates as Hendrie's edition. In some copies the types are much damaged, implying heavy wear.

Lord Byron's Don Juan. With Life and Original Notes, by A. C. Cunningham, Esq. and many illustrations in steel

1852. C. Daly. 8vo. Red stamped Victorian cloth, decorated in gilt. The notes claim to contain stanzas omitted by Byron, but all are forgeries. The name Cunningham is probably intended to mislead readers into believing that the book was prepared by Allan Cunningham, a well known writer and editor. Daly's pirated edition of Shelley's *Poems*, 1844, claims to have been edited, revised, and corrected by 'G. Cuningham' with illustrations by 'G. Standfast', a name which reminds the unwary customer of the illustrator Clarkson Stansfield.

N.d. 1850s onwards. London. Milner and Compy. 16mo. Engraved title with vignette and portrait in addition to printed title. Price 1 shillings. Tightly printed with scarcely a space between the stanzas. Pirate, but legitimate later. Milner kept the book in print for the rest of the century, occasionally changing the title page and the cloth cover.

After *Don Juan* finally came completely out of copyright, it continued to be reprinted as a separate book, mainly in cheap editions, alongside the many official editions of Byron's collected poetry. Milner prepared an edition of the full version, including the preface, but he and others also continued to reprint the old incomplete version from their stereotypes.

N.d. c. 1860. London; Walker and Co. 12mo. Small print, with six stanzas to the page, each page encircled with a black line, and stanza numbers summarised at the foot of each page. Only one copy known.

N.d. c. 1864 and later. London; C. H. Clarke. 2 shillings. A yellow back.

During the 1870s the publication of a number of books about Byron's marriage encouraged a number of publishers to reissue *Don Juan*.

N.d. 1874. Routledge and Sons. 24mo. Small print, with five stanzas to the page, but pleasantly produced in emerald gilt cloth.[56] 4,000 copies printed.

1875. Chatto and Windus. 2 shillings. 2,000 copies were printed, using the stereotypes made by Morris in about 1829. The plates were kept until 1906.[57]

N.d. c. 1900, but perhaps earlier. Published for the booksellers. 16mo. Six-and-a-half stanzas per page, numbered. Poor quality paper. Stereotyped.
Shows that the poem continued to be reset, not just run off from plates, for extensive reprinting right through the nineteenth century.
In the last decades of the nineteenth century *Don Juan* is available from John Dicks at sixpence, perhaps the cheapest-ever price for a work of this length.
In 1926 the book is published with erotic 'art' illustrations, including some of female nudes with pubic hair. More than a century after its first publication *Don Juan* is still pushing at the textual limits set by the law.

[56] Date and print run from Routledge archives.
[57] Production book for 1875, Chatto and Windus archives, Reading.

EARLY PLAY QUARTOS. INDICATORS OF PRICE AND EXTENT OF
CIRCULATION

The remark in the bookseller's address in *Troilus and Cressida* (1609) appears to refer to the
actual price.

'Among all these is none more witty than this; and had I time, I would comment upon it,
though I know it needs not – for so much as will make you think your *testern* [slang for
sixpence, i.e. 0.5 of a shilling] well bestowed – but for so much worth as even poor I know
to be stuffed in it.'

	Prices (shillings)	Print runs
1628. For Chapman's *Bussy d'Ambois*, a quarto tragedy printed in 1607	1.5	
Probably a premium price for book which was no longer in print[1]		
1628. For two recently printed or reprinted plays[2]	the two: 1	
1628. For three older plays by Middleton and Dekker, no longer in print	the three bound: 3	
Probably a premium price for books which were no longer in print[3]		
1629. Edward Heath pays 6 shillings 'ffor ten playbooks', implying an average price per printed play at that time of under half a shilling[4]		
1629. For a recently printed play by Heywood[5]	0.66	
1637. Bookseller's bill, '2 playes of Henry 4th' suggests that 4to versions were still available at 0.5 shillings each[6]	the two: 1	

Printed play texts appear to have circulated nationally through the chapman network.
'Plaies out of this Citie are like wenches new falne to the trade, onelie desired of your
neatest gallants, whiles th'are fresh: when they grow stale they must be vented by Termers
and Cuntrie chapmen.' From 'To the Reader' in the anonymous *The familie of love* (1608).[7]
'Termers' was a name given to those who only came to London occasionally, such as
lawyers for the legal terms, a group of whom Davenant wrote in 1673 'to cry Plays down is
half the business Termers have in Town'.[8] The quotation implies that termers sold their
copies of plays, presumably when they returned to the country.

Possible evidence of print runs

1613. Decker's *A Strange Horse Race*

[1] McKitterick, 'Ovid' 216.   [2] *Ibid.*   [3] *Ibid.*
[4] Quoted from a manuscript by John R. Elliot Jr, 'Four Caroline Playgoers', 189, in *Medieval and Renaissance Drama in England* 6 (1993).
[5] McKitterick, 'Ovid' 216.
[6] Mary Elizabeth Bohannon, 'A London Bookseller's Bill, 1635–1639' in *The Library* (1938) 440.
[7] Quoted by Douglas A. Brooks, *From Playhouse to Printing House* (2000) 48.   [8] Quoted in *OED*.

Appendix 12 (*cont.*)

'A thousand palats must be pleased with a thousand sawces; and one hundred lines must content five hundred dispositions.' In 'Note to the Readers', in which Dekker compares writing to cooking. The comment may indicate that print runs of 1,000 and 500 were normal for new literary works.[9]

1639. The first archival record I have found. Benson is   1,500
given permission to reprint an old play printed in
1629 and never entered.[10]

THE MOVE TO EXPENSIVE FOLIO

1619. Pavier, as leader of a consortium of printer/publishers who own quarto texts, reprints some Shakespeare quartos under a false date.

1619. Upon receiving a letter from the Lord Chamberlain, the Stationers' Company decides that 'no playes that His Majtyes players do play shallbe printed without consent of some of them'.[11] This decision seems to be a preliminary step intended to permit the publication of Shakespeare's dramatic works in a collected edition.

1622. *Othello*, the last of Shakespeare's plays to be first published in 4to, published after having been entered in 1621.

1623. *Mr William Shakespeares Comedies, Histories, & Tragedies*, first folio edition. Jaggard.[12]

	15 unbound, 20 bound	unlikely to be over 500
At the latest count about 220 copies are known still to exist, about half of which came from libraries of noblemen and well-endowed institutions.		
Print run for a folio published by Jaggard at about the same time.[13] 1619. Brooke's *Catalogue and Accession of Kings, Princes . . .*		500
1632. Shakespeare second folio[14]	18.5	na
A price in 1638 probably bound[15]	22	
Ownership of the intellectual property rights was now spread among a range of printer/publishers		
A copy sold in 1678[16]	16	na
1664. Shakespeare third folio	na	na

[9] *The Non-Dramatic Works of Thomas Dekker*, edited by Alexander Grosart (1885) iii, 311.

[10] *The Tragedy of Albovine.* Jackson 325. The figure for the edition may be for the maximum allowed rather than the actual number of copies planned. The play was not reprinted.

[11] Jackson 110.

[12] Prices based on prices noted in some surviving copies and an account book of Sir Edward Dering. See Anthony James West, 'Sales and Prices of Shakespeares First Folios' in *Proceedings of the Bibliographical Society of America* (1998), quoted by Blayney 25. Much of the information is consolidated in Anthony James West's book, *The Shakespeare First Folio, The History of the Book* (2001) i.

[13] Mentioned in William Jaggard's 'The Printer' in Vincent's *Discoverie of Errours* (1619) *STC* 24756.

[14] Quoted by Blayney 26, and West, *Shakespeare First Folio* 11.   [15] *Ibid.*   [16] Wheatley 231.

Appendix 12 *(cont.)*

Contains a further seven plays, mostly not by Shakespeare. Some copies dated 1663 do not contain these plays		
A copy sold in 1678[17]	28.5	
A copy sold in 1684[18]	15.5	
(Works of *Sir William Davenant*, a folio of plays of similar size)[19]	24	na
1685. Shakespeare fourth folio	more than 18	na
1686. A price at auction[20]	18	
1688. Copies being auctioned in quantities within the trade, an indication that sales at the full price had been disappointing.[21]		

Shakespeare part of a 'folio canon' of English literature

1695. English authors published in folio format. '*Shakespear*'s Plays, *Beaumont and Fletcher*'s Plays, *Ben. Johnson*'s Works, Mr *Cowley*'s Works, Sir William *D'avenant*'s Works, Mrs *Phillip*'s Poems, Mr *Chaucer*'s Works, Mr *Spencer*'s Fairy-Queen, Mr *Milton*'s Paradise Lost and Regain'd, Mr *Killigrew*'s Plays'. A bookseller's advertisement.[22]

c. 1700. Shakespeare 'fifth' folio, seventy pages of the fourth folio reset and reprinted[23]

1705. New copies of Shakespeare's plays in folio, that is of the 1685 edition, still being advertised.[24]

1623–1774. The intellectual property rights in the folio texts of Shakespeare's plays pass to a succession of firms operating perpetual intellectual property rights.

1660. Establishment of the theatre duopoly, limiting the performance of plays to the two Patent Companies, Drury Lane and Covent Garden. The performance rights in older plays, including those of Shakespeare, are divided, in effect creating two distinct monopolies in the theatrical performance of Shakespeare's plays.

---

[17] West, *Shakespeare First Folio* 70, Wheatley 231.   [18] Wheatley 231.

[19] 'Catalogue of Books printed for John Starkey' in *The Works of Sr William D'avenant Kt* . . . (1673).

[20] West, *Shakespeare First Folio* 70.

[21] *A Catalogue of Latin, French, and English Books, to be sold in numbers, to the Booksellers of London and Westminster, by Auction: on Tuesday next, being the twenty fourth of this Instant April; at the Bear in Ave-Mary Lane near Ludgate Street, By Benjamin Walford* (1688). Copy in Cambridge University Library. This includes under 'English Books in folio'. '*Shakespears* Works'.

[22] Advertisement of books 'printed for, and sold by Francis Saunders' inserted in *The Temple of Death* (second edition 1695), Ac.

[23] See Eric Rasmussen, 'Anonymity and the Erasure of Shakespeare's First Eighteenth-Century Editor', in Joanna Gondris, ed., *Reading Readings, Essays on Shakespeare Editing in the Eighteenth Century* (Madison 1998) 319, commenting on a discovery made by Giles Dawson in 1951, and ignored since then.

[24] Wellington's advertisement list in *All the Histories and Novels Written by the late ingenious Mrs Behn* (1705), Ac.

Appendix 12 *(cont.)*

CLAMP-DOWN ON BALLAD VERSIONS AND ABRIDGEMENTS

Titus Andronicus, of which a ballad version was composed at the same time as the play

1594. *Titus Andronicus.* Entered to John Danter on 6 February 1594, 'a Noble Roman Historye of Tytus Andronicus', no author named, and as a separate entry, for which a separate registration fee was paid, 'the ballad thereof'.[25]
The date when the ballad version was first printed is not known but may have been soon after.
Titus Andronicus was the first of Shakespeare's plays to be entered in the Stationers' Register. None of the printer/publishers who registered the first printings of other plays by Shakespeare, or who obtained the intellectual property rights from other printer/ publishers, registered ballad versions, at any rate in the surviving registers.

1602. 'A booke called Titus and Andronicus', that is the play text not the ballad version, reregistered to Pavier in 1602, on assignment, from the then owner Millington, an entry which may imply that the ownership of the intellectual property in the play and in the ballad version had already diverged by that time.

1620. The ballad version is reprinted in the third (first surviving) edition of *The Golden Garland of Princely Pleasures*, which appears to be a collection of ballad versions already printed.

1623. When the owners of the intellectual properties in the 4to texts of the plays agreed to allow publication of *Mr William Shakespeares Comedies, Histories, & Tragedies, Titus Andronicus* was included in the arrangement but the ballad version remained in separate ownership.

1624. 'Titus and Audconmus' is noted in the re-registration of a large number of old ballads made on 14 December 1624 to confirm the ownership of the recently established Ballad Partners.[26]

1655. Ballad version re-entered to the Ballad Partners as 'The history of Tytus Andronicus'.[27]

Late seventeenth century, the earliest extant copy of a prose chapbook, date of first composition unknown. It was 'printed for' E. Wright,' one of the Ballad Partners. The version was also 'printed by and for A[lexander] M[ilbourn]', another of the Partners.[28] By 1685 ownership had passed to William Thackeray.[29]

1698. Listed among the contents of the Ballad stock, held by the Ballad Partners.[30]

1754 and **1764.** Listed as available as a chapbook version in Dicey's wholesale ballad trade catalogues.

Romantic period. Disappears in the mass extinction

---

[25] Arber ii, 644. See also Jonathan Bates, ed., *Titus Andronicus*, Arden Shakespeare (1995).
[26] Arber iv, 131.   [27] Arber, *Transcript* ii, 37.   [28] Reprinted in the *Roxburgh Ballads* i, 392,
[29] *Bagford Ballads* ed. Joseph Woodfall Ebsworth (Hertford 1878–80) i, lxi. The reversal of the previously held view that the chapbook was a source of the play, has implications for our reading of the play, e.g. that it need not be regarded as set in the late empire of Theodosius, and that, unlike many of Shakespeare's other plays, it has no obvious single source.
[30] Reproduced in facsimile in W. G. Day, editor, *The Pepys Ballads* (1987) v, 446.

Appendix 12 (*cont.*)

Romeo and Juliet

1596. What appears to be a ballad version is entered.[31] No trace has been found, either at the time or later, and it is possible that it was never printed.

1597. First printing of the play for Danter, who is known to have commissioned ballad versions of other plays which he owned.

Possible explicit documentary evidence for the sudden cessation of ballad versions of Shakespeare's plays

1596. Thomas Millington is fined by the Court of the Stationers' Company 'for printinge of a ballad contrarye or order'.[32] A later hand has added a sentence, later deleted and unfortunately not dated, whose words were read by the 1930 editor as 'Md the ballad intuled The taming of a shrewe. Also one oth(er) Ballad of Macdobeth'.[33] If, as has been suggested, the entry is a modern forgery, the forger was highly perceptive in his choice of the title, 'a shrewe' and of the date. The forger also knew that the fine would refer to only one ballad and that the ballad of 'Macbeth' had gone unpunished. A reference in William Kemp's *Nine daies wonder*, 1600, to his meeting a 'penny poet' whose 'first making was the miserable stolen story of Macdoel, or Macdobeth, or Macsomewhat' tends to authenticate the whole entry and its gloss.[34] If so, it would show that Millington's offence was to print a ballad version of a text which belonged to another, that Shakespeare's *Macbeth* may have been performed before 1600, and that the clamp-down on ballad versions extended to ballads of works which had not been printed.[35]

King Leir and his Three Daughters, a play of which a ballad version already existed before Shakespeare's play was written, and of which the ballad version continued to be reprinted until 1774 and for a short time later

1594. *King Leir and his Three Daughters* registered. Whether the entry refers to the old play of that name or to the ballad version is not certain[36]

1605. Shakespeare's play *King Lear* registered. No ballad, chapbook, or abridged version is known to have been printed until after the abolition of perpetual copyright in 1774.

1620. Ballad version of *King Leir and his Three Daughters* reprinted in the third edition of *The Golden Garland of Princely Pleasures*

---

[31] 5 August 1596, To White 'these twoo ballades the followinge, viz. The one intituled. A newe ballad of Romeo and Juliet'. Arber iii, 68.

[32] Greg and Boswell 55.

[33] Although I have not examined the manuscript, I would conjecture that, whether or not the entry is a later forgery, the writer intended 'Vt [for videlicet] the ballad intituled'.

[34] Quoted by Nicholas Brooke, ed., *Macbeth*, Oxford Shakespeare (Oxford 1990) 59.

[35] The *Taming of A Shrew*, according to the entry of 2 May 1594, belonged to Peter Shorte, Arber ii, 648. The 1596 edition implies on the title page that it then belonged to Burbie, with no indication that Millington had a share in the ownership.

[36] 'The mooste famous Chronicle historye of Leire kinge of England and his three daughters', Arber ii, 649. See also R. A. Foakes, ed., *King Lear*, Arden Shakespeare (1997) 90.

Seventeenth century. The *King Leir and his Three Daughters* ballad version probably continued to be available, although no copies are known to have survived.

1725. Included in *A Collection of Old Ballads*, a formal publication of their own properties by the then intellectual property owners.[37]

1764. The ballad still listed as available from Aldermary Churchyard, as part of the chapbook canon. Copies exist.[38]

1807. Lamb's *Tales from Shakespear*, published by Godwin. 'King Lear' was among the tales which were sold separately. This is the first abridged version of any of Shakespeare's plays since the ballad version of *Titus Andronicus* of 1594.

c. 1830. A version from the old ballad, preserving the spelling 'Leir', still being reprinted by Marshall, one of the successors to Dicey, in Newcastle, but with the availability after 1774 of newly composed abridgements from a wide range of texts, that may have been the last.[39]

Did Richard Johnson compose the ballad versions?

The author of the ballad version of *Titus Andronicus* and of *King Leir and his Three Daughters* may have been Richard Johnson, the author, or compiler, of *The Seven Champions of Christendom*, another long-lived pre-1600 text, first printed by Danter. The title page of *The Golden Garland of Princely Delights*, 1630, in which the ballad versions of *Titus Andronicus* and of *King Leir and his Three Daughters* are printed, describes them as 'Being most pleasant songs and sonnets to sundry new tunes now most in use. The third time Imprinted, enlarged and corrected by *Rich Iohnson*'. To a modern reader, this formulation might imply that Johnson was the editor who did the enlarging and correcting, but the same formulation is used in books written by Thomas Deloney, another abridger, compiler, and writer of ballad versions, in editions first printed long after his death.[40] The title page of the 1598 4to version of *A Pleasant Conceited Comedie called, Loues Labors Lost. As it was presented before her Highnes this last Christmas. Newly corrected and augmented* by W. Shakespere should not be read as an acknowledgement of Shakespeare's authorial revision, but as an indication that the book is a new edition intended to supersede an earlier printed version of which no copy has survived. Johnson is also named as author or compiler of *The Crowne Garlande of Golden Roses* (second edition, first surviving, 1631) a collection of shorter ballads in similar style.

The willow song, evidence for its being privately owned

1565. 'A ballett intituled I am not the fyrsty that hath taken in hande the Wearinge of the Willow garland &c' entered in Stationers' Register. This appears to be an allowed variant of the main willow song.[41]

---

[37] For the status of that collection as a publication by the copyright holders see chapter 17.
[38] Listed in *ESTC*.   [39] Copy in CUL.
[40] For example, *The Pleasant Histories of John Winchcomb* (1626), is described on the title page as 'Now the tenth time Imprinted, corrected and enlarged by T. D.' Reproduced in facsimile by Mann 1.
[41] Arber i, 270.

Appendix 12 *(cont.)*

1578. The main song included in the printed miscellany, *A Gorgeous Gallery of Gallant Inventions*, one of the printed anthologies whose proliferation may have helped to precipitate the clamp-down.[42]

1689. Listed among the Ballad stock in 1689.[43]

SHAKESPEARE'S PLAYS, PRICES, AND PRINT RUNS

Although most of the following information on prices and print runs has not previously been made available, I make no claim to be comprehensive. In some cases the information in the archives is not easy to reconcile with other records.[44]

High monopoly period

Quarto and duodecimo versions of single plays

1660s until Rowe's edition of 1709. An intellectual property right to print certain plays in 4to, especially *Hamlet, Macbeth, Othello, Julius Caesar*, and *King Lear* continued to exist, apparently as a result of the negotiated agreements for the publication of the first folio of 1623.[45] Prices appear to have doubled from those charged before the closure of the theatres.

1676. *Hamlet*	I	na
1703. *Hamlet*[46]	1.5	2,000
1720s. *Hamlet, King Lear, Othello, Macbeth*[47]	I	2,000
From 1660. Adaptations of Shakespeare's plays by later writers, all of which qualified as newly created intellectual properties[48]	I	na

---

[42] Seng 192.

[43] 'Give me my willow garland' and 'Willow Green'. Reproduced in facsimile in W. G. Day, editor, *The Pepys Ballads* (1987) v, 448 and 450.

[44] Among the descriptive bibliographies which include useful information, particularly on publishing history and prices, are William Jaggard, *Shakespeare Bibliography* (Stratford 1901) and H. L. Ford, *Shakespeare 1700–1740* (Oxford 1935).

[45] For example, Wellington's advertisement list of 1727, in a copy of Lee and Dryden's *Oedipus*, Ac, mentions these two plays as available in 4to, in addition to *Hamlet, King Lear* and *Othello*, 'in twelves'.

[46] Price from *Term Catalogues* iii, 380 (1703). Edward Arber, ed., *The Term Catalogues, 1668–1709 A.D.; with a number for Easter Term, 1711 A.D. A contemporary bibliography of English literature in the reigns of Charles II, James II, William and Mary, and Anne* (1903–6).

[47] Prices printed on title pages, for example of *Hamlet*, printed by J. Darby, for A. Bettesworth . . . and F. Clay (1723). See also quotations from booksellers' catalogues in Fredk. J. Furnivall, *Some 300 Fresh Allusions to Shakespere* (n.d. c. 1880) vi. An advertisement of 'Books printed for A Bettesworth' in *Vida's Art of Poetry* (1725), Ac, offers among 'Plays on a neat Elziver Letter' price 1 shilling each, *Hamlet, King Lear*, and *Othello*. The print run is implied by the 1737 trade sale catalogue. 'Shakespear's Plays, by Rowe, Pope or Theobald, 92 Sets and a Half out of 3000. N.B. When Mackbeth, Othello, Julius Caesar or King Lear is printed, this Share produces 185 in 2000.'

[48] See Hazelton Spencer, *Shakespeare Improved* (New York 1927). Some were entered in the Stationers' register. Prices of the altered *King Lear* and *Richard III* 1699 and 1700 from *Term Catalogues* iii, 128, 173.

Newly written plays[49]	1.5	na

From 1661 until Rowe's edition of 1709, a group of booksellers produced a printed catalogue of English plays, including all that had ever been ascribed to Shakespeare, 'all of which you may buy or sell'.[50] About a dozen plays which were first published in the folios, including *As You Like it, Twelfth Night, The Winter's Tale, Coriolanus,* and *Antony and Cleopatra,* had never been made available individually. At that time, unless they were dealing in second-hand Shakespeare 4tos over fifty years old, or manuscript copies, which seems unlikely, many of the customers must either have gone away empty-handed, or been sold plays broken from the folios. One of the booksellers concerned, Thomas Johnson, later moved to the Netherlands where he reprinted plays, including many by Shakespeare, offshore for illicit sale in England.[51]

1711. Price in England of Shakespeare's plays, sold individually, printed offshore in the Netherlands.[52]	0.5	

R. Walker's edition

1731. End of the transitional period established by the 1710 Act. As a printer for Tonson the publisher, the main 'proprietor' of the Shakespearian plays, Walker could know how wide the margin was between Tonson's costs and his prices. He decides to take some of the market, offering attractively printed editions, each with an engraved frontispiece, at a third of the monopoly price.

Individual plays, one published every Thursday.[53]	0.33 each	na, large
Tonson and the other 'owners' while refusing to have the matter decided by the courts, drive Walker out of business by predatory pricing.		
Tonson's predatory price	0.25	
Then down to a penny[54]	0.08	
Tonson's price after Walker is driven out of business	1	
Extra-statutory monopolistic element in the price	0.7 (70 per cent)	

1734 and **1735.** Tonson's 12mo edition, nine volumes including *Poems,* in which each play was given a separate title page so that they could be sold both as a set and individually.[55]

Pericles[56]	1	8,000
Cymbeline[57]	1	10,000
Antony and Cleopatra[58]	1	10,000
Two Gentlemen of Verona[59]	1	10,000

[49] Examples in *Term Catalogues.*

[50] *An exact catalogue of all the comedies, tragedies, tragi-comedies, opera's [sic], masks, pastorals and interludes that were ever yet printed and published till this present year 1680* by Francis Kirkman (1680). Wing notes editions of 1661 and 1671. See also quotations from booksellers' catalogues in Furnivall, *Some 300 Fresh Allusions* vi.

[51] A full list with prices in Edmund Smith, *Phaedra and Hippolitus* (1711), Cambridge University Library.

[52] *Ibid.* See also Ford 48.

[53] Price, '4d. with the Frontispiece' printed on title page of *Richard III* (1734).   [54] Ford 43.

[55] Bowyer ledgers 2101, 2103, 2105, 2106.

[56] Bowyer ledgers 2101. 10,000 copies were also printed of the spurious *London Prodigal.*

[57] Bowyer ledgers 2105.   [58] *Ibid.* 2103.   [59] *Ibid.* 2106.

Appendix 12 *(cont.)*

When Walker was driven out of business, the 'proprietors' then raised the price, but appear shortly afterwards to have stopped selling individual plays altogether, keeping the unsold stocks as a strategic reserve with which to again flood the market at predatory prices if another similar challenge were to be mounted.[60]

1773. *Hamlet.* Jennens's edition.[61]   na   750

Summary of minimum price of buying an individual Shakespeare printed play

Before the 1623 folio	0.5
After 1623 until early eighteenth century	
Except as part of the folio editions	mostly not available
1730s. Tonson's price	1
Walker's price, attempting to exercise his statutory rights	0.3
Tonson's predatory price	0.25
Tonson's price after Walker is driven out of business	1
After 1730s	
Except as part of multi-volume sets	mostly not available
1774. Perpetual intellectual property forbidden	
c. 1780. Outsiders break the monopoly	
After 1780. Many editions, e.g. 1785 *Macbeth*.[62]	0.5
1821 onwards Dolby's (later Cumberland's) *British Theatre*	0.5
The early numbers sold 14,000 copies[63]	
1832. 'Penny Shakespeare'[64]	0.33
1880s. Various cheap editions, some as low as[65]	0.25
Later nineteenth century, Dicks's edition[66]	0.08

Collected plays

Rowe

1709–10. Rowe's edition, six volumes, 8vo with plates[67]   30   na

---

[60] See chapter 8. For the practice of keeping of stocks in reserve, ready to flood the market, identified as a feature of cartels under potential challenge, see Rotemberg and Salone 73–97.

[61] Bowyer ledgers 4965.

[62] Charles James Longman, *The House of Longman 1724–1800, A Bibliographical History* (1936) 341.

[63] Thomas Dolby, *Memoirs* (1827) 119.

[64] Advertised in *The Tourist, or Sketch Book of the Times*, 8 October 1832, Ac. The 'penny' is the price of the series in parts, not the price of a complete play.'

[65] *English Catalogue* (1891).

[66] A penny. Full list of Dicks's 614 plays, beginning with *Othello*, on covers of Peake's *Frankenstein* (n.d.), Ac.

[67] Price from *Term Catalogues* iii, 654 (1709).

Appendix 12 (*cont.*)

Largely a reprint of the 1685 folio, at a higher price. The publication of this edition, with a named editor, enabled the then owners of the Shakspeare copyright to prolong their period of ownership under the transitional arrangements of the 1710 Act.

1714. Second edition, including *Poems*, nine volumes,   27   2,500
12mo[68]
Individual plays were apparently not available to be bought separately

Pope

1725. Pope's edition, six volumes, 4to   126 to subscribers   750
Of which 140 sets were still unsold in 1767.[69]
Can be regarded as a move back to the top of the demand curve including a misjudgment of the demand to be expected at such a high price, even with the name of Pope.

1726. Dublin, eight volumes, 8vo. An immediate offshore   28   na
reprint in smaller format and far lower price.[70]

1728. Second London edition, ten volumes, 12mo   30   na

1731. Pope's edition, nine volumes, 12mo, Knapton   na   na
Probably tranched down even further.[71] Knapton had leased the intellectual property rights from Tonson.[72]

Theobald

1733. Theobald's edition, eight volumes, 8vo, Tonson[73]   42   1,360

1739. Dublin, seven volumes 12mo. An immediate   na   na
offshore reprint in smaller format and far lower price.[74]

1740. Second London edition, eight volumes, 12mo[75]   28 or 30   1,500

1752. Third edition, actually second reissued with new   na   na
title page[76]

1762. Eight volumes, 8vo[77]   24   1,500

---

[68] Edition size implied in trade sale catalogue, 10 November 1757. Assignment document by Robson, a publisher, 1768, in Robinson archives, transcribed by Bentley. Price from advertisement of 1715 in Ford 15.

[69] Timperley 716. Lowndes viii, 2259.   [70] Price from advertisements in Ford 57.

[71] BL catalogues describes this edition as 12mo.   [72] See Geduld 145.

[73] The phrase 'Copy Right' was used in the contract between Tonson and Theobald dated 26 October 1731, transcribed from a manuscript in the Bodleian by Peter Seary, *Lewis Theobald and the Editing of Shakespeare* (Oxford 1990) 215.

[74] Ford 28. Since there were only 134 subscribers Ford thought that the edition size could not have been above 200, but, having been assured that they could cover their costs by subscription, the publishers might have produced more copies for illegal export to Great Britain and the British colonies.

[75] The *Catalogue of Most Esteemed Books* (1751) gives price of 30 shillings.

[76] Print run for this edition implied by trade sale catalogue 1755.

[77] Print run from assignment document by Robson, a publisher, 1768, in Robinson archives, transcribed by Bentley 109. Price from *A Complete Catalogue of Modern Books* (1766).

Appendix 12 *(cont.)*

1767. Eight volumes, 12mo[78]	na	1,500
1772. Eight volumes, 12mo	na	na
1773. Eight volumes, perhaps the same edition[79]	na	2,000
c. 1777. Eight volumes[80]	28	na
Before 1766. An unidentified edition, nine volumes, 18mo[81]	18	2,500
Total for all Theobald editions[82]		12,860

Hanmer

1744. Hanmer's Oxford edition, the text largely taken from Pope's edition, in defiance of the claimed perpetual copyright, six volumes quarto. Hanmer took no fee and paid for the illustrations.[83]	210	600 sets
1751. Price of the six volume edition[84]	30	

Other editions

1747. Another edition, Knapton, nine volumes, 12mo	na	na
1770. Six volumes, 'royal quarto'[85]	126	na
1745. Six volumes, 8vo	na	na
1747. Osborne's edition in defiance of the claimed perpetual copyright[86]	na	2,000
1751. Nine volumes, 12mo	na	na
1760. Nine volumes 12mo	na	na

Warburton

1747. Tonson's Pope and Warburton edition. Eight volumes, 8vo[87]	48	2,500

[78] Trade sale catalogue, 18 August 1767, Jacob and Richard Tonson. 'Two editions in the press, one of Theobald's 12mo. 1,500'.

[79] Strahan archives. Figures are for volumes vii and viii.

[80] Price in 1786 from *General Catalogue*, 1786 and the same in 1799 from *London Catalogue*.

[81] Price listed in *Complete Catalogue* (1766). For the print run, in the catalogue of the trade sale of 18 August 1767, it is noted that Tonson had 1646 in 2,500 of the 18mo in nine volumes.

[82] Lowndes viii, 2260, from Tonson archives since lost.

[83] Harry Carter, *A History of Oxford University Press* (1975) i, 303.

[84] Price in the *Catalogue of Most Esteemed Books* (1751).   [85] Price from *London Catalogue* (1799).

[86] Hernlund 104 from Strahan archives.

[87] Print run from Ackers ledger, 219, 296, 315, volume viii only. Price from *Catalogue of Most Esteemed Books* (1751).

Appendix 12 (*cont.*)

Never reprinted. Seems to have been a misjudged attempt to move back to the very top of the demand curve at a time when cheaper 'pirated' editions were still available.

1751. Catalogue price[88]	30	na
1747. Dublin, 8 volumes.[89] An offshore piracy	16	na

Scottish editions, taking advantage of the fact that the terms of the 1710 Act were not frustrated in Scotland

1753. Hugh Blair's edition, *The Works of Shakspeare, In which the Beauties observed by Pope, Warburton, and Dodd are pointed out*		
Edinburgh, eight volumes, 8vo	na	na
Reprinted 1761, 1767 (ten volumes 12mo), 1771, 1795, 1797, with changes as the London editions fell out of statutory copyright.		
1764. Donaldson's eight-volume edition on sale in London.[90]	16 bound	?1,000
1752 to **1766.** Foulis of Glasgow's edition from Pope's second edition[91]		
Eight volumes, 8vo	32	na
Sixteen volumes, foolscap 8vo (small format)	16	na
Each play has a separate title page presumably to enable it to be sold individually		

Samuel Johnson

1765. Johnson's edition, eight volumes	48	1,000
1765. Second edition[92]	na	750
Commercially disappointing although Johnson himself was financially well rewarded		
1766. Dublin. Ten volumes. An offshore piracy	na	na

---

[88] Price in the *Catalogue of Most Esteemed Books* (1751). Dibdin 801 quotes a price of 18 shillings.

[89] Price from *Proposals for Printing by Subscription The Works of Shakespear in Eight Volumes* (Dublin 1747) BL. The price appears to have been 16 shillings for everything or about a shilling more if paid for in instalments, half bound.

[90] *A Catalogue of Books printed for Alexander Donaldson, Bookseller in Edinburgh; and sold at his shop near Norfolk-street, in the Strand, in London, and at Edinburgh; Also by the Booksellers of Great Britain, Ireland, and America* (Edinburgh 1764) 19. Cambridge University Library Munby d.157. For his print runs, see the quotation in appendix 1, 469.

[91] The trade prices are given in *A Catalogue of Books, Being the Entire Stock in Quires of the late Robert and Andrew Foulis* (Glasgow 1777) copy in Glasgow University Library; the retail price from Philip Gaskell, *The Foulis Press* (1986) 273.

[92] Bowyer ledgers 4559,

Appendix 12 *(cont.)*

Capell

1767. Capell's edition, Ten volumes. 8vo.[93]   42   1,500

Capell provided a clean readable text, with his commentary, *Notes and Readings*, published between 1779 and 1781 at 63 shillings in 4to

Jubilee edition

1768. An edition finely printed by Baskerville of   na   2,000
Birmingham, nine volumes, 8vo, prepared at the
suggestion of Garrick and sold at Stratford during the
Shakespeare Jubilee. Published in defiance of the
claimed perpetual copyright.

Offshore piracy

The Plays of Shakespeare from the text of Dr S. Johnson, with prefaces, notes, & c, of Rowe, Pope, Theobald, Hanmer, Warburton, Johnson (and others, including Capell)

1771. Dublin. Twelve volumes 16mo, or seven volumes in   na   na
thirteen parts

An example of how Dublin offshore reprints could offer the most up-to-date editions in small format at cheap prices

Johnson and Steevens

1773. Ten volumes, 8vo[94]   60   na
1778. Second edition, ten volumes, 8vo[95]   70 bound   1,200
1780. Supplement[96]   18   na
1785. Third edition, ten volumes, 8vo, revised by Reed[97]   70 boards   1,200

Malone

1790. With Malone's historical account, eleven volumes,   88   1,200
8vo[98]

1790. With Malone's historical account, seven volumes,   21   1,200
12mo[99]

Reprinted offshore in Dublin 1794, sixteen volumes, 12mo

[93] Trade sale catalogue, 18 August 1767, Jacob and Richard Tonson.
[94] Zachs 283 from Murray archives. The Longman copyright ledger i, 172, gives 1,500 copies.
[95] Longman, *The House of Longman* 340.
[96] Zachs 326 from Murray archives. The Longman copyright ledger i, 172, gives 1,500 copies.
[97] Zachs 369 from Murray archives. Price from *General Catalogue* (1799).
[98] Zachs 369 from Murray archives.   [99] *Ibid. General Catalogue* (1799) gives price of 157.5 shillings.

1793. Fourth edition, Steevens's own, fifteen volumes.[100]	135	1,200
1794. Reduced to[101]	103 or 130 bound	
1803. Fifth edition, Johnson and Steevens, revised by Reed, twenty-one volumes, 8vo[102]	na	1,250
1813. Sixth edition, twenty-one volumes, 8vo[103]	132	1,250
1821. Unnumbered edition, twenty-one volumes, 8vo	132	na

Jennens

1773. Jennens's edition of some individual plays[104]	na	750

Bell

1773/75. Bell's edition, five volumes, 12mo[105]	15	4,500

'No fewer than 8,000 copies were sold in one week.' Lowndes[106]

Text from Johnson and Steevens. Illustrated. This was the John Bell whose edition of *The British Poets* precipitated the decision of the London booksellers to commission Samuel Johnson to prepare a rival series. See chapter 7 and appendix 6.
The engraved illustrations were available separately, 'to bind up with any edition of Shakespeare' or 'for ornamental furniture' at various prices depending upon the quality of the paper. Cheapest 0.5 shillings each.[107]

1786–8. Bell's edition reprinted, seventy-six parts at 1 shilling, or in twenty volumes.[108] Said to be the first edition of Shakespeare sold in parts	60	na
Copies sold of the first number, *The Tempest*, according to Bell[109]		3,000
1804. Reprinted by Cawthorn, sold in fortnightly parts	60	na

---

[100] Catalogue sheet of Hamilton's *Capital Books, Wholesale, Retail, and for Exportation, constantly on sale at the Shakespeare Library* (1794). Copy in Bell and Bradfute archives SL 138/9.
[101] Longman copyright ledger i, 172. *Virtue's Almanac* (1874) says 1,500.
[102] Murray archives. A costing is reproduced in (Richard Duppa), *An Address to Parliament on the Claims of Authors to Copyright, by a Member of the University of Cambridge* (1813) 22.
[103] Bowyer ledgers, 4965. *Hamlet* and others.
[104] Bowyer ledgers 5024, 500 royal, 2,000 crown, and 2,000 fine, based on quantities of paper used. This is a much larger figure that the 1,300 on ordinary paper and 134 subscribed, noted by Colin Franklin, *Shakespeare Domesticated, The Eighteenth Century Editions* (1991) 32, no source given.
[105] Lowndes viii, 2262.
[106] Advertisement issued while the series was still not all published, in a copy of Bell's *British Theatre*, Ac.
[107] Lowndes, viii, 2262.   [108] See Morison 6.
[109] To judge from figures for his edition of the novelists.

Appendix 12 *(cont.)*

Some monopoly breakers' editions produced in London as soon as it was clear that the 1774 decision would stick

1770s and **80s.** Harrison's *Theatrical Magazine*[110]	cheap	many 000s
1784. Stockdale's one-volume edition, with explanatory notes and life[111]	15 carriage free anywhere in Great Britain	na

THE MARKET VALUE OF THE SHAKESPEARE COPYRIGHT

High monopoly period, prices rising strongly

Prices obtained for sales of shares in the perpetual copyright at the closed book-trade auction sales, or by private transaction within the cartel. The prices paid (given in pounds, shillings and pence) were the cost of being allowed to participate in the publishing of the work to the extent of the shareholding, excluding all the costs of manufacture etc., which were shared by the partners in accordance with their relative shareholdings, and were influenced by the likely timing and cash flow from expected new editions. The figure for total value represents the market capitalisation of Shakespeare seen as a rentable property in conditions of monopoly in which the supply to the market was carefully controlled.

Individual plays

An intellectual property right to print certain plays was held independently of the property rights in Shakespeare's dramatic works.

1763. *King Lear* A ninth share £2/15/0.[112]
implying a total value of this right of   £24.75

1763. *Hamlet.* An eighteenth share £2/17/0.[113]
implying a total value of this right of   £51.3

Dramatic works

1707. 'A moyety of Mr Shakespiers playes' and at least 130 other properties £140[114]
implying a total value of   a small fraction of £280

---

[110] Advertised in *New Books printed for John Stockdale* inserted in *A Sketch of Modern History* (1799), Ac.

[111] Marked catalogue, 21 April, 1763.

[112] Receipt by Charles Corbett bought on 21 April 1763. Upcott collection iii, 57.

[113] Noted by Giles Mandelbrote, in 'Richard Bentley's Copies' in Hunt, Mandelbrote, and Shell 67. See also Terry Belanger, 'Tonson, Wellington, aand the Shakespeare copyrights' in *Studies in the Book Trade in Honour of Graham Pollard* (Oxford Bibliographical Society 1975), although no prices are given.

[114] Quoted from an assignment document in the Folger Library by Giles E. Dawson, 'The Copyright of Shakespeare's Dramatic Works' in Charles T. Prouty, ed., *Studies in Honor of A. H. R. Fairchild* (Columbia, Miss. 1946) 25.

1709. Half share in twenty-five plays with approximately 380 other properties £100[115]
implying a total value of   a small fraction of £200

1734. Offer of £200 to Walker to cease from printing the plays[116]
implying a total value of   much more than £200

1737. '*A Ninth of the following Copies* . . . Shakespear's whole Works, *third*; *And a right of printing separately*; Julius Caesar, *third*; Macbeth, *third*; Othello *whole*; Hamlet whole.'
£25, with others.[117]
implying a total value of   less than £675

1737. A ninth of a share with the same rights (with others) £13[118]
implying a total value of   less than £351

1737–8. A sixth part of five-ninths of a share with similar rights, but excluding *Hamlet*,
£10/10/0[119]
implying a total value of   less than £340

1741. A ninth of a third share of Rowe, Pope, and Theobald, £16/5/0[120]
implying a total value of   £439

1756. Forty-six in 2,500 £30[121]
implying a total value of   £1,630

1759. 'Lintot's copies.' One sixth of five-ninths of a third.
'The purchaser of this Lot is entitled to a share in some
plays when printed single' £53[122]
implying a total value of   £1,717

1760. Two other shares of one sixth of five-ninths of a third, each £53[123]
implying a total value of   £1,717

1761. One twelfth of five ninths of one third £21[124]
implying a total value of   £1,361

1762. Fifteen-and-a-quarter in 2,500 £7/17/6[125]
implying a total value of   £1,291

1763. 'Wellington copies'. One sixth of five-ninths of a large portfolio of properties which
includes one-third in editions of Shakespeare by Rowe, Pope, Theobald &c. £106[126]
                              total value of not easily calculable

1765. 'Feales's copies'. One-ninth of a portfolio mainly consisting of a ninth of
Shakespeare's whole works plus a right of printing separately *Julius Caesar* one ninth,
Macbeth one ninth, *Othello*, one third, and *Hamlet* one third plus 'Heppinstal's copies'
(Not identified but, since they are not listed, they are unlikely to have been extensive)
£42/15/0[127]
implying a total value of not much less than   £3,462

---

[115] See Geduld 194.   [116] Marked catalogue, 17 November 1737.
[117] Marked catalogue, 22 December 1737.   [118] Marked catalogue, 23 February 1737/38.
[119] Marked catalogue, 20 August 1741.   [120] Marked catalogue, 5 February 1756.
[121] Marked catalogue, Lintot copies, 26 April 1759.   [122] Marked catalogue, 8 January 1760.
[123] Marked catalogue 29 September 1761, as amended in manuscript.
[124] Marked catalogue 9 December 1762.   [125] Marked catalogue 21 April 1763.
[126] Marked catalogue 8 January 1765.   [127] Marked catalogue 8 January 1765.

Appendix 12 *(cont.)*

1765. Another with exactly the same rights sold at the same sale £37[128]
implying a total value of not much less than   £2,997

1767. Twenty one-thirtieth shares of Tonson's share, which was about 65 per cent, were floated for £60 to £61.5 each[129]
implying a total value of   £2,838

1768. Forty-six in 2,500 in 8vo, 12mo, &c. £20[130]
implying a total value of   £1,087

(1769. The Shakespeare Jubilee at Stratford)

Pretender or expiring copyright on Reed's edition which remains in copyright

1776. A sixtieth £22/5/0[131]
implying a total value of   £1,335

1778. Two shares of a sixtieth each £9/15/0[132]
implying a total value of   £1,170

1781. A sixtieth £7/17/6[133]
implying a total value of   £472

1783. A sixtieth £9[134]
implying a total value of   £540

1783. A share of fifteen-and-a-quarter in 2,500 £7/7/0[135]
implying a total value of   £1,202

1783. A share of 46 in 2,500 £17/10/0[136]
implying a total value of   £951

1792. A sixtieth, £16/16/0[137]
implying a total value of   £1,000

1792. Another share of a sixtieth sold at the same auction, £18
implying a total value of   £1,080

Before **1794.** A sixtieth, £10/2/0, and a one-hundred-and-twentieth share, £5/0/0[138]
implying a total value of   £600

1794. A hundred-and-twentieth £6[139]
implying a total value of   £720

---

[128] Marked catalogue, 26 May, 1767. Strahan copyright ledger, BL add. mss. 48,804, notes £60/17/2.
[129] Marked catalogue, 13 October 1768.   [130] Strahan archives, BL add. mss. 48,804.
[131] Nicols ledger. See also Zachs 283.   [132] Zachs 369.   [133] *Ibid.*   [134] Nicols ledger.
[135] *Ibid.*   [136] Marked copy, 22 March 1792.
[137] From a page from a trade catalogue photographically reproduced in Shaylor 192, unfortunately not easily legible and no date given. However, the paucity of entries, and the names of publishers who bought shares, seems to require that the date is later than the sale noted in the previous entry but before Vernor amalgamated with Hood in 1794. For the dates when the various publishers were in business see Ian Maxted, *The London Book Trade, 1775–1800, A Preliminary Check-list of Members* (1977).
[138] Zachs 396.   [139] *Ibid.*

1794. Two-hundred-and-twentieths £12[140]
implying a total value of £720

1796. Two-hundred-and-twentieths £16/5/0.[141]
implying a total value of £975

Value of intellectual property in texts of Shakespeare without any paratextual editorial material

After **1774** nil

The editor of Shakespeare as a commercially valued creator of new intellectual property

Fees paid to successive editors.[142]

1709–10. Rowe	730
1714. Hughes adding to Rowe	567
1725. Pope	4,352
Fenton	614
Gay	717.5
Whalley	240
1733 and later. Theobald	13,050
Plus 2,000 shillings from a nobleman for his dedication	
1746. Warburton	10,000
1765. Johnson, first edition	7,500
1765. Johnson, second edition	2,000
1767. Capell	6,000
1791. Malone[143]	4,000
1803. Reed. Revision of Johnson and Steevens	6,000
The proof corrector	2,000
1821. Boswell[144]	20,000

SOME EDITIONS AFTER THE BREAKDOWN OF PERPETUAL COPYRIGHT IN ENGLAND, INCLUDING SOME NEWLY EDITED EDITIONS WHICH QUALIFIED FOR COPYRIGHT PROTECTION

Many editions of Shakespeare's plays besides those listed below are recorded as published before 1830. The following is a provisional sample only and some double counting may have occurred.

---

[140] *Ibid.*
[141] *Ibid.*
[142] Timperley 716. Some of the payments are confirmed by contemporary documents. See, for example, Kathleen M. Lynch, *Jacob Tonson, Kit-Cat Publisher* (Tennessee 1971) 132.
[143] Bentley 93. Perhaps an advance only.   [144] Dibdin 807.

Appendix 12 (*cont.*)

1786–91. Rann's edition, Oxford, six volumes 8vo[145]	48	na
1786. An edition, nine volumes 18mo, the cheapest available from the mainstream London industry at this time[146]	18	na
1788. Nichols's edition, seven volumes, 12mo	na	na
1791. Bellamy's edition, eight volumes	na	na
1796. 12mo[147]	na	1,500
1797. Seven volumes, imperial 8vo	73.5	na
1798. Nine volumes, 18mo[148]	22.5	2,000
	plus extra copies on fine paper	500
1800. *The Plays of William Shakespeare* Thirty-eight numbers individually dated, illustrated, making twelve volumes[149]	na	2,000
1802. Boydell's illustrated, folio, eighteen parts, nine volumes, ninety-five engravings, folio	756	na
Price in 1818, nine volumes folio	756	na
with additional plates	1,880	na
1803. Symonds's Shakespeare's *Plays*[150]	na	4,000
1803. Nine volumes, 18mo[151]	27	2,000
The same in ten volumes, royal demy	45	1,000
The same in ten volumes, 8vo	70	500
1804. Sharpe's edition[152]	na	4,000
An edition before 1807, nine vols, 32mo[153]	18	na
1805. Chalmers's edition.[154] 'super royal'	na	250
'royal'	na	500
'demy fine paper'	na	1,500
These were sold in 700 numbers		
'demy inferior paper'	na	1,000

---

[145] Colin Franklin, *Shakespeare Domesticated, The Eighteenth Century Editions* (1991) 43. Price from *London Catalogue* (1799).

[146] *General Catalogue* (1786). Perhaps one of the Theobald editions.

[147] Longman copyright ledger i, 172. Perhaps the same as one of the other pretenders' editions.

[148] Longman copyright ledger i, 172. Price from *London Catalogue* (1799).

[149] Print run from John Nichols, ledger of purchase and disposal of copyrights 1769–1815, CUL, add. 8226.

[150] Whittingham archives.

[151] Longman copyright ledger i, 172. Price from *New London Catalogue* (1807).

[152] Whittingham archives, BL add. mss. 41,901.

[153] Advertised in *New London Catalogue* (1807). Perhaps an earlier edition still available, although none is recorded in such a small format.

[154] Longman impression books.

Appendix 12 *(cont.)*

Instead of tranching down the publishers issued this new edition simultaneously at a wide range of prices		
Reprinted 1811, 1818	na	na
1823[155]	na	1,000
1826. Eight volumes[156]	na	1,250
Prices of Chalmers's edition in 1831[157]		
Eight volumes 8vo	72	na
Eight volumes with plates	96	na
In one volume	14	na
Some other recorded prices and edition sizes		
Before 1806. Oddy's (a fringe publisher) pocket edition, nine volumes.[158]	16	na
1806. Manley Wood's edition, fourteen volumes, 8vo	126	na
large paper	152	na

'Besides the very heavy expence of fine paper and superior printing, more than two thousand guineas have been expended by the Proprietors in embellishments.' preface

1807. Ten volumes, 8vo	na	na
1807. Douce's *Illustrations to Shakespeare*[159]		1,000
1810. Ten volumes 18mo[160]	30	3,500

1813. 'Cabinet' edition printed by Whittingham, in series, with 230 woodcuts. Text of Johnson and Steevens, with life specially written by John Britton

Each play 1 shilling, the whole in seven volumes.[161]	38	na
1817. Another edition[162]	42 in boards	2,000
1817. Individual plays published in sets of three at fortnightly intervals, for Sherwood, perhaps the same	na	2,250
The print run for the later plays was reduced to 2,000		
1821. Three volumes, 12mo	18	na
Bound in one volume	15	na
1820s. Jones's edition, one volume, 8vo[163]	15	na
1823. Jones's *Diamond Shakespeare*[164]		
32 weekly numbers at 0.5 shillings or 16 parts at 1 shilling.[165]		4,000

---

[155] Strahan archives.   [156] Strahan 48,846.   [157] As advertised in *London Catalogue* (1831).

[158] Advertised in copy of Oddy's edition of (Sterne's) *Sentimental Journey* (1806), Ac. Oddy was the name of the firm specialising in cheap reprints later called Jones.

[159] Longman impression books. Confirmed by Richard Taylor archives.

[160] Longman impression books. Price from *London Catalogue* (1818).

[161] As printed on the paper covers of *Hamlet*, (1813), Ac.

[162] Whittingham 41,926. Advertised in list of Sherwood, Neely, and Jones, December 1817, in copy of (Smiths') *Rejected Addresses* (1818), Ac.

[163] Advertised in copy of *The Mirror and Lounger* (1827), Ac. Other advertisements give 16 shillings.

[164] Whittingham archives.   [165] Advertisement in a copy made up from numbers, Ac.

Appendix 12 *(cont.)*

Compiled from the editions of Rowe, Johnson, Steevens, and others, Double columns. The tiniest achievable print size.

1823. One volume stereotyped[166]	16	na
1822. *Juvenile Shakespeare*, plays abridged and adapted to chapbook size	na	na
1823. Eight volumes, octavo[167]	na	1,750
1823. Ten volumes, 18mo[168]	na	2,500
1825. Tegg's prices, twelve volumes[169]	42 discounted from 63	na
Six volumes[170]	16.5 discounted from 30	na
1825. Ten volumes, 18mo.[171]	na	2,000
1826. 'Plays and Poems.' One volume, 'English classics,' bound in cloth, with forty illustrations[172]	36	na
Without illustrations	15	na
1827. Another edition, 12mo, with woodcuts[173]	na	7,000
1827. Another edition, Demy 32mo[174]	na	5,000
1833–7. Five editions printed for Tegg, totalling[175]		6,000
1837. Eight volumes.[176]	72	1,000
1826. Ten volumes royal, 18mo[177]	na	2,000

Bowdler's *The Family Shakespeare, in which Nothing is added . . but those Words and Expressions are omitted which cannot with Propriety be read aloud in a Family'* Editions of 1818, 1820, 1822, 1827, 1831, 1843, 1847, 1852, 1860, 1863, 1865. Price tranched down from 94 shillings to 63 shillings and 30 shillings.[178]

1846. Cheapest price advertised by the London industry[179]	7	

Dodd's *Beauties of Shakespeare*, an anthology

1757. The only Shakespeare anthology permitted by the owners of the intellectual property in the plays.

---

[166] Strahan archives. Price from *London Catalogue* (1832). Commended by Dibdin 808.
[167] Strahan archives.   [168] Strahan archives.
[169] *A Select library of Books . . . now offered at greatly reduced prices, By Thomas Tegg* in Locke's *An Essay on Human Understanding . . with notes. 25th edition* (1825), Ac.
[170] *Ibid.*   [171] Whittingham 41,925.
[172] Advertisement of 'English Classic Library', inserted in copy of Ovid's *Epistles* (1826 but sold later), Ac.
[173] Whittingham 41,925.   [174] *Ibid.*   [175] Clay ledger 1289/3/3/3.
[176] Strahan archives. Price from *London Catalogue* (1832).   [177] Whittingham 41,926.
[178] Prices from *London Catalogue* (1846).
[179] *Ibid.* A Tegg edition, probably the one volume edition in tiny print stereotyped.

Appendix 12 (*cont.*)

As with the main Shakespeare texts, the monopoly private ownership could not be enforced after 1774, and the title was reprinted by several publishers at falling minimum prices. Other anthologies were also published in competition. Some archival records, showing its popularity as part of the old canon in the romantic period.

1810. Whittingham's edition[180]	8	2,000
1818. Tegg's edition[181]	na	4,000
1821. Another Tegg edition[182]	na	4,000
1824. Another Tegg edition[183]	na	3,000
1824. *Walker's classics* edition[184]	na	4,000
1826. One volume by a consortium, stereotyped, first impression[185]		4,000
1838. Another impression[186]		2,000
Many later editions, including stereotype editions in Victorian times by Warne, Milner, and others	lowest 1	na
1915. The stereotype plates of the Warne edition are sent for melting[187]		

Victorian period

Innumerable editions published at a wide range of prices. For example Longman, eight volumes, stereotyped[188]

1837, 1847, 1856	each impression 1,000

Longman, one volume Galignani style, stereotyped[189]

1846, 1853, 1863	impressions of 1,500, 1,500, 1,000

The following are some recorded print runs, from the many editions of the English poets in formal series, among whom Shakespeare was usually included along with the poets of the romantic period. All stereotyped.

Gall and Inglis of Edinburgh[190]

1864. Two volumes	2,000
1864–1906. One volume	9,000
1871–94. 16mo	61,000

Routledge's *British Poets*

Cumulative production, 1882–1902, at various prices[191]	81,000

---

[180] Whittingham 41,925. [181] *Ibid.* [182] *Ibid.* 41,926. [183] *Ibid.*
[184] Longman divide ledger 8. [185] *Ibid.* [186] *Ibid.* 9. [187] Warne archives.
[188] Longman archives. [189] Longman archives.
[190] Gall and Inglis impression book. Figures rounded including overcopies. See also appendix 13.
[191] Routledge archives. See also appendix 13.

Appendix 12 *(cont.)*

Frederick Warne editions

Albion and Imperial (expensive) editions, 1875 to 1892, then apparently discontinued	15,000
Lansdowne (middle price) Shakespeare 1869 to 1893, then apparently discontinued	67,500
Chandos (cheapest) (Cut off date, not known, perhaps 1920s)[192]	344,000

The Lansdowne and Chandos editions were made from the same plates

The 1891 London trade catalogue listed about two dozen editions of the complete works available in print at that time at a large variety of formats and prices, plus innumerable other shorter editions, anthologies, bowdlerised versions, adaptations, and texts intended for schools.[193] At that time Routledge was selling about 3,000 copies of the complete works a year, Warne about 6,000. In 1895 an impression of 10,000 of the Macmillan Globe edition is recorded.[194]

The long fall in minimum prices, both nominal and real, appeared to have culminated in Dicks's edition, first available in the 1870s, when the complete works, with 36 newly drawn illustrations, could be bought for 1 shilling in cloth or 0.5 in paper. But by the 1890s, many individual plays were available at one penny (0.08 shillings) obtainable nationwide by sending postage stamps.

1894. Temple Shakespeare[195]   250,000 annually
                                                                  100,000 annually to United States

Pocket size. Continued until 1934, when a new edition was published[196]

---

[192] Arthur King and A. F. Stuart, *The House of Warne, One Hundred Years of Publishing* (1965) 5.

[193] *English Catalogue of Books* (1891).   [194] Macmillan archives, BL 55910.

[195] Shaylor 342, from trade sources.

[196] *The House of Dent, 1888–1938, reissued with additional chapter* (1928) 273.

Appendix 13 The romantic poets in Victorian times

Gall and Inglis of Edinburgh. *Family Edition of the Poets*

1853 until 1890s.[1] The first canonising series when the poets of the romantic period began to come out of copyright under the 1842 Act. Made from stereotype plates, in a range of bindings in leather and cloth at different prices. Some versions had 'Red Rule' borders. In the *Landscape Edition of the Poets*, each page printed over a tinted romantic engraved view of Edinburgh, Venice, Rome, or the desert and the jungle.[2] A few editions were gorgeously bound with a cameo window and flowers on the front cover. The series enjoyed its largest sales in the 1870s and ran until the mid 1890s. Cumulative production, rounded, excluding overcopies, between the date of first publication and the ending of the series.

Longfellow, 1855	101,000
Scott, 1853	91,000
Byron, 1857	80,000

The Life of Byron scarcely mentions *Don Juan*, and it is omitted, along with *Beppo*, from the text.

Burns, 1859	70,000

'In this edition of Burns the more Objectionable Passages and Pieces have been excluded.' Advertisement

Cowper, 1853	70,000
Milton, 1854	70,000
Moore, 1859	66,000
Wordsworth, 1857	51,000
Goldsmith, 1856	45,000
Campbell and Coleridge, 1856	20,000
Campbell, 1874	12,000
Coleridge, 1874	10,000
Hemans, 1876	26 000
Pope, 1860	23,000
Kirke White, 1855	19,000
Crabbe, 1854	17,000
James Montgomery, 1861	17,000
Herbert and Heber, 1860	14,000
Young, 1866	9,000
Tupper, 1874	8,000

Nimmo of Edinburgh *Editions of the Poets*

Mid and late Victorian.[3] 'Red-Line', 'Crown', and 'Popular' editions, in a range of bindings in leather and cloth at different prices between 12 and 3.5 shillings.
Longfellow, Scott, Byron, Moore, Wordsworth, Cowper, Milton, Shakespeare, Thomson, Pope, Burns, Beattie and Goldsmith, *Humorous Poetry, Ballads*. No production figures found but likely to be comparable to Gall and Inglis.

[1] Gall and Inglis impression book. Other information from advertisements, e.g. in Moore's *Lalla Rookh*, n.d., Ac.
[2] Advertisement in Herbert and Heber, n.d. (c. 1882), Ac.
[3] Advertisement in Thomson, n.d., Ac. Another, 1869 in Byron, Ac. Plus additions from another in *Books and Authors*, n.d., Ac.

Appendix 13 *(cont.)*

Routledge's *British Poets*

Begun in the late 1850s, and sold strongly in the 1870s and later. Made from stereotypes in double columns in small type, usually illustrated, at a range of prices eventually as low as the 'Poets for the People' series at 1.5 shillings. Many smaller selections and individual poems by Scott, Byron, Moore, and others were also published. Cumulative production, 1859 to 1902, with date of Routledge's first edition,[4] rounded.

Longfellow, 1850	see below
Burns, 1858	137,000
Byron, 1859	116,000
Moore, 1859	116,000
Scott, 1853	111,000
Wordsworth, 1858	91,000
Milton, 1855	87,000
Cowper, 1855	50,000
Hemans, 1872	51,000
Campbell, Herbert, Hood, Goldsmith, Pope	below 50,000
Bloomfield, Chaucer, Coleridge, Herbert, Montgomery, Shelley, Southey, Spenser, Kirke White, Whittier	below 30,000
Bryant, Crabbe, Dryden, Leigh Hunt, Keats, Landon, Rogers	below 10,000

Moxon's *Popular Poets*

Edited by William Michael Rossetti, each with illustrations by Ford Madox Brown, Thomas Seccombe, and other Pre-Raphaelite artists. Begun 1870, by which time the authors were all either out of copyright or the residue of the copyright was owned by Moxon. 'Red-Line' and other editions, in a range of bindings in leather and cloth. In order published. No production figures found but advertised soon after first publication as having sold over 100,000 copies.

Byron, Longfellow, Wordsworth, Scott, Shelley, Moore, Hood, Keats, Coleridge, Burns, Tupper, Milton, Campbell, Pope, Cowper, *American Poets*, Hemans, Thomson, Whittier, Lowell, Young, Shakespeare, Keble's *Christian Year*, Poe, Leigh Hunt, W. M. Rossetti's *Lives of Famous Poets*, Scott's *Minstrelsy*, Dodd's *Beauties of Shakespeare*, Poems of Ireland. In 1870 when Moxon went out of business, the stereotype plates were taken over by Ward, Lock and Co., and production continued under the name of *Moxon's Poets*, later renamed the *Popular Poets*.[5]

Ward, Lock and Co's list[6]

'Standard series'. 5 shillings, bound in half calf. 'People's Standard Library'. 2 shillings, cloth gilt. No production figures found.

Byron, Longfellow, Wordsworth, Scott, Shelley, Moore, Hood, Keats, Coleridge, Burns, Tupper, Milton, Campbell, Pope, Cowper, *American Poets*, Hemans, Thomson, Whittier.

---

[4] Routledge archives.
[5] Edward Liveing, *Adventures in Publishing, The House of Ward Lock, 1854–1954* (1954) 47.
[6] Advertisements in copies of Byron and Shelley, Ac.

Appendix 13 *(cont.)*

Some of the plates were later taken over by Collins of Glasgow who published nineteen volumes of 'Grosvenor Poets' until the 1920s.[7] The plates also appear to have been used to produce editions for sale in the colonies, some under local imprints. In some editions of Byron and Shelley the plates have become so worn that many words of the text can scarcely be read.

Warne's lists[8]

In 1865 Frederick Warne, who had been a partner of Routledge, set up in business on his own, taking some titles, and presumably also the stereotype plates, with him.[9] His series of reprints of English classics, prose and verse, was kept in print until the great melting for armaments of 1914–18, and others until another melting in 1937.[10] Warne also published many new books for children which later became the firm's speciality. The texts of all the editions of the poets seem to have been set from the same stereotype or electrotype plates, and manufactured for the different series with differing quality of paper, with or without the red line, and in a rich and rapidly changing selection of different bindings. The texts were updated and prefaces altered from time to time, and the illustrations replaced by others. In a few cases, for example the verse works of Scott, a new edition was prepared and new stereotype plates manufactured, but, at least until 1914–18, the plates were mostly repaired and updated. All the better-selling authors for which there is a surviving record show a large initial surge, a continuing demand through the 1870s and 80s, and a rapid falling away in the 1890s and later. This follows the patterns seen in the other series. *The Albion Poets*. 3.5 shillings. Twelve titles were also available at the time of the 1887 Jubilee even more expensively as *The Imperial Poets*. The firm also offered *The Padded Poets*. 'A selection of . . . Our Most Popular Poets choicely bound in padded Algerian Levant' (i.e. bound like Bibles and prayer books). *The Lansdowne Poets*, with notes, portraits and illustrations. Large crown 8vo, extra gilt, 3.5 shillings, 8 shillings morocco. *The Chandos Poets* small 8vo, 1.5 shillings in stiff wrappers, 2 shillings in cloth gilt. The following lists of production numbers, from incomplete archives, cover various commencing dates from 1868 through until 1895, after which no production information is known, although some of the editions continued to be produced for some decades later.

Imperial and *Albion* (more expensive) editions

Burns	22,000
Hood	9,500
Byron	8,500
Wordsworth	8,000
Moore	6,500
Elizabeth Barrett Browning	6,500
Shelley	1,500
Information on the others not available	

---

[7] Keir 189.   [8] Warne archives.   [9] King and Stuart 1.
[10] Advertisements in copies, Ac, with further information from Warne archives. For the melting of 1914–18 see chapter 21.

Appendix 13 *(cont.)*

Lansdowne Poets (middle range)

Scott	65,000
Burns	57,000
Byron	43,500
Milton	42,500
Wordsworth	38,500
Hood	36,500
Burns	35,500
Moore	34,000
Cowper	28,500
Shelley	13,000
Pope	11,000
Gems of National Poetry (anthology complied by Laura Valentine)	11,000
Book of Authors (anthology of sayings of authors, modern *sententiae*)	7,000
Gray, Beattie, and Collins	6,500
Sacred Songs	5,500
Montgomery	4,500
Heber	4,000
Percy's *Reliques of English Poetry*	2,000
Dryden	1,000
Schiller	1,000
Information on the others is not available	

Chandos Poets (cheaper range)

Ultimately 154 titles. 1.5 shillings in paper (few copies in this form survive) and 2 shillings in cloth. Total sales of the whole series exceeded five million.[11]

Shakespeare	340,000
Byron	125,500
Eliza Cook	64,500
Moore	56,500
Hemans	39,000
Shelley	34,000
Cowper	32,500
Campbell	15,750
Book of Authors (an anthology of sayings, modern *sententiae*)	6,000
Dryden	3,000
Montgomery	2,500
Longfellow 1865–1900 see below	
Shakespeare see appendix 12	
Information on the others not available	

[11] King and Stuart 5.

Exaggerated claims for sales of Longfellow

Routledge's claimed sales to 1900[12]
Poetical works   390,000
Individual works   326,000
of which *Hiawatha*   37,000
Although the figures were supplied by the firm, they cannot be reconciled with the
information in the surviving archives.
Warne's claimed sales of all editions, 1865–1900[13]   410,919
This figure too cannot be easily reconciled with the (incomplete) information in the
surviving archives.

Newbery Classics. 1880s and 1890s[14]

Published by Griffith Farran, London. Crown 8vo. Gilded cloth covers. About 600 pages
each volume, double columns, tiniest print, no illustrations or introductions. Price
2 shillings.
Longfellow, Scott, Mrs E. B. Browning, Hood, Moore, Wordsworth, Shakespeare,
Campbell, Byron.

Finch's *Standard Classics*

Turn of the century.[15] Ecclesiastical style, with gilt and limp leather
Browning, Elizabeth Barrett Browning, Burns, Byron, Campbell, Eliza Cook, Cowper,
Goldsmith, Hemans, Hood, Keats, Longfellow, Lowell, Milton, Moore, Pope, Scott,
Shakespeare, Shelley, Tennyson, Whittier, Wordsworth.

Sands's *Apollo Poets*

1890s, no prices found.
Scott, Longfellow, Milton, Byron, Burns, Wordsworth, Moore.

Macmillan's *Globe Library*

1885.[16] Cloth 3.5 shillings. A successful attempt to provide a series, of better quality in
terms both of text and readability, than was available from any of the publishers who were

---

[12] From a letter sent to Gohdes by the firm dated 23 February 1939, quoted by Clarence Gohdes,
'Longfellow and his authorised British Publishers' in *PMLA* 55 (1940) 1165.

[13] Quoted by Gohdes 1179 from a letter sent to him from the firm 31 January 1939 but, like the figures
for sales of Longfellow given by their rival Routledge, looks like an exaggeration. The Warne archives
show other examples of such exaggerations. For example, frequent advertisements claim that sales
of the novels of Silas Hocking, one of their bestselling authors, had exceeded one million although
the surviving archives suggest a lower figure.

[14] Advertisement in copy of *The Poetical Works of Lord Byron* (n.d., but, from presentation inscription,
not later than 1893).

[15] Advertisement in edition of Wordsworth, n.d., Ac.

[16] Advertisement in copy of Clough, Ac.

Appendix 13 *(cont.)*

locked into their old stereotypes. Some texts were newly edited from manuscripts and early editions. Stereotyped in a clear type, the series was kept in print for many decades, and probably helped to hasten the fall in sales of the versions produced by other publishers from inferior stereotypes. Why Byron was not included is not known. The series is said to have sold 20,000 copies in the first few months alone.[17]

Shakespeare, Scott, Burns, Goldsmith, Pope, Dryden, Cowper, Malory, Virgil, Horace, Milton, Spenser.

Poetical Works of Scott, edited by F. T. Palgrave[18]   51,000

The print runs of the others are not available although it is possible that some could be reconstructed from the Macmillan archives in the British Library.

Cassell's *Miniature Library of the Poets*

1880s, each in two volumes in a tiny case 2.5 shillings. A curiosity, like the Diamond Poets of the 1820s noted in appendix 6, scarcely suitable for reading, but an indication of how the competitive pressures on costs and prices pushed at the limits of manufacturing technology.

Burns, Byron, Hood, Longfellow, Milton, Scott, Sheridan and Goldsmith, Wordsworth, Shakespeare.

List of Milner of Halifax, *The Cottage Library*

Mid 1870s. Milner had begun his business by reprinting Burns and non-copyright Byron, and as a chapman taking his stock round the towns and villages of Yorkshire, hiring a shop for a week or a stall for a day. His huge business eventually included a long list of works in prose and verse, including many religious and conduct books first published as long as two hundred years earlier. Sales seem later to have been mainly to the newly literate working classes in the industrial north of England with a large export trade to the colonies. Many dozens of titles at around 1 shilling each.

Cumulative sales of poets, 1837 to 1895, rounded[19]

Burns	183,000
Byron	127,000
Milton	85,000
Pope's *Homer*	69,000
Bloomfield	66,000
Longfellow	63,000
Moore	58,000
Cowper	52,000
Wordsworth	29,000
Shelley	22,000
Dryden's *Virgil*	18,000
Scott	17,000

---

[17] Charles Morgan, *The House of Macmillan, 1843–1943* (1944) 76.
[18] Total impressions before 1935 quoted by Simon Eliot, 'To You in Your Business' in Elizabeth James, ed., *Macmillan: A Publishing Tradition* (2002) 24, from archival records.
[19] Wroot 169.

Appendix 13 (*cont.*)

Hemans	13,000
Thomson	12,000
Kirke White	10,000
Coleridge	8,000
Butler	4,000
Heber	4,000
Keats	4,000

Nicholson of Wakefield's *Cottagers Library*

A rival to Milner's *Cottage Library* which it closely resembles.[20] Mid and late Victorian. Mainly out of copyright novels, religious and conduct books. 1 shilling, Poets included Milton, Burns, Byron's *Select Works*, Longfellow.

'New and Popular Editions of the Poets'

Dunn and Wright, Glasgow and London, no date but probably end of nineteenth century. Double columns. Fine thick paper and strong cloth 1 shilling. Paper 0.5 shillings.[21] Longfellow, Moore, Burns, Byron, Scott, Cowper, Campbell.

John Dicks's *English Classics*

1870s and later.[22] Complete poetical works, small print, double columns, all extensively illustrated with works by late Victorian artists, bound in cloth or paper. Mostly 0.5 shillings in paper; 1 shilling in cloth. Postage for mail order from London 0.17 shillings and 0.25 shillings, for which payment could be made by sending postage stamps to be bought at any post office. In order advertised.
Shakespeare, Byron, Pope, Goldsmith, Hemans, Scott, Longfellow, Milton, Cowper, Wordsworth, Burns, Moore, Thomson, *Arabian Nights*, Bunyan's *Pilgrim's Progress*.
'A series of Complete Unabridged Works of the most popular Writers. Profusely Illustrated, neatly printed, and stitched in coloured paper. Pronounced to be the cheapest books ever published.' Advertisement.

	Shillings
Don Juan by Lord Byron	0.5
The Lady of the Lake by Sir Walter Scott	0.17
The Siege of Corinth by Lord Byron	0.08
Lalla Rookh by Thomas Moore	0.25
The Corsair by Lord Byron	0.08
Marmion by Sir Walter Scott	0.17
Childe Harold's Pilgrimage by Lord Byron	0.17
The Vampire by Lord Byron (not by Byron)	0.08
Poetical Works of Percy Bysshe Shelley, c. 1892	0.5
Scott's *Waverley Novels*, thirty-two volumes	0.25 each
Whole set in seven volumes	14

[20] From advertisement in Ac.
[21] Advertisement of the firm's list in copy of Cowper, Ac. No copy of the paper edition has been seen.
[22] Advertisments in editions of Byron, of Shelley, and of Longfellow, Ac.

Appendix 13 (*cont.*)

Everyman's Library

Begun 1906. Planned to be 1,000 volumes. Still continuing.
'We had to print at least 10,000 of each volume to cover the bare cost, and in many cases – notably of Shakespeare and Dickens – as many as 20 or 30,000. For my fixed determination was to make it a democratic library at the democratic price of one shilling.' J. M. Dent, the founder.[23]
For some print runs of Mary Shelley's *Frankenstein* see appendix 9.

Anthologies

	Print runs
Poets of the Nineteenth Century	
1856. A fine illustrated gift edition	
11,000 in 1856–57, 4 reissues before 1885[24]	
Chandos Classics edition 1885 to 1892[25]	12,250
Gleanings from the English Poets	
1862. Gall and Inglis, until 1893[26]	51,000
F. T. Palgrave, editor, *The Golden Treasury*	
1861. 9,000 in 1861, by 1884	61,000
Warne's *Modern Readings and Recitations*, 1886 to 1895[27]	12,500
Warne's *Gems of National Poetry*	
Chandos Poets series[28]	1,500

UNIVERSITY EDITIONS, SCHOOL BOOKS, AND BOOKS AIMED AT EDUCATING THE POOR

Clarendon Press *English Classics*

1890s, a series of short books, each edited by a well-known name, with scholarly notes. Mostly 2.5 to 5 shillings, some titles available more cheaply as school books.[29] Chaucer, Langland, Spenser, Marlowe and Greene, Shakespeare, Milton, Dryden, Pope, Thomson, Gray, Goldsmith, Cowper, Burns, Keats's *Odes*; and *Hyperion* book 1, Byron's *Childe Harold*, Shelley's *Adonais*, Scott's *Lady of the Lake, Lay of the Last Minstrel, Lord of the Isles, Marmion*, Campbell's *Gertrude of Wyoming*, Wordsworth's *White Doe of Rylstone*.

Chambers's *English Classics*

1880s, paper covers, a few pence each.[30] Shakespeare, Chaucer, Burns's *Cotter's Saturday Night*, Byron's *Childe Harold; The Prisoner of Chillon; The Siege of Corinth*, Campbell's *Pleasures of Hope*, Coleridge's *Ancient Mariner*, Cowper's *Task*, Dryden's *Virgil*, Goldsmith's *Deserted Village* and *The Traveller*, Gray's *Odes* and *Elegy*, Hemans's *Select Poems*, Macaulay's *Armada, Ivry, and Evening*, Milton's *Paradise Lost; Paradise Regained;*

---

[23] *Memoirs of J. M. Dent* (1928) 126.
[24] Figures quoted by Sabine Haas, 'Victorian Poetry Anthologies' *Publishing History* (1985).
[25] Warne archives.   [26] Gall and Inglis impression book.   [27] Warne archives.
[28] Warne archives.   [29] Advertised in copy of Pope, 1896, Ac.
[30] Advertised in copy of Byron's *The Prisoner of Chillon*, Ac.

Appendix 13 *(cont.)*

Comus; Samson Agonistes; L'Allegro, Il Penseroso, and *Lycidas,* Pope's *Essay on Criticism; Essay on Man,* Scott's *Lady of the Lake; Lay of the Last Minstrel; Lord of the Isles; Marmion,* Spenser's *Faerie Queene,* Thomson's *Seasons,* Wordsworth's *Excursion; Odes to Duty, Immortality, &c; The Brothers; Tintern Abbey, Happy Warrior,* &c.

Arnold's *British Classics for Schools*

1890s, each with introduction and notes. 1 shilling and 1.5 shillings.[31]
Macaulay's *Lays of Ancient Rome,* Scott's *Lady of the Lake,* Milton's *Paradise Lost* I and II, Milton's *Paradise Lost* III and IV, Byron's *Childe Harold,* Scott's *Marmion,* Scott's *Lay of the Last Minstrel.*

Macmillan's *English Classics* for schools, with notes[32]

Late Victorian, mostly 1 shilling. Poets include Campbell, Cowper, Dryden, Goldsmith, Gray, Milton, Scott, Shakespeare, Spenser, Tennyson, Wordsworth, selections from Wordsworth, Byron, Shelley, Lamb, and Scott.

Cassell's *National Library*

1880s. An educational series. Weekly volumes, 0.25 shillings; or on cloth 0.5 shillings. Eventually ran to about 200 titles, mainly prose but including Shakespeare's plays. Average sales were said to have been 30,000 per volume over twelve years. After the first 150 titles, Cassell claimed that over 300,000 copies had been sold 'which would fill twenty four miles of bookshelves'.[33]

Masterpiece Library. *The Penny Poets* and *Penny Popular Novels*

Begun 1893, originally monthly, price 1 penny (0.08 shillings), 'may be had of any newsdealer or direct by post . . . for 6s, the whole series of 48'. The series was later extended, each book available individually for three halfpence, post free. Some recorded sales. Macaulay's *Lays of Ancient Rome* 166,000 by 1894, 196,000 by 1895; Scott's *Marmion* 150,000 by 1894.[34]
'The most efficient agency that has yet been devised for making our best literature familiar to the mass of the nation'. Lord Salisbury, the prime minister.

---

[31] Advertisement in copy of *Marmion* (third edition 1899), Ac.
[32] Advertisement in copy of Gray's *Poems* (1895), Ac.
[33] Simon Nowell-Smith, *The House of Cassell, 1848–1958* (1958) III.
[34] Advertisements in surviving copies, Ac.

Bibliography

(Place of publication is London, unless stated otherwise.)

MANUSCRIPT ARCHIVES OF PUBLISHERS, PRINTERS, AND BOOKSELLERS

Adlard, printers, a ledger c. 1825–32, Bodleian.

John Bagford, notes and transcribed papers, made in the early eighteenth century. BL, Harleian mss. 5,892–5,998.

Bell and Bradfute, booksellers and publishers in Edinburgh:
  Five ledgers, mainly of retail sales, 1788–1829, with other incomplete early records, NLS.
  Eighty-five ledgers, 1788–1820, with some later, Edinburgh City Archives, with a few other ledgers transferred from Edinburgh Central Library.

Richard Bentley, publishers, almost complete archives, with some papers relating to Henry Colburn and Colburn and Bentley, BL. Microfilm includes copies of papers held elsewhere.

A. and C. Black, owners of the Scott copyrights, minute book, NLS.

William Blackwood, publishers, substantial archives, NLS.

Booksellers' autographs, mainly eighteenth century. Bodleian ms. Eng. misc. c. 134.

E. Burns to James Watson, letters, BL add. mss. 46, 345.

Cadell and Davies, publishers. Letters from authors and others: Bodleian and NYPL.

W. and R. Chambers. Extensive archives, NLS.

Chatto and Windus, publishers, archives, Reading University Library.

Richard Clay, printers, incomplete archival records from 1819. Lowestoft Record Office.

William Clowes, printers from 1803, a ledger of orders, 1810–15, Clowes Printing Museum, Beccles, Suffolk.

Archibald Constable, publishers, substantial but incomplete archives, NLS.

Dent/Dutton, archives held at University of North Carolina, Chapel Hill.
  Some figures relating to *Everyman's Library* kindly supplied by Professor Mark Reed.

Evert Duyckinck, bookseller, printer, and publisher in New York, archives 1795 until 1820s. NYPL.

Robert Fleming and Patrick Neill, printers and law stationers in Edinburgh, two ledgers 1764–73 and other papers, seventeenth to twentieth centuries, NLS, Dep. 196.

Gall and Inglis, publishers, 1844 until 1960s. Impression book listing all the publications of the firm, with every edition, impression, and print run. In the possession of the author.

Daniel Graisberry, printer in Dublin, ledgers of print orders 1777–1806, Trinity College, Dublin.

John Harris, children's bookseller, a ledger, 1825–43, Guildhall Library, London.

Thomas Harrison, printer, order ledger, 1821–35, City of Westminster Archives.

Hookham and Carpenter, booksellers, publishers of novels, and circulating library owners, two ledgers of the 1790s. Public Record Office, Kew, C104/75.

Houlston, publishers and booksellers, some papers 1827–61, BL.

Joseph Johnson, publisher, letter book 1795–1810. Pforzheimer collection, NYPL.

Kincaid and Bell, booksellers and publishers, two letter books, 1764–72, Bodleian.

Longman, publisher, substantial archives from 1790s with a few earlier records. Reading University Library.

Macmillan, publishers, full archives, BL.

Daniel Midwinter and Aaron Ward, valuation 1732, BL add. mss. 44,849.

John Murray, publishers, archives, including those of firms taken over, in the possession of John Murray (Publishers) Ltd.

John Nichols, ledger of purchase and disposal of copyrights 1769–1815, CUL add. mss. 8226.

Oliver and Boyd, printers and publishers in Edinburgh, substantial archives, NLS.

An Oxford bookseller, ledger of sales, and hiring of books, 1819–23, Bodleian.

Sir Richard Phillips, some records among the Longman archives, Reading University Library.

George Routledge, general publishers in Victorian times and later, publication registers. Library of University College, London.

Society for the Promotion of Useful Knowledge (SPUK), archives. Library of University College, London.

Stationers' Company. Typed transcription of the unpublished confidential ledger known as Liber A. Pollard papers 304, Bodleian.

Stationers' Company. Registers of copyrights, 1710–86, Stationers' Hall, London. Registers of copyrights, 1842–52. Public Record Office, Kew.

Timothy Stevens, bookseller of Gloucester, four late-eighteenth-century sales ledgers, Gloucester Public Library, described by Paul Kaufman, 'A Bookseller's Record of Eighteenth Century Book Clubs' in *The Library* (1960).

William Strahan, eighteenth-century printer and publisher, with papers of the successor printing firms in the nineteenth century, including Spottiswoode, BL.

John Taylor, publisher and bookseller. Various papers, Derbyshire Record Office, Matlock. Extensively quoted by Chilcot. Nine commonplace books, Berg collection, NYPL.

Richard Taylor and Company, printers, later scientific publishers, archives, St Bride's Printing Library, London.

Upcott. Copyright assignment documents 1712–1822 collected by William Upcott, BL. Others, Bodleian.

Frederick Warne and Co., publishers. A large, though incomplete, collection of books published by the firm in the Victorian period dispersed from the firm's property room, many with archival summaries relating to their intellectual property status, costs, successive print runs, and disposal of stereotype plates. In the possession of the author. Some others were seen and noted before they were dispersed.

Charles Whittingham and Co., London printers and publishers, archives, BL. Other papers, NYPL.

Woodfall's accounts. BL add. mss. 38,169. Quotations from their ledgers now lost in *Notes and Queries*, 1855.

TRANSCRIBED ARCHIVAL SOURCES, AND PRINTED
WORKS CONTAINING ARCHIVAL INFORMATION

A Ledger of Charles Ackers edited by D. F. McKenzie and J. C. Ross (Oxford 1968).

Arber, E., *A Transcript of the Registers of the Company of Stationers of London, 1554–1640* (1875–94).

(Bennett and Clements) Hodgson, Norma and Blagden, Cyprian, *The Notebook of Thomas Bennet and Henry Clements* (Oxford 1956).

Bentley, G. E. Jr, 'Copyright Documents in the George Robinson Archive: William Godwin and Others 1713–1820' in *Studies in Bibliography* (1982).

Besterman, Theodore, *The Publishing Firm of Cadell and Davies. Select Correspondence and Accounts 1793–1836* (1938).

(Bohun) S. Wilton Rix ed., *The Diary and Autobiography of Edmund Bohun* (Beccles 1853).

Bonnell, Thomas, 'Bookselling and Canon-Making: The Trade Rivalry over the English Poets, 1777–1783' in *Studies in Eighteenth Century Culture* (1989).

(Bowyer) Maslen, Keith and Lancaster, John, eds., *The Bowyer Ledgers* (1991).

(Burney) Hemslow Joyce *et al.*, eds., *The Journals and Letters of Fanny Burney* (1972–).

John Cheney and His Descendants, Printers in Banbury since 1767 (Banbury, Privately printed 1936).

Christianson, C. Paul, *Memorials of the Book Trade in Mediaeval London* (Cambridge 1987).

The Correspondence of Robert Dodsley 1733–1764, edited by James E. Tierney (Cambridge, 1988).

Dorne, John, bookseller in Oxford c. 1520, *Daybook* edited by F. Madan (Oxford 1885). See also Bradshaw, Henry, 'A Half Century of Notes on the Day-book of J. Dorne' in *Collected Papers* (1889).

Eliot, Simon, *Some Patterns and Trends in British Publishing, 1800–1919* (1994).

Ford, Worthington Chancey, *The Boston Book Market 1679–1700* (Boston 1917).

(Godfrey) *Garrett Godfrey's Accounts c 1527–1533* edited by Elisabeth Leedham-Green, D. E. Rhodes, and F. H. Stubbings (Cambridge 1992).

Gomme, George Laurence, ed. *The Gentleman's Magazine Library, Being a Classified Collection of the Chief Contents of the Gentleman's Magazine from 1731 to 1868* (Boston n.d., c. 1868) Volumes entitled *Bibliographical Notes* and *Literary Curiosities*.

Greg, W. W., *A Companion to Arber* (Oxford 1967).

Greg, W. W., and Boswell, E., *Records of the Court of the Stationers' Company, 1576 to 1602* (1930).

Hackwood, Frederick William, *William Hone, His Life and Times* (1912).

Harrison, James, *Printing Patents, Abridgements of Patent Specifications Relating to Printing 1617–1857* (1859 and 1878, reprinted 1969).

Index to Titles and Proprietors of Books Entered in the Book of Registry of the Stationers' Company from 28 April 1710 to 30th December 1773 n.d. [1910].

Kaser, David, ed., *The Cost Book of Carey and Lea, 1825–1838* (Philadelphia 1963).

Kaufman, Paul, *Libraries and their Users, Collected Papers in Library History* (1969).

(Knox) 'Henry Knox and the London Book-Store in Boston 1771–1774. Transcriptions of Correspondence by the Editor' in *Proceedings of Massachusetts Historical Society* (June 1928).

McKitterick, David, '"Ovid with a Littleton"; the Cost of English Books in the Early Seventeenth Century' in *Transactions of the Cambridge Bibliographical Society* (1997).

Maslen, Keith, *An Early Printing House at Work, Studies in the Bowyer Ledgers* (New York 1993).

Samuel Richardson, Printer of London (Otago 2001).

Maxted, Ian, *The London Book Trade, 1775–1800* (1977).

The British Book Trades 1731–1806, A Check-list of Bankruptcies (Exeter 1985).

Mayo, Robert D., *The English Novel in the Magazines 1740–1815* (Evanston 1962).

Plomer, Henry R. *Abstracts from the Wills of English Printers and Stationers from 1492 to 1630* (1903).

Plomer, H. R., Bushbel, G., H., and Dix, E. R. McC, *A Dictionary of Printers, and Booksellers who were at work in England, Scotland, and Ireland from 1726 to 1775* (1968).

Raven, James, 'The Export of Books to Colonial North America' in *Publishing History*, 41 (1997).

London Booksellers and American Customers (Charleston, SC. 2002).

Rouse, E. P., 'Old Halifax Circulating Library, 1768–1866' in *Halifax Antiquarian Society Publications* (1911). The original minute books are lost but Rouse's notes and transcriptions are preserved in Calderdale District Record Office, Halifax.

Schoenbaum, S., *William Shakespeare: Records and Images* (1981).

Select Committee on the Copyright Acts, Minutes of Evidence Taken, House of Commons (1813).

Select Committee on the Copyright Acts, Minutes of Evidence Taken, House of Commons (1818).

Select Committee on Dramatic Literature. Report. House of Commons (1832).

Stockdale, Eric, 'John Almon and the Stockdales 1760–1840', typewritten copy. BL add. mss. 71220.

Stoker, David, 'William Procter, Nathaniel Ponder, and the Financing of *Pilgrim's Progress*' in *The Library* (2003).

Thompson, Ralph, *American Literary Annuals and Gift Books* (New York 1936).

A Transcript of the Registers of the Worshipful Company of Stationers From 1640–1708 A. D. (1914).

Tryon, Warren S., and Charvat, William, *The Cost Books of Ticknor and Fields* (New York 1949).

Voet, Leon, *The Golden Compasses: A History and Evaluation of the Printing and Publishing Activities of the Officina Plantiniana at Antwerp* (1969–72).

Vogt, George McGill, 'Richard Robinson's *Eupolia* (1603)' in *Studies in Philology* (1924). A transcription of a manuscript in the BL.

Wills, Elizabeth Carter, *Federal Copyright Records, 1790–1800* (Washington, DC 1987).

Wroot, Herbert E., 'A Pioneer in Cheap Literature, William Milner of Halifax' in *The Bookman* (March 1897).

Zachs, William, *The First John Murray* (1998).

LIBRARIES' AND INDIVIDUALS' MANUSCRIPT ARCHIVES AND OTHER COLLECTIONS OF MANUSCRIPTS RELATING TO BOOKS AND READING

Albums and commonplace books, author's collection and others in private and institutional collections.

Bolton Caledonian Book Club and Bolton Union Book Club. Bolton Central Library.

Bristol Library Society, archives. Bristol Central Library.

Chambers lending library account book, 1828–29, NLS 341/413.

John Clare, his papers and his books, Northampton Public Library.

Eclectic Book Society, Minute Book, Guildhall Library, London.

Halifax Circulating Library, incomplete archives, Calderdale Record Office.

Leake Family papers, Hertford Record Office.

Luddenden incomplete archives, Calderdale Record Office.

Kirkcudbright Public Library, incomplete archives, Hornell Museum, Kirkcudbright.

Royal Literary Fund. BL.

Wigton Subscription Library, archives, Hornell Museum, Kirkcudbright.

Wright's Royal Colonnade Library, Brighton, Subscription Book. Brighton Public Library.

RARE AND EPHEMERAL PRINTED SOURCES

Advertisements. Late-eighteenth-century and early nineteenth-century books in their original unbound state, British, offshore, and pirate, in which titles are advertised, with their prices, on the covers, Ac.

Announcements and prospectuses. Reading University Library.

Publishers' and booksellers' ephemeral print, papers of Gillyat Sumner, Bodleian.

Copyright Papers, 1774. Legal documents, petitions, and papers, Bodleian. 40. Jur. x 136.

Pamphlets relating to the law on copyright deposit. London Library P127.

Federation of Master Printers, *Members Circulars*, 1914–18. St Bride's Printing Library, London.

John Johnson collection of printed ephemera. Bodleian.

Lauriston Castle chapbooks, NLS.

Subscription Libraries. Printed catalogues of the main city subscription libraries. Private collection.

BOOK TRADE CATALOGUES

A Catalogue of Latin, French, and English Books, to be sold in numbers, to the Book-sellers of London and Westminster . . . By Benjamin Walford (1688). CUL.

A Catalogue of Most Esteemed Modern Books, That have been Published for Fifty Years past, to this present time, With the Prices Affixed (1751). Bodleian, CUL, Ac.

A Complete Catalogue of Modern Books Published from the Beginning of the Century to 1756 (1756). Bodleian.

A Compleat Catalogue of all Books and Pamphlets Published for Ten Years Past; With their Prices (1760). John Rylands.

A Catalogue of Books printed for Alexander Donaldson, Bookseller in Edinburgh (Edinburgh 1764). CUL.

A Complete Catalogue of Modern Books Published from the Beginning of the Century to the Present Time, With the Prices Affixed (1766). BL.

A Catalogue of Books, Being the Entire Stock in Quires of the late Robert and Andrew Foulis (Glasgow 1777). Glasgow.

A General Catalogue of Books . . . Printed From the Year MDCC *to* MDCCLXXXVI *. . . With their Sizes and Prices* (1786). Bodleian.

The London Catalogue of Books . . . With their Sizes and Prices (1799).

The Modern Catalogue of Books . . . Containing the Books which have been Published in London since the year 1792 (1803).

The New London Catalogue of Books (1807), Ac.

The Modern London Catalogue of Books (1818), Ac.

Lackington, Hughes, Harding, Mavor, and Jones, *General Catalogue of Books for the Year 1819* (1819). Other catalogues at various times.

The English Catalogue of Books, published at intervals during the nineteenth century.
A Select Library of Books . . . now offered at greatly reduced prices, By Thomas Tegg bound in a copy of Locke's *An Essay on Human Understanding . . with notes.* 25th edition (1825), Ac.
The London Catalogue of Books Published in London . . . 1810 to 1831 (1831).
The London Catalogue of Books Published in London . . . 1814 to 1834 (1835).
The London Catalogue of Books Published in Great Britain . . . 1831–1855 (1855).

BOOK TRADE CATALOGUES. POPULAR LITERATURE

[Conyers] *Books Sold by G. C. at the Ring in Little Britain.* Bound in R. Green[e], *The Pleasant and Delightful History of Dorastus and Fawnia* (n.d., not earlier than 1698). Newberry.
A Catalogue of Maps, Histories, Prints, Old Ballads, Copy-Books, Broad-Sheet and other Patters, Drawing-Books, Garlands, &c Printed and Sold by William and Cluer Dicey, At their Warehouse, Opposite the South Door of Bow-Church in Bow-Church-Yard, London (1754). Bodleian. Another version, 1764, Glasgow, probably also a unique survivor. Unlike the 1754 version, quotes prices.
John Bew, 'Chapmen's Books' printed list in a copy of *The New History of the Trojan Wars* (n.d., late eighteenth century), Ac. Summarised in appendix 4.
Cheap Books published by Milner and Company (n.d. late Victorian). Bound in copy of Scott's *Poetical Works* (n.d. late Victorian), Ac and in other Milner books.

CLOSED BOOK INDUSTRY MARKED AUCTION-SALE CATALOGUES WITH ACHIEVED PRICES MARKED IN MANUSCRIPT

Catalogues of London sales, from 1704, Longman's copy. BL, c170 aa 1. Another set, xeroxed from original in the John Johnson collection, British Library, Cup. 1259 e 4. Other copies in the possession of John Murray (Publishers) Ltd.

ONLINE DATABASES

Early English Books online.
National Register of Archives.
Reading Experience Data Base.
Library History Data Base.
British book trade index.

PRINTED LISTS

Aldis, H. G., ed., *A List of Books Printed in Scotland before 1700* (1904, updated 1970).
Biographical Dictionary of the Living Authors of Great Britain and Ireland (1816).

Boyle, Andrew, *An Index to the Annuals* (Worcester 1967).
Brown, Philip A. H., *London Publishers and Printers c. 1800–1870* (1982).
Case, Arthur E., *English Poetical Miscellanies 1521–1750* (Oxford 1935).
Catalogue of Five Hundred Celebrated Authors of Great Britain Now Living (1788).
Clarke, John, *An Essay upon Study, wherein Directions are given for the due Conduct thereof, and the Collection of a Library* (n.d. 1737).
Corpus of British Mediaeval Libraries (ongoing).
Dibdin, T. F., *The Library Companion, or The Young Man's Guide and Old Man's Solace in the Choice of a Library* (second edition 1824).
Dickson, Robert and Edmond, John Philip, *Annals of Scottish Printing* (1890).
Evans, Charles, *American Bibliography, A Chronological Dictionary of all the Books, Pamphlets, and Periodical Publications Printed in the United States of America from the Genesis of Printing in 1629 down to and including the Year 1820* (Chicago 1903).
Garside, Peter, Raven, James, and Schöwerling, Rainer, eds., *The English Novel, 1770–1829: A Bibliographical Survey of Prose Fiction Published in the British Isles* (Oxford 2000).
Goodhugh, William, *The English Gentleman's Library, or a Guide to the Formation of a Library of Select Literature* (1827).
Jackson, J. R. de J., *Annals of English Verse, A Preliminary Survey 1770–1835* (Garland, New York 1985).
Romantic Poetry by Women, A Bibliography, 1770–1835 (Oxford 1993).
Jackson, William A., *Records of the Court of the Stationers' Company, 1602 to 1640* (1957).
Johnson, C. R., *Provincial Poetry, 1789–1839* (1992).
Livingston, Carole Rose, *British Broadside Ballads of the Sixteenth Century: A Catalogue of the Extant Sheets and an Essay* (1991).
Lowndes, William Thomas, *The Bibliographer's Manual of English Literature* (new edition 1857–64).
Michael, Ian, *Literature in School, A Guide to the Early Sources, 1700 to 1831* (Swansea 1999).
Munby, A. N. L., General editor, *Sale Catalogues of Libraries of Eminent Persons* (1971–5).
Neuburg, Victor E., *Chapbooks, A Bibliography* (1964).
'The Diceys and the Chapbook Trade' in *The Library* (1969).
Popular Literature, a History and a Guide (1977).
Nichols, John, *Biographical and Literary Anecdotes of William Bowyer* (1783).
Illustrations of the Literary History of the Eighteenth Century (1817–31).
Literary Anecdotes of the Eighteenth Century (second edition 1812).
Raven, James, *British Fiction, 1750–1770, A Chronological Checklist* (Newark, NJ 1987).
Rollins, Hyder E., 'An Analytical Index to the Ballad Entries (1557–1709) in the Registers of the Company of Stationers of London' in *Studies in Philology* (1924).
Roxburghe Ballads The, edited by C. H. L. P. Hindley (1873–4).

(STC) *A short title catalogue of books printed in England, Scotland and Ireland: and of English books printed abroad 1475–1640/ first compiled by A. W. Pollard and G. R. Redgrave,* (second edition, revised and *enlarged* 1976).

Sadleir, Michael, *XIX Century Fiction, A Bibliographical Record* (1951).

Simmons, R. C., *British Imprints relating to North America, 1621–1760: A Checklist* (1996).

Todd, William B., *A Directory of Printers and Other Allied Trades in London and Vicinity, 1800–1840* (1972).

Todd, William B., and Bowden, Ann, *Tauchnitz International, Editions in English 1841–1955* (1988).

Sir Walter Scott: A Bibliographical History, 1796–1832 (Oak Knoll, Delaware, 1998).

Watt, Robert, *Bibliotheca Britannica* (1824).

Weiss, H. B., *A Catalogue of Chapbooks, and Broadside Ballads in New York Public Library* (New York 1936).

Welsh, Charles and Tillinghast William H., eds., *Catalogue of English and American Chapbooks and Broadside Ballads in Harvard College Library* (1961).

Wing, Donald Goddard, *Short-title catalogue of books printed in England, Scotland, Ireland, Wales, and British America, and of English books printed in other countries, 1641–1700*/compiled by Donald Wing (second edition, revised and enlarged New York 1982–1998).

PRINTED BOOKS AND ARTICLES

GENERAL

The History of the Book in America i: *The Colonial Book in the Atlantic World* (*CBAW*) edited by Hugh Amory and David Hall (Cambridge 2000).

The Cambridge History of the Book in Britain iii: *1400–1557*, edited by Lotte Hellinga and J. B. Trapp (Cambridge 1999).

The Cambridge History of the Book in Britain iv:*1557–1695*, edited by John Barnard and D. F. McKenzie, with the assistance of Maureen Bell (Cambridge 2002).

Allan, David, 'Book Culture in the Scottish Enlightenment' in *The Library* (2002).

[Almon, John] *Memoirs of a late Eminent Bookseller* (1799).

Altick, Richard D., *The English Common Reader, A Social History of the Mass Reading Public 1800–1900* (Chicago 1957).

Writers, Readers, and Occasions (Columbus, Ohio 1989).

Areopagitica Secunda; Or Speech of the Shade of John Milton on Mr Sergeant Talfourd's Copyright Extension Bill (1838).

Armstrong, Elizabeth, *Before Copyright: the French Book-Privilege System 1498–1526* (Cambridge 1990).

Authorship and Publication, A Concise Guide for Authors (1883).

Ashton, John, *Chap-Books of the Eighteenth Century* (1882).

(Austen) *Jane Austen's Letters,* collected and edited by Deirdre le Faye (third edition 1995).

(Bagford) Ebsworth, Joseph Woodfall, ed., *The Bagford Ballads* (Hertford 1878).

Barker, Hannah, *Newspapers, Politics, and Public Opinion in Late Eighteenth Century England* (Oxford 1998).

Barnes, James J., *Authors, Publishers, and Politicians, The Quest for an Anglo-American Copyright Agreement 1815–1854* (1974).

Free Trade in Books (1964).

(Bell) Morison, Stanley, *John Bell, 1745–1831* (Cambridge 1930).

Bennettt, H. S., 'Notes on English Retail Book Prices, 1480–1560' in *The Library* (1950).

English Books and Readers 1475 to 1557 (second edition, Cambridge 1970).

English Books and Readers 1558 to 1603 (Cambridge 1965).

English Books and Readers 1603 to 1640 (Cambridge 1970).

Bentley, Richard, see under Gettman.

(Black) *Memoirs of Adam Black*, edited by Alexander Nicolson (second edition 1885).

The Black Book or Corruption Unmasked (1820).

(Blackwood) Mrs Oliphant and Mrs Gerald Porter, *William Blackwood and his Sons* (Edinburgh 1897 and 1898).

Blagden, Cyprian, *The Stationers' Company, A History* (1960).

Blakey, Dorothy, *The Minerva Press, 1790–1820* (1939).

Blanning, T. C. W., *The Culture of Power and the Power of Culture, Old Regime Europe 1660–1789* (Oxford 2001).

Blayney, Peter W. M., *The First Folio of Shakespeare* (Washington, DC. 1991).

Blunden, Edmund, *Keats's Publisher, A Memoir of John Taylor (1781–1864)* (1936).

Bowyer, W., *Biographical and Literary Anecdotes of W. Bowyer, and of Many of his Learned friends* (1782).

Brack, O. M., Jr., ed., *Writers, Books and Trade, An Eighteenth Century Miscellany for William B. Todd* (New York 1994).

Bradsher, Earl L., *Mathew Carey* (New York 1912).

Britton, John, *The Auto-Biography of John Britton* (1849/50).

Brown, Richard D., *Knowledge is Power, The Diffusion of Information in Early America, 1700–1865* (Oxford 1989).

(Byron) *The Complete Miscellaneous Prose*, edited by Andrew Nicholson (Oxford 1991).

The Complete Poetical Works of Lord Byron, edited by Jerome J. McGann (Oxford 1980–1993).

Byron's Letters and Journals, edited by Leslie A. Marchand (1973–82).

Capp, Bernard, *Astrology and the Popular Press, English Almanacs, 1500–1800* (1979).

Carnie, R. H., *Publishing in Perth before 1807* (Dundee 1960).

Carpenter, Kenneth E., *Books and Society in History* (1983).

Cavallo, Guglielmo and Chartier, Roger, eds., *A History of Reading in the West* (1999).

Chambers, William, *Memoir of William and Robert Chambers* (12th edition with supplementary chapter 1883).

Chandler, James, *England in 1819* (Chicago 1998).

Chew, Samuel C., *Byron in England, his Fame and After-Fame* (1924).

Chilcott, Tim, *A Publisher and his Circle: The Life and Works of John Taylor, Keats' Publisher* (1972).

Christie, William Dougal, *A Plea for Perpetual Copyright* (1840).

Clair, Colin, *A History of Printing in Britain* (1965).

Clegg, Cyndia Susan, *Press Censorship in Elizabethan England* (1997).

Clive, John, *Scotch Reviewers* (1957).

Clowes, Alice A., *Charles Knight, A Sketch* (1892).

Cochrane, J. A., *Dr Johnson's Printer, The Life of William Strahan* (1964).

Cole, Richard Cargill, *Irish Booksellers and English Writers, 1740–1800* (1986).

Coleridge, *The Collected Letters of Samuel Taylor Coleridge*, edited by Earl Leslie Griggs (Oxford 1956–1972).

Collet, C. D., *History of the Taxes on Knowledge* (1933).

Collins, A. S., *Authorship in the Days of Johnson* (1927).
   The Profession of Letters. A Study of the Relation of Author to Patron, Publisher, and the Public, 1780–1832 (1928).

Collins, firm of, see under Keir.

Conway, Moncure Daniel, *The Life of Thomas Paine* (one-volume edition 1909).

(Constable) *Archibald Constable and his Literary Correspondents* (Edinburgh 1873).

Cooper, Thomas, *The Life of Thomas Cooper Written by Himself* (1872).

Creech, William, *Edinburgh Fugitive Pieces . . . by the late William Creech . . . to which is Prefixed an Account of his Life* (Edinburgh 1811).

Cruse, Amy, *The Shaping of English Literature* (1927).
   The Englishman and his Books in the Early Nineteenth Century (1930).
   The Victorians and their Books (1935).

Curry, Patrick, *Prophecy and Power, Astrology in Early Modern England* (Princeton 1989).

Curwen, Henry, *A History of Booksellers* (n.d. 1873).

Davidson, Cathy N., ed., *Reading in America* (1989).

Darnton, Robert, *The Literary Underground of the Old Regime* (Cambridge, Mass. 1982).

Darnton, Robert, *The Forbidden Best-Sellers of Pre-Revolutionary France* (1995).

Darnton, Robert, and Roche, Daniel, eds., *Revolution in Print, The Press in France 1775–1800* (Berkeley 1989).

Darton, Harvey, *Children's Books in England* (Cambridge 1932).

Daunton, M. J., *Progress and Poverty, An Economic and Social History of Britain 1700–1850* (Oxford 1995).

David, Paul, *Intellectual Property Institutions and the Panda's Thumb* (Stanford 1992).

Deloney, see under Mann.

Dent, J. M., *The House of Dent, 1888–1938* (reissued with an additional chapter 1928).

Dolby, Thomas, *Memoirs* (1827).

Dooley, Allan C., *Author and Printer in Victorian England* (Charlottesville 1992).

Doughty, D. W., *The Tullis Press, Cupar 1803–1849* (Dundee 1967).

Dunlop, John, *The History of Fiction* (1814).

Dunton, John, *The Life and Errors of John Dunton, Citizen of London* (1818 edition).

[Richard Duppa], *An Address to Parliament on the Claims of Authors to Copyright* (1813).

Duval, Gilles, *Littérature de colportage et imaginaire collectif en Angleterre à l'époque des Dicey (1720-v. 1800)* (Bordeaux 1991).

Edwards, Mark U. Jr, *Printing, Propaganda, and Martin Luther* (Berkeley 1994).

Eisenstein, Elizabeth, *The Printing Press as an Agent of Change* (Cambridge 1979).

The Printing Revolution in Early Modern Europe (Cambridge 1983).

Elfenbein, Andrew, *Byron and the Victorians* (Cambridge 1995).

Engelsing, Rolf, *Der Bürger als Leser, 1500–1800* (Stuttgart 1974).

Everest, Kelvin, ed., *Shelley Revalued* (Leicester 1983).

Farrer, James Anson, *Books Condemned to be Burnt* (1892).

Feather, John, *The Provincial Book Trade in Eighteenth-Century England* (1985).

A History of British Publishing (1988).

Publishing, Piracy and Politics. A Historical Study of Copyright in Britain (1994).

Febure, Lucien, and Martin, Henri-Jean, *The Coming of the Book, The Impact of Printing 1450–1800* (original French edition 1958, English translation 1976).

Feinstein, Charles, 'Changes in Nominal Wages, the Cost of Living, and Real Wages in the United Kingdom over Two Centuries' in Scholliers, P. and Zamagni, V., eds., *Labour's Reward, Real Wages and Economic Change in 19th and 20th century Europe* (Aldershot n.d. c. 1995).

Finkelstein, David and McCleery, Alistair, eds., *The Book History Reader* (2002).

Fontaine, Laurence, *History of Pedlars in Europe*, translated by Vicki Whittaker (Durham, NC. 1996).

Forry, Steven Earl, *Hideous Progenies, Dramatizations of Frankenstein from the Nine-teenth Century to the Present* (Philadelphia 1990).

Fox, Adam, *Oral and Literate Culture in England, 1500–1700* (Oxford 2000).

Foxon, Frederick W., *Literary Annuals and Gift Books* (1973).

Fraistat, Neil, 'Illegitimate Shelley: Radical Piracy and the Textual Edition as Cultural Performance' in *PMLA* (1994).

Frasca-Spada, Marina and Jardine, Nick, *Books and the Sciences in History* (Cambridge 2000).

Frost, Thomas, *Forty Years Recollections* (1880).

Reminiscences of a Country Journalist (1886).

Gadd, Ian Anders, ' "Being like a field" Corporate identity in the Stationers' Company 1557–1684' (unpublished D. Phil. thesis, Oxford University, 1997).

Geduld, Harry M., *Prince of Publishers, A Study of the Work and Career of Jacob Tonson* (Bloomington 1969).

Gent, Thomas, *The Life of Mr Thomas Gent, Printer, of York* (1832).

Gettman, Royal A., *A Victorian Publisher, A Study of the Bentley Papers* (1960).

Gill, Stephen, *Wordsworth and the Victorians* (1998).

Gillett, Charles Ripley, *Burned Books* (New York 1932).

Gilmont, Jean-François, ed., *The Reformation and the Book*, translated by Karin Maag (Aldershot 1998).

Gilmore, William J., *Reading Becomes a Necessity, Material and Cultural Life in Rural New England, 1789–1835* (Knoxville 1989).

Gohdes, Clarence, *American Literature in Nineteenth Century England* (Carbondale, Ill. 1944).

Goodrich, S. C., *Recollections of a Lifetime* (New York 1856).

Graham Dougal, *The Collected Writings of Dougal Graham, 'Skellat' Bellman of Glasgow, edited by George MacGregor* (Glasgow 1883).

Grant, James, *Portraits of Public Characters* (1841).

The Great Metropolis, by the Author of 'Random Recollections of the Lords and Commons' Second Series (1837).

Green, Ian, *Print and Protestantism in Early Modern England* (Oxford 2000).

Greg, W. W., *The Shakespeare First Folio* (1955).

Licensers for the Press, &c. to 1640 (Oxford 1962).

'Richard Robinson and the Stationers' Register', in *Modern Language Review* (1955).

Gregory, Benjamin, *Autobiographical Recollections* (1903).

Griest, Guinevere L., *Mudie's Circulating Library and the Victorian Novel* (1970).

Groom, Nick, *The Making of Percy's Reliques* (Oxford 1999).

Halasz, Alexandra, *The Marketplace of Print, Pamphlets and the Public Sphere in Early Modern England* (Cambridge 1995).

Hansard, Luke, *The Autobiography of Luke Hansard, written in 1817*, edited with an introduction and notes by Robin Myers (Wakefield 1991).

Hansard, T. C., *Typographia* (1825).

Hansard, T. C., ed., *The Parliamentary History of England from the Earliest Period to the Year 1803, xvii: A. D. 1771–1774* (1813).

Harlan, Robert Dale, 'William Strahan, Eighteenth Century London Printer and Publisher' (unpublished Ph.D. thesis, University of Michigan 1960).

Harrison, James, *Printing Patents, Abridgements of Patent Specifications Relating to Printing 1617–1857* (1859 and 1878) (reprinted 1969).

Hirsch, Rudolph, *Printing, Selling, and Reading, 1450–1550* (Wiesbaden 1974).

Hodgson, Thomas, *An Essay on the Origin and Progress of Stereotype Printing* (Newcastle 1820).

Houston, R. A., *Literacy in Early Modern Europe* (1988).

Howe, Ellic, *The London Compositor, Documents Relating to the Wages, Working Conditions, and Customs of the London Printing Trade, 1785–1900* (1947).

Hughes, Thomas, *Memoir of Daniel Macmillan* (1883).

Humphreys, A. L., *The Private Library* (1897).

(Hutton) *Life of William Hutton . . . Written by Himself* (1816).

The Importance of Literature to Men of Business: A Series of Lectures Delivered at Various Popular Institutions (1852).

Isaac, Peter, ed., *Six Centuries of the Provincial Book Trade in Britain* (1990).

William Bulmer, The Fine Printer in Context 1757–1830 (1993).

Jackson, Holbrook, *The Fear of Books* (1932).

James, William Louis, *Fiction for the Working Man* (Oxford 1963).

Jerdan, William, *The Autobiography of William Jerdan* (1852–53).

Johns, Adrian, *The Nature of the Book: Print and Knowledge in the Making* (1998).

Johnson, Edgar, *Sir Walter Scott: the Great Unkown* (1970).

Johnson, F. R., 'Notes on English Retail Book Prices, 1550–1640' in *The Library* (1950).

Johnson, Joseph, see under Tyson.

Jordan, John O., and Patten, Robert L., eds., *Literature in the Marketplace* (Cambridge 1995).

Judge, Cyril Bathurst, *Elizabethan Book-Pirates* (Harvard 1934).

Keir, David, *The House of Collins* (1952).

(Kelly) R. C. Fell, *Passages from the Private and Official Life of the late Alderman Kelly* (1856).

Kernan, Alvin, *Printing Technology, Letters, and Samuel Johnson* (Princeton 1987).

Kerr, Robert, *Memoirs of the Life . . . of William Smellie, late Printer in Edinburgh* (Edinburgh 1811).

Kewes, Paulina, *Authorship and Appropriation, Writing for the Stage in England, 1660–1710* (Oxford 1998).

Kewes, Paulina, ed., *Plagiarism in Early Modern England* (2003).

King, Arthur, and Stuart, A. F., *The House of Warne, One Hundred Years of Publishing* (1965).

[Kirkman, Francis] F K, *The Unlucky Citizen* (1673).

Klancher, Jon, *The Making of English Reading Audiences, 1790–1832* (Madison, Wis. 1987).

Kluber, George A., *A New History of Stereotyping* (New York 1941).

Knight, Charles, *The Old Printer and the Modern Press* (1854).

Passages of a Working Life (1864).

Shadows of the Old Booksellers, with a preface by Stanley Unwin (1927).

Korte, Barbara, Schneider, Ralf, and Lethbridge, Stephanie, eds., *Anthologies of British Poetry, Critical Perspectives from Literary and Cultural Studies* (Amsterdam and Atlanta, GA 2000).

(Lackington), *Memoirs of the Forty Five First Years of James Lackington* (thirteenth edition, corrected and much enlarged, n.d., c. 1810).

Leavis, Q. D., *Fiction and the Reading Public* (1939).

Lectures on Mental Improvement, Burnap's Lectures to Young Men; Channing on Self-Culture; Original Thinking; Channing on the Elevation of the Labouring Classes (Derby n.d. Victorian).

[Lee, John] *Memorial for the Bible Societies in Scotland* (Edinburgh 1824).

Lehmann-Haupt, Hellmut, *The Book in America* (1952).

Linton, W. J., *James Watson, A Memoir* (Manchester n.d. [1880]).

Linton, William James, *Memories* (1895).

(Linton) Smith, F. B., *Radical Artisan, William James Linton, 1812–97* (Manchester 1973).

(Lister) *I Know my own Heart, The Diaries of Anne Lister, 1791–1840*, edited by Helena Whitbread (New York 1992).

Liveing, Edward, *Adventures in Publishing, The House of Ward Lock, 1854–1954* (1954).

Lockhart, J. G., *Memoirs of the Life of Sir Walter Scott, Bart.* (one-volume edition 1842).

[John Gibson Lockhart] *John Bull's Letter to Lord Byron* edited by Alan Lang Strout (Norman, Okla. 1947).

Love, Harold, *Scribal Publication in Seventeenth-Century England* (Oxford 1993).

Loewenstein, Joseph, *The Author's Pen, Printing and the Prehistory of Copyright* (Chicago 2002).

Lowndes, John J., *An Historical Sketch of the Law of Copyright* (1840).

McCalman, Iain, *Radical Underworld, Prophets, Revolutionaries and Pornographers in London 1795–1840* (1988).

McDougall, Warren, 'Smugglers, Reprinters and Hot Pursuers' in Myers and Harris, eds. *The Stationers' Company.*

McFarlane, Gavin, *Copyright: the Development and Exercise of the Performing Right* (1980).

McKenzie, D. F., 'The Economies of Print, 1550–1750' in *Produzione e Commercio della Carta e del Libro secc. XIII–XVIII.* Istituto Internazionale di Storia Economica (1992).

   Making Meaning, 'Printers of the Mind' and Other Essays, edited by Peter D. McDonald and Michael Suarez (Amherst 2002).

Mace, Nancy A., 'Litigating the Musical Magazine' in *Book History* 2 (1999).

McGrath, Alister, *In the Beginning, The Story of the King James Bible* (2001).

McKitterick, David, *A History of Cambridge University Press* i: *Printing and the Book Trade in Cambridge, 1534–1698* (Cambridge 1992).

   A History of Cambridge University Press ii: *Scholarship and Commerce, 1698–1872* (Cambridge 1998).

Macmillan, see under Hughes.

Mann, Alastair J., *The Scottish Book Trade 1500–1720* (East Linton, 2000).

Mann, Francis Oscar, ed., *The Works of Thomas Deloney* (Oxford 1912).

Marotti, Arthur F., *Manuscript, Print, and the English Renaissance Lyric* (Cornell 1995).

Marston, E., *Sketches of Some Booksellers of the Time of Dr Samuel Johnson* (1902).

[T. J. Mathias] *The Pursuits of Literature* (seventh edition, revised 1798).

Maugham, Robert, *A Treatise on the Laws of Literary Property* (1828).

Merriam, Harold G., *Edward Moxon, Publisher of Poets* (New York 1939).

Michael, Ian, *The Teaching of English from the Sixteenth Century to 1870* (Cambridge 1987).

Miller, George, *Latter Struggles in the Journey of Life* (Edinburgh 1833).

Millgate, Jane, *Scott's Last Edition* (1987).

Minto, John A., *History of the Public Library Movement in Great Britain and Ireland* (1932).

Mitch, David F., *The Rise of Popular Literacy in Victorian England* (Philadelphia 1992).

Mitchell, B. R., *British Historical Statistics* (1988).

Mokyr, Joel, *The Gifts of Athena: Historical Origins of the Knowledge Economy* (Princeton 2002).

Moran, James, *Printing Presses* (1973).

    Clays of Bungay (Bungay 1978).

(More) Roberts, William, *Memoirs of the Life and Correspondence of Hannah More* (third edition, revised with an additional preface 1835).

Morgan, Charles, *The House of Macmillan, 1843–1943* (1944).

Morison, Stanley, *John Bell, 1745–1831* (Cambridge 1930).

Moritz, Carl Phillip, *Travels in Several Parts of England in 1782* (reprinted 1924).

Moulton, W. F., *The History of the English Bible* (n.d.).

Mumby, F. A., *The House of Routledge 1834–1934* (1934).

Murray, John, see under Grant, and Smiles.

(Lindley) Tieken-Boon van Ostade, Ingrid, ed., *Two Hundred Years of Lindley Murray* (Münster 1996).

Myers, Robin, ed., *The Stationers' Company, A History of the Later Years 1800–2000* (2001).

(Myers) *The Book Trade and its Customers, 1450–1900: Historical Essays for Robin Myers*, ed. Arnold Hunt, Giles Mandelbrote, and Alison Shell; introduction by D. F. McKenzie (Winchester 1997).

Myers, Robin and Harris, Michael, eds., *Development of the English Book Trade, 1700–1899* (1981).

    Fakes and Frauds (1989).

    Spreading the Word: The Distribution Networks of Print, 1550–1850 (1990).

    Censorship and the Control of Print in England and France, 1600–1910 (1992).

    The Stationers' Company and the Book Trade, 1550–1990 (1997).

Newbery, see under Welsh.

Newcomb, Lori Humphrey, *Reading Popular Romance in Early Modern England* (New York 2002).

Nichols, J., *Literary Anecdotes of the Eighteenth Century* (1812–16).

Nowell-Smith, Simon, *The House of Cassell, 1848–1958* (1958).

Papali, G. F., *Jacob Tonson, Publisher* (Auckland 1968).

Patten, Robert L., *Charles Dickens and His Publishers* (1978).

Pearson, Jacqueline, *Women's Reading in Britain, 1750–1835: A Dangerous Recreation* (Cambridge 1999).

Perkins, David, *Is Literary History Possible?* (Baltimore 1992).

(Phillips) *Memoirs of the Public and Private Life of Sir Richard Phillips* (1808).

Phillips, James W., *Printing and bookselling in Dublin, 1670–1800* (Dublin 1998).

Plant, Marjorie, *The English Book Trade* (third edition 1974).

(Pollard) *Studies in the Book Trade in Honour of Graham Pollard* (Oxford 1975).

Pollard, M., *Dublin's Trade in Books, 1550–1800* (1989).

Potter, Esther, 'The London Bookbinding Trade: From Craft to Industry' in *The Library* (1993).

Pottinger, David Thomas, *The French Book Trade in the Ancien Régime, 1500–1791* (Cambridge, Mass. 1958).

Prince, John Henry, *Life, Pedestrian Excursions, and Singular Opinions* (1806).

'The Printer's Devil' in *Quarterly Review* (December 1839).

Raumer, Frederick von, *England in 1835* (1836).

Raven, James, *Judging New Wealth, Popular Publishing and Responses to Commerce in England, 1750–1800* (1992).

Raven, James, ed., *Free Print and Non-commercial Publishing since 1700* (Aldershot 2000).

Raven, James, Small, Helen, and Tadmor, Naomi, *The Practice and Representation of Reading in England* (Cambridge 1996).

Rees, Thomas, *Reminiscences of Literary London from 1779 to 1853* (1896).

Remer, Rosalind, *Printers and Men of Capital. Philadelphia Book Publishers in the New Republic* (Philadelphia 1996).

Renier, Anne, *Friendship's Offering* (Private Libraries Association 1964).

Rhys, Ernest, *Everyman Remembers* (1931).

Richardson, Alan, *Literature, Education, and Romanticism: Reading as Social Practice, 1780–1832* (Cambridge 1994).

Richardson, Brian, *Printing, Writers and Readers in Renaissance Italy* (Cambridge 1999).

Rivers, Isabel, ed., *Books and their Readers in Eighteenth-Century England* (Leicester 1982).

Books and their Readers in Eighteenth-Century England: New Essays (Leicester 2001).

Rivington, Septimus, *The Publishing Family of Rivington* (1919).

Roberts, W., *The Bookhunter in London* (1895).

Robinson, Charles E., 'Percy Bysshe Shelley, Charles Ollier, and William Blackwood' in Kelvin Everest ed., *Shelley Revalued, Papers from the Gregynog Conference* (Leicester 1983).

Rogers, Shef, 'The Use of Royal Licences for Printing in England, 1695–1760: A Bibliography' in *The Library*, seventh series, 1, 2 (2000).

Roper, Derek, *Reviewing before the 'Edinburgh'* (1978).

Rose, Mark, *The Invention of Copyright* (1993).

Rose, Jonathan, *The Intellectual Life of the British Working Class* (Yale 2001).

Roston, Murray, *Biblical Drama in England* (1968).

Rotemberg Julio J., and Salone, Garth, 'The Cyclical Behavior of Strategic Inventories' in *Quarterly Journal of Economics*, 104: 1 (1989) 73–97.

Rouse, Richard H., and Rouse, Mary A., *Manuscripts and their Makers* (2000).

St Clair, William, 'The Impact of Byron's Writings: An Evaluative Approach' in *Byron, Augustan and Romantic*, edited by Andrew Rutherford (1990).

Saunders, David, *Authorship and Copyright* (1992).

Scherer, F. M., and Ross, David, *Industrial Market Structure and Economic Performance* (third edition Boston c. 1990).

Schofield, R. S., 'The Measurement of Literacy in Pre-Industrial England' in *Literacy in Traditional Societies*, edited by Jack Goody (1968).

Shaylor, Joseph, *The Fascination of Books with Other Papers on Books and Bookselling* (1912).

Shenfield, John H., and Stelzer, Irwin M., *The Antitrust Laws, A Primer* (American Enterprise Institute Washington DC. fourth edition 2001).

Shephard, Leslie, *John Pitts, Ballad Printer* (1969).

Sheridan, Thomas, *Lectures on the Art of Reading* (1775).

Sherman, William, *John Dee, The Politics of Reading and Writing in the English Renaissance* (Amherst 1995).

Silver, Rollo G., *The American Printer, 1787–1825* (Charlottesville 1967).

Siskin, Clifford, *The Work of Writing* (Baltimore 1998).

[Charles, Shillito], *The Country Book Club, A Poem* (1788).

Smellie, see under Kerr.

Smiles, Samuel, *Memoir and Correspondence of the late John Murray* (1891).

Smith, Adam, *An Inquiry into the Nature and Causes of the Wealth of Nations*, general eds., R. H. Campbell and A. S. Skinner, textual ed., W. B. Todd (1976).

Smith, Charles Manby, *The Working Man's Way in the World* (1857, reprinted 1967).

(Smith) Maxwell, Sir Herbert, *Life of the Right Honourable William Henry Smith* (1894).

[Robert Southey] 'Cases of Walcot v. Walker; Southey v. Sherwood; Murray v. Benbow, and Lawrence v. Smith' in *Quarterly Review* 27, (1822), 123.

[Michael Sparke] *Scintilla, or A Light Broken into darke Warehouses* (1641). Reprinted by Arber, *Transcript* iv, 35–8.

A Second Beacon fired by Scintilla (1652).

Spedding, James, *Publishers and Authors* (privately printed 1867).

Spinney, G. H., 'Cheap Repository Tracts: Hazard and Marshall Editions' in *The Library* (1939/40).

Spufford, Margaret, *Small Books and Pleasant Histories* (1981).

Steer, Francis W., *Scriveners' Company Common Paper 1357–1628* (1968).

History of the Worshipful Company of Scriveners of London (1973).

Stewart-Murphy, Charlotte, A., *A History of British Circulating Libraries* (Newtown, Pa., 1992).

Strahan, see under Cochrane, and Harlan.

Strathesk, John, ed., *Hawkie, The Autobiography of a Gangrel* (1888).

Sutherland, J. A. *Victorian Novelists and Publishers* (1976).

Talfourd, Thomas Noon, *A Speech delivered . . . in the House of Commons . . . on A Bill to Consolidate the Law relating to Copyright* (1837).

Taylor, John, see under Blunden, and Chilcott.

Tebbel, John, *A History of Book Publishing in the United States i: The Creation of an Industry, 1630–1865* (1972).

Tegg, Thomas, *Remarks on the Speech of Sergeant Talfourd* (1837).

Terry, Richard, *Poetry and the Making of the English Literary Past* (Oxford 2001).

[James, Thin] *Reminiscences of Booksellers and Bookselling in Edinburgh in the Time of William IV. An Address to a Meeting of Booksellers' Assistants* (privately printed, Edinburgh 1905).

Thoms, William J., ed., *A Collection of Early Prose Romances* (1828).

Thomson, Robert S., The Development of the Broadside Ballad Trade and its Influence upon the Transmission of English Folksong (unpublished Ph. D. thesis, University of Cambridge 1974).

Thompson, James Westfield, *The Mediaeval Library* (Chicago 1939).

Thompson, Ralph, *American Literary Annuals and Gift Books* (New York 1936).

Timperley, C. H., *A Dictionary of Printers and Printing* (1839).

Tinsley, William, *Random Recollections of an Old Printer* (1900).

[E. Topham] *Letters from Edinburgh Written in the Years 1774 and 1775* (Dublin n.d. c. 1776).

Townley, James, *Biblical Anecdotes* (1813).

'A Traveller'. 'Facts relative to the State of Reading Societies and Literary Institutions in the United Kingdom' in *Monthly Magazine* (June 1821).

Turner, John R., 'Arrowsmith's Royalty Ledger,' in *Publishing History*, 48 (2000).

Tyson, Gerald P., *Joseph Johnson, A Liberal Publisher* (Iowa City 1979).

Vincent, David, *Bread, Knowledge and Freedom. A Study of Nineteenth Century Working Class Autobiography* (1981).

Literacy and Popular Culture: England 1750–1914 (Cambridge 1989).

Vizitelly, Henry, *Glances Back Through Seventy Years* (1893).

The Vocal Library: Being the Largest Collection of English, Scottish, and Irish Songs, ever printed in a single volume (1824).

Watt, Tessa, *Cheap Print and Popular Piety, 1550–1640* (1991).

Webb, R. K., *The British Working Class Reader, 1790–1820* (1955).

West, William, *Fifty Years Recollections of an Old Bookseller* (Cork 1835).

Welsh, Charles, *A Bookseller of the Last century . . . John Newbery* (1885).

Wheatley, Henry B., *Prices of Books: An Inquiry into the Changes in the Price of Books which have occurred in England at Different Periods* (1898).

Wiener, Joel H., *Radicalism and Freethought in Nineteenth Century Britain, The Life of Richard Carlile* (1983).

Wiles, R. M., *Serial Publication in England before 1750* (Cambridge 1957).

Williams, Jane, *The Literary Women of England* (1861).

Williams, Raymond, *The Long Revolution* (1961).

Wilson, Frances, *The Courtesan's Revenge, The Life of Harriette Wilson* (2003).

Wilson, Harriette, *Memoirs of Harriette Wilson* (1831). Stockdale's eight-volume edition, with much detailed additional information about the trials for piracy and libel. BL.

Winger, Howard Woodrow, Regulations relating to the Book Trade in London from 1357 to 1586 (unpublished Ph.D thesis, University of Illinois 1953).

Wolf, Edwin, *The Book Culture of a Colonial American City* (Oxford 1988).

Woudhuysen, H. R., *Sir Philip Sidney and the Circulation of Manuscripts 1558–1640* (Oxford 1996).

Wrigley, E. A., and Schofield, R. S., *The Population History of England, 1541–1871, A Reconstruction* (Cambridge 1997).

Wroth, Lawrence C., *The Colonial Printer* (New York 1931).

Index

I have included topics, themes, and arguments as well as significant mentions of persons, firms, and titles of books, although not fictional characters, and have grouped them in ways that I hope will prove helpful to readers. As far as the appendices are concerned, however, since many authors and titles are mentioned only once, often as part of a list, I have been more selective. I have, for example, indexed many individual titles under broad headings such as 'travel books'. Since the printed works by the many modern authors on which I have drawn are listed in the footnotes and bibliographies, I have included only a selection in the index. My hope is that these arrangements will help readers to find their way, to follow lines of inquiry, and to assess the conclusions without overloading them with unnecessary duplication.

Voltaire, 85, 313, 352, 369, 535, 670
his *Philosophical Dictionary*, 336

Wakefield, Gilbert, 259
Walkley, Thomas
printer/publisher, 153–154
Walker, Victorian publisher, 335
Walker, A., stereotyper, 184
Walker, R.
printer/publisher, attempts to exercise
statutory rights, 92, 113, 154–155,
699–700
Walker, W. S., boy prodigy, 509
Walker's Classics, 113, 130, 204, 473, 506, 507, 532,
713
Waller, Edmund, 525–534
Walpole, Horace, 537, 598
his *Castle of Otranto*, 537
Walvin, James, 258, 562
Wanton Wife of Bath, 341
war, *see* romance, women
Warburton, William, editor of Shakespeare, 155,
702–703
Ward and Lock, publishers, 417, 444, 519,
716–717
Warne, publishers, 25, 417, 430–432, 444, 519,
601, 713, 714, 717–718, 725
Warton, Thomas
his *History of English Poetry*, 127
Watson, James, publisher, his list, 679
imprisoned, 310, other references, 196, 312,
314, 317, 318, 395, 660
Watt, Tessa, 80
Watts, Isaac, 131, 515, 668
Waverley novels, *see* Scott
Wedderburn, Robert, bookshop assistant,
imprisoned, 314
Weissman, Steve, 510, 657
Wellington, Duke of, 308, 311
Wesley, Charles, 73
West, Anthony James, 145, 694
West, Jane, writer of conduct literature,
publication, 657
West Indies, 36, 215, 218, 257, 375, 380, 455, 619,
647, 665
Westall, Richard, artist, 134, 620
Whelan, Tim, 561
Whittaker, publishers, 128, 171
Whittingham, printers and publishers, 134, 168,
532–533
White, James, of Boston, bookseller,
381
White, Henry Kirke, 217
Whitefield, George, 377
Whittier J. G., 399, 716, 719

Whole Duty of Man, 92, 515
Wigton Subscription Library, 251, 671
Wilde, Oscar, 370
Wiffen, translator of Tasso, 399
Williams, Raymond, 85, 86, 88, 439
Willow song, in Shakespeare's *Othello*, 153–154,
491, 697–698
Wilson, Kilmarnock printer, 585
Wilson, Andrew, stereotyper, 206, 515
Wilson, Frances, 32, 657
Wilson, Harriette, publication, 657–658
other references, 181, 223, 322, 337, 677,
678
Wilson, John, 211, 590
Wither, George, 45, 493
Wits Commonwealth, 71
Wolfe, Charles, author of *The Burial of Sir John
Moore*, 227
Wollstonecraft, Mary
publication, 658–660, limited impact, 132,
other references, 7, 162, 179, 259, 277–280,
337, 389, 400, 509, 543, 547, 569, 622, 657,
668, 679
women
as readers, 4, 227, 344, 413, 632, 660, in book
industry, 47, 60, 96, 108, 483, attempts to
control women's reading, 280–284, as
authors, 172–174, 195, 215–216, 230, 366, no
women verse writers in old canon, 128, as
novelists, 174, 244, 474, celebrators of
domestic affections, 215, 220, 608, and the
imperial enterprise, 227–229, ideal women
in neo-chivalric romance, 226-227,
subverted by *Don Juan*, 323, and war,
215–216, 227, 287, compilers of
commonplace books, 224–232, readers of
Don Juan, 227, 335, 688, members of
commercial circulating libraries, 242–244,
members of reading societies, 249, 252,
409, suffragists, 366. *See also* readers
woodcuts, *see* illustrations
Woodfin, A.
poorly paid author, 173
Worcester Library, 248
Wordsworth's family, 158, 202
Wordsworth, William
publication, 660–664, in Victorian times,
715–723, not regarded as a romantic poet in
his time, 212–213, continues the old canon
ideologies, 213, 234, 285, 661, and
Galignani, 299, 300, 302, high book prices,
201, personal beneficiary of state measures
against reading, 310–311, and intellectual
property, 43, 206–207, and popular
literature, 79, 114, 346–347, 350, in